TALKING FOOTBALL
(HALL OF FAMERS' REMEMBRANCES)
COMPLETE SERIES

———————

AUTHORS: DAVID SPADA &
ELLIOTT HARRIS
EDITED BY MELINDA SPADA

TALKING FOOTBALL
(HALL OF FAMERS' REMEMBRANCES)
COMPLETE SERIES

Table of Contents

ABOUT THE AUTHORS

David Spada is a successful attorney whose dream was to become a sports talk show host. Elliott Harris is a former Chicago Sun-Times Quick Hits columnist who has covered the world of sports for decades.

David and Elliott teamed up in 2011 to host the sports podcast "Sports & Torts" on talkzone.com. "Sports & Torts" was a finalist for Sports Podcast of the Year in 2013 by the website podcastawards.com. David and Elliott interviewed over 210 Hall of Famers from the world of football, baseball, and basketball. They are pleased to share their interviews with 138 Pro Football Hall of Famers who talk about their careers in this book.

Chapter 1

Charley Trippi

College:
Georgia

Career History:
Chicago Cardinals (1947–1955)

1968 Inductee Pro Football Hall of Fame

College Choice
A Coca-Cola man was an alumnus of Georgia, and he played football there. He talked me into taking a trip to Georgia. When I did, I was impressed and I stayed. I was a halfback at Georgia when I played there. Winning a championship, that's the thing you play for. It's something you live with the rest of your life.

Bidding War For Services After College
Back then, the leagues were bidding for talent. Even during the war, they had people coming around saying, "We'll give you a hundred dollars a month until you sign your contract and it won't count against your salary." I stayed away from that because I promised Charles Bidwill, the Owner of the Chicago Cardinals that I was going to sign with him regardless of what the other league offered me.

I went to New York and talked to Dan Topping and another gentleman. They made a good offer to me for both baseball and football. I signed with the Atlanta Crackers to play baseball and I got a better bonus. I got a $10,000 bonus to play in AA ball. I had a good year. I hit .336. Then they wanted to sell me to the Boston Red Sox after that. I made up my mind. I just couldn't compete in both sports. The wear and tear was so hard because you're active every day. You have to perform every day. It's tough when you have to perform every day.

Plus, I didn't have much of a family life. I was away from home four months a year back then. I decided I was going to throw in the towel on baseball and just concentrate on football with the Cardinals. I always had ambitions of playing big league baseball, but as it turned out, the money in football was so attractive that I decided I'd stay with football. The thing that escalated the price of football players was the formation of the American League back then. They were bidding for talent. Then, it got to be about money. As it turned out, it was in the best interests for the ballplayers back then.

Back in 1945, there were two leagues competing for talent, the American League and the National League. It put me in a good negotiating position. I ended up with the Chicago Cardinals. Back then, the National League was more established than the American League. Plus, Charles Bidwill was very generous with my contract. He gave me a four-year contract for $100,000, and I was perfectly happy with it.

When Mr. Bidwill drafted me, we sat down and in five minutes he said, "What do you want?" I said, "I want a four-year contract for a hundred thousand dollars."

He said, "You got it." I didn't even worry about the American League then. I was happy with what I received from the Cardinals, so I didn't give them an opportunity to beat the price I got with the Cardinals. You see, the American League was just beginning to get established. I wanted to be with a team that was well established and in the game to stay.

When I signed with the Cardinals, Mr. Bidwill said he had a green backfield, which was comprised of Paul Christman, Pat Harder, Elmer Angsman, and me. That was his greatest ambition—to have a green backfield. He had a vision, with the green backfield, that we were going to win the NFL Championship, which we did. Unfortunately, Mr. Bidwill never lived long enough to see his team win it.

1947 NFL Championship Game Against Eagles
I had a good day. We played on a frozen field. We played in tennis shoes. I had a 50-yard run from the line of scrimmage and I ran back a punt about 65 yards. I scored two touchdowns. I never anticipated playing in tennis shoes and I never anticipated scoring a touchdown with tennis shoes. It worked out pretty good. We got better traction with tennis shoes. We went out to warm up with football shoes and we couldn't stand up on the frozen turf.

It wasn't my idea. It was a necessity. We couldn't stand up with cleats. We took them off as soon as we got on the field. We stood up and then we're falling down. We always had tennis shoes in our bags so we all resorted to tennis shoes to play.

Playing Multiple Positions
I started playing in high school, where I did everything. I played defense. We had the single wing back then. I was a tailback, I threw passes, and I punted. It just came natural to me so it continued on into college and then into professional football. To me it was just another thing really.

1948 NFL Championship Game Against Eagles
We won our division and played in the Championship again against the Eagles in Philadelphia. The night before the game we had a big snowstorm. The ballplayers had to get the tarp off the field. As we got the tarp off the field the snow kept coming down. We had a hard time trying to play a football game under those conditions.

Greatest Thrill In Football
Well the greatest thrill I ever got out of football was playing in the Rose Bowl. I played in the Rose Bowl in January of 1943. I got to play 59 minutes. It so happened we had a football player by the name of Frank Sinkwich, who was a real good football player. We had a scrimmage out there before the game. He got hurt. He couldn't play. During the course of the game we brought the ball down to the one-yard line. We called a timeout so Sinkwich could come in and score. He scored with a bad ankle. We allowed him to finish his career on top of the ledger.

Chicago Cardinals vs. Chicago Bears Rivalry

Anytime you have two teams in the same city there's a big rivalry. We had some tough games with them. They were a good football team. I can't remember ever losing to the Bears. The Bears built up a lot of football traditions over the years. They've had great football teams. Of course the people of Chicago recognize the Bears as the number one football team in the city. As it turns out, we were pretty competitive. Every time we played the Bears we did pretty good against them. I think the league put pressure on the Cardinals to move. They didn't want two teams in the same city. I think they bought out the territory from the Cardinals so the Cardinals could move to St. Louis. There was some money exchanged between the league and the Cardinals back then.

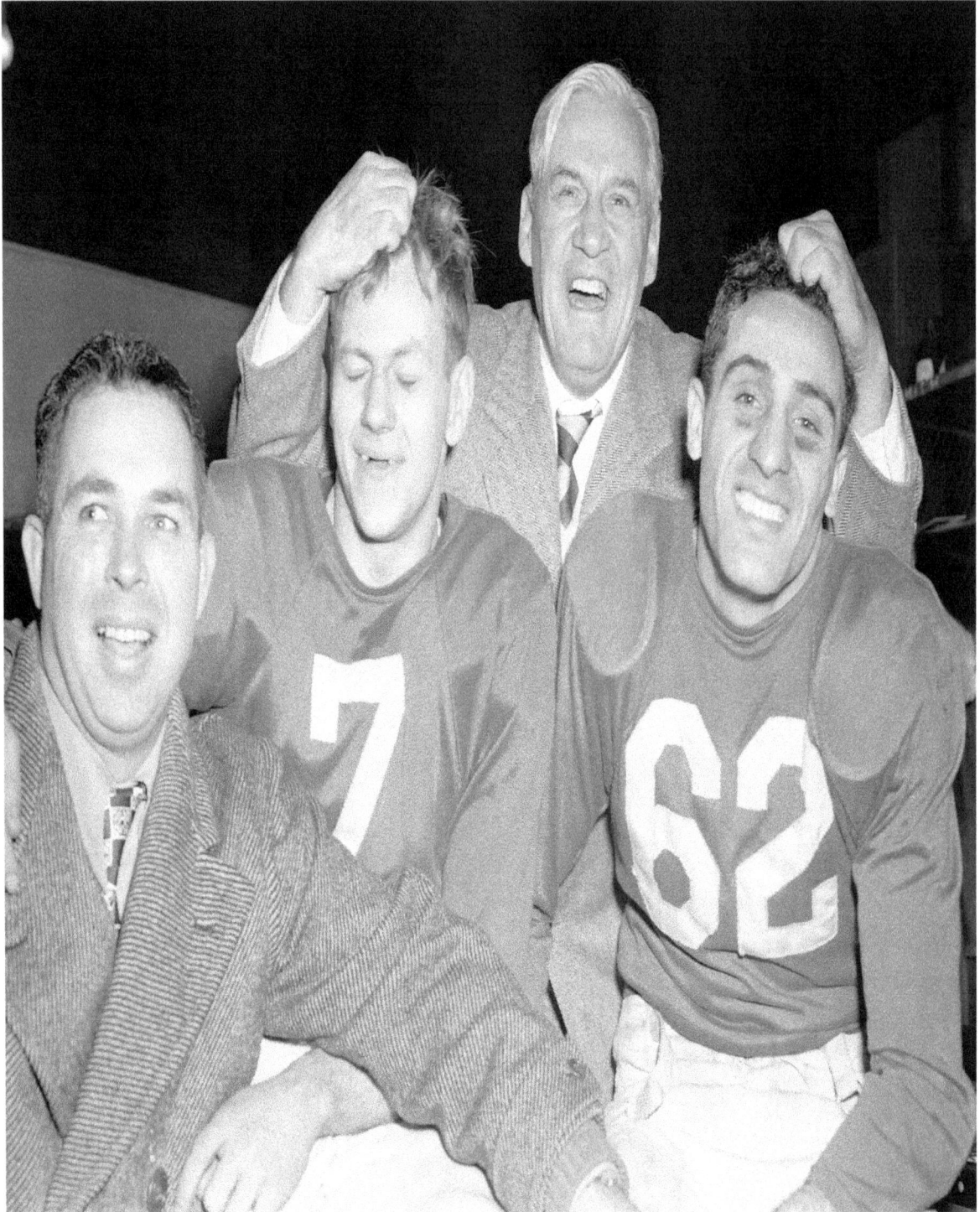

Chicago Cardinals coach Jimmy Conzelman grabs the hair of running backs Charley Trippi, right, and Elmer Angsman as assistant coach Phil Handler, left, grins after the December 28, 1947 National Football League Championship game.
Photograph copyright Associated Press

Chapter 2

Art Donovan

College:
Boston College

Career History:
Baltimore Colts (1950)
New York Yanks (1951)
Dallas Texans (1952)
Baltimore Colts (1953-1961)

1968 Inductee Pro Football Hall of Fame

Notre Dame

You know, it's a funny thing. When I was at Notre Dame, I was better than maybe half the tackles there. When the war was over, I met a coach from Notre Dame in California, and he asked if I was coming back to school. I explained that I wanted to, but Frank Leahy had his pets and I wasn't one of them.

I had a fight with one of his pets. A tackle was holding me and I kept saying, "Hey, don't hold me, okay? If you can't block me, don't hold me." He did it a couple more times. Finally, I got sick and tired of it and gave him a couple of punches. Then we got into a real fight. Leahy came over and told us to shake hands. I said, "I'm not going to shake hands. He doesn't like me and I certainly don't like him." That was it. I think that was my ticket out of Notre Dame.

My mother was in shock, but I'll tell you the truth, I really wanted to go to Fordham. It was a ten-minute walk from my house and I was always a Fordham fan. In fact, I use to watch them practice in the afternoon. The coaches and priests used to let us watch practice. I was just happy. So, after the war I saw the Fordham Athletic Director and he said, "Look, we're disbanding intercollegiate football, so if I were you, I'd go to Boston College." Then, I made up my mind, and went to Boston College.

Draft

We had guys come in who were first round draft picks and not know what football was all about. We had a guy we took in the 19th round, Raymond Berry, and look how he turned out.

You don't know about a football player till they get on the field. Believe me. The Giants drafted me, but I wanted to stay in college for two more years. I hoped after that, if I was lucky, somebody would draft me. That's why the Colts drafted me in 1950. On Sunday morning I'm leaving the Bronx to come down to Western Maryland to go to Colts training camp. I came out of church, which was right across the street from where I lived. My father sees my car packed with my two pair of pants and about four changes of underwear. He said, "Where are you going?" "I'm going to Baltimore." "What are you going to do in Baltimore?" I said, "I'm going to try out for the football team." My father said, "Are you crazy?" Then, he hollered up to my mother, "Mary, those big guys will kill him down there!" He was wrong. I'm still alive.

Eating

They used to say, "Hey, run around, Donovan. You're killing the grass." If I told you the truth, I never worked out in the off-season. I never ran. I never did anything. The first day of fall practice was the first time I ran around a field, because I figured I had to conserve my energy.

A friend of mine called me and said, "Hey, when you die I'm coming up there to the funeral and I'm going to give the undertaker $1,500 to cut your stomach open and see all the junk in there."

I think in 13 years I did 13 pushups. I was told when I was playing by a member of the team I had to start working out better.

I said, "Do you want a defensive tackle or do you want a gymnast." He said, "Alright, don't worry about the pushups."

There was nobody who could beat me eating hot dogs. I loved hot dogs. I went home one time and on my way back, I went through the Holland Tunnel. There was a guy selling hot dogs on the roof of a real fancy truck. I ate so many that I ran out of money and I had to stop eating them. The next time I found the guy and stopped for some hot dogs, was about four months later. He told me he didn't know who I was or where I came from, but he really missed me. I was the best customer he ever had.

We had a lot of great times, a lot of great stories. These guys today just don't have the fun we had. I think it was the greatest time in football history because the guys grew old nicely and we just had more fun, seriously.

Don Joyce and Gino Marchetti had a chicken-eating contest at training camp. I bet on Joyce and somebody bet on Marchetti. There were four of us betting and we bet a $100 a piece. It was a Sunday afternoon, and we ate a typical Southern Maryland meal, chicken, mashed potatoes and peas. Gino starts eating the chicken, but Joyce, he's eating the chicken, the mashed potatoes and the peas.

I said, "For crying out loud, Joyce, don't worry about the God damn potatoes and the peas. Eat the chicken."

Marchetti gets to about, I guess, 18 pieces of chicken, and I said, "Joyce, one more and we win." He said, "I'm still hungry." He ate, I think, 26 pieces of chicken.

We didn't care if he blew up or not. We won the bet. He reached into his pocket and picks out three pieces of Saccharin and dropped it in his iced tea. He was watching his weight.

For four months in 2012, I didn't have one beer. I had a bladder infection. I was told I had cancer in my bowel so I couldn't have beer. I had to give up the Schlitz and the hot dogs. The only Schlitz I had in four months was the one I had with the doctor in the hospital. His boss caught us and he nearly got fired.

Early Colts Teams

We knew we were getting better before Johnny Unitas came. We had a couple of quarterbacks who were real good. One time we played Green Bay and they were pretty good, but we beat them.

We got on the bus up in Green Bay and Gino Marchetti says to me, "Hey, fatso, how good do you think we are?"

I said, "Gino, I think this is the beginning of a good football team." It certainly was since we had Weeb Ewbank.

Gino said, "He's a weasel, but he's a good coach." And that was it.

Playing The Chicago Bears At Wrigley Field

It was fun playing at Wrigley Field, and it was fun playing against the best. They had that old time band out in center field. They used to play a lot of marching songs, and we would march onto the field. We'd make like we were marching with their music. We all got a great kick out of that.

Les Richter

We were playing the Rams out in the LA Coliseum in 1954. Les Richter was supposed to be a tough guy and now we're playing him out there and Don Joyce is our kickoff man. He kicks the ball and the next thing you know we're running out to get onto the field. Joyce is standing in the middle of the LA Coliseum and Richter is lying down on the ground.

Joyce has got Richter's helmet in his hand. I said "What the hell did you do now, Joyce?" He says, "I was only protecting him."

He claims that Richter kneed him. He ripped Richter's helmet off and hit him in the face with his own helmet. I swear to God. We're standing there looking, and Richter's got his hands over his face, blood coming out through his fingers. They almost threw Joyce out of the League.

Bobby Layne

He was a hell of a football player and he was a real character. We're playing him here in Baltimore and we were putting a lot of pressure on him. We had heard about his shenanigans and everything. In the third quarter we rushed him and three of us were lying on top of him. He's screaming and hollering and I said, "God damn, Bobby, you're breath! You must've had a hell of a night lastnight."

He looked at us and said, "Hey, I had a few at halftime."

Lenny Moore

The best football player I ever saw on the field was my teammate, Lenny Moore. He could do anything. He could've been an All-Pro defensive back. The guy was amazing, absolutely amazing.

1958 NFL Championship Game At Yankee Stadium

I got a great kick out of it because I lived 4 miles from the stadium and when I got introduced, everybody, including all my neighbors booed me. It was a great day, great day. You know what, if you really want to know the total truth, we didn't know what the hell was going on. We didn't know there was overtime or anything else.

When we tied the score, I said, "What are we doing next?" The official had to tell us. I think he had to tell, Weeb Ewbank, our Coach, what was going to happen after that. I thought we were so much better than the Giants and I think we were.

I said to Gino Marchetti when the Giants went ahead, "Hey, Gino, if we lose this God damn game, it will be the greatest tragedy because we're so much better than these guys." He said, "You know, Fatso, you're right." We got lucky and won.

Frank Gifford did not make a first down on two occasions. The first time Marchetti and I made the tackle. Big Daddy dropped over and he broke Gino Marchetti's leg. The second time was in the overtime. Gino wasn't even in the game. He was sitting under the goal post watching. The fellow who came and stopped Frank was Ordell Braase from South Dakota. He was another fine football player. He grabbed Frank Gifford and stopped him.

Frank was screaming, "I made that. I made that!"

I said, "Hey, Frank. You didn't make it. Why don't you stop the bullshit?" And that was it. He and I have been friends ever since.

Joe Schmidt
I was happy I played with a great football team with a great bunch of guys. I think the greatest thing that I ever heard a guy say about the Baltimore Colts was from a great linebacker from Detroit, Joe Schmidt.

He said to me, "You know what? I wish I had played with you guys. You guys really had a lot of fun and you were good." He's another great friend of mine. I made a lot of great friends playing.

Johnny Carson
Mr. Carson was something else. He was a real gentleman. In fact, I was on his show a couple of times. The first time, I was sitting in a room thinking, "What the hell am I going to do here all by myself and nobody to talk to?"

Then a guy knocks on the door and says, "Listen, the people alongside of you, they don't have enough room in their room. Can I open the door and let them in? They're going to be on the show." I said, "Sure, go ahead."

He didn't tell me it was a lady from the San Diego Zoo with all these Goddamn animals. I opened the door and here come snakes and other animals. I'm from the Bronx. I don't know anything about animals.

The second best thing was Johnny Carson's band. Doc Severinsen and the whole band congratulated me and Doc said, "You should be on at least once a week."

Cooking with Julia Child
I didn't know who Julia Child was and I said, "Where are you from, Ms. Child?" I thought the way she talked she was from England.

She said, "Cambridge." I said, "Cambridge, England?" She said, "No, Cambridge, Massachusetts." I told her I went to Boston College and I used to go over to the square there and drink beer in Cambridge. She said to me, "I don't drink beer." I said, "You're missing something."

She was a nice lady, and to tell you the truth, we got drunk. It was on The Letterman Show and David Letterman also got drunk. We were drinking cognac and at the end of the show, the three of us went in the back of a small convertible and I couldn't get out. So, they had to stop and get her out first.

I said to her, "We'll stay here all night. I don't care. I laughed my rear end off. It was fun."

Walter Cronkite
I was sitting in a room before I went on with Johnny Carson and a guy says to me, "Hey, there's a man out here and he wants to meet you." I went out and it was the great TV announcer, Walter Cronkite. He was a war correspondent.

I said to him, "You wanted to meet me?" I couldn't believe it. He said to me, "Young man, don't ever change. Just tell the truth and you'll be okay."

To me, that was the nicest thing that anybody ever said to me. I couldn't get over it. Walter Cronkite, saying to me, a defensive tackle, that he enjoyed me.

I said, "Mr. Cronkite, thank you very much. That's the best thing anybody every said to me."

Book "Fatso"
My wife is the one that wanted me to write a book, not me. Listen, I'll tell you the God's honest truth. I'm an Irish Catholic, and the only book I have ever read in my life was the Catechism going to Catholic school. I'm telling you the God's honest truth.

What can I say? I just was lucky to play with great football players, and I had Coach Weeb. The guys who played alongside of me, Marchetti, Don Joyce, Ray Krouse were just fine football players.

Don Shula
Don Shula, another teammate, and I bought a house and we lived together. Shula then was as wild as we were. I'm serious. We'd get in the house and we'd wrestle, those two guys against me. They'd get me down, and start walloping my ass and I'd be laughing so hard, I couldn't do anything. They just beat the hell out of me, but I loved it.

Photograph copyright Associated Press

Chapter 3

Chuck Bednarik

College:
Pennsylvania

Career History:
Philadelphia Eagles (1949-1962)

1967 Inductee Pro Football Hall of Fame

First Contract
I got a $3,000 bonus, and a $7,000 contract, which totaled out to $10,000. In those days, that was pretty good money.

Nickname
After practice, I used to sell concrete. That's where I got the nickname, 'Concrete Charlie'.

Background
My parents came from Czechoslovakia, and I was born into poverty, in Bethlehem, Pennsylvania. My life was tough. I started playing football at Bethlehem High School. In those days we played both ways. That's the way football was in those days. Today it's pussycat football.

Fingers
I've got crooked fingers. When I shake the hand of a little kid I'll say squeeze it, and I go "Oink, oink." The finger on my right hand is wired and it goes way out there. The kids say, "Oh," and run away.

Philadelphia Eagle Chuck Bednarik after his famous hit on New York Giant Frank Gifford on November 20, 1960. Photograph copyright Associated Press

Chapter 4

Y.A. Tittle

```
College:
Louisiana State

Career History:
Baltimore Colts (AAFC) (1948–1949)
Baltimore Colts (1950)
San Francisco 49ers (1951–1960)
New York Giants (1961–1964)

1971 Inductee Pro Football Hall of Fame
```

College Choice

Marco, Texas is my hometown. It's about 20 miles from the Louisiana border. I got scholarships to the University of Texas and LSU. My brother had lived in New Orleans, Louisiana. That is why I went down there. It was a good decision, I think.

LSU

LSU had a good team. We went to the Cotton Bowl in 1946 and played against Arkansas. We beat Alabama and all the Southeastern Conference schools during the season. I enjoyed it a lot.

Cotton Bowl Against Arkansas

The score was nothing-nothing. It's not too big an honor to not even score a point and be most valuable player. We made 19 first downs and Arkansas made 2. We played on ice. We just played in tennis shoes because we could not stand up in cleats. We could not score. We would get down around the 25, 30-yard line and it was solid ice. Nobody could stand up. We could not get across the goal line. It was nothing-nothing.

On a day like that you have to learn how to palm the ball a little bit. I took thumbtacks and I filed them down really low. Then I put them on my right fingers and thumb tips. Then I wrapped tape around my fingers. It was illegal to do that but at least I could puncture the ball with the thumbtacks a little bit and get a little friction. It was against the rules but I got away with it. I put tape around all the fingers on my left hand so the referee would not be suspicious.

I will tell you a little secret. I used those thumb tacks to my advantage. Some of those bigtackles would get me and twist my arm and pinch me and do everything else. I had my weapon too. I had those thumbtacks. I could put my hand up under their elbow and run my hand up and down. I scratched the heck out of them. They did not know that until the game was over and they thawed out. They were so cold they did not feel it. I should not tell you that. I got my revenge.

Baltimore Colts

Baltimore drafted me. I went to the All American Conference and I played under a legendary football person. Cecil Isbell was the coach. He was a passing type coach. He had been an All-American at Purdue, I think. He believed in the forward pass. He encouraged me to become a good player, and taught me some of the skills of the forward passing game.

Baltimore folded financially and collapsed. We were redrafted. The Baltimore players were put in the college draft. We were redrafted like college players. I was San Francisco's first draft choice. I went to California. I played here ten years and got married, raised a family, and went into business. I am still here and I like it.

Frankie Albert

For the first couple of years I played behind Frankie Albert. He was good for me because he gave me some of the skills of quarterbacking. He was a very confident person. I do not want to be critical of him, but he was not a great thrower. He was a run around quarterback. He had good knowledge of the game and good leadership qualities. I learned a lot from Frank. He was a good friend. He and Fran Tarkenton invented the bootleg.

Alley Oop Pass

That was not an invention, that was if you can't find anybody open just throw it up in the air and let RC Owens jump for it. That did not take very much skill.

R.C. was a basketball player in college. He could really jump, rebound, get the ball, and get up high in the air. I was trying to throw the ball away one day out of the end zone. I threw it too short. R.C. jumped up in front of about five people and pulled it down. I gave him credit for it. He said he could do it every time, so I started doing it. We could not think of anything to call it. If I got in a huddle I would say, "Okay R.C. Alley Oop." That was the name of the play, R.C. Alley Oop. That took a lot of skill. You could do it. I could do it. My wife could do it. Throw the ball high up in the air and let R.C. jump for it. Players from the opposing team would try to get under the ball to try to intercept the pass and they would end up bumping into each other. R.C., he would swoop in at the last second between them. He would come down with a big hyper finish from the air and he would gobble the ball up.

R.C. said he liked the ball to wobble a little bit so he could judge it better. He did not want a tight spiral. He wanted it to wobble. I did not want to throw a wobble because you are proud of your ability to throw the ball with a tight spiral, and things like that are pretty. He came down with about three or four Alley Oops. I learned how to throw a nice wobble.

Trade to New York Giants

I had to make a decision as to whether I was going to quit playing. I had already played a long time in football before I was traded. I was married and had a young family. My wife's mother said she would help out with my two young children at that time when I went back to New York for training camp. That made it possible for me to play some more.

15

Million Dollar Backfield

My only problem with the million-dollar backfield was keeping track of who carries the ball three times or four times. I would try to make it even so that nobody would get mad. I had Hugh McElhenny, Joe Perry, and John Henry Johnson. They were something else.

Joe Perry carried it most of the time. He had a lot of stamina. McElhenny was never in condition too much. He could not carry the ball like Joe Perry, or as many times as Joe Perry. It worked out fine. McElhenny was a runaround type of guy. He would run right in, change his mind, go back to the left, back to the right. He did not want to carry the ball 25 times a game like Joe did. He could not because he was too exhausted, I guess.

I was a little bit jealous of them. But listen, I was the quarterback and my job was to win the games. If we could win the game with me throwing two passes, that was fine. It did not make any difference to me. All I wanted to do was just win. With Joe Perry, Hugh McElhenny, and John Henry Johnson, boy I could not make too many mistakes. The short passes I would throw to McElhenny and swing passes to John Henry. I had an opportunity to throw short in games for a lot of yards.

Let's put it this way, I did not, at the time, appreciate Red Hickey. He was a tough guy. Later, I learned to appreciate what he gave. He was a good football coach. He had talent. He had good skills. He knew a lot about the game and he was a demanding type of person. He was not popular with some of the players at the time. We learned to appreciate his talent.

Going to New York was an opportunity for me. My wife wanted me to go there because she wanted to go to stage shows. That is one of the reasons she wanted me to go. She was the best thing that ever happened in my career. I got recognition in the New York papers, the largest press in the world, and also the entertainment industry. We had a good team back then. We won the Eastern Conference four or five times in a row. That was a great break for me.

John Brodie

I am not sure John Brodie would have beaten me out with San Francisco. I am joking I am not trying to make a case about that.

John Brodie was a great quarterback. There was no question. He had a good arm and good knowledge of the game. He turned out to be a great pro.

He was a great golfer but there was a rivalry. When two quarterbacks are equal in talent, there are going to be rivalries. There is going to be choosing up sides by teammates with some teammates pulling for one guy and some pulling for the other guy. It did create a problem with the team. Some of them were Tittle fans and some of them were Brodie fans. It was not a healthy thing. It was okay, but not the way it should be.

New York Giants

I know I had great years in New York. I know that when I came back to San Francisco to play against the 49ers after two years of being traded to the Giants. Boy, I turned it on. I had my big day.

Giants quarterback Charlie Conerly did not welcome me with opens arms at first, but we later became good friends. His wife and my wife were very close friends. After Charlie's retirement we became good friends. I saw him. He lived in Mississippi. He did not hold any anger toward me to his credit.

Throwing Seven Touchdown Passes Against Redskins In 1962
I think my best game as a pro was against the Washington Redskins in 1962. I threw seven touchdown passes. I forget how many yards but I think it was probably the best day I had in pro football.

I did not have any secret. I just had some great receivers. I just kept throwing. I was not shooting for a record; in fact, I never even knew I had broken a record till after the game was over. They told me I had broken the record. We would score and they would score. Then we would score again and they would come back. We would get ahead but they would come back again. I had to keep throwing so I ended up breaking the record accidentally.

Giants Offense
I had Frank Gifford and Kyle Rote. Kyle was a great player. But it was not like the million dollar backfield. I do not think in the history of pro football that a team had three running backs of that caliber.

Scrimmage
We did not scrimmage that much. Once a season starts you do not knock down scrimmages too much. You do not want to get any ball players hurt. In training camp, we would scrimmage. We had all out game type scrimmages. We had Sam Huff and Andy Robustelli. They were all on that defense. All the stars were defensive players.

Reason For Losing Three NFL Championship Games In A Row
I do not know any reason. Except I do know this, the games that we played, the championship games, the field should not have been played on. There was ice and snow. Ice, ice, and more ice. From the quarterback standpoint, you could not hold on to the football. You could not throw the ball; you had to sort of sidearm it and sling it because the ball was frozen. I am not trying to make an excuse. I am very disappointed I did not have any championship winning games. At least I got there many times. That is more than some quarterbacks could say.

Uniform Number
I wore number 64 before they changed the rules for numbers. Quarterback numbers were in the '60s originally. Frankie Albert was number 63 originally and then he was 13 after the change. I was 64 and when they changed I became 14.

Picture Of Him Kneeling On Field & Bleeding
I do not remember what I was feeling then because I was out. I did not know where I was. I think the score was 0-0. I am not sure. No one can score on an ice and snowfield. I got knocked coo-coo. That is a famous picture. You do not see my winning touchdown passes you just see me sitting there like I am praying to the good Lord.

Favorite Receivers

In New York, I had Del Shofner and Frank Gifford to throw to. Frank Gifford was a running back and I threw a lot of passes to him when he would come out of the backfield. I mean running and catching the ball. Del Shofner was a flanker and very fast receiver. He was my number one target in New York at first. In San Francisco, I had a number of guys to throw to like Hugh McElhenny. I threw it at a lot to running backs out here because we had Joe Perry, John Henry Johnson, and Hugh McElhenny.

Allie Sherman

Allie Sherman was a very creative coach, sort of ahead of his time. He sometimes had problems getting along with some of the ballplayers. He was very good to me. I liked Allie and he was, I will not say ahead of his time, but he was very progressive in his thinking. He believed in throwing the ball and we did that. He created a lot of new ideas.

There was some, I will not say disappointment, but some resentment. Allie was a new coach with new ideas. A lot of the team were Tom Landry players. They idolized Tom Landry. They always compared Allie Sherman to Tom Landry. I did not play when Tom Landry was there.

Movie "Any Given Sunday"

Oliver Stone contacted me and wanted to know would I play a cameo role in the film. I did not say too much. I did not do too much acting. I did a lot of coaching in the movie. When they got down to the end, they cut my words out because they paid you residuals on how much speaking you did. I remember saying, Send in the kicking team. That is about all I did. I was a great actor. Clark Gable would have been jealous of me.

Decision to Retire

First of all, I played on so many good teams. So many teams that won. For some reason, the New York Giants management or Allie Sherman, I do not know whether it was Allie or not, but they traded lots of the players away. We went from the top to the bottom in a hurry. I was 30 some odd years old and it was not time for me to start all over again and recharge the batteries anymore. I played 17 years and that was longer than anybody had ever played. It was time to quit, I guess. I will tell you the truth, I really was not finished. I could still throw better than any of the other quarterbacks they had.

They had a lot of quarterbacks that came long after me. We played what you called an Exes Game, where the old timers came back and played against the new team. I came back as an ex, an old timer. I ripped them apart. A quarterback is not like a running back. I do not have toworry about my legs giving away on me. I did not have any knees that hurt. Nothing was wrong with my knees. Nothing was wrong with anything. My arms were still as strong as ever. I could still throw a ball 80 yards in the air when I quit. I could have played longer but my wife did not want me to. She thought it was time for me to hang it up. Sherman had traded a lot of players away. They were not going to be the New York Giants of old, they were rebuilding.

I mean, I quit when I had a lot of good years left. I had some great years in New York, and then we had a bad year so I decided to hang it up mainly because of my pride. Then when I went to the 49ers training camp the next year I got to coach the 49ers backfield. I was coaching, but the coaches were throwing the ball especially when we were working on our defense. I would throw and I was just ripping the defense apart. I was the best quarterback on the field, and I wanted to come back because the coach of 49ers said, If we can get you released from New York, would you play for us? John Brodie was ruled ineligible for some kind of a gambling bet. The Giants gave me the okay to go ahead and play if I wanted to, but my wife said no. She said "You've had a great career and the 49ers are not going to be as good of a team as you used to play for. You're going to lose a lot of things you want to remember, and don't do it." Anyway, she was my quarterback so she commanded me not to.

Pro Football Hall of Fame Induction
That was one of the great honors of my lifetime. When you are selected as one of the great players like Knute Rockne, Don Hudson, and all the other great players that is a great honor. There are still not too many quarterbacks in the Hall of Fame. It was a great honor and still is a great honor.

Name
My dad was Yelberton Abraham too. He was called Abe Tittle. I can't imagine him giving me my name. Yelberton Abraham Tittle Jr.

Yelberton Abraham was not my fondest name. Nobody ever knew my name. In high school or college, I kept it a secret. I was always just YA.

1963 NFL Championship Game
Well, you know I'm not going to make excuses because the Chicago Bears had a great team. But we were really a high scoring team in the league at that time. I felt we could win in Chicago. We had been playing on good fields and with weather that was presentable and we were going to Chicago to play in the championship game. Now we're playing in ice and snow and mud. We weren't quite as adjusted to that type of weather as the Bears were. They had a great team; don't get me wrong. We had Sam Huff, Frank Gifford, and Andy Robustelli. We had some wonderful players.

When I walked out I said, I hope I never see Chicago ever again. I don't want to ever think about cold weather ever again and the Chicago Bears is a dirty word.

New York Giant Y.A. Tittle squats on the field after being hit during a game against the Pittsburgh Steelers on September 20, 1964. Photograph copyright Associated Press

Chapter 5

Gino Marchetti

College:
San Francisco

Career History:
Dallas Texans (1952)
Baltimore Colts (1953-1966)

1972 Inductee Pro Football Hall of Fame

Decision To Play Football
My family came from Italy and lived in West Virginia, where they worked in the coal mines. Eventually they moved to California to work in the steel mills. That's how we got to California. I settled in a little town called Antioch, where the population was only about 3,500.

My mother and father being from Italy, they didn't know much about football. When I started to play I had to fight them all the way. They didn't want me to play. They were afraid I'd get injured. They weren't very happy with me but I held something over their head. I said, "If I don't play football, I'm just not going to school. When I'm 16, I'm out of there."

They signed me up and they let me go out for Antioch High School. An interesting thing about that is when I was going out for football there, they had 24 uniforms. I didn't make the team but I still wanted to play. A friend of mine was the equipment manager of the football team. He gave me a pair of pants, shoulder pads, and I practiced with the team for the whole year, not going to any games, not being able to play, but I just tagged along you might say. Then my second year, I played a little and then third year I started to improve. That's where it all really started.

Enlisting in the Army
One day I left Antioch High School to go home, picked up my girl, and out of the blue I said I'm joining the Army. At 17, I started the paperwork to join the Army. My mother and father didn't like that so I gave them that same spiel, if you don't let me join I'm not going to school. They let me join and I joined the Army in 1944. From there I went to Mississippi and then I joined the 69th Infantry Division in Europe. That's where we got into action. I know they always say that I was in the Battle Of The Bulge. I was in part of it but by the time I got there, the bulge had been stopped and we started moving forward. Going into the Army was good for me because it gave me discipline and really, really kept me in shape. I think for every kid today, if they spent a year when they got out of high school in the service it would be good for them. I was over there for two years. I had enjoyed that.

College Choice

When I got out of the Army, I went back to Antioch and I wanted to play some football. I never thought of playing professional football because I wasn't that big. I organized a semi pro team and that was tough because you had to go around to the grocery store, the liquor store, the bars, and collect money for the uniforms. We did that and we had a pretty good team. My brother, who was a better football player than me, played on the team. One day, we were driving to the Bay Area to play a team in San Francisco. As we were leaving the town, I noticed a red Chevrolet by my mother's house, so we stopped to see who it was. Inside the house, was a line coach from Modesto Junior College and Johnson, the head coach of their football team. They talked to my brother. They really wanted my brother to go to that college, so he committed to Modesto Junior College.

As we said our goodbyes, I shook the line coach's hand and he made a joke. He said, "You look like you're big enough to play. Why don't you come up?" I said I would, and I went there. My brother made first team right away. It took me about three weeks, and then I was recruited by Joe Kuharich and Brad Lynn to go to the university and play football. Then I went up to the University of San Francisco and things worked out well there. Then I ended up being drafted by Baltimore.

The first guy I met and the guy that really trying to get me in The University of San Francisco was a guy by the name of Brad Lynn. I don't know what school he went to. I can remember the day I was working in the bar and I was tending bar and all of a sudden this guy comes in with a suit and a tie. I wondered what he wanted because in that little town, most were working guys, guys going to shifts and coming home. He introduced himself. I said, "What are you doing here?" He says, "We'd like you to come up to USF and try to play football for the University of San Francisco. At that time I was smoking a cigarette. I'll never forget I put that cigarette out because I didn't want him to think I was smoking. I reported to the University of San Francisco on the following Monday and went in to meet Joe Kuharich. At that time I was riding motorcycles and me and my friend drove up to San Francisco and went in to see Joe and he wasn't very impressed with me I guess because motorcycles drivers or riders have a bad reputation. We didn't have a bad reputation but I had a leather jacket on which everybody had to have if you were riding a motorcycle. You bought a leather jacket and on a leather jacket, the more zippers you had the better it was. You felt really cool. I had 17 zippers, one zipper on top of the other. Anyway, the meeting between Joe and I didn't go very well because I wasn't the Notre Dame type I guess that he was used to when he played there and he also coached a little there. Brad Lynn talked him into it. Brad Lynn said, "You don't whether that kid can play football."

We went out and Joe Kuharich was practicing the USF team from about I think January to June. There were full-scale scrimmages on Saturdays. I happened to go on this one particular day. It was on a Saturday and he got me the equipment and I worked out with them. Then when we went to scrimmage. He put me into the scrimmage. I wasn't dumb. I knew that they were going to try to run me, run over me, run inside, outside, or just to see if I had any ability at all. After that practice, Joe Kuharich told Brad Lynn, "You bring him in." That was my lucky day.

University of San Francisco

Most of the schools we were playing, the bigger schools had players play only on offense or defense but little schools like the University of San Francisco, we played both ways. We played Stanford once and Cal but most of opponents were all little Catholic schools like St. Mary's, Santa Clara, and that type.

We had nine guys off that one team that went into the professional level and made NFL teams. Our backfield at that time was Ollie Matson who is in the Hall of Fame. Ed Brown was the quarterback. Scooter Scudero was the other halfback and then there was Bob St. Clair, Dick Stanfel and one of the best football players on that team, I've said this a trillion times, was Burl Toler. He was a black athlete and he was a damn good one. He was probably the best athlete of all of us. Burl was drafted when he was a junior. We had some pretty good studs I guess.

Some of those guys, like myself, and there were a couple other guys I can't think of who were from the service. That's where a lot of the leadership on the team came from because the guys in the service were a little older than everybody else and realized how lucky we were to get another chance to play. We kept working pretty hard.

Burl Toler

I definitely think he'd have been a hall of famer, no question about it. I'd never seen a big guy, particularly on offensive. He had great balance. He had legs about the size of birds. He wasn't built that strong but he was strong and he played offensive tackle and he played middle linebacker and did an excellent job. He was the only one of us that started the all-star game mainly because when you go to those all-star games, a lot of times they got Big Ten coaches, Pac Ten; they got all the big schools and here you are from USF. The coaches always took care of their guys. On the first or second play in the college all-star game, the Rams ran a sweep around his side and he took everything down, stopped the play but the problem is he didn't get up. He tore up his knee terrible. In the locker room after, I was standing there talking to Kuharich and Burl was coming out of the shower and I said, "How do you feel, Burl?" He said, "I don't know. I don't think I'm going to make it." He took a step and his knee just went. He fell completely down. He never did recover from that knee injury. They didn't have much experience in those days on torn ligaments and that type of thing. That's what he had. That ruined his professional career. He would've been in the tops. He was voted captain, one of the greatest individuals you'll ever meet.

Team Turning Down Chance To Play In Bowl Game

The thing that led up to it is our senior year, we were undefeated and we were coming up to the last big game on our schedule and that was against the College of Pacific. They had Eddie LeBaron. He played four or five years as a pro. He was a quarterback and they were undefeated. We played them and we beat them 47 to 0 or something like that. We really gave them a whooping. Then the bowl representatives came down to the locker room after the game. I don't know whether they were looking at us, or College of Pacific because they were awfully good also. The way we manhandled College of Pacific that afternoon I guess they decided to take us. The only problem they had, they wanted us to go and leave Burl Toler and Ollie Matson our black players at home. When they asked me about it, I said, "Hell no. They're a part of this team." I was the captain too. I said, "If they don't go, we don't go, I don't go. I don't care." The whole team took that approach that we would not go without the whole team. What was really great about it is that everybody stood together on it. You didn't hear one guy upset saying we should go, we'll never get another chance, or that type of stuff. Never heard it. When we said we weren't going, that was it. The subject was dropped, and we never regretted that decision. That's they way things go.

It was tough in those days for black athletes I guess. I never knew that because in California it was never really a problem. Professionally, it was tough on them because a lot of places where we went down south to play, the black athletes had to go into a different part of town to stay than where we were. We couldn't stay together. We didn't like that. I didn't like that but there was nothing we could do about it.

Draft

I never thought that I could ever make a professional team because of my size. I was tall, 6'5 or 6'6 but I only weighed 215 to 220. People think during the early years of professional football players weren't big. I'll tell you one thing, they were big. They drafted guys because of their size or whatever. They drafted me and I only weighed like I said, 220. When I reported to camp, I used to, when they had weigh-ins put a 10 pound weight in my jockstrap so I'd weigh 230-235. They'd look at me a little better I guess. Eventually I could throw away the weight. I made it and it wasn't a very good season. We were terrible but I got to play.

We moved to Baltimore and the fans were great to us. I think our team was great to the fans too because we used to out and sign autographs every night practically and do those types of things that other teams would never do.

Baltimore Colts Defense

We had a great defensive team I think mainly because we didn't blitz much. We could rush the passer and we could cover the run and screens and really, really play well. The defense had Art Donovan who of course is in the Hall of Fame. Then there was Big Daddy Lipscomb, who was 6'7" and about 300 pounds. We had a guy named Don Joyce, Ordell Braase, who was an excellent defensive end, and I. We had a great middle linebacker in Bill Pellington. We got everything done that we wanted to do in a game just with those guys. We didn't have to blitz. Some players are lucky if they play with a team who blitz almost 40% of the time. That gives you a lot more chances to get sacks. We played a regular defense and we got a pass rush and everything else. Offensively, you couldn't find a better receiver than Raymond Berry, a better halfback than Lenny Moore, L.G. Dupre was there at fullback, and Johnny Unitas played quarterback. He was as good of a quarterback as ever played the game. Not only that but he was one of the nicest guys that we had on our team. I shouldn't say it like that because every guy on our club was really, really nice. There was no dissension. We all got along good and it was a lot of fun. I didn't make much money but it was a hell of a lot of fun playing in Baltimore.

Weeb Ewbank

When I reported to the Texans, they had a coach named Jimmy Phelan and I don't know if he ever knew what football was. We worked hard but never saw a film. Our meetings were short. It was just a poorly run organization. As a matter of fact, we only stayed in that town five games and they declared bankruptcy. We were a traveling team then. We lived in Hershey and stayed at the Hershey hotels and would go to work every day and then play all of our games.

Art Donovan's Diet
Art Donovan's diet was hamburgers, hotdogs, Jewish bologna or whatever they call it, spaghetti and pizza. That was his diet. I've never seen him eat a salad or vegetables. That was his dinner. Them days, what they did was weigh you in every week. They would weigh you in and give you a weight to be. We'd get a letter during the off-season telling you report to camp ready to hit and do this and do that and by the way, we want you to report at 240. I had a weight of 240. I was 20 pounds under. That's why I went in with the weight in my pants. Arty, he weighed about 286 but during the weigh-in, he would starve himself until he reached a weight that they wanted him at 277. What was tough about that, they'd never tell you what day that they're going to weigh you on. So the guys who had a weight problem, hardly ate until they got weighed in. During the weigh in of course, Arty weighed in at 277 but by the time we got to the game on Sunday, he was probably 285. They pumped themselves up with food or liquids.

Colts Players Chicken Eating Contest
Art Donovan tells all these stories over and over and each time he tells a story, he gets one part from there, over here, one part from over there. He is always funny but he may tell the same story five different ways. Don Joyce was the champ of the eating contests, of eating period. We were talking and we just ate a lot of chicken. We weren't having any contest because I would never challenge him because I could never beat him.

1958 NFL Championship Game
You got to love that game because it made professional football. It made it because that was the only game in NFL history that ended up in a tie. The thing that was funny about that is when the game ended in a tie, we didn't know, the coaches didn't know, and I guess the ownership didn't know what are we going to do. You can't end a championship game in a tie. It has never been done. Then that's when the word came down because Commissioner Bert Bell was at the game and he said, "We'll play and the first score wins." That's what we did. As far as the greatest game ever played, I really didn't think it was. I think there were a lot of mistakes made. I think Frank Gifford fumbled two or three times. We fumbled twice. The ending was exciting.

They proved on the big screen that Frank Gifford was stopped short of a first down. Some scientist that had a way of measuring, taking measurements with a laser light went through the whole play, where Frank went down and where the yard line was before. He was nine inches short. Frank always tells me "You know Gino, I made that first down." I said, "Frank, who's got the ring? We got the ring." That shut him up a little bit.

The newspapers in New York were on strike. I'll tell you this, I think if that game was played in Baltimore, it would've been great for us but it would have never got the coverage that the New York press and radio and television gave it. That's what pushed it over the hill, man. After that, the next season, all the stadiums that were half full or three quarters full the previous season were all full. Tickets were starting to get hard to get. New York made it. The players gave me the game ball.

Bob St. Clair

Playing against him was a strange feeling. At USF we'd hit each other every day and then have a couple beers. We were pretty good friends and then professionally it was completely different. I wouldn't talk to him before a game. He wouldn't talk to me. It was just all business. It wasn't all laughing.

You go to some of these games now, they hate each other. We never did that. It was a serious, serious situation. I played a game without talking. If he held me I'd kick him or something. After the game, we'd see each other. If he had a couple hours to spare we would go and have a couple beers and talk a little bit about the game or whatever and then he'd go back to San Francisco and I'd go back to Baltimore. I would never pat him on the butt and tell him he did a good job.

Pete Rozelle At University of San Francisco

I'd say he was as good as our best player. He couldn't be more polite to us. If we wanted something, we'd ask him, he fought like hell to get it. He was just a hell of a nice guy.

The only thing, this is just kidding, the only thing I really didn't like about what he did; one day they called, Ed Brown, Ollie Matson, and me to Joe Kuharich office. Coach Kuharich wanted to see us. He talked to us and said, "I just want you guys to know that we're going to play Florida this week and it's up in New York."

He said, "We've decided that we're going to push Ollie Matson for All-American." We went to New York. Ollie received the kickoff, and almost ran it all the way down for a touchdown. He had a super game. He really deserved everything that he got. The thing that Pete Roselle gave him was The Catholic All-American Plaque.

About four or five days later, Pete Roselle wants to see me so I go up and see him. He said, "Gino, here." He reaches in the drawer and gives me my plaque. I said, "Oh, thank you," and walked out. When he gave it to Ollie, man they must have had 15 guys from the press. I thought it was funny.

Pro Football Hall of Fame Induction

I felt great. Where I came from, the things that I had personally gone through, and I had not really planned on being inducted. Some guys say I'm going to do this, I'm going to do that, or I'll be this. I never had any goals. It just seemed like where my right foot went, my left foot followed. I just never planned on going to USF, never though I'd play at a professional level, and never thought I'd be in the Hall of Fame. It's just been a great, great, great ride. What can you say? The people, the fans, the players I met really, really made it a goodfeeling.

Three Retirements From Football

The first time I came back I don't know mentally if I was ready to retire. I didn't report to camp because I was going to stay retired. I didn't stay retired for one reason … Don Shula was named the coach. He wanted me to be a player coach so I said okay. I came back for that.

Then the second time I thought the team was ready maybe to go for another championship. I had retired and the guy that was supposed to take over my position was Don Thompson. They weren't happy with what he was doing so they called me back. I felt good that they wanted me but I really didn't want to come back because I didn't want to play the game. I didn't want to be, what's that quarterback from Green Bay that retired 30 times or whatever his name is. I didn't want to play that game. I didn't do it. Then after about three or four exhibition games, Thompson wasn't making them happy. They called me back. Shula had called me back and at that time I was still pretty much in shape. The Colts were so good to me. I couldn't say no, so I did it.

The last time I came back was in 1966, when Shula was going for the championship. Everybody was hurt so he asked me if I would come back. I was still in pretty good shape. I had been out of football for a year and a half. It was halfway through the season when he asked me to come back. So I went back and that was it. That time when I went home I said to Shula, "Don't call me anymore."

Don Shula
We knew that he was going to be a Hall of Fame coach. Everybody knew that because hell, when he got traded to Baltimore, he practically coached the defense. Charlie Winner, Coach Weeb Ewbank's son-in-law, was the defensive coordinator and didn't know a hell of a lot about the professional way of doing things. Shula used to teach him. We knew that Shula would become a very fine coach. As a player, he was not a great player but capable because he was so smart that he knew the patterns of the opposition we were playing and all that. He was a good player but he didn't have the speed like a lot of the guys had, but he did a damn good job and mostly because of his abilities to know the defenses.

Comparing Weeb Ewbank & Don Shula
When Weeb came in, he brought organization and Weeb was a very, very smart offensive planner, game planner, recruiter, and drafter. He knew everything from A to Z about football, which made him successful. He had one major flaw and I told him this. I'm not saying anything behind his back. I told him that he was too nice.

He didn't like Alan Ameche. Nobody knew why he didn't like Alan. Alan knew he didn't like him. For some reason, he didn't like him. He would pick players that he didn't like and it would be obvious.

Eventually players on the team start to loosen up because they knew that, like me for instance, I could probably do what I wanted to do and Weeb wouldn't have said anything to me. If the third stringer made a mistake and John Unitas made that same mistake, he would chew the third string quarterback out but wouldn't say anything to John. That type of stuff just doesn't go. Eventually the football players will take advantage and they did after five or six years. He lost his job coaching with the Colts and if you look at his record when he went to the Jets, after five or six years he lost his job there because those guys did the same thing. They're making money and having a lot of fun. You just have to control them. He just didn't do that.

Don Shula, on the other hand, he would chew you out if you made a mistake. He didn't care who you were. He lasted longer as a head coach. The players might not have liked him. They would tell you this as I would tell you. I didn't like a lot of things he would do, but I had the respect for him. I didn't have quite the same respect for Weeb as a head coach as I did Shula. Shula was tough. The good thing about it, he always forgot. It's like the old saying, if you forgive, you got to forget it. You can't carry it around with you every day. You just got to let it go.

Baltimore Colt Gino Marchetti with Head Coach Don Shula. Photograph copyright Associated Press

Chapter 6

Jack Butler

College:
St. Bonaventure University

Career History:
Pittsburgh Steelers (1951–1959)

2012 Inductee Pro Football Hall of Fame

Pro Football Hall of Fame Induction
To be quite truthful with you, I never even thought about it. That was not one of my priorities. It's an honor and it's a privilege and all that, but I just look at it like I was fortunate enough that I had the talent to play the game and I enjoyed playing the game. I had a lot of fun and it was great. The rest of it was a bonus that's thrown in. I never thought about it and that's all there is to it.

St. Bonaventure
I love the city of Pittsburgh. I was born and raised here and went to St. Bonnies, which is only like a four-hour drive from Pittsburgh. I went there and had a great time. I moved back to the city and I plan on staying here the rest of my life.

I never played high school football. I wasn't that big. At that time, I was probably 5'10" or 5'11" and 160 pounds. Now I went to St. Bonnies, I was only 17, and got to be 6-foot and 200 pounds.

My father was a friend of Mr. Art Rooney, who owned the Pittsburgh Steelers Ball Club. I just finished high school. I was talking to Mr. Rooney and he said, "I know some people down at Virginia Military Institute. That's a good school and you ought to go to VMI."
I went home and my father said, "Well, okay, yes, that's alright." I'm thinking, I don't want to go to a damn military school. I said, "I don't want to go to VMI. It's a military school and I don't want to be a soldier or anything."

I went back and saw old Mr. Rooney and told him I didn't want to go to VMI. He said, "My brother is up at St. Bonnie's, Fr. Silas Rooney, the athletic director at St. Bonnie's." He said, "That's a nice little school. You want to go to St. Bonnie's?" I said, "Yes, that'd be fine. Anything's better than VMI."

So I went to St. Bonnie's. I didn't know where it was. I didn't know anything about it. I went up there and that was all there was to it. It was a nice little school, nice campus and everything, and I thought it was great.

When I went there, I happened to be put in a room with two other guys and they were both scholarship football players. That's all they talked about. They talked me into going out for football. I went over with them. The equipment manager had a tablet with everybody's name on it. I'm behind these guys and we're training. He looks at the list, and said, "You're not on this list. Hit the road."

I left and I happened to bump into Fr. Silas Rooney, the Athletic Director. He told me to go back down the next day and I did. They gave me a uniform and that was the beginning of it all.

I had no position. I never played the game before. They put you in a big long line. The scholarship football players, they knew who they were. Then there were a lot of walk-ons and things, and I was like a walk-on, whatever you want to call it. We're just standing in a long row and he'd come along and ask you what you played. The guy next to me was an offensive lineman and he said, "I'm an offensive lineman." I'm next in line. He said, "What do you play?" I didn't play anything. I told him I was an offensive lineman. They looked at me and said, "You'll never make it." I was probably about 170 pounds or something.

I sat around for weeks and weeks then a guy got hurt and they called for a defensive back. Nobody went in. They called again and again. I finally walked over and the guy said, "I thought you were a lineman." I said, "No, I'm defensive back." He said, "Get in there." That was it.

You just learn. You watch other people. I remember when they passed out the uniforms; I didn't know you put the pads inside the pants and everything. I had to watch them and I did the same thing they did, and put the pads on. I didn't know what they were. It was a brand new experience, everything.

I just watched. Whatever they did, I did. When the guy wanted a defensive back and nobody went out, I went out. I just watched the guy on the other side. Where he'd lined up, I lined across from him. You chase a guy, cover a guy, I knew that much. You just learn by watching and trying to do it.

Draft

I was not drafted. We weren't a big school. I graduated and I went home. I was going to go back to school. I was in graduate school, my last semester, and I was going to go back and get a master's degree.

Then that summer, the general manager of the Pittsburgh Steelers, called me up and asked me to come downtown. I went and met him. He asked me if I wanted to try out for the team and I told him, "Yes, fine. I'll try out." I was in his office and he pulled out a contract. He said, "Sign it." I said, "Well, how much will I make if I make the team?" He told me, $4,000. I told him I'd like to make $5,000. He said, "Sign the contract." In other words, sign the contract or get the heck out. I signed the contract.

I made $4,000 as a 21-years-old. I thought I was making an awful lot of money. That was plenty of money then I guess, for a young guy who still lived at home and had no expenses. Wow. I was in good shape.

Pittsburgh Steelers

They were still playing the single-wing and I didn't even know what it was. I never saw it before in my life. I never even heard of it. When I went to training camp, they were lining up in an unbalanced line. I'm looking at it and I'm trying to figure what is this thing. I'm a receiver. I thought I was a receiver anyway. I'm thinking, there's no way in the world I can make this team. I'm not that big.

I go to Coach John Michelosen who was the head coach at the time and I said, "I'm quitting. I don't understand this single-wing formation. I don't understand it. I don't know how to play it. I'm a wide receiver. I thought I was a receiver. I'm going to go to Detroit and I think I can make the team there because one of my coaches in college is now a coach with the Lions in Detroit."

This coach told me to come to Detroit and he thought I could make their ball club. I told Coach Michelosen, I'm going to quit. I'm going to go to Detroit. He said, "You can't do anything until I cut you. You're under contract. That's it. You can't do a thing until I let you go."

I said, "When will you let me go?" He said, "I don't know. Just go out and do the best you can. I don't know." I figured I'm not going to make it anyway so I figured the hell with it. I will go all out. I'm hitting anything that moves. I'm doing everything. I made the damn team. I never thought I would with the single-wing. Then he changed me over to a defensive back.

It was better than trying to be an end on a single-wing, on the short side. Those other guys were as big as the tackles. They were big people. Like I said, I'm probably 6-foot. I was probably at that time maybe 190 pounds.

It was the second game of the season and we were playing the 49ers at Forbes Field. I'm just sitting on the bench. I thought I'd never get in the game. A guy gets hurt so Coach Michelosen says, "Butler, you get in there." I go in and at that time, I was playing different positions. In fact, I was like the third defensive end. He had Bill McPeak, and I was like the third defensive end and I played a little bit of defensive back during practice and things. He says, "Get in there." I go in and there's Howard Hartley, a defensive back who is hurt. I come back out and I say, "Coach, Howard Hartley's hurt. He's a defensive back." He said, "I know who's hurt. You get in there. That's when I become a defensive back."

They had some receivers who could run like heck, too, but I knew one thing. Nobody got up behind me in that game. I played so deep they couldn't get behind me. They caught a bunch in front of me, but they didn't get behind me. Of course, that was the first time I was playing defensive back. They weren't going to score a touchdown on me. Oh, well. Those were the good old days, I guess.

Intercepting Passes

I think it's all instinct. You know your game. I think that was probably one of my best assets. I thought I had pretty good instincts for the game. I believed I could always catch the ball.

When I was in school, I was a wide receiver at St. Bonnie's and I thought I should've been a wide receiver. I still think I should've been a wide receiver. I could catch the ball; everything turned out well though. Being a defensive back was altogether different.

Ted Marchibroda & Jim Finks

Ted Marchibroda and I went to school together at St. Bonnie's. I was a year or two ahead of him. When I came to Pittsburgh, he came the following year or something. They drafted him and he came down to St. Bonnie's and we were friends all through college and everything.

Jim Finks was a good quarterback. He was smart and so was Ted. I'm not saying he was smarter than Ted or anything, but Jim Finks was smart. He handled people. He had a great personality. He could get people to do things, but he didn't have a real rifle of an arm. His passes were more of a floater. He had good accuracy, but he didn't have a lot of fire on the ball. Ted Marchibroda didn't either. Some guys could really throw the ball in fact some threw too hard. Ted and Jim were good solid quarterbacks.

John Unitas

John Unitas is also from Pittsburgh. He went to the University of Louisville. I remember driving back to camp with Johnny. The coach said we could bring our cars back because we were going to break camp. It was toward the end of training period and getting down to the final cuts. We're driving back and John says, "I think they're going to cut me." I said, "No, I don't think so, John. They never gave you a look yet. They never put you in any games."

He could throw the hell out of the ball. He'd stay after practice and I used to stay out and run past the defender just for the heck of it.

We got back from Pittsburgh, where we had played a preseason game. We were going to break camp that following week. We get back, and as we were walking over, here comes the head coach, Walt Kiesling. He calls John over and cuts him right then and there. He could've done that in Pittsburgh. Now John had to take a bus all the way back to Pittsburgh. He went to Baltimore and turned out to be one of the great quarterbacks in the league.

He never had a shot. He never got in a pre-season game and he didn't even practice. He didn't do much. I used to stay after practice and just run past the defender even though I was a defensive back. He'd throw the ball. He'd stay out there for hours just to get some time in. They didn't do anything with him and then they finally just cut him. Baltimore picked him up and wow that was it.

BLETSO

I went to Buffalo in 1960, as a coach and was on crutches. I couldn't do the job and I go to the owner and tell him, "Hey, you're paying me. I can't do the job. I'm on crutches and the doctors say I'm going to be on these for a long time. How can I coach, you know what I mean? Being on the field. There's no way."

I went back to Pittsburgh and I got into personnel. Detroit, Pittsburgh and Philadelphia formed a group called LESTO and they broke the country into areas. Each team put in two guys. They broke the country into six areas, and you covered all the schools in the area and made reports. The reports went to all the teams. Then they made me in charge of it.

Then I got Miami, Chicago, Baltimore to join and we end up calling it BLETSO. Then we got the Vikings to join. We put a V behind BLETSO for the Vikings and called it BLETSO-V and that's how it all came about.

I never really found a player. I happened to be in charge of it. I would go out with a guy for maybe two or three days. I would visit each one of them in the spring and in the fall. I would see how they went out and how they met the coaches and handled themselves. I would get all the reports back and read all the reports. Then we computerized everything. I never really went out and scouted guys and wrote guys up.

NFL Combine
In fact, we started the NFL Combine. Each team was bringing players in to give them a physical. Pittsburgh would bring guys in from the West Coast, give them a physical, and they'd go home. Then maybe Detroit would bring them in for a physical. They were doing all that.

I'm thinking that's kind of stupid. Why don't we bring the players in one place and get all the teams to join it rather than the teams doing that stuff individually. We would have it at Indianapolis and use their dome out there and each team would come with their own doctors and examine everyone they want to examine and work them out. We did and everything went great. It had to be about 1963 or 1964 when we started it.

Wonderlic Tests
We gave them. I didn't like them personally. That doesn't mean a player can't play football. We had to do it, but I don't know about it.

Scouting
A lot of it's natural; instinct and things. You play the game and you have to like to play the game and want to play the game. Those intrinsic things are important. Some guys have a lot of talent and you look at them, you work them out, you bring them to Indianapolis, they're in their shorts and they're built great, and they could run like hell, they could do everything, but they can't play football very well. They look great and everything. They look good, but they're not football players though.

Some guy looks the opposite and you say, "Holy man, the guy's a good football player. He may have stumpy legs and he may be a little overweight, but you think, 'Well, man, he can't be …'" Then you find out he's a better football player than those other guys.

Photograph copyright Associated Press

Chapter 7

Hugh McElhenny

> College:
> Washington
>
> Career History:
> San Francisco 49ers (1952-1960)
> Minnesota Vikings (1961-1962)
> New York Giants (1963)
> Detroit Lions (1964)
>
> 1970 Inductee Pro Football Hall of Fame

College Choice

I was at USC on an extension. I lasted two months. My job was to water the quad where the Trojan horse is along with some flowers. I had to water that three times a day. Well, I did that for two months, but I never got my $65 and that's when I quit and I went to Compton J.C.

Washington paid me the most money. I can't really remember how much. My wife would. We had just got married on March 19, 1949. Her father wouldn't okay the marriage because I didn't have a job. I had just got out of Compton Junior College after having an outstanding year. The University of Washington propositioned me to go up to school. They made it possible for me to provide for my wife and get a college education. So, I went to the University of Washington.

I don't know how I got the money, but I got a check that was never signed by the same person each month. When I turned 21, I worked at the racetrack as a ticket taker and then my last two summers, I worked for Rainier Brewery. I was a public relations goodwill person. My job was to entice grocery stores, bars and restaurants to use Rainier Beer.
One of the first assignments they gave me was on 1st Avenue and Seattle; I guess a low-income type area. So I'd go into the bar and introduce myself and say can I buy you a beer. I would offer everybody a beer. They gave me $100 to buy the beers and to influence the people to buy Rainier Beer. I made ten stops along there. I never had a beer myself, but when I was through, I came back to the office and gave them $100 back since no one made me pay for them.

I ended up keeping the $100. After I gave it back to them, they gave the money back to me. It kind of went like that.

Washington

Well, they had a new coach, Howie Odell. It was just like going to any other school or any other football program. They treated me very well. The practices were very difficult. It seemed like our practices were always on muddy fields, very seldom on a dry field. But it's amazing. I don't remember really playing a rainy game in the three years I played at the University of

Washington. The only rainy days I had on a football field were at the University of California and Southern California.

Don Heinrich

Don Heinrich was kind of a quiet type of guy, a very confident individual. He was, for a young age, very intelligent about the game of football. He knew how to handle it. He had separated his shoulder my senior year. So he didn't play. He was an All American 1950 and '52. He had a separated shoulder in '51. He was just a natural. He was a good thinker, never got frazzled. He was just a solid quarterback. He ended up coaching in the pro ranks for some 20, 22, 25 years.

Draft

I could have gone into pro football back in 1949 after I finished one year at Compton J.C. The Los Angeles Rams, Hampton Pool didn't talk to me. He called my dad and wanted to meet my father. So Hampton came to the house and I was there. He offered me a contract at that time. I was still a minor so that's why he was talking to my father. He offered me, at that time, $10,000 to play for the Rams.

Of course my dad was very flattered and all that, but he turned Hampton Poole down. He said I was too young and would go to school. He wouldn't let me play.

The Rams were the team I always wanted to play for. In high school I was a ticket taker at the Los Angeles Coliseum for the Rams, UCLA, USC games, so I was really attached to the Rams. I was disappointed.

I was the eighth or ninth pick in the first round by the 49ers. I was hoping the Rams would choose me as their first choice, but they ended up getting the bonus choice and they took Bill Wade, a quarterback out of Vanderbilt.

It's hard to remember how it all came down. I played in the Hula Bowl. That's when they picked 15 outstanding college players in the United States and played against a few of the pros. I had an outstanding game and Frankie Albert was the quarterback for the Hawaiian team.

I guess Frankie had influence. He talked the 49ers into drafting me and that's how I got drafted by the 49ers, the influence that Frankie Albert had.

Rookie Year

I just came back from the College All Star Game in Chicago. Bob Toneff, who was the 49ers second draft choice, and I came back. We played the game on Friday night. Saturday we came back to San Francisco. The 49ers were playing the Cardinals at Candlestick Park. They gave us a uniform, suited us up, and we just kind of watched the game. It was sometime during the 4th quarter and Frankie Albert called a timeout. He came over to Buck Shaw and said put me in. I remember standing there and Buck says, he doesn't know the plays. He said, "That's okay, I have a play for him."

So I go into the game and just like old sandlot football, Frankie got down on his knees in the huddle and he drew what every player should do. It happened to be a 49 pitch and I went 38 or 40 yards for a touchdown.

The Chicago Bears game my rookie year I scored five touchdowns and two or three were called back. I broke the cardinal rule; you don't handle a punt within your own 10-yard line. You take the chances of it going in the end zone for a touchdown. I just caught it and it happened to work out and I went the distance for six points.

Nickname "The King"
Back in Chicago, after the game, everybody huddles around and the coach has a few words to say and so forth. Frankie Albert has the game ball and he says, "Hugh, we chose you as player of the game. Joe Perry you're still The Jet; Hugh, you're now The King, King Of the Halfbacks." And that's how he nicknamed me.

My Speed
In high school I held a world's record, 14 seconds flat in the high hurdles. I think I had the world's record in low hurdles; 220-yard lows at 21.6. I never ran the 100. I anchored a relay, high hurdles, low hurdles and the broad jump.

The University of Washington thought that I would participate in track, but I was never a really smart guy. I had all I could handle getting through school and playing football. If I ran track and football, I probably wouldn't have lasted three years at the University of Washington.

Pay In College
The three years I was in school, with my wife and I working we made more than $7,000 a year. It was great. The conference was checking on me every year. One time the conference came and asked where I got my car.

At Los Angeles Coliseum Relays in high school during my senior year I won the high hurdles, low hurdles, broad jump and our team took 4th in the relay. It was the last meet of the year and my mom and dad were waiting for me to come out of the coliseum. My mom, of course, gives me a big hug and a kiss and my dad, he just looks at me and smiled. He went to shake my hand and in his hand were the keys to my mom's car. It was a 1948 Dodge.

Supposedly he gave me the Dodge, but the thing is, they never took it out of my mother's name and when I drove up to Seattle to enter school, I was getting parking tickets and I never thought much about them. Anyway, I never paid for a parking ticket. My mom was getting the bill. They paid my parking tickets for two years.

Million Dollar Backfield
I certainly was just a player. John Henry Johnson, he was up in Canada. He was playing somewhere up in Canada in 1952. They brought him down in 1953. It was Y. A. Tittle, Joe Perry, John Henry Johnson and myself. John Henry only played with us for two years before they traded him away. So the Million Dollar Backfield was 1953 to 1954.

Of course over the years, we all became Hall of Famers. But the story was, as I understand it, the Million Dollar Backfield was named because the 49ers were for sale in 1952. With Y.A., Joe, John Henry and myself, we started filling the stands. So therefore, Tony Morabito decided not to sell and he kept the club. The Million Dollar Backfield meant us selling tickets and so forth. That's kind of how it came about.

Reason For Not Winning A Championship

I hate to say it because there aren't many of them alive anymore, but we just never had a good defense. We could score on everybody, but we had trouble-keeping people from scoring on us. Offensively, Jesus, for 12 games, I never carried the ball more than 15 times in a ball game as a 49ner.

Today, all these records that are being broke, geez, they're carrying the ball 20, 25 times a game. The percentages are the more you carry the ball the more opportunity you're going to have to make yards. The biggest problem, I think, was Y.A. Tittle. How does he share it? How does he share Joe Perry carrying the ball, me carrying the ball, and John Henry Johnson carrying the ball? That must have been a tough job for Y.A. I don't remember us ever talking about it, but if I were a quarterback, I would be thinking that. Who's productive today? It's tough for a quarterback to make decisions with three guys like us in the backfield.

Alley Oop Pass

That was an accident. Y.A. will tell you this too. The first Alley Oop was only maybe good for 20 yards for a touchdown. The ball slipped out of Y.A.'s hand and went high in the air and oop, R.C. Owens out jumped Jack Christiansen and Yale Lary, and caught the ball. That's how it came about. It was a fluke ball that went up in the air and R.C. Owens out jumped the other two players. So they went and then started practicing that during the week, because R.C. Owens could jump high and had good hands.

Frank Gifford

Frank Gifford and I became very, very, very good friends. Frank and Maxine were married. Peggy and I rented an apartment in the same complex. Peggy and I just had a baby, named Karen and two weeks later, Maxine had Jeff. We were in the same complex and so we became very close. We'd get together for lunch and dinner and potluck and that sort of thing for three or four months.

I was coming to play in the College All Star Game and Frank and I roomed together. Then we played in the East-West Shrine Game, we roomed together there. Then when I went back to New York to play for the Giants, he took me in. I roomed with him during training camp with the Giants. We were friends, he'd come to our house for dinner; we'd go to his house for dinner.

Then, of course, when I left New York, we all went different ways and we more or less lost contact. The only time we'd really seen each other was going back for the Enshrinement at the Hall of Fame. He doesn't make it every year and I certainly don't either. But I consider him a great friend and he's always been very kind to me. He always spoke very well on my behalf. He's just a great guy.

I knew when I was rooming with him with the Giants; he would be practicing and doing things for his radio show. He had a talk radio show at that time. Let's see, that's back in 1963. I consider him a great friend.

1963 NFL Championship Game

That was really disappointing. I can't remember too much. I took the second half kickoff and got to midfield and I made a move and I slipped on the ice. The defensive back was Roosevelt Taylor and he nailed me. But, he was the last guy. If I had gotten by him, it would have been six points. That probably would have been the difference in the game. We lost 14 to 10 or something like that.

1961 Trade to Vikings

As a matter of fact, I was very unhappy. I can't really say what I think of Red Hickey. He was the worst coach I was ever around. Today, they could sue him for harassment. The way he treated some players, it was just terrible. The way he talked to them and so forth. I was supposedly considered one of his favorites, but we didn't get along. So I was very happy to be traded. I thought maybe I still had a couple good years in me, if I didn't get hurt. But to sell me for $15,000 that was a real insult to me. Red Hickey did that.

Norm Van Brocklin

He was a tough coach; I liked Dutch. He was tough on everybody, but he was really fair. If he didn't like something you did, like forgot your helmet, he'd come by and flick you in the head with his fingers. I really learned from Dutch in our meetings, like scouting for how we were going to play the team coming up, and so forth. I learned a heck of a lot from him and I understood more. I think for the first time I really understood what my position was supposed to be on a football field.

It seemed like before it was memorize the number, go to the direction and let your instincts take you wherever you want to go. I learned from Dutch that there were more things I could do to better myself and help the team.

Howard Cosell

I'm not saying this to offend anybody, but when I went into the Pro Football Hall of Fame, Howard Cosell came up and shook my hand. He was at Compton J.C. a couple years before I was, as a Public Information Director. He put his arm around me and whispered in my ear, "You are now the last of the Great White Hope." What does that tell you?

He was terrific. I think he had a lot of respect for me. That's the way I felt, the way he treated me, the way he talked to me, and the way I'd be invited to things. He chose me to toss the coin at Super Bowl XIX in San Francisco. Of course, I didn't get to toss the coin. I had to tell President Reagan to please toss the coin.

We didn't talk much about anything when I went to Seattle. It was hard to try to bring pro football to the city of Seattle. Then he couldn't be close to me. We'd go to various meetings and he'd look at me, but he wouldn't wave or say anything. He couldn't have any direct contact with me.

Fran Tarkenton

It was obvious he was a scrambler. He was quick on his feet. He wasn't great with straight-ahead speed, but he was a good scrambler. Dutchman would have him work out with weights and throwing, developing his arm so he could throw the deep ball. He was accurate with the short ball, but you have to throw the ball further than 30 yards. I remember that. Certainly Fran went on and learned how to throw a ball more than 30 yards. He was great.

Pro Football Hall of Fame Induction

When I look back at my induction, and now we're celebrating the 50th anniversary of the Pro Football Hall of Fame, I can't believe it. Forty-three years ago when I went into the Hall, there were about 50 or 60 Hall of Famers at that time. God, we stayed in a motel. My mom and dad were there, my wife and my daughters. It seemed like we were scattered all over the place.

I remember it being fun because you had time to greet and see the other players that were in the Hall of Fame and that were going into the Hall of Fame. The day I went back for my 40th anniversary, I hardly knew anybody. They've all mostly passed away. There were maybe four or five that I would see that I remembered and played against, but when I went in the Hall of Fame, it was very simple. It was very close and very caring.

Today, it's a big show. It's a big deal in Canton and I'll tell you, the City of Canton, they do a fabulous job of handling all of us celebrities. I wish I could go back there and experience the first year I went in.

Secondly, one thing I disapprove of today is, all these speeches. Everybody thanks their brother's cousins, Uncle Jack and Bill and Bob, and they go on and on and on. It's obvious that anybody who goes into the Hall of Fame cannot properly recognize all the people that contributed to their success. I get blown away when all these guys get up there and spend a half hour talking about a bunch of B.S. That's the only thing that frustrates me now. When we went in, we thanked our parents.

Photograph copyright Associated Press

Chapter 8

Don Shula

College:
John Carroll

Career History:
As Player:
Cleveland Browns (1951–1952)
Baltimore Colts (1953–1956)
Washington Redskins (1957)

As Coach:
Detroit Lions (1960–1962)
(Defensive Coordinator)
Baltimore Colts (1963–1969)
(Head Coach)
Miami Dolphins (1970–1995)
(Head Coach)

1997 Inductee Pro Football Hall of Fame

College Choice
When I got out of high school, all of the veterans were getting back from the service. They were getting all of the scholarships and I couldn't afford to go. I decided to stay out and work a year then go to college. I bumped into my old high school coach and he said, "Don't do that. You might not ever go." He said, "I know this coach at John Carroll who is looking for talent. I'll recommend you." He did and that's how I got to John Carroll.

I knew that Carl Taseff went to Cleveland East High School. When we were freshmen together at John Carroll, we got to be roommates and then became friends, lifetime friends. Carl was a great guy, a great football player.

NFL Draft
Actually, playing at John Carroll was right in the shadow of the Cleveland Browns. My senior year, we played Syracuse University in Cleveland Stadium. Paul Brown and his whole staff were there scouting Syracuse. We ended up winning the game. After that, Carl Taseff and I were drafted by the Browns.

Being selected was the furthest thing from our minds. As it turned out, I'm in this game when we beat Syracuse and we both had big days. That's the game that impressed Paul Brown and his coaching staff.

Paul Brown
Paul Brown was just a great coach, a great teacher. He just covered every possibility. There wasn't anything that he didn't prepare you for.

15 Player Trade
I was going to grad school in the off-season. I had some time between classes. I picked up the newspaper, opened the sports page, and my picture was on it. What's my picture doing in the paper? I looked and it said a trade, 10 for five, with the Colts. That's how I found out about it.

Weeb Ewbank
Weeb Ewbank was like a Paul Brown disciple. He used pretty much the same playbook and covered all the details. He was a great football coach.

Decision to Start Coaching
I played for seven years. When it became apparent that I was coming to the end of my career, I started to look at the possibility of getting into coaching. I was recommended to the new head coach at the University of Virginia, Dick Voris. He hired me over the phone.

Blanton Collier
Blanton Collier was just a genius of a football coach. I doubt if he ever played the game. He just was the guy that studied the game and was a great teacher, a lot like Paul Brown.

Becoming Colts Head Coach
Gino Marchetti was their captain and a great football player, a Hall of Famer. Carroll Rosenbloom loved him. Rosenbloom said to Marchetti that he was going to make a coaching change and asked, "Whom should I hire?" Marchetti said, "Why don't you look into this young guy, Don Shula?" Rosenbloom said, "You mean the guy who played here who wasn't very good? Then he said, "Yeah, but he's a good coach."

I was in Detroit with the Lions at that time. Rosenbloom called and said, "You've been recommended. I think you're ready for the job." I said, "The only way that you'll find out is if you hire me." He liked that answer and hired me.

The toughest thing was coaching the guys who I played with and the guys I played against. Now, all of a sudden, I'm up there and I'm their head coach. A lot of them were much better players than I ever was when I was a player. I had to convince them every meeting, every practice that this was the right thing to do and I knew what I was doing. Eventually, they bought into it.

Johnny Unitas
Johnny Unitas was unbelievable. The guy was tough mentally and tough physically. He could make the big plays in the big games. The guys were proven players. They were guys that were winners. You put them out there and they know how to win.

Leaving the Baltimore Colts for the Miami Dolphins
It was tough to do it. I love Baltimore. I love the fans and a lot of the things that were connected to Baltimore and the Colts. Miami was a great opportunity, a relatively new franchise with some very good players.

Achievements
I know the perfect season when we won all the games, 17 of them. It was a year to remember. I had a lot of great games to remember, but nobody had ever won 17 before.

There are a lot of things that I'm very proud of. I'm proud of the games I won as a coach, the perfect season, and back-to-back Super Bowls.

1985 Game vs. Bears vs. Dolphins
That's the best half of football I've ever been associated with. We had 33 points at halftime against a great Bear defense. It ended up we won the game handily. That ended up being the only game that the Bears lost that year. They ended up winning the Super Bowl.

Dan Marino had a great quick release and he did what he wanted to do with the ball. He had great decision-making skills. We put him in situations where their safeties had to cover the slot receiver who at the time was a great slot receiver.

Johnny Unitas, Earl Morrall, Bob Griese, & Dan Marino
They had great talent. They were hard workers, had knowledge of the game, and were great competitors. You have to have all those things going for you when you accomplish everything that they did.

Earl Morrall
You never expect somebody to step in and do what Earl Morrall did. After Bob Griese went down, he led us to the championship game. Then, Griese was healthy again. I had to make a tough decision as to when I could put Griese back in, because Earl had been playing so well. Earl was a temporary quarterback and Griese was a quarterback here and now, and also in the future.

Coaching Key
When you have an arm like Marino, you want to put him in a position where he can use his great ability. Every defensive coach in the league would have congratulated me if I had Marino hand the ball off and not use his great arm. Coaching is all about analyzing your talent and putting them in a position where they can best use their talent.

David Woodley
We're in the Super Bowl with David Woodley. He was an athlete playing quarterback and Dan Marino was a quarterback playing quarterback. We got the most out of Woodley. Thinking back, he was a great competitor and that helped us win a lot of games.

Preparation For The Super Bowl
You use all of your experience and you try to use that and understand the pressures, the importance of the game, and how hard you worked to get there. You want to make sure that, when you get there, that you are ready to play the best game of your season.

Pro Football Hall of Fame Induction
That's just a great, great feeling to be recognized for your career and to go in there with so many people that have meant so much for the game, the hall of famers, and the people that were going in with me in that class. It's just a very, very special time in my life.

Greatest Player
You'd have to, I guess, have Jim Brown up there as one of the greatest players, if not the greatest player, then Otto Graham. I have so much respect for Otto. When he was a quarterback for the Browns, all he ever did was win championships. I've been around a lot of great players. My players here in Miami, like Dan Marino and the way that he threw the football, and all the excitement he brought to the game.

Baltimore Colts Head Coach Don Shula with Johnny Unitas. Photograph copyright Associated Press

Chapter 9

Doug Atkins

College:
Tennessee

Career History:
Cleveland Browns (1953-1954)
Chicago Bears (1955-1966) New
Orleans Saints (1967-1969)

1982 Inductee Pro Football Hall of Fame

Mike Ditka & The 1963 Season
It was in 1963 when he ran for that touchdown. If he hadn't scored that touchdown, we wouldn't have been in the championship. During the 1963 season, we had the last game, and we were tied with Detroit. He caught a touchdown. We kicked the field goal. We won. That put us in the playoffs.

Tennessee
I gave up basketball my sophomore year at Tennessee when I couldn't play both basketball and football. It was all football after that. It was my choice too.

Football was easier to play than basketball. In basketball you're traveling all over the place. Football is not quite as long and you're not on the field as long. You don't play as many games. You can just play those and get them out of the way.

Robert Neyland
Robert Neyland was one fine coach. He was a service man but he was a good football coach. That's why you can win with good people. That was a long time ago, back in the '50s.

Paul Brown
Paul Brown didn't like me. He sent me to Chicago. That was fine with me. I had some problem and I was out for a while. He just replaced me with some other guy. First of all, I had some kind of reaction. I had a sore throat and they give me something I had a reaction to. I lost about 20 pounds real quick there and I had a bad knee anyway for a little bit. When I lost all that weight during my second year, I finally played a game and I got benched. He put a guy named Massey in there, Carlton Massey. The second year, I don't know how many games I played before I got benched. I went down to probably about 230 pounds or something. It was my stomach or something. It was probably the best thing. The first year I couldn't do anything wrong and the second I couldn't do anything right.

Trade to Bears
I knew it was coming that year before it happened. He put somebody in there and took my place. It didn't make any difference. You got to go where you got to go.

Difference Between Paul Brown & George Halas
It was a little different. I was with Paul Brown with the Cleveland Browns first and he was just a completely different coach than George Halas. George Halas had been around so long. He started out in the old days. I got there and things were a lot different. Our drills in Cleveland were quick and to the point. We got Mondays and Tuesdays off which I liked with the Cleveland Browns. Unless you had an injury, then you had to show up. Our practices were not over an hour and 45 minutes on Wednesday and then they'd taper it down. We did things fast and quick and when the time was up, we'd be off the field.

With George Halas it'd be one more play, one more play. We'd probably be out there three hours by the time we got done because he didn't have anywhere else to go except the office. It was enjoyable for him to be out there. They had a bunch of old coaches. We never picked up any new coaches, any new blood until we got George Allen. It was the same old people.

We had weigh-ins. That was probably the toughest part of the practice. He set your weight, what he thought you were supposed to be. We'd line up like cattle and he'd put us on the big scale and weigh us every day instead of one day a week. We'd go to the heat baths and the whirlpools and everything and sweat it off. Then right after he'd weigh us, we'd make our weight and then we'd put the weight back on. We had a small dressing area downstairs. Then you went upstairs to get taped and everything was in a little room up there.

Coke At Halftime
During halftime of the games, we would always get a Coke. Dave Whitsell was sitting on a corner and someone came by with a Coke in his hand. Whitsell grabbed that Coke. He wouldn't turn it loose. They were fighting over that Coke, and finally Whitsell jerked it out of his hand and took a big chug of it and he spit it out. Guess what the problem was? That Coke had bourbon in it. He was carrying it to George Halas. That was his drink during halftime. That was the best interception he ever made.

George Allen
When we got George Allen, it helped us a lot. He did things a little different. He put us in different positions and it changed a whole lot of things. We got to change at times but you just can't do things one way one week, and do something different the next week. We got in this basic defense and things we could do off of that. When we had the other coach there, he had all this stuff. It would take all day to write it down. He had you going four places in one play. It's hard to do. George Allen was a fine coach.

Detective Agency
George Halas had the Burns Detective Agency following us. They would follow us after we left practice. They followed us as we went home. If Halas thought we were going somewhere else, he'd have us follow there. We found out later on that we were being followed.

He had a lot of tricks I'll tell you. George Halas had to know what everybody thought about the team. The detectives would follow us to a beer joint or most of the time we went to a bar at a hotel. They'd have that detective come in and ask us questions. This went on for a while and we finally found out.

One time I thought I was talking to the insurance man. He asked what do you think about Halas and I told him some things that weren't too nice. I answered all of his questions. Halas called me and told me what I said. He said "I want you to drive to my office after practice." He knew I wouldn't go downtown to his office. I said, "I'm not about to drive downtown after practice and talk to you."

I said, "You live at the Edgewater Beach Hotel right up from me how about just stopping by and seeing me?" He did. He stopped by, came in the door, and took his hat off. I was sitting there in a t-shirt. He looked at me and he said, "That's not your body. God gave that to you." I said, "Yeah it's a businessman like you to use, abuse, and trade, and do anything you want." He said, "If you don't get out and drink anymore, I'll give you until the end of the season."

Jim Parker
Jim Parker from Baltimore was a real tough player. We had a pretty good time out theretogether. The first year I beat him pretty bad, and then he got a little smarter. He weighed about 290. He had a good team with him in Baltimore with Johnny Unitas, and a good blocking line. You had to go through him. There wasn't anywhere else to go. The other linemen were doing their job too. We had tough times with him.

Trade to New Orleans
It got a little tiresome in Chicago. I had three good years in New Orleans. I was hurt the second year. I got a little injured, but I enjoyed playing there. I had a good coach and it was different. We had a pretty good team. We played pretty good, but we didn't have enough players to do that good in New Orleans. We had some pretty good players, but we just weren't quite good enough.

Mike Ditka's Fight in Practice
The regular defense was on the sidelines. Our substitutes were in there working against the offense. The defense had a guy named Moon Mullen. He was a little defensive halfback. We noticed that there was a little scuffle between Moon and Ditka and we were cheering for Moon Mullen to get him "Get him Moon!"

They had a little encounter there and I think Moon just swung at him or hit at him or something, and then Mike Ditka swung at Moon. Moon dodged it and Ditka fell down, and it looked like Moon punched him. His hands were going when he swung. The team gave it to Ditka. Ditka jumped up and said a little off colored word and walked off. Moon Mullen weighed 180 pounds and big old Ditka weighed about 220. That was something.

Pro Football Hall of Fame Induction
It was nice. I had to wait a long time but it didn't make any difference. I don't know why it took so long. People got different ideas. Sometimes they like some people better than others. I don't

know. Like, why did Ditka have to wait so long for anything? He should've got in right away. He was a good football coach too. We needed him when Halas was there with his group.

George Halas & Finances
Back in those days when George Halas started, I didn't realize how tough he had it until I started reading a few books. When I read what they had to do back in the old days it was rough. He almost lost the club a few times. Halas and his whole family had to work. It was really a tough thing to do. He had about three brothers, and they all lived in the same place. He worked all the time and borrowed money.

One of the stories I read, was how one day Halas was working and after work he was going to play a baseball game somewhere in Chicago. Where he had to go, he had to take a boat with his team. That day he wasn't on time for the boat. The boat took off without him and it sank. Everyone on the boat died. His life was saved. They were a working group of people. I understood him after I read some of the books.

Retired Number
In New Orleans, they retired my number. But, when they sold the team, the new owner gave my retired number to one of his players. That's the way that some men do business. They're tricky.

Chicago Bear Doug Atkins tries to recover a fumble by Green Bay Packer Jim Taylor.
Photograph copyright Associated Press

Chapter 10

Mike McCormack

College:
Kansas

Career History:
New York Yanks (1951)
Dallas Texans (1952)
Cleveland Browns (1954-1962)

As Coach:
Washington Redskins (1965-1972) (Assistant coach)
Philadelphia Eagles (1973-1975) (Head coach)
Cincinnati Bengals (1976-1979) (Assistant coach)
Baltimore Colts (1980-1981) (Head coach)
Seattle Seahawks (1982) (Head coach)
Carolina Panthers (1993-1997) (President and GM)

1984 Inductee Pro Football Hall of Fame

College Choice
Don Faurat came down and offered me a scholarship to Missouri, but so did George Sauer from Kansas. The proximity of Lawrence to Kansas City is about forty miles, and it's about 150 to Missouri.

Oklahoma did not come after me, to tell you the truth. I had several offers, but none from Missouri or Kansas, until it was in the paper that Bear Bryant invited me down to Kentucky and was going to offer me a scholarship. Then all of a sudden Missouri and Kansas got interested. I went to a Christian Brothers school and was offered a scholarship to St. Mary's in Moraga. Thank God I didn't take that because they dropped football the next year. Things worked out pretty well going to Kansas.

Kansas
I played in '48, '49, and '50. 1947. My freshman year was 1947, but freshman were not eligible. We couldn't even play freshman ball. We were The Big 6 in '47, The Big 7 in '48, and The Big 8 in '50. We grew, but at the same time, that whole time, we were called Oklahoma and the seven doors. We finished second to Oklahoma once and third to Oklahoma twice.

NFL Draft

The draft was not anywhere as big as it is now. The Kansas City Star had a sports editor who was definitely anti professional. He thought the professionals were the big fat guys with the big fat cigars in the back room. When the draft came, there was a small piece added in a box on the sports page that said area boys drafted. John Kadlec, Ed Stephens, and I were the only ones drafted from Missouri. I really didn't know anything about being drafted. About six weeks later, one of the assistant coaches came to see me while I was coaching at Kansas. He wanted to sign me then. Pro football was not what it is today.

The New York Yanks drafted me, and then I was inducted into the service. I went into the Korean conflict. While I was gone, the New York franchise moved to Dallas, but I never played in Dallas. Then Dallas folded. They became a ward of the league and then they became the Baltimore Colts in '53. I was traded from Baltimore to Cleveland in '53. While I was in the service, I heard the Cleveland—Detroit game on Armed Forces Radio. It was the game where Detroit came from behind and beat Cleveland. I had just been notified that I was Cleveland's property at that time, so I took interest in that game. Then a year later I was out of the service and joined the Browns and we won a world title.

15 Player Trade

Don Shula and I still laugh about how he went from Cleveland to Baltimore. Five Colts were traded; it was Tom Catlin, Don Colo, Herschell Forester, John Petitbon, and I. We all played for the Browns. Only three of the ten players that went from Cleveland to Baltimore played for Baltimore. They were Bert Rechichar, Don Shula, and Art Spinney.

Art Donovan

Art Donovan and I were teammates. In fact, three of us were single, Art, Don Colo, and me. They called us the big three and we kind of hung around together. Art Donovan, of course, he was the son of a famous fight referee. We would go to his folk's home and have dinner.

Paul Brown, Vince Lombardi, & George Allen

I've been associated with three, in my mind, three great coaches: Paul Brown, Vince Lombardi, and George Allen. All three of them were entirely different. Paul was a teacher, he taught us everything every year for the nine years I was in training camp there. We would start off with our stance, how to drive off the stance, and the steps to take. In my mind, he was a great teacher. Vince Lombardi was a driver. He made you think. He worked you so hard he made you think you were better than the other team. And then of course, George Allen relied on experienced veterans, the old timers. He wasn't much of a teacher. All three of those coaches were successful.

Otto Graham

Otto Graham came back in '55. He had made Paul a promise that if they needed him he would come back one more year. So in training camp, we were 0 and 6 and Otto joined us. We won the title in '55 as we did in '54. He was a great athlete. He was also quite the tennis player and golfer, almost a scratch golfer. Plus, he could throw the ball extremely well and he was a great teammate.

Switch from Defensive Line to Offensive Line
Well, you have to go back almost to New York. Kate Smith and Dan Topping owned the New York Yanks before they gave it up. So during that season we wound up starting with 32 players and we wound up with 23 because they hadn't made any money for five years. They sold the club to the Miller brothers, but the Millers weren't going to add any more players than necessary. I wound up playing seven games, as a linebacker and an offensive tackle. That's how many players were cut. I had played both ways in college. When I joined the Brown's, Bill Willis, another Hall of Famer, retired and Paul asked me to play the middle line. That amounted to middle linebacker, nose tackle but I would drop out a lot of times in pass coverage. I enjoyed playing defense. In fact, I played defense on goal line situations for quite a few years.

Paul Brown
Paul was one who was not very complimentary. You did your job and he respected you for that, but he never gave much praise. We were playing the Philadelphia Eagles in '54, ahead six to nothing and late in the game they got the ball on the three-yard line. The only time that Paul singled me out, I made a tackle for a one-yard loss on first down. I made a tackle for a one-yard loss on second down. Third down came up and the offense was nervous and jumped offside. So it was fourth and seven and then I knocked down a pass. It was one where I dropped out as a linebacker, and knocked down a pass in the end zone and we won the game six to nothing. Paul always gave me credit for winning the game, and having him give me credit in front of the whole team, was the highlight of my career with Cleveland. Stealing the ball from Bobby Layne was good, but that was just one play and I didn't get many accolades from Paul.

Bobby was a notorious rounder. You can go any place and when you start talking about Bobby Lane, they're going to have stories about him.

Radio Helmet
Paul Brown had the first radio helmet and I don't know whether it was banned. He rotated guards and he tried to use a radio helmet. We tried it in the Rubber Bowl in Akron, Ohio. George Ratterman was the quarterback at that time, and all of a sudden he gets a perplexed look on his face and he looks over at Brown and calls time out. Then he goes over and tells Paul, "Paul, I'm getting directions for cabs to go pick up somebody. They've got the wrong channels." That ended the radio helmet at that time. That was in 1956.

Jim Brown
Jim Brown reported to training camp. He was 6'3" and 230 pounds. He had a 32-inch waist, and thighs about 21 inches in circumference. What a physical specimen, he was just a great athlete and could run fast and strong. It didn't take long before everyone was impressed with Jim Brown.

Bobby Mitchell
When Bobby Mitchell was traded to Washington, they put him at the right position as a flanker. He was a heck of a running back and a great compliment to Jim Brown. Jim was a quality running back for the Browns at that time. Bob was a fine compliment to him.

Len Dawson

The Browns were going to draft Lenny Dawson, but instead, they drafted Jimmy Brown. Later on when the Steelers cut Lenny, the Browns picked him up and signed him. Then Paul cut him, but I don't know why because Lenny was a fine player.

Chuck Noll

Chuck Noll was another one who played offense. He played right guard when I played right tackle and then he went on to be a linebacker later on in his career. We used to call Chuck, Newton because he was smart. Anything he wanted to talk about, he spoke about with authority.

Lou Groza

Lou is something else. We had quite a few Hall of Famers, but Lou was my mentor. He played left tackle and he was just the grand old man of the Browns. He just took care of every young guy.

Gino Marchetti

Gino Marchetti was my nemesis. I go back to the time I was singled out earlier in that Philadelphia game. We played the Colts in Cleveland, and after the game Gino had a field day. He really played well. Paul Brown looked at me and said, "Michael, I hope your parents didn't see the game you played the other day; they would really be embarrassed." A few years later we played the Colts and I had a good day against him. Of course, we had Jimmy Brown by that time, and we featured the running game as the pass. Gino was the best pass rusher I think I have ever seen.

Decision to Retire

I went to training camp and there was no maternity leave for players. So I was in training camp when my wife had our first girl. We had two boys and another girl. They were all born in the summer, so I told her when she got pregnant again, I wouldn't leave. I just decided it was time.

Joining Seattle Seahawks Front Office

Well, yes it was quite an experience and I credit the Nordstrom's for that because I felt sure I could do the football end of it but they made me President and General Manager. I was worried about all the business details and things like that, but they said that based on their store experience they wanted store managers rather than one of their merchandisers to run their stores. They wanted a football guy to run their football team. I was pleased they had that much confidence in me, and things just went well. They were fortunate to hire a great coach in Chuck Knox, and the rest is history.

First Coaching Job

I went into coaching when Otto took a coaching job. Otto asked me to join him because I had been coaching in the east—west area in the College All-Star Game with him and we hit it off as far as being former teammates in Athens. So when he asked me to join him with the Washington Redskins I didn't think a thing about it.

Joining Carolina Panthers Front Office

Jerry Richardson said he would like to talk to department heads in Seattle because Seattle was the last expansion franchise prior to 1995. I said fine and so Jerry spent about three days with us and then he left and thanked me, of course. Then the new Seattle ownership fired me, they said I was too much like the Nordstrom's so they let me go. Jerry called and he said, Mike, I want to thank you for allowing me to come and visit with all your department heads, and this and that. He said, "I came back and told my partners that we were going to go for the expansion team, but the only problem was I knew the guy I wanted to run it, but he already had a job." He said, "You don't have one now, will you come down?" So I was out of work that year for two weeks and then I joined the Carolina Panthers. Between Jerry, Mark, his son, and me, we got the franchise and expanded it. That was, the most fun I'd ever had because we hired the whole organization. We built the stadium, dealt with state legislators, and the league offices. It was quite an experience. I really enjoyed it. It's just sad that it came so late in my life.

I'm tickled with this and the fact that we went to the championship game in our second year. We lost to Green Bay up there, but it was really a great experience and a lot of good young kids made that franchise and made it a better franchise.

Pro Football Hall of Fame Induction

The induction is a stage and you think about so many things that happened in your lifetime. There are so many people that had a piece of it. I think we had to deal with it ourselves when we were there. We had a coach that came over and he was a basketball coach and he was supposed to coach all sports. I'll never forget him saying, "Mikey, I don't know a damn thing about football, but I can make you run and I can make you a better athlete, if you would do my basketball drills."

I can remember skipping rope and doing things like that. My senior year they hired someone else who was a good football coach. He came in and I think he perfected whatever I became as far as a football player. It was my senior year that got me scholarship offers and as they say, the rest is history. I was thinking of those people and so many that helped me along the way at the induction.

Best Player Ever

I would say Jim Brown was the best athlete I ever saw. The best play, gee there were so many, you know when you play that long. I would have to go with of all the players that I've played with and again Jim Brown. The best lineman would be definitely Gino Marchetti.

Photograph copyright Associated Press

Chapter 11

Frank Gifford

College:
Southern California

Career History:
New York Giants (1952–1964)

1977 Inductee Pro Football Hall of Fame

College At USC
We were in the early days of television and everything I did early on was filmed in black and white. It was vastly different.

These days, athletes play under a microscope, not only the way they play but also the way they live. It's a totally different world.

NFL Draft
I was kind of surprised. I didn't even know that they were drafting that day. I got a phone call from Braven Dyer, a sports writer for the L.A. Times, and he said, "What do you think about going to New York?" I said, "Well I had a great time." He said, "No, you've been drafted by the Giants." I said, "I don't play baseball."

I was only half-kidding because I didn't even know they had a professional team quite honestly. I mean pro football wasn't that big and I wasn't planning to play professionally. I had a pretty good career going. I was doing a lot of stunt work, studying acting, and I was under contract at Warner Brothers at the time. I got married as a senior and I thought, well I'll just go and play football for one season, check out New York, and see the Statue of Liberty and the big buildings. That was back in 1952 and I'm still here.

Acting Career
I did a lot of stunt work. John Wayne was actually a football player at USC. A lot of times USC was able to recruit players by getting them in as screen extras by the screen actor's guilds. On our days off or on our vacation, we would get jobs. They were making a lot of military movies after the war, so there was a big demand for soldiers as extras. It was a good way to supplement our income, which wasn't very much. I enjoyed it and started getting seriously involved studying acting. At one time I was under contract with Warner Brothers. They gave me an ultimatum a few years later. I had to pick football or acting. That year I was the MVP in the NFL. My coach said, "Here's what we will do, don't worry about your contract with them, we'll take care of that, you come and be with us."

Position Change in NFL

I played both ways at USC. They couldn't figure out what to do with me. My senior year I was strictly on offense and we had a pretty good football team. I had a big year. I made All-Coast, All-American, and I was up for the Heisman. It was all new to me. I'd never been in that kind of limelight before. I got that call from Braven Dyer when I was on my way to go skiing in January of 1952. Getting drafted by New York turned out great for me. I got to know the Mara family. They're still good friends of mine.

Transition from California to New York

It wasn't that big of a deal. New York is a very small town really. It just has a lot of numbers. If you live in Manhattan, it's only a few miles long and half-mile wide or maybe a mile at the most. The people are very warm and friendly, and it has a great, great history that I got deeply involved in. I made so many lifelong friends. I'm really blessed. I can't imagine what might have happened had I gone to some other place. I was blessed and fortunate that it was New York.

1958 NFL Championship Game

Well, if I hadn't fumbled a couple of times it wouldn't have been called the greatest game ever played, it would've been a wipeout. I fumbled one time on the way in to score. We were in scoring territory at that time. Then I fumbled another time out of scoring territory. So, I was a big plus for Baltimore that day.

Johnny Unitas was a legendary NFL quarterback. Think of all the players that played in that particular game. It went down in history as a great football game. It was the first game that ever went into overtime. Of course, we lost in overtime and that was a historic thing in itself. It really defined pro football but more importantly, it was nationally televised. Up until that time, there had been only a few games that were nationally televised. When they got the ratings they were astonished. The ratings were just incredible. Something like 75-80% of the television sets in use in the country had been watching that football game. The West Coast had a lot of viewers because it was televised later. It had a 1 o'clock start. That game had a huge effect on the entire NFL in terms of television broadcasting.

In overtime, we had the first possession. We didn't get the first down, so we decided to punt rather than go for it on fourth down with about a yard to go on our own 35-40 yard line. I always thought we should have gone for it because everyone was exhausted at that point. Johnny Unitas and Raymond Berry teamed up on that memorable drive. They came down the field and it was a great performance. There was no question to me that Johnny was one of the greatest quarterbacks of all time and Raymond Berry was one of the greatest receivers. Alan Ameche wasn't bad either.

We didn't know quite what happened. First of all, we ended up tied. Neither team knew what to do. The officials actually didn't know how to go about it either. They didn't know how much time they would have before they would kick off for the overtime, or if they would flip a coin, or who would receive first. We did flip a coin and our team received first. There was one possession by us and then one possession by them. Ameche scored from the two-yard line and that was that.

I vividly remember that play of 47 power. I carried the ball on third down for about a yard. You can make a big deal out of it because Gino Marchetti broke his leg on that play. There was a big pile up on the line of scrimmage. I was fairly positive, I didn't even look at the yard markers, that I had made the first down. The referee came running in and grabbed the ball. Marchetti was screaming like a panther. His bone was actually coming out of his leg. He was obviously very seriously hurt. They were unpiling everybody and they never bothered to put where they marked the ball. Years later I talked to a couple of the officials that were involved in it and they felt the same way. We didn't get a fair mark on it. I'd been playing football a lot of years at that point and when I turned the corner and turned it up field, I had a good block. I broke it back in to the inside. To this day I think I made the first down. I'm not going to make a big issue out of it and I didn't at the time because it would've looked like sour grapes and I knew they weren't going to change it. I've said it and I've written about it. Whether or not we would've gone in to score or to kick a field goal, I don't know, but at least it would've been a different kind of an outcome.

Art Donovan

Arty is great. Art is a big old pudgy guy. You come up to the line of scrimmage and look over and see those guys like Arty Donovan and Gino Marchetti, they were a great football team. If you think about today, what do we have 32 franchises playing football and 50 man rosters? When I played, there were 12 teams that played and we had 33 man rosters. All the good players were being used. There was nothing that you had to have to fill out a roster. If you go down Baltimore's lineup, several of them who I mentioned previously were unbelievable. I feel the same way about our backfield of Alex Webster and me. We both played in many Pro Bowls. Charlie Conerly, our quarterback, was a great quarterback. We had great personnel. It just wasn't as diluted as it has become over the years.

New York Giants Defense 1958

Tom Landry was a player coach at the time and he went on to become a Hall of Fame coach with the Dallas Cowboys. Sam Huff who was the middle linebacker and Andy Robustelli were just extraordinary guys. It was a memorable game and I think it helped define pro football as having arrived in the eyes of the public.

Jim Lee Howell

I was surprised that Mr. Mara made the big decision to hire Jim Lee Howell. I think he hired Jim Lee Howell, who didn't know much about football, because he was a disciplinarian and he had been in the military. They had a bunch of guys who, I wouldn't want to use the word wild, but they were borderline. There were a lot of returning serviceman and guys that were tough to discipline. Jim Lee Howell could handle these guys much better than Vince Lombardi. Tom Landry was a player coach. I think that he made the move for those reasons. Of course Lombardi went to Green Bay and put together a Hall of Fame career. Tom went to Dallas and he put together a Hall of Fame career there.

Decision to Retire

My head hurt and I didn't want to hang around like a lot of other guys. More than that, I started working in 1958, my last season, in local television doing local news. I did network radio with Phil Rizzuto, and I knew what I was going to do. I had a place to go. A lot of guys at that time, like I said, had returned from the military. When they left football they didn't really know what they were going to do. I knew what I was going to do and I couldn't wait to do it.

I played 12 years. That was long enough. There was a change in coaches. Allie Sherman replaced Jim Lee Howell and that was a disaster. Not personally, but he arrived with the football team just coming apart. Guys were retiring, guys didn't like him, and I knew when it was time to get out.

Chuck Bednarik

I keep trying to tell people that I had a spinal concussion. They didn't have the CAT scan in the 1960s when I got the famous hit by Chuck Bednarik and was lying on my back in the field. Years later, I start getting a lot of numbness and tingling in my arms. By then, the CAT scan was available and I went to see a specialist. The technician who did the scan asked me what year I was in an automobile accident. Bednarik wasn't a car, but I had multiple fractures of the vertebra in my neck. It's a good thing I decided to take a year off because had I gone back and tried to play it may have been much worse than it was. Taking that year allowed everything to heal. People remember me for only as getting hit at that point, but I came back and played four more years and I went to the Pro Bowl again as a wide receiver. That injury didn't define my career, it was just a dramatic thing that people kept replaying over the years. In fact, I think it was on a postage stamp in Philadelphia.

Favorite Position to Play

I just loved to play. I played as a defensive back and I doubled up a couple of times as an offensive back too. I was a tailback in the single wing when I came out of USC. I made All-American as a tailback. I could run and I could pass, I could block and I could catch. For several years I was the leading receiver and the leading rusher with the Giants. I just loved to play football. I don't think that I could've had the career that I had if I was playing today. Everything is so specialized today. I just loved to play.

Don Meredith

Don Meredith was a wonderful friend. He really was. He was an incredible guy. We got to know each other on Monday Night Football and we stayed friends after that. He was one of a kind. His life was far too short.

Kyle Rote

Kyle Rote could've done anything he wanted to do. He was a dreamer. He was an artist. He was a remarkable person. He would've been an unbelievable football player. He was fantastic at SMU and one of the people that inspired me to go in to professional football. I happened to be listing to the radio when Kyle and SMU were playing Notre Dame. It was the most fascinating radio call I'd ever heard. He was drafted number one by the Giants; the year before I was drafted number one and he got hurt that season in training camp. They were going to play me on defense and so that was the reason I went over to the offense. Kyle had torn his knee up and never did recover from that. He limped through a pretty long career with the Giants and he made the Pro Bowl a couple of times. God only knows what he would've been had he not torn that knee up before his first football game.

Howard Cosell

Howard Cosell told us he was a lawyer. I wouldn't want him representing me. Bless his heart; he's gone on to that great gridiron.

He was okay. He really was. He had a great mind. His name was really Howard Colon and at the time he felt that there was a great prejudice against him coming into the broadcasting world. He was defensive about everything and Lord knows he might have been right about a lot of things at that point of time. He could be very difficult but there were things that he was brilliant at. He had a remarkable memory. He had a way of interviewing that few people did. It was more of an interrogation. He arguably was one of the first people, at least in radio and television, who wasn't kissing up to somebody when they interviewed them. Howard asked the questions that other people wanted to know the answers to. He was one of the first people to do it. Now they all do it.

Being a Traffic Cop in the Booth Between Howard Cosell & Don Meredith

Well, at times but I never felt that way. I've heard that over the years. Don like I said was one of my dearest friends and we lost a real beauty in him. He didn't miss much; I can tell you that on the way out.

Monday Night Football

I don't think that there is destination television any more unless there is a moon launch or something like that. There's just too much out there. Everything seems so focused now. There's nothing that crosses over the demographics and reaches out to an entire country like Monday Night Football did. A lot of people tuned in to watch it because they had never heard anyone like Howard Cosell. A lot of them wanted to see what Don Meredith was going to do to punch through that balloon, that arrogant guy that was on TV. They didn't even know what football was about. Some people tuned in to watch the game itself. There was so much that surrounded it. There will never be a circumstance like that again because everything is covered night and the day. It's just a world of difference. I said many times, we had the best of times, we really did.

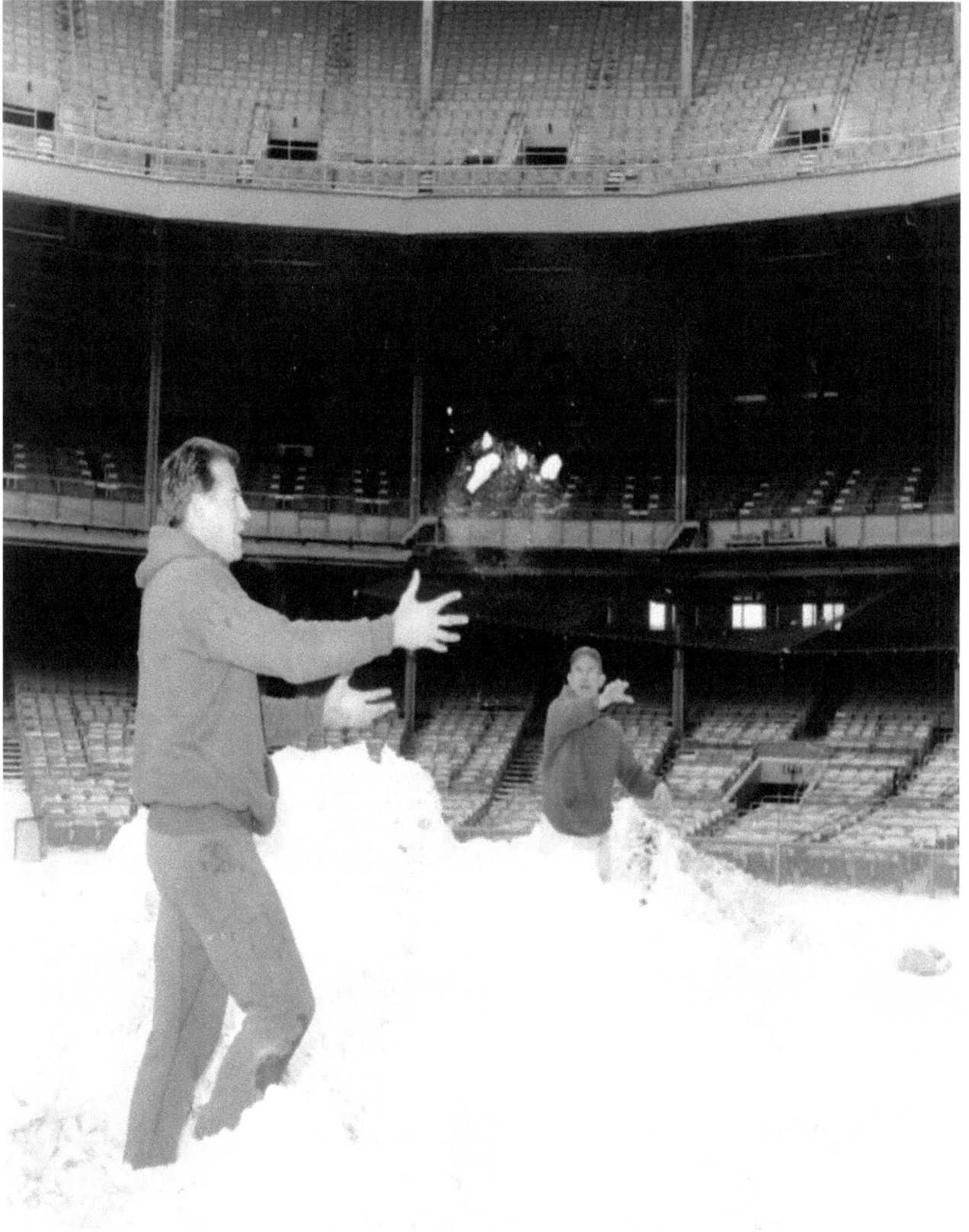

New York Giant Y.A. Tittle passes a snowball to teammate Frank Gifford. Photograph copyright Associated Press

Chapter 12

Yale Lary

College: Texas A&M Career History: Detroit Lions (1952-1964) 1979 Inductee Pro Football Hall of Fame

College Choice

First of all, Texas A&M scouted me in high school. I had several offers, the Naval Academy, Notre Dame, University of Texas, A&M, TCU. I chose Texas A&M.

Jim Brown

I played against Jim Brown for several years. He made a classic statement about me. We played him in championship games and beat him every time. He said, "Well, I never did know if Yale was going to block me or tackle me." He gave me a nice compliment. He's very friendly, and we've remained friends for a long time.

Texas A&M

It was just a military school, so to speak. It was an all-boys school, when I went there. They had a lot of returnees from World War II. I went down there in 1948, and graduated from there. I'm glad I did. I got my commission down there and went during the Korean War. I served for two years. That took two years out of my professional career, but I came back alive. That's the most important thing.

NFL Draft

At the time, professional football wasn't very popular in Texas. They got to see the Thanksgiving game with Green Bay and Detroit. I wanted the challenge. I was honored that Detroit drafted me as high as they did. I was their first draft choice they kept. That's quite an honor to be their first pick. I was very flattered for the choice that they made. They made it for a pretty good reason, I guess, because I had a fabulous career up there.

I went up there just to make some money. I was just married and needed to have a job. I could have had a job when I graduated from A&M, but didn't want to. I could have been a coach in high school or maybe college, I don't know. I was thrilled to death to make the team.

Bobby Layne

Bobby Layne was the best. His famous saying was he never lost a game. He just ran out of time. I believe that. He was by all means the greatest.

He was a competitor. He pitched at University of Texas and never lost a game. I don't think he lost any football games either; not very many. He was just a great competitor. He was naturally talented.

Buddy Parker
Buddy Parker kept to himself. When he said something to you, you better pay attention because he didn't speak too much. He was very worried about everything including the team and the individuals. He was a fabulous coach. He won a lot of games and championships.

How he Became a Punter
During World War II, I was at a military football game. I was in junior high school, 12 or 13 years old. Army was playing another branch of the armed services at a high school football stadium. When the football was kicked for the extra point, it went over the fence and I caught the ball. I started punting it in the street. It just came natural.

Jack Christiansen & Jim David
We played together quite well. Instinctively, we knew what one was going to cover; if he could or couldn't cover. We just worked together and played together well.

NFL Championships
It was wonderful, a real thrill to the team. Of all the teams, you're the best team up there and that's saying quite a bit. It's quite an honor. Especially when you didn't have all those teams. It was quite a thrill. We won the world championship three times in '52, '53, '57.

Buddy Parker Quitting & George Wilson Taking Over as Head Coach
We didn't believe it when we went to the 'Meet the Line' banquet in downtown Detroit. Buddy Parker got up and said that he quit. That was a real shocker to us. What can you do? George Wilson was a good coach.

Joe Schmidt
Naturally, he was a great ballplayer and just a tremendous leader. He could get everybody together and raise their spirits. Joe Schmidt was an inspiration.

Doak Walker
Doak Walker was just a wonderful man. He was always nice. He could do everything: run, pass, kick field goals, and extra points. I always wanted to be like him. I could do a few things like him, but not many.

Favorite Moment in the NFL
I guess winning the world championships was my favorite NFL moment. That's what you're there for. I just wanted to make my family proud of me—my lovely wife and my two children. Of course, I was pleased with my performance and was thrilled to receive the honors I got.

His Speed
I was pretty fast. In high school, I was ten flat. They never timed me in the professional ranks. I was fast enough to return a few kickoffs or a few punts. I had some good moves, and I was fast.

Doak Walker wasn't really fast either, but he had the ability to find that little gap. I did too on several of them.

Bobby Layne
I don't think there's any question that the stories about Bobby Layne were magnified. He was a real good friend of mine. A lot of writers have to write about these popular individuals and they picked him. He was very outspoken and didn't hide his activities. He was a great ballplayer who was noticed for every win.

Dick "Night Train" Lane
Dick "Night Train" Lane had to replace Jim David. When Jim David retired we needed somebody over there and Lane was available. He was a great defensive back. It's hard out there. Your all by yourself and you're a cornerback and spread in that way, and there's a receiver out there, one-on-one. He was a good one.

Pro Football Hall of Fame Induction
I didn't expect it or plan on it. I was very honored, of course. I started to feel like I deserved it when I looked back on my career.

Toughest Quarterback
Johnny Unitas was probably one of the toughest ones. Norm Van Brocklin was really tough too. None of them were easy.

Favorite Player Growing Up
My favorite player was my dad. He played football at the same high school I did, North Side High School. I didn't have a favorite college player. I was too busy playing high school ball. I played every sport there was in high school.

I made all conference in baseball for Texas A&M. We went to the World Series. I made a home run in the World Series and we beat Ohio State 3 to 2. Marty Karow coached me at A&M and then he went to Ohio State. It kind of gave me a thrill to hit a home run against him in Omaha.

Paul Hornung Naming You The Best Punter in NFL History
That's flattering. We didn't have the domes like they have now and all that stuff. We had to play in ice, sleet, snow, and rain. The elements weren't favorable. I feel like I did the best I could do at the moment. I'm proud of what I did.

Career
I played in Detroit with Doak Walker, who is one of my favorites and was one of my very good friends. I knew Sammy Baugh, of course. I played against him one year before he retired in Washington.

Retirement from NFL
I was offered several opportunities to fly over to Detroit on the weekends and punt, but I declined. There's no question that I could have played a lot more. I could have played defensive back, I thought for a couple of more years. I could have punted for no telling how long.

Photograph copyright Associated Press

Chapter 13

Bob St. Clair

> College:
> University of San Francisco
> Tulsa
>
> Career History:
> San Francisco 49ers (1953–1963)
>
> 1990 Inductee Pro Football Hall of Fame

College Choice

There were other colleges I could have gone to, but I was married at the time and the University of San Francisco was giving me a housing allowance to live off campus instead of living on campus. It was home and we were raising a family. At that time we had one child, and my wife was pregnant. A lot of the guys who were from out of the area or weren't married would live in the old barracks they had on campus. I would get the equivalent of the value of that. It wasn't very much, but it was something.

College Team

We thought we were pretty good once we started winning and beating other teams. We had a lot of confidence. We had a great coach, Joe Kuharich, who later coached for the Redskins. There are three of us in the Pro Football Hall of Fame, Gino Marchetti, Ollie Matson, and me. There's a fourth in the Hall of Fame who was from our class, our publicist, Pete Rozelle.

Coach Kuharich had two cement posts that were wrapped in canvas and cushioned. It was enough for just one person to get through. We'd get in a three-point stance on each side and he'd hike the ball. We battled our way through using our hands. It was almost like a fistfight.

Ollie Matson

The interesting thing is he was such an offensive threat, yet he made All-American on defense his last year 1951. Isn't that something?

He played both offense and defense. We all did in those days.

Burt Toler

When Pete Rozelle became the Commissioner, he made Burl Toler the first black NFL referee. I remember going out on the field and I'd come out behind Burl and hug him. He turned and looked at me the first couple times and said, "No, you can't do that. You can't do that."

1951 University of San Francisco Football Team

I think man for man we could have beat anybody. I really do. We never really had a chance. No one would play us. The year before, we had played Stanford and Cal and they had beaten us. We almost beat Cal that year. They went to the Rose Bowl in 1950. So in 1951 we thought we'd be able to play them again. No way. They didn't want any part of us. It had nothing to do with having black players on the team. Not here on the coast. It was just that they felt that we were that good and it's a no-win situation for them. They were supposed to beat us, and if they lost it would be really a black eye to them.

1951 Orange Bowl Not Allowing Black Players from University of San Francisco to Play
We were going to play Georgia Tech in the Orange Bowl but when we got the invitation the coach said, "Well, what do you guys want to do? Do you want to have a meeting?" We said, "We don't even have to have a meeting, Coach. We're not going to go for this. This is crazy. We're not doing this."

We didn't care what color they were. What the hell? That was a slap in our face. Obviously they wanted us to lose, we thought. Evidently the Bowl Committee, and this was very prevalent in those days had that kind of attitude. In fact, I think one of our officials was told that this is very common in the south at all the bowls. They don't accept black players.

They're making a movie about our team. Gino and I are going to be in it. I have already filmed some parts of it in San Francisco at Kezar Stadium where they named the field after me. They filmed the old locker room and some nostalgic stuff. I played 189 games there.

Bob St. Clair Field at Kezar Stadium
It was a real honor to have the field named after me. I mean, usually you have to be dead before they name anything after you. I looked in the mirror the next morning after the naming and said, "Geez, do I look that bad?"

Transfer to Tulsa University
I went to Tulsa University my last year because that was the only team that would recognize a transferee. USF had dropped football because they couldn't afford to field a team anymore after we refused to play in the game. There would have been enough funding to last for a few years if we played in that game. What happened was I went back to Tulsa University. They would recognize me as a transferee without having to sit out a year. That is what I was interested in and I played the year back there.

NFL Draft
I was finished at Tulsa when I was drafted by the 49ers. I received a call from the owner, Tony Morabito and he said, "Bob, we are so happy to have you, a local kid, playing. You went to Poly Technic High School, University of San Francisco and now with the 49ers." He said, "You're a perfect fit here. We're going to give you a little more money than we do the average rookie. We're going to give you $5,500." I said, "Well, I'm sorry, Mr. Morabito, I can't accept that."

The only reason I said that was because the guard drafted next to me had just signed a contract with Green Bay for $6,000. So, I thought that was the figure and I didn't want to look like a piker. He hung up the phone. I had to wait a week back in Tulsa before he called me back. He said, "Listen, St. Clair, you better be as good as you think you are. We're going to give you the extra $500.

Diet

I eat raw meat. Even today I eat raw meat. I don't cook red meat at all. In fact, I'll go in a restaurant and order a rare chicken and they'll look at me and have me sign a release. Ever since I was a little kid I can remember my grandmother in San Francisco chopping meat at the chopping block in the kitchen. When she was chopping up meat, the dog and I would be looking up at her waiting for her to throw a piece of meat. She'd give the dog or me a piece. I'd always be fighting that damn dog trying to get as much as I could away from him. I just acquired a taste for raw meat. The thing is, my favorite food is raw liver. I still like it today. You can't get it in a restaurant but I'll buy it at the store or a butcher shop. Every once in a while I really enjoy that.

I can remember when the rookies first came into camp when I was playing. I was the captain of the team and on Thursday night we would have liver at training camp. I would get my raw liver, put a napkin over it, and walk over to where the rookies sat. Most of the rookies sat by themselves in training camp. I'd sit with them and I could see the expressions on their faces.

They'd look at me and think, "What the hell is the captain sitting with us for? Jiminy Cricket." Then I'd take the napkin off and there'd be blood all over the plate, and I'd start chewing on the liver. Most people don't know raw liver tastes and sounds like an apple; it crunches. I'd exaggerate it naturally and let a little blood drip down my chin. All of those guys would get the hell away from me. They would get up and leave, saying, "I'm not as hungry as I thought I was."

Nickname the Geek

There was a movie that came out when I was playing called Nightmare Alley, with Tyrone Power. He was called the Geek in the movie. His character was part of a circus side-show and ate live chickens. They would throw him a live chicken and he would rip it apart and blood and feathers would be everywhere. That is where I got my nickname. A guy said of me, "That's the Geek" and it stuck.

Y.A. Tittle

I thought I'd died and gone to heaven when I was drafted by the 49ers and I came back to my hometown. I had gone to high school in San Francisco; I played at the University of San Francisco, and then with the 49ers. The day I went to training camp Y. A. Tittle was assigned as my roommate. I thought it couldn't get any better until I slept in the same room with him for a couple of nights. He's an asthmatic and he wheezes at night. No one wanted to be his roommate because they couldn't sleep very well. I had to come up with a plan because the training team told me I looked a little sleepy. They wanted me to make the team.

The next night the coach, Buck Shaw, came down and was talking with Y.A. about the next days practice. He said, "Practice tomorrow at eight o'clock." As he was leaving the room he said, "I'll turn out the lights." I said, "No coach, let me."

We had beds on the opposite side of the room and there was a little sink. I got up and I played like I was getting a drink of water. I said, "I'm going to get a drink of water."

I faked it and then I turned out the lights. Then I turned the corner went to Y.A.'s bed. I reached under the covers and kissed him on his bald head. Then I patted him on his ass, and whispered in his ear, "Goodnight, Y." He never slept a wink all night. He told the whole team I was gay.

San Francisco 49ers Y.A. Tittle, left, Hugh McElhenney, right, and Bob St. Clair in the middle.
Photograph copyright Associated Press

Chapter 14

Joe Schmidt

```
College:
Pittsburgh

Career History:
Detroit Lions (1953–1965)

As Coach:
Detroit Lions (1967–1972)

1973 Inductee Pro Football Hall of Fame
```

NFL Draft

I was disappointed, not from the standpoint of coming to Detroit, but I didn't really think I had much of a chance to make a championship team. They just won a championship the year before. I really wanted to play for the Pittsburgh Steelers. They had told me through the grapevine that they were going to draft me. So I was planning on being a Pittsburgh Steeler. I came from Pittsburgh. That is where I went to school.

I was excited about the possibility of being a Pittsburgh Steeler. As I listened to the draft on the radio the rounds went by and eventually the Lions drafted me. I thought I'd go up there, give it a shot, and see what happened. Everything turned out for the best. I played on some great teams and with some great football players. I have had an extremely exciting life here in Detroit.

I had an older brother who played for the Steelers. He played at Carnegie Tech in Pittsburgh. He played for one year before he had to go into the service. I always felt that's where I belonged. I was anxious to play professional football, naturally, and especially in my hometown.
If you take the point where the Allegheny and Monongahela Rivers join the Ohio River and you go down the Ohio River, and you take a radius of about 30 miles within that point, you have some great football players. Joe Montana and Johnny Unitas lived about a mile and a half from where I grew up. Then there was Mike Ditka, Tony Dorsett, and Dan Marino, Jim Kelly who played for Buffalo, and of course Big Joe Namath. There are quite a few Hall of Famers within that area. I would say there are probably 10 to 15 guys from Pittsburgh, Pennsylvania that are in the NFL Hall of Fame.

Running Backs Who Gave Us The Most Trouble

I don't know who gave us the most trouble. Probably the running backs that we played against gave us the most trouble. There is a whole list of guys including Jim Brown. We played the Browns quite frequently. I always looked at Rick Casares as a great football player from the Bears. The 49ers had Hugh McElhenny and Joe Perry. During that time most of the 12 teams had pretty good running backs. At least one of whom who was pretty damn good. The guys I mentioned always gave everybody trouble.

Bobby Layne
Bobby Layne gets credit for a lot of things that really never transpired. There are all kinds of stories about him. I don't want to paint him as a choirboy or anything of that nature but he liked to go out and have a good time. When he stepped on the football field in practice and in the game he was all business. He enjoyed himself. He would always drag a couple guys around with him to a few places. That was his mentality.

In spite of that he was always prepared to play. He always knew what he had to do. He always played up to expectations. Like everybody else he had bad games, naturally. He set the pace for everybody. He wanted everybody to play to the maximum. I know of a couple times during the course of his career where somebody wasn't blocking properly on the offensive line and he would stop the game and go over and tell Coach Buddy Parker, "Get so and so the hell out of the game. He's not playing."

Of course at that particular time we only had 33 guys on the team. So we didn't have the luxury of taking some guy out and putting another guy in. He said, "If he keeps it up and he doesn't start blocking, I am coming the hell out. I am not playing." He expected everybody to perform properly.

Alex Karras
Alex Karras was quiet. He wasn't much of a practice player. He was a game player and was a good player. In my opinion he should be in the Hall of Fame. Being that he had some problems there with gambling and so forth, I think that is the thing keeping him out of the Hall of Fame. Alex had very quick hands and quick feet and he was very strong. When he played I don't think there were too many guys who could block him.

Radio Headsets
Radio headsets were new to football. The receiver was in my helmet and my defensive coach would call the plays. A lot of times he would take his time. The offensive team would be coming up to the line of scrimmage and I had to get the defense set. So I would call it and he would get a little upset.

He had to do his job and I had to do my job. If the play wasn't in on time, I had to do what I thought was best. We got in a few contests about that. It was something they were experimenting with. I would prefer to call my own defenses. He felt that it was necessary for him to be involved with it. So I had to go along with it.

Transition from Player to Coach
It was difficult to tell you the truth. I was only on the staff for six months prior to becoming head coach. One year I was a player and the next year I was a coach. Everybody I coached, or everybody on the teams I played with, were good teammates and good friends. Coaching friends at times was difficult. I had to make some adjustments and cut some teammates. We had rookies coming in and I had to replace my former teammates. It was difficult from that standpoint. Everybody was watching me, naturally, at all times. So it was a little touch-and-go at times, but I think we were able to handle it. It got a little tight at times. Of course when you are coaching everything doesn't go properly. So you have to make adjustments accordingly.

Chuck Hughes Death During Game

Unfortunately at that time, physicals and things of that nature were not adequate. They didn't do the extensive testing that they do today. Chuck Hughes whole family had congenital heart problems. That wasn't really established when he was getting a physical. Of course, he kept it quiet.

The game was against the Bears. He wasn't a starter but he was always walking next to me asking for me to put him in. We were losing in Tiger Stadium against the Bears and I put him in.

It was the end of the game. I got him a pass and he ran down the field. It was like a long pass pattern. He came back and then he ran another one. Then he came back and he dropped down. He died right there on the field. It was quite an experience, for the whole team, the whole organization, and of course, his family. It was difficult to move on.

I still think about that every football season and I think about his family. It is difficult to erase that from your mind. It was an unfortunate thing. I guess these things happen in life. That naturally put a damper on our season that year. The whole team flew down and went to the services in his hometown in Texas.

It is difficult to get the team back to thinking about the game when something that drastic happens. We didn't have anything like grief counseling. It was hard to get over. I don't like to use that as an excuse for our season, but it affected us.

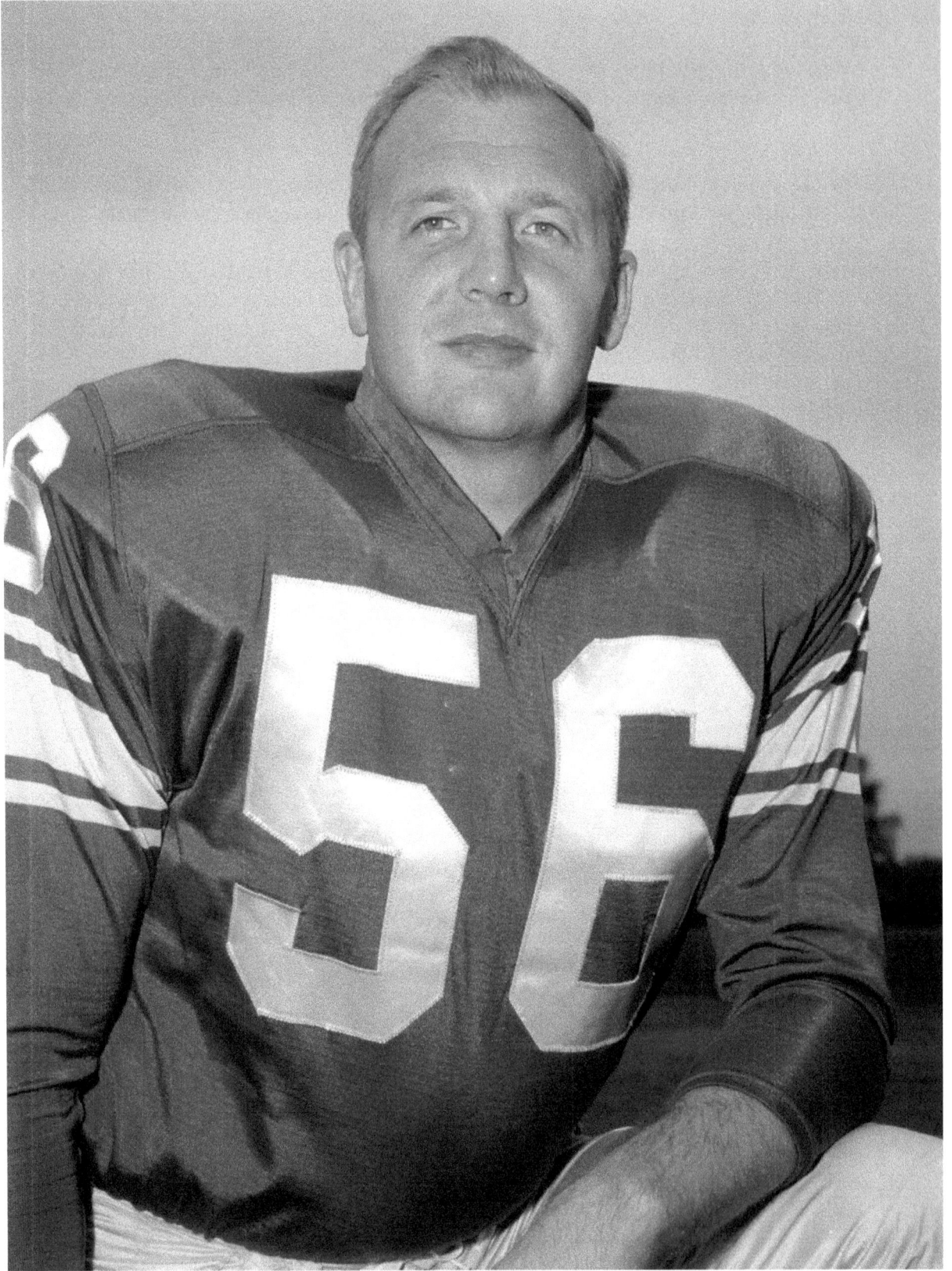

Photograph copyright Associated Press

Chapter 15

Raymond Berry

College: Southern Methodist Career History: As Player: Baltimore Colts (1955–1967) As Coach: Dallas Cowboys (OE) (1968–1969) New England Patriots (1984–1989) Detroit Lions (QB) (1991–1992) Denver Broncos (QB) (1992) 1973 Inductee Pro Football Hall of Fame

High School
I wasn't big enough or good enough to play in high school. By the time I was a senior there wasn't anyone else there, so I got a starting position at 150 pounds. I was about 5'10" in those days, but I had size 12 feet. My nickname in high school was skis. There wasn't any snow in Paris, Texas either.

College Positions
My junior and senior years I was the left end and we ran the Straight-T Formation, with no split receivers whatsoever. We went both ways, playing offense and defense.

I was the left defensive end, which in today's terminology would be an outside linebacker. I was on the end of the line, but I played in the three-point stance most of the time. Forrest Gregg and I played side by side for two years together. We played both offense and defense in those days. We didn't throw the ball any, we just ran the ball from a Straight-T Formation and played good defense. I loved to play defense. I was a natural defensive player. That was what I liked to do. I didn't know anything about being a receiver. I didn't get introduced to the passing game until I got into pro football with Baltimore.

College
I caught 33 passes in two years, my junior year and my senior years. We just didn't throw much at all. We ran the ball and played defense.

Draft
I'll put it this way. If Baltimore thought I was a future Hall of Famer they certainly underpaid me. I made $10,000 in my first two years and I was one of the higher paid guys.

As a matter of fact, I was a 20th round draft pick. That was the year they drafted 30 players. They took me on the 20th round after I finished my fourth year in college. I was a junior college transfer so I actually went five years to college and my junior year at SMU was my fourth year in college, I was eligible for the draft so they drafted me in the 30th round. They drafted me to play offense.

Baltimore Colts

It wasn't fun whatsoever. I was expecting to get cut at any time. The only thing that saved me and actually, it's the only reason why I ever got to play in the NFL is I happened to arrive in Baltimore at the right time, at the right place, with the right people. I happened to arrive in Baltimore when they had no veteran receivers. I arrived in Baltimore when that team had only been in existence for one year. They had no veteran group and they had no veteran receivers.

My rookie year there was 13 rookies that made the team out of a 33-man roster. I couldn't have made it anywhere else I would have gone in the league. They didn't have anybody so I got to play. I got to be a starter and I played 12 games. I ended up catching a tremendous number of passes. I caught 13 passes in 12 games. That was my production. I didn't know my butt from first base about running pass routes, about getting away from man to man coverage. I didn't know anything about the passing game and how to get open or anything. I did have a natural pair of hands and I could catch and I could run and jump. I was 185 pounds that was my credentials.

Johnny Unitas

If you had seen Johnny Unitas and me in training camp in 1956, you may have gone away sobbing. We were two pitiful cases of football players. Fortunately, we had a coach named Weeb Ewbank who saw something nobody else did. He saw something that we didn't know anything about and I'm glad he did.

John made the team as a backup quarterback. That was 1956, Johnny's and my second year. The Steelers cut Johnny the year before. He made the team as a free agent quarterback because we needed a backup to George Shaw. George Shaw was a number one draft pick who played my rookie year. I think he was rookie of the year in the NFL. He was a great athlete. He got a severe knee injury around midseason of that year.

We were playing the Chicago Bears in Chicago and George got a severe injury. Unitas came in and he threw a touchdown pass on his first completed pass. The touchdown went to the Chicago Bears though. That was his first completed NFL pass. A defensive corner out there for Chicago, who probably got a raise in salary in the following offseason, picked it off. If you had been a close observer that day, you may have picked up something that nobody, I don't think, really recognized. That was John a free agent trying to hang on in the NFL, who never gets to play, finally gets to play, throws a touchdown pass to the Bears on his first play and then the rest of the game, he just goes about his business like nothing ever happened.

What you were getting was insight into this guy's mental toughness, competitiveness, and confidence. He had it in spades. That was a real tipoff, because it didn't faze him a bit. He went about, had a very decent day, and the Chicago Bears ended up being world champions that year.

When I came back for my second year, I was due to be replaced. They had drafted two All Americans for my position when I came to camp. It was just a matter of time before they were going to give me a bus ticket out of town. I didn't have anything in my life but football. It was the most important thing in my life and I loved to play. My world was getting ready to end. Johnny Unitas came as a free agent. He'd already been cut the year before and he loved to play football. He didn't have anything else on his mind but that.

We were two highly motivated players who loved to play, wanted to play and didn't want to leave. One of the things that you need to understand is that in this highly organized day of modern football, I don't know how many coaches even allow time for players to work on their own after practice. Every place I coached after I left the game as a player and started coaching, the head coaches got so carried away with what they're doing that they didn't allow any time for a receiver and quarterback to go out there and work on their own.

A lot of coaches don't even want them working on their own. They're afraid something will be out of their control so they don't encourage it. Instead, coaches discourage it and just don't allow it. Weeb Ewbank was totally the opposite. He had learned under Paul Brown with the Cleveland Browns. Paul Brown always allowed his receivers and quarterbacks to spend as much time on the field on their own after practice as they wanted. Weeb saw great results from that, those great Cleveland Browns passing games of the Paul Brown era.

He encouraged it, allowed it and gave us a time to do it. We stayed out there as long as we wanted to. We worked and got to know each other. We developed timing that you just couldn't get any other way. I realized there is a confidence factor involved in this. Something clicks in the quarterback's head when he works with a receiver on that type of the basis for a long period of time. He gets to the point where he just knows that receiver, he knows when he's going to break, he knows the timing of his plays and he has great communication with him and great confidence.

In the heat of the game, I think without question, the quarterback will invariably go to the receiver he knows is going to be where he's supposed to be, when he's supposed to be there. I think that's exactly what happened with Unitas. We worked as one. We were a unit. I know in games Unitas was given the responsibility of calling plays. Weeb Ewbank recognized an instinctive play caller in Unitas. He let John call the plays.

I wasn't old enough or mature enough to understand, but Unitas would call on me on some plays because he knew I was going to be where I was supposed to be and he knew I was going to catch it.

Art Donovan
Art Donovan is a totally different case. He couldn't do anything, but eat and play football. He could play football well and he certainly could eat. He couldn't run, but he didn't have to. Playing defensive tackle if he could just take three steps one way or the other that's all he needed.

Lenny Moore

The result of Lenny Moore's work after practice with Johnny Unitas ended up exactly the same as it was with me. I think that this type of after work practice was one of the reasons we won two World Championships in Baltimore. Look at the games we played against the New York Giants defense, which was the leading defense in the league. Key plays were plays we had perfected, talked about, and worked on after practice until they were automatic. In the heat of the game, those things just came up and happened. It wasn't an accident. That after practice work with the quarterback allowed us to gain confidence with him. That was the key to our success.

Frank Gifford & 1958 NFL Championship Game

I've heard Frank Gifford talk about bad spots in the 1958 NFL Championship Game. I think he really believes that. I looked at the film very closely and I really disagree with him. I don't think the official missed the spot of the ball at all. I think Frank hit the ground and bounced. I think where Frank bounced to was not where the spot of the ball should be put, but actually when you hit the ground that's where the ball should be spotted. The bounce doesn't count after that. I don't think any of us realized the significance of the game. I don't think we were old enough to understand at all. I don't think we had a clue. I think we were just thrilled to death that we were able to win the game and be part of the history and the significance of it. I'm not saying that nobody understood it. I think there were some people that did. I think the man that really understood it and this came to me years later as I began to piece together the chain of events was Bert Bell.

I think the man that really understood the significance of that game immediately was Bert Bell, the Commissioner of the League. I saw him after the game. I can't remember exactly what the circumstances were, but I saw him face to face, very shortly after that game was over. The memory of his face that day will be with me forever. Bert Bell had tears in his eyes and he was crying. I saw his face and then went on about my business, but that picture of him with tears in his eyes stayed with me. Years later I'm beginning to put it together. Bert Bell understood that this league, that he had been nursing for several years and doing everything he could to bring it to prominence, he knew that his baby was born.

The rulebook had been structured. Someone realized that in a championship game, they had to have some policy for a tie game. I don't know who came up with the rule, but it was in the rulebook. Of course, nothing like that had ever happened. Nobody even knew about it.

The head referee in that game was a veteran referee and he knew the rule. I remember being out on the field when that game ended in a tie. We all thought the game was over. We went to our benches thinking it was a tie game. We didn't know anything about overtime. Nobody had ever talked about it. That official came over to the bench and explained to Coach Ewbank the procedure. That's when we realized we were going to keep playing.

I don't know if any of us realized the significance of sudden death. All we knew was that we were going to keep playing. We went out on the field and when we got the ball, we went about our business without realizing the significance of what was happening. I know that the Giants won the toss and got the ball, but our defense stopped them. They punted and we were 80 yards out. We knew this was no longer going to be a tie game. We weren't fighting the clock anymore. We were 80 yards out and it's a 17-17 game.

Unitas comes in the huddle and he just methodically starts mixing run and pass. He moves the darn football 80 yards and when we get into field-goal range, a lot of people later on had this big question why didn't you kick the field goal? I was out there on the field with Unitas watching him; I was under his spell without even realizing it. Weeb Ewbank had given Unitas authority, the free rein to call the game. In this particular situation, the last thing on his mind was getting a field goal. He's going to put that ball in the end zone. He just mixed run and pass. I think it was 13 different plays, five or six passes, seven or eight runs, and move it all the way in. Alan Ameche went in for the final three or four or five yards to score. As soon as that happened, the game was over and we all turned and started running toward the clubhouse. There wasn't any extra point. The official explained the first team that scores, wins. Ameche scores, the game is over 23-17.

I didn't realize at the time, but without question, that game was the greatest game that I ever played. As I said, I wasn't doing anything. We had a very basic, simple offense. I had about four or five pass plays and that was all we had. We weren't doing anything complicated. This simplicity was the genius of Weeb Ewbank.

He made the decision about how many plays he was going with, and that's all he did. I played under him and we used to beat a bunch of teams because we could execute. That was Weeb Ewbank's philosophy. He had very few plays, but we knew how to run them. Over the years I've came to realize that it takes a genius to keep it simple.

Pickup Game In Central Park Against Giants
As an assistant coach I kept working out and running in Central Park for several years. When we got the word that they wanted to reenact the game in Central Park, I was still able to run pretty darn good. The Giants weren't the only team that was five or six years older than when we had played them in '58.

All the players were getting older. Out there on the field that day, I could run darn near full speed. John Unitas and I hadn't been on the field together in about six years.

We started running those routes and it was like there hadn't been any break. I was telling him this is how I can get open on and he'd call it. We'd run it and complete it. It was a replay of the earlier game in a way. It was very interesting to me that this several year gap happens, and Johnny Unitas and I stepped onto the field that afternoon and he was putting the ball right on the money. We were like when we were playing. You would have never figured that could be the case.

His Phenomenal Hands
This is how it works. First of all, I think you're born with it. I think it's a physical gift at birth. I think it has something to do with heredity. For example, my dad was only 5'8" and probably weighed about 155 pounds, but he had big hands and big feet. I ended up being 6'2" and 185,

and I got big hands and I got them from my dad. From the time I started playing football, I could catch the football without even thinking. It was just a natural gift.

When I got to the professional level and was catching the fastballs at the speed with which Johnny Unitas was throwing, I found that I was dropping footballs that I should have been catching. Very early in my years with Unitas, I started practicing catching like I'd never done before. I really studied catching all the different type of catches. I ended up with a list of 12 different situations in the short ball, and six different situations in the long ball. There are 18 different drills. You've got lowball, highball, behind you, too far left, too far right etc. I just started drilling and I would catch 60-70 balls. I'd go right down that list catching three or four of each type.

It was drill and repetition. It's the exact same thing you do when you take a typing course in high school. At first, you don't know anything about typing. Your hands have never been on a typewriter, but you complete an exercise that you go through every day. Drill and repetition, drill and repetition and by the time the semester is over, you know how to type and you'll never forget it. I see the same parallel in catching. If you perform catching drills like catching the high one over your left shoulder over and over, then more than likely in a game, you'll catch the high one over your left shoulder.

His Footwork
There were a couple of things that helped me with my footwork. I ran track every year I was in college for five years. I worked with the sprinters, doing whatever they did. I developed speed and quickness during those years. Of course, there was a lot of heavy speed work I did over and over to get faster. At some point, I developed these drills for footwork. I would backpedal and backpedaled fast. Then I'd be backpedaling and I would twist to my left and go three or four steps, crossing over. Then I'd twist to my right and crossing over.

I had a whole routine of quickness drills that I developed. I did those on a regular basis, especially in the offseason. I did them over and over. There's no question my speed began to increase because I was still growing physically. When I went into professional football I was still growing. Two years after I started playing professional football, I probably finally leveled off.

During the first two years I played, I spent the off seasons working out. I worked out February through July, when we started training again.

I was running and doing all these agility and quickness drills, but I couldn't find anybody to throw to me so I had a hard time working on catching. I had the footwork, the quickness, and the speed. I was getting such a high level of conditioning and strength that I hardly ever got injured. I went through most of my pro career without even getting hurt.

Pro Football Hall of Fame Induction
I was coaching; I believe I was at the University of Arkansas in 1973, when I got word about it. It was the first year I was eligible for the Pro Football Hall of Fame. I wasn't surprised. In my sixth or seventh year in the league, I broke the NFL record for receptions and then broke the record for yardage. When I retired as a player, I held the record for the most passes caught in a

career. I think I had the most yardage gained through receiving in a career. So when the time came, I knew pretty well I was going to be put in the Pro Football Hall of Fame. I wasn't really surprised.

Toughest Defensive Backs

There were five or six tough defensive backs that were the toughest. I played 13 years so I came up against some great ones. Right off the top of my head, there was Abe Woodson of the 49ers. By the way, two of the four or five I'm going to name were 100-yard dash sprint champions in the Big 10.

Abe Woodson came from Illinois. I think he won the 100-yard dash in the Big 10 track. He had tremendous speed. When he came to the 49ers, they put him over in the corner. I faced him twice a year, at least five years in a row. He tried to cover me conventionally for a while. He really introduced the bump and run on me. He walked up on me. The first time he did it, he just got right in front of me like a yard off.

He didn't understand though that he was not keeping me from getting inside on him. The first time he did it, we just completed a bunch of passes inside. The second game of that season then he walked up there on me and he got inside of me. He was going to cut me off from getting inside. That puzzled me for a few quarters. I couldn't figure out exactly what I should do because the guy could run. He was right up on me and I didn't know what to do.

Eventually what I realized was we had to beat him deep. That's what we had to do every time he walked up there. I'd give him three or four moves in the first five yards. Then, we timed a deep pass that I could catch fading away toward the boundary. He had a hard time covering that one, but I couldn't get anything short on him so we just had to go deep.

Irv Cross was the next guy I think about. Irv brought a whole different problem to me because that guy was big. Abe Woodson only weighed about 175 pounds. Irv Cross weighed about 195, and had won the 100-yard dash in the Big Ten. He tried to cover me conventionally the first time or two I played and I ate him alive. He walked up on me and started taking me on at the line of scrimmage. He gave me a fit trying to get away from him. When we had the collision, I lost it and then I tried to outrun him. He won the race. For a couple games there, I had one heck of a time trying to figure out how in the world to get open on this guy.

Dick Lynch of the New York Giants was another one that he was very smart and he studied you, but he also crowded you. He came up and he crowded you and he'd take you on early. You just couldn't run conditional patterns on him. He knew what he was doing and he could run. He wasn't real big either, so when collisions came, I didn't walk away with anything worse than a tie and sometimes I'd win the collision. With Irv Cross, I couldn't win the collision.

Jesse Whittenton of the Green Bay Packers came along with Lombardi's teams. He was tough to get away from because he was another guy who would line up five or six yards deep, but he only backpedal a yard and he'd just walked squat. When you got down there, he was sitting there waiting on you. He took away all your conventional stuff. It took me a while to figure out how to beat Jesse. Going deep on a guy like that was the thing we did. John and I were pretty good at timing a deep ball so we did have something against him. Those four guys were very challenging.

Coaching

I'll tell you the formula for coaching is enjoying coaching first and foremost. If you get great players, you enjoy coaching.

When I inherited the New England Patriots job, I'd been out of coaching over two years. I was living in Boston and working. I had a friend there that had a business and he had hired me and I was working for him. I was making a living outside of coaching. I wasn't even thinking about ever getting back in it again. I had been fired too many times. I was tired of it.

The Patriots fired Ron Meyer right in the middle of the season. That was 1984. I get this phone call. Understand, I've been out of coaching now for two, two and a half years. I'm making a living. I'm personally happy. I know enough about the coaching profession, and no I am not missing it. Pat Sullivan gives me a call and says, I'd like to come over and talk to you. He came over at the house and talked and he said, "We're going to fire Ron Meyer." They had six games left on their schedule that year. He said, "I'm offering you the job."

I said, "Pat, I'll call you in the morning, with my decision about it." I thought about it long and hard because if you had been in the coaching business long enough you knew the drill. I was tired of getting fired and moving. I thought about it and I thought I think I need to do this. I gave him a call and said, "I'm coming over. I'm coming to work." I drove over there and walked in as the new Head Coach of the New England Patriots with eight games left on their schedule. I hadn't been in coaching for two and a half years. I didn't know anybody on the coaching staff except maybe one guy. It was Ron Meyers' staff.

I knew about six veteran players on the team, all the rest of them were new ones that had been brought in since I had been let go two years prior. This is a Thursday and we have a game against the Jets coming up on Sunday there in New England.

That's how I got back in the coaching business. I didn't have anything to do with it. I started looking at this football team and trying to get familiar with the players. Everywhere I looked was talent and depth. I thought to myself this football team has got everything you need to make a run for a championship. They got depth. They have two quarterbacks, Steve Grogan and Tony Eason both of them you could win with. With a 16 game schedule in the NFL, you better have two quarterbacks because trying to get one of them through a season healthy is a major accomplishment.

We had four great wide receivers and two fine tight ends. We had an offense line that was as good as anybody could hope to have and depth there. Then on defense, we had four great corners that could cover anybody man to man, three great safeties and a slew of linebackers and we had good defensive linemen. This team was loaded. I thought to myself what have I inherited here? This team can run with horses. That's the team that I inherited with eight games left. I started learning and getting familiar with the personnel. I think that during that eight game stretch we won four and lost four if I remember right.

Super Bowl XX

By the off-season, I realized what we had. When the season ended, I told the coaching staff, all of which had been brought there by Ron Meyer, "I'm going to hire my own coaching staff now. Any of you guys can apply for the job and I will hire some of you. When it's all over and done with, you're going to be on my staff." There was about two or three of them that did apply and I kept them. There was two or three of them that left.

The good part about it was I knew this team was ready to win if we could just keep it simple. The biggest problem you got with taking over a new team is the learning process that a team's got to go through to learn the system. You just can't operate at full physical ability when you're trying to learn and you're in learning mode. The first year a lot of times is not productive because you just can't go on all cylinders.

The special teams coach I kept so we didn't have to change the special teams system. The defensive coordinator was Rod Rust and I kept him so we didn't have to change our defensive system. Their offensive system was not good enough to win in the NFL and I knew it after I took a look at it. I hired a new offensive staff and in the off-season we installed a new offense. When training camp came, our biggest problem was on offense and it showed up in our early games. I think that after six or eight games, we were playing five hundred football, but then they began it to get it. We got on a roll and won eight or nine in a row to get to the Super Bowl.

When we went to the Super Bowl, we had a first year offense and it was A, B, C. I'm not real sure if it was even C, but it was A and B. It was that simple and that basic. The theory was and it wasn't just a theory because I'd been around long enough to know that if you've got great players, don't confuse them, let the physical abilities flow. If you put too much on their minds, it isn't going to work. I knew I had great players. I didn't want to screw them up. It went A and B and it did us well all to the Super Bowl.

The problem with an A and B offense when you come up against a PhD defense, you've got a problem. We couldn't score against the Chicago Bears. They had a defense they had been putting together for five years. They had a defensive minded coach over there named Buddy Ryan that was as good as it got in the NFL. They had a great defense with great personnel and a great defensive scheme. Our little A, B deep offense just was not up to handling a PhD defense so we couldn't score and got our butts beat.

Best Defenses Of All-Time

There's no question about Buddy Ryan's defense. All you have to do is look up the numbers. Looking at the NFL since the '50s, I would rank the Chicago Bear defense in 1985, in the top four or five that I've ever seen. When ranking the Pittsburgh Steelers, I'd look at the defenses under Chuck Noll. They had a great defensive coach up there, Bud Carson. I would say that was the best defense I've ever seen.

I would put Tom Landry's Dallas Cowboy defenses in that ranking too. George Allen with the Washington Redskins was a defensive genius. He was with the Chicago Bears when they won the World Championship. Then he went on to be a head coach. Playing against George Allen's defense was a full day's work. Those are four or five of the best. Buddy Ryan is as good as any of them.

George Allen

You had your work cut out for you when you were playing George Allen's teams when he was with the Bears, Rams, or Redskins. He was an absolute defensive genius. No question about it. Buddy Ryan's defensive scheme was right there with him. I'll add Tom Landry, Bud Carson, and Chuck Noll to that group also.

I had the privilege of facing all of those guys. I was with Forrest Gregg and the Cleveland Browns for two years. One year, we had to play the Steelers twice. I saw them up close and personal for two years. They had personnel and a scheme; it was just a great defense. If you want to have a nightmare as a receiver, just go up against Mel Blount all day.

Best Player All Time

Jim Brown and Johnny Unitas were the best. They are in a class all by themselves. Jim should have been outlawed. He was something.

We played in Baltimore in 1959, and won the World Championship that year. We played Cleveland in Baltimore another year and Jim Brown scored five touchdowns. They beat us 35-28.

Photograph copyright Associated Press

Chapter 16

Forrest Gregg

College:
Southern Methodist

Career History:
Green Bay Packers (1956–1970)
Dallas Cowboys (1971)

As Coach:
San Diego Chargers (1972–1973) (Off. Line)
Cleveland Browns (1974) (Off. Line)
Cleveland Browns (1975–1977)
Toronto Argonauts (1979)
Cincinnati Bengals (1980–1983)
Green Bay Packers (1984–1987)
SMU Mustangs (1989–1990)
Shreveport Pirates (1994–1995)

1977 Inductee Pro Football Hall of Fame

College Choice
SMU was in the Southwest conference and they were probably as good as Texas at that time. My high school football coach went to SMU and he encouraged me to go. He felt I would like it there.

I played both ways. I played what we called inside tackle on both lines. I did a lot of pulling and double-teaming. I played all sports in high school. I played basketball, baseball, and was on the track team.

NFL Draft
The Packers drafted me in the second round in 1956. I wasn't sure where Green Bay was. I had to get the address and then check. I thought it was up in Minnesota or somewhere like that, or Illinois. I didn't know. I found out quick where they were. The Packers weren't very good around that time.

Early Years with Packers
It was a change because a lot more pass blocking was required. It was great. There were a lot of outstanding football players. Competition was fierce.

When I got to Green Bay they weren't sure where they were going to play me. They didn't know whether they were going to play me on offense or defense. I got to play a little bit of defense during training camp. We opened with the Bears that year. The Bears beat us. I think I played about three plays on defense and I played on special teams. I really wanted to play defense. I thought I could play defensive end.

I was drafted in '56 and went into the Army. I was in the Army in '57 and missed one full season and one game. I first met Willie Davis when we played football together at Fort Carson, Colorado. He got out of the Army before I did. He went back to the Cleveland Browns and was traded to Green Bay the next year.

Green Bay had a terrible season in '58. That was the year before Lombardi came. We were 1-10-1.

Vince Lombardi
After the '58 season was over, I went back home to Dallas and got a job. I also finished school. I needed three credit hours to finish my degree. When I went back to school, I got a job working with the school. I heard that they had fired Scooter McLean who was the Head Coach and hired some guy named Vince Lombardi, an assistant coach from the New York Giants. I didn't know anything about him.

I went to some SMU sports functions in downtown Dallas in the spring of '59. I ran into a friend of mine named Donnie Goss. Donnie had played for the Cleveland Browns and was traded to the New York Giants. Donnie asked me, "You know anything about that Lombardi that they hired in Green Bay?" I said, "No I don't Donnie. Do you know anything about him?" He said, "Yes, he's a real bastard." That was my first knowledge of Vince Lombardi.

I went to training camp and didn't unpack my bags right away because I didn't know if I was leaving. Lombardi turned out to be the greatest coach of all time. He was a disciplinarian. As Henry Jordan said one time, "He treats us all the same. Like dogs."

He was tough but fair. He treated everybody the same. It didn't matter who you were. Bart Starr, Paul Hornung, or some other player, were all treated the same. If you didn't perform up to his expectations you heard about it. I think one of the things that made him great, was he expected to win. He had great expectations of every player. You thought, if Lombardi thinks that I'm good enough to do this, I must be. That's the kind of guy he was. He was a good football coach, a knowledgeable coach. We had a physical team. He expected us to win.

We had a challenging football team. That was basically the thing; you look back, not necessarily at the starting positions, but at the team. It was basically the same team that went 1-10-1. The talent was there. What needed to happen was we needed to be put together. Like I said, he had great expectations of us and would not accept less.

Not one player ever got away with anything as far as breaking the rules were concerned. You just didn't get away with it. If you missed meetings, you were fined. If you were late for a meeting, you were fined. If you were late for curfew and you were caught, you were fined.

Paul Hornung
Paul Hornung respected Vince Lombardi. Paul was great football player. He was a team player.

Vince Lombardi Calling Forrest Gregg The Best Player He Ever Coached
I can't even begin to tell you how I felt. Of all the great players that he coached in Green Bay, New York, and Washington; for him to say I was the best player he ever coached made me feel very humble.

Favorite Moment in NFL
I think probably one of the biggest games we ever played was the '61 NFL Championship game against the Giants. We had a pretty good high school team but we never won our district. We never got into the playoffs. When I was at SMU we had a lot of fine football players. We never got into the playoffs or went to a bowl game.

I remember going out onto Lambeau Field in 1961. Jerry Kramer had been hurt earlier in the season. They moved me from right tackle where I'd made All-Pro, to right guard taking Jerry's place while he was hurt. I remember being introduced and running out on the field for that game. It was an awesome feeling. We were able to score pretty well that day and we beat the Giants. At that time it was called the World Championship.

Super Bowl I
The big thing about Super Bowl I was the uncertainty of the competition that we were playing against. We met some of those guys playing for the Kansas City Chiefs coming out of college, but there were a lot of them we didn't know. The only thing you could tell about them was their size. We would watch them play against teams who we didn't know anything about. We didn't know how good our competition was. Going into that game, we were picked to win. We were representing the old guard, the National Football League. We were expected to win. We were able to pull it off and that was awesome.

I never saw as much media in my life as we saw during that week prior to the game. We went to Santa Barbara, California and worked out. We were playing the game in the Coliseum. We had the media following us all week long. There were television and newspaper reporters, the Associated Press, radio, you name it, they were there.

Chicago Bears vs. Green Bay Packers Rivalry
It was never like any other game playing the Bears. Vince Lombardi wanted to beat George Halas but he wanted to beat everybody.

As far as the Bear's defensive linemen, the one I remember most of all was Ed O'Bradovich. Ed and I banged heads together usually three times year; because it seemed to me, we always played the Bears in preseason and twice during the regular season. Ed and I competed against each other. We were both about the same age. He was one of my favorite players. He wasn't a dirty football player but he was a tough football player.

Comparing Ray Nitschke, Bill George, & Dick Butkus
Ray Nitschke said he was the better player. He was my teammate and I'd have to agree with him. Dick Butkus said he was better and Bill George said he was better. Don't ask me to pick because they're all great football players. It was fun playing against them because I knew I was playing

against the best. One way to measure yourself is how you stand up against the other guy when you're playing against the best.

Year with Dallas Cowboys

That was a great year for me. Dallas had been to the Super Bowl the year before I got there. After I had retired from Green Bay, I moved to Dallas and was selling sporting goods. Dallas had a bunch of offensive lineman get hurt during training camp. Tom Landry called me and asked if I would be interested in playing. I remember getting my football shoes and reporting to their training quarters, which was north of my home in Dallas. I went in the locker room with my football shoes in my hand, and those guys looked at me like, what in the world is this guy doing here.

On the way to my locker, I ran into Herb Adderley who I played with at Green Bay. We got to talk. Then I ran into Bob Lilly. We knew each other well and he was a welcome site to see. Knowing that you've got great players like those guys on your team makes you think, we have a chance to win, and we did.

Tom Landry was a great football coach. Tom was one of the most knowledgeable football coaches I ever had. Offense or defense, he knew the p's and q's of both sides of the ball. He was a good teacher and the system that he used was a lot like the system in Green Bay. Lombardi had been the offensive coordinator with the New York Giants and Tom had been the defensive coordinator. They both adopted that Giants way of doing things. That wasn't totally strange to me except the Dallas offense was much more complicated than Green Bay's.

Coaching Career

I always wanted to coach. I had a job opportunity in sporting goods. It was a way to making a good living. I always thought in the back of my mind that I would like to coach. I guess one of the things that I thought was, I can't be Vince Lombardi. I'm not like him. If that's what it takes to win in football, I don't know whether I can do that or not. Then go out and play for a guy like Tom Landry, who was similar in a lot of ways to Vince, but not the disciplinarian. Tom had expectations of his players also. I think that's one thing that I think they both learned from Jim Lee Howell in New York. There was a lot of peer pressure with the Cowboys. I guess that's the best way to describe it. If you were the starter you were expected to perform with a winning attitude and a winning performance. I never was a starter there but I noticed the players. If you didn't perform well in a game, some guy beat you and sacked the quarterback, you're teammates looked down their nose at you. I would say that was one of the differences in Lombardi and Landry.

I thought I couldn't be like Vince Lombardi and win because you've got to be yourself. I thought there's Tom Landry who was exactly the opposite as Vince Lombardi and he won, so he was himself. He wasn't anybody else and didn't try to be anybody else. That's the same way it was with Vince.

I thought well if that's the case then maybe I've got a chance to win as a coach. That's what put me in the direction of coaching. I knew after that season that I probably wouldn't play anymore or maybe shouldn't play anymore. I started looking for a coaching job when that season was over. I got an offer for a line-coaching job at San Diego.

Raymond Berry

Raymond Berry and I played side-by-side in college. I played left tackle, he played left end. He was also at that time playing both ways. Raymond was a smart ball player. He looked at the other people's offense and figured out what they were trying to do. He also did that on the other side of the ball. I never had to worry about a player getting around the corner before I would have a chance to make a tackle. That was good for the team and good for me. Raymond was a tough and physical football player. He grew up in a football home. His father was a high school coach in Paris, Texas and had been there most of Raymond's life. Raymond grew up in a football family. He also had great hands.

Pro Football Hall of Fame Induction

I never felt that I would be in the football Hall of Fame. I strived to be the best that I could be. I wanted to win football games for Vince Lombardi. I thought about the Hall of Fame but I didn't know whether it would ever happen or not. There are very few people that make it. I just don't know what the numbers are right now. Last time I counted there's not a lot of players inducted into the Pro-Football Hall of Fame. It's just a dream come true.

Ed O'Bradovich

Recently I have been diagnosed with Parkinson's disease. One of the nicest letters I ever received was from a guy named Ed O'Bradovich who wrote me a letter and gave me a lot of encouragement in fighting this disease. There are some things in your life that you'll never forget. I won't forget that letter that I got from Ed and the encouraging words that he gave me. I just think that he's a big old guy, he was a tough football player, and played every down to the best of his ability.

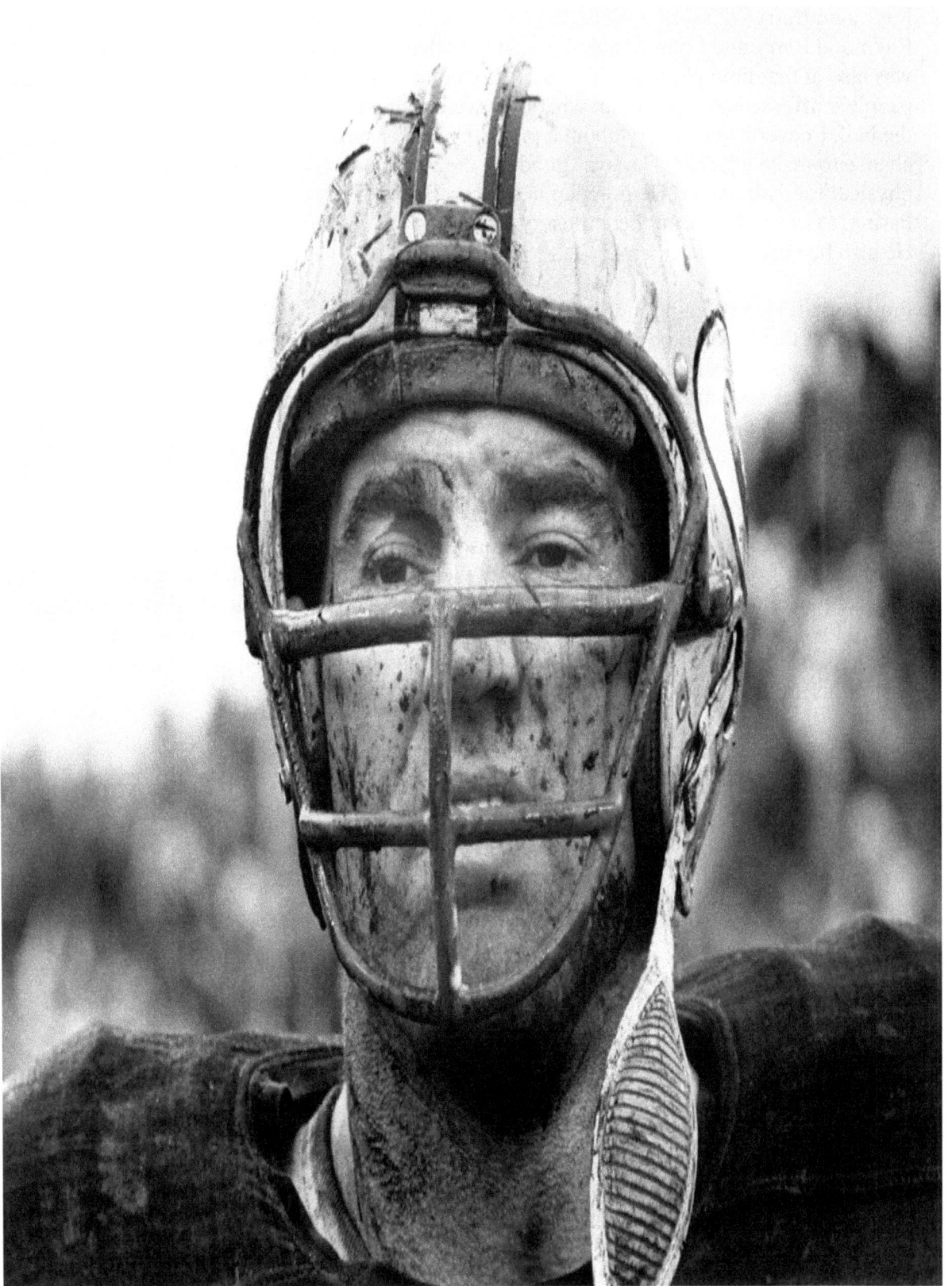

Photograph copyright Associated Press

Chapter 17

Lenny Moore

College:
Penn State

Career History:
Baltimore Colts (1956–1967)

1975 Inductee Pro Football Hall of Fame

College Choice

I wasn't really thinking about college. My brothers enlisted in the service and I thought I'd do the same. They enlisted in the service because that was one less mouth to feed at home. They would get allotment checks and send them home to help out with expenses. I didn't see anything down the road. I just took it year by year. My high school coach, Andy Stopper, stayed after me and encouraged me to go away to school.

Next thing you know, it was my senior year of high school and colleges were calling me. Thank God, as I said before, for Andy Stopper. He said, "Lenny, you've got to go away to school. You need that college education."

Then prayerfully he said, "You'll do well with the football team. I'm not concerned about the football side because I know that you're going to be all right there. So I'm going to stay after you and hope that you go away to school."

The high school line coach was a guy named Bob Perugini. Bob Perugini went to Penn State, and that's when the door opened up for me. We just kept it right in line, and that's where I ended up.

Rip Engle

Rip Engle was my college coach. Bob Perugini and Andy Stopper, opened up the gates for me at Penn State.

Joe Paterno learned from Rip Engle. That I know. In fact, Joe had even said before his death, that he learned what he knew from Rip Engle. Both of them were at Brown University. Rip Engle was the head coach at Brown University, and Joe Paterno was his quarterback. Joe was all set to go to law school. When Rip took the Penn State job, he brought Joe with him. That's how Joe ended up at Penn State. They had a father-son type of relationship. Rip just kept Joe under his wing. Joe learned Rip's disciplines and coaching style. He tried to keep the same thing going when he became head coach in the '60s, after Rip retired.

Penn State in the Mid-'50s

For men of color at Penn State, which was predominantly a white university, there were some things that were very difficult to deal with because there were certain places I couldn't go. Aside from that, there was no place to get a haircut. We had to learn where we could go and where we couldn't go, and what we could do and what we couldn't do. A lot of our time was spent in the dorms; I'll put it that way.

Baltimore

The same racial issues were everywhere and very difficult to deal with. When I got to Baltimore, black athletes basically had only one area to go for entertainment, and that was Pennsylvania Avenue. Pennsylvania Avenue was just about the only street that was wide open to us, where we could seek entertainment and places to eat, without going through the race process.

I checked with a lot of the older guys like Ollie Matson, Marion Motley, and Buddy Young. Those guys were there way before me. I'd ask them how they dealt with things, especially when I went out of town. You couldn't go anywhere if your hotel was downtown. You couldn't go to the movies; you couldn't go in certain stores, and things like that.

That was pretty common in most of the major cities. You just had to deal with it. You were confined to the hotel. There were a few places we stayed on the outskirts of town. That way the team could stay together without splitting up. That was typical all over the league.

We also knew that number of black players allowed on certain teams was going to be limited. We talked to each other about situations, and how it was going and how we were dealing with it. It was always keep your mouth shut, do what they tell you to do, and just be cool.

I thank God like I said, with the atmosphere, the separation of blacks and whites; you never knew what was going to happen down the road. You just didn't know. You couldn't just relax and think, everything is okay, because it wasn't okay. It was about being careful and watching yourself, because you didn't know what was going on. We would check with the other guys of color on the other teams. They were going through the same things.

It wasn't until years later that you heard that every team was given a quota of how many black athletes could be on a team. You weren't able to go over that number. Of course, we didn't know that. We always did the best we could and prayed that we became a part of the team. That was the way it was.

Baltimore Colts Teammates

It was about whatever God-given abilities we had, that Raymond Berry had, and that John Unitas had. That really encompassed the team because we knew, regardless of what the situation was, once the game was over, they went their way, we went our way. You know what I mean. That's just the way it was during that time, but we knew that we had to come together as one and play to the best of our abilities. There was no separation on the team, just business as usual.

I played against Alan Ameche in college when he was at Wisconsin. I didn't know anything about Raymond Berry until we played for the Baltimore Colts. I realized that collectively, we grew together as one team. That was very, very encouraging because we knew we needed each other. We also knew that for us to move ahead, we had to give the best we had, whatever our abilities were. For me, it was a lot of praying. I did a lot of praying and hoping that everything was going to work out for the best.

I knew nothing about Johnny Unitas. I knew nothing about any of them, with the exception of Ameche. All I knew about him came from when I played against him. As far as their backgrounds and things of that nature, I knew nothing about them at all.

We had to work as a team, but once the whistle blew, they went their way; we went our way. That was unfortunate because we didn't get a chance to really know each other during those early years.

Spats Nickname
When I was in college, Rip Engle's Penn State team was what you would probably call Plain Janes. They had plain uniforms, plain everything. Just simplicity. No dressing up, so to speak. The backfield guys couldn't wear low-cut shoes. If you looked at other teams, most of those backfield guys wore low-cuts. Rip's backfield guys had high-tops, just like the linemen. Everybody was dressed the same. Rip Engle wanted everybody to be the same.

Bob was a backfield guy who had hurt his ankle. Of course, with the high-top shoes and stuff, he had to get his ankles really taped up. I just strapped myself down with high-tops. Of course, they made comments. What are you doing with that tape on your shoes? I said, "Well, it makes me feel good", as I taped it on the outside. It did make me feel good. I just kept doing it.

Now what I did was, as they would tape the guy's ankles, there was always a little bit of tape left on the roll that they would throw in the trash. So they couldn't get on me about using tape. I would maybe grab about a half a dozen of those rolls and tape my shoes.

Of course, that became a fixture with me, even when I got in the pros. I did the same thing. I said, "I'm not wearing low-cut shoes. I'm wearing high-tops." A lot of the backfield guys looked at me and said, "Man, what are you wearing them old shoes for?" That's what I did. It's just something I learned in college and I just kept it going.

Johnny Unitas
Fortunately for me, I had the opportunity to go to quite a few Pro Bowls where they always had the top quarterbacks. I was able to see some of the top quarterbacks in the league and compare them to Johnny Unitas. I said, "Man. Johnny is better than these guys, or at least he's as good as, if not better than, a lot of these guys." He just didn't get the publicity or have that kind of publicity until we grew as a team. Going into our second year, we got into the playoffs. Then of course '58 we were world champions, and '59. The rest is history as far as Johnny U was concerned.

He was a guy that, whatever ability he had, he used it and took it to a different level. He pushed himself. Johnny was his own man. He learned. He watched a lot of film, which is the key to really knowing the game from the inside out. Not only that, he had the great Raymond Berry with him. Both of them watched films like crazy. Nobody else on the team really watched films other than when we had our meetings, because when practice was over, boom, everybody hit the locker room, and we were on our way home. That's the way it was.

Raymond Berry

Raymond Berry came to me, and I never ever forgot it and said, "Lenny, I've been watching films. Based upon what I have seen from the films we need more of you in our offense." I was wondering, what in the heck is he talking about. I said, "Weeb Eubank is our coach. He's the one that calls the shots. He's the one that gets us in position." He said, "You can catch, so why can't we use you a little bit more often as a wide receiver?"

We started working on pass patterns and running pass patterns and he told me, "You're going against the great Dick Night Train Lane!" I'm looking right at Raymond the whole time. He said, "Night Train Lane knocks the hell out of people. He's one of them guys, he will throw that form at you and you've got to learn to get away from him. But in the meantime, he's giving himself up, Lenny. There are certain patterns I've got that we can do against a guy like Night Train. That's how I ended up being a wide receiver as well as being a running back. Running back was something I always did.

Also, fortunately for me, I went both ways in college. In college, I was a defensive back as well as being a running back. Now, at Penn State, we didn't throw the ball that much, but at least I learned how to tackle. I learned how to cover, as a defensive back would do. I learned how to bring punts and kickoffs back and that kind of thing. I was a good special teams man because I did it all the way through college.

Coming into the pros, putting me in other positions wasn't a handicap for me. It wasn't hard for me to make the adjustment. Thanks to Raymond Berry, who was the one that came up with the idea to use more of me in the wide receiving position. This opened it up for him, as he was the wide out on the other side of the field. That's how all of that happened.

He told me, "Lenny, John is not going to throw the ball to you unless you work with him." What that meant was to stay after practice and work with Johnny on running pass patterns to get the timing down. Raymond said, "Johnny's got to have the confidence that he knows where you're going to be and how you're going to cut on certain patterns. Never cut on your inside foot, because you'll be out of balance. Make sure that you cut on your outside foot if you're going to make a sideline cut. Make sure your outside foot is your plant foot."

He was so right, because when I started practicing these patterns and things like that, I understood exactly what he was talking about, to get the body in sync so that you would have your hand-and-eye coordination together. All that came from Raymond. He worked with me on running pass patterns and things of that nature. That's how I learned.

Johnny Unitas started the drill that most pro teams use today, in 1958. They called it the "two-minute drill." Nobody did that but Johnny U, and that was back in 1958. That was something that we worked on just for the 1958 NFL Championship, because nobody did any kind of a two-minute drill. You'd get right up to the line of scrimmage and he call the plays right up on the line. Other teams didn't do that. Guys would always break out of the huddle and the quarterback would get up and call the plays. We didn't huddle.

1958 NFL Championship
There was confusion when the game was over, because we were tired and nobody knew what to do. The referees and the officials weren't sure what to do. They called their own huddle and were trying to figure out what to do. They talked to the head coaches, and decided that we needed to play another quarter and try to work it out.

The officials decided that whichever team scored first, won the game. Other than that, they weren't sure exactly what to do. They weren't sure if we should play a complete quarter or end the game once one team scored. They made their decision, and the rest is history. Gino Marchetti got hurt in that game, and they took him off the field in a stretcher.

Art Donovan, Big Daddy Lipscomb, & Roger Brown
It was unusual to see guys that big. Big Daddy was about 280. Donovan was about 275. That was huge for defensive linemen. Most of the defensive linemen were 240, 245, maybe 250, at the most. When you had guys like Donovan and Big Daddy Lipscomb and Big Roger Brown, from the Detroit Lions, weighing about 300 pounds, that was an unusual.

Gino Marchetti
Gino Marchetti was as active as any defensive end could possibly be jumping over people, getting around people, and just lightning fast. He developed the position. Most guys that came after that learned from Gino. That was it, because most of the time, most of the linemen took care of their own territory and then released, but Gino was fast.

You had offensive tackles trying to block Gino. Man, that was a job and a half for them, because there was nothing they could do to hold him up. Gino was that good, that fast, and that strong jumping and getting around.

Pro Football Hall of Fame Induction
The only thing I thought about it was, 'Gosh, what an honor,' when I got in. You had to wait like five years to be eligible. During my third year of eligibility, they said I just missed out, and then I didn't make it the fourth year. I think I got in the fifth year. I think that's the way it happened. But no, it's just a question of getting in. Man, with such a high honor as that, wow.

Jim Brown Best Player Ever?
Well, when you say, "Best player ever," that's a heavy subject, to say "the best ever." Jim Brown's is in that category. I could probably say that he's one of the best.

Jim Brown was something else. No question about that. When you start mentioning good or top running backs, Jim Brown is right there. Rules have changed over the years and the way things are done, but Jim, no question, is up there among the tops.

Affiliation

Definitely I am an ex-Baltimore, not Indianapolis, I am a Baltimore Colt. I don't support the Indianapolis Colts. I am a Ravens fan to the nth degree. The Ravens are my team.

I was working for the Colts at the time that they left Baltimore, in one of the front-office jobs doing public relations. You could hear the talk going around that Bob Irsay was thinking about moving the team, but nobody really mentioned how serious he was. The next thing you know, boom. Here come the trucks and everything was gone. He was a very, very unusual man, to say the least, in his way of doing things.

We're not Indianapolis Colts. We are Baltimore Colts alumni. That's who we are. When they left, they left. I can't give enough kudos to the fantastic Art Modell. What a tremendous, tremendous gentleman. I grew as I got to know him. He was that grand of an individual. You could see, everything he did was one for all, all for one. Fortunately for us, Carroll Rosenbloom was a great man also.

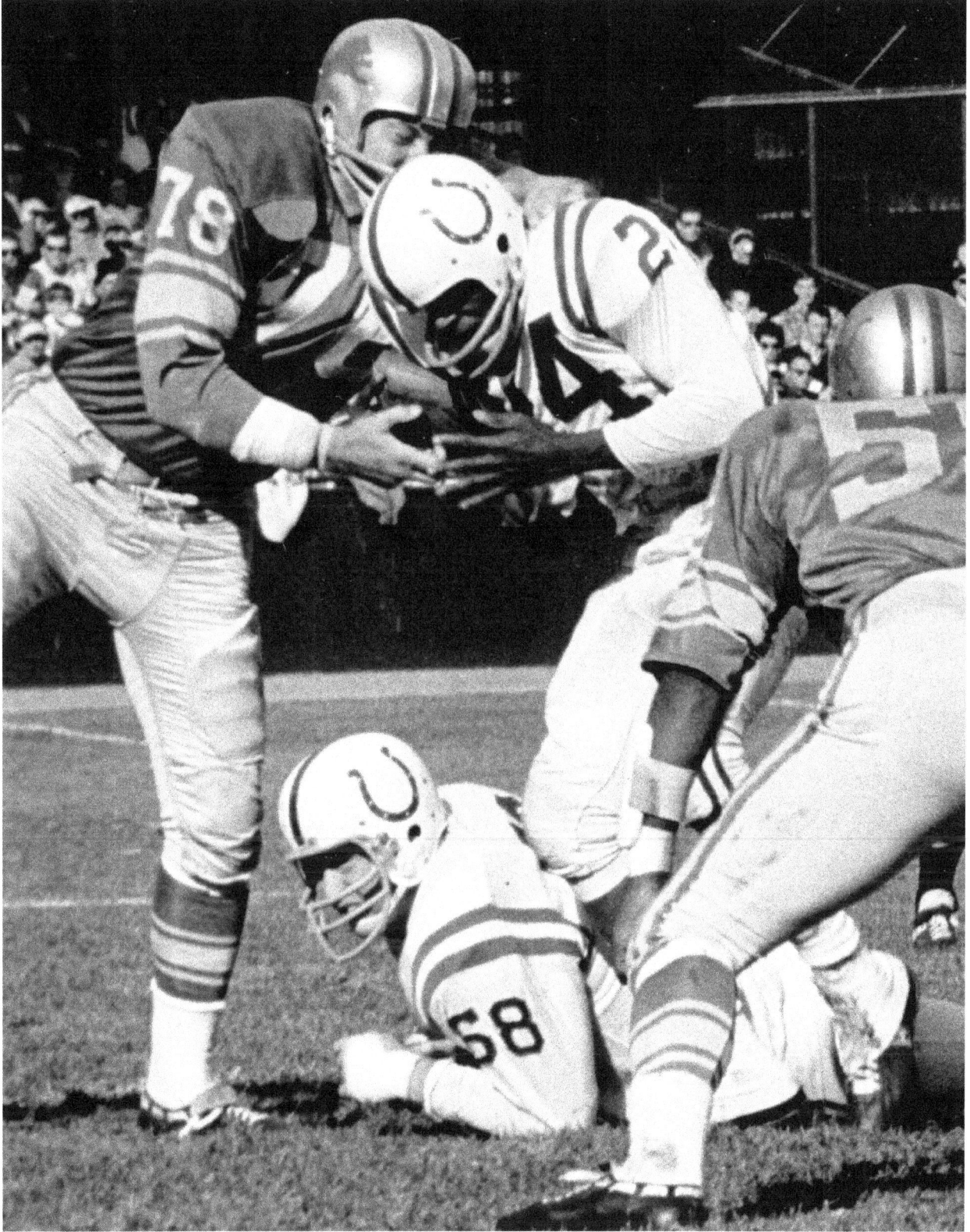

Baltimore Colt Lenny Moore is met by Detroit Lion defensive end Darrius McCord.
Photograph copyright Associated Press

Chapter 18

Bart Starr

College: Alabama Career History: As Player: Green Bay Packers (1956–71) As Coach: Green Bay Packers (1975–83) Head Coach 1977 Inductee Pro Football Hall of Fame

College Choice

I grew up in Montgomery, Alabama. My Dad was in the military so we lived all over the country. In my final years of high school, he was able to stay in one location for a few years so I was able to stay in the same school.

I met this beautiful lady whom I'd fallen in love with in when I was a senior in high school. I stayed at the University of Alabama because I discovered that she was going to go to Auburn. Originally I was planning to go to Kentucky and play for Coach Bryant. I thought to myself, if I go to Kentucky, and she goes to Alabama, I'm going to lose her. I call it the greatest audible of my life. I chose to go to Tuscaloosa where I could get an old jalopy or something, so I could drive to see her and at least keep that relationship alive. It turned out to be a great decision because I married her.

The University of Alabama is an excellent school and I knew that going in. I really enjoyed it. I was in the business school there. It was just super fun and a great challenge. I enjoyed all four years.

Draft

I didn't know that much about Green Bay. I knew where it was obviously, but I wasn't that familiar with it. It was a joy and an honor and the longer we stayed there the more we came to love it even more. It is a tremendous community. The people are fabulous and I'm not exaggerating. They're as great you'll find anywhere. They were inspired by that low round draft choice. I was going to prove to them that I was worth it. I understood why I was a low round draft choice. At any rate, I'd worked extremely hard. I'd never worked so hard in my life before going to that first Green Bay Packer training camp.

We weren't a powerhouse, but I just wanted to get into the NFL and to play there. The more reading I did about Green Bay, the team franchise, the community, the more I was falling in love with it. I could hardly wait to get up there.

Packer Offense

The way plays were called how they were established and what the rationale was and so forth and so on was a change. That too led to an excitement, a challenge, because it was something a little different than what you had perhaps been associated with somewhere else.

I enjoyed our offense because it was solid. The offense was solid because it was based on the run more than the pass. In those days, we had some very strong runners. Obviously, we were taking advantage of that and we had some excellent offensive linemen.

By having that as a core, our passing game was very effective. We could run play-action passes as though it was going to be a run and pull back and pass and so forth. It offered a great challenge for us and it was a very strong challenge for our opponents.

I didn't know the size of the playbooks that some of the other teams had. We were very strong and very solid. We had everything built around a core of plays. We obviously had excellent alternate plays off of those core plays. What we had that was very strong on Coach Lombardi's part was the core of an offense that was so sound and so solid that it was unbelievable. We were very, very proud and pleased with it.

Being a Backup in Green Bay

You want to play and you understand why maybe coaches are going with someone else. They have different reasons. They know more about the other person and so on and so forth and they're staying with them. I felt that it was a challenge each day in practice. You wanted to perform better so they would see you as a possibility of working into that starting slot.

Vince Lombardi Hiring

We didn't have any idea at all. We were just interested and reading a lot about him and following him and so forth, but no, we had no idea at all because we had not been exposed to him that much.

It changed immediately because when he held his first meeting with us I could tell within 15 seconds that this man was truly going to be special. The way he approached the meeting, he had about 10 or 12 of us, a mixture of offense and defensive players.

His approach was so solid, so sound, so simple, and direct that you couldn't wait to get to the next little piece he was going to talk about. I'll always remember our first meeting because after we were in it for about 45 minutes we took a break. I ran a short distance down the hallway there in the Packer office building where we were holding the meeting and got on the pay telephone and called my wife back in Alabama. All I said to her was, "Honey, we're going to begin to win."

The championships were not all because of him, but primarily because of him because leadership starts at the top. You have to have strong leaders if you're going to accomplish anything. Obviously you have to have the people with you that form the team. That's what that leader does because he's going to get great assistant coaches, good players and so forth. They build an organization. It was so obvious, as I said, from that first meeting that we were going to change and going to win. That's when I was so pumped.

Losing the first and only championship game he ever did was difficult on him, he moved on immediately after it because that was typical of Coach Lombardi. It was a disappointment so he used that as a plus, as a tool for building, rebuilding and going on and winning the next ones.

Super Bowl I
It was exciting, very challenging, and thrilling. We were just blown away and honored to be in it. Little did the traditional NFL people know how strong that game was and how good the Kansas City Chiefs were because I can tell you unequivocally the Kansas City Chiefs were an outstanding team.

I think that we were very strong as a team because we had been together for longer than they had been. We were able to handle them quite well. I don't think enough people realize how tough every play was. The Chiefs were good and we didn't just run all over them and so forth, and blow them out of the stadium. That was just not the case at all. The Chiefs were very well coached, extremely talented group, and we had a fierce competitive game going on, which we knew going in.

Coach Lombardi had done a great job of preparing us for it. We didn't over look it and didn't just think that this was a secondary kind of league that we were playing. He saw how good the Kansas City Chiefs were.

He was typically a sound and thorough coach. He was extremely well organized. Lombardi was very, very well prepared, and thorough in his approach of handling different people in different positions throughout the team.

Paul Hornung
Paul was quite a gentleman. He was vibrant, alive, and despised curfews. He and Max McGee, I don't know if they ever made two curfews the whole time they played with the Packers. Coach Lombardi fined the heck out of them and went on about his business because he knew how good they were.

Max McGee Super Bowl I
Ironically, I saw Max McGee the morning of the game and knew that he had been out all night. I was going down to pick up a paper the morning of the game. I was walking toward the front desk to pick it up. On my left was one of the entrances of the hotel and walking through, and this was at 7 a.m. the morning of the first Super Bowl is Max McGee. My thought was oh my God, here we are in the biggest, greatest game of our lives and this guy has been out all night. He had been but you saw what he did. He just played like gangbusters during that ballgame.

Bob Skoronski Not Being Inducted Into Pro Football Hall Of Fame
I can tell you one player that is very, very deserving and I think it is disappointing he is not in. I root for Bob Skoronski each year and write about him each year. He was our offensive captain and our left tackle, blindside tackle, for me. He was a fabulous, fabulous tackle. Flip that over

and on the right side was Forrest Gregg. Forrest Gregg went into the Hall of Fame with me in 1977. If you looked at the grades on Monday morning following ballgames the marks for Bob Skoronski and Forrest Gregg were almost identical.

I'm not sure how the selection committee is structured, but I'm obviously very biased. I've seen others who have gone into the Hall of Fame since we went in years ago. With no disrespect to them, many of them are good, but I have yet to see an offensive tackle or lineman go in there that's anywhere close to what Bob Skoronski was.

Most people unfortunately don't have a clue because of all the media that was directed toward Forrest Gregg, and deservedly so. He deserved it. Bob Skoronski also deserves it.

Ice Bowl

We were very confident because the lead play on short yardage in that ballgame was a wedge play, meaning you had two linemen somewhere up front coming together with a wedge against a single defensive player. With no disrespect to anyone we ran the wedge play on one of the defensive players with the Cowboys. We had run it two or three times. We had run it once before we scored and had gained yardage on it then. We knew the play would work. It was very, very strong.

The Cowboys developed a submarine technique where their linemen charged so low you couldn't block them. All you could do was fall on them except for one defensive lineman who was so big and tall he couldn't get down that low. His charge angle was up and you could just knock him back. We'd seen it, we'd done it, and we did it out on the field.

Unfortunately, the ground was so slick and so hard it was tough to get footing to make it go. That's why we scored on that play that we called because we got enough footing and got in. Rather than give the ball to the fullback, whom we had used on that play, and him slipping and sliding on the ground that was so hard, I was upright. I could shuffle my feet and then lunge in. That's why we called that play when we did.

Coaching Green Bay

It was very tough and very demanding and a very poor mistake on my part. I don't think that you can get into something and do it successfully unless you prepare well for it. I had not prepared to coach. I had no ambitions to be a coach. I was delighted to be where I was and what I was doing.

I think if you're going to be a coach you work your way up the ladder until you have earned the right and earned the experience to be a good head coach. I hadn't done any of that. As a result, I was not that successful. It was an embarrassment for me.

Pro Football Hall of Fame Induction

I was extremely honored and humbled by my induction. It's truly a unique honor when you're in something like that.

Favorite Moment In the NFL

I think my favorite moment that I had in the NFL was in the Ice Bowl and what that game meant to us. We had prepared so diligently for it and then to play under those conditions and along with those fellows. I am not exaggerating the ground was as hard as this desk that I'm sitting here tapping on right now. I don't know how we were able to do what we did or what Dallas did as well. It was very, very, very difficult to play that day.

It's a great challenge in a situation like that. I think that you call on your strengths and you have to have the right attitude. I personally feel that next to God, attitude is the strongest word in our vocabulary. I think in a situation like that, your attitude in a game where the ground is just almost frozen, and it is so cold it's unbelievable, that your attitude is going to be a very, very strong asset.

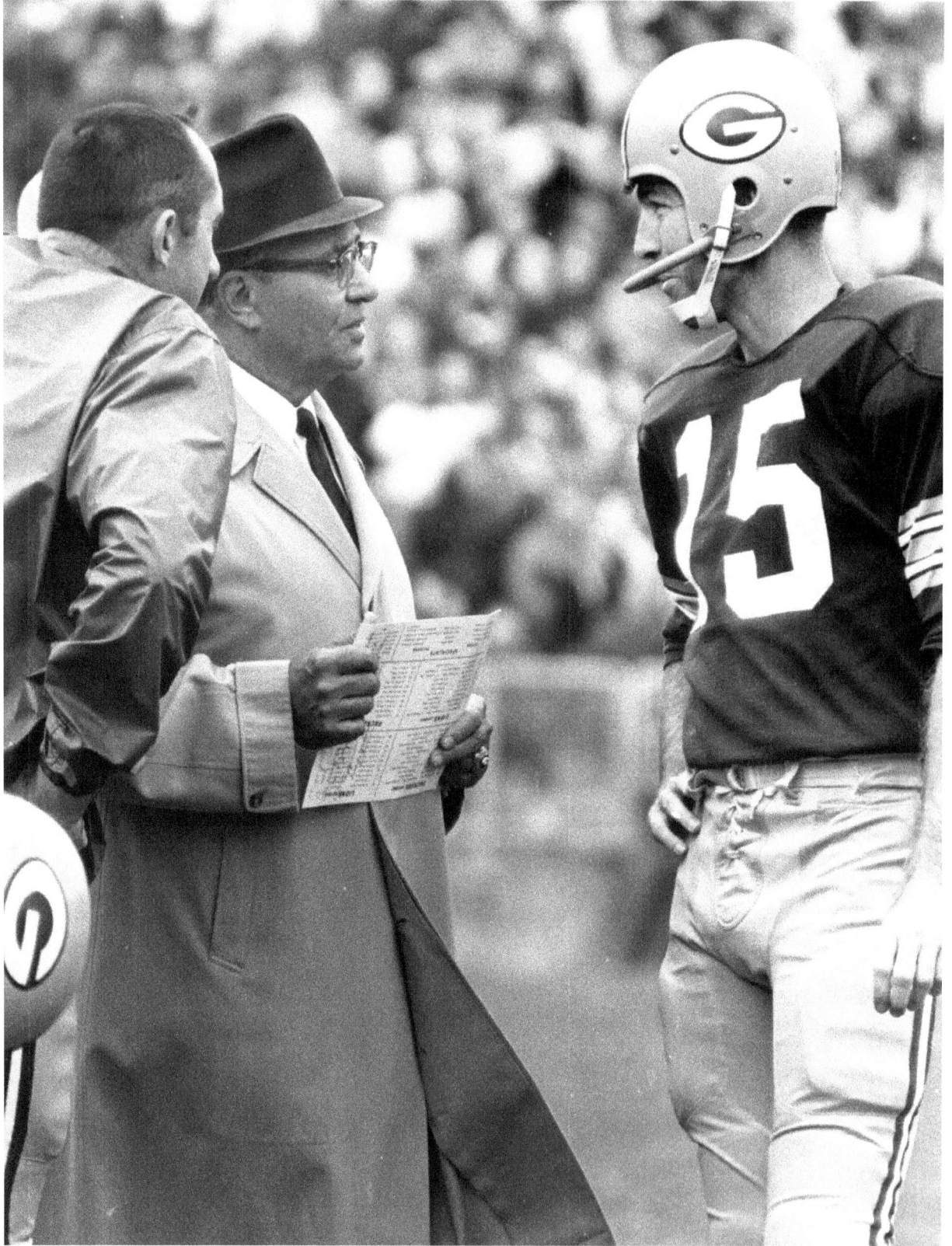

Green Bay Packer Bart Starr talks with Head Coach Vince Lombardi. Photograph copyright Associated Press

Chapter 19

Willie Davis

College:
Grambling State

Career History:
Cleveland Browns (1958-1959)
Green Bay Packers (1960-1969)

1981 Inductee Pro Football Hall of Fame

College Choice
Actually, I went to Grambling State because of the coach more than anything. Coach Eddie Robinson, who as you know before he passed away, turned out to be the winningest coach ever. You'd only need to spend a couple of minutes with him to know why. He was the most dynamic man. He could make you feel like you were his only child for a moment, and the next moment he could make you realize that kickin' your butt was the best thing for you.

I was playing football in the South. Very, very few of the southern schools in the SEC and other places were integrated. I never played against a team that had white players on it until I went to Cleveland.

Grambling
At Grambling Coach Eddie Robinson insisted that you not suffer in any situation for not getting the right information, the right style, or the right everything. He made it a point to make sure that every Grambling player was up-to-date. When I went to Cleveland, I didn't feel like I missed anything that any white player possibly would have done because I had covered it at Grambling. Buck Buchanan & Willie Brown are in the Pro Football Hall of Fame from Grambling and there are a couple others that skip me right now. Coach Robinson, at one time, had 13 players in the pros at the time. He truly was a coach probably ahead of his time.

First Training Camp With Cleveland Browns
Frankly, I didn't know what to expect. I was a little bit fearful of some of the challenges, but once I got there, I got acclimated. It's football any way you look at it. I remember Coach Eddie Robinson telling me when I was up at camp (he used to call me Big Dave), "Big Dave, how is it going?" I said, "Coach, it's going okay, but I feel like I spend half the time explaining where Grambling is." He said, "What?" I said, "I feel like I spend half the time with the players and the other half with other people explaining where Grambling is." There was a pause, and he said, "Well, let's give 'em a couple weeks. They'll know. They'll know." I never forgot that because he was right. Within a month or so, everybody could appreciate Grambling.

Comparing Eddie Robinson & Paul Brown

Coach Paul Brown felt, we can show you, we can teach you, but we can't do it for you. He believed there was a certain amount you had to bring to the game, to practice, and everything else. I would say Coach Robinson had a similar opinion, but he would hand-feed you a little bit along the way. Coach Brown would say, "Hey, get out there and do it." And, he expected you to do that.

Otto Graham & Bart Starr

Otto Graham obviously had to have coaching along the way, but I think his mindset just led him to kind of always be reaching for that next level. He was always reaching for that next opportunity to do it better.

Many times I've said that if there was a player that in my mind reminded me of Otto Graham, it was Bart Starr. They had very similar habits and behavior. There was no one that wanted victory any more than Bart.

Trade to Green Bay Packers

My trade to the Green Bay Packers turned out probably to be a mistake for Cleveland to the extent that I went on and had the career that I had, but I never held it against Paul Brown. I just went out and tried to kick their butts and make sure that he remembered.

In fact, my Browns teammates used to tease me in training camp telling me if I didn't like it in Cleveland, they could always send me to the Siberia of football in Green Bay. Believe it or not, when I went to Green Bay, I could sense what players in Cleveland and other places would think. It was just not a team that was focused or was prepared each Sunday to go out and win. That's where Vince Lombardi came in. He changed all of that. With him, you went out every Sunday, or whatever day the game was, prepared to win.

Vince Lombardi

I have said this before, and I'll say it as long as I live that there's no question in my mind Vince Lombardi created more diversity in the National Football League than any coach ever. He brought black players in not thinking whether they were black or white. He was thinking can you play football and make us a better football team? Then we want you on our team. I think to the very end he felt that he had accomplished something.

Position Change from Offensive Line to Defensive Line

There's no question that I was better-suited playing defense because of my intensity and my speed. There were a lot of things that Coach Paul Brown just didn't recognize that Coach Vince Lombardi immediately saw and put in place.

Vince Lombardi Only Losing One Playoff Game As A Head Coach

He would probably say, "We didn't lose that game; time didn't permit us to win." He was right about the 1960 Championship. No question in my mind. That game ended with us down on about the 15-yard line. Give us another couple minutes and we would have scored. We probably would have won the football game. I always adhere to his thought that in some instances we didn't lose that game; time didn't permit us to win. They stopped Jim Taylor and Chuck Bednarik sat on him until the time ran out.

Sacks
It's probably unfortunate they didn't keep track of sacks. There's no question in my mind I would have been someplace north of 150-160.

Deacon Jones
Deacon Jones was a great rusher, but I can tell you that he had great support with Merlin Olsen, Rosey Grier, and Lamar Lundy. Many times a quarterback didn't have a place to go. Deacon, with his great speed and quickness, could get there. I know this: The times we played the Rams I remember one game they beat us. There is no question in my mind over the series that we played when I was there; I had more sacks than Deacon.

Five Championships
The five championships that I was a part of each had a special place. That first championship we won in Green Bay when we beat the New York Giants, was the sweetest because it was Vince Lombardi succeeding. It was the Packers succeeding. It was all the things that we probably wanted to accomplish in Green Bay at the time. It was a great feeling.

That championship clearly was a great moment in Vince Lombardi's life. Even in a private conversation he told me how much it meant for him to succeed. There's no question that as we went on and won other championships ... the first two Super Bowls were important to us ... but I'd have to go back and say that the victory against the Giants in the NFL Championship was probably as big as any.

Green Bay Packers Running Game
Our running game at the time was probably equal to our passing game. We threw when the situation required us to throw, but I think what we were all about was if we needed to move the ball we could run it. Jim Taylor and Paul Hornung probably were two of the best players of their time back then. They just wouldn't be denied.

Cleveland Browns Running Backs
When I left Cleveland, I talked about what a combination Jim Brown and Bobby Mitchell should have been. I still think about what would have happened, if Ernie Davis had lived, with Jim Brown. You probably would have the record books today full of information covering the two of those guys.

Jim Brown
When people ask me could Jim Brown have played today, and it's almost like I have to look at them and say, Are you serious? Jim Brown as far as I'm concerned could have played in any era of football, including now, and anytime before.

Super Bowl I
It was kind of a strange game. In some ways we went into the game very conservative and very concerned that we did nothing to encourage Kansas City, and that was totally due to Coach

Vince Lombardi. He sat us down one day and he said, Don't forget that when you look at their team roster, they have some of the same All-Americans and everybody else that you played against. I would say by game time he had us very concerned. We went out and to this day I will remember at halftime when we all had a moment to refresh, he got us together. He said, "I just want to say a couple things. You went out and played 30 minutes of football, and you adjusted to the Chiefs. Now I want you to go and play 30 minutes of Green Bay Packer football and let's see can the Chiefs adjust to you." It was almost like he couldn't have been more profound. He said it, you had a sense that he felt it, and all at once we were a different team in the second half.

Favorite Play
I had that one tackle on Johnny Unitas when we beat them over in Baltimore the year that we won that second championship I believe it was. I hit Johnny Unitas and he fumbled. They called it the million-dollar fumble. I always laughed. I said, Well, that's interesting. It was a million dollar fumble that was done by probably a $10,000 guy.

Baltimore Colt Johnny Unitas, watches Green Bay Packer Willie Davis, New York Giant Sam Huff, and New York Giant Frank Gifford jump off a tank during their visit to U.S. Installations in Saigon, South Vietnam on Feb. 15, 1966. Photograph copyright Associated Press

Chapter 20

Tommy McDonald

College:
Oklahoma

Career History:
Philadelphia Eagles (1957-1963)
Dallas Cowboys (1964)
Los Angeles Rams (1965-1966)
Atlanta Falcons (1967)
Cleveland Browns (1968)

1998 Inductee Pro Football Hall of Fame

Favorite Quarterback
Norm Van Brocklin, Sonny Jurgensen, Roman Gabriel. Gosh, I was blessed. Absolutely blessed. I was in the right spot at the right time thanks to the good Lord. You know, God is my quarterback.

I had two great quarterbacks, Sonny Jurgensen and Norm Van Brocklin. It was great being there with them. We won the 1960 Championship against Green Bay and Vince Lombardi, Bart Starr and all of those guys.

Recipe for Success
God gave me good speed and good hands. Sports Illustrated put me on their cover in 1962 for having football's best hands! When that happened, I thought I better prove that I have the best hands. I used to squeeze clay to make my fingers strong. It really strengthened them. I was really lucky that made my fingers and hands strong.

My speed helped me too. I won the 100-yard DASH and the 220-yard DASH when I was in high school. I got a scholarship to the University of Oklahoma. I got about five scholarships offered to me from SMU, TCU, Texas, Oklahoma, and Colorado. I looked at SMU and Texas Christian, but I decided on Oklahoma because Bud Wilkinson said something that really hit home with me.

He said, "Now Tommy, if you're just coming here for football, I don't want you to come. I want you to come here to get an education because the education is going to last for the rest of your life. Football is only going to last for four years." I got to thinking, other coaches were thinking about the four years I was in school, but they weren't thinking about what happens to me afterward. That helped make my decision. What a beautiful decision. I went to Oklahoma and we never lost a game!

Bud Wilkinson

I won 10 games my sophomore year, 10 games my junior year, and 10 games my senior year. I made All-American at the halfback position. We played Notre Dame and beat them 40 to nothing. Paul Hornung was on that team.

Pro Football Hall of Fame Induction

I can't get over even getting into the Hall of Fame because I'm only 5'9". Nowadays, if you're only 5'9", they don't even want to give you a scholarship to college. You're told you're too little or you're too small. You have be 6'2" or 6'1" or something like that. But, low and behold, I was able to do that with Oklahoma.

The Eagles drafted me. During my rookie year with the Eagles, in 1957, our receiver broke his arm. They put me out there to see how I could do and I scored two touchdowns. They said, "Tommy, you're halfback days are over. You're going to be a receiver from now on."

That was really great. Low and behold, God just let me be in the right place on the right team. I'm very big on God because he's my quarterback every day. Every day is game day in life. You're either on God's team or the devil's team.

Chuck Bednarik

I'll tell you one thing, I wouldn't want to be hit by number 60, old Chuck Bednarik. He's just something else.

Mike Ditka

Mike Ditka, I love that guy. I would love to be on his team and have him coach me. Jiminy Christmas, what a desire that guy has. I'm so glad that he got in to the Hall of Fame too. In fact, he even beat me in the Hall of Fame. He got there in 1988; he beat me by 10 years, 1998.

Being Last Non Kicker to Not Wear a Facemask

I didn't wear a facemask, because I didn't want that bar to be in front of my face and in my eyes. I wanted to be able to see very clearly when that ball was coming into my hands and everything like that. I played for the Eagles for seven years before I got traded to the Dallas Cowboys, and that wasn't really good. They didn't really throw the ball a lot even though they had Don Meredith. I told Tom Landry after the season was over, "Coach, I'm out of here because you run the ball all the time. I'm a receiver; I want to be involved in the game a little bit. I would like to have one or two catches a game!"

Baltimore Colt Bobby Boyd defends Los Angeles Ram Tommy McDonald. Photograph copyright Associated Press

Chapter 21

Sonny Jurgensen

> College:
> Duke
>
> Career History:
> Philadelphia Eagles (1957–1963)
> Washington Redskins (1964–1974)
>
> 1983 Inductee Pro Football Hall of Fame

College
When I was at Duke we went up and played Ohio State and beat them. We beat Nebraska in the Orange Bowl. It was a good football program at the time. We didn't throw the ball. I only threw it 53 times my senior year in college.

The only people that were throwing the ball in that area were the guys in Georgia. They probably threw the ball more than anything else. I really thought about going to school there. It would have probably facilitated my professional career, because you know in that era you played both ways. I played safety. I was leading the nation in interceptions at one time, playing safety, but it was a different style of football then.

Early Years with Philadelphia Eagles
I started four or five games my rookie year and was 1-3. We beat Cleveland, Pittsburgh, and Washington Redskins in my three wins. Norm Van Brocklin wasn't there in 1957 when I went to Philadelphia. He came in 1958 as our quarterback.

He was there '58, '59 and '60. We weren't very good in '58. We only won two games. We won seven in '59, and we won the championship in '60. After he retired, he became a coach. Then, before we got on the field in 1961, Buck Shaw retired. Nick Skorich took over as Head Coach in '61, and we won ten games that year. We had a big year offensively.

NFL Draft
I learned a great deal. We didn't have a flanker and we didn't have a wide receiver when I was at Duke. It was a different style of football.

The Eagles offensive coordinator was the man who came to Duke to work with me because we hadn't thrown the ball a lot. He put me through a lot of drills that they do with quarterbacks. They still do them today, throwing different types of passes. That's why I was drafted in the fourth round. I was fortunate to get with the Eagles. They drafted, Jimmy Harris an All-American quarterback from Oklahoma at that time. They were looking for quarterbacks. They needed to get some people in that position and let them grow. I had the opportunity to be mentored by Van Brocklin, who was a legend. I learned a great deal from him about touch, looking people off, and just learning to play the position.

My colleague's coach actually recommended me to the Eagles. He said, "Boy, he's going to make a very good safety in the league." I said, "What? If you put me at safety I'm not going to last a week up there."

Chuck Bednarik

Chuck Bednarik was on my team. He was a great football player and a great leader, on the Eagles football team. He was the face of the Eagles until Van Brocklin came, and then you had two faces of the Eagles. It was great to be around people like that. The Eagles had an outstanding defense and legends of the game on it. He was quite a football player.

He was a perfectionist and an instinctive football player. So many times in playing, the defense was designed to do one thing and he would just do it. Bednarik's instincts would take him to the football and he would be going the wrong way, but he would make interceptions and go back the other way. He was a great instinctive player and obviously a very physical, dominating player in that era.

Quarterbacking

You use psychology, and all quarterbacks did, in the huddle. You know who wants the ball in a crucial situation whether it's a running back or a receiver. You could be a running back who just got a stinger on the play before that, and he'd want a break for a play. You know, just block or something instead of giving him the ball; that he just hurt a shoulder or something.

The receiver is the same way. Can you beat this guy? We need to move the chains. Can you run this pass pattern? He'd say, "Yeah, I'll get him." You ask a lineman the same thing. We need a first down. Can you get this guy? Can you block him? And the running back ... you know, that's where the game was on the field. I mean, we were drawing plays in the dirt! Yeah it was a great. I'm glad I played in that particular era.

I had great receivers in Philadelphia too. Tommy McDonald, Pete Retzlaff, and Bobby Walston. Charley Taylor came in as a running back and he was great. I think Charley Taylor would have been in the Hall of Fame even if he had to play defensive, like if he had played cornerback. He was a great athlete. He started out as a halfback, but he was an undisciplined runner because he was running by the lineman instead of giving them an opportunity to block. They made him a receiver and he was a great receiver. The job of the quarterback, to this day, is to get the ball in your skilled player's hands and give them the opportunity to make plays. The quarterback can't do anything with a ball in his hand except get it to a skilled player; whether it's a running back or receiver.

I broadcasted games for the Washington Redskins after I retired. I've been in the radio booth since 1981. I did games when I retired in '74, working with CBS Sports. I still sit and look at defenses. You're reading defenses before the snap of the ball like you did as a quarterback. I think it helped me playing defense.

Bobby Mitchell

Bobby complimented Jim Brown. He was a great football player. He was so fast. You just got the ball in his hand as quickly as you could and let him do the rest. He was capable of going the distance at anytime. Cleveland also had a tight end who was an undersized tight end, even for that era, but he was an exceptional one with Jerry Smith.

Tommy McDonald

Tommy McDonald was about 5'10". He was a great receiver. If he could touch the ball he was going to catch it. He didn't drop many passes. He was a halfback coming out of Oklahoma who they made a receiver. He was fun. We came in together. He was drafted in the third round. The Eagles drafted me in the fourth round. We were very close friends, and still are to this day. I still see him. We had a lot of fun playing.

Favorite Receiver

The guy who was open, the guy who could get open, and the guy you knew you could depend on in a crunch. It was the guy that would make the catch when you needed it the most and was going to give you a 100%. Charley Taylor was probably the best athlete overall. He had strength, size, and speed. He was a devastating blocker, just a complete football player.

Toughest Defensive Player

The toughest defensive players were the ones who put your lights out. I don't think so much of individuals. I think of teams, like the Bears. The Bears were a great football team in that era. You also had the Giants. The Giants were a very sound football team. You know, when you consider the fact that they had Tom Landry coaching defense and Vince Lombardi coaching offense, they were difficult to play. Obviously the Browns played great team defense. The Giants were just getting into the flex defense that Dallas made very famous later on. The flex defense had four defensive linemen; two on the line and two were back. It was really a gap defense, everybody was responsible for a gap and they played it. The Giants had great players in Andy Robustelli, Jim Katcavage, Rosey Grier, Dick Modzelewski, and Sam Huff. I mean, the people that they had were great football players. You know, when you're playing against people like that, it was very difficult. Then with The Bears having Doug Atkins and Larry Morris and the people that they had there, it was difficult to play them and you had to battle them.

99-Yard Touchdown Pass

I think that touchdown pass was against Dick Butkus. I remember him chasing Jerry Allen. It wasn't a very long pass. In fact, I threw it about 30 yards but, they were in single coverage and Butkus ended up on the back coming out of the backfield. I just remember Dick chasing Jerry Allen. He wasn't going to catch him down the sidelines and I was thinking to myself at the time, 'I hope he doesn't spike the ball. If he does, Butkus is libel to kill him. He'll beat him for that touchdown.' And I said, "Please don't spike it. You don't want to get killed down there."

Butkus was a great football player. The intensity that he had on every single play was incredible. You didn't play anybody better than Butkus.

Dick Butkus, Chuck Bednarik, Sam Huff

People like Dick Butkus, Chuck Bednarik, Sam Huff, yes, they all need to get to anger management class.

It was a classic matchup when the Giants faced the Browns. Jim Brown & Sam Huff both won when they played. They both knew whom they were playing against and it was great to watch, especially when you weren't a part of it.

Jim Brown

Without question, Jim Brown was the greatest running back I've ever seen. I played with him in the '64 Pro Bowl, and he was head and shoulders above everybody else, in my opinion, all time. I can remember being at Duke University and my football coach told us to go up and watch Jim Brown's lacrosse game. We said, "What?" He said, "Go up and watch his lacrosse game. Duke's playing Syracuse."

And we went up to watch and saw Jimmy Brown play lacrosse and he just ran up and down the field knocking people over and they had to change the rules of lacrosse because of the way he played. They changed the rules because he was just devastating. He was an All-American Lacrosse player and he was the best, best I'd ever seen at that game.

Jim was so much stronger than all the running backs. In talking with him over the years about running the football, he was so smart knowing where all the lines of pursuit were coming. He could go around the end and be making cuts, anticipating where the pursuit angles were coming from the defenders. He didn't have to look, he knew where they would be and that's what made him exceptional. You can go back and watch. Every time you saw him running the football you know it is something special.

Favorite Coach

Vince Lombardi was head and shoulders above the rest. I played for nine different head coaches in the 18 years that I played. It's very interesting when you hear today and you've heard of in the past of coaches with 700-page, 400-page playbooks. Vince Lombardi was the only coach I played for that simplified the game of football. We had few plays and it wasn't how many plays you could run, it was how well you ran each play. So, it's a matter of execution. If you execute, you don't need a lot of plays. It's making those plays work against any defense and that was Lombardi's philosophy. He didn't have a lot of plays, but what you did, you did right. He simplified the game, the keys, the passing game, and reading double coverage and zones and what have you. It made the game fun. In 1969 I had more fun and worked harder under him than any year in professional football.

I don't care where he was coaching he would have been and was a leader. He knew how to motivate. He'd have been successful at anything he did and he proved that.

He also coached high school basketball. He knew nothing about basketball. We had books and I think they won. He was just a leader and knew how to coach and was a great communicator.

I talked with Paul Horning, Bart Starr, Boyd Dowler, Max McGee, and other players that had played for Lombardi before he came to Washington and they said, "You will love him. You will love him because of the intense preparation you go through, you're never surprised on the field." It was great preparation. It was really fun and I knew we were very fortunate to have him for any length of time. We unfortunately only had him for a year.

Photograph copyright Associated Press

Chapter 22

Sam Huff

College: West Virginia
Career History:
New York Giants (1956–1963)
Washington Redskins (1964–1969)
1982 Inductee Pro Football Hall of Fame

Early Life
I went to college at West Virginia. I went to grade school outside of Fairmont, West Virginia. Then I went in West Virginia to Morgantown for high school.

My dad, my brothers, everybody went to work at Consolidated Coal Company. Consolidated Coal Company owned the house, and they owned the coal under the ground. Consolidated Coal Company owned everything. I did go down in the coal mines with my dad, and they had a big machine underground called the Sam Huff Special, named after me.

One day in the mine I said, "Dad, we got to get out of here. This is like a time bomb." He said, "Oh, I knew you would say that because you want to go to New York, and Washington and West Virginia … all of that. This is what I do." I said, "Dad, let's get the hell out of here." And we did. We got on this big elevator and we got out. That mine exploded and killed 93 miners. Ninety-three. Unbelievable. I knew every one of them. But that's the life you live.

Every linebacker would tell you, if you have the ball, we're going to take you down, that kind of talk. Joe Schmidt had it, Bill George had it; all the great ones had it. When they got Chris Hanburger he was the outside linebacker and I was the middle linebacker. Nobody broke through the line, because when they got to the line we got them. Both of us hit them. That's what people want to see. They want to see a contact sport called football and that was the sport we played back then. I loved it then, and I love it now. I broadcast now and it's great. I get paid for broadcasting. I mean, how do you beat that?

Switching To Defense Upon Joining Cowboys
Tom Landry switched me to defense. Tom Landry was a coach in New York for the Giants. After I played in the College All-Star game in Chicago, I went to New York to meet Tom Landry and the Giants staff.

We had Jim Lee Howell as Head Coach who was from Arkansas and loved to yell and scream like a lot of coaches do because they don't know what the hell your name is. Jim Lee Howell used to say, "Hey, you! Hey, you!" Lombardi just looked at me and he said, "What the hell is going on with you?" I said, "That guy is yelling at me." This kind of stuff goes in to the game that America loves.

Well, Landry took a little gamble on me because I came from the all-star game and I could run. I basically hit people even in practice. I knocked Jim Brown out. I knocked Jim Taylor out. Practice to me was just like a game. You came in my territory, I was going to deck you, and I did. That's what got me to where I am today, attitude, toughness, and a great coach by the name of Tom Landry. My other great coach was Vince Lombardi. Now, let me tell you something. It doesn't get any better than that.

Baltimore Colts
John Unitas called everything for Baltimore. Those big tackles, they didn't know what was going on. They just knew to grab the defensive end and hold him.

1958 NFL Championship
Football is football. There's only one ball. Follow the ball. You have to have guys who take leadership in the locker room and on the football field. There are very few great coaches like Tom Landry and Vince Lombardi.

The Colts were a great team. That was a great match up between the two of us. It was a great game. Everybody got his money's worth at Yankee Stadium. There were Giant fans and there were Colt fans. That was a great contest.

I thought every game I played was the greatest game ever played. You go out there and you get hit. You get knocked down and you look up and here's a little guy about 135 pounds or something that blocked you. You just get up and you say, "Do that again and you aren't going to go home. Okay? I'll see to it." You put him on a train and send him to some place in New York.

Time Magazine Cover
I was the best player they could find for the cover of Time Magazine. I was the first and only one. People came to me and said, "We have a problem!" I said, "What's the problem?" They said, "Well, you're supposed to be on the cover of Time Magazine." I said, "Yeah. When do I have to do it?"

They were going to do it when they got rid of that monkey on the satellite. I said, "You mean to tell me I'm a football player and I tackle people and I got to answer to a monkey?" Honest to God. The monkey died and I'm on the cover of Time.

The guy from Time came to my locker at Yankee Stadium. I'm telling you stuff that nobody has asked before. He came to my locker. He said, "Sam, we got a problem." I said, "What are you talking about you got a problem?" He said, "Well, you're supposed to come out on Time Magazine." I said "Yeah, what's wrong with that?" He said "Well, there's a monkey that on the satellite and if that monkey dies, you are okay, but if that monkey lives, he's going on the cover." I said, "You mean to tell me I play football here in New York and I got to answer to a damn monkey?" Honestly, I'll tell you. The guy said, "Yeah, well." The monkey, he got lost and I was printed on the cover of Time Magazine. That's New York for you. It really is. It's the greatest city. To me, it's the greatest city in the world.

Jim Brown
Jim Brown was big and strong. I could take him down, and I did. I took down Jim Taylor too. They were great guys and great runners. We were blessed to have teams like the Giants and the Baltimore Colts and everybody else. Football is America's game.

Trade From New York Giants To Washington Redskins
It was the dumbest thing that ever happened to me. I was set with my family in New York, out by LaGuardia Airport and I gave them everything I had. I was on television with Howard Cosell. They made the mistake. We had a great team with great players and great coaches, playing in Yankee Stadium. We were champions. We played the best against the best all the time. That was the saddest thing, I think, other than death of my family, that's ever happened. To be traded. You're like a piece of equipment then. The Giants made a mistake when they started getting rid of people. They got rid of both Tom Landry and Vince Lombardi. Landry was defense, and Lombardi was offense. They were great. Why would they let them get away? That's where the Giants made their biggest mistake ever, in my opinion.

Howard Cosell
Howard Cosell was a yeller. He was like a fan. He loved television because it made him look good and he could yell and scream. He kept us on Monday Night Football with his yelling and screaming.

Vince Lombardi
Well, the best against the best. We played against the Green Bay Packers where Vince Lombardi was, when I was with the Giants. Lombardi was the best. He was like all of the great coaches. When he yelled, you moved. You got out of the way. He was a yeller and a screamer. The Giants had Tom Landry and Vince Lombardi as coaches and didn't hire either one of them. That was awful.

Chuck Bednarik Hit on Frank Gifford
That was the greatest hit I've ever seen. I mean Frank Gifford caused that himself. You're trained defensively to take a pass drop and Chuck Bednarik did. You're trained not to go underneath the linebacker. You're trained to go behind them because there's a seam in-between the linebacker that the quarterback would throw the ball to you. Well, Frank came underneath two linebackers for the Philadelphia Eagles at Yankee Stadium and was running toward the pitcher's mound, because we shared that stadium. Bednarik hit him. It was the biggest hit I've ever seen. He clotheslined him. He flipped him in the air. Gifford came down, hit his head on the ground and fumbled the ball. The Eagles recovered it with two minutes to go in the game. I thought Gifford was dead. They carried him off the field on a stretcher and took him to the Yankee Stadium locker room.

I thought Chuck Bednarik killed Gifford. I walked over and Gifford was shaking. It was near the cut out on the field, I guess. I looked down at him and he was shaking. I told the umpire, "You got to be careful. I think he's going to die." That was the biggest hit I think I've ever seen on a football field

The Eagles recovered the ball and just ran out the clock. We went in the locker room and we were getting undressed. Andy Robustelli was on one side of me and they brought a body out of the trainer's room, covered up on a gurney with a sheet over it. I said, "There goes Gifford, he's dead. He's dead. Bednarik killed him!"

It wasn't Frank; it was a policeman who was working the game. He was so excited he had a heart attack and died. This all took place at Yankee Stadium. I thought it was Frank. It wasn't Frank, but unfortunately somebody died. Frank was already at the hospital. He was hit so hard he was knocked out. Frank missed the entire next season.

Frank was a heck of a ballplayer, but he made a mistake going underneath Bednarik. I would've done the same thing. Bill George would've done the same thing. Dick Butkus would've done the same thing. Butkus would've acted like Bednarik did, slamming his fists and all that kind of stuff. It was terrible, but it was football and you have to say, "That's the way I would've hit the guy too."

Frank is still alive. Frank is still Frank. I'm glad he's alive. He's a good person. He's a great person and he was a great player. We had some great players there, and Frank Gifford was one of them.

Chuck is a good guy but he liked to let everybody know how tough he was. Goes around hitting people. Hey, it's okay to hit somebody. Just make sure they have their uniform on. But, I'm not sure he knew that.

Pro Football Hall of Fame Induction
I made it. That's all you have to say. That's all you can say. When a coach tells you something, you do it or he'll get rid of you. That's the way you feel. It's a great event in Canton, Ohio. When you see people like Bobby Layne and Chuck Bednarik there; you see guys from every team who were on those football fields. Then here you are in Canton, Ohio and you're in a parade. It's something special.

Toughest Ball Player Went Up Against
There were two. Jim Brown and Jim Taylor. They were great. You're standing up. They're down in a three-point stance and you know that quarterback's going to hand that ball off because he doesn't want to get hit. Hand it off to Jim Brown and boy, you got to take him down quick or he's going down for a touchdown. Jim Taylor, from Green Bay, would hit you up to try to run over you. I took them both on.

Yankee Stadium & Mickey Mantle
I got a chance to play for the Giants in Yankee Stadium. I shared a locker with Mickey Mantle. It doesn't get any better than that. You could ride the train from downtown New York, where we all lived, to Yankee Stadium for a quarter. Hell, that was a lot of money then. You make do with what you got.

Favorite Player Growing Up

Frank Gatski was my favorite player. He played for the Cleveland Browns. Gatski was ahead of me in West Virginia. We played against each other. That's the kind of games that America has. You go out there and you play and you beat each other up, but you're still friends.

Most Memorable Play In Career

The game when I hit Jim Taylor in New York has to be my most memorable play. I hit him so hard I damaged his helmet and mine. Mine came down and split. The umpire said, "Sam, for Christ's sake, you destroyed your helmet!" And I said, "Well, for Christ's sake, get me another one."

The trainer saw what was happening. He got a new helmet and brought it out to me. He took the old one and threw it away. I had a new helmet. The helmet is like a military helmet, somewhat, I guess. Your helmet fits tight and it's got a strap underneath so you don't lose it. That helmet becomes a weapon in some people's mind. It's a weapon, because he's going to hit me with his helmet and I'm going to hit him with mine. That's the way the game was played.

Most of the guys on defense were pickups at one time or another. Frank Gifford came from California and he liked to be in Hollywood. Football is football. You put us on the field and people are going to get hit, people are going to get hurt. I hit Jim Brown and probably knocked him out. I hit Jim Taylor and probably knocked him out. I hit them so hard they had to get new helmets, too. So, there were three new helmets. I had a new helmet, Jim Brown had a new helmet, and Jim Taylor had a new helmet.

Success is success. I could hit people, I could tackle people, and I could cover people. A great linebacker, like Joe Smith, was one. He was the big guy in Philadelphia. We basically have our group. We played hard and we hit hard. That's what people pay to see. If they go to a prizefight, they want to see somebody box and hurt somebody. If you're in New York at Yankee Stadium, we're going to hit you down on the field. That's the way the game is played and it's okay. It's a great game. It's America's game.

I did my job. I dented a few helmets of my own hitting Jimmy Taylor and Jimmy Brown. It's like a car collision. You have a wreck but both sides are going to get hurt.

Tommy McDonald

Tommy never came over the middle. He ran the up pattern. It was a corner pattern but he didn't come over the middle. He was a good player.

Football in the 1950s

The Bears have always had good linebackers. Somehow they like that bad weather in Chicago. Those were such great days in the '50s with the Chicago Bears and the New York Giants. Sports were different then. Now, these guys make a play and what do they do? They bump their rearends together and pump their shoulders together and show their muscles. If you did that with us, one of those linebackers would walk up there and punch you in the mouth.

Todays Players Celebrating After a Catch
I'll tell you what I'd do. I would take the 15-yard penalty and knock him into the stands. So would Chuck Bednarick, Bill George, Joe Schmidt, and all of us linebackers. We wouldn't put up with that crap. Excuse the language but that's true.

Well, that's because of coaching. Coaches control that. You would never do that with a Tom Landry or Vince Lombardi. These coaches allow that to go on. You just don't do that. You have to have control of these guys. There are about 100 of them. You throw a fine on them or cut their pay or get rid of them.

Jack Kent Cooke
Jack Kent Cooke drafted three quarterbacks in one year, Heath Shuler, Trent Green, and Gus Frerotte. Now, I live five minutes from Mr. Cook and you know I'm broadcasting and everything. He called me into his office and said, "I want to know, because you were a player, about these quarterbacks." He said, "We offered Heath Shuler a contract and I think it was about $500,000. The kid is just coming out of college. Sam, he's not going to report unless I give him a million. What do you think about that?"

I said, "Well, Mr. Cook, you drafted three quarterbacks and you've got to get your number one draft pick into practice and get him going. Why don't you talk to his agent?" Now they all have agents, but we were not allowed to have one. They all have a lawyer and advisor and so forth now. I said, "Why don't you talk to his agent and tell him that he's the number one choice. If he takes you to the Super Bowl, you'll give him a million dollars."

You know what he said? "Get the hell out of my office! I am not giving anybody a million dollars." He doesn't show up and they start out with Gus Frerotte. I'll never forget this. It was against the New York Giants at FedEx Field. He ran like a quarterback draw or something and goes into the end zone for a touchdown. He got so excited that he ran his head into the stadium. I remember saying to Sonny Jurgensen, "I'm glad that was a quarterback instead of a linebacker because I'd never hear the end of it." He knocked himself out. I mean, things happened in Washington that were unexplainable sometimes.

The Violent World of Sam Huff on CBS
Oh well, I was wired for sound. They put a backpack on my shoulder pads and covered it up with sponge rubber. I had a microphone on the front of me. They recorded everything. That was CBS News. That was not CBS Sports. They recorded every hit that I made and every play that was called, and that was the big sounds. You know, it was award winning. That pack that they put on my back was a little over a pound. If you're playing, like I was playing, I was on all the special teams as well as the middle linebacker, it weighted me down a little bit but I was young and I was able to handle it. It was great. I didn't know how important it was. I just did what they asked me to do.

That was one of the deals that I made. You edit the film and cut out the bad language and they did that. It was really first class. CBS did it and they did such a great job. It won all kinds of awards. I was the first guy ever wired for sound. It was magnificent and it helped me get another raise of about 500 dollars.

I was in New York at the time and when you're in New York, all those big corporations there went to see the Giants play at Yankee Stadium. Now Yankee Stadium doesn't exist anymore. It's a different world. But, that was a great time in sports. As far as I'm concerned the '50s and the '60s made it what it is today and they are reaping the benefits of it.

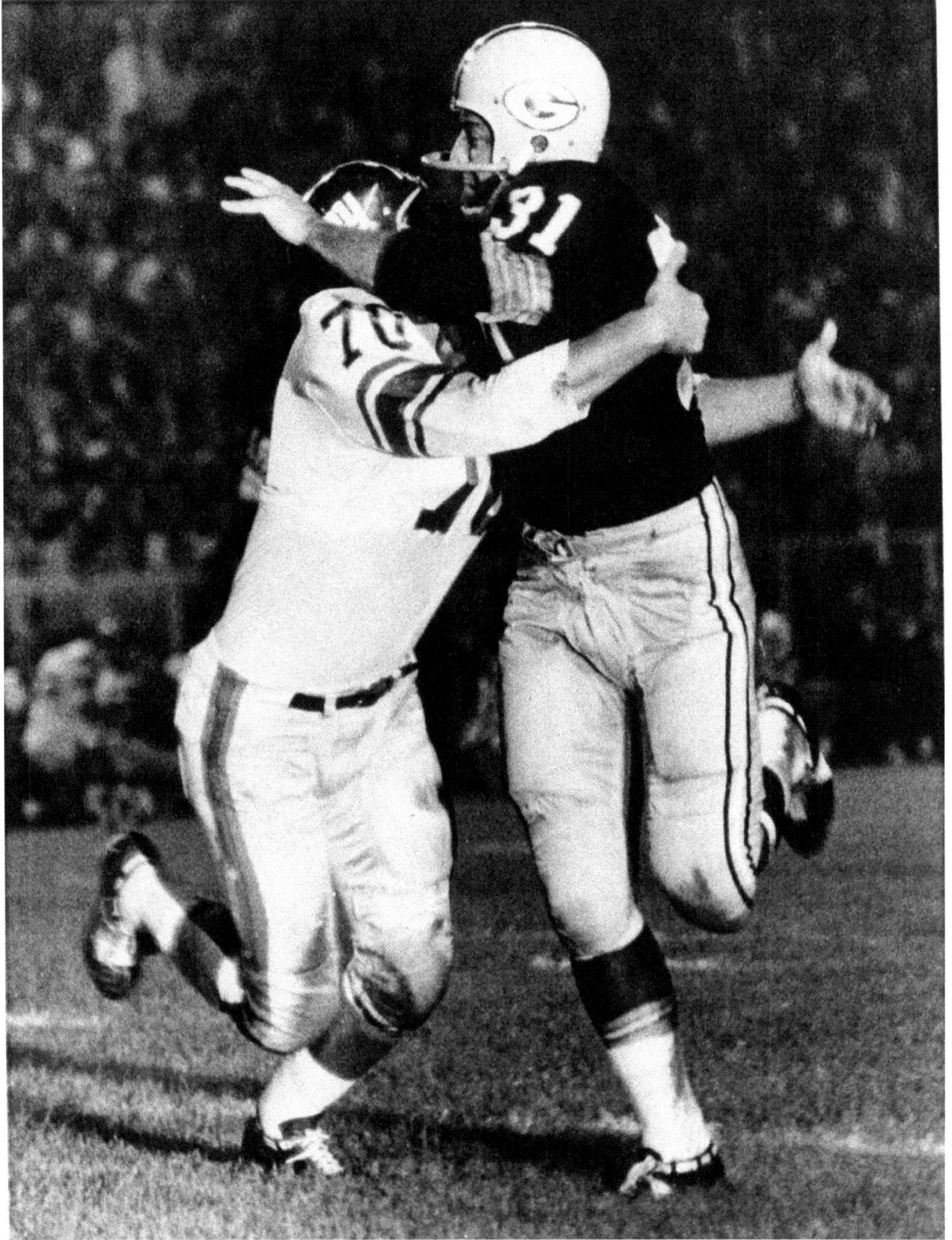

New York Giant Sam Huff puts a crushing hit on Green Bay Packer Jim Taylor.
Photograph copyright Associated Press

Chapter 23

Don Maynard

> College: Texas
> Western
>
> Career History:
> New York Giants (1958)
> CFL Hamilton Tiger-Cats (CFL) (1959)
> New York Titans/Jets (1960-1972)
> St. Louis Cardinals (1973)
> Los Angeles Rams (1973)*
> WFL Houston Texans / Shreveport Steamer (1974)
>
> 1987 Inductee Pro Football Hall of Fame

College Choice

I went to Rice University first and I stayed down there a year. Then I transferred to Texas Western College in El Paso. I was home sick, lonesome, and 585 miles from home. I went home five times the first semester and rode a Greyhound bus 585 miles. Each time I went home, I went home to stay, but my brother got on my case and I went back. Eventually I stayed and transferred my hours to Texas Western College. I was a redshirt out there during spring training and then the next fall. Being on the redshirt team I did everything. I played quarterback and so forth. When I got eligible as a sophomore, I stepped into the starting lineup and was a starter for three years. Back then you played both ways. Defense was my claim to fame, but I did pretty well on offense, too.

NFL Draft

The Giants drafted me and I belonged to them. I went to the Giants in '58 and we wound up going into the sudden death game with the Colts. I ran kickoffs back and I did punt returns. I was probably one of the most versatile players on the team besides the great Frank Gifford.

First Training Camp

My first training camp was in Salem, Oregon. The name of the college was Willamette University. In training camp, there's not too much going on.

Accommodations During Season

I lived in the same hotel as Frank Gifford and Charlie Connelly. There were about 18 Giants that lived at the Concourse Plaza Hotel. We went to workout every day. We had to be in our seats and ready to go at 12 o'clock. Then we had meetings and practice. After practice we got home about 5:30. Like I say, many families lived in the hotel.

The Concourse Plaza Hotel was one of the old established hotels. It was about two or three blocks up from Yankee Stadium and across from the Polo Grounds. They had apartments in the hotels. You could have a one-room efficiency that had the kitchen on one wall and the couches made into beds. If you had kids, you might have a one bedroom. Maybe if somebody's got more, they might have a two bedroom. There were all kinds of suites, but they all had a full kitchen and bathroom facilities.

Everybody was pretty close. I think we only had three rookies on the ball club, so the veterans were real close. That was my first year in '58, that they put 35 players on the roster.

1958 New York Giants
The enjoyment is you played your position. You did what you were told to do on the field and that was it. We probably had the most players ever from one team to have made it into the Hall of Fame.

Vince Lombardi
Vince Lombardi was a great coach. He was probably as great as he was back then with the Giants as he was later with the Packers. A lot of his greatness carried over and that's why he became the head coach at Green Bay. The nice thing about him and Tom Landry was they expected you to know the system, and they wouldn't tolerate a mistake. There weren't any mistakes made. I think I made one, one time in a ballgame. I was supposed to fake up into the line a little bit. Charlie Connerly was throwing a delayed flare or swing pass to the back, and I missed it. That was the only mistake I made in 16 years of pro football.

1958 NFL Championship Game
We were tied with Cleveland in the Eastern Division and played them in a playoff. We beat them and went to the championship game. Years later, I knew if we just showed up we were going to get the losers share and if we played a little harder, we could wind up with the winning share. The Baltimore Colts had a great team led by Johnny Unitas, Raymond Berry, and some other great players who wound up in the Hall of Fame. That game probably had more Hall of Fame guys in it than any game that will ever be played. When we went into overtime, it proved which team was the best team. That day Baltimore was the best.

Whatever Frank Gifford said and whatever the film showed regarding Frank Gifford and him missing the first down, the nice thing about film, a lot of times it answers the truth. Frank said the officials missed him getting the first down. He had carried the ball and that's the play that one of the Colts, Gino Marchetti, broke his leg on and there was a lot of confusion going back and forth with the officials in trying to get a trainer out to the injured player. I'm sure he's seen it a lot more times than I have, but whatever he said was probably true.

Being Cut by Giants Before 1959 Season
That was in 1959 during training camp. Vince Lombardi went to Green Bay and Tom Landry went to Dallas after the 1958 season and the Giants brought in a guy named Allie Sherman. He had been on the Giants scouting staff and he had been a coach. He's the guy that cut me. I never dropped any balls and never said anything to anybody. They kept somebody in the place of me. I could have probably run backwards faster than that guy could run forward. When a coach

doesn't like you, then you've got a problem. The nice thing about Landry and Lombardi was that they always kept the best ballplayer. It wasn't the case with Allie Sherman. It tickled me years later when he became a head coach and he probably lost a bunch of games.

I played under nine head coaches and 42 assistants. I only complain about one, and that's Allie Sherman. As time went on, I found out that I knew a lot more about football, especially about the passing game, than he'd ever know.

I got released by the Giants and instead of going home, I made contact with the Hamilton people and decided to just run up there and play. I could play as a wide receiver and also go both ways. They had 12 Americans; most of the 12 Americans went both ways, except the quarterback position.

After I went up there, I learned that Lombardi had picked up my option in Green Bay. I had already played a couple of games before they finally tracked me down. I mentioned to Vince Lombard that I was getting to play up there. Under contract rules, I would have had to go back to Green Bay, but Lombardi was nice enough to say, "If you're doing okay, I won't contest the agreement between the Canadian League and the NFL." So I stayed there and went to the Grey Cup. We lost to Winnipeg in the Grey Cup. A coincidence, 20 some years later my son wound up coaching for Winnipeg. They won the Grey Cup and were also runner up. He has a ring a lot bigger than my Super Bowl ring.

New York Jets
In 1960, the American Football League was founded. When I played in Canada, I didn't sign a contract to go back until the next year. When the American Football League was founded, I wound up being the first New York Titan that was signed. The Titans later became the Jets. I stayed with the Jets for 15 years.

The Green Bay Packers had given me my freedom, a free release so to speak, and they wouldn't contest it. I wanted to play with the New York Titans because they hired Sammy Baugh as coach. I had played against him when he was a coach my three years in college and I played for him in the Blue-Grey game. I knew he was going to throw the ball a lot. His key receiver coach was Bones Taylor. Bones told me they were just going to have me play offense, wide receiver, and that's the way it turned out there.

I think we were the number one or two teams in the league in yardage gained. I was right up there one or two from the top with the most receptions. We had a good passing attack.

Sammy Baugh
Sammy Baugh was the greatest guy. He's probably the greatest football player who ever played. People talk about Jim Brown being a great player. I came up with a point deal with players. Let's say offense is 10 points, defense is 10 points, and punting is 10 points. Sammy Baugh was All Pro offense, All-Pro defense, and his punting records probably still stand. He had 30 points compared to somebody else that might only have 10.

Jim Brown's a nice guy and a great runner, but on defense, I think he only played a little bit of defense in one game. He didn't run kickoffs or punts back, except maybe one game or two. Sammy Baugh was a great player, but he was also a great coach. He knew the offense, the defense and the passing game. It was great to be able to be indoctrinated into football under his ability. I played against him three years in college and I knew he was going to throw the ball. That's probably the main reason I came back to the states for the first year of the New York Titans and it was a lot of fun.

Joe Namath

Joe Namath played in the Bowl game against Texas. Naturally I watched TV and ball games. I could tell he was a great quarterback and then the Jets drafted him. He came to camp and I told him, "I'm going to make you a lot better quarterback and you're going to make me a great receiver. We're going to talk on every play in practice as we set up our passing offense."

Joe got to camp and we discussed a lot of things. I already knew he was a great ballplayer. I said, "We'll visit and we'll discuss the routes. I rounded my patterns off and that was a little bit different than some people were taught. It's like driving a pickup. When you drive a pickup, if you're going to turn 90 degrees to the right, you slow down. Me, I'm going to round mine, my pass pattern. Namath and I had one busted play in the 11 years we played together.
He called the plays in the huddle. I taught Joe something that I've never known a coach to teach. Joe calls a play. Let's say I'm going to run a 5-yard out. He knows I'm going to run a 5-yard out, but as he drops back in the huddle the defensive back comes up on me. As I call it, they used to call it bump and run. I call it the crowd. He's crowding me up on the line of scrimmage.

Instead of me running a 5-yard out, I'm just going to slide to the outside and I'm going to run a go pattern and he would just lay the ball up. I said, "Joe, don't read me. You already know what you told me to do. You read the defensive back. If he stays back 5-yards, I'm going to do a 5-yard out. If he comes up on the line of scrimmage, I slide to the outside and I'll run a go and we've got six points."

We went to the Super Bowl. Baltimore's defense doubled and tripled me the whole game. Namath wasn't going to throw the ball over to me, he just looked over and I'm out so wide, they've got to double and triple me so why even risk a throw over there? He threw about eight of the passes to Sauer, Mattress had three, Snell had maybe four or five, and Boozer had three or four.

Joe was just going to go to the guy who was open. Like I say, why risk throwing the ball to me when there were three guys guarding me? That worked out great. I always kid people and say, "I had the best seat in the house. I knew I wasn't going to get thrown to, but I had a job to do to entertain, the linebacker, a cornerback, and maybe a safety. It worked out real good."

Joe Namath's Prediction That Jets Would Win Super Bowl

We didn't even think about it. Matter of fact, all week long Pete Lammons said our defense was number one in the league and we had an offense that nobody was going to stop. We weren't worried about the Colts at all. We just did one thing. We didn't make any mistakes. As a result, that's the way it went and the game went a certain way. In the fourth quarter, I think it was 16-0, and Namath never even threw one pass in the fourth quarter. We just ran the ball down their throat. We had two of the greatest runners in the league, Matt Snell and Emerson Boozer. They did okay. As a matter of fact, I don't have some of the stats in front of me, but Matt gained over 100 yards. They never did slow him down.

His Speed

I don't know if anybody was faster than me. Many say they were a certain speed and they ran on a nice turf. I could run. I started out at about a 4.3 with full football gear on a grass field. We usually had our timing after a hard day's work out. Like I said, I never got caught from behind that's all that really matters.

Jersey Number 13

I chose 13 and even had it written in my contract with the Giants because I had worn it in college. The number 13 was a great part of my life. My dad was born on the 13th, my sister was born on the 13th, and I married a lady who was born on the 13th. I had 13 in college and I went to 13 schools growing up, five high schools. The Super Bowl victory was the 13th of the year. I just had all kinds of other 13's. I don't have my little chart in front of me to rattle off a whole bunch of deals, but I went to the Blue-Grey game and they never had a 13 in their history. I said, "I have to have 13 if I'm going to play in your game." They got me a jersey with a 13 on it.

I played for 13 years. "M" is the 13th letter of the alphabet. My mother and dad always called me Donald Maynard, which has 13 letters between my first and last names. I was number 139 going into the Hall of Fame. It's got a 13 in it and if you multiply 13 times 3, it will equal the 39, the end of that number.

Pro Football Hall of Fame Induction

I met some great guys playing football. All of the guys I was in the league with, were deserving. As a matter of fact, I remember when we got to Canton, there was a big sign up that said exit number 13. When I saw the number 13 on that exit I said, "Well, I guess I'm supposed to be here." That worked out pretty good.

Philosophy

I never thought past the game that I was playing. A lot of times the only thing I'd look for on the schedule was when we might be going to Dallas to play them since it was in the state where I was raised. As a matter of fact, playing in the AFL championship, we played Oakland in New York. After the first half when we came in at halftime, I just said, "Men, if you want to go to the Super Bowl, you've got to win this game. The Super Bowl is in the future and it may not be there. We've got to go out there and play the second half like it was the only game we were playing." We did and we came back and beat Oakland. We all got to go to the Super Bowl.

If you want to go out there, it's just another ballgame. We're going to get paid the loser share just for showing up. If we go out there and play real well, we get the winners share. Somebody said they gave you a dime. Then one guy said you get a check. I said, "I don't want a check. I want all my money in dimes. I want to see it. It worked out pretty good."

144

Favorite Moment

The big pass that made a lot of difference to me was in the playoff game against Oakland. In the third quarter, I said to Joe Namath I've got a wide one when you need it. It was late in the quarter. They got ahead. I ran a long go pattern and Joe told everybody in the huddle, "All right let's be careful. We're going to go for it. I need a little extra time, I just need for you to block them."

The wind was blowing about 50 miles an hour. I went down the right side, straight down the right side on a go pattern or post pattern and the ball was thrown at the post and I was behind the guy by about 3 or 4 yards. Then the wind caught the ball and if you're looking at a clock, I was going to catch it about 10 o'clock up there as you look at the clock as you run down the field. The wind caught the ball and it moved the ball over to the 11 and then 12 and then 1 o'clock or 2 o'clock right there. I caught it for 59 yards and went out of bounds at the 6-yard line. My momentum and direction carried me out on the 6-yard line or I could havescored.

Then Joe called a couple of plays. He called a pass play to be on the right side, but then as the formation changed, the defense changed, instead of me being the number one option, now I'm number four in order of catching the ball. He went to the left looking to George Sauer and then Pete Lammons and then Bill Mathis and then to me. You could see him brace himself real strong. He threw the ball to me and I had done my delayed route to come open as the fourth receiver. He threw the ball and I caught it just about waist high and I just huddled it in and wound up and caught it for a touchdown. That put us back ahead of the Raiders and the defense held the Raiders down intercepting a ball I believe. We beat them for the AFL Championship to get to go to the Super Bowl.

Singing Career

That was a great time. As a matter of fact, later on Bake Turner recorded a song "Is Anybody Going to San Antone", and it was climbing the charts like mad. Our buddy Charlie Pride recorded it and he took it to number one. I think it was number one for about 20 weeks. Bake was a great entertainer. Getting on the Johnny Carson show and a couple other special event things that we went to, worked out really good. The other great thing is we got paid for it.

End of Career

I didn't call it a career. The last eight years I played, I didn't miss a pass. They brought in a couple of other guys. Weeb Ewbank brought in his son-in-law as an assistant coach and they just released me. Then I went to the Cardinals and after that, I went to the Rams. I told the Cardinals coach I wasn't going to be a messenger boy, sending plays in and out. I'm going to play regularly or you can cut me or trade me. The Cardinals released me.

I told their coaching staff what was kind of wrong with some of their ball players, the organization, and passing routes before I left. Then Don Coryell did pretty good there. After that he went to, I believe, the Chargers, but that was about it. The politics got in there and so I didn't go back out to the Rams, which I should have.

Pro Football Hall of Fame Induction

I was real proud and glad. Joe Namath had gotten in a couple years before, I think. I went in '87. It's an honor to get in, but the main thing I felt good about was I was always in my mom and dad's hall of fame and my brother and sister's. Those were the main things with me and then naturally, my wife before I lost her.

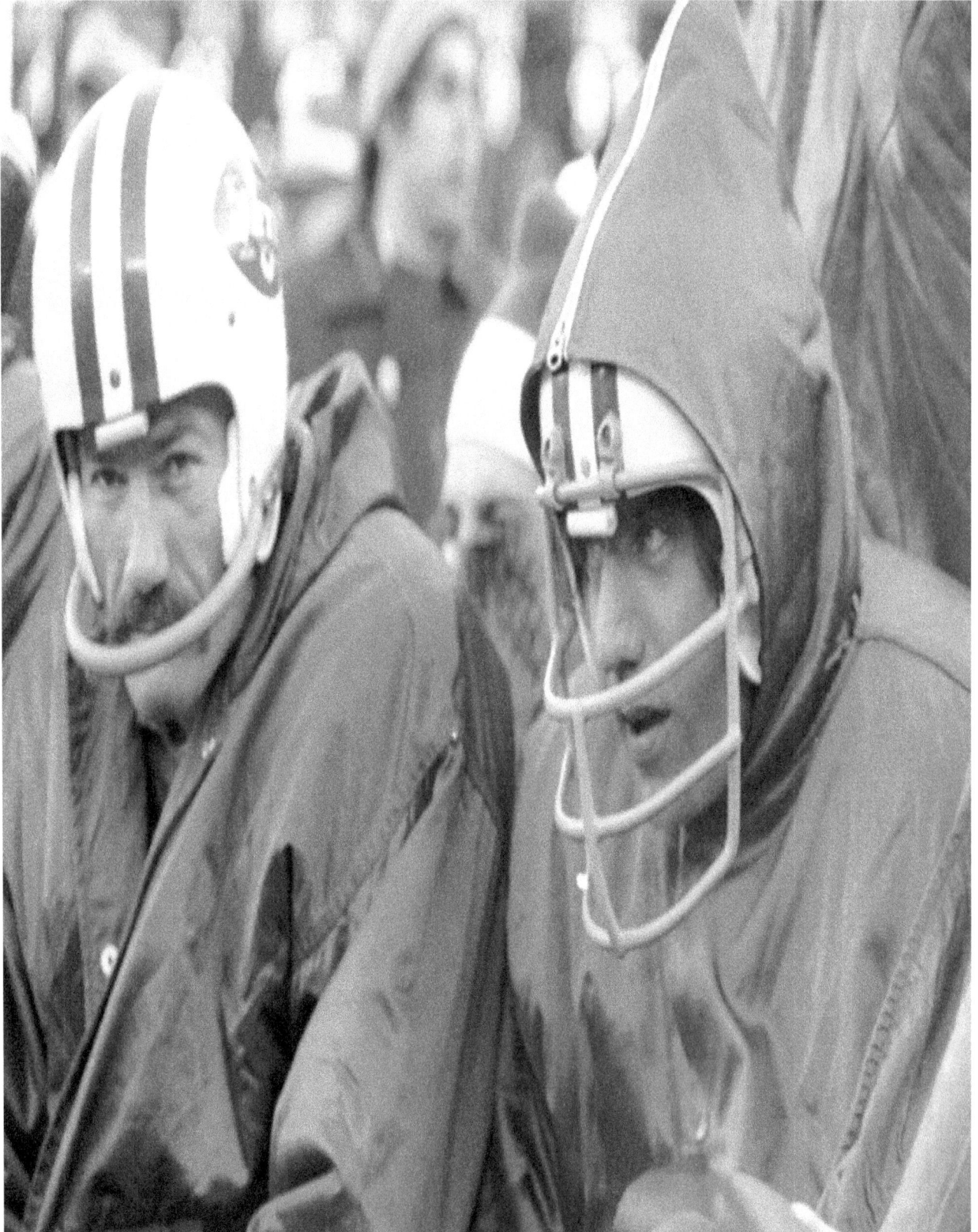

New York Jet Don Maynard left with Joe Namath
Photograph copyright Associated Press

Chapter 24

Bobby Mitchell

College:
University of Illinois

Career History:
Cleveland Browns (1958-1961)
Washington Redskins (1962-1968)

1983 Inductee Pro Football Hall of Fame

<u>College Choice</u>
It was the times. In the '50s I couldn't go to the University of Arkansas so I had to go east. Quite a few of us did that. You look at the Southwest Conference at that time or the Southeastern Conference at that time and African Americans weren't on any of those teams. The Big Ten had a long history going way back with African Americans. I didn't have much to do with my college choice. My mother, spoke to someone she knew in my hometown and he was an Illinois graduate. I didn't even know any of this, although I was around. He and the freshman coach at the university at the time had been roommates at Illinois. They had been following me all along. When everything opened up east and west in '54 with the Brown vs. Board of Education decision, I went from five scholarships to something like 36. So, that's what happened. A lot of the schools opened up for blacks. They directed me to Illinois. To tell you the truth, I wanted to go to Grambling with Eddie Robinson.

All the black schools recruited me and none of the white schools recruited me. As I said, in '54, when the new school decision of Brown vs. Board of Education a lot of the schools opened up for blacks, that's when I got all of my scholarships at the last minute and had a lot of offers. My family had already decided I was going to Illinois. I didn't even know where it was. I said where is that? I had never been out of the south. I didn't know anything. So, that's how it happened. I ended up there not because I wanted that or that they had pursued me. It was really word of mouth and they gave me an opportunity so I took it. But, I was virtually controlled on that by my momma because I personally was going to Grambling.

Well, the one good thing I did that I often talk about, was go to the University of Illinois. I don't think that I could have made the Grambling football team. They had so many great football players because the guys couldn't go to white schools. They were just stacked up at those black schools. You couldn't get in to Florida, A&M, Jackson State, or Tennessee State. They had so many great athletes. I don't know what would have happened if I had gone to Grambling. Of course Eddie Robinson and I laughed about it for years. He had some great players, super, super players. So, I don't know what would have happened.

All of us coming out of Arkansas that year, the big time players, went east and my best rival and friend from Little Rock, Arkansas went to Michigan. He was an All-American at Michigan and he was everything up there. Another one of our guys from Little Rock went to Wisconsin. He probably was the first black quarterback out there, Sidney Williams. Michigan State got Smitty and different guys just went all over the country. They all did quite well. They all got great honors in their careers. I've always thought that I was the one that had the least chance of being a star because I didn't think that I was on the level of those guys but it worked out pretty good.

Grambling Pro Football Hall of Famers Willie Davis, Buck Buchanan, Willie Brown, & Charlie Joiner

Those are all good friends of mine. They all did real well. Willie Davis and I played together at Cleveland for a year and then he went to Green Bay. Later on, Willie Brown and I, if Al Davis could have pulled it off, would've been in Oakland together. We had some great guys come out of there. There were tons of other guys who did well in pro football. None of them are in the Hall of Fame, but several of them said they were good enough to get in the Hall. We had some great guys come out of Arkansas.

Draft

Well, you know the strange thing about it … I didn't know anything about pro football. I had never even watched a pro football game. All the time I was at Illinois I had never thought about pro football because I wasn't that good of a player at Illinois. Ray Nitschke wasn't either. All of us just came along at the last minute. I knew nothing about pro ball. I knew nothing about the Cleveland Browns. I was not contacted about pro football until the season was just about over my senior year. That's when a scout approached me and told me that Paul Brown of the Browns was interested in me. He wanted to know if I was interested.

I was sort of interested. I think that I had watched one game because J.C. Caroline went to the Bears and he was always playing defense and special teams. I wanted to watch him because I got to know him my freshman year at Illinois. That's the only reason I watched that one game. It wasn't on my mind. It was not even a part of my thoughts or anything like that. In fact, I didn't think that I could even play. I didn't think that I was good enough to go any further with my football career because I had become so enthralled with track. I was enjoying my track career at Illinois. I forget about football.

Let me say this, one of the things that has always disturbed me is that I didn't give it my all to the University of Illinois and the coaches because I never cared that much about football. I cared about track. I had a great sophomore year in football the last half of the season when I got a chance to play. When I played I had three, four, or five really great games my sophomore year. I got hurt my junior year. My senior year I was running well at track and didn't care. So, it was kind of a crazy, crazy, crazy career, college wise. So, I wish now that I had given my all for them because they could've used it. We didn't win very many games.

College All-Star Game

I thought that I might get a chance to go to the Senior Bowl because they selected Ray Nitschke and I think another receiver from Illinois. No blacks could play in the senior bowl that year so I couldn't go to it.

Later on, I was asked to go to the East-West game in San Francisco. Paul Brown had a friend who was coaching in the game invite me so that he could get a look at me. I had a very good game. I was shocked. When I got back to school, I found out that Paul Brown had also called Otto Graham who was the coach of the College All-Star team, to see if he could get me into the game. He wanted to look at me further. That's how I got invited to those two games.

The running back at Notre Dame had hurt his knee. Because he got hurt, Otto put me in his spot for Paul Brown and that's how I got into that game. I had never been outside as a receiver and they put me outside. I broke out and went on to have a tremendous game. That started my career. That's when the league was much smaller.

Cleveland Browns

I was in a fog after being drafted. I knew nothing about nothing. I was just being pushed along by people saying, "Now go here, and do this, and do that." Paul Brown sent me a contract and told me to read it, sign it, and get moving. After I had that game, the very next day, I had to report to training camp with the Browns.

It was the strangest feeling to walk into that dressing room at training camp. By then I had gathered some names, like Lou Groza and Jim Brown. I had to walk in that locker room and my eyes were running around. I was actually looking at these guys that I had been hearing about. I thought, what am I doing here? This is the Cleveland Browns and these are the greatest guys. It was a real shock. I had that great game but it just dawned on me that I could play with these guys.

I had to earn my way in training camp because they had a lot of good running backs when I got there. I was the rookie. They had a lot of veteran guys. Back then, there weren't very many teams. All of those teams had guys stacked up in positions waiting for an opportunity. A lot of them had already played for two, three, four or five years. So, you're up against a veteran player and trying to get a slot. I was just like a little kid. I didn't know what was going on. I was just running around. What settled me down was Paul Brown putting me in the same locker with Jim Brown. I didn't think that I had the right to be in that locker room with Jim Brown. But, the team accepted me. What saved me again was my speed. He didn't have anybody on the team that could run like me, speed wise. They had great players. I think that there was no doubt of my speed and that helped me.

Jim Brown

Well, for me, he was super because he kept me grounded and I just followed his lead. We were running mates and we were running buddies off the field. For four years we virtually lived together. So, we were very close.

Trade

Nobody was able to beat Green Bay. They had two big running backs, Jim Taylor and Paul Hornung. That always bothered Paul Brown because he had Jim Brown. He thought I was too small to go up in the middle, which wasn't true, but that's how he felt. He didn't run me in the middle that much. I had to get my yardage elsewhere. I think that had a lot to do with it.

Coming out of school that year was a young man who was big and built like Jim Brown and had some of Jim's speed. His name was Ernie Davis. I think that Paul Brown felt that he would go to the Redskins. They had the first pick that year and got Ernie, but Ernie didn't want to go there because of the situation of no blacks being there. It all worked out for Paul in that sense. He made the deal with the Redskins and said that they had to take a black and I guess they decided I would be a good one to have because I had beat them two or three times. So, the deal was laid that Ernie Davis would go to the Browns and I would go to the Redskins along with some other people. That's the way it went.

Ernie Davis got leukemia that summer and of course never got a chance to play. I really think that he would have been a great player.

I had been in the service when I was traded. Back then, the draft was in December so I was in service when everything went down. I really didn't know anything about the trade. It was told to me. I got out of the service just before training camp. That was the last year that the Redskins trained in California. George Preston Marshall always went out there to hang with the movie stars during the summer, so he would take the team out on the train and they'd train at Occidental College.

I went out there to hook up with the team. I remember, because I was a little late from the military. Bill McPeak was the head coach and I walked up a hill to the football practice field. When I got up the hill, nobody was there. This shocked me because with Paul Brown's team, you better be up there 30 minutes ahead of him. I couldn't believe there were no players there. It was probably five minutes before practice was going to start. That shocked me and then right away I thought that's why they didn't win but one game last year.

Bill and I were standing there talking waiting for the players and he said, "Bobby, you know I don't have a great offensive line. I've got a good quarterback in Norm Snead. What do you think about (I'm sure that he and the coaches had talked about this.) going outside as a receiver?"

I had never been a receiver and knowing that he didn't have a good offensive line, I didn't want to get killed either. I said, "Yeah, I'll try it." That's basically how that happened. From day one I went outside. The craziest thing about it was we didn't even have a receiver coach. I was basically coaching myself. I did a pretty good job for me to make All-Pro.

Another fortunate thing was back then, we had six preseason games. I needed all six of those games to get used to Snead and for Snead to get used to me, because we were training ourselves. Fortunately, by the last preseason game we began to find each other. That was just before the season so we went on and had a really good year.

1st Black Player with Redskins
What I went through, I wouldn't want for anyone. I think that if I had gone to the Redskins fresh out of college, there was a chance that I would've never made it because I couldn't have mentally handled all the things away from the game. It was a pretty tough town at that time. There were so many places you couldn't go. So many things you couldn't do. Because I had already been in the league for four years, I was kind of a seasoned veteran, and I had been

virtually raised by Jim Brown. So, I had a stronger mind and I withstood a lot of the things that were going on. I don't think that I would've been able to make it if I had come fresh from college.

I think Ernie Davis was smart for refusing to go. I don't know if he would've been able to handle all the other things away from football. I had had four years of experience that helped me. I was able to disregard things and think about my family. It was pretty nasty at times. The players were great, but everybody around us was not. It was a pretty tough time.

They got blacks coming into the stadium which none had before. George Preston Marshall got financially better and the team was better. The rah, rah, rah was better. Everything just went topside. The only thing was that the black guys had a tough time.

George Preston Marshall
People wonder about him because of his reputation and what it was like, but there was not much contact with him other than when I first met him. We talked and finely agreed on a contract. After that, I really didn't see him that much. I would see him once a while since he was the owner. Players don't spend that much time around owners. Today they do a little more because everybody is a publicity hound, but back then you didn't see owners that much. The coaches didn't want them around anyway because they wanted to control their players and their team. So, I never really had that much interaction with George Preston Marshall. I was like everybody else. I was hearing about him and I'd see him and he would speak, but I didn't have much interaction with him.

Being Switched To Wide Receiver
Otto Graham always said I was his best runner because he knew me from the Browns. He didn't like not being able to use me in the backfield. When he would bring it up, I would refuse it. So, what he would do was wait until the game would start and then send in a play for me to go to the backfield. Well, every time he'd do that, I'd either break it for a touchdown or for a very long run. This was really playing right in to his hands, that he was right. I was his best running back. But, I had gotten used to being outside as a receiver and I liked it. I didn't want to go back in the backfield. The guy that I watched all the time, Lenny Moore, who went from running to receiver and then back to runner, popped his kneecap. I was thinking about that as soon as he went back to the backfield. I didn't want to get hurt back there and ruin my career. But he insisted on it and so I had to run in the backfields sometime and play outside sometimes. We would try to harness Charlie Taylor's speed and quickness, but he was too fast for the linemen. He didn't know how to adjust to it. It was better for Charlie to go outside where he could go on and cut loose. Of course he went on and was one of the greatest receivers.

No one wanted to decide where I should be. I was returning punts and kicks. I was too versatile.

Pro Football Hall of Fame Induction
Reporters talked to me about why it took me so long to get into the Hall. It was that all of my votes were being split up. A certain number of reporters wanted me in as a runner, another group as a receiver, and others wanted me in as a special teamer. Finally, they agreed to combine it all.

When they did that, I went right in to the Hall. My chances were getting hurt because I was too versatile.

When you're name comes up as a possibility you're excited. Then it took nine years to get in. That's what happened in my case. It's year after year of being disappointed, which as you know today, is happening to so many guys.

You're on that list each year and you never can get in. You get close but never in. Each year that you don't get in, there are great players coming up.

On Not Being Named A General Manager

When you're ahead of your time, you can't be bitter about something like that. I was never bitter about that. I knew all along that it wasn't going to happen even though I knew Mr. Cooke respected me very much. He called on me too many times to do things that he would normally ask other people in the hierarchy to do, so I knew that he respected me and he respected my brain power. He was no different than most of the owners in the league at that time. Who wanted to be the first to make that move? I never expected it to happen, though. It never really bothered me. It bothered other people. It bothered people in the organization. It was something that I didn't have to get because I had learned as an assistant general manager I had all the power that I needed.

Washington Redskin Bobby Mitchell makes leaping catch over St. Louis Cardinal Norman Beal. Photograph copyright Associated Press

Chapter 25

Len Dawson

College:
Purdue

Career History:
Pittsburgh Steelers (1957-1959)
Cleveland Browns (1960-1961)
Dallas Texans/Kansas City Chiefs (1962-1975)

1987 Inductee Pro Football Hall of Fame

College Choice

I had a very good senior year athletically at Alliance High School. I was First Team All-Ohio in football and basketball, so there were a lot of colleges after me. Of course, I'd heard a great deal about Ohio State, growing up in Ohio. I had an interesting conversation with Woody Hayes, the Ohio State Head Coach. He told me what the offense was going to be like. He said, "You're going to be under the center, and there'll be three backs behind you. When you take the snap, you step into the line of scrimmage. Then you're going to go down the line of scrimmage, and we're going to option off of the defensive end."

I said, "What do you mean by that?" Woody said, "Well, we're not going to block for you. If the defensive end comes after you, you pitch it back to the halfback that is coming by. Or, if the defensive end looks like he's going for the halfback, then you run with it."

I was thinking, my health is going to be in the hands of a defensive end. I know what's going to happen. I will be coming down the line of scrimmage without anybody blocking for me, and they're going to rip my head off. I said, "No, I don't think I like that."

I visited Purdue, and talked with the Purdue coaches. They talked about passing the football and that got my attention. One of the main reasons I went to Purdue University is that I just liked the coaching staff there. Hank Stram was the assistant coach at Purdue. I liked Purdue's style of football, because that's how I played during high school.

Stu Holcomb was the head coach and he had several assistant coaches. Hank Stram was one of the assistant coaches. Bobby DeMoss was another assistant coach. He played quarterback in college. He was the freshman coach. They had some other assistant coaches as well.

First Two Games Playing At Purdue

I got off to a tremendous start playing at Purdue. My first game was against Missouri and I started that game. I ended up throwing four touchdown passes against Missouri. The Missouri coaching staff didn't know Purdue had somebody that could throw the football. The next week, we played in South Bend, Indiana, against some religious school down there (Notre Dame). Paul Horning was on Notre Dame. I ended up throwing four more touchdown passes. I had eight touchdown passes in two weeks.

Playing Football At Purdue In The 1950s
Playing football at Purdue in the 1950s was nothing like it is today. Today it seems like the players are there the whole year playing football, whether it's football season or not. I was there to get an education too. I didn't know anything about professional football at that particular time. I was a young man, and it was an opportunity for me to get a college degree. I was a pretty good student too. I really wasn't thinking about professional ball.

NFL Draft
I didn't know I was going to be drafted in the first round by the Pittsburgh Steelers. I didn't know much about the draft at that particular time. It's not like it is today with all the hype and everything else. There were no scouting combines.

Some of the coaches at Purdue had played professional football. They knew about some of the teams and their owners. After the Steelers drafted me, one of the assistant coaches who had played for the Steelers, took me to Pittsburgh to meet the ownership and the coaching staff.

Pittsburgh Steelers
In 1956, the Detroit Lions won the NFL Championship by beating the Cleveland Browns. The Lions were going to have a luncheon before they went to training camp and Buddy Parker, the Lions head coach, told the players, "Now listen, I don't want anybody above the mezzanine floor of the hotel because there are going to be some hospitality suites by corporations there. There will be drinking going on, so let's get this luncheon over with. Bank them, and we will get on and try to defend our championship."

Buddy got on the elevator and instead of stopping at the mezzanine it went all the way up to about the 15th floor. The elevator doors opened up to a suite there. He saw a couple of his players having a totty. So when they asked him to speak he said, "Listen, I can't control these guys anymore. I quit."

They thought he was joking, but he wasn't. So, he left. Then Art Rooney, the Pittsburgh Steelers owner, called Buddy and said, "Listen, Buddy, Walt Kiesling is a friend of mine. He is the coach here, but he has some health problems. Would you consider coaching the Steelers?"

Buddy said yes, and came over from Detroit to Pittsburgh. He had never played a rookie in his life, and particularly a quarterback. So, he made a trade for Earl Morrall, who was with San Francisco, and I was Earl's backup. The next year they made a trade for Bobby Layne in Detroit, and I was his backup for two years. I didn't get to play.

It wasn't anything like what they do today because today, teams work with the players that are drafted. The team works on the player and explains to him what he has to do and what he can or cannot do.

I was just kind of on my own. There were not too many coaches, just a couple of assistant coaches. It was not like it is today where they have a quarterback coach, punting coach, etc.

Trade To Cleveland Browns

When I was traded to the Cleveland Browns the problem was that Milt Plum was their starting quarterback at that time and they had Jimmy Brown and Bobby Mitchell as their running backs. Head Coach Paul Brown was going to run with Jimmy and Bobby, and why wouldn't you with those two guys? So, I didn't get to play in Pittsburgh like I didn't get to play in Cleveland.

I was in Cleveland for two years and hadn't played, so I went to Paul Brown in June of 1962, and asked him to put me on waivers. Paul agreed and placed me on waivers.

Nobody picked me up. I found out, after talking to coaches afterward, that the reason was the coaches were on vacation at the time. June was the time of year that the assistant coaches had off before they went to training camp. Several coaches told me that had they known I was on waivers, they would have at least brought me in and taken a look at me. I said, "I'm glad you didn't." The reason I was glad they didn't was that Hank Stram was in Pittsburgh, where I was living at the time, at a coaches' conference. He had lunch with me and could see that I wasn't happy not getting any opportunities for five years in professional football. I had been with Pittsburgh for three years and with Cleveland for two years, and really hadn't played for either team.

Hank told me he'd just acquired the head-coaching job with the Dallas Texans in the newly established American Football League. He said, "Geeze, if you get through waivers, I'd love to have you on my team." I got to thinking, well I'm going to ask Paul Brown to waive me since I knew I wasn't going to get any playing time the next year. I asked Paul Brown to put me on waivers and he did. I went through waivers.

I just wanted a chance to play. Then, I contacted Hank Stram and we got together. I thought Hank Stram was one guy that knew about me because he worked with me at Purdue University for four years. If anybody was going to give me a chance to play, it would be Hank Stram, and it worked out that way.

Jim Brown

Jim Brown was phenomenal. I've never seen anything like Jim Brown. He never stepped out of bounds and the defensive backs weren't that big in those days. He was about 230 or 235 with great speed. They'd want to wait until he was even with them, and then they would jump on his back. Well, hell, when he's even he's leading.

Hank Stram

Hank Stram wasn't afraid to do something different. He was always working on things, like offense in particular. He was always working on something that had a better chance to move the football and score some points. He had a great personality. He got along with most everybody. He was going to find a way to develop an organization or find a way to win football games.

More Passing In American Football League Than NFL

There was more passing in the American Football League than the NFL. I think the reason why was that when the AFL got started, they had to do something to make it a little more interesting to get people to buy tickets and watch their football games. The Chicago Bears and all of those teams in the NFL that were so terrific back in that era, were basically running teams who passed sometimes. Then the AFL came along and started throwing the ball all over the place.

Play Calling With Kansas City Chiefs

I called the plays on offense for the Kansas City Chiefs. Hank and I would get together on the sidelines when I wasn't in the game. We would talk about what was going on, what ideas he had, and what ideas that I had. I was basically the guy calling the plays in the huddle. It's not like I had a new offense; I was running the plays that Hank had been working on all week long.

Dallas Texans Move to Kansas City

I was still living in Pittsburgh when we won the AFL Championship. Hank called me and said if I was thinking of moving to Dallas, don't do it because Lamar Hunt is going to move the team. Hank didn't know exactly where the team was moving to, though.

In 1962, our training camp was in Dallas. Now, imagine the weather in Dallas in August. It's a hot place. You can hardly walk on the sidewalk because the heat just goes right through you. I was concerned about where training camp was going to be in 1963. Hank said, "Leonard, we're going to go north of Kansas City for the training camp." So, I said, "Okay!"

Hank had a sense of humor. He didn't tell me north meant 15 minutes north of downtown Kansas City, Missouri, where it's hotter than hell up there at that time of the year, too.

Kansas City Chiefs Toughest Opponent

When people ask who our toughest opponent was, the San Diego Chargers would be one that comes to mind. They had some good players like Ernie Ladd and some of those big, old, tough 300-pound guys that could move around. They had a good offense and defense. Lance Alworth was there and John Hadl was a quarterback who threw the ball all over the place. They had a very good team. They were in our division, so that was the team that we had to beat to get into the playoffs.

AFL-NFL World Championship Game Later Known As Super Bowl I Kansas City Chiefs vs. Green Bay Packers

The AFL-NFL World Championship Game was a big event for us. I believe it was a bigger event for us than the Green Bay Packers because they had won championships before and they had good football teams in the past. It was a situation where I thought we were in awe of the Green Bay Packers. I had some players on my team say that some players on their team were their heroes. I said, "I don't think this is going to work out too well," but that was just that game. After Super Bowl I, things really evened up.

We had never been involved in anything like a championship game. I was just one of the guys who didn't make it in the National Football League. After that game, we proved that we belonged in the NFL. Our guys were just in awe that we were there, in Super Bowl I.

There was a whole section in the stadium where there were just four people. It wasn't as if the game was a sellout or anything like that. Super Bowl I was nothing like it is today. For us, we were playing with the best in professional football, the Green Bay Packers. I think that maybe we gave them too much respect because we still had to play a game.

Kansas City Chiefs Linebackers Bobby Bell, Willie Lanier, & Jim Lynch
Even though the starting offense didn't practice against the starting defense, I would rely on our linebackers Bobby Bell, Willie Lanier, and Jim Lynch by asking them after I threw a pass in practice, if they would have been there to stop the pass. Most of the time they said, "Yeah Lenny, I think I could have been there." But every once in a while they said, "Lenny, you had it." It gave me an idea of how I had to play and how quickly I had to release the football.

Think about the Super Bowl we played against the Minnesota Vikings. There were five guys who are now in the Pro Football Hall Of Fame that played in that game for Kansas City. Buck Buchanan, Curley Culp, Willie Lanier, Bobby Bell, and Emmitt Thomas, played in the defensive secondary. We had a defense. That was a mismatch really. All we had to do was not screw it up. We had the guys to make us win, and we did.

I knew as the quarterback that I could call some plays that were on the edge of being good, or maybe not so good, since I knew that our defense was going to hold up against the opponent. It was great for me.

Super Bowl IV
We went to New York for the playoffs in '70, to play the Jets who had won the Super Bowl the year before. Otis Taylor made the big play there. He came to the sidelines. I know this doesn't happen anymore because the quarterback has a telephone in his ear, or you know, whatever that is, getting instructions from somebody. Otis is drawing—I have a photograph of it—a play in the dirt of what he thought he could do against the Jets. We use to create formations. One we would create was a slot formation. When we did that we had both wide receivers on the same side. He said, "If you go on a quick count, I can get down the field because it's not a cornerback that's covering me there. It's the free safety and I can beat him."

We had a goal line stand. Namath threw a ball into the end zone incomplete, but the referee threw the flag and it was interference on us and first and goal for the Jets. Our defense was Willie Lanier, Buck Buchanan, Bobby Bell, and those guys. The Jets settled for a field goal. As we were going on the field after we got the kick off, Otis said, "Are you going to call that play?" I said, "No, no I'm not. I'm not going to call it right now." I waited until we were in the huddle so everybody could hear me. Using my sense of humor I said, "Well hell yes, I'm going to call it."

He was absolutely right. The wind was swirling there, and if you didn't get a good release on the ball, the wind would take it and move it wherever it wanted to. I let it go and I thought dog gone it, I threw it too far. But he had different gears in him so he caught up to it, took it inside the 10, and the next play we scored a touchdown. That was the difference in winning and losing that game.

The next week we went to Oakland to play them. They had beaten us twice during the regular season. We beat them and he came up with the big play in that game. Man, a marvelous catch. And then in Super Bowl IV, he made the catch, just a little hitch pass, but he broke a tackle and scored. Those were the three biggest plays because I am talking about three teams. The Jets, Oakland, and Kansas City had great defenses that year.

Rivalry With Oakland Raiders

After you played against the Oakland Raiders a time or two, you knew that you better brace yourself because they would challenge the rules of the game sometimes. We had a very tough team, so we had guys who could give it back to them. With Ben Davidson, you didn't turn your back on him because he could take a cheap shot at you. I think that and Al Davis may have had a lot to do with our rivalry with the Raiders.

The Raiders were the team that Hank wanted to beat because if you beat them, you were going to have a good chance to win the championship.

Decision To Retire

I played for 19 years. I didn' t necessarily play all that much my first five years, but for 14 years I was a starting quarterback. I just knew it was time to retire. Goodness, I was 40 years old my last year, and I didn't have the same enthusiasm as I did when I was in my early '20s. Besides that, I was involved in broadcasting at that time too.

Sportscasting Career

Jack Steadman was the General Manager of the Kansas City Chiefs. Jack went to the general manager of KMBC TV, which is a television station in Kansas City, and said, "Listen, we have to have sports on the ten o'clock news. KMBC didn't have any sports on at ten o'clock. What KMBC would do is have the anchor give the baseball team's score, or KU, or MU, or K-State, and that was it. Jack Steadman was interested in selling tickets. He said, "We've got to have a sports guy on the air." The general manager of KMBC said, "Well, I've been thinking about it but I don't have anybody in mind. Do you?" Jack said, "Yes, I do. Our quarterback, Len Dawson." Naturally, the general manager asked, "What kind of experience does he have?" Jack said, "Don't worry about it. He can handle it." This happened without Jack ever talking to me.

I would get through with Chiefs practice at five o'clock, be on the six o'clock news, go home and have dinner with my family, and come back and do the ten o'clock news. Somebody else put together the material, but I did the sportscast for about ten years before I retired.

Then NBC and CBS both contacted me about working for them. I decided to work for NBC. Then HBO called and I got involved doing the program, "Inside the NFL."

Lamar Hunt

Thank goodness for Lamar Hunt all the time. Lamar loved sports, loved football, and started the AFL. Just think about the number of people who had an opportunity to perform, where otherwise there wouldn't have been that opportunity. He was something special.

Pro Football Hall Of Fame Induction

I grew up in Alliance, Ohio, which is about 18-20 miles from Canton, Ohio. When I was in high school we played against Canton McKinley, which had a strong high school football team for years and years in the state of Ohio. Massillon, Ohio is out there too, where Paul Brown got started. I never thought or dreamed about being in the Pro Football Hall Of Fame. It's the greatest honor that you can have, period.

There are three Pro Football Hall Of Famers who are in as players and broadcasters. They are Dan Dierdorf, Frank Gifford, and I.

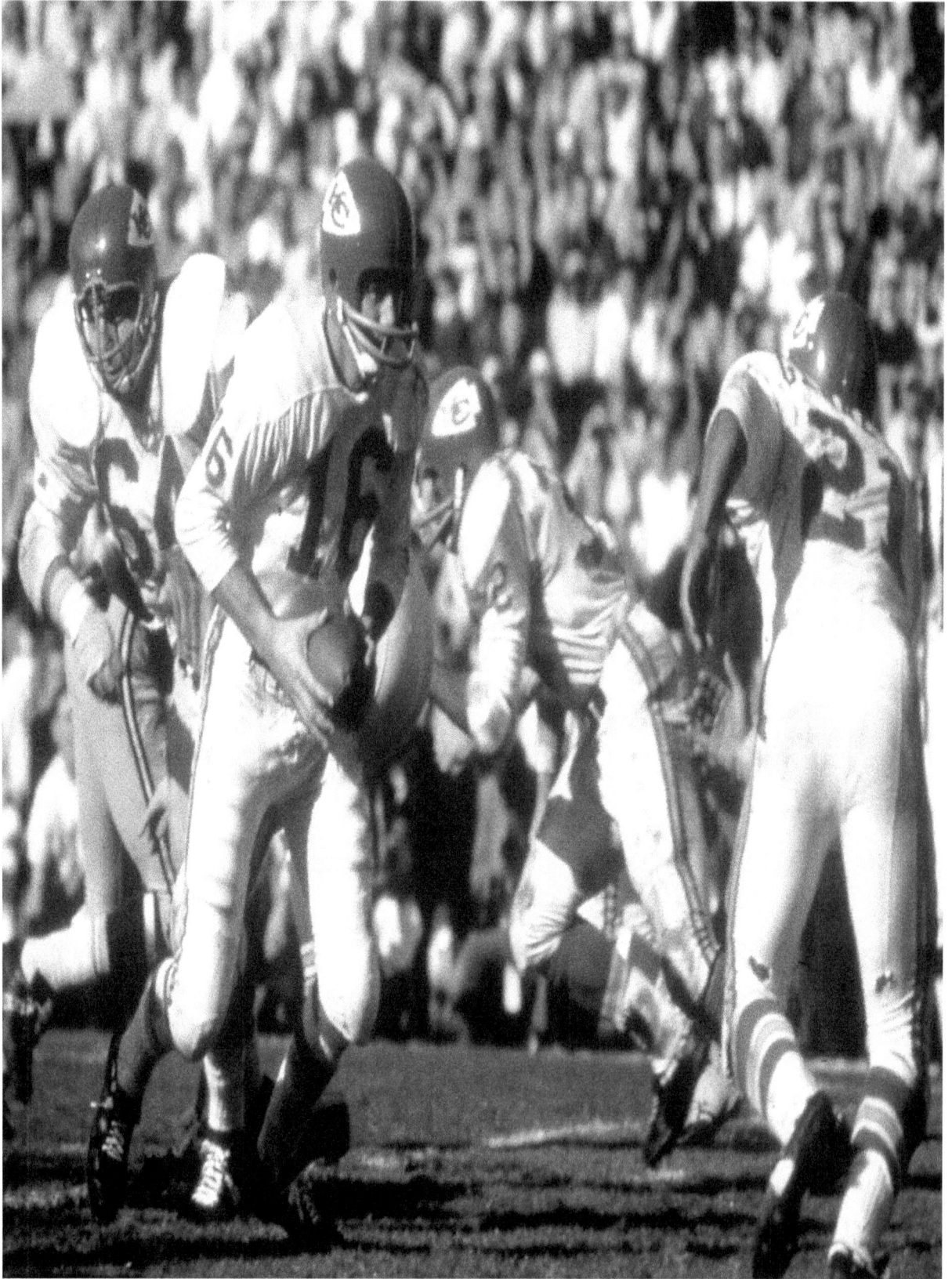

Photograph copyright Associated Press

Chapter 26

Paul Hornung

```
College:
Notre Dame

Career History:
Green Bay Packers (1957-1962, 1964-1966)

1986 Inductee Pro Football Hall of Fame
```

College Choice

I actually wanted to go to Kentucky. I loved Bear Bryant. I got to know Babe Parilli; he was kind of like my idol in high school. I really hadn't thought about Notre Dame until they got into the picture. My mom, being a very strict Catholic gal, really wanted me to go to Notre Dame. Back in those days, athletes went to the college that their parents picked and that was the case for me.

I wasn't unhappy with it, for heaven's sakes. It's one of great places of all time. I had gotten to know Babe Parilli and Bear Bryant. Bear Bryant cleared the way with Adolph Rupp. He was the coach of basketball. I wanted to play basketball. I was All-State in basketball for two years. I don't know if Coach Rupp really liked the idea of giving me a chance to play with the basketball team, but I think Bear Bryant asked him to and he said okay. When I met with Coach Rupp and Coach Bryant, I kind of decided that I was going to go to Kentucky and try to play football and basketball. But my mom wanted me to go to Notre Dame, so case closed.

If you grew up in Kentucky, basketball is really the number one sport. It always has and always will be. We went to the state championships my senior year. I was All-State my junior and senior years, so I wanted to play. I did play a year at Notre Dame. I played when I was a sophomore. I made the team and was going to play my junior and senior years, but Terry Brennan, the coach at Notre Dame said, "You know Paul, it is too important for you to maintain your grades. If you play basketball and it is going to take you away from your studies, I would really appreciate it if you didn't." So I gave up basketball after my sophomore year at Notre Dame.

Positions Played at Notre Dame

I played quarterback my senior year all the way. I didn't play halfback. I think I was a real good defensive football player. I was a safety. I was second in the team with tackles, first in interceptions, and I played 60 minutes a game. Those were the days when you played 60 minutes; you played offence and defense of course. I enjoyed both parts of the game. We were two and eight for heaven's sakes. The only real bad point in my four years at Notre Dame was to have to remember that. Terry Brennan was the coach. They let him go a couple of years after that. I think that season dominated their thinking as far as Notre Dame was concerned about keeping Terry Brennan as coach.

Frank Leahy
The first day I was there, he called me up and said, "I want this guy to take you over to practice kicking." It was Johnny Lujack for heaven's sake. What a thrill. Then he had Lou Groza, helping with kicking drills, come in from Cleveland. I was ecstatic. To know that on my freshman team I was going to be tutored by Johnny Lujack was very, very important. He and I became great friends. He still shoots his age in golf. He is unbelievable. He is a hell of an athlete.

I enjoyed it. I enjoyed my four years at Notre Dame. I wouldn't take them back for anything in the world.

Nickname "The Golden Boy"
Tom Fitzgerald, a writer for the Courier, nicknamed me that. I had a real good day in the spring game against the seniors and veterans from the pro league who would come back. I was a sophomore quarterback. Ralph Guglielmi was to be the number one quarterback with Tom Carey, who is now president and owner of Hawthorne Race Track. I was a sophomore and Gugliemi and Carey were seniors.

Winning A Heisman Trophy On A Losing Team
You really got to have some talent to do that. It has never been done since and probably never will be. I was in the top four or five when I was a junior. So I was kind of like the favorite. Jim Brown was right there with me. He got the highest votes behind me when I was a junior, so we were kind of the top two that they thought were going to beat John Brodie and Len Dawson. Tommy McDonald from Oklahoma was sensational in those days. Out of the top ten football players that came out of that year, when I was a senior, I think that all of them are in the College Hall of Fame and eight or nine of them are in the Pro Football Hall of Fame. It was a pretty good year.

The '57 College All-Star Game
He was a pain in the ass, Otto Graham. He didn't like me at all. He didn't like Notre Dame. Here was the Heisman Trophy winner from the University of Notre Dame going to Chicago. We had great quarterbacks on that team. We had Len Dawson and John Brodie. Otto Graham ran the offense. I told Curley Lambeau the Head Coach, "I will never forgive you. Here I am the number one pick of the draft, going to Green Bay and I don't start this game."

I was pissed off. He started Brodie and he didn't do anything. Then he put me in. He had Jim Brown, and he didn't even start Jim Brown. He didn't start Jim Brown and he is former Cleveland Brown. Well, he was really pissed, Brown was.

So when we got in in the second quarter, I called Brown's play six times and I threw him four flat passes and we scored a touchdown, the first one. Brown said, "God damn, you going to give me a break a little bit?" I said, "Nope. You are going to get it every time." So at halftime Brown said, "I'm suiting up. Come on lets go change clothes, I'm not playing for this guy."

So, it wasn't Curley. He relinquished all of his power to Otto on offense. He said, "I'm starting you and Brown after halftime." I said, "I don't know about Jimmy, but I'm not playing anymore, I'm finished. I'm afraid I'm going to get hurt Curley." I lied to him of course. He knew it. Jim

Brown didn't play either. Brown refused to play. So we sat on the bench. Of course we got beat in the second half, not because of that, they were a better football team.

NFL Draft
I knew I was going to be a high pick. It didn't bother me. Shit like that doesn't bother me. If it happens it happens. I'm not looking forward to being number one in this or that. I have been very lucky in my career, being at Notre Dame, winning the Heisman and all of that, then being named the MVP of the NFL. I couldn't have had a better career in football for heaven's sake. I got to play under the greatest coaches. Vince Lombardi stood above the whole bunch, the best guy in the world for that. I look back on my career with great pride and I am happy.

Bonus Pick.
They had a bonus pick then, just like they do in basketball. You pick, you get the bonus pick then you are out of the pick. The rest of them are in. It runs through the whole league. There were two teams left in the bonus pick at that time. It was the Packers and the Chicago Cardinals.

That is where the franchise was. Back in the '50s, the St. Louis Cardinals were the Chicago Cardinals and they played at Comiskey Park. I wanted to be picked by the Cardinals because I had so many interests in Chicago, having gone to Notre Dame. I was going to go right into business with a couple of Chicago people, so I was kind of hoping to be picked by the Cardinals. Of course, the Packers picked me. I played in the All-Star game and went to Green Bay for 11 years.

I enjoyed my time with the Packers because of Lombardi. Lombardi changed it all around for Green Bay. He was one of a kind. I was a Green Bay Packer for those years.

First Packers Training Camp
It was fine. I didn't know where I was going to play. Curley Lambeau had set the stage for me, arriving at Notre Dame not having played that much in the All-Star game, the questions and all of the publicity. Of course, I didn't get along with Lisle Blackbourn. When I say I didn't get along, I didn't like him. I didn't think he was worth a shit, and he wasn't.

He played me halfback one week, but he wouldn't tell me until Saturday. We are going to use you at fullback this week. We are going to use you at halfback. What kind of a coach is that? I didn't even work out during the week at the position that he was hoping for me to play. So, I had a very poor rookie year as far as I was concerned. I didn't enjoy it whatsoever. I was establishing a pretty successful business in Louisville so I was actually thinking, to hell; I'm not going to put up with this guy all my life. I will just get out of it, and go on into real estate.

Then of course Vince Lombardi came and changed the whole thing. Not too many quarterbacks come out having made making All-American in college who make All Pro at another position in the NFL.

Vince Lombardi
Vince Lombardi took over. He was disciplined. He came in that first day and told us who was boss and we were going to do it his way or it was the highway. Either enjoy it or get your ass out.

We all bought into it. After what we had been through the first two years when I was there, it was ridiculous. I was ready to hang it up. He talked me out of that and said that I could be a hell of a football player in his offense. He told me how he was going to use me throwing the football and running the football. He said, "I think you are athletic enough to block, so right now you are my halfback. If you don't screw it up, you are going to be successful in this league." And, I believed him.

Jerry Kramer
Name me one team that has 12 guys in the Hall of Fame. We should have 13. It's absolutely ridiculous that Jerry Kramer is not in. He was better than all of the guards in the league in his day.

He is not in the Hall of Fame, because of Alex Karras. See, Karras should have kept his mouth shut about killing Jerry Kramer because Karras was sensational. He was one of the greatest players I ever played against period! He was unblockable. Jerry Kramer couldn't have blocked him. He was the best guard in the league and he couldn't block him. You shouldn't hold that against one guy all his life. Some of these reporters, it just shows you that they don't know shit about football. To keep him out is ridiculous.

They kept me out. There was a guy in Baltimore who used to solicit votes against me. You wanna keep your mouth shut when you gotta vote. You do not need to talk to anyone else. It is kind of an unwritten law with the guys who vote on the Hall of Fame. This guy was adamantly against me. Now, there is somebody who has been adamantly against Jerry Kramer, and just because he had a hard time. He will tell you he had a hard time against Alex Karras. Alex Karras was the best tackle I played against.

There are other tackles that he would take care of who are in the Hall of Fame. It just pisses me off that Jerry is not in there. But, we have 12 guys off our team in the Hall of Fame. No team can even come close to that.

Dave Robinson
Dave Robinson was unblockable. Nobody blocked him. He also was on our team, a team that had many guys in the Hall of Fame. Writers get tired of voting for Packers. I can understand that to a point. But, believe me, I had to go up and block against him. I knew what kind of linebacker he was. I watched him practice and nobody was as good as he was.

Mike Ditka & Gale Sayers
I played against Mike Ditka. There was no better tight end that played the game than Ditka. If you played safety against Ditka, you were in trouble. You had to always know where he was, because when Gale Sayers would reverse his field, those poor safeties and defensive backs down there, they better know where Ditka was. It was kind of brutal. You would watch the film and all of a sudden Gale would switch gears and go somewhere else. Incidentally, when he first walked off Lambeau Field up in Green Bay, I grabbed a hold of him said, "Gale, you've got to work hard. Stay straight baby because you are going to be the best football player in this league, period." He did turn out to be that. I still think he is the best runner I have ever seen, period. Nobody is close.

Dick Butkus

I am going to tell you a great story about the Bears. This is a true story; a lot of people don't know this. When Vince Lombardi first took a look at Dick Butkus at his first game in the exhibition season, he said, "Oh he is a little bit deep. Look at him. He is back there about six yards. He is six yards deep of middle linebacker. Now I know he makes the tackle here, but the guard misses him, the tackle misses him but yeah he kind of upset the whole … but we are going to be able to take care of this guy, he is too deep, and he doesn't get over there real quick. I know he got there and he stopped the play, but … "

We were leading the league in rushing at the time and I was running the ball about 12 or 13 times. Jimmy Taylor was running the ball about 25 times and we were gaining about 200 yards a game rushing. We played the Bears the first game against Butkus. I ran the ball about 13 times and I gained about 12 yards. Jimmy ran the ball 22 times and he normally was leading the league in rushing at the time, about 150 a game, Jimmy ran the ball 22 times and gained 44 yards. Butkus made like 24 tackles.

Chicago Bears Linebackers

Before that we had to face Bill George, so you know, we were kind of used to pretty good middle linebackers. George was one of the greatest linebackers of all time, who played before Dick. Anyway, Doug Atkins was unblockable. After Lombardi saw that, he said, "Look, he was sitting back there, you missed him, Forrest Gregg everybody misses this guy, he must be something special." And that is what Lombardi said after the first time and of course, what the hell, he did prove that he was special. It's ridiculous what he did. The film that I saw last week of Dick Butkus was the damndest film of a football player that I have seen as a linebacker. He killed people.

Rick Casares

Rick Casares was something. People do not realize what a tough son of a … I saved Ray Nitschke's life once because Nitschke broke Casares ankle. Casares never forgot. Casares said, "I'll get him." Casares dared Nitschke outside up in Appleton Wisconsin and of course Nitschke wouldn't go, he isn't going to go because Casares would have killed him.

I saw Casares hit a few people and it worried me to death. I thought he killed a guy on Rush Street one night. I mean, the guy made a remark about Casares girlfriend and Casares unloaded on him and his face disintegrated, just disintegrated. I jumped down and I pulled Casares off of the guy, or Casares would have killed him. Casares was unbelievable. Nobody was as tough as that, nobody fooled with him.

Photograph copyright Associated Press

Chapter 27

Jim Taylor

College:
Louisiana State

Career History:
Green Bay Packers (1958-1966)
New Orleans Saints (1967)

1976 Inductee Pro Football Hall of Fame

College Choice
I got invited to go to other colleges. I made a couple of trips to other colleges to visit them. I came back home and said, "No. I'm going to stay in Baton Rouge, here at Louisiana State University." I wanted to be in my hometown in Baton Rouge.

LSU Teammates
Billy Cannon and Johnny Robinson who later played defensive back for the Kansas City Chiefs were teammates of mine. When Johnny went to Kansas City the AFL was just coming into existence. The AFL's Houston Oilers and Owner Bud Adams also courted Billy Cannon. Later on he went to Oakland Raiders where he ended up for most of his career. He was a running back at the college level and they moved him to tight end with the Raiders.

I was a middle linebacker in college. I probably had better games playing middle linebacker than I did running the ball. We just ran between the tackles and threw short passes.

Green Bay Packers
Green Bay's a special place and I stepped right in. When you're blocking big defensive ends or blitzing linebackers your job is to protect your quarterback. It's the job of moving up and maturing and becoming a more polished player. In the NFL you just play one position, either the running back position or fullback. Paul Hornung, who had come to the Packers the year before, was the halfback and I was the fullback. Ron Kramer came from Michigan as a basketball player and tight end and stepped right in and played tight end.

I didn't play running back. I was on special teams and Scooter McLean came from the Detroit Lions as the head football coach. You got to see the whole, big picture. Then Vince Lombardi came the following year, in '59. When I got there in '58, we won one game. It was a learning experience where you had a very weak team and lots of older players. Then, we got it right. The next year we got Willie Davis and we got some others that we traded for. Henry Jordan was picked up by the Packers. In the first year we had one victory. My first year, I only played in games in California. We left Detroit after we played our Thanksgiving Day game and went on to California to play L.A. and San Francisco. I think they realized the coach was going to be gone so I was put in to be the running back in both those games. We didn't win but I gained over a hundred and some odd yards in both games but we lost them. I had the feeling I think I can play professional football as a running back.

I wasn't involved in the social life in Green Bay. I came to the Green Bay Packers to play football in that little town. I'm a pretty straight shooter. I really dedicated myself to training and fitness and I said I'm going to be the best physical conditioned player on this football team because I knew I was going to get the ball twenty-five, twenty-eight times game in and game out. I knew that my fitness level had to be at its peak.

Vince Lombardi
Vince Lombardi came to Green Bay and he knew what he wanted to do, how he wanted to coach his team, and how he wanted to lead them. We had some decent talent because we got some good draft picks in the first year or two. We were in the championship in 1960. It was his second year, I think. We were 7-5 his first year. We were 1-10-1 was my rookie year and the second year were 7-5. The next year we were playing the Philadelphia Eagles in Franklin Field for the championship of the National Football League. It was a pretty swift and short turnaround. It's a big step up in class knowing that you moved up towards the top to compete against solid football teams. Now, you have to leave the outhouse and try to move closer to the penthouse.

It was amazing. Lombardi was an assistant coach at the high school level and then at Army. After that, he went on to the New York Giants. He knew what he wanted to do with his experience working with different coaches and teams. When he got to Green Bay, he said this is the formula, and this is the format for playing championship football. He started to put together personnel for all the positions. Now, we've got 11 players in the Pro Football Hall of Fame. You could see the tradition and the history of the Green Bay Packers being established after Lombardi arrived. He had a great team and a great concept of teamwork on both sides of the ball. He just wouldn't let anyone be bigger than the team. Everyone was expected to play, do his job, and be a very tough and good football player.

Winning NFL Rushing Title in 1962 The Only Year Jim Brown Didn't Win it During His Career
I won the rushing title in 1962, with outstanding blocking and outstanding coaching, and me making my contribution with the football.

Paul Hornung was there but I think he was injured, so we had Elijah Pitts and Tom Moore filling in for Paul. The offensive line was very explosive. I was able to read our offensive linemen's blocking and then maximize the yardage on a play. I just got acclimated. It's a matter of making really quick decisions and having split vision to be able to see the blocking and things. I was quick, had good balance, and tried to stay low and do things as an instinctive type of a runner.

We knew we had some good backups with Tom Moore and Elijah Pitts. We might have had some other players and running backs that we could plug in when we had injuries to our first teamers.

I was so fortunate and lucky I didn't miss too many games. I didn't have too many injuries in my whole career. All my joints now, my ankles, my knees, my hips, my shoulders, and all are functional. I didn't have any procedures or surgeries in my 10 years at the professional level.

Ray Nitschke
Ray Nitschke was a great player and very aggressive player. He just led our defense. They were so strong. People haven't given the Packer defense all the credit that they deserve. People talk about Bart Starr, the receivers, Paul Hornung, and myself but the defense had outstanding players. They were just solid because game in and game out, they would just get the job done and kept teams from scoring. They just shut them down.

After First Championship Did The Packers Players Think It Was The Start Of A Dynasty?
A dynasty? I don't think so. I don't know that. We really wanted to follow Lombardi. We needed and wanted leadership. We were just starving for leadership. The Hornung team, I think, we went 1-10-1, the worst in Packer history. It was just a complete turnaround because the personnel were there. It's just a matter of getting the players to work together and maximize their ability. With the talent we had and the players looking to Vince Lombardi for leadership and motivation it all come together. The 12-2 or the 11-3 seasons were pretty good seasons with young players with Lombardi only being with the team for two or three years. It started from the grassroots and it started to build and it went real fast because the talent was there and the leadership was there and the productivity and the results were evident.

Max McGee
Max McGee was a different type of player and he was phenomenal. He was a good competitor. I remember seeing him play at Tulane in his college days. He was a running back at that level at that time and moved to the wide out in the NFL.

Max McGee's nickname was Paper Head. He wouldn't really stick his head in there to make a whole lot of blocks. He was a good competitor with great hands and a good leader on our team because of his humor.

Green Bay Packers Attitude
Back in those days, the egos and all about me attitude did not exist. Our football team was not individually hungry to be on television on in the newspaper. They just wanted to be team players and do their job. That is my attitude, sitting here in my house today. I wanted to play football and be the best football player. I didn't worry about the money or about the publicity or whether I'd get All-Pro or this or that. That wasn't the mentality of our football team or myself. Today's players have a little different perceptive and have a little different attitude than our football team.

Forrest Gregg, Fuzzy Thurston, Jim Ringo, Willie Wood, Herb Adderley, and Willie Wood, these people came to be orientated with the team concept. It's just so hard for anybody intoday's generation to understand that. You can tell today's generation over and over and over and it just doesn't resonate, it doesn't penetrate to their perceptive. You see where I'm comingfrom.

That and that the game itself on the field is no different. They still play with four to five second intervals on either side of the ball. Once the quarterback calls the play and snaps the ball, it's thousand-one, thousand-two, thousand-three, thousand-four, play's over with. You have a team actually playing only 12 to 13 minutes out of a three-hour game. This is what the average fan cannot possibly comprehend and this is the way football is played. That is some of Lombardi's inspiration and the leadership that he instilled in our Packer football team that this is the way it's played, with explosion, whether it's a running play, a passing play, it does not matter. Once the play's over with, you go off the field.

Nobody wants to talk about what the basis of the game is. The game of football is explosion and doing your job and blocking, tackling, and moving those chains. Running and picking up whatever yards are needed to move the chains. The average fan cannot possibly understand or comprehend what I'm saying.

Vince Lombardi's Speech Prior To Super Bowl I
It was to go back and do what we did all week. We worked on first down and we worked on explosion. We worked on getting ourselves mentally tough to play the game against the opponent. We were looking at films all week of the opponent evaluating and looking at their players. They're going to block either on the run or pass.

Once the game is over on Monday morning you start to look at where you broke down and what it cost you and if you lost, it's amplified. With winning and exploding, by going 12-2 and 13-1 you're not as concerned but you still have to go back home and recoup and work on your weak points and your breakdowns. Lombardi tried to get you to be perfect, which is impossible. He required you to block 100% on the pass and a 100% on the run.

It's just that you're there to do your job and you love the competition. That is the point. Just forget about the media and all this talk and all this crap. Let's put the ball on the field. This is the only thing I had in my head. Let me hit these guys. Give me the ball. See? Now, you see, you're excited about exploding and doing your job for the fans to enjoy you making field goals, touchdowns and winning. That's the ultimate thing. We have our 11 players on offense and 11 on defense. Here again, fans cannot understand that either. You can write, you can talk, and I could preach this over and over and over and the fans would not understand it.

New Orleans Saints
I came home to New Orleans, Louisiana, and joined their expansion team and that was it. I made my choice to play with that team and at the end of that one season, I said I would go into scouting and radio and continue to fulfill my contractual agreements. I wasn't disturbed that this could possibly happen after one year of playing. There wasn't anybody in the dark. There wasn't any living in denial that my career was coming to an end. I was willing to accept it and move on.

Induction Pro Football Hall of Fame
It seriously a great feeling to be inducted into the Pro Football Hall of Fame and be recognized by your peers. It's just a wonderful feeling and your just cherishing the moment. You just kind move on. It's like scoring a touchdown or having the winning catch. It's just a real gratifying, self-satisfying feeling that you achieved or competed. The ultimate is to do the best job you can do and being inducted is giving you that recognition. Then, you move on. I mean, that's it. Put it behind you and then continue to climb more mountains.

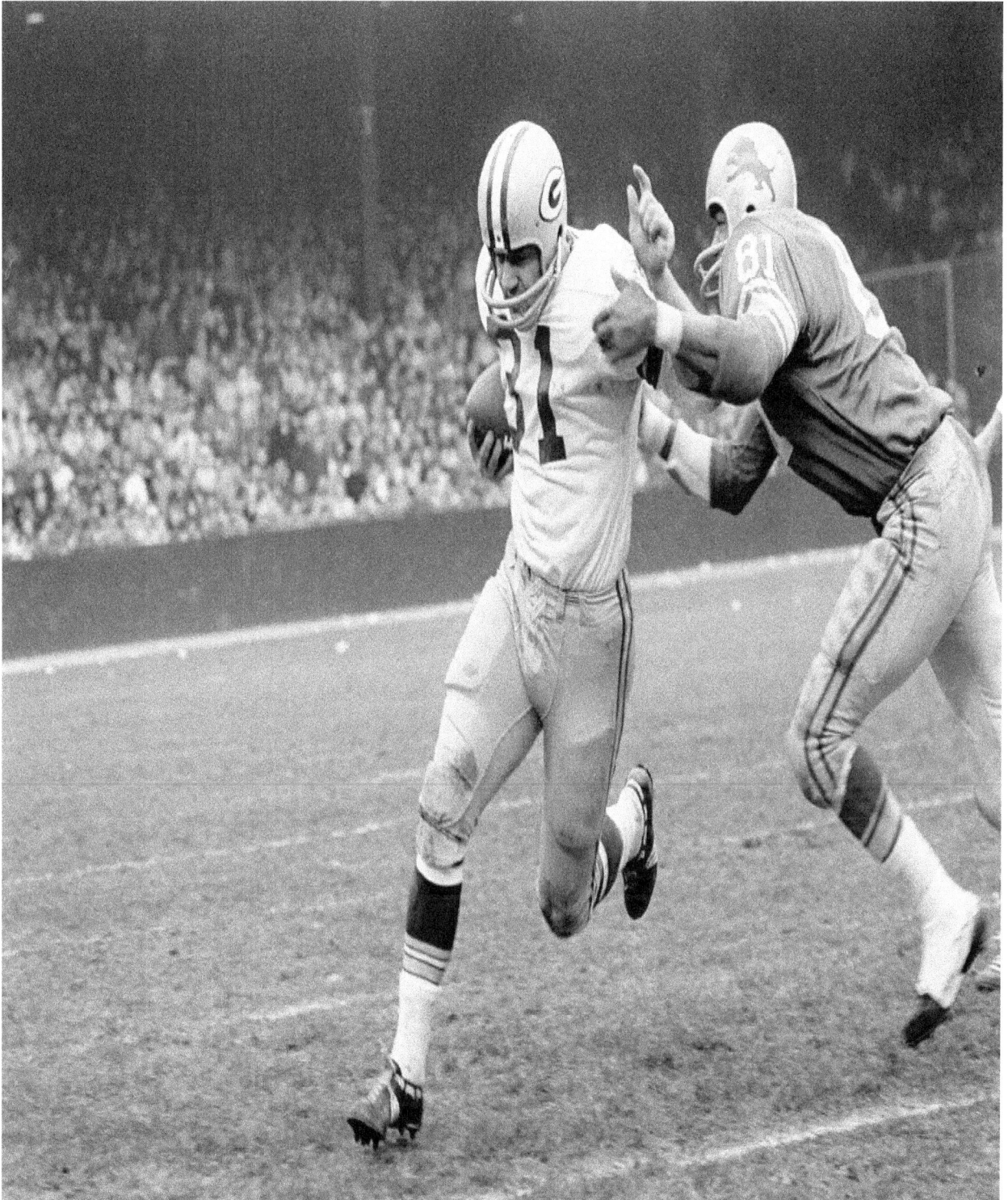

Green Bay Packer Jim Taylor is brought down by Detroit Lion Dick Lane. Photograph copyright Associated Press

Chapter 28

Jerry Kramer

College: Idaho Career History: Green Bay Packers (1958-1968) 2018 Inductee Pro Football Hall Of Fame

College Choice
I had a chance to go to Washington State, University of Washington, and a couple other schools. My dad had a business in Sandpoint, Idaho, and some of the business people were encouraging him to have me go to the University of Idaho.

I was visiting University of Washington and the coach took me out on the field and introduced me to the team in the middle of a scrimmage. He also took me to dinner. He had a boat and wanted to take me fishing up the West Coast and into Canada. He said they'd fly my folks to every home game for three years. So, I called my dad and told him the offer. My dad said, "I don't need to fly to a home game. I need to go to a game I can drive to. You get home. You're going to Idaho."

I start thinking about it and realized that if I went to Idaho, I'd probably play a lot. The better I play, the better I'll get, and the more I play, the better I'll get. Idaho played Oregon, Oregon State, Washington, and Washington State at that time, so it was a pretty good schedule. They were competing against some really good schools, so I decided I would go to Idaho and keep peace in the family, in the little town of Sandpoint.

College
Idaho was fantasyland for me. Going to college was not on my radar through high school and all of a sudden it jumped up in the form of scholarships. No one had gone to college amongst my six brothers and sisters. My older brother had gotten married and went to work. My older sister got married. So it was quite an experience for me.

I joined a fraternity and became a Sigma Nu. That was another part of college that was unknown to me. It was a wonderful experience. I had a great time in college. I just loved it. I had great pals, both on the football team and in the fraternity. So many became lifelong pals. Everybody was young, optimistic, and full of fun. It was a wonderful time.

I really enjoyed college. The games were kind of long and arduous. We would average 59 minutes a game. We would be out for five or six minutes the last game of the season and that would make it 59 minutes because we played damn near every snap both ways. We had three or four other kids that played professional football. Wayne Walker, Tony Anderson, and Jim Prestel played in the NFL. Bobby Dillinger played in Canada. Jim Norton played in Houston in the American Football League [at that time]. So, there were some pretty good players but just not very many of them on the team.

College All-Star Game
I played in the Senior Bowl. Wayne Walker and I played in the East-West Shrine Game and the College All-Star Game. That was really a wonderful step between college football and professional football because kids from Ohio State, Notre Dame, Michigan, West Virginia, and from all over the country were on our team and as opponents on the field. So it was a huge thing for us, maybe one of the bigger things in our lives up to that point. Otto Graham was our coach at the College All-Star game and John Sandusky was my line coach.

Playing in the College All-Star Game was a huge thrill. We beat the Detroit Lions and put them on the skids for 50 or 60 years, whatever it's been now. My pal Wayne Walker never got over it. He really had a hard time with my success and his lack of success. He thought I was lucky, and I was.

The College All-Star Game was a big start for me. If you can play against those guys in the game, and those are the kind of guys that are going into the league, you can probably play in the league. It was a defining moment for us in terms of our confidence.

John David Crow, Jin Ninowski, Jim Taylor, and Joe Nicely from West Virginia, and Dan Currie, Bobby Mitchell, and Charlie Krueger from Texas A&M were on the college team. Charlie Krueger was about three days late getting into training camp for the game. Charlie's wife would call every 15 minutes and say, "Is Charles Kruger by y'all?" I'd answer, "No, ma'am. Charlie is not here." She was calling literally day and night, until he arrived. For the rest of the camp we were all messing with him, "Is Charles Kruger there?"

I wrote about this in *Instant Replay* during the 1967 season. In 1968, we were playing the San Francisco 49ers in Green Bay and Charlie was playing defensive tackle against me. I went into this mental thing to prepare for a game. I got angry and generated a manageable intelligent anger that got my juices flowing. It was kind of like, I'll show that son of a … It kind of helped me get ready to play. I didn't want to talk to anybody, didn't want to look at anybody, and didn't want to have any conversations. I just wanted to work on my mind and my emotions. I was out on the field and was going through all of this. I didn't look at anybody. I finished my warm-ups and I went back into the locker room for the last two or three minutes of pregame conversation. I was going up the steps and I felt this presence right behind me, almost brushing me. The voice leaned up against my ear and said, "Is Gerald Kramer there?"

I said, "God damn you, Charlie. You just destroyed me." He knew it too. He read *Instant Replay* and knew what I was doing and what I was thinking, and he just destroyed my preparation. I enjoyed the hell out of him and John David and all the guys. It was just a fun, fun time.

Wayne Walker
Wayne Walker and I drove to the College All-Star Game together. I had a little Chevy convertible with baby blue seats and top. We gave ourselves ten days to get ourselves from Boise, Idaho to Chicago, Illinois. Seven days out we're in West Yellowstone. So we had to kick it in gear. All the way back from Chicago Wayne is saying, "I'm going to play for the World Champion Detroit Lions with Joe Schmidt, Roger Zatkoff, Jim Martin, and Bobby Layne, and

you're going to Green Bay." He busted my ass all the way from Boise to Chicago with that noise. He was tickled to death to be going to Detroit.

I had gotten a little more publicity than Wayne in college. Wayne played as much as I did and he was a hell of a football player. He had a wonderful career, but he kept comparing his career to mine. In the NFL I won championships and Wayne didn't, so he was always a little feisty with me. He was a little fussy about Green Bay; he had a difficult time with it. It worked out just fine for me, but Wayne had a problem with it.

John Sandusky

I had an interesting deal with John Sandusky. He told me that I wasn't going to make the Green Bay Packers. He said, "You'll be able to play, but you just won't make the Green Bay Packer team." I looked at him kind of funny. He said, "They got five veteran guards returning." So, I'm going well okay. I go to Green Bay. Scooter McLean is our head coach and he calls me into his office and says, "What in the hell is wrong with you?" I said, "What do you mean, coach?" Well you're looking out in the crowd, you're giggling, you're playing grab ass, you're not watching the scrimmage; you just don't seem to be engaged. I said, "Well, I'm waiting to be traded." He said "You're what?" I said, "My college All-Star coach told me I'd be traded. He said I wouldn't make this team, so I'm waiting to be traded." Coach McLean said, "Well I didn't draft you to trade you. You're starting Friday night." So that gave me a couple of days to think about what he said.

It was an interesting final cut. We were down to 37 guys on the club and we were going to keep 36. There was another guard named Kenny Gray, who later played with the Cardinals. It came down to one of us would make the team. Kenny had been there the whole camp. He was playing defensive tackle and making himself valuable. He was a good football player and a good guard. I saw him the day that I got the news that I was going to make the team and be a Green Bay Packer. I'm down at the cigar store, picking up some magazines and he's across the street from the store when I come out. He hollers across the street, "Son of a bitch, you had a no cut contract, didn't you?" I go, "What's a no cut contract?"

After he was released, he went to St. Louis and played for ten or twelve years. He wore the number 64 down there. He was a good football player, and I believe he was an All-Pro at some point.

Detroit Lions

The whole Detroit team has a problem with the Packers. We beat the Lions in Green Bay, 9-7, in Lombardi's first or second year coaching Green Bay on a field goal winning kick. Our kicker kicked it like 50 yards, unobstructed, and we won the game in the last few seconds. The Lions' quarterback, Milt Plum, had thrown an interception. The Lions' players were just going crazy in the locker room. They're throwing garbage cans around, breaking shit, and just going nuts. The Lions thought they had us beat during the game.
We went to the playoffs six or seven times and the Lions didn't. They were in the same division as us. They had good reason to be angry with us.

Vince Lombardi

Everything changed when the Green Bay Packers hired Vince Lombardi as Head Coach. The Packers players were having fun before Coach Lombardi arrived. We were just tickled to death to be professional football players. We were drinking beer, hanging out, bullshitting, and just enjoying every aspect of being professional football players. We did very little conditioning. Our conditioning consisted of waving our arms and making our fingers go up and down.

Scooter McLean, our head coach, would play gin with Paul Hornung, Max McGee, and one of the other guys. In 1958, we were 1-10-1. After about the fourth loss or so, it got so painful to go downtown that we started staying in the locker room to have our celebrations.

Players would take their babies and go home, check everything out, and get the baby sitters stabilized. We would come back to the locker room with our wives and bring a bottle. We had a coke machine, an ice machine, and a juke box in the locker room. There must have been 20-25 couples. We'd kick the socks and jocks out of the way and dance; have a party and have a few drinks. We weren't going downtown, but we were still having a hell of a good time. Local folks in Green Bay wanted to know what the hell was going on.

Coach Lombardi laid it out in his first meeting. He said, "I've never been a loser and I'm not about to start now. If you're not willing to make the sacrifice to pay the price to support your team and do the things you need to do to win, then get the hell out. The three things in your life should be your God, your family, and the Green Bay Packers. That's it. We're going to work harder than we have ever worked before. There are planes and trains and buses leaving here every day. I have a five year contract and some of you may be on the team."

He laid out the kind of work we were getting into pretty clearly. We didn't believe him until we got on the field and people started losing consciousness. We would just kneel over them, throw water on them, move them off to the side, and keep on going.

After one practice Leon Crenshaw showered, got on the bus, and went back to Saint Norbert. While he was standing in the cafeteria line, he lost consciousness and crumpled over.

There was a scout from the St. Louis Cardinals on the sidelines by the tower one day. I came out of the scrimmage and he looked at me and said, "Jerry, I have never seen anything like this. I have never seen anybody work like how you guys are working." He said, "If we did this in St. Louis half of the guys would quit and the other half would be dead."

It was extreme conditioning. You knew that the spark in Lombardi was what really made the difference.

Prior to Coach Lombardi we had good football players who were fast, and had all the qualifications and characteristics necessary to play the game. We didn't have a fire, a burn, a direction, or a spark in us. Coach Lombardi put that spark; that fire, and that drive in you. He said he coached 40 individual people, not a team of 40 people.

Coach Lombardi told me, after chewing me out unmercifully, that I was going to be one of the best guards in football. Herb Adderley came off the field one day and Coach Lombardi ran up to Herb and said, "Herbie, you have just played the finest game I have ever seen a cornerback play. You take that with you whenever you walk on the field in the future. Carry that thought with you." Herbie said, "For the rest of my career, whenever I walked on the field, guess what I remembered." Coach Lombardi found out when and where you were most vulnerable and he would either pat you on the back, chew your ass, or both.

The one thing that was really consistent and interesting about him is he never left a practice without re-establishing communications. He chewed me out for jumping offsides. He came in the locker room looking for me. He patted me on the shoulders and re-established communications.

That was part of the brilliance of him. You'd know, okay he chewed me out, but I made a mistake. Maybe I should have been chewed out. I'll be a little more focused next time and maybe I won't make the mistake. If he thinks I can be really good, maybe I can, maybe I can be something special. So he was the magic of it all. It was the emotional package that he brought that he created in each and every one of us that made the difference.

Green Bay Packers Only Losing One Playoff Game Entire Time Vince Lombardi Was Head Coach

This will not happen again not under the current rules. The NFL looks for competitive balance today with the salary cap, the ability of players to move from team to team, and with so many of the rules today made to create an even field for everybody. Obviously today there are eight to ten teams that seem to be in the mix all the time.

A team can't keep an offensive line together for ten years. A team has to pay players too much and doesn't have enough money to pay all their offensive linemen if they are going to pay the quarterback what he deserves or what he can get as a free agent. The eight-year veteran is as expensive as hell and a team can't afford him, so it's more difficult today to build a dynasty.

Last Drive Of "Ice Bowl" Dallas Cowboys vs. Green Bay Packers

We've heard or read of a lady being able to lift a car off of a baby—that is like the Green Bay Packers last drive in the "Ice Bowl". We [Green Bay Packers] got the ball with four and a half minutes to go. We were on the 35-yard line. We had 65 yards left to go to score. It was minus 57°outside and we were freezing our asses. We made a minus nine yards in our previous 31 plays.

Bart Starr got in the huddle and said, "Alright, let's go." That's all he said. The generation of emotion, the drive, the hunger, the want, the burn, the fire, whatever the hell you want to call it, kicked in and everybody on that team felt it and made a contribution. We went down the field to score and win with 13 seconds to go. You can get a guy with legs, you can get a guy with size, and you can get a guy with speed, but give me a guy with heart.

Ron Kostelnik

Ron Kostelnik joined us during my third or fourth year with the Green Bay Packers. Ron had a little bit of a dunlop coming over his belt and he was not well defined. He looked chubby, rather than muscular. I looked at him and said, "Boy, this kid is not going to be here long." Well he started nine years for us. They couldn't measure his heart, his want, or his fire.

Why Played Injured

I played with broken ribs for the team not for the money, not for the coach, but for the guys. I played with a 103° fever, a busted thumb, concussions, detached retinas … all kinds of shit. But, I didn't play for the coach; I played for the guys.

Bart Starr

There was a single moment in Bart Starr's career that changed our opinion of him, and I believe it changed his life. We were playing the Bears. The nasty Bears with their nasty middle linebacker Bill George. Our coach told Bart to throw the ball deep. He would throw it underneath, and the safeties were coming up threatening to intercept Bart. Our coach said, "Just throw the damn thing as far as you can throw it. I don't care if you complete it or not, just throw it down the field."

So we've got a pass play and Bart goes back to throw and throws the ball. Our tackle stops and turns around and watches the ball. Bart and I are also watching the ball. Bill George is not watching the ball. Bill takes about a five-yard run and hits Bart with a forearm, right square in the mouth and knocks him backward about five yards. Bill says to Bart, "That ought to take care of you Starr." Bart Starr responded, "F— you, Bill George. We're coming after you."

Bart's upper lip was split all the way up into his nose. Blood is flowing down the front of his jersey. I said, "Bart, you better go to the sidelines to get sewed up." He said, "Shut up and get in the huddle." I said, "Yes sir. Yes sir, Mr. Starr."

Bart took us down the field in eight or nine plays for a score. Then he went to the sidelines like the rest of us and they laid him down on the bench. We weren't as delicate as these young boys today. They put about 11 stitches in Bart's upper lip and he went back into the game the next time we got the ball. He never missed a play.

The only question really about Bart up to that point was his toughness, was he tough enough to play. That game answered that question very loudly and very completely. For the rest of Bart's career I never doubted Bart Starr. He became our leader.

Many times I thought I had a play that might work and I'd talk to Bart about it. One time Bart said, "Well Jerry, talk to the other guys, see what they have to say. Do they think it will work?" So from that point on, I would go to either Jim Ringo, Ken Bowman, Fuzzy Thurston, Forrest Gregg, Bob Skoronski, Bill Curry, or whoever the hell was in the game and I'd say, "It looks to me like this play would work for us. It looks good from my standpoint, what do you think?" They would say, "Yeah, Jerry. I think it will work. Yeah, yeah, yeah."

Then I would go to Bart and I'd say, "Everybody thinks it will work, so if you need it, this play is available." Bart showed that fire and he was bright. He did things I don't think people often do.

We were playing the Bears again. We had a cadence where when we would get to the line of scrimmage, it was a set, a single digit number and a double digit number and a series of huts, as in, two, 48, hut, hut, hut. Bart had said that if the quarterback repeats the snap count, say it's on two and he comes up to the line of scrimmage and he says, "Two," then it's a brand new play and the next double digit number is the play, and it goes on the second hut.

So we call this play on one and Bart comes up to the line of scrimmage and breaks the huddle. He comes up to the line of scrimmage and he says, "Set, two, 46," and the whole Bear defense moves shifting over to our right (their left). The Bears were going to kill our play. They were going to overwhelm our play. We had no shot. The next thing I hear is "hut." Bart called it on one actually. Bart came up and said, "Two 47." So it's supposed to go on the first hut and the play is dead, dead, dead. I'm thinking, "Jesus, I got this. Unless I hear a hut, I've got to block this 280 pound idiot across the line of scrimmage from me or Bart if changes it, I may have to pull left."

It's bad to be in that state. It's tough to anticipate, tough to get a good start, and tough to do everything. Bart said, "Easy, hold it, one 36, hut." There wasn't a missed assignment; there wasn't a single guy that was out of focus. We were waiting on Bart to change the play and Bart knew that. Bart knew his game and he knew our game. He was just a bright, intelligent, human being and was tough as nails. Zeke Bratkowski said one time, "You may think Bart's a sweetheart, but he'll cut your heart out if he has to."

Jim Taylor Leading the NFL In Rushing Being Only Time In Jim Brown's Career Jim Didn't

The Green Bay Packers really were a team. We wanted the team to win and individual accomplishments weren't made out to be that big of a deal.

We would have a game against the Cleveland Browns and everybody knew that Jim Brown was having a war with Jim Taylor and Taylor was having a war with Brown. So we may have given a little more, but we didn't have a lot extra to give. We were playing with everything we had. We were happy when Jimmy came out ahead. We thought that reflected on us and we were proud.

Jim Taylor & Paul Hornung

There was always a feeling our running game was pretty much our bread and butter, so we were running most of the time. Passes were mixed in to confuse our opponent.

Jim Taylor and Paul Hornung were different types of runners. Jimmy was more brutal; a brute force. Hornung was more cerebral. Hornung would see a defensive back and he would know that I had to block the defensive back. He would be under enough control to get at the magic point when the defensive back had to make a decision, and if he didn't, I was going to kill the defensive back. Hornung would be in a position where he had to move. At that instant, he would take a step to his left and make his shoulders and his whole body, look like he was going that way. The defensive back would commit and come in to try to make the tackle. Hornung was setting me up for the block and then he would go the other way. They were different runners, but both of them were sensational.

If they each rushed for 100 yards a game, then we were happy. It was always more of a team thing than an individual thing. We sure as hell were aware and happy about it.

Toughest Defensive Lineman

There are about five defensive linemen that I remember very well as being the toughest. Leo Nomellini, a great football player on the San Francisco 49ers, helped me out a great deal by putting his right foot back when he was going inside, and putting his feet parallel when he went outside. I picked that up my first year playing against him. From that point on, I knew everything that Leo was going to do and it made a huge difference in my blocking.

Art Donovan was a shaker and a matador. Most defensive tackles will come straight at you, bully you, try to run over you, or take you back to the quarterback. They'll use strength and aggression on you. Artie would stand up and shake. He would get his belly going side to side and he'd wait for you to make a lunge at him. Then he would step aside or grab you and push you in the direction that he'd want to go. Then he would go around you. I didn't understand that those kinds of tackles played in the NFL. The first time that I played against him, I wanted to hit him after the game to make sure that he was real. He was an education. All you had to do with him was wait on him. He couldn't shake forever. He had to make a move and when he made his move, you would move. You had to have patience.

Charlie Krueger played for the San Francisco 49ers, but he was from Texas. He was 6'5" and weighed 265. He was lean. He brought it all day and all night. He never slowed down for a play. He didn't take a half a play off. He didn't take a quarter of a play off. He just never let up.

The top two defensive linemen in my book were Merlin Olsen and Alex Karras. Merlin had great work ethic. He had great physical capabilities. He was 6'5".
I got Merlin and Doug Atkins on the scale one day at the Pro Bowl. They were giving me some crap about something and I said, "You two, get over here. I want to see what you weigh." They both got on the scale for me and one weighed 296 and one weighed 300. They were both listed at about 265, but that was a long way from reality.

Merlin never quit either. Merlin was going to be there until tomorrow night when you played against him. If you were going to try to whoop him, you better bring a light and a lunch, because it was going to take a while.

I was a finalist for the Pro Football Hall Of Fame in 1997. I still remember Art Daley calling me and doing a story about me. I said, "Well, Alex didn't play his heart out against Atlanta or the some of the other teams that weren't doing well that year. He played his heart out against Green Bay. He was fiery, angry, emotional, and he played his ass off. He was a hell of a football player." Art hung up from me and called Alex. He told Alex, "Kramer said you maybe didn't play all that hard against Atlanta and some of the lesser teams, and that you had a lot of animosity towards Green Bay. You had a lot of passion and a lot of fire; you were a different player." Alex said, "I'd say he's about right."

Alex was a wonderful football player. Alex had a low center of gravity. Merlin was 6'5". Tall boys got the strength up above. I don't think Alex was under 6'0", but it felt like he was 5'10" and 285. He just had a low center of gravity and he was really strong. He worked out all the time. He had a background in professional wrestling so he had the fire and the burn. He was a hell of a player.

Block On Jethro Pugh For Bart Starr On Game-Winning Quarterback Sneak In Ice Bowl
I had watched game film of the Dallas Cowboys' three previous games before our game. In their first game I saw Jethro Pugh was playing high in their goal line defense. The Cowboys defensive linemen put their noses about ten or twelve inches from the field. Bob Lilly would charge straight ahead and come low. You couldn't move him with a Caterpillar D9. Jethro was supposed to stay down low too.

The next game it's the same thing and the game after the same thing again. So I mentioned this to Coach Lombardi. I told Coach Lombardi, "We can wedge two if we have to." Coach Lombardi said in his most conversational, social voice, "What?"

I said, "I think we can wedge two if we have to." He said run that back to me. So I ran it back about four times to him. Coach Lombardi said, "That's right, put it in the red zone two."

I had no dream of that play being called on the one-yard line with 15 seconds to go. I thought Coach Lombardi might call it when we were on offense in the middle of the field or in the second quarter. I thought maybe we don't use it at all or we don't need it. I didn't think a lot about it.

We were a different team when we came down the field on that final drive against the Cowboys. Every guy was playing his ass off. So, now it was my turn. I knew what I needed to do and I prayed that Jethro was going to do what he did the last three weeks. So I find a little divot, almost like a golf divot, where my left foot would go. Normally I drove off my right foot. My right foot is back so I get more push off my right foot. My left shoe just snuggled into that divot so it acted like a starting block. I had a really good start when I came out of the crouch. In difficult situations, there are three things you really need to do. Keep your head up, your eyes open, and follow through. All I thought was, it's my responsibility since I suggested the play. It's on my back now, so let's get the job done. I kept my eyes open. Jethro came up and I put my face in his chest and everything worked out.

Green Bay Packers Rivalries
Coach Lombardi knew that the Green Bay Packers fans considered the Chicago Bears the ultimate rival. Coach Lombardi would say, "I'm going to go out there and beat those Bears. I want you to tear them up today. You guys beat the Bears and I tickle old man Halas' ass." Then Coach Lombardi would giggle a little bit.

We would have practice on Wednesday, Thursday, and Friday, and players would wear different jersey numbers when it was Bears week. I might wear number 12 and Bart might wear number 75.

Coach Lombardi would say, "Who's that guy down there? That's one of Halas' spies. Go see who it is. Go get his ID, show me who it is."

He was always using little gimmicks to get us interested in the game and pumped up about it. When I look back it was so silly. Could you imagine the Bears scout saying to Coach Halas, "They've got the fourth string playing quarterback. Number 75 is the quarterback this week." Not likely, you know. But it kind of got us going. It gave us a little lift, a little boost, and a little more animosity towards the Bears.

I think probably the Dallas Cowboys rivalry was more personal. Coach Lombardi and Coach Tom Laundry of the Cowboys didn't always agree on things when they were assistant coaches with the New York Giants. In the 1958 NFL Championship Game, Lombardi wanted to go for it on 4th down and Laundry wanted to punt. I believe there was always a personal thing there for Lombardi with Laundry.

Writing Book *Instant Replay*

Generally, I think the team's response was pretty positive when my book *Instant Replay* came out. The book had come out a week or two before training camp. We were in training camp and the book was getting a lot of conversation. I had a record that I liked to play before I went to sleep or as I was going to sleep called, *One Stormy Night*. The sound from the record was thunder, rain, and pitter-patter. It was mood music, kind of. I was playing the record and Gale Gillingham and Forrest Gregg were right across the hallway from me at Saint Norbert. I heard some stirring around in the hall. Gilly had gotten a glass, gone down to the john, and come into my room. He threw the water up on the ceiling so it was really raining. Gilly and Forrest were giggling their asses off. They thought it was really funny. Willie Davis was my roommate that year, and we didn't think it was quite as funny as they did. Willie said, "Be careful Forrest. Jerry will put that in his next book."

Forrest said, "That damn book. That's all I hear about. Everybody wants to know about that book. That damn book." He said, "I'll tell you one thing, Jerry. You were dead honest." I thought that was as high of praise as I could receive. He was not only my teammate; he was my linemate. He communicated with me like a brother. We were pretty close. When I saw something that was different I'd say, "Forrest, got it." When he'd see something he'd say, "Jerry." I'd say, "Yup."

That's all we'd say when an odd situation came up. So, I thought that was high praise from Forrest. I think generally the guys really enjoyed the book. It's been so much more than a book for me. I still get letters from people who are inspired by it. They took the Lombardi principles and it worked for them.

I met with the publisher, his people, and my agent in New York. I asked the publisher, "How many books do we need to sell to do good?" He said, "Jerry, 7,500 to 10,000. Sports books don't sell traditionally, so I think if we do 10,000 books, we will do well."

I never dreamt of ever writing a book or even being close to someone who wrote a book. I started to think that I had to use some big, long, flowery words that an author would use, and that I had better increase my vocabulary. I was having thoughts like that. That went on for two or three days. Then I thought, "Who do you think you're kidding? I mean, come on. It is what it is and you are who you are. So just be as dead honest as you can be about it. Tell it exactly the way you see it and you think it is or could be. Be precise about what you say, because you're going to have to defend it. Be ready to defend it. If they don't like it, they don't like it, but at least you put it down the way you saw it to be and the way you thought it was." That was my final thought on that.

Playing Kicker & Offensive Line

Kicking puts a little pressure on you. It's a little bit of a different deal. You're all alone. The whole stadium is watching you. You can't think about all those things. You've just got to think about keeping your head down, following through, hitting the ball properly, and getting everything right. There was always a little nervousness with the kicking part of things. As an offensive lineman, my Momma didn't know what I was doing on the line.

People hardly ever saw you unless it was the Ice Bowl block or something like that. The big part was that you went unnoticed. That's what you really preferred as an offensive lineman—to go unnoticed. Kicking I felt was a responsibility and not a celebration. I wasn't tickled to death when I made a kick. I was relieved I had been able to do what the team wanted me to do. The last kick I made in Yankee Stadium in 1962, I knew exactly where we were and I knew that if I made that kick it would put the game pretty much out of reach.

The wind was blowing like hell. I aimed ten yards outside the right goal post and I kicked the ball. I hit it pretty solid and it came right down the middle of the goal post. I knew that they were asking me to do something and I had to get it done. I was more relaxed and pleased that I was able to make the kick than I was celebrating about the kick.

AFL-NFL World Championship Game "Super Bowl I"
We didn't give the Chiefs as much credit as they deserved in the AFL-NFL World Championship Game. We had no information about anybody they ever played. We had no way of judging them and their opponents. We watched films. We were watching a film one evening and two of their safeties ran into each other. Obviously one of them went the wrong way. They knocked each other down and were flat on their butts. One of the Green Bay Packers, Max McGee, starts doing Looney Tunes noises. We were giggling and laughing about it.

We thought the games would be in descending order of difficulty. That maybe the Rams would be the most difficult since they had beaten us three weeks before. The Cowboys would be right behind them since they had a good football team. Then we thought, we got the AFL-NFL World Championship Game and that will be the easiest game of the playoffs.

During the first quarter of the Championship Game we found out that there were some pretty damn good football players on the other side of the line for the Chiefs, including E.J. Holub, Ernie Ladd, Bobby Bell, Johnny Robinson, and Willie Lanier.

So we kind of checked our gear at halftime and buckled our hats. We came out of the locker room with a little bit of a different attitude, a much more serious attitude, and took care of business. We were not really that uptight or worried prior to the game. I think we were more worried at halftime than we were at the beginning of the game.

Green Bay Packers coach Vince Lombardi rides on the shoulders of tackle Forrest Gregg and guard Jerry Kram (64) after defeating the Oakland Raiders in Super Bowl II. Photograph copyright Associated Press

Chapter 29

Jim Brown

College:
Syracuse
Career History:
Cleveland Browns (1957–1965)
1971 Inductee Pro Football Hall of Fame

College Choice

I had a mentor, Judge Kenny Molloy from Manhasset. He also went to Syracuse. He took an interest in all of the kids out in Manhasset. He helped a lot of us tremendously. He wanted me to go to his alma mater and made arrangements for the people in the city to pay my way in and send me there on trial. It was a fiasco in the beginning, but it finally worked out. It wasn't because of him that it was a fiasco. I don't think Syracuse wanted me at that time, but since he wanted me to go there they followed through. I really had to prove myself about five times. Now I'm a real good alumnus of Syracuse.

I just wasn't one of the choices of at least some of the coaches there. Head Coach Ben Schwartzwalder was a different kind of guy. They had another African American there by the name of Avatus Stone. He was a quarterback, but he left them and went to Canada and played football. I think he had a lot of resentment. We had something in common being of the same color. I didn't know the guy. They had problems with having African American players there that were independent individuals. I ended up being the only African American player on the team.

I love ball sports and I tried to play as many as I could. At Syracuse, football and lacrosse were my two main sports. Lacrosse was a game I loved because the coach was a great coach and his son and I were really good friends. We're friends today. We went undefeated in our senior year, which was really good. It's a great game that has a Native American background. It was created by the Native Americans and used to be Canada's national sport. A lot of people never knew that. Now I think it's the fastest growing sport in this country.

Why I Chose to Play Professional Football

I had a better shot at being a professional football player than any other sport. I took advantage of it. I had nine years as a member of the Cleveland Browns that were very successful and very happy years. I never really played for money. I never did anything for money only. As I've said, I'm an all-around athlete because I love pretty much all sports. I was also a decathlete. When I was a senior in high school I finished 5th in the nation, which I was very proud of because I had no coaching.

Paul Brown
Paul was a very creative individual. He was a visionary. He was a great pioneer for professional football. He created certain things like the playbook and the facemask. He was an individual that was sometimes misunderstood, but I liked playing under him because he was a very strict disciplinarian. Everybody was afraid of him so the team really stuck together and concentrated on playing football, which was what I really liked.

Paul relied on me a lot and I loved it. I wanted the ball and I got it enough to be a very successful running back.

On Being Called Greatest Football Player Ever
I'm going to be real honest with you. I don't live my life based on trophies, awards, or opinions. I respect a lot of opinions. I have my own. When your teammates or opposing players feel that you are a great competitor, that's a good compliment. That's a solid compliment because they usually won't tell anything or say anything that they don't believe. I can take that, accept that compliment to a certain degree but I usually know what I can do, what I can't do. I really know how I performed. I'm my greatest critic. I don't think anyone has ever heard me say that I'm the best at anything, because I think that we shouldn't try to judge ourselves. There are too many variables in a team sport. If it was boxing or something like that it would be different, but in team sports you depend upon each other. Lebron James has proven himself to be a great team player and I love him for it because people overlook the greatness of a team player. Magic Johnson, Larry Bird, and Bill Russell, are the types of individuals that I like because they understood team sports and how important the last guy on your team is, because he might be the difference in winning and losing.

1964 Browns Team
We had a good team and everybody participated in that '64 game. We beat the Baltimore Colts and they were like a Hall of Fame team. They had many Hall of Famers on the team. The great Johnny Unitas was the quarterback, Raymond Berry was there, John Mackey was there, and "Big Daddy" Lipscomb was there. It was an unbelievable team and we beat them twice. I think they lost by three touchdowns and we had individuals that did their jobs tremendously and we were able to shut them out. Once again the offense got all the credit but the defense didn't allow them to score a point. That just goes to show you that sometimes the media or public opinion isn't always what we see as players. We have a great appreciation for the contribution of others that a lot of times, the general public doesn't even see.

Sam Huff
Sam Huff made a lot of tackles. Sam was a great middle linebacker for the Giants, and he was very smart. Sam was a good friend of mine, a good advocate for professional football, and played on some really great Giant teams. He was a leader on those teams and I always had great respect for him and great respect for his abilities.

Playing Defense
I did play defense in college. I was a decent safety in college. All throughout my athletic career I played defense but as a pro we didn't. We played one way and that was good enough for me

because in professional football you have to really concentrate and it was difficult to play both positions.

Speed
I was fast and my speed was combined with my balance, strength, and power. I had a combination of things that all worked together. You might be the fastest guy in the world but if you don't use it properly, it doesn't really materialize into anything. I was fast enough. I never got beat in a 40. I always worked on my starts as a high school football player because my coach wanted me to. It gave me an advantage because I could get out of the blocks real quick. It always helps in professional football if you can really accelerate quickly. It's a great asset to have.

Larry Wilson
Larry Wilson's number was 8. Now how would I remember a guy's number? When I first came in contact with him, he tackled me and I didn't know where he came from. I looked down, and the number 8 was on his jersey. I went back and asked my teammates, who wore number 8. He put a hell of a tackle on me because that guy was too small to stop me but he did. He caught me around the ankles and I said, "You know, we're going to have to watch out for him." Then two plays later he did the same thing. I said, "We are really going to have to watch out for him because he can really play. I think he was one of my favorites because he was a smaller guy but very good at tackling big guys like me, getting low, wrapping our ankles up. When your ankles are wrapped up, you can't employ too much power. I've always had a lot of respect for Larry.

Retiring at Height of Career
Leaving football was not hard for me at all because I am a well-rounded person. I'm a college graduate. I'm an activist. I've been an activist all of my life. I have an organization now called Amer-I-Can. We work in schools across the country. We work with violence across the country. I got Earth, Wind, & Fire their first record contract. I've done many, many things in my life. I've been an entrepreneur in many ways and I try to be as much of a humanitarian as I can be. I have a very well rounded life.

I took an interest in doing other things rather than just being an athlete. To me it was the wise thing to do. I knew that my legacy would be based on the fact that I had left at age 29. We won the championship in 1964. I was MVP of the league in 1965. The legacy stands very tall because I did leave at the height of my career.

People stay too long. There's no reason to stay that long. It's only a part of your life. You should not put too much importance on it. Your education is going to ultimately prove to be the best thing you can acquire. If you do not understand economic development then you're going to have a problem. I think of all the money that the players make today. After three years most of them declare bankruptcy, which is a shame.

Gale Sayers
Gale Sayers is a dear friend of mine. He is a wonderful human being and a very smart young man. I love him. I have nothing but respect for him. You have to manage your money especially if you make a lot because the more you make, the more trouble you can get into. The one thing that will always be a major problem is taxes. In your financial planning you have to take taxes

into consideration very strongly. If it's not in your plan properly, it can back fire on you later. Once you're in trouble with the IRS, you're really in trouble.

Regardless how much money you make, you have to really manage it properly. You must consider your taxes, and any kind of deferred payments have to be allowable. You have to be very careful with your investments. Very few players manage their money correctly. Very few agents can really tell players the truth because players will fire the agent if he is not just talking about making more money. In order to really be successful you have got to live off an allowance. Each year you have to decide what it is that you can live off of, pay the proper taxes, and have the balance that you need. When people make a lot of money they think they can just spend a lot of it.

Decision to Become an Actor

It was an opportunity that knocked on my door. I was offered a part in a movie because I was a football player and had some notoriety. After I did that part, I decided to get an agent and he got me a part in "The Dirty Dozen", which was a tremendous hit. I got good reviews. It gave me the chance to have a high profile profession that paid me a lot of money? I tried it. I had an opportunity to break down a few doors, break down some taboos and I had a lovely acting career.

The movie 100 Rifles was quite an experience because it was the first time that an African American male had a major love scene with a Caucasian female. There was a lot made of Raquel Welch and I doing it at the time. It was like breaking down doors. I enjoyed it because I felt, not only was I making money, I had a chance to do something different. I felt I could probably open up opportunities for people that deserved opportunities. I looked at it that way and did some meaningful films.

My favorite actor was Al Pacino. Al Pacino is a great actor, a Hall of Fame actor, and a great guy. I had a couple of real scenes with him. Yes, I had the pleasure of working with him on some meaningful scenes. With him being such a nice guy, it was just a great experience.

Fred Williamson

I appreciated Fred Williamson's intelligence. Fred was a producer and a director and he did a lot of small films, which I acted in with him. I have admiration for his ability to understand the business and cut a niche out in the business for himself. As far as competition, I only compete with myself. I never got into competing with other people. This whole "best" thing, I think is it's a weakness to go around talking about you are the best at something. Your performance speaks for itself, your actions speak for themselves and if you're confident with yourself you don't have to really get into, 'Who is the best?'

Photograph copyright Associated Press

Chapter 30

Jim Otto

College:
Miami

Career History:
Oakland Raiders (1960–1974)

1980 Inductee Pro Football Hall of Fame

College Choice

When I was a senior in high school I had 48 university scholarships. Miami was one of them, but I hadn't really thought that much about Miami until I had visited Minnesota, Wisconsin, Northwestern, and some other schools. I think it was 30 below zero when I left Wausau, Wisconsin. I visited Miami in February. When I got to Miami, it had to be about 75 degrees.

I couldn't believe it could be so cold in one spot and so nice and warm in another. Everything smelled fresh because everything was so green. For a country boy from Wisconsin, it was really just a dream that I never thought would come true.

When it came time to go away for two days in August, I went to Minnesota. We got there in our old car, and the next morning we turned around and drove right back to Wausau. I think we had about 20 dollars from my parents. I was able to make it with gas money all the way down to Miami.

Northwestern recruited me just before Ara Parseghian was hired as head coach. I was recruited the spring of 1956, during my senior year in high school. Wisconsin and Minnesota had two great teams as well. I would have played in Rose Bowls if I had gone to either one of those two schools.

Miami is hot and humid, and the college was on probation. I really had to think hard before going there. That held me back from going there to begin with, but then I looked at their schedule for the four years that I would be there. The University of Miami would be playing schools in the Atlantic Coast Conference, Southeast Conference, Southwest Conference, and the Big Ten. I'd be exposed to a lot of different types of football, and I'd play against almost every conference in America.

Weight Training

Jim Ringo was probably the premier center when I got out of college. He was with Green Bay and weighed about 245. They might have thought he was a little small. When I got out of college, I weighed 217. I went to training camp and lifted weights, and weighed 240 my rookie year.

I gradually worked my way up through weight training. There weren't too many athletes doing weight training in those days, but I believed in it. I studied kinesiology in college and understood how I could build muscle, strength, and quickness. I did a lot of weight training and working out to the point where I worked my way up to 276. That was the biggest I was.

Nobody believed I would get that big. A lot of the teams tried to acquire me from the Raiders. When Mr. Davis came in 1963, he wouldn't let me go for anything.

Early Years With Raiders
I didn't know what I was getting into because it was a step up in the pros. In 1960, the American Football League wasn't that good. We didn't have that good of football players to begin with. It took a couple of years for guys like Al Davis, Sid Gillman, and Hank Stram to really start recruiting and signing some better players into the league.

Even though I had hopes that I would be a part of that all along, I just wanted to play. The National Football League didn't draft me. They said they were going to draft me, but when draft day came, the NFL didn't draft me. I just wanted to play football and get the chance to play with Oakland. Playing in Oakland was the best thing for me because I grew up there. I grew up there, got big, and I learned how to really play football.

Let's just say that in 1960, '61, and '62, we were kind of the doormats of that league. My first year with the Raiders we only won a couple games.

It was tough, it was really tough, but I new that there was a light at the end of the tunnel. If I played hard and got my teammates to play hard, and we had a coach that we had faith in, then we would be good. Al Davis did that for us, so I was happy while I was there.

I used to think that maybe they would trade me, but it never happened. There were teams trying to trade for me, but the Oakland people wouldn't let me go. When Miami got their franchise, since I was from the University of Miami, the Miami Dolphins would have liked to have me there as a player. They would have liked to have a University of Miami player on their team, but Al Davis wouldn't let me go. I didn't mind it. I loved the entire time I was in Oakland; I'm still an Oakland boy.

Al Davis
As a coach, Al Davis was far superior to anyone. I think Sid Gillman was an excellent coach for the San Diego Chargers. He was a very fine coach, and so was Hank Stram. But, Al Davis put so many innovations into football while he was coaching and he did so many different things while coaching players. He was excellent at working with wide receivers, like Lance Alworth, who is in the Pro Football Hall of Fame. He worked with him in San Diego. He also worked with Fred Biletnikoff and a lot of our wide receivers and offensive linemen, like me.

He would come up to me during the practice and say, "Jim, just move your right foot a little bit more to the outside and then drive off of that foot." He had different little things he'd help everybody with, actually.

We played in some games where it was very similar to what Baltimore did recently when they got a direct snap from the center and ran around the end zone to run the clock out.

The very first time we did that, people thought we were nuts. I predicted Baltimore would do it when I saw the situation they were in. I said, "They better take the ball on a direct snap and run the clock out." I was kind of excited about that. Al Davis did a lot of things that were innovative.

I know that Al Davis also had the help of Ron Wolf, who was an outstanding football person as well. He was a big help to Coach Davis.

Tom Flores
I didn't envision Tom Flores ever coaching the Raiders when he was playing. I knew Tom was a football person. He knew what he was doing out there on the field. His first three years in the league he didn't do that well because he was sick. After his illness he came on and showed what he could do. He had a football mind and he had a mind for coaching and it was no surprise to me that he became the Raiders Head Coach and then later on with Seattle.

Look at both Tom Flores and Jim Plunkett. They're both Hispanic, and you don't like to think that's what holding them back from being named to the Hall of Fame. The selection committee for the Hall of Fame, I wouldn't want to say they are racist or anything like that, but I think a lot of them thought that Tom Flores and guys like Tom were tutored so heavily by Mr. Davis that it wasn't really their ability to do what they're doing. They were getting it from Mr. Davis.

I think that's unfair because even back a few years ago when John Madden went into the Pro Football Hall of Fame, the selection committee wanted to put him into the Pro Football Hall of Fame as a football related person, not as a coach. I was very, very upset about it. I went to the Hall of Fame for one of the selection committee meetings and I sat before all those people and really called them out and told them what I thought about the situation. John Madden was a football coach and the greatness of the Raiders at that time was because of John Madden.

Raiders Going From Doormat To Successful
It was fantastic. A football player loves good coaching and he will respect the coaches, because it's important for a coach to take you all the way. You saw the two Harbaugh brothers coaching in the Super Bowl and prior to that, everything they did throughout the season. These are the kind of coaches that a real football player loves to play for. Players would give their shirt off their back to play for a guy like that.

Back in the day when Jon Gruden was a Raiders coach, every young guy in the National Football League would have liked to have been with the Raiders at that time. When you get a coach who has the ability, the desire, and the drive like the Harbaughs, Gruden, and Davis, it's like a dream come true to play for him.

First Raiders Super Bowl
They said it was going to be a lot of hoopla, and there was, but I didn't let that stuff bother me. I didn't get into that at all. All I knew was I'm a kid from Wausau, Wisconsin, going against Lombardi's Packers; Ray Nitschke, those guys in the inside, that's what I was after. That's what

I prepared for and I'm very proud of the way that I played against them. Vince Lombardi complimented me on my play, but we lost. But I was after a win, not a compliment.

Toughest Defensive Player Went Up Against

If you go to the Pro Football Hall of Fame and look at my era, the middle linebackers and the defensive tackles that are in there, were pretty darn good. You got Bob Lilly, Joe Greene, Ray Nitschke, Dick Butkus and all these different inside guys; linebackers. There were some great ones in there and those were the guys that I had to prepare to battle for.

To get the notoriety of the Hall of Fame or All Pro, you've got to be able to handle guys like that and I'm proud to say that I did a pretty good job at that.

Success Of Raiders Offensive Line

It was the weightlifting we did, but there was just an awful lot of pride and poise in those guys and we worked hard together at practice. We wanted to be the best. Gene Upshaw and Art Shell had tremendous pride in themselves, and naturally I was very proud of my team. I tried to exude that pride out there on the field every day in practice and every Sunday in the game.

It was something that I think Mr. Davis instilled in us; the pride, the poise, the dedication, the commitment to excellence, all those things that you've heard about over the years, that was the Raiders. That was our Raiders team.

Favorite Quarterback

I didn't have a personal favorite quarterback. When George Blanda took a snap from me, I knew we were going to do something special. I knew that he had a plan to complete some passes; get in position to get a field goal or get in position to get a touchdown. When Ken Stabler was in there we knew that it was going to be bam-bam; you're going at it, let's go. There was a lot of commitment and pride out there.

It was the same with Daryle Lamonica. Lamonica was a super athlete. We practiced hard. Teams today don't practice like we did back then. To be successful, a team has to work on it. Look at the 49ers and the Ravens in the Super Bowl. Those guys worked hard for the last couple years. Jim had two playoffs and John had five playoffs in a row.

You don't get there if you don't work hard. Every team out there has to work hard if they want to get to the big time.

Injuries & Physical Problems

I had my leg amputated a couple years ago due to football injuries and nobody really said, "Jim, I'm sorry. What can we do for you?" There was no insurance for dismemberment or anything like that. As far as concussions are concerned, I think it's being overplayed a little bit. I've had probably about 25 concussions, more than that when I played, and I'm not complaining. My wife thinks I'm a little goofy at times, but every wife thinks that about her husband.

I don't have Alzheimer's. Doctors have examined me and they said I'm not going to have Alzheimer's. I do have some cognitive problems, though. A doctor I saw in Southern California is concerned about some of the cognitive tests that I didn't do well on, but I feel very good about it. I'm going to go along. I punished my body playing football like we all do, but some of these guys, I think, are just looking for a handout after they get through playing. They're looking to get a paycheck from some insurance, or someone who is going to pay off the guys that do have some memory problems.

I played 308 straight games and hurt my knee; well, that's an understatement. I hurt my knees and I kept going. In 1974, I thought, wow, it's getting kind of tough out here, and yet I made Second Team All Pro after all those years. In my 16th year of football I had a feeling in my knee that I didn't like. It didn't seem as though I would be able to play up to the standards that I had played to all this time, and I just didn't want to be the guy who's hanging on out there.

I didn't make much money at all. I think the most money I made was $70,000 a year, in my 16th year of pro football. You've got Flacco talking about $20-$27 million now. I wouldn't mind hanging around with him and being his water boy or something. I think they're just making a lot out of this thing. Sure, we all have memory loss to a certain extent. You can't think of a professor's name, where you went to college, or sometimes your wife might ask you to pick up a loaf of bread and you bring home a pound of cheese instead. That's no big deal as far as I'm concerned.

We've been playing football for many, many years and there have been a lot of headaches and a lot of concussions out there. I've had amnesia for three days. I didn't know who I was or where I was, but I can still remember when it happened. As long as I can remember when that happened, and that's been a lot of years ago, I think I'm in pretty good shape. I wish guys would quit crying so damn much. If they would have had some strength and been a decent football player to begin with, they wouldn't be crying right now.

I hit with my head all the time. I would lead with my head. That's the first thing I would hit the opponent with, then my forearms, then my shoulders. I blocked the way I was taught to block and that's the way I was taught. I tried to be a perfectionist at my trade and that's what I did every time. You get headaches doing that.

I had a concussion three weeks ago. I was in a wheelchair because when I take my leg off at night to sleep, I have to have a wheelchair to get me to the restroom. I was in a hotel and I backed up with the wheelchair in my room and it tipped over backwards. I hit my head right on the tile floor. It sounded like a coconut broke open and I had a headache for about four days; so I had a concussion. What the hell, I've had a lot of concussions.

There I was, I didn't feel too good for about four or five days. My wife and I are in this hotel; we're off having a holiday and visiting and I got a headache. Big deal. I probably got hit in the head that time harder than most guys ever get hit in the NFL. I was a little dizzy for a while, but you've got to suck it up and get off your backside.

Bill Bergey
John Madden is chewing me out from the sideline. Bill Bergey was a rookie and Bill was setting up his defensive line to free him from me. I couldn't get a free shot at Bill Bergey, and Bill was

making some tackles. Madden was kind of hollering at me, "Otto, can't you get that rookie?" Then there's Bergey, he's saying, "Yeah, Otto, can't you get that rookie?" I said to myself, you're damn right I can get that rookie. I went after him and put him out of the game.

John Madden
John Madden was only about a year and a half older than me. I had tremendous respect for Coach Madden, as did the rest of my teammates. He wanted the game played a certain way and we played that way for him. He was demanding. He would demand that we play the game that way and that's what we would do. He was like one of the guys, but he was also a taskmaster and he wanted the game to be played that way. We all loved John Madden. He was a great guy to play for.

Al Davis
I normally called Al Davis, Coach. When I would come up to him, I would usually address him as Coach, whether we were in the office or on the field. Then there were times when I would refer to him as Mr. Davis. On the field and in football, I'd call him Coach Davis.

Greatest Football Player
I think that person has yet to be seen. As far as I'm concerned, you've seen a lot of great football this past football season and in past years. We see great football players, great plays—fine young men doing well for football. Football is a way that we can communicate with people to be good leaders, good Americans, and be great football players. I think the greatest football player is yet to be seen.

Reflection On Life
You look back and you say, gee, Johnny Unitas died young. Gee, so and so left us too soon. Ray Nitschke was a tough son of a gun. How come he had to die so young? I had my 75th birthday and I sat with my grandchildren and I just said, "Children, can you believe Grandpops is 75 years old? I don't feel it, but I am. We've been really blessed that I've been able to be here this long with you guys."

I've been able to lead a wonderful life. I will always be very thankful for the big hits that I got, some of the big hits that got me, the victories, the celebrations afterwards, and all that stuff. I'll always remember that.

Pro Football Hall Of Fame Induction
The day I was notified that I was going into the Hall of Fame, I had an idea. People told me that I was up for it that year, but I was at my ranch. I had a pair of bib overalls on, and I was all full of dust and dirt. I guess it was in January when they made the announcement that I made it. I raise walnuts and I have thousands of walnut trees. I just was going to work like I normally would, even on the day of the selection. I just went to the ranch and did some work.

The phone rang at my ranch manager's house and his wife came out and said, "Mr. Otto, you're wanted on the phone." So I went to the phone and there they were and they said, "Jim Otto, you've been selected to the Pro Football Hall of Fame." I said, "Oh, boy. Wow, what do I do now?"

Anyway, they made arrangements for my wife and everybody so we could go to Hawaii where they would make the announcement. It was very, very exciting for a kid that was told that he couldn't make it in the pros because he was too small. I went out to prove that I could do it. It was a very, very exciting time.

Photograph copyright Associated Press

Chapter 31

Ron Mix

```
College:
USC

Career History:
1960–1969 Los Angeles/San Diego Chargers
1971 Oakland Raiders

1979 Inductee Pro Football Hall of Fame
```

College Choice

My first choice was UCLA, but only USC offered me a football scholarship, so the decision was easy. Parents who are raising teenagers should just encourage them that if they are really falling in the love with the sport and you put the time in, good things will happen. It doesn't necessarily mean you end up in the Pro Football Hall of Fame, but you'll be very pleased with yourself.

In high school I was a very late developer. I didn't become a starter until my senior year because the starting end was injured. I really liked the game, though, so I decided I was going to keep trying and I came up with a plan. I was going to start working out right away, as soon as the season was over. The plan was to go to a Junior College for two years and then go to UCLA. That was my dream school. It just happened.

Our league was playing an All-Star game against another league, and the head coach of the All-Star game from our league was my football coach. All of the really good ends that year were juniors.

The coach was literally stuck with me. I bet he thought he'd never see the words All-Star and Ron Mix in the same sentence.

I had been working out for months since the football season ended. I grew taller, I gained weight, my speed increased, and I started lifting weights. Lifting weights was something all coaches frowned on, but I couldn't understand how it could be bad to be strong. I was really one of the few people that were lifting. By the time of the All-Star game that summer, I was the star of that team. USC happened to see me and offered me a scholarship. I was so thrilled. I couldn't believe I got a scholarship to USC. I was almost embarrassed because every one of my high school teammates during my Senior year were better football players than me prior to my improvement. I told myself I was going to make USC look good. I was going to work out year round. I was going to moderate my life on and off the field to become a great football player.

My plan included lifting weights year round; something that really nobody was doing. I wasn't going to have a single alcoholic drink. I wasn't going to eat any sweets, because at that time, coaches said sweets were very bad for you, and no soft drinks. I didn't do any of that stuff.

I know objectively that I could have had a beer now and then. I could certainly have candy now and then. Every time I consciously refused to do it reminded me of what my goal was. I continued to progress and finally my senior year I was Captain of the team, made All-American, and was the number one draft choice of the Baltimore Colts. The Boston team had also chosen me in the new league. They traded me to the Los Angeles Chargers because I said if I had to go back East, I definitely wanted to play for the Colts, not a new league.

Willie Wood
It was interesting. You've got to remember the times those were. This was in the late '50s. Willie and I were Captains of the team at a time when 99 ½% of the fraternities would not permit us to be members because of Willie being black and me being Jewish. Our white Christian teammates decided we were the right guys to lead them and made us their captains. It's an example of how sports have been one of the most influential reasons for race and religions barriers falling down.

Al Davis and Mel Hein at USC
I was an end my first two years at Southern Cal and Al Davis was my position coach at end. Then my eyes started going bad so I couldn't see the ball. Not a good thing for an end. They switched me to tackle and my coach was a Hall of Fame center from the New York Giants, named Mel Hein. He was great.

Coaches at that time acted like mad fools. Everyone was screaming and yelling. There were no limits to the amount of time you could be on the practice field in those days. We were on the practice field 2 ½ to 3 hours. Every drill was full speed contact. Coaches screaming and yelling all the time; except for Mel Hein and to a lesser degree Al Davis. They were a little more cool and collected.

Notre Dame
To show you how petty I am, when I was at USC we lost to Notre Dame all three years. I still can't get over it. I root for them to lose at everything. I still can't get over it. I'm Exhibit A that men never grow up.

Monte Clark
Monte Clark was a terrific guy, an outstanding football player, and extremely funny. Back then he could do impressions. He did Al Davis perfectly. Monte was a pleasure to have as a teammate.

Al Davis Not Being Hired As USC Coach
I would think Al Davis was probably upset. He had a grand opinion of himself but it was justified. He was an outstanding coach even then; he was so young. When I first met Al it was in the locker room and I was doing leg lifts on the bench. I was standing on the bench and going up and down to build up my legs. Al came over and said, "Do you lift weights too?" I said, "Yes I do, although the coaches don't recommend it, but I think it's important." He said, "I do too." I

thought he was a player. He looked that young. Then he introduced himself as the coach and it surprised me.

Al was a terrific, terrific guy. He did more for former players than all other owners combined. That's not an exaggeration. He gave more former players jobs in coaching, in scouting, and in the front office, than any other owners combined. There was never a time when I brought it to his attention that one of his former players needed some financial help, that he didn't come through.

Mike & Marlin McKeever

I could not tell the McKeever twins apart. They were truly great football players. The McKeever twins and I were the only ones who were lifting weights on that team. USC didn't even have a weight room. We worked out at a gym in Inglewood, California, which is about 15 miles away from the USC campus.

This is going to seem so immodest but we were so much stronger than everybody else, including anybody we played against. It was like a total mismatch. It was unbelievable. We could military press over our heads 300 pounds. We all weighed about 225. Guys we'd play against would be anywhere from 190 to 250. What a bunch of confidence it is to know that if you wanted to, you could pick them up and military press them.

Being Drafted By the Baltimore Colts In the NFL Draft And Not Signing

I wanted to stay on the West Coast. That was my preference. I wanted to start off in the NFL not the AFL. I think I could have broken the starting lineup with the Baltimore team. I'm very confident that I could have.

I only intended to play a couple of years to get enough money to buy a car and a house. The USC practices were 2 ½ to 3 hours; constant contact, all sorts of pressure all of the time. I didn't play a skill position so I never touched the ball. It's not like you're having fun. All you get out of the game is the satisfaction of doing a good job. My gosh, it was so difficult. I decided I was going to play two more years in the game.

Then in the NFL, both leagues, you no longer played both ways. You didn't play the whole game. It was so easy. Playing offensive tackle was honestly just so easy that I couldn't believe it. Also, because I worked out year round I was in great shape. Anyway, I found the joy in the game again.

1963 AFL Championship Game

You know what? The score was misleading. We beat them worse than that. The game wasn't that close. It was complete domination. What's interesting is that everybody played his "A" game. You don't get that. It was unbelievable. Keith Lincoln had something like 347 total yards running and catching passes. Lance Alworth had about 120 yards receiving. Paul Lowe had over a hundred yards rushing. It was just amazing what we did.

The defense was unreal. We had two defensive linemen that really don't get enough historic attention, Earl Faison and Ernie Ladd. For about a four-year period of time those guys played the game in their positions as well as anybody has ever played and I mean right up to the present day. Ernie Ladd was 6'9" and 340; Earl was 6'5", 280 and they were great, great athletes. Absent injuries cutting short their effective careers, they'd both be in the Pro Football Hall of Fame.

Nickname "The Intellectual Assassin?"
I got that nickname from my offensive line coach, Joe Madro. He came up with it because I was going to law school at night while I was playing and I had an aggressive style of playing for an offensive lineman. I did a lot more attacking than just dropping back. At the time I thought it was kind of silly and contrived. Now I really like it.

Only Two Holding Calls In Entire Career
I didn't hold. I really didn't. I really wasn't being facetious when I asked those referees how they made the mistake. Those were two bad calls. Here's the thing, this will sound holier than thou, but I don't know how you can take satisfaction in doing a good job if you cheat. That's the way I felt.

Joe Madro, my line coach, used to tell his offensive linemen when anybody held, "You know what? You're never going to make 15 yards on offense in your whole life. You never touch the football!" That was always ringing in my ear. I'd never really gain 15 yards so I shouldn't cause the team to lose 15 yards.

Deacon Jones
We played against each other three times. The first time I give to him, but then the next two times I give to me. I think I figured out the head slap. I figured out when he'd reach out to slap or attack. The next two times I thought I played very well against him. In fact, after the second time I played against him, the Cleveland Browns played the Rams the next week. Monte Clark saw the films and called me. He said, "Ron, that's the best I've ever seen anybody play against Deacon Jones." Deacon would never concede that he was beat.

I heard him on the radio once and they asked him who was the toughest offensive lineman he ever faced? He said, "I don't know because I never faced just one. They always put two people on me."

Deacon was such a terrific and funny guy, but he'd never admit that anyone ever beat him.

Jack Kemp
Jack Kemp was a terrific quarterback and he did a great job. Jack was an interesting guy. He became a U.S. Congressman and he was on the ticket to be elected Vice President of the United States. When I played with Jack, he was far more conservative than he eventually turned out to be as his thoughts progressed. For instance, he believed that we should do away with Social Security. People should just take care of themselves.

I remember Jack and I had as discussion about that. I said, "Jack, it just doesn't work. My Mom and Dad were divorced when I was four and my brother was five. We were on welfare the whole time. When my Mom did work, it was making twenty-five cents an hour as a waitress. Are you telling me that if someone like her had a chance to spend a dime on her kids or put it away for her retirement, she should put it away for her retirement? It wouldn't happen."

Anyway, Sunday comes and we were playing the Houston Oilers. It was 98 degrees in San Diego. It was hot and they were a tough team. At halftime, we're walking to the locker room and I hear Jack say, "Ron! Ron I want to talk to you." I think he's going to ask me something about the game. Instead he's says, "I've been thinking about what you said and you're right about Social Security." I said, "Jack, we're in the middle of the game. I'm exhausted. What are you talking about?" He was so obsessed with politics and public affairs. That was like Exhibit "A" of how obsessed he was. It was the middle of a football game he's thinking about our discussion.

Tobin Rote
Tobin Rote had an immediate grasp of the game and was so slick. His arm was going away. He made Lance Alworth famous because he'd throw those big floaters that would fall short and Lance would have to come back and jump like a deer. Dare I say jump like Bambi, which was Lance's nickname, to catch the balls. By the next year Tobin's arm was just completely gone and John Hadl had to take over. John needed that year to develop.

Sid Gillman was a brilliant coach. John Hadl just had it and Sid saw enough of him in college that he felt he could play quarterback. John's passing skills just developed and kept improving every year. It was my recollection of how John developed into a quarterback that made me think Tim Tebow would develop into one. Boy was I wrong. The guy can't throw.

Toughest Defensive Lineman
Deacon Jones was as great player. Bubba Smith was outstanding. Kansas City had a terrific guy named Jerry Mays. The New York Jets had a terrific end named Gerry Philbin. For a short period of time, Denver had a terrific end named, get this, Rich "Tombstone" Jackson. You know what? The truth is everybody's tough. Football is the hurt business. It's impossible not to have a giant collision on every play. Everybody's tough.

Sid Gillman
It was thrilling because we felt we'd score any time. We had explosive people like Lance Alworth, Don Norton, Keith Lincoln, Paul Lowe; gosh I can't even remember everyone. And there were terrific running backs, like Dickie Post and Brad Hubbard. At all times we had the threat of the deep pass because of Sid Gillman's offense.

My San Diego Chargers Number Being Unretired By Gene Klein When I Went To Raiders
I complained to Pete Rozelle and Pete ordered them to re-retire it. Then two years later they brought it back and by then I was tired of the whole thing so I didn't do anything about it.

Pro Football Hall Of Fame Induction
I'm not sure I really appreciated it immediately. When I was first called up about it I was just thinking another honor. That's somewhat blasé but I didn't really think about it. I didn't really understand it. I didn't have a full appreciation for it until that first luncheon took place when I was inducted.

Every year there's a luncheon just for the players. The players stand up and say something about themselves and talk about interesting things in their lives and what was important to them. To hear the guys talk so elegantly. Great legends of professional football, like Gino Marchetti and

Paul Hornung, there are so many of them. It just came to life for me. I thought wow; I'm in the Pro Football Hall Of Fame with Jim Brown, Gino Marchetti, Bob Waterfield, and Norm Van Brocklin. I must be as good as them. There's not that many of us in there.

USC Treatment Of Athletes During His Time
I think USC started flirting with that preferential treatment again after those penalties. Let's see if we can get away with something. I know we'll give certain guys the cool jobs during the summer. The McKeever twins' jobs were at the studios. They were the most recruited two players in America. Their jobs were at the studios. The rest of us were called "Plunking Iron." We were working construction. We would carry these very heavy iron bars that would then be set to tie in grids before they laid the cement. They treated us a little differently than McKeever twins.

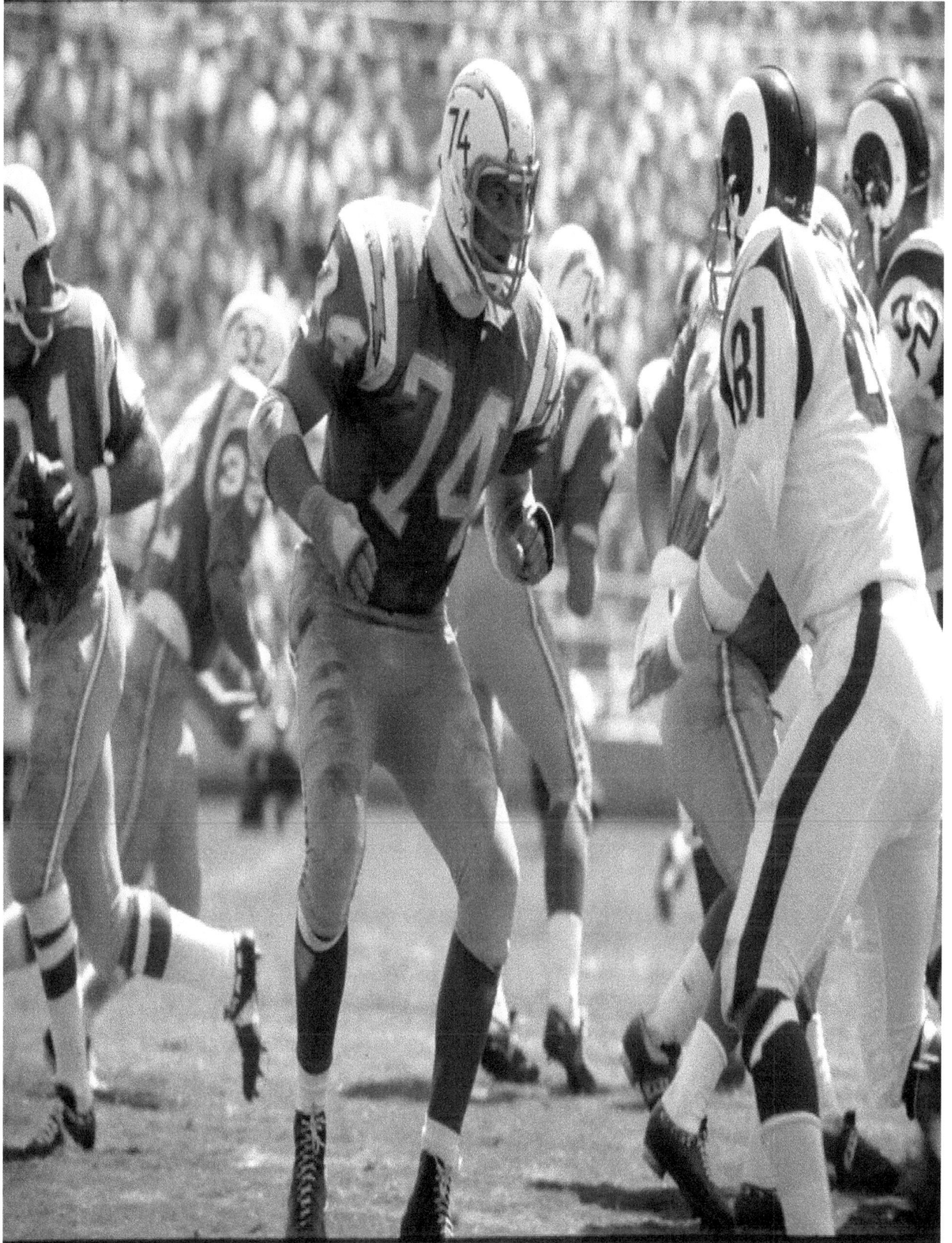

Photograph copyright Associated Press

Chapter 32

Larry Wilson

College: Utah

Career History:
St. Louis Cardinals (1960-1972)

As coach/executive:
St. Louis Cardinals (1973-1976) (Director of Scouting)
St. Louis Cardinals (1977-1987) (Director of Personnel)
St. Louis Cardinals (1979) (Interim Head Coach)
Phoenix Cardinals (1988-1993) (VP and General Manager)
Arizona Cardinals (1994-2002) (VP)

1978 Inductee Pro Football Hall of Fame

College Choice
Well, I'm really closer to Utah than I was to any place in Idaho. It was a situation where my father felt like I would do better at Utah, as far as getting an education, and we went that way. I really didn't care to get too far away from home.

NFL Draft
It was an exciting time. That's quite a few years ago now. Back then, the draft was not that big a deal. They called you and said that you were drafted. I was excited about it. I was very happy that things worked out. Actually, the Buffalo Bills and the Cardinals drafted me. I signed with Cardinals for five hundred dollars more.

My whole career, we trained in Lake Forest. They kept our training camp there so we were around Chicago. We always scrimmaged the Bears a couple of times. We also played in the Armed Forces game all the time and a Pre-Season Game with the Bears.

First Training Camp
I really didn't have expectations, to tell you the truth; I kept my suitcase packed all the time. I was drafted as a Running Back. They had John David Crow, and we had a crew of running backs. They traded Dick 'Night Train' Lane to Detroit, and that made a spot open in the Secondary. So I got moved over there, bounced around, and then they moved Jimmy Hill out to the corner. I got to play safety, and things worked out pretty darn well.

Safety Blitz

We played a lot of man for man defenses. We blitzed a lot and the coach always tried to come up with one extra guy they could block. I remember when we first did it back in New York. The coach said, "Larry, when you get in there, jump up, cover up your number, and run back to huddle, so they won't know who you are. Red Dog was just blitzing the outside linebackers. We were called the Wild Cat … kind of got that nickname.

Jim Brown

Well, the key was to get on Jim Brown and hold on. You never worried about getting hurt with Jim Brown. He was a guy who could slip and slide. Since he had a great running ability, you really never got a clear shot at him, and so you never worried about getting hurt by him.

Jim Brown, to me, was the epitome of football then. He just did so many things, and he is one of the guys that really made the game great.

St. Louis Cardinals Rivals

Back then we were in a Division with Philadelphia, New York, Cleveland, and Dallas, so we had some pretty good rivals. I think that our main one was Dallas. When they came in, it was always a big game for us. And, we loved playing in New York too.

Favorite Interception Of His 52

I wish I could remember that far back. I was a running back when I was drafted. I enjoyed getting the ball and running with it. I think what it proved was that I was on the right side of the ball; or I couldn't have been a running back in the League.

St. Louis Cardinals Secondary

Our secondary, I think, was one of the better ones in the business with Roger Wehrli, Jerry Stovall, Jimmy Hill, and Billy Stacy. We had some good defensive backs. Back then you played man for man most of the time. We played very little zone, so it was a challenge for everyone; but overall, I thought we had as fine a secondary as it was in the league.

Johnny Roland

Johnny Roland was one super football player and just a marvel. You're really fortunate to get a good guy like Roland who really wants to play the game, enjoys playing, has fun, and is a part of the team. That's the whole key to all of this, getting it all together, and doing your job.

Johnny Unitas

I think Johnny Unitas was absolutely a phenomenal player. I sit back and marvel, and think about the times that I got to play against him. He was as good as everybody said he was. I think that there were a lot of fine people. You're talking about the Jim Browns, and the whole slew of them.

Best Receiver

The best pass receiver that I ever played against was Paul Warfield. Paul could play in today's game and be a superstar like he was when he played. I just think he is a phenomenal guy and what a great player he was. He was very quick, had good size, and I tell you what, he was a mean bugger. All those things added together made him a real problem when he was out there. We spent a lot of time trying to figure out how to cover him. We got it done now and then, but most of the time he whopped us.

I think back to that time. We didn't get a chance to play against a lot of people in the American Conference, but at the end of my career, we were playing against the Miami Dolphins, and we had a change in coaches. We were playing against the Dolphins and a guy by the name of Larry Csonka who was a big fullback at that time, and our coach said, "We've got to stop Warfield." They had Larry Csonka carry the ball. I tell you what, he ran over me so many times, I couldn't count them.

Jim Hart
Jim Hart was a tremendous quarterback; he had some size and could really throw the ball well. I don't think he got the credit that he was due. We had another guy who played early on, but when Jim came in he just took over and made our team a much better football team.

Joining Front Office
After 13 years I was beat up bad. I thought there's got to be something else to do in this world, so I knew it was time to quit.

I always wanted to coach, and I got an opportunity a couple of times, but overall the Front Office was also an interesting situation. It was the time when computers were starting to move into the game, and getting those set up, getting the scouting program in, and taking the coach's work and getting it computerized, was always something that I was interested in. I enjoyed my time in the Front Office.

The draft has become a circus right now. There are so many things going on, they know everything about you. The thing they can't do though, is really tell what kind of a player you are going to be when you get there. That's all in the heart, and boy, the hardest thing to do is to figure out which guy is going to be the guy that goes out and gets to be a part of the team, and makes a real impact for you.

The toughest job of all is to predict which guy is going to come in and be the player that he should be. The guy who is willing to pay the price, to be a part of the team, to know that he's one of 11, not just one out there. Then, you have to put together a team that plays together and plays hard together; that's the real key to getting some success. You've got to have guys that can do their job and do it well.

Raymond Berry & Johnny Unitas
Raymond Berry was another guy that you just marvel about. He didn't have the great speed, but he certainly would run his routes well. He took advantage of everything, and could catch the football. He and Johnny Unitas were a part of unit that played exceptionally well together, and consequently they were winners.

Cardinals Move To Arizona

It was slow to start with. Arizona was basically a Dallas Cowboy area for television, so there were a lot of Cowboy fans here. I was amazed at how quickly they accepted us, and supported the team out here. The greatest thing that happened there is when we got our own stadium. We have a beautiful stadium here and one that, I think, everyone in the community enjoys. I just think people enjoy coming out and watching the game.

The interesting thing here is that this city is about 90 percent Chicagoans and 10 percent Minnesotans, so we have to win them over. I was just laughing because the neighbor next door has got a cockeyed Chicago Bear flag hanging in her yard, and I'm always on her about getting it out of there.

Pro Football Hall Of Fame Induction

I was so excited I was flabbergasted, and I enjoyed that. That is one of the real highlights of my career; I'm so gratified by being there.

Photograph copyright Associated Press

Chapter 33

Jimmy Johnson

College: UCLA Career History: San Francisco 49ers (1961-1976) 1994 Inductee Pro Football Hall of Fame

College Choice

The main reason I chose UCLA was the fact that my brother Rafer had chosen UCLA for his college sports career. Rafer was a senior in high school when I was a freshman. I watched his career as it progressed, and was very excited that I had the opportunity to go to UCLA.

My decision to go to Santa Monica City School for my first year of college boiled down to, from my point of view as an athlete, it giving me an opportunity to work against a tougher level of football player. As a freshman at UCLA, I would have only been playing against freshman from other schools. Also, the freshmen at UCLA only played five games during the season. In addition, Santa Monica City School gave me an opportunity to up my game in a couple of academic classes.

College Coaches

Red Sanders was Head Coach at UCLA, and I was expecting to play under his tutelage. Unfortunately, he passed away.

George Dickerson took over when Coach Sanders passed away. That created a monumental pressure, recruiting and what not, on Coach Dickerson.

He had a nervous breakdown from the recruiting wars, trying to talk high school players into coming to UCLA. Billy Barnes took over and was at UCLA for my last two years of college.

Playing On Offense & Defense In College

I actually preferred to play on offense. In the single wing formation that we used at UCLA, I was in the wing back slot. The wing back slot didn't really get to carry the ball that much. From that position I would be flanked out and become a part of the passing game. I would run a reverse a couple of times a game.

In the wing back position on any given play, I was usually scraping along the line and blindsiding offensive linemen.

Playing Against USC

USC was definitely our biggest rival. It was a monumental situation for someone like me. I went to UCLA via Kingsburg High School in the Central Valley. Kingsbury was a very small high school and we played in front of very small high school crowds. Playing against USC was a very overpowering experience. What I think worked in my behalf was the fact that I went to Santa Monica City College my freshman year.

I had a very nice season at Santa Monica City College, both academically and in sports. It gave me a chance to play three sports for one more year. I played football, basketball, and ran track and field. That was the first time I ran track and field.

Running Track & Field At UCLA

When I left Santa Monica City College I no longer played competitive basketball. I actually was not going to run track; but was just going to play football at UCLA. UCLA had a renowned coach by the name of Ducky Drake. Ducky convinced me that if I stuck with track and field, I could be a world-class runner by the time I got out of UCLA.

I took him at his word and participated in track with the football department's good wishes. I didn't have to attend spring football training I just ran track. Ducky's words rang true as I had a pretty fantastic track and field career.

Not Qualifying For 1960 US Olympic Team

It was absolutely devastating not qualifying for the 1960 Olympic team. That was probably the most devastating situation for me because my brother was going to be on the team competing. I had progressed during my last two track seasons in college to a world premier level. I was running good times at UCLA under the tutelage of Coach Ducky Drake. I was really primed to make that Olympic team.

After the NCAA finals, which were held at UC Berkley, I ran in some AAU meets and ran some really phenomenal times. The Olympic trials came down to that last big meet which was held at Stanford University. I won a couple of prelims at the trials. I got to the finals as the number one seed. I had a middle lane, right smack in the middle of the track.

I led the race for seven hurdles. I hit the seventh hurdle and nicked the eighth hurdle but regained my balance. I was in a photo finish. Now when you're in a photo finish, you find out the results right away.

Back then, they had to develop the film and make a decision. It wasn't a real quick process. There was a lot of waiting around until I got the final results of the race. It was a photo finish between Hayes Jones, Jerry Tarr, Lee Calhoun, and me. I didn't qualify for the Olympics.

There went my aspirations to become an Olympian. In my mind, I went back to what Ducky Drake had told me when I was a sophomore at UCLA. He told me that if I worked at it, I could become a world-class hurdler. I was one step short of making the 1960 Olympic Games.

Draft
There was talk that I was going to be drafted. I just continued on with my college life at UCLA, not really thinking that I would be drafted.

A lot of things happened for the dominoes to fall into place. The 49ers had sent out feelers to try to find out if I would be interested in playing for them. That was a no brainer. Of course I was interested. Later on I found out the L. A. Rams and the San Diego Chargers were also interested.

Sid Gillman
Coach Gilman was a real cheerleader in reference to my situation. I had several meetings with Al Davis and Coach Gilman in Los Angeles.

There were a lot of ifs and buts in what the Chargers and the 49ers were going to do. The morning of the draft, I was having breakfast with Sid Gilman and Al Davis in their hotel suite at the Stanford campus. It was all lined up, if such and such is still available, then this will happen and this will happen.

As it turned out the 49ers had three first round draft picks that year. They had the Pittsburgh Steelers number one pick, the St. Louis Cardinals number one pick, and their own. They ended up using a first round pick on me. With their other two first round picks they got Billy Kilmer and Bernie Casey.

Al Davis and Sid Gillman were very excited about the possibility of me playing for them and I was equally excited. There was a little overlay of aw shucks, when the 49ers drafted me. I finished my breakfast with them and went back over to the campus to continue my preparation for the East-West game.

Red Hickey
It was hard to understand where Coach Hickey was coming from. With his military background, he treated the team from top to bottom like we were recruits in the Army. He had a very tough approach and would let you know exactly how he felt. That was one good thing about him.

If you were on his down side, he would verbally let you know. In the middle of a practice he'd stop the practice and he'd use all of these red-hot words. He would just jump all over the perpetrator on the team that had made a mistake. It was almost like he was steaming.

College All-Star Game
I played in the East-West Shrine Game, Coaches All-America Game in Buffalo, New York, and then I went to Chicago to start preparing for the College All-Star Game. The Philadelphia Eagles were the previous season's NFL Champion, so that was who we were going to face off against in the game.

We practiced at the Northwestern College Campus in Evanston, Illinois. I was strictly an offensive end on the team. I had real good speed and good hands. I was beating a lot of guys out there in one-on-one situations.

There was a defensive back, Elbert Kimbrough, who had also been drafted by the 49ers, like me. I was having a really super day during one practice. Elbert had to cover me on several occasions. Billy Kilmer was the quarterback. On a post pattern, I beat Elbert really bad and I was just waiting for the ball to come to me since Billy had thrown a floater. While waiting for the floater, Elbert made up the yardage that I had beat him by and really took me out with a tremendous tackle. I dislocated my wrist and broke my arm. They put my arm in a cast and I was not able to be a participant in the game.

Rookie Season With 49ers
I went to the 49ers training camp with a broken arm. It was apparent that I wasn't going to be able to play on offense my rookie year. The 49ers team physician, Dr. Lloyd Milburn, told me if I wanted to play my rookie year that he would take my dislocated left wrist and re-work the bones by using pressure.

He operated on me on two different occasions, attempting to put the wrist bones back in position. It was readily known I wouldn't be able to play on offense. I recovered well enough that with proper protection on the wrist, I was able to play a defensive back for the 49ers.

I've surprised myself with my ability in man-to-man coverage. A lot of times I had inside help from our outside linebackers, and some deep help from the free safety. For the most part, I was on my own in figuring out the opponent's wide receivers.

Many times I was in a flanked out position with the receiver, 20 yards from the line of scrimmage with very little help. Even with a broken arm, I learned a lot about myself as a man-to-man cover guy during my rookie year. Those first few years I was an excellent man-to-man guy and that worked in my behalf as my career got rolling along.

After a few seasons, I could hold my own against a premier wide receiver like Charley Taylor of the Washington Redskins, knowing that I wasn't going to get a lot of help from my teammates. During my career, quarterbacks would not throw my way. During a game I may have gotten two balls thrown my way. Quarterbacks would work the other side.

Gale Sayers Knee Injury Against 49ers
Kermit Washington, being a real tough tackler, caught Gale Sayers when Gale was making a cut. Gale was making a real sharp cut, changing direction and unfortunately Kermit's shoulder pad and helmet hit Gale right on the knee and hyperextended the knee with such force that Gale's knee broke down.

Toughest Receiver
I never categorized a wide receiver as the best. I knew that every Sunday my game plan was going to be full just trying to take care of the wide receiver I was matched up against.

There were a lot of wonderful wide receivers. If there was one guy that I had an affinity to work against and be competitive, it was Tommy McDonald. Tommy played on the Philadelphia Eagles and later on in his career with the L.A. Rams. In a highly competitive football game Tommy would do a few comical things on the football field and I couldn't figure out why he was doing those things. The main thing was just to stay close to him. He had great speed and jackrabbit like moves.

We were playing the Rams and Tommy ran a pattern on me, and I blocked it. Tommy ran another one and I blocked it. When you block a pass pattern, you tend to want to lounge a little bit, get up slow, and feel good about the fact that you just knocked a ball down. On that first pass pattern that I blocked, Tommy jumped up from the ground and ran just as fast back to the huddle as he was running on the pass pattern.

I thought he was doing that to psych me out. In order to be in position, I jumped up just as fast as he did, and ran back towards the line of scrimmage with the same vigor and speed that he had run the pattern. I found out later in that game that was just the way Tommy was, like a little jackrabbit.

Jack Christiansen Being Named 49ers Head Coach
Jack Christiansen had been my defensive backfield coach with the 49ers, so I was a little bit sad to lose him as my defensive back coach when he became our head coach. He worked very closely with me in deference to my ability as a defensive back. Red Hickey got fired as head coach. Coach Hickey was such a tyrant. He had us all walking on our heels. If a player was walking down the hallway in the dorm and saw Hickey down the hallway, he would rather go the other way so he wouldn't have to run into Coach Hickey.

When you would see him in the hallway, it was a very high tension, stringent situation. Almost everyone tried to avoid eye contact or speaking with Coach Hickey as they moved about the dorms. He made it really difficult.

The players loved Coach Christensen. Everybody wanted to win for him. We had been under the iron fist of Coach Hickey for so long that I think the players, as much as they wanted to win for the coach, just couldn't quite put their nose to the grindstone because of Coach Hickey.

When Coach Christiansen was named head coach, players started doing silly things like not being on time, missing a meeting, and not getting treatment. We just couldn't get a victory. The harder we tried the less likely it was that we'd get a victory. I think the reason for us not winning under Coach Christiansen was that is was like a bunch of guys getting out of jail or out of the Army; all of a sudden you are able to just spread your wings and fly on your own. There were a lot of infractions the players committed. Things that they could have done easily, they just didn't do. The team just didn't play the type of ball that Coach Christenson deserved as head coach.

Dick Nolan
Dick Nolan brought in a whole different regimen. It was very much together. Everyone knew what he had to do to be a part of a winning effort, from the front office right on down to the water boy. Everyone got onboard. We were primed to do a two hundred percent job all day every day. Coach Nolan was an easy head coach to be around. He was a great guy.

Coach Nolan had the complete package with his coaching staff and with each individual. He had a personal relationship, or as close as you could get. Players felt Coach Nolan was their buddy.

You would never walk up and throw your arms around his neck or give him a bear hug, but that's the way you felt about him. You knew what he was trying to do; the avenue he was taking it. We all knew that we were potential champions.

Pro Football Hall Of Fame Induction
When I found out I was being inducted into the Pro Football Hall Of Fame it was pretty monumental. I experienced a lot of disbelief. I didn't think it was going to happen. I didn't think that I could garner the votes necessary. My family and I were very excited. I think what made it even more exciting was the fact that local media came by my house to talk about it.

It was almost like I had an extension of my career. There was a lot written about me being chosen. A lot of people said a lot of nice things on my behalf. I was beside myself. I was extremely happy it finally happened.

My family and brothers and sisters were extremely ecstatic. The letters I got congratulating me really brought it to the forefront. It was a long road, but I was very happy that it finally became a reality.

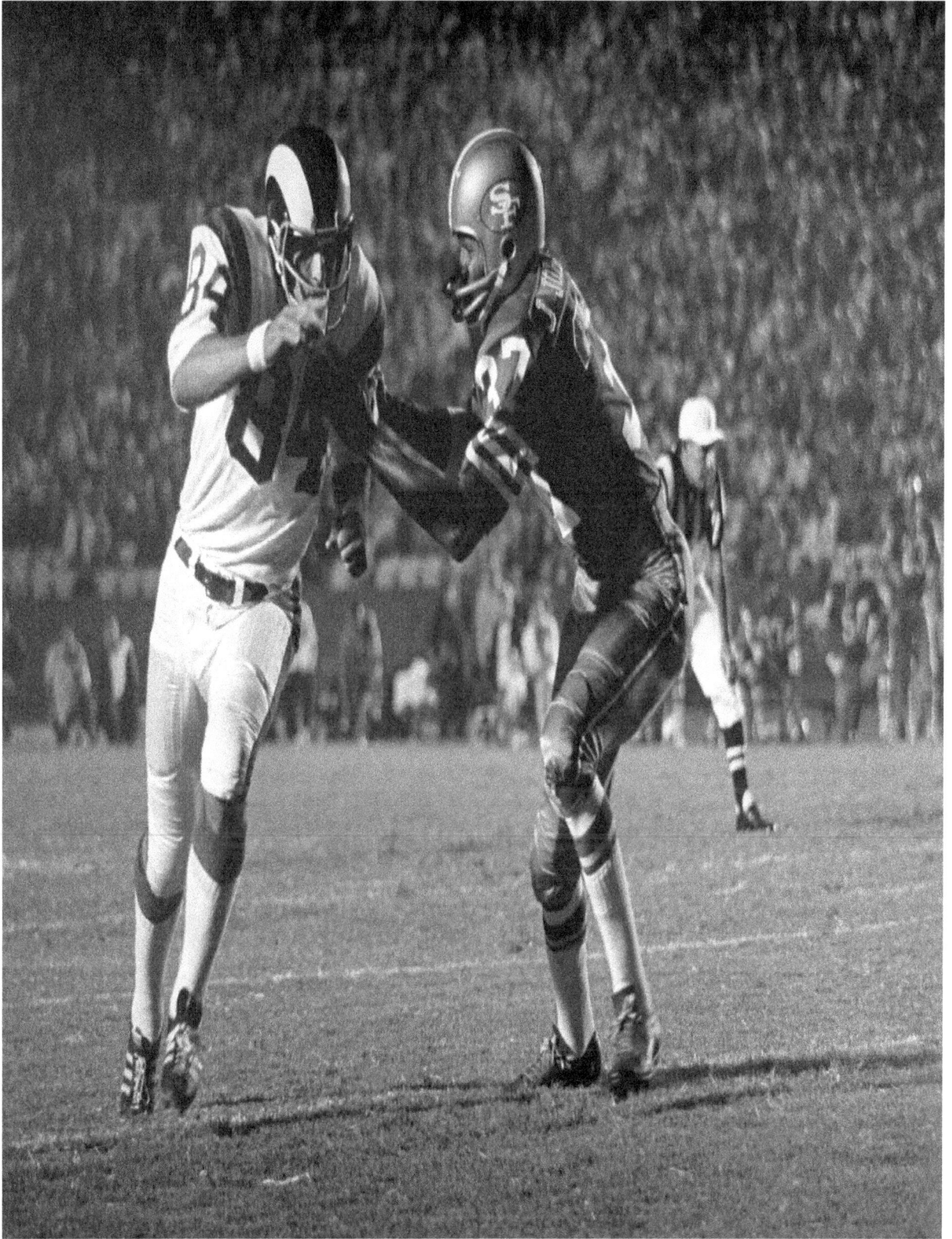

San Francisco 49er Jimmy Johnson plays bump and run coverage on Los Angeles Rams wide
receiver Jack Snow. Photograph copyright Associated Press

Chapter 34

Deacon Jones

College:
South Carolina State
Mississippi Valley State

Career History
Los Angeles Rams (1961-1971)
San Diego Chargers (1972-1973)
Washington Redskins (1974)

1980 Inductee Pro Football Hall of Fame

Best Defensive Lineman Of All Time
That's a question that's, I guess, forever in the people's mind about who's that and who's this. But I think if you get down to a situation where you could put the actual facts in the middle of the table, you'd understand, I'm talking about facts on everybody, not just the guys that they decided to talk about in 1982. You put my facts down the way they were accounted for, and you'll find out who the best ever was.

NFL Not Keeping Sack Totals Until 1982
It always upset me because every team in the National Football League kept their own stats. They started on a league level recording sacks officially in 1982, which I think is embarrassing. The point is they got the facts in the book. We got them in the book.

I got my facts right here in George Allen's 1967-68 playbook. I was paid per sack; they didn't let me count. I tore this league apart for six years straight. I mean total domination. I'll go right there. I'll give them the rest. I'll take six years out of the mid part of my career in the 1960s and I'll go with those numbers. I'll go with those numbers and I'll tell you what, you'll make them fold that stuff up and burn it up. Because if you're going to measure it on total sacks, total pressure, total tackles, there isn't anyone real close to me.

1967 & 1968 Seasons
Well, I don't think that anybody ever had a performance like me. I also had six sacks in 1967 in the postseason and you add that together. That's total domination.

I backed that up the next year with 24 sacks. These are stats that the world hasn't heard about. You look at me in 1967 and '68, and see if anybody ever totally dominated the game with pressure on the quarterback. I had 100 unassisted tackles that year, along with 26 sacks. Now tell me that doesn't scare some people.

Also, I got paid $500 a sack. So I made my money. I didn't even discuss my years I had 10 sacks or 12 sacks. I would have been embarrassed to go ask the man for any money.

Draft

They made you earn the money. It wasn't given up front. My rookie year, I was probably in the best condition I've ever been in. I was really scared to death when I came up here. I had never played against a white guy before. I had never played integrated football. So I had all these fears. I had the fear of going someplace that I had never been, which was that level of football. So I had all that pressure on my mind and I was a 14th round draft choice. After I got there I found out that the Rams draft people who were on the freeway going home when they drafted me. So I walked into camp with one thing on my mind man. I'm going to whip some heads. That was all I had going for me. I got to run everywhere on this football field. When the coaches blew the whistle, I got to run. I got to get in front in every drill. I got to get in front, and then get back in line, then get in front again. I gotto make   somebody see me. That violence in my game came out because of that. I learned the tougher you are out here, the better football player you are.

Accomplishment

One thing is certain. I got a chance to get all the frustration out man. I have no reason to be covered in anything anymore. When I left the game man, I stayed until I wanted to get out and I felt like I had done what I had to do.

Photograph copyright Associated Press

Chapter 35

Billy Shaw

College:
Georgia Tech

Career History:
Buffalo Bills (1961-1969)

1999 Inductee Pro Football Hall of Fame

College Choice
I was born in Natchez but I was raised in Vicksburg. My parents moved to Vicksburg before I was two years old, and my idol in grammar school was a high school player by the name of George Morris. George Morris was Mr. Football in Mississippi. George Morris went to Georgia Tech and he became an All-American. Coach Dodd said that he was the best football player that he ever coached. George Morris got into my life while I was in high school, and he led me in that direction. That's how I got from Mississippi to Georgia Tech.

Cookie Gilchrist
Cookie Gilchrist was probably the best football player I ever played with, not the best athlete, but what a great football player he was. He did some placekicking and it was in a pinch in 1962.

Cookie was one of those rare individuals as far as a football player. He could have played guard, because he was our size. He could have played linebacker, he could have played anywhere on the defensive line. Just a phenomenal player, and he took that competitiveness in his lifestyle outside of football. You didn't push him around.

NFL vs. AFL
The caliber of the player was certainly different. My situation, going to Buffalo, was similar to college because we were not one of those AFL teams that threw the ball. We ran the ball possibly two out of three times. We were more like an NFL team back in that day. We weren't like the San Diego teams or the Denver teams, and later on in Namath's career, the New York teams that threw the ball all the time. I did not regret not playing in the NFL.

Draft
My last year in college was 1960, and my coach was Bobby Dodd. The Bills of the AFL drafted me number two. I was talking to the NFL, particularly Gil Brandt of the Dallas Cowboys. They wanted to play me at linebacker, but I'd never played linebacker. Of course, I would never have been picked ahead of Bob Lilly, who was their first choice, and a great, great, great player.

I went to Coach Dodd to get his advice and he told me sign with the AFL. You're going to be playing the position either on the defensive side or the offensive side of the ball that you are used to, and that's where he thought that my career should be. I actually signed with the AFL before the NFL draft. The Dallas Cowboys went ahead and drafted me anyway, I think in the 14th round, 184th player picked, thinking that the AFL was going to fold and they would have my rights. I never, ever looked back. I enjoyed playing in the AFL. As time went on, the teams got better, the league got better, and I just enjoyed it.

Jack Kemp

Jack Kemp took command. You didn't cough or sneeze in that huddle. Jack came to us in the latter part of 1962, and we knew immediately that he was a different guy. He was one of the most intelligent people I've ever been around. His conversation was always geared toward the political arena, and we knew that he was going to be special.

I believed in Jack. At that particular time in my life, I was not a Republican. I was a Democrat, and we never argued about it. We talked at length about what one party believed and then what the other party believed. He was an intelligent person.

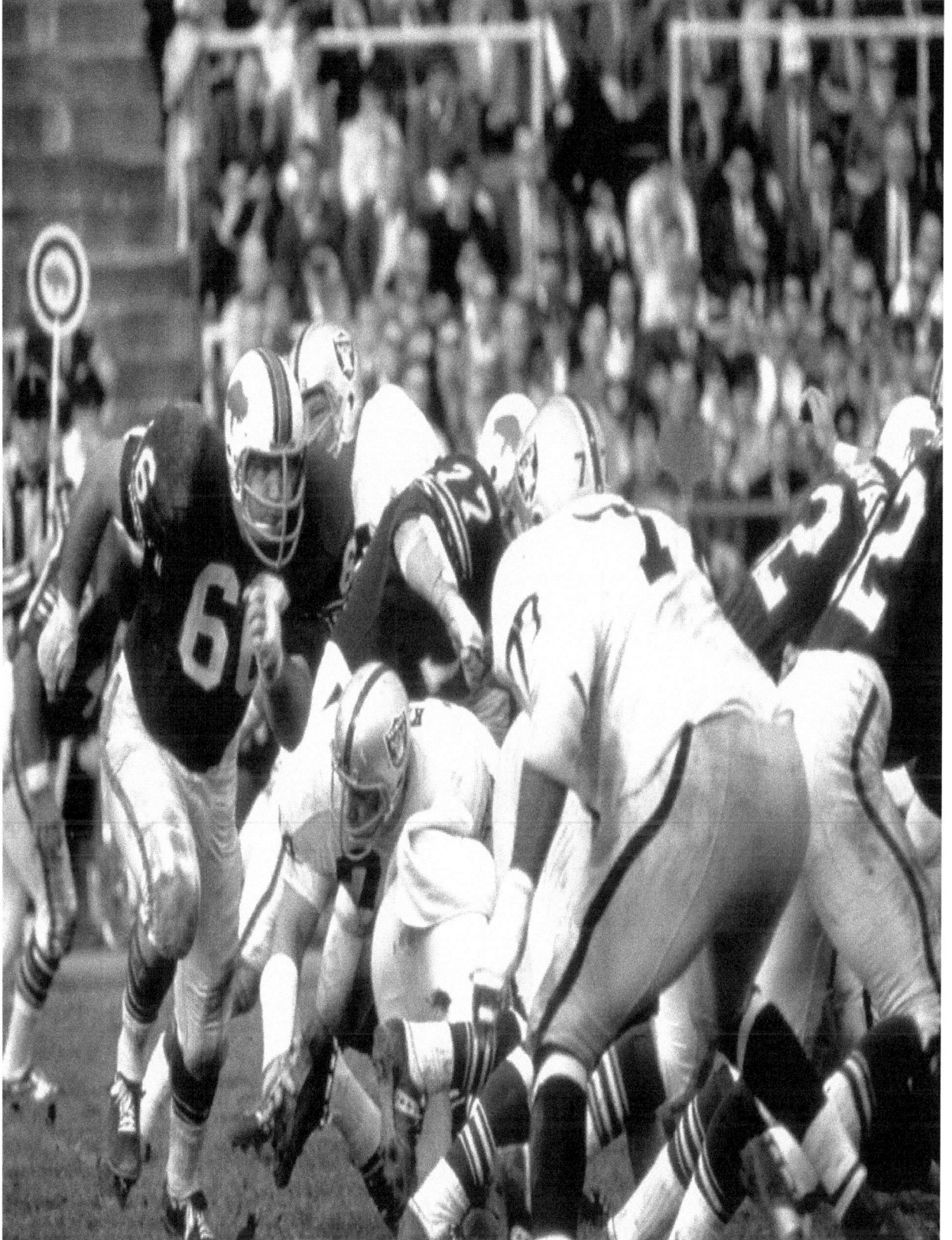

Photograph copyright Associated Press

Chapter 36

Herb Adderley

College:
Michigan State

Career History:
Green Bay Packers (1961-1969)
Dallas Cowboys (1970-1972)

1980 Inductee Pro Football Hall of Fame

Vince Lombardi Not Being Named New York Giants Head Coach
The New York Giants hired Allie Sherman. They said that Vince Lombardi applied for the job. For some reason they bypassed him and decided to hire Allie Sherman and got Lombardi a job in Siberia. That's what they called Green Bay at the time. They sent him up to Green Bay. I think Green Bay had only won maybe one or two games previous to Lombardi getting there.

Tom Landry
Tom Landry made a lot of coaching decisions that cost the Cowboy games. Not only with his play calling but also with the personnel. In the Cotton Bowl, Don Perkins was running like Jim Brown. We couldn't stop Perkins. Perkins was running inside the tackles. He didn't even come around my side, he would run inside the tackles and he got the ball down to the 20-yard line. All of the sudden, Landry decided to take Perkins out of the game and put in Dan Reeves. Reeves had two bad knees and I could walk faster than Reeves could run. Landry changed his game plan and started throwing the ball instead of running. If Perkins had stayed there, I guarantee you, that game would have been tied. We would have gone into overtime, and it might have been a different outcome. Because of Landry's coaching, decisions, and his personnel moves, it cost them games before I got there and it cost them games by the time I got there. I saw it firsthand.

Dave Robinson
The first time that Dave Robinson met Vince Lombardi was after the All-Star game when the All-Stars played against the Pro Champions at Soldier Field. When Dave was on that team, they'd beat us in that game. Lombardi was livid, man. Dave had time to take a shower, get dressed, and come over to our locker room.

He was feeling good with a big grin on his face coming to the locker room, and he heard Lombardi chewing us out. We didn't even have time to take our pads and stuff off because Lombardi was chewing us out for that game. This went on for about 45 minutes. I don't know what Dave was thinking when he came in, but that was his first encounter with Lombardi.

The College All Stars had a good team. They had some great players on that team. I don't think we took anybody for granted. It's just a case of them making some good plays. I guess you could say they won the game or maybe they outplayed us.

Move To Defensive Back With Packers

When I was at Michigan State, I was the number one draft choice as a running back out of all the Big 10 running backs. When I got to the Packers, Paul Hornung (a Hall of Famer), Jim Taylor (a Hall of Famer), and Tom Moore (drafted out of Vanderbilt), were all there. The year I got there, Elijah Pitts came along with me. We had four or five running backs. Lew Carpenter was also there. With all of those running backs, and I knew my chances were almost nil. I played special teams and played behind Boyd Dowler at wide receiver and at running back a little bit too in practice.

In Detroit on Thanksgiving Day of my rookie year, Hank Gremminger got hurt in the second quarter. At halftime Vince Lombardi said, "We got an emergency situation and we're going to put our best athlete out to play the left corner." I'm just sitting on the bench thinking about running the kickoff back in the second half. He comes over, puts his hand on my shoulder and said, "Herb, just do the best you can."

I looked at him and I say, "Who, me?" He said, "Yes." By that time, everybody was getting up and walking out of the locker room for the second half of the game. I didn't even have time to find my helmet. I was so nervous that I had to go back and get my helmet.

I had never practiced the position, and end up intercepting a pass and setting up the winning touchdown. I guess that's when he thought that I could play defense, because I could play both sides of the ball, and I went right back to offense. I never played another down on defense until the Championship Game when we beat the New York Giants, 37 to nothing. The last two minutes, he told me again, "Go out there for Jesse Whittenton." This was on the right corner. I intercepted a pass. The only two times I played as a defensive back I intercepted a pass, so I guess he decided in 1962 that he'd switch me over.

It takes a lot of athletic ability. I have God given athletic ability. I played four sports in high school. Basketball was my favorite sport. It wasn't any problem for me to make the adjustment. All I had to do was learn how to tackle.

College Choice

Number one, Clarence Peaks was my idol when I was in high school. I only played two years of football in high school because I played basketball. It was my favorite sport. I ended up playing football for a couple of years and my high school coach said, "Hey look, you're going to have the ability dude. Go to a big time school and maybe get yourself a scholarship." He started to ask me during my senior year, where I wanted to go and I told him about Clarence Peaks at Michigan State. He said, "Look, I know Duffy Daugherty." He knew Duffy from some coaching clinics they were having around the country. He said, "The only thing I can do is give him a call and let him know I got a blue chip ball player and let's see what he says." That's how the whole thing got started. I wanted to go to Michigan State because of Clarence Peaks. That's where the number 26 originated.

He was my idol. When I got there, he met me at the airport, and showed me around. He was a senior. In fact, he was the number one draft choice of the Philadelphia Eagles, my hometown. When I got to Michigan State, for some reason, they gave me 26. I said, "Hey, if you can emulate Clarence Peaks, you're going to be a great player." That's how the whole thing started with Michigan State. I went on as a walk-on. I had to make the team. I didn't get a scholarship.

I went to all integrated schools in Philly. My elementary school was Fitler Elementary School was an all integrated school. I also went to Roosevelt Junior High School. It was also integrated, and there were never any problems. Then I attended an all-boys high school in Philly, Northeast High School. We had a variety of ethnic groups playing sports.

Michigan State had probably more black All-Americans than any school in the country. You had Don Coleman, Clarence Peaks, Leroy Bolden, Ellis Duckett, and Jim Ellis just to name a few. All these guys were All-Americans, and they had a chance to play because Michigan State didn't go for segregation. They wanted to play the best ballplayers.

Segregation At Michigan State & Green Bay

The first time I really experienced segregation after coming out of Philly was in East Lansing, Michigan, because they didn't allow black people to live in East Lansing. All the black people that lived off campus had to live 10 miles down the road in Lansing, which is the state capital. That included the professors at Michigan State University also. I think it was in 1959, that the NAACP started picketing, but eventually it got to be okay. My senior year, I lived right on the street, Grand River Avenue in East Lansing, where the school's located, so things changed.

When I got to Green Bay, it was an all white town. It really wasn't a big deal because that's the way East Lansing was when I got there. There were fewer people in East Lansing than the 68,000 people in Green Bay. I really didn't have to make an adjustment. The small town blues didn't get me, coming from Philly with millions of people then going to East Lansing, a small town. Green Bay was easy for me to make the adjustment to.

There wasn't any social life at all in Green Bay. The social life at Michigan State, because they had quite a few black co-eds, wasn't a problem. In Green Bay, being single, your social life was just socializing with the guys or just going out to Speeds or to Tropicana or my brother's place and having a Budweiser or your adult beverage of choice.

We had to drive 112 miles to get a haircut in Milwaukee because Vince Lombardi didn't allow any facial hair or long hair, whether you were black or white. We had to keep ourselves in good physical shape and looking well, suit and tie on the road all the time. That's the way it was.

Being out at restaurants or wherever in a small town, people will come over and say hello and ask for your autograph. Nobody ever came to me and said, "We don't want you dating white women. Or, we don't want you talking white women." That never happened the whole time I was there for nine years.

Dallas Cowboys

When I got to Dallas, they had Mel Renfro, Cornell Green, and Jethro Pugh on defense. They had three black guys on defense. With Green Bay, we had seven on defense. In Dallas, they moved me to the corner; put Cornell Green at strong safety. Mel Renfro would have been the greatest free safety of all time because of his speed, his athletic ability to play free safety, and to help the cornerbacks. Tom Landry didn't want Mel playing free safety because he wanted Charlie Waters or Cliff Harris, two white guys in there to play free safety.

Mark Washington was drafted out of Morgan State. Mark was a great athlete and a natural cornerback. Mark could have played the right corner with the help of Cornell, Mel, and me. We would have had four black guys for the first time in history in the NFL secondary, but Landry didn't want to get that in his legacy. He didn't want any part of that.

In other words, Landry didn't want to put the best players on the field. I think that he made the choices because of the color of skin rather than the contents of the character and athletic ability.

It cost him some games before I got there and it cost him some games while I was there.

Man, I don't know what they would have done to him. I know one thing, the president of the United States got shot down there and killed. No telling what might have happened.

Bill Cosby

Bill Cosby and I grew up together in Philly, and he did the forward in my book. We're still friends to this day.

Fat Albert was a guy that we grew up with by the name of Bobby Martin, and he came to Green Bay a couple of times. He's about 350. He did play football in high school but he kept getting heavier and heavier, and he could hardly carry his weight around.

Man, we did all kinds of things in the neighborhood. Most of Bill Cosby's act comes from just the natural stuff that happened in the neighborhood when we were growing up. When Bill Cosby was a student at Temple University, they had a standup comic contest at a place called Underground in Philly. It was Underground because you had to go down steps, like if you're going down for the Subway.

Johnny Carson was doing "The Tonight Show" at that time, and he just happened to be at the Underground and he heard Cos. Then Cos got his break because Carson called him and said, "Look, why won't you come over to the show." That's when Cosby got started with a standup comic act. Fat Albert is still showing all around the world in different languages.

Cosby was a natural athlete in high school just like me, and we competed against each other. We went to different high schools. He went to Germantown High School, but we competed against each other in track, basketball, and baseball, and we played on the same local basketball team at the Boys Club. There's a picture of us. Cos was 16 and I was 14. We played on the same team. There's a picture in my book and, it points out Cosby and I being friends back in the day.

I was all-city in every sport. I don't think Cos was all-city in any of the sports, but he was a good athlete. In fact, he played halfback at Temple.

Mike Ditka

My senior year at Michigan State, we played Pitt in Pitt Stadium and Mike Ditka was on that team. Mike Ditka went both ways. He was a great athlete from Aliquippa, Pennsylvania. I was a running back like I had mentioned, and Mike Ditka was like a spy. He was playing linebacker and defense depending on where I lined up. He was hitting me on every play where I had the ball that night.

Finally, I think it was in the third quarter, I told Fred Arbanas, "Look. Next time Ditka does that, I'm going after him." He said, "I'm with you." Ditka did it one more time. As he was walking away, I hit him in the back of the head with a forearm and it started a brawl. Both benches emptied. Mike Ditka and I both got thrown out of that game along with a few other guys because the coaches and everybody were on the field trying to break us up. The game was on national TV, my senior year in 1960, and the game ended up in 7-7 tie. From that day on, I had no respect or love for Mike Ditka.

When he got with the Bears it even lessened because the Bears were our most hated rival. Ditka and I never forgot what happened at Michigan State in the Pitt game. We used to be going after each other when we were playing against each other in the pros.

When I got traded to Dallas, we ended up being teammates for three years. Obviously we spoke, but we never got to be great friends. He never invited me over for dinner. I couldn't tell you his wife's name. He never introduced me to her. We didn't socialize or anything, but we got along. That's about all I can say as far as Ditka is concerned.

Green Bay Packer Herb Adderley prepares to hit Dallas Cowboy
running back Don Perkins.
Photograph copyright Associated Press

Chapter 37

Bob Lilly

College:
Texas Christian

Career History:
Dallas Cowboys (1961-1974)

1980 Inductee Pro Football Hall of Fame

College Choice

I grew up about 100 miles west of Fort Worth, where TCU is located. My dad's hero was Sammy Baugh, who grew up pretty near where I grew up. When dad was a young man, he went to watch Sammy Baugh. Dad started taking me down when I was in about the eighth grade. We went to a couple of games a year. Even though I visited many other campuses, for some reason, I guess because of my dad's love for TCU, I went to TCU.

We had a seven-year drought in Throckmorton that started in 1950. We were farmers, basically. Dad also had some bulldozers, which he used to build ponds, terraces, oil field roads, and things like that. By 1955, we were on the verge of being totally broke. In fact, I think we were, but Dad still worked. He had to go out of state to work.

In 1956, my mother and dad had called all of the relatives we had all over the country for work. My mother had some kinfolk in Oregon. Her cousin found Dad a job up there, so we sold everything we had. We had a 1952 Studebaker and a homemade trailer and we put what we could get on it, and moved. We were like the Beverly Hillbillies going to Oregon.

I went to Pendleton my senior year. It was a much bigger school, a 4A school, rather than a 1A. We went to the semi-finals in football, basketball, and I went to state in track. I think I made All-State in football and Second Team All-State in basketball. It turned out to be a blessing in disguise. I didn't really want to leave my kinfolk and my friends. It was kind of a lonely ride to Oregon.

I got a postcard from Allie White, who was an assistant under Coach Abe Martin. We didn't have a phone, so they had to call the coach. I visited schools in the Northwest, but when I got the one-cent postcard, they offered me a four-year scholarship to TCU with 10 dollars a month for laundry.

My dad had a mild heart attack by that time. I heard him talking about coming back and I think that's another reason I wanted to go to TCU. My grandmother was still alive, and they came back. My dad convalesced with Mom and they lived with my grandmother for about a year until Dad got well. Anyway, I started my career at TCU.

Draft

My senior year in college, I made All-American and the Dallas Cowboys, Dallas Texans, and Houston Oilers came into existence. I was drafted by the Cowboys and the Texans.

I asked Coach Martin what I should do. He said, "I like the people that own both teams. They're very nice people. But the NFL has been around quite a while and I think you would be wise to go with them if the money's about the same."

It didn't make a lot of difference. I think my salary was $11,500, or maybe it was $10,500. I can't remember. For the first two or three years that I was with the Cowboys, I thought, "I can't believe I'm getting paid to do something I really love."

I thought of signing with Lamar Hunt and the Texans at first, because when they started the AFL, they had a different way of drafting people. They tried to draft locally so they would have a lot of interest. There were a lot of Southwest Conference players that I knew personally and knew them well. Some All-Americans signed with the Texans.

I really didn't have any close friends other than Glynn Gregory, whom I had played against at SMU. Don Meredith was there; I played against Don. I used to go out and eat hamburgers with the Texans more than I did with the Cowboys the first couple of years.

The Cowboys didn't have a draft the first year, which was my senior year in college. They did have a draft the next year, and I was fortunate to be the number one draft pick.

I am very happy that I stayed in Dallas. I'm happy that I went to TCU. My dad and mother got to come down with my brother and sister, to watch the college games. They also were able to come to Dallas to watch the Cowboy games at home. I had extra tickets sometimes. My dad would bring my uncles too, which was nice. I really enjoyed that. I'm happy that that's the way things worked out.

Positions

I started out as defensive end. Tom Landry wanted me to play left defensive end, because I was really quick off the ball and I was left-handed. He just thought that would be ideal, but I had never played defensive end. I always played defensive tackle. Playing defensive tackle is kind of like playing middle linebacker. There's somebody who's going to hit you every play. It's really a perfect position for people who are very quick and strong enough to withstand the zone blocks and the double-team blocks. I fit right in there.

I moved during the middle of my third year, to defensive tackle. I went to the Pro Bowl after my second year as a defensive end, but I didn't like it. I hated it. There was no action. It was like you just sat waiting around out there, but in the middle, you've got to be alert or get killed.

Early Years Of Cowboys

We had training camp a long way from home all the years that I played with the Cowboys. The first year, I think we went up to Minnesota, to St. Olaf College. We had training camp there for seven weeks, but two of those weeks I was in Chicago at the All-Star game. The next year, we went somewhere up in Michigan and had frost every morning. We were also gaining weight. Tom Landry was working us to death and we were gaining weight anyway. Then we moved from there to Thousand Oaks California for my last 12 years.

We were always gone six weeks. It was quite an adjustment to leave your family and everything. The first few years in California, up until we started making money, nobody had enough money to rent a TV or a car. Maybe one or two of the guys would rent a car and we'd all cram in there as best we could. We only had Sundays off, so Saturday nights you could go to a movie and could be in at midnight. The rest of the time, it was 11 o'clock lights out with coaches checking the rooms.

It was a $100 fine if you were late turning your lights out. If broke a rule again, your fine doubled. If you were overweight a pound, it was 25 bucks. If you were overweight a pound the next time, it was 50 bucks. That's the way it was back then, as far as our living conditions. We had good food and dorm rooms the whole time I played. It was pretty austere.

By the time we were under Coach Landry for a couple of years, we were always early. Willie Townes, who I really felt sorry for, had a glandular problem and a weight problem. Sometimes they fined him as much as he made in the game when he was weighing in. There were little fines. Most people didn't really get fined that much.

One time Jerry Tubbs, who was our linebacker and eventually became our linebackers' coach, was fined. Jerry was from the neighborhood where I grew up. Jerry lived in Plano, and he came not far from where we were practicing. They had a power outage in Plano and Jerry had an electric clock like everybody else did. Jerry was a player coach at the time, so here he comes, late.

Coach Landry said, "Jerry, I'm sorry, but I'm going to have to fine you 50 bucks."

Jerry said, "Coach, I don't think that's right. Our power went off." Coach Landry said, "I'm sorry, but you guys need to go buy a mechanical clock as well as electric."

One time, Craig Morton had a wreck. He missed practice or he was late for the bus to go out of town to play. Coach Landry fined him for being late. He said, "Coach, I had a wreck, I couldn't do anything." Coach said, "You need to start earlier."

Coach Landry wasn't a mean person. He was a very nice person, but he meant what he said. Whenever he said something, that's the way it was. I think for that era, it was a good way to do it.

Transformation To Super Bowl Champion
It was a transformation and it was a long process, but my first year, I didn't know what to expect. We had some good players that they'd gotten out of the pools, but they didn't have a draft. Meredith was there, and so was Eddie LeBaron. He was very good and very smart. We had some other players that were also good. Most of them were toward the end of their playing careers. We didn't have the speed that we got in the next few years.

The draft my second year was a really good draft. We drafted a lot of good players, Cornell Green, George Andrie, and Dave Edwards. All of those guys played about 14 years. I don't even remember who they all were, but anyway, a bunch of really good football players. We had Meredith and Perkins already, and then we started getting people like Mel Renfro in about 1963, and Lee Roy Jordan somewhere around 1964. We started building a team.

By 1963, our defense was planned pretty well. Our offense was still sputtering a little, but by 1965, we had a seven and seven record. We lost up in Pittsburgh in the seventh game. We played 14 league games. In the seventh game, Coach Landry ordered everybody out of the locker room, and told us that he was proud of our 110 percent effort. Landry was proud of us as people, because we'd done everything he'd asked. He said, "I thought I would be a good coach in the NFL, but maybe I'm not a good coach." Then he teared up and said, "I love you guys."

That was the last year that we didn't perform well. We had a winning season every year from then on. The next year we had the opportunity to go to our first Super Bowl. We played Green Bay and lost. We had the ball on the one-foot line, had a penalty, and Don had an interception. We lost our shot at that. The next year was the Ice Bowl. Then we had three years where Cleveland beat us. Then we came back and went to the Super Bowl and got beat by Baltimore.

Finally, the 1971 team went to Super Bowl VI. I think it was in New Orleans, and it was in January. That was really a highlight. We had gradually and slowly built a team that was performing on a championship level, but we just couldn't quite seem to get the job done. We had all kinds of names that people gave us, like "Next Year's Champions" and "Bridesmaids of the NFL", and I don't know what else. There were several. "Can't win the big ones," or "Cowboys can't win the big ones."

But we finally did it that 1971 season. It was like we'd had a 100 pound weight lifted off each other's back. I'd never seen people so happy. It was a great experience. Roger Staubach had come and taken over as quarterback. He was a great leader. He guided the Cowboys for several more years. Anyway, it was just a wonderful evolution. I'm really happy that I got to go through that, because it made me understand a lot more about how hard it is to be successful in life and in other things besides football.

Coach Landry taught us a lot of things in a business way, because he had several degrees. He was very smart, but he was also a businessman. We had goals and we set goals. We learned how to do all this. If we had some faction of our game, or some element of it that was going downhill, then that's when we stayed after practice and we worked on it for 30 minutes. In a few weeks we had that corrected.

We were a good team. We weren't a dynasty, but we were in the playoffs a lot of years. The Cowboys went to three more Super Bowls after I left. They won one of them and lost two to Pittsburgh.

29 Yard Yack Of Bob Griese In Super Bowl
It seemed to me all I was doing was chasing Bob Griese from behind and Larry Cole was kind of helping me a little. Then, finally I caught him because I could outrun Larry and Bob. I'm not

sure I could outrun Bob Griese, but I think I could. Anyway, it was a big play. I don't think it really affected the outcome of the game that much. It was a big play for me, because I'd never had a sack that long before.

Super Bowl VI
The Miami Dolphins had a great team. I'll never forget watching them. We watched hours and hours of games. We were very worried about the running game. The thing was, we had the flex defense. We could stop the run pretty well, but we didn't know if we could stop them, because they were running the ball about 65 percent of the time. They were making about 240 yards a game and wearing everybody out. They had a great team. Of course, the next year they proved it when they won all of the games.

It wasn't as easy as it looked. They had opportunities. We took it away from them and shut their running game down. Then they had to go to the passing game. They just weren't used to being a passing team, and our coverage was good enough to stop Warfield and some of the other guys,

Career
I really enjoyed my career. I think it was a perfect setup to go to TCU and then go 30 miles away and play the rest of my career.

That was 18 years of my life right there in Fort Worth and Dallas. You establish a lot of friends. Your kids grow up in a pretty stable situation, where they don't have to move around all the time. I think I've been blessed.

Induction Cowboys Ring of Honor
I didn't know anything about it. I knew that they were going to have a Bob Lilly Day, and at halftime they sent me back out to the middle of the field. I thought, "They're probably just going to give me a plaque." I had no idea. I went out there and all my teammates were down there on one side. They had a brand new Pontiac station wagon. Our team doctor had given me a bird dog with a cage, and my teammates gave me a Browning shotgun because they knew I loved hunting birds.

Then they made big speeches, and they pulled a flag off of the top of the stadium. There was a blue stripe running around Texas Stadium. Finally, they got the rope loose, and there it was. Bob Lilly, had number 74, and I don't know what else. They announced the Ring of Honor, which was a shock to me. I was shocked to get a shotgun, a dog, and a Pontiac station wagon, and then be in the Ring of Honor.

Nickname Mr. Cowboy
Roger Staubach was the one that pinned that on me. I asked Roger one time, and I think what he told me was he was watching our films quite a bit. Whenever we played the game, it was filmed very inclusive, it wasn't split up defensive and offense like it is now. He would watch offense and he would watch the defense. One day after a couple of years, he said, "I think you're Mr. Cowboy," and that's how it got started, as far as I know. I didn't have anything to do with it.

Dallas Cowboys, America's Team

Being America's Team was the worst thing that ever happened to us. Because where we went, people were trying to kill us. We hated that name. We hated for the Cowboys to be called America's Team, and I'm glad that I was toward the end of my career when I started getting the nickname Mr. Cowboy, but it has grown on me since then.

End of Career

Actually, I don't think I ever felt like I was slowing down. I knew that I was breaking in guys like Harvey Martin and Ed Jones, and I loved them; they were great defensive ends. George Andrie was a great defensive end in my opinion. Larry Cole was a great football player. We had really good athletes, but these guys were just getting bigger and faster.

I hurt my neck probably about the seventh or eighth game of my 14th year. I woke up thinking it was a crick, but it ended up that I had a bulge disc, and I couldn't sleep at night. I was taking aspirins and I got a bad ulcer. I couldn't hit anybody with my head. It just hurt too much. I figured I don't want to go out of this league on a sorry note. I played and started all the games that year, but I wanted to leave while I was ahead, while I was on top, and I did. That's the reason I quit after 14 years.

Coach Landry tried to get me to come back but I told him, "Coach, I wouldn't be very good. I'd be an embarrassment." He said, "You can help these younger guys." I said, "I don't think so. I physically can't do it." That's the reason I quit.

I finally explained that to him. My wife helped me. He used to come by and have coffee with us in the morning and talk about it. I knew better. I'm glad I did what I did. It has never quit hurting, either.

Tom Landry

Coach Landry was very stable. He never had what you called real highs or real lows. He was always businesslike and everything, but he had his principles, and I don't think I ever heard him say a curse word. A lot of coaches will cuss the players or they will cuss something, which is fine. That is part of football. That's just the way it is. He was a good example to all the guys. All the guys that played a long time for Coach Landry, I think he made better people out of them. I think they had a lot better sense of how to accomplish things, like how to actually start a business and how to set it up.

Also, he was very successful in business in the Dallas area, and we saw that. Back in those days, it might have just been the era, but I think because he was a Christian man and he controlled himself, that we had that same type of control among the players. There weren't many prejudices. There just wasn't a lot of friction or conflicts.

In the meetings, we always watched the film together, because it wasn't split up. It was all on one reel. We would watch the game and the kicking team they had a separate camera for the kicking team, so we did get to see that separately.

Anyway, when we had a really bad game, he would come in and he would be very serious. We knew that we were going to be running a lot of wind sprints. He would run that film back and forth. If he had a good game he would praise you some times and if you had some bad plays he would get on you for that as well. If we lost as a team and we didn't do very well at all, we made a lot of errors—that's what he really hated, was errors.

He would run that play back and forth about 20 times. We hated that more than anything, because our teammates watched us get flattened or something. That was his way of getting out of control. If you were creating problems as far as being part of the team, he would call you in and tell you about it, not get mad, just tell you bluntly. He would say, "This has got to stop, or you're going to have to move on."

He was very good with players when they would get toward the end of their career too. He would want to keep them around another year to train the younger people coming up. A lot of guys got to play another year probably after they should have quit, like I could have done. I just didn't feel right about it. I knew that I wouldn't be able to help my teammates.

Anyway, Coach was a wonderful man. He was very involved with the City of Dallas, in the Fellowship of Christian Athletes in Dallas, as well as other business, and all kinds of charitable things with his wife Alicia. Both of them were involved. They were wonderful people. Coach Landry was a wonderful man. After we all retired from football, I would go see him from time to time or be in a golf tournament with him or something like that. He was so down to earth and so nice and pretty glib, but when you were playing football for him, it was a little more serious.

Jerry Jones
I think most of the players were shocked that Jerry Jones didn't notify Tom Landry prior to hiring Jimmy Johnson. What I found out later was that Jerry ended up having to negotiate with Bum Bright, who was the owner after I'd gone. I didn't know Mr. Bright very well. I think what happened was Jerry was negotiating with Bum Bright and they made a handshake deal. The snake had got out because Jimmy Johnson had come to town and they were eating in a restaurant in Dallas, and the people put two and two together with the media there.

Sure enough, there had been a handshake sale, and he went ahead and hired Jimmy Johnson. That was announced. Then somebody said, "Nobody's told Coach Landry." Jerry said, "Oh my goodness," so he flew down and told Coach Landry. I'd never heard Coach Landry say one bad word. I heard him say, "I wish I'd had known this a while back because I have put so much effort into this next season and I hate to miss it." That was about it. He said, "I've been ready to retire for two years. I knew that the ownership can change at any time, and things like this are possible." Jerry came down and apologized for the way it was handled, and that's fine with me. He never said another word.

Being Called Greatest Defensive Tackle in NFL History
I don't get a big head, because I don't think I was. I think there's been many, but it is a compliment. I appreciate it, but I don't think about it. I don't dwell on things like that. There's too many different circumstances. I think there have been many great tackles, so we'll just let it go with that.

Interest In Photography

My senior year in college, I was on the Coaches All-American Team, which was sponsored by Kodak back then. They gave each of us a camera and film. By the way, there were only about 13 guys on the team back then because we played both ways. They usually had a couple of guys like the kicker and somebody else who would be a backup for the quarterback to play on defense or something. Anyway, I got an automatic camera. They also gave us 200 rolls of film with mailers to send them back to Kodak, and they would send us the pictures free.

After that, I got to go to several All-Star games, the Hula Bowl being one of them. I took a lot of pictures over there. I wish I could find them, because I actually took some pretty nice pictures. I took some at the Shrine Game, and then some in Buffalo. I played an All-Star game up there. I went to Chicago and played in that game. We played the winners of the seasons before, the College All-Stars versus the pros. I took my camera with me.

My second year, I had dark room. I had a real dark room from that point until about 1992, when we moved and I didn't want to build another one. I started going digital, although I still went down to the camera store to print my own prints on their equipment and paid them for the use of the equipment. I do it all digitally now, and I really enjoy it. It's a fun thing to do. I'm getting older and I don't do it as much as I used to, but it's been a really nice hobby for me throughout the years. I took all my teammates and their children's pictures. Some of my teammates have come back and told me they wouldn't have had any pictures of their kids if it hadn't been for me. Anyway, it worked out pretty good.

Dallas Cowboy Bob Lilly takes on Los Angeles Ram Tom Mack.
Photograph copyright Associated Press

Chapter 38

Mike Ditka

College:
Pittsburgh

Career History:
As Player:
Chicago Bears (1961-1966)
Philadelphia Eagles (1967-1968)
Dallas Cowboys (1969-1972)

As Coach:
Dallas Cowboys (Asst. Coach) (1973-1981)
Chicago Bears (1982-1992)
New Orleans Saints (1997-1999)

1988 Inductee Pro Football Hall of Fame

College Choice

I visited Notre Dame; I visited a lot of places but really I wanted to be a dentist and that's what my high school coach wanted me to be. That's why I went to Pittsburgh. They had one of the best dental schools in the country and they had a great football program. They'd play Michigan State, Syracuse, Penn State, Miami, and Notre Dame. They played them all. We had a national schedule that we would play all the best teams. That's why I went. That really is the main reason.

College Stats vs. Rookie Year With Chicago Bears

My first year in pro football, I caught 56 passes for over 1,000 yards. You know, it's crazy. What'd I have, 12 touchdowns? I don't know what it was, but it was crazy. I caught 12 passes my senior year in college and I caught 56, I think, my first year in pro football. That's a pretty big jump.

College All Star Game

My head coach for the College All Star Game was Otto Graham. He coached a number of the All Stars in those years and he had a really good staff. Dick Stanfel, who coached for me with the Bears, was on it. A lot of good guys were on it. It was really a good staff. They were good people.

Pittsburgh

We dodged Syracuse. It was close, it really was. We couldn't score a lot of points. We had a good defense, we played hard on special teams, and we ran the football on offense, but we just couldn't score a lot of points. We weren't a high scoring offense, so if we were going to beat somebody, we were probably going to beat them seven to nothing or fourteen to seven or ten to seven, or something like that. That's basically what it was. We ended up with four wins, three ties, and three losses one year. The losses were by five points or something, not very much. I think Penn State beat us the last game, thirteen to three. That's basically all I remember.

We had a lot of good players. That recruiting class that came into Pit when I was a freshman was one of the best recruiting classes ever. We had a different quarterback every year. We never had one quarterback all three years. It was hard because there was not a whole lot of stability to that position, but they didn't put a lot of emphasis on that position really, because all we did was hand the ball off.

Draft

Houston offered me a lot of money at that time. Here is what it came down to. I had a great respect for George Blanda and the Houston Oilers and the whole AFL, but I said, "If I'm going to play football, I'm going to play in the best league there is. I'm going to play in the National Football League," and I did. That was my decision. I went to the Bears. I'll never have any regrets about it ever.

I talked to the 49ers a lot, I talked to the Redskins a lot, and I talked to Pittsburgh. If I were to have played for any of those teams I would have been a linebacker, no question about it.

When the Bears drafted me and I went to Chicago and was told that I was going to play tight end. You had to say what the heck is a tight end because most people didn't know and they never really used them to catch the football. Because of a guy named Luke Johnsos, who was the position coach for me with the Bears, and George Halas they really created that position and they got me to play it and a lot of good plays were set up for me.

We had a great outside receiver, Johnny Morris, myself, and we had a great running back in the beginning with Willie Galimore. We had some good players, we really did. We were a pretty darn good football team, but don't forget in the early '60s. The Packers were really great. In 1963, we broke through and we won the Championship and that was a big deal. I feel I played against some of the greatest teams in NFL football, including the Packers in the '60s.

Rick Casares

Rick Casares was pretty special, I mean, I've never seen someone play a game with a broken bone in his ankle. He taped it up. I don't know how he did it, but he played, and he played really good. He was a fullback, nothing flashy. He would knock you right on your back. He could run, he could catch, and he was just a great football player. We had Willie Galimore and Casares in the same backfield. We had Billy Wade at quarterback. He played great quarterback for us in those days. He had been with the Rams earlier but he came to us and he played great. He was a great guy.

I look at our defense and we had Doug Atkins, Stan Jones, and Bill George. They're all in the Hall of Fame. We had Richie Petitbon, Larry Morris, Joe Fortunato, and Fred Williams. We loved him. All of these guys can't be in the Hall of Fame. We had a great group of guys. I can't remember them all now because I'm getting old. We had J.C. Caroline who played for us at that time. He was a cornerback. Bennie McRae came in and played cornerback for us and he was really good.

We had Bill Brown who was drafted number two. I was drafted number one by the Bears. He played with the Bears before he went to Minnesota. The reason he could play was because of Casares. Bill Brown was a great football player, a great professional football player for the Vikings.

Chicago Bears Winning 1963 NFL Championship
You think there would be a lot more championships, but there aren't. A lot of the other teams stepped up and became very good, the Colts especially, there were other teams too, like the Browns. You're always caught in the moment. I mean you don't look to the future but you always say well, there'll be a lot more good years, but there aren't. It was the same when I coached. When you hit that magic moment, you think there's going to be more of these, but there's no guarantee about anything. The fact that we won one was great. We had the critics that said we should have won more than one. We probably should have, but we didn't. We were a good football team. We won a lot of football games but we only won one championship. In life, you're judged on your championships, not your wins.

1963 NFL Championship Game Between The Chicago Bears & New York Giants
Well, it was bad field, but both teams played on it. There's no question about that. Were the Giants a good team? Yeah. Were they a better team than us? They had a better offensive team than we did, we were a better defensive team and defense wins football games. The field just wasn't good. I mean none of the fields were good at that time of the year anyway. The grass was all gone. You were playing on dirt. In this case, we were playing on mud and dirt. It wasn't very good, that's true, but it was a very good football game. I think that year our offense had an average score of fourteen points a game and we won the Championship. Our defense on average was giving up ten points a game. The score that game was fourteen to ten. That's pretty crazy, but that's basically what it was. We might have scored maybe a few more points and made it to seventeen, but that game was very close, very hard played. It came down to our defense making a couple of big plays, interceptions, and knocking Tittle out of the game. There were a lot of interesting things that happened in that game.

George Halas
You've got to understand that George Halas and George Preston Marshall, these guys started the National Football League. They persevered. They robbed Peter to pay Paul. They didn't make any money in those days. Then they developed it and created a great, great sport.

Halas persevered through a lot of things. He had another business on the side. George was old school, he was tough, he was tight, and he should have been. I mean that's just the way it was. It was his money, he made it, and he had a right to spend it the way he wanted to. He wasn't a guy who was going to throw it around needlessly or overcompensate players, that's for sure.

I got along with him in the beginning. I really did, but after a while he got tired of my act and shipped me off to Philadelphia. That was okay. I have no apologies for anything that I did in Chicago. I enjoyed all those years. I played as hard as I could for the Bears.

Trade To Dallas Cowboys

My life changed when I went to Dallas, I'll be honest with you, when I met Tom Landry it really resurrected my career, resurrected my life as a person, and I really learned to play the game the right way in Dallas because they played as a team. As a member of the team, there was no ego involved in Dallas. I was just trying to help the football team win games. Anybody who says that there's no ego involved in sports is lying because we all have one. I can honestly say that in Dallas, it all changed because of Coach Landry. I spent four wonderful years playing there, then spent ten more years there, as an assistant coach. That's where I really learned the game of football.

Tom Landry

Tom Landry was a Christian. He and Lombardi were so similar. They were two people who were driven by three things: faith, family, and football. They were both the same. Both were very devout religious men, with strong beliefs, who were also big family people. I mean tremendously they're families are first and then football. That's basically their life. They didn't have a whole lot of other things going on outside of that. That's why they were good at what they did. Tom would never swear, but I did hear one slip out when I was an assistant coach.

Roger Staubach

Roger Staubach was a winner, period. He's a leader, he's a winner; he was a guy that should have been a quarterback and he finally did get to quarterback and we finally did win the Super Bowl. That's as simple as I can put it. When it comes to leadership and the guy you want to go into battle with, you want to go in with Roger.

When you talk about what a quarterback is, I don't care about raw emotions. I don't want to hear that. I want to hear about your leadership. I want to hear how you play under pressure, the respect you get from your teammates by the way you play the game. Staubach had all that.

New York Giants Not Hiring Vince Lombardi As Head Coach

It was New York's loss and Green Bay's gain. I think it was meant to be. Vince Lombardi was meant to go to Green Bay, Wisconsin, the smallest NFL city in the country, and win, and win big. He made many fans from all over the country. I still go everywhere and people still say, "You know, I'm still a Packer fan." I understand that.

Revolutionizing Tight End Position

I didn't revolutionize anything. All I did was play the position and they threw me the football. I really loved to run with the football after I caught it. I had a lot of success doing that. I'd run up over people stiff-armed. I didn't care. I was having fun. They just started throwing the ball to the tight end at that time and I happened to be the guy in Chicago they were throwing it to. After that, the tight end became a very integral part of every offense because people would double on the outside guy and there you'd end up with a linebacker on you, basically, as a tight end. If you couldn't beat a linebacker, you shouldn't have been playing.

Process Of Being Hired As Chicago Bears Head Coach

In 1982, Tom Landry called me in and said, "Mike, Coach Halas wants to see you." I said, "What about?" He said, "I think he wants to hire you to coach the Bears." That's what really happened. I said, "What do you think?" to Tom. Tom said, "I think you're ready." That's basically all we said. He said, "Good luck!"

Process Of Being Hired As An Assistant With Dallas Cowboys
I was in a business in Dallas with some guys and we were making pretty good money. We had a couple of nightclubs. We opened one in Houston, one in Shreveport, and one in Oklahoma City. We were making good money at that time and we were pretty successful. That's what I thought I was going to end up doing.

I was in this place in Dallas when Tom Landry called me and he said, "Can you come in and talk to me?" I said, "Sure, coach." I drove up there to talk to him. He said, "Have you ever thought about coaching." I replied "I have to be honest with you, I never thought about coaching ever! Not for one minute, not for one second. I never thought about it." He said, "Well, I think you'll make a good coach. I'd like to hire you to coach the special teams and the receivers." I said, "Okay, oh boy."

Now I've got to make a decision and give up all this whatever you call life it was. It didn't take me long to make the decision, though. I made that decision and I went to work for I think, the greatest man I've ever known, I really do. It was the best decision I've ever made. I'm so fortunate to have been in that position, to meet somebody like that, and then do something like that.

Drafting Jim McMahon
Actually, when we were drafting him, George Halas said, "Why do you want to draft him?" I said, "Because he's a good leader, he's a great quarterback, and he's smart." He said, "He's got no arm. He's small and he can't see out of one eye." I'm telling you, he said all this. I said, "Coach, I still want him." He said, "Okay, you want him, we'll draft him." Then we drafted him.

Whether you like him or you don't, Jim McMahon was the best thing we did at that time withthe quarterback position. He played the position with courage, with brains, and he was a leader of our offense. That's as simple as I can put it.

Jerry Vainisi & Bill Tobin
Jerry Vainisi, Bill Tobin, and I worked together. Bill was our Director of Player Personnel, Jerry was our General Manager, and I was a Coach. We worked together. We drafted and put in place what we thought we needed for that football team to make it successful. I'm very proud of that.

I love Jerry Vainisi. Did he have the football background? No. Was he a football man? Yes, and George Halas knew that. That's why he hired him.

Sustaining Only Loss During 1985 Season To Miami Dolphins
Play every game one at a time. You don't worry about that stuff. You just play them one at a time. We played Miami and we got beat. We got beat by a better team. We got beat by a better coach that night. There's no question about it. But we learned from it. We could have fallen apart, but we learned. We learned that we had to do certain things a certain way. We went down to Miami with a pretty cocky attitude and they just whipped us, period. That caused us to

refocus, and as a result of that, I think we became a much better football team to finish out the year. The records in the playoffs show that. We were pretty dominant.

George Halas Retaining Buddy Ryan As Defensive Coordinator When Hiring Mike Ditka As Head Coach

There was a transition and I couldn't control that. Buddy Ryan wanted to keep the defensive staff, and I said fine. I hired the offensive staff. Buddy was a great coach. He was great for our defense. Our players loved him and he was the reason we had a great defense. It was Buddy. I'm not going to blow any smoke at anybody. There was some animosity, but I think a lot of that was a little overstated. There was none on my part; I know that. Anyway, when we won, we won. I knew when we won that Buddy was going to leave. I knew that. He should have had a chance to have a head job, and he did. Did the Bears miss him? Heck yes, they missed him. His players really related to him.

Walter Payton Not Scoring A Touchdown During Super Bowl

I realized it after the game, not during the game. That's something I regret. Walter Payton was probably the greatest football player I've ever seen. I said I scored a touchdown in the Super Bowl, he can have mine, and I really mean that. It doesn't mean anything. In the end, the only thing that matters is if you win or lose. It hurt him. It was my fault. It was an oversight on my part because it would have been very easy to hand him the football, just as well as the other guy.

Comparing Jim Brown & Walter Payton

I didn't play with Jim Brown; I played against him. Was he great? Absolutely. He was probably as great as anybody. I can only deal with what I know, and I know that the way Walter Payton was on and off the field, the leadership and camaraderie he provided for his teammates, and the way he treated the fans and the media, he was special.

Now, I think the whole package is what counts. Was Jim Brown a bigger back? Yeah. Was he stronger back? No. Did he have bigger heart? No. Maybe he did some things better than Walter, but I don't know what they would've been. I've always said that Gale Sayers was as good as anybody who ever played the game. Don't forget he only played six years and then he got hurt. I mean my goodness; there are a lot of great running backs. I don't even want to get into all that, but I'd say, in my opinion, I've been around some of the greatest ones. How good was Paul Hornung? How good was Jim Taylor? These guys were great football players. They were versatile; they did everything. I don't know that Jim Brown handled a football. Walter walked, caught, and ran … everything. I'm not knocking anybody. Believe me, I have the utmost respect for Jim Brown. I think he's maybe one of the top three players that ever played the game. I'm just saying, I was close to somebody that I thought was the epitome of greatness, and that was Walter.

Pro Football Hall Of Fame Induction

I'm very honored to be in the Hall of Fame. I have so much respect for the Hall of Fame, what it stands for, and the guys in it. It wouldn't have changed my career if I didn't make it into the Hall of Fame. I played the game the only way I knew how and I enjoyed it. Some people may not have enjoyed the way I played it. I can't help that. I played as hard as I could for as long as I could. It's a wonderful reward. Were there better tight end receivers? Yes, absolutely. Were there better blockers? Yes. I did both of them pretty well.

Mike Ditka looks over film with University of Pittsburgh Coach Johnny Michelosen. Photograph copyright Associated Press

Chapter 39

Jackie Smith

College:
Northwestern State

Career History:
St. Louis Cardinals (1963-1977)
Dallas Cowboys (1978)

1994 Inductee Pro Football Hall of Fame

College Choice
I wasn't recruited at all to play football. I went up there to run track and they said they couldn't give me a full scholarship for track. They said if you just go out for football and don't quit then we can give you a full scholarship. That's how I got into football.
I ran the high and low hurdles, mile relay, javelin, and the discus.

Transition From Track To Football
At times I did both track and football but you benefit from one to the other as far as the workouts. The type of condition that you get from the workouts really carries over. It was nice to be able to do both because one sort of complimented the other and helped me stay in shape for each sport. It was tough to do it.

The last year I was there during track, I worked on getting in shape and trying to do things more directed towards football. I found a guy who played football at Northwestern State, named Charlie Hennigan, who had gone on to play with the Houston Oilers of the American Football League. I went to a camp he was running when I was drafted and had him help me. I worked out with him in the afternoons.

I didn't miss much of spring football practice. I didn't miss much of anything. They found some way to make it work because there were a lot of guys that played football and ran track. It wasn't a very big school, so everybody had to do everything if we were going to have a team at all. That's sort of the way it went.

Charlie Hennigan
Charlie Hennigan taught me the basic fundamentals of running a pass pattern. At that time the League was running mostly man-for-man defense so it necessitated the receiver being able to run straight at that guy and beat him on a pass pattern. That's really what we concentrated on. The efficiency of those steps that Charlie taught me really worked well throughout my whole career. What Charlie taught me really allowed me to make the Cardinals.

I see him periodically when I get back to Northwestern at some events. I always make sure that he knows how much I appreciate him. He was the reason I made the Cardinals, with his expertise and his ability to teach me to run those patterns and teach me a little bit about them as far as the footwork was concerned. That's the truth because they make it on such a slim edge sometimes every little bit helps.

I continually talk to people about how Charlie Hennigan should be in the Pro Football Hall Of Fame, but he played such a long time ago. He still has some records in his name that he did back then as a receiver. A lot of people have never seen him. I'm not going to stop putting in my two cents worth about him and about his contribution to the League. I'm hoping somebody will listen one day.

Draft

I didn't expect to get drafted by either the NFL or AFL. I was surprised as hell. I was like, what are you talking about I got drafted in the tenth round? I was the most surprised guy in the world when that happened. I thought they had made a mistake and so that's how we left it. But it worked out okay.

Being Named A Starter With St. Louis Cardinals

Taz Anderson got hurt and that's when I got to play. Tight ends were bigger then and I was only 205 pounds. So I was really a receiver and that was the reason I got to stay there. I could jump in at tight end if need be, but I was really a receiver so that's actually what happened. When Anderson got hurt I got in there and got massacred for the rest of the season and figured I'd have to gain weight or get a gun or something to keep on playing.

Evolution Of Tight End Position

It has definitely changed. It's a different deal than it was. Now tight ends take a five or ten yard split with nobody in front of them. They have a wide-open look at the defense and a quick read on where they're going. I think even as old and beat up as I am, I could run a couple of pass patterns today. I'm even more scared now than I was then, so I would be running like hell.

Playing For St. Louis Cardinals

It was fun. It was a great time to play because of the time and place it was. Nowadays I wouldn't even know if I would've made the team because they have so many ready-made tight ends coming out of school that are used to playing the same type of offense formations. I'm lucky to have done it when I did.

I didn't care what I did. I just wanted to make the team. I wasn't really that concerned. I was also damn surprised. I was in shock for the first year that I even made the team so that was a surprise to me. I was willing to do most anything just to stay around.

Head Coach Wally Lemm

Wally was fine. He wasn't a big fan of mine. He didn't think that I should have made the team but the offensive coach at the time, begged him to let me stay. He said that I think I can make a tight end out of him sooner or later. Thanks to him I was able to stick around for a little while until I could get my bearings in the league.

Head Coach Charley Winner
Charley was just glad to be there. He was glad to be there and he's a nice guy.

Head Coach Don Coryell
He made a difference and made some changes that really modified our offense. We were glad he came along; really glad he came along.

He'd already been established. That's the reason we got him. Then he brought some good guys with him who went on to be successful in their own rights.

Cardinals Drafting Joe Namath
The Cardinals management didn't ask us to be involved in the negotiating process, but Mr. Bidwell was not about to pay the asking price for us to get Joe Namath. Mr. Bidwell almost had a heart attack when he heard it. That was just the Cardinals. That's the way the Cardinals operated.

Playing Philosophy
Listen, any of those guys can hit. If they couldn't hit they wouldn't be there. It's a question of just giving them a chance to do that and it's much better to be the hitter instead of the one getting hit.

The trick is not to give them a good shot and then trying to hit them as hard as they hit you so that you kind of neutralize them a little bit. I'm certain there are plenty of guys that could tackle me. I'm sure that there were. That did happen a lot. Well, I tried not to let it happen. I just wanted to make sure I got in as much as I could out of each play. That was really my driving shield.

Pro Football Hall Of Fame Induction
I was elated. I was surprised and it was under some interesting circumstances, but I was really very elated and so was my family. They were tickled to death about it. It was a nice thing to happen.

Photograph copyright Associated Press

Chapter 40

Mick Tingelhoff

College:
Nebraska

Career History:
Minnesota Vikings (1962–1978)

2015 Inductee Pro Football Hall of Fame

College Choice
I grew up on a farm in Nebraska. The only school that gave me a scholarship was the University of Nebraska.

Nebraska
I played my sophomore year some, and then I think I started my junior and senior years.

We ran the ball a lot and yeah, it was fun. We won quite a few.

NFL Draft
The Vikings were the only pro team that contacted me. I was very happy that they did and they wanted me to move to Minneapolis and play for the Vikings. I said, "Fine, I will."

First Training Camp
I had just gotten married. We drove out there together and looked at the stadium and around the area. I came from a very small town in Nebraska and we were in the big city in Minneapolis. There were a lot of things to look at.

Coach Norm Van Brocklin
He was a very good coach. You didn't want to make him mad, though. His nickname was Stormin' Norman. He got mad all the time, and he was real strict coach.

Fran Tarkenton
Fran the Man is what we called him. He was from Georgia. He was very good. He could run. Fran could really run. We'd have the guys blocked. It was good playing with him because he was a very smart guy, too. He's really fast and quick.

Coach Bud Grant
Bud was a very good coach and when he came in, he did it his way. Bud was a real strict coach. I don't think he ever smiled.

Minnesota Vikings Defense
The Vikings defense was very good. They were great defensive guys and we had a real good defense. We had a real good team, actually.

Vikings Super Bowls
I wish we had won one. We didn't, but we made it to the Super Bowl. I think we beat some of the teams we played in the Super Bowl in the regular season, but we didn't beat them that day.

Dick Butkus
We called Dick Butkus "Dickie Doo" to try to tease him. You didn't want to tease him too much because he would get mad. He was a very good player and we roomed together during the Pro Bowl out in LA one year. Dick was a good guy, a very good guy.

Playing In 240 Consecutive Games
I was lucky. I never got hurt. No one was hitting me. I was going after them and I was trying to block so no one was trying to block me. I think that's one of the reasons.

Photograph copyright Associated Press

Chapter 41

Bobby Bell

College:
Minnesota

Career History:
AFL Kansas City Chiefs (1963-1969)
NFL Kansas City Chiefs (1970-1974)

1983 Inductee Pro Football Hall of Fame

College Choice
The thing is, Minnesota did not recruit me. I wanted to go to North Carolina but at that time, blacks could not go to North Carolina. I played in the All Star Game as the quarterback. I was a quarterback in high school. When I went to the All Star Game for the black schools in Greensboro, some of the coaches from North Carolina and up North, like Michigan and Notre Dame, came to watch us play. Jim Tatum, the head coach from North Carolina, saw me play.

When I went in to the game to play, the guy already had three good quarterbacks from Triple A schools. He said, "Well, you can play." They had me playing halfback. When they finally put me in the middle of the first quarter and I started running the ball, I think I scored at least two or three touchdowns, and I got Most Valuable Player of the game. He ended up calling Coach Warmath at Minnesota and said, "Hey, there's a kid here who lives next to the mountain in Shelby, that's a hell of a football player. You need to put him up there. I guarantee he'll make it."

I didn't know this until after the fact that he made a promise to Coach if they'd take me. They'd never seen me. I found out years later that he told the coach if I couldn't make the team he would pay for the scholarship.

As a freshman at Minnesota, I played quarterback. Then, I was moved to offensive tackle and defensive end. I went both ways.

It was a culture change, a big culture change for me when I ended up in Minneapolis, Minnesota. Back then it was probably two percent black in the whole state of Minnesota. I went from one culture in North Carolina, to Minnesota where I'd walk around campus and didn't see anybody black except Sandy Stephens, Judge Dickson, Bill Munsey, and Bob McNeill. We had five black players on the team. That's all I had socially with blacks at that time. It was a big shock.

The thing is, when I went to Minnesota, I wanted to play baseball. I was a better baseball player than I was a football player. At that time, Minnesota was a Big Ten champ and a National Champion in baseball. I wanted to play baseball. When I ended up going there and getting off the plane for the first time, I asked the football coach "Can I play baseball too?" He said, "Oh, yeah." I told my Dad, I would love to go to Minnesota.

Going to high school and elementary school, the whole school was 168 students and I'm going to a big university. At that time I guess it was 35,000 students. I'd never seen that many people in one place. I told my Dad, "Listen, I would like to go here." He said, "Hey, if that's what you want, go for it." I say this all the time; my dad is the one that drove me. He just kept saying, "Son, you can do it. You can do it."

Back then, most of the people in Shelby graduated from high school, went to college for a couple of years, came back and got a 40 hour job, got married, had a family, and that was it. That's what they were doing, but I wanted to do something better. I wanted to go beyond that. My dad worked at a textile mill in Shelby where they would take cotton and turn it into yarn, then turn it into cloth.

The owners of the mill lived up at the country club. I used to cut their grass and take care of their house. Their kids went to militaryschool, and when they'd come back, they'd invite me into the house. I'd go in there and look at the yearbooks. I thought that was the greatest thing in the world.

My dad never finished school, he just barely went to three grades and that was it. He worked. I always went back to him and said, "Dad, you should see this book, man, this yearbook and stuff. You think that I will be able to do that some day?" My dad always said, "Yeah, you can do it, son. Go for it."

People always ask me, "What's the biggest thing that ever happened to you, Bobby? Was it going into the Hall of Fame? Going into the College Hall of Fame? Being the Outland Trophy? Being third in Heisman?"

I say, "Well, no the Pro Football Hall of Fame, that's the top of the pyramid." I say, "The biggest thing for me, guys, is that you know my dad always was a driver of me. He was always on my side. He told me to go for it. The biggest thing is that the first time that I played varsity football at Minnesota and they had Father's Day there, my dad and mom came to the school. He had an opportunity to see his son play in front of 65,000 people. It was a nationally televised game; it was like my dad went to school there. For him, that's one of the highlights of my life, of playing. I had the opportunity to go to school and my parents got to come see me play like the other kids. The people from the mill, the owners of the mill, saw I had the opportunity to go to a big school."

My father always walked up the street and back, and people would holler, "Pink, saw your son on national TV, on the Johnny Carson show, on the Ed Sullivan Show, man, the Big Ten Champs, man he's awesome, he's awesome." My dad walked down the street, just like a king. So for him to see that and for me to have that opportunity for him do that, to go to Minnesota, to go to the Rose Bowl and see it, the biggest game in the country, that is the top of my pyramid. The other stuff, the awards, is good too but to have the opportunity to see my parents come to Minnesota, on Father's Day at Minnesota, it was just awesome.

My Dad passed away but I still can see him walking that day with his big coat, his hat on, and an overcoat on. It was just unbelievable.

Shelby was a small town. I played six-man football. We didn't even have enough men to play eleven-man. Nobody really saw me play in high school until I got to the All Star Game and these coaches saw me play. You've got Shelby tucked next to the mountain, right in the mountains there; you played little bitty towns, that was it. You didn't get exposed like some of these other players did. I saw Grambling play at A&T one time in college in North Carolina but I wasn't exposed to a lot of that stuff.

I played basketball and I played football. We played basketball and football in high school. That's it, no baseball. We had a baseball boys club and I had a chance to play with the White Sox on their farm team. They came through Charlotte and I was playing up there on a field. They wanted to offer me a baseball contact. My dad said, "I thought you wanted to go off to college."

Nobody actually saw me. When I got really exposed was when the late Jim Tatum from North Carolina saw me and called coach Warmath. Coach Warmath brought me to the campus. They hadn't seen me play one down. He went on the word of him and that's what happened.

College Career
Sandy Stephens was a quarterback from Uniontown. He was the first black All-American quarterback. The whole thing is Coach Warmath, God rest his soul. He brought me into his office my sophomore year. At that time, freshmen could not play varsity football. He had me running the freshman year at quarterback and the next year he brought me in the office and said, "Hey listen, this is what I got to do. We've been losing, losing, losing, but I want eleven of my best players on the field at the same time. I want you to be part of that." I said, "Hey coach, not a problem." I'd have played any position. Then he said, "I'm moving you to offensive tackle." I laughed at him and said, "Oh come on, coach." He said, "Yeah, I'm moving you to offensive tackle." I said, "Wait a minute." I laughed. I thought he was kidding and the nose guard joked. He said, "That's what I want to do because I want my best players all up on the field at the same time. Now we can go both ways." I said, "Well, are you serious?" He said, "Yeah." I turned around and I looked at him and I said, "Ok, coach. I've never played tackle but I'm coachable. If you've got somebody to teach me how to play tackle, I'll play tackle." That's how it happened.

I was so nervous when I went out to play my sophomore year, I didn't see my name. We had 13 teams suited up. I walked out and I looked down there. I figured he's got to be kidding; I might be an end. I looked down there and I didn't see an end. My name was nowhere on the charts. Halfback, no name, quarterback, that was out. We had three quarterbacks. I looked there for four. I was sitting there and Coach Crawford, who was the line coach, came out and said, "What's wrong with you?"

My heart was beating out of my chest because I thought maybe he'd let me go and send me back home. I thought I was gone. I said, "Coach, my name. You forgot to put my name. Am I on anybody's team?" He said, "Well, hell bell, look over there on the tackles." I went down to tackles and I went all the way down to the thirteenth team. I was on the thirteenth team tackle. I went out there and I had no idea what I was doing.

For the first three or four days I was getting beat like a pom-pom. Then I told the coach, "You got to stay out here and tell me, show me, coach me. Teach me how to play tackle because I'm going to play it." At that time, my sophomore year, it was all junior and senior teams. The first two teams were juniors and seniors. They said there wouldn't be a sophomore that makes the team. I said, "I'm going to make the team." On the first day we played, I was the only sophomore. I started at offensive tackle and defensive end and never gave up the whole time. It was one of those things. I could have been a quarterback or a running back; I didn't care what it was. I wasn't going home. I'd have played any position I told him. I probably played every position out there. I even centered the ball. I even centered the ball on field goals and extra points. I also did that in the pros, too.

I centered the ball for the extra point on center relief. I snapped the ball for Joe Wilson. I had to stay. I wanted to play.

The more you play, the more you're involved in the game. From us, blacks going to Minnesota, it was a moving thing for the blacks across the South. Everybody started watching us play at

Minnesota, the Big Ten, we were on national TV all the time. We won the Rose Bowl two years in a row, National Champs, and Big Ten Champs. We were on TV and everybody was trying to figure out this all black backfield. It was all black. How'd they win the National Championship? They said we couldn't do it. Rose Bowls and Big Ten Champs … they can't do it. We had a pow wow. We were beating everybody.

From that we started the next year by kind of recruiting Carl Eller from North Carolina & Lou Hudson for basketball. I was the first black basketball player at the University of Minnesota. A lot of people didn't know that.

Draft
At that time I'd have said the Vikings were after me. They were saying that I was too small to play offensive tackle and defensive end. They said I was too small. Minnesota drafted me in the second round and Kansas City got me in the seventh round. Montreal drafted me also. Everybody thought I was going to go to Minnesota because I played at the University of Minnesota. Minnesota drafted me, but at that time, Norm Van Brocklin was the coach there and I was telling him, "Hey, I'd like to play here but I want a three-year contract. You've got to give me a chance. Not a one-year, I want a three-year." I wanted him to guarantee it because I didn't want to be jacked around. He kept saying, "Yeah, we're going to give you a three-year and they didn't." They wanted to give me a one-year, two-year, three-year contract, but they didn't want to guarantee me.

Lamar Hunt came up, but I never talked to any of the coaches from Kansas City. Lamar came to Minnesota and met with me. I took him out and to get some ice cream. He wanted to know where he could get some good ice cream. I took him down to the University to a good ice cream place and he told me, "Hey, I'd like for you to be part of my organization." He asked me what it was going to take and we went back and forth and I said, "I don't know. If you want to sign me, just tell me."

I ended up signing with Kansas City but my contract was written down as Texas. That was the year they moved, 1963. I asked him, "Hey, we aren't even going down there, aren't we even talking to the coach?" When we came to terms it was a long-term contract. He didn't have the contract at the time we agreed; he shook my hand. The next morning I was flying to New York to be on the Johnny Carson and Ed Sullivan shows for the All- American thing and shook his hand. Lamar went with me to New York.

That's how it started with Lamar. Everybody thought I was going to the Vikings. I'm kind of glad I did go with the Chiefs. People ask me tall the time if I would change anything going from Shelby and the high school six-man football team. I wouldn't change anything. That ride from Shelby to Greensboro, Greensboro to Minneapolis, I wouldn't change anything there. How many guys can say that they won the state championship in football and basketball in high school? How many guys can say they won the American Championship and Big Ten Champs? How many can say that they were a College All-Star in 1963? The College All-Stars beat the Green Bay Packers in '63. I was on that team.

College All-Star Game
When I got out of college and went to the All-Star Game, I went up there as a defensive end and offensive tackle. Otto Graham was the coach. For some reason he called the Minnesota Viking Coach, Norm Van Brocklin, and said, "This Bobby Bell's not a tackler. He weighs about 215, 218 soaking wet. This guy can't play."

He made me leave the offense and defensive end. He told me to go down there with the linebackers. He said, "You can't play up here, man, go down there." I changed again. I changed positions like toilet paper. I went down to the linebacker crew. The linebacker crew was Lee Roy Jordan, Dave Robinson, and Lee Roy Caffey. I went down there and had no idea what the hell I was doing. I went down there and played linebacker. I ended up starting as a linebacker for the first time.

I must have pissed him off or something. I have no idea why he sent me down there. I sat there and watched those guys and learned what to do. That's how I learned and got in the game. I almost got Most Valuable Player.

I don't know what I did to piss him off, but he swore up and down. One of the things that bothered him was that I got a no-cut contract with the Chiefs. Back then a lot of coaches didn't like that. They didn't give out no-cuts. Van Brocklin wouldn't do that.

Even after I ended up playing left linebacker, Lee Roy played the middle and Dave Robinson played the right, we all kind of changed positions but we ended up playing linebacker. Right before the game started, they go to introduce the Green Bay offense and they said, "Oh, we wanted to introduce you all to defense." We lined up on the sidelines and the coach came up to me and said, "Hey, Caffey's going to be in and he's should be standing here." I said, "Oh, I thought I was on the starting defensive linebackers." He said, "Yeah, but Otto said he wanted Caffey to be in." They introduced him. He goes out there and he plays three plays and the coach says, "Man, you got to get in there. I played the rest of the game."

It's just strange the way things happen. For a long time, Otto didn't say much to me. Then he came when I was playing with the Chiefs, against the Jets. Otto was coaching the military. After the game Otto walked into the locker room straight to my locker and said, "Hey Bell, I wanted to apologize to you about some things. I want to let you know that you are a hell of a football player." I said, "Thank you." He turned around and walked away. That was it. From that moment on, every time I saw him at a function or something like that he would acknowledge me. He'd be the first one to come up to me, and say, "Hey Bell, come here, I want to introduce you to somebody."

That was my trail, my learning process from high school learning how to adjust, and learning how to change with the different organizations. I learned a lot. By playing quarterback, I learned how to play defense. I talked to Willie Lanier. We talked all the time when we were in the game. We were like coaches on the field. When we played defense we didn't have a platoon. We had eleven guys out there. The offense came out and changed the formation. We'd check off and we'd have to play. That's why I ended up playing defensive end at times, then I moved back and played linebacker. I could play route cornerback or I could play safety, it didn't make any difference. We just used the personnel that we had on the field.

Black Football Players
Willie Lanier was the first black middle linebacker. We had a lot of firsts. We were just awesome. Yeah, he was the first middle linebacker, and they said he couldn't do that. That's what a lot of black quarterbacks who played college ball heard. When I was at Minnesota, we recruited Tony Dungy. Jimmy Raye went to Michigan. A lot of these guys came to Big Ten schools because they saw us play back in the '60s. We got a lot of players to come out of the south and go up north to start playing at the big schools. That's when they started branching out all over the country.

Hank Stram
Coach Stram was an awesome, great coach. He was, as they say, before his time. He had the offense, the defense, big players, small players, wide players, and quick players. He wanted to win. He was a coach that didn't care whether you were blue, black, green, orange, or white. He just wanted to know if you could play football. That's the way he was. He cared about you as a man. He looked at you like a man. He respected you and you respected him.

I talked to him up until the day he passed away. The first thing he'd ask me was, "How are you doing? How's your family doing?" That was the type of coach. I would go down and visit him at his place and I'd be in his swimming pool.

After he left the Chiefs and went to New Orleans, he kept in contact with all of his players from Kansas City. I talked to him once or twice a month all the time. That's the way the coach was. If he found out a player living in Kansas City had a problem, he would call me or somebody in Kansas City and say, "Hey guys, you need to check on so and so. I heard that so and so might …" That's the way he was until he passed away. He was the coach.

If you had a problem, you could go into his office and talk with him. If something came up, he'd call you in his office and ask you point blank, "What's the deal here? Let's straighten this out." That's the way he was. He was a hands-on coach.

We came out with the spread offense and everybody thought, you can't run that stuff, you can't do that. We came out with the triple stack, three lineman and four linebackers, and we were told we couldn't do that stuff. Everybody wanted to run the 4-3. The spread offense, they had to rename it, was called the West Coast. We were running all that stuff back then.

When we came out in the first Super Bowl, the coach said, "Hey, we can beat these guys. The only reason we lost that first game is because we turned the ball over to Green Bay." We turned the ball over twice in that fourteen-point loss. That was the game right there. You can't do that with a veteran team like Green Bay.

We just wanted an opportunity to come back and play in another Super Bowl. We knew we had a great team. That's when we played against the Minnesota Vikings and we were the underdog by 17 points. We felt like, hey, no way. Coach said, "They're good, but we can beat them. We got a better team." We were the wild card that year. We went back to New York and beat the Jets. The Jets thought that they were going to go back to the Super Bowl.

Oakland beat us twice that year. Stram said, "We beat the Jets and we got to go back and beat Oakland. There's no way they going to beat us a third time. We had too good of a team."

Coach, always came up with something new. He always felt like he had to keep everybody fresh and strong. We were the first team, I think, with Gatorade; we were the first team that had a weight coach.

Coach Stram had everybody lifting weights and stretching. We had quick guys. We had strong people. That's why we ended up playing Minnesota. We basically crossed the line and man-held the guys up there. We had running backs that were bench-pressing 250, 240, 260.

Coach Stram was just out in front of everybody. If there was anything new, he wanted to experiment with it. He wanted quick guys. We had a racquetball court inside the stadium. He said, "I want you guys to learn how to play this game." I already knew how to play racquetball from Minnesota. He had lineman in there because you're moving quick, quick steps. He had us playing tournaments and stuff like that. He came up with stretches, all kinds of different things like that. If it was out there, he wanted to know about it.

Max McGee in Super Bowl I
Fred Williamson was our left cornerback and I was a left linebacker. I asked, "Fred, why are you running your mouth?" He was just talking, "I want to do this and do that."

Freddy knew that I was a linebacker. If any plays came my way he knew I was going to take it out. Freddy would come up and jump on the pile or something. One time I cleaned out everything, but then Donny Anderson hit Freddy in the head and knocked him out. I went over to him and said, "Freddy, hey man, get up." He said, "Man, leave me alone." He was taken over to the sideline. I said, "Hey Freddy, what's up, man?" I know Freddy. I see him all the time. I talk to him a lot. He tells everybody he broke his leg or something like that.

That wasn't the problem. We lost that game because of the two turnovers. One was an interception and then a fumble or something. They got the two turnovers and 14 points, and that was the game. Going into halftime we were ahead and we turned it over.

Super Bowl IV

We went into that fourth Super Bowl and there was no way we were going to lose. There was no way. We were going to shut them down. We felt we had the best defense and they could not keep up with Mike Garrett, Wendell Hayes, Frank Pitts, and Otis Taylor. Those guys were so quick and fast, man, they were like horses when they ran, like thoroughbreds all over. Minnesota started off getting beat, and we hit them with the short stuff. If they wanted to pitch on the quarterback, we would do the in around reverse on them. We would keep them off balance all the time. That's what the coach wanted.

Coach Stram was a great coach. He should have gone into the Hall of Fame a long time before he did. Everybody thought that he made fun of the team by calling the plays on the sideline. The NFL film brought cameras down there. Bud Grant said he wasn't going to put the stuff on. They went over to Coach Stram and asked, "Can we mic you up? We want to tape everything. We got cameras here, and we want to use them." Coach said, "Do it. Don't tell anybody." He called the plays off the sideline, sent them in with the clock running and all. A sixty-five-toss sweep is in there, like it was a script. He called the play and it worked. Everything he used, worked.

Kansas City Chiefs Players

I'm kind of prejudice. I think we had the best linebackers. If I had a choice of picking people, I wouldn't change it. I would pick Willie Lanier and Jim Lynch in a heartbeat. If I picked a linebacker, that's who I would pick. Unbelievable. I loved it. We got to the point where we knew each other. We knew the capability of Willie and Willie knew the capability of Jim Lynch and me. We knew what we could and couldn't do. We compensated for each other. That's what you do, you compensate.

Same way with the defensive cornerbacks, Jimmy Marsalis, Emmitt Thomas, Jim Kearney, and Johnny Robinson. It was like having five or six coaches on the field. We'd come up to the line and look around. You wouldn't have to call a time out. You'd check out, say hey man, check out, man, man. We talked to each other.

1969 AFL Divisional Game Versus Jets

They had Matt Snell coming in there and Joe Namath takes it in there and pulls it out. Joe says, oh no, he's going to go for this fake; he's going for it. He came out of there and I said, nope, here I am, Joe. I stopped him right there on the seven, eight line. He came up to me and said, "God damn it, Bell. There's no way. How do you?" He just got the ball out, didn't even give it to us. He was just going to drop it. We stopped them and we beat them. That was a big play right there. Lanier would stop and say, "Hey man, we can't let them score. We can't let them score."

Joe Namath

Actually he was one hell of a quarterback as far as I'm concerned. He came to Kansas City one time and it stands out in my mind. He threw the ball three times, the same way. We didn't stop the ball twice on it. Same play. The third time, it's a touchdown. He said, "God darn it, I knew that thing would work." I mean, he sat there and picked them out. He called the plays up there; he'd pick them out. I don't know what he was thinking about or what they'd seen, but here's a guy saying that hey man.

Let's go back one step and say that's one of the things about quarterbacks. Peyton Manning right now, kind of reminds me of Joe Namath. He'd come up to the line and he'd chill out. Peyton Manning comes up and looks at it and studies things. He thinks oh this isn't going to work here, and he tells everybody. That's the guy. I would have loved to play with Peyton Manning, Joe Namath, and Johnny Unitas.

I played against Johnny Unitas and I thought he was a good. I think I made the first sack on Monday Night Football against Johnny Unitas. Joe Namath, I tell you he's one of the greatest quarterbacks in the Hall of Fame.

Approach To The Game

I approached the game in the same way that I did my homework. I'd know some of the things that a player liked to do.

Every time I got a new contract, I'd always end up playing maybe two years of the contract duration and they'd extend it. I always walked into his office and say, "Coach, the reason I want you to pay me is because I'm going to give you the ball two and a half times a game, with a turnover. You hear me? I'm going to give you the ball. I'm going to get an interception, make a fumble, or create a fumble or two interceptions, a game. I'm going to turn the ball over to you. My goal is to give it to you two and a half times a game. Some games I might get three, one game I might get less. But, I'm going to average two and a half times."

I said to the Coach, "You need to get another player to do that. If you're doing that, making a turnover four times a game you'll win the game." I walked out of his office.

Pro Football Hall of Fame Induction

At that time, back in 1983, I didn't even know I was up for it. Pete Elliot, who played against me in college when he was at Michigan, was President of the Pro Football Hall of Fame. I didn't even go to the Super Bowl that year. That was the one year I missed going to the Super Bowl. Pete Elliot called me to let me know they voted on it. The way they do it now, everybody knows for almost a whole year that is up for going into the Hall of Fame. Back then, you didn't know. They went into a room to decide. They'd go in and say this is this and you wouldn't even know until Saturday who was eligible for it and then they'd pick.

I had no idea until I got a message from Pete. My son, Bobby Junior, was playing at Missouri. I called him up and said, "Bobby, are you sitting down? I just got a call from Pete Elliot and he said I've been inducted into the Pro Football Hall of Fame." Bobby's roommate at Missouri was Willie Davis, the son of Willie Davis who played for the Packers. Willie went into the Hall of

Fame the year before me. Bobby Junior and Willie Junior were roommates at Missouri and played football at Missouri.

That's how I found out. Pete wouldn't let anybody else call me because he was a friend. He said he wanted to call me.

I went in 30 years ago and I got the opportunity to meet a lot of the guys that I read about in books. I got to meet them, personally. Marion Motley and I became great friends. John Henry Johnson, Joe Perry, and I did so much as a family. We got to know each other and our friendship is unbelievable. It's a fraternity that we join. We're all here together, we played against each other; we had a lot of fun, now we're on the same team. You're on a team now that you can't be trade from and they can't cut you from. We're all the same. It's not one is better than the other; we're all the same and that's how we try to treat it. We're all Hall of Famers.

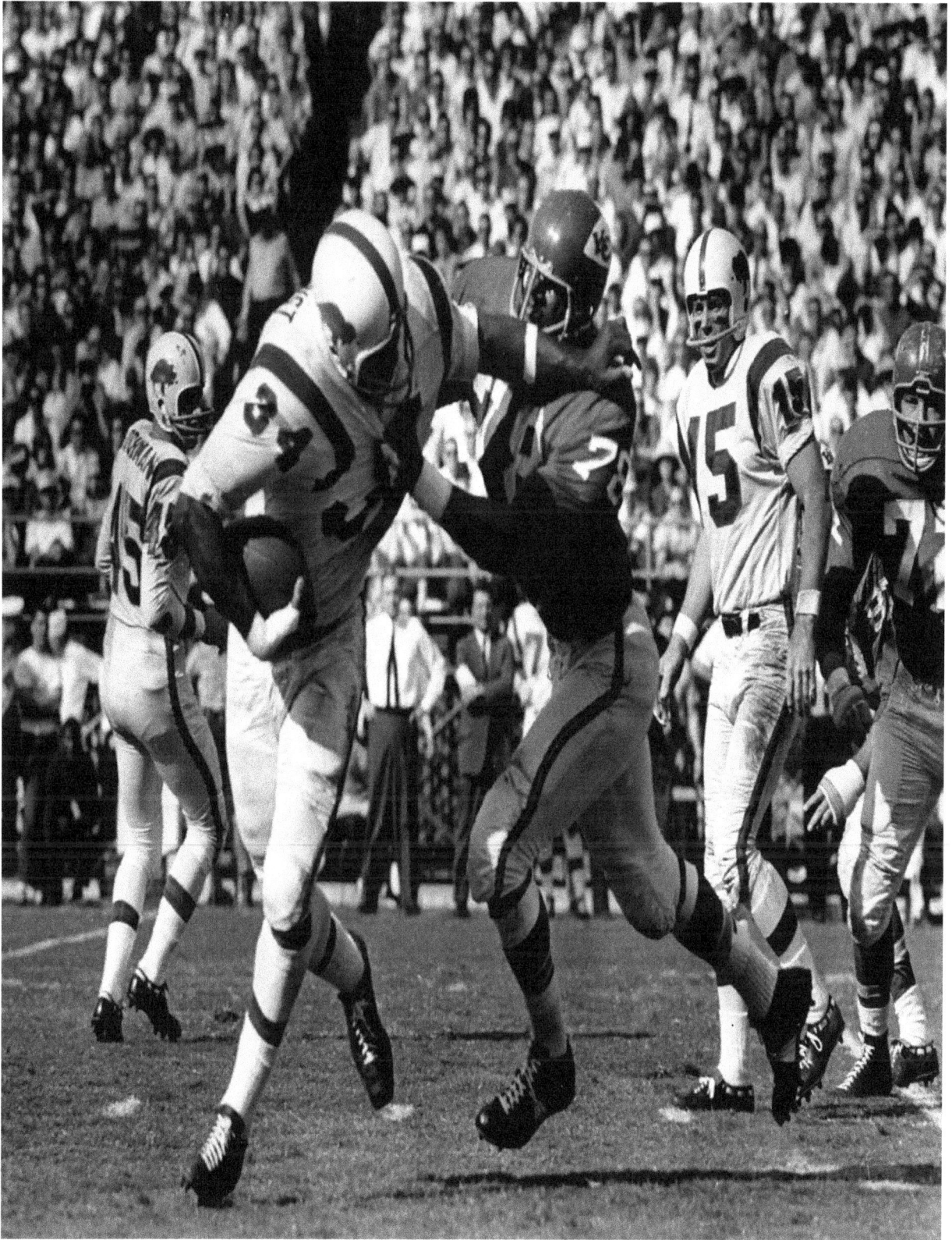

Kansas City Chief Bobby Bell grabs Buffalo Bill Cookie Gilchrist. Photograph copyright
Associated Press

Chapter 42

Lance Alworth

```
College:
Arkansas

Career History
San Diego Chargers (1962–1970)
Dallas Cowboys (1971–1972)

1978 Inductee Pro Football Hall of Fame
```

College Choice

I was going to Ole Miss. I got married and they told me I had to come on a baseball scholarship rather than a football scholarship, so I decided to go to Arkansas.

Baseball was an awful lot of fun. I enjoyed playing it, but football was, particularly playing outside receiver, a lot of fun.

In baseball they give you a glove to catch with. It's a lot of fun. I played center field and enjoyed it. At that time I think the Yankees, and a couple of other teams were interested. I almost signed during the summer but my dad said, "No, you need to go get a college education." He was smart and right. My hat goes off to him. He was a great father.

Arkansas

It was a different type of football than people see these days. We didn't throw the ball very much. It was just a running game and a defensive game. Coach Frank Broyles started smaller teams, playing with smaller guys even up in the front. We were quick and fast, but not big. Whenever we ran into a big team that was fast, sometimes we had a lot of problems.

Other than that, it was great. It was a great time. I think we won or shared three Southwest Conference Championships in a row. I can't complain. It was a great life.

I went to law school for a couple of years. I just decided I didn't want to be an attorney after seeing how much time you had to spend in the library.

Coach Frank Broyles

He's a great guy, a great coach, and I really enjoyed playing for him. Whatever honors they gave him, he deserves more than that.

He had a big stand out in the middle of the field, where practice was filmed from everyday. I think he's the one that started that. He really coached from up there.

We had a lot of outstanding coaches on the field, but Coach Broyles was the mastermind. He stayed away from the guys a little bit.

Ron Mix

Ron's certainly a great attorney, but he had a lot more patience than I did in law school. I was ready to get in and get out. Ron was always right there, very studious, very strong, a great teammate, and a great football player.

Pro Football Draft

The Chargers drafted me. I was their number two draft choice I think, and they traded for me. I was drafted number one in San Francisco, and I can't say that I talked to them one time. At that time you didn't have any agents. I met with the San Francisco people on my way back home.

First thing the San Francisco people asked me was, "What do you want?" I said, "I talked with the AFL guys. I'd like a no-cut contract." They said, "We don't give no-cut contracts." I said, "Thank you very much." I walked out of there and never talked to them again.

When I signed that year, I signed with the Chargers. Al Davis was really the reason that I ended up in San Diego. He recruited me to San Diego and I loved him. I still love him to this day. He was a great man and a great coach. I have nothing but positive things to say about him. They gave me a $10,000 bonus and $20,000 a year for 2 years. A lot of money, huh?

Move To Wide Receiver With Chargers

When I came in, that's what they wanted me to play. It was really funny because when they started the draft, Kansas City had called me and said, "Look, we'd like to draft you. We want you to play defensive back." I said, "Hmm-mm. I'm going to law school if you draft me to play defensive back. I don't want to play defensive back." They didn't draft me but the Chargers did, so I got a chance to play the outside receiver.

"Bambi" Nickname

Charlie Flowers, a guy from Ole Miss walked in to training camp. He walked around a little bit, went out and practiced a bit, came back in and said, "Well, you know you got big brown eyes, you run like a deer, you got short brown hair. We're going to call you Bambi." I just ignored it because I didn't like it, but it sort of stuck. For the first couple of years they called me Bambi. Then for three or four years they called me Bam; Bam this, Bam that. In my seventh year when they called me Mr. Alworth, I knew that I was an older player. That's really how it happened.

Sid Gillman

Sid was a genius. He was an offensive coach. All the stuff that you see today, and all the stuff that was run by San Francisco and San Diego in the '70s and '80s was all from Sid Gillman. He invented the West Coast offense. They didn't call it that at the time, but he's the guy that was responsible for it.

Differences Between AFL vs. NFL

We didn't throw the ball very much. Nobody did in those days. I think if you look back in history, it shows you that the AFL probably threw more than the NFL did in those days.

I wish I were playing now because they throw almost every down and I love it. That's fabulous. I love watching it. They used to be able to hold a little bit more.

Toughest Cornerback
Willie Brown from Oakland was like 6'2" or 6'3" and he was fast. He played hands on. He could come up and play right in front of me. He could hound you from the moment you left the line of scrimmage. He was just fast. I really enjoyed playing against him. He was a great player.

John Hadl
John had a great arm. Unfortunately, John hasn't gotten into the Hall of Fame. If anybody deserves to be there, he does. You check his stats against people that are in there now and he's right in the middle of the stats. It's really a shame that he hasn't. John had great timing. He was a great athlete, a great guy, and a great leader. I had to tell him all the time I was open, but I think all receivers say that.

Al Davis
Al Davis called me one training camp when I was trying to get a raise of $5,000, from $30,000 to $35,000. He said, "Hey, I just traded for you. Sid Gillman will be calling." I'd been going before and Sid had given me all kinds of problems about a $5K raise. He said, "What kind of raise do you want?" I said, "Five grand." He said, "No problem. I'm trading for you."

I expected to have Sid come up and call me for my playbook. A guy came up and called me and I went in to see Sid. Sid looked up at me and said, "What did you want?" I said, "Thirty-five thousand." He said, "You got it." He didn't trade me. He didn't take the trade.

I don't think he would've traded me. At that point in time I was right in the middle of my career and I was doing pretty well.

1963 Championship Game
It was a game during the season we played the Boston Patriots who beat us I think, 7-6 or 10-7, or something like that. Sid Gillman put together a great game plan for the Championship Game. We went in and played and almost ran them off the field because of the great game plan that Sid had. It was all based around our fullback and Keith Lincoln. Keith had a fabulous game; one of the best of all time. I have to say the 1963 team was probably the best team I played on during my career.

We offered to play the Chicago Bears who won the NFL Championship. They wouldn't play us. I think we could've beaten them.

Dallas Cowboys
It was pretty different. When I got there, Coach Landry told me, "I traded for you to block. If you block, we'll win the Super Bowl." I said I would. I did and we won the Super Bowl.

It was a big change for me. It looked like on paper that the Cowboys threw the ball a lot, but they threw to backs and tight ends. They very seldom threw to outside receivers. It was a real adjustment for me mentally trying to get ready to play the game.

That was the reason why I retired after two years. I couldn't get myself to go work out during the offseason because there wasn't anything to work for. All I did was block. I enjoyed doing it because it was part of the game, but it wasn't the real reason for playing.

I went back one time and told Coach Landry, "Look, all I have to do is look like I'm going to run and turn and run straight down the field and we'll got a touchdown." He looked at me and he said, "When I go deep, I'm going with Bob Hayes." I looked at him and never spoke to him again about being open.

Roger Staubach
Roger was a great quarterback. Roger was a lot like the kid going to the Browns, Johnny Football. Roger was that type of football player. He was a great one. I can't say anything but good things about him.

Having Al Davis Present Him At Hall Of Fame Induction
I wouldn't have had anybody else. Al was a special guy in my life. He was the real reason I went to the AFL. He was the one guy in pro football that I respected more than anything. To this day, I hold that respect and awe for him and appreciate all that he did for not only me, but for everybody that played for him. He was just a super, super guy and meant a lot to me in my life.

Pro Football Hall Of Fame Induction
It's really funny because I got a call five years after I played. I was out trying to make a living and doing things and they called to tell me I was voted into the Hall of Fame. I thought they were just calling to tell me that I was on the list or something. I hung up the phone and told my wife at the time. I said, "Let me call my dad and tell him." I called my mom and dad and I realized at that moment what it meant because I couldn't get it out to tell them. It meant so much to me. All of a sudden I realized that all my life I had spent trying to prove to my dad that I was that good. My dad always told me no matter how good you are there's always somebody better and don't forget it.

Wide Receiver Position
When I played, it was sort of a new position. There wasn't anybody you looked at who ran patterns or watched that closely because there wasn't that much of it at the time. It's not like it is today.

Most 200 Yard Receiving Games In A Row
That's a long time ago so I should be real proud of that record, I guess. We didn't throw that much, but when we threw it we did it pretty well. We had great players and great coaches. We had some great guys, an outstanding quarterback, and the system made it work.

AFL Players Who Should Be In Hall Of Fame
We've been trying to get John Hadl in. Nobody seems to back us up and that's really a shame when you look at all his stats. Charlie Hennigan's should be in too.

The thing about it is now we're getting where we put too many people in. There are a lot of those guys who deserve it, too. There are just too many. There are just an awful lot of people getting in.

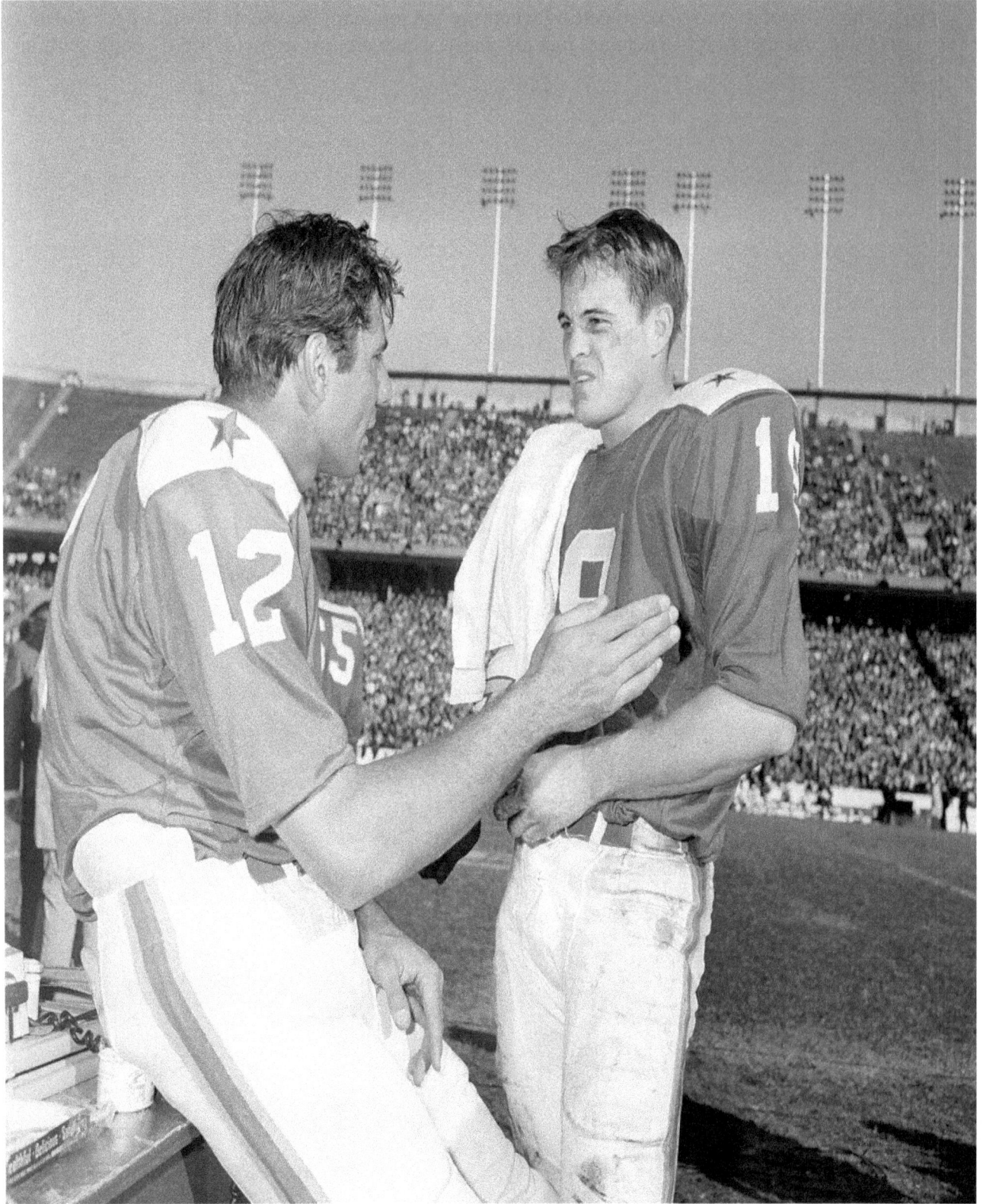

Left New York Jet Joe Namath talks to San Diego Charger Lance Alworth. Photograph copyright Associated Press

Chapter 43

Willie Brown

College:
Grambling State

Career History:
As Player:
Denver Broncos (1963–1966)
Oakland Raiders (1967–1978)

As Coach:
Oakland Raiders (1979–1988)
Long Beach State 49ers (NCAA) (1991)
Jordan High School (Los Angeles) (1994)

As Administrator:
Oakland Raiders (1995–present)

1984 Inductee Pro Football Hall of Fame

Al Davis' Loyalty To Former Players
At one time we had 15 former players employed by the Raiders. That is one thing about Al Davis; he always took care of his players. He'd make sure they were okay and he'd find a position for them. I think it's great. I've been here 41 years, and everything is fine with the organization and me. I'm pretty sure we'll be the same with Mark Davis. Mark Davis understands the process and what Al was doing. He knows how Al handled the players and Mark feels the same way.

When you play for the Raiders you feel right at home. Everybody in the organization understands once a Raider always a Raider, and that's the thing we like to live by. When you've been in this organization, you understand the organization. You understood Al Davis when he said certain things and did certain things.

Eddie Robinson
Eddie Robinson was demanding and understood the game of football, period. He taught you to play many positions. When I was at Grambling I was a starting tight end or a starting linebacker. Sometimes he would put me at halfback, and sometimes he would put me at wide receiver. He was very aware. He had the knowledge to see and understand that the players he brought into Grambling had a lot of talent, and they could play at that level. I've told a lot of guys that the starting team from Grambling for three or four years was really great. The starting team that I played on was bigger than any pro team.

Not Being Drafted

Not being drafted really wasn't difficult. I never had my eyes set on playing pro ball. I had other goals in mind. Number one was to get my education, get my degree, and coach in high school. That was my main goal, to go back and to start coaching in high school. We had so many great ballplayers on the team my senior year, that a team was coming in trying to sign whoever they could sign. Buck Buchanan was the number one draft choice that year. So I knew that if I wanted to play, I had an opportunity to play. The Houston Oilers came in and offered me a contract. It wasn't much of course. I believe they only offered me ten thousand dollars and I signed. I saw the competition that I was matched up against playing the defensive back position when I got there. I had played college football as a linebacker, and as a tight end. My first day of training camp, they stuck me outside on the corner. I didn't know anything about playing corner of course. But I picked it up fast.

Interception Of Fran Tarkenton's Pass In The Super Bowl

I got winded after I got into the end zone with all the players rushing onto the field, patting me on the back, throwing me around, and jumping up and down. That's when I really got tired. The run wasn't bad because I was in pretty good shape at the time. You know it's a thing that you do every day in practice.

Toughest Receiver

People always ask me who the tougher receiver was. I tend to look at the guys that I played against who are in the Hall of Fame, of course. Guys like Paul Warfield, Lance Alworth, and Charlie Hennigan. I have a lot of respect for those particular guys. When I played against Lance, he was a guy who hustled on every play. He would do the same thing, so you had to pay attention to him because he was tough. Paul Warfield ran very good yards. One time I was covering Paul and he jumped up in the air and changed directions while he was up in the air. I was like man, what in the world are you doing to stop him. So I stopped playing tight cover. I was the first one to start playing bump and run because I knew the receivers couldn't get by me because of my size. I was just as fast as they were, so I decided to play end tight. That's how I played Paul.

Fred Biletnikoff

I covered Fred Biletnikoff. Fred stayed away from me because he knew I could beat the hell out of him when I played bump and run. So Fred stayed on the other side. He didn't want any part of me and I probably didn't want any part of him either. Fred was small, but he had very big, good hands. That was the thing about Fred, if you threw it anywhere near him, you knew that he was going to catch it. So yeah, we had many battles in practice but the majority of the time Fred stayed away from me. He stayed on the opposite side from me.

Favorite Moment In Career

I have a lot of favorite moments because my career was good. I mean every game, every week; I had something good happen to me. So I guess to cap it off, it would probably be the Super Bowl when I ran an interception back for 75 yards to score a touchdown. That was probably one of my highlights. The other time was when I intercepted four passes in one game and I had one other, which would have been five, but the referee called roughing the passer or something like that. Things like that kind of stick out.

Houston Oiler Ken Burrough hangs on to Oakland Raider
Willie Brown. Photograph copyright Associated Press

Chapter 44

Nick Buoniconti

College:
Notre Dame

Career History
Boston Patriots (1962–1968)
Miami Dolphins (1969–1976)

2001 Inductee Pro Football Hall of Fame

College Choice
I had a couple of good influences for that. One was Angelo Bertelli who was the Heisman Trophy winner I guess in the '40s. He was from West Springfield, Massachusetts, went to my high school, and lived nearby. He was just a great all-around athlete. There was another man who went to my high school, who graduated two years before me. His name was Joe Scibelli. Joe ended up not finishing at Notre Dame, but he influenced me to at least take a visit out there. Being a small kid from an Italian family, living in an all-Italian neighborhood and not really being exposed socially to some of the finer things in life, I was really enamored when my father and I took a trip out there. I just became enamored with the entire situation, the history of Notre Dame and the boundaries of it. My father saw it and the thing that sort of captured us was the golden dome. My father saw the golden dome in all it's splendor and the beautiful bay, and he said, "This is where you're going to school," and he helped me make the decision and I never regretted it.

College Coaches
My freshman year, I was recruited by Terry Brennan and his staff. He had a great bunch of assistant coaches too. At Christmas time of my freshman year though, they let Terry Brennan go. I felt this was not a great decision on the part of the university because I thought Terry Brennan was a very good coach and I really liked his assistants. I really enjoyed being with those people.

The university went out and hired Joe Kuharich, an excellent Notre Dame guy. He had been coaching with the Washington Redskins. The next three years under Kuharich were probably as grim as anybody could ever have in major college football. He just didn't understand how to coach young players. He tried to bring a pro system into a college atmosphere. His work ethic was demeaning of the players and it was not a pleasant experience. Our record showed it, too. In the three years that I played under Kuharich, I think we won 12 games. Winning 12 out of 30 is not a great record.

The great thing that Notre Dame did for me was something that can never be replaced. It gave me the opportunity to grow socially, but at the same time, to respect how my family brought me up. I was taught to respect my elders and enjoy life. My time at Notre Dame also taught me social graces. It was a great experience.

You build friendships at school that never go away. Not only that, you're part of the Notre Dame family. When you're part of the Notre Dame family, you are a part of that family for life. That's why when good things happen for Notre Dame we all rejoice. It is a great school. The great tradition lives on; it's just a wonderful.

College Positions

Notre Dame had me playing offensive guard because we had to go both ways back then. You had to be able to play both offense and defense. So I played offensive guard and linebacker and every once in awhile I would go down in the three-point stance to make the defense calls. I normally played linebacker for ND and unfortunately at the time, I was the only All-American my senior year on the team. It was the College Football Coaches All-American Team and wasn't the Kodak Team. Since it wasn't the Kodak, team I'll never forget it. I was passed over for guy from Colorado, who had a 4.0 average and was an engineer. That kept me out of the College Football Hall of Fame. That's the only Hall of Fame that I'm not in. I was a first team All-American, but it wasn't on the Kodak team.

Draft

I had the choice to go to the Patriots in Boston, which was 90 miles from my home, or go to Calgary, which was 3,500 miles from my home. It was not a difficult decision to make. Number one I didn't want play in the Canadian Football League, and number two I got to be close to home.

I was drafted in the 13th round by the Patriots so it was not like I had a layup going there. I had to make the team. It was a long climb, but obviously I got lucky and I made the team. I spent seven great years there. I love Boston and I love the people. Everybody still thinks I'm coming back. They still can't believe that I'm living in Miami. It's remarkable. I made such great friends on the Patriots, Gino Cappelletti, Larry Eisenhauer, Houston Antwine, Jimmy Hunt, Bob Dee, Babe Parilli, Larry Garron, and Ron Burton. It was just a great team. It was just a really solid bunch of guys and it was just wonderful to be part of it.

Trade To Miami Dolphins

Obviously what ended up happening was Mike Holovak was fired and they brought Clive Rush in from the New York Jets. Clive's claim to fame was that he coached Joe Namath and Namath beat the Baltimore Colts in the Super Bowl. He said that I was making too much money. I think I was making, $30,000 a year and I was going to law school at night. I was going to get my degree in 1968. After got my law degree, he got there and said to me, "What we really don't need is an attorney for the defense." He basically traded me for nothing. He traded me for Kim Hammond, John Bramlett, and a fifth round draft choice. I was one of the best players on the team. He got nothing for me.

Don Shula

I was there one year before Don Shula. George Wilson was the coach. Things didn't change until Shula got there. When he became coach, things dramatically changed.

He had unbelievable assistant coaches. The assistant coaches were Monte Clark on the offensive line, Bill Arnsparger as the defensive coordinator, Mike Scarry as the defensive line coach, Tom Keane as defensive back coach, and Howard Schnellenberger as the receivers' coach. It was a super bunch of assistant coaches. You put all those guys together in one room and you're going to come up with a good game plan every game. You may not win every game, but it's not because of the game plan. Maybe we didn't execute the game plan, but it was just a stellar group of assistant coaches. The great thing about Don Shula is that not only did I learn a lot about football from Don, but also he really is the most highly principled individual I've ever been around in the game of football. I took those principles into my business life and it really helped me succeed. He's just a super, super leader.

Joe Thomas
Joe Thomas traded for me. He traded for Paul Warfield. He made the Larry Little trade. Then you follow him up with Bobby Beathard and then George Young. If you look at the transition within the Dolphin franchise, you can understand why during those years the team was so good.

Joe also traded for Marv Fleming. He picked up Wayne Moore on waivers. He picked up Jim Langer on waivers. He picked up Bob Kuechenberg on waivers. You've got Langer, a Hall of Famer, and Kuechenberg who should be in the Hall of Fame. It's a travesty that he's not in the Hall of Fame. I still to this day don't understand that. Then you have Wayne Moore who was just a great tackle for us. Along the way he picked up Doug Swift, our stunning linebacker, Mike Kolen was drafted. All in all it was a pretty good way to reap the harvest.

The No-Name Defense
Tom Landry was preparing for the Super Bowl against us and he looked at the roster and said, "You know, these guys are nothing but a bunch of no names." Someone picked it up in the paper and that's how we got tagged with "The No-Name Defense". We really embraced it because we weren't the Purple People Eaters and we weren't the Fearsome Foursome. We were The No-Name Defense and it was something that I think we all embraced.

1972 Miami Dolphins
No one expected us to go undefeated. That was not our goal. Our goal was to get back to the Super Bowl. We had embarrassed ourselves so much the year before getting slaughtered by the Dallas Cowboys. I believe it was 24 to 6 or something like. It was very embarrassing, so our whole objective was to get back to the Super Bowl and the wins just sort of happened. The key to any team having a great record is having someone, either offensively or defensively, step up to make an incredible play and that's what happened to us game after game. Someone stepped up. Manny Fernandez kicks off the ball, takes the ball from the quarterback from the Bills and helps win the game. I intercept Joe Namath on the goal line to help win the game. Paul Warfield makes a great catch against Cleveland in the playoff game that sets up the winning touchdown. I can go on and on about every game that we played. Someone stepped up and made an incredible play to help us win. All of a sudden you look up and you're 14 and 0, and you're in the playoffs. It really wasn't something that we played for; it's just something that just happened.

Pro Football Hall Of Fame

When you're talking about 273 players who played the game being in the Hall of Fame, that's the epitome of success. That's recognition by your peers. You were good enough to be in a select group. I'm in the Patriots Hall of Fame. I'm in the Dolphins Hall of Fame. I'm the Italian Hall of Fame in Chicago, which is an honor, but the NFL Hall of Fame is the epitome of success.

Miami Dolphin quarterback Bob Griese, left, and Nick Buoniconti
Photograph courtesy Associated Press

Chapter 45

Dave Robinson

College:
Penn State

Career History:
1963-1972 Green Bay Packers
1973-1974 Washington Redskins

2013 Inductee Pro Football Hall of Fame

<u>Vince Lombardi</u>
Vince Lombardi Jr. said that Wellington Mara and his dad were very close. Marie Lombardi, Vince Lombardi's wife told me Wellington Mara called Vince in his office and said, "Vince, I know what you want to do. I'll tell you what. New York City is not ready for an Italian head coach. If I were you, I'd take the job in Green Bay." She said that Vince vowed at that time never to lose to the New York Giants, and he never did. That was the end.

The other thing he told him was Allie Sherman was going to be the next head coach. He was of after Tom Landry left being an assistant coach.

I don't know how the true this story is because I've heard it about three or four times in different places, but the Giants received a kickoff in overtime and they went down the field. It was fourth and one. Lombardi told Jim Lee Howell, the Giants Head Coach, "We should go for it. Any good team can make one yard." Tom Landry said, "The odds are against it. We should punt the ball and let my defense hold them." Vince was adamant they should go for it. Jim Lee Howell went with Landry and they punted the ball. The other team got the ball, marched down the field, scored and beat them. Lombardi always felt that he was right.

Fast-forward another 18 or 19 years. On December 31, 1967, we were on the one-yard line, third and goal, with 16 seconds to go in the game. We call timeout; Lombardi goes in and tells Bart Starr to go for it. Mel Renfro told me that Tom Landry told him, "Play the outside. The only play they could run is a bootleg or a pitch out or an option play. They got to have something where they can throw the ball to kill the clock."

Some of the defensive guys from Dallas were playing to the outside, soft, which made the block a lot easier on Jethro Pugh, who was trying to get outside to stop a sweep that was going to come right up the middle. We made it. Vince Lombardi felt vindicated at that moment. He beat the Dallas Cowboys right up the middle. That's how it was.

One of my greatest plays happened the year before that down in Dallas. They had fourth and two with 52 seconds left. What did he run? He ran a bootleg with Don Meredith. Similar situation there, but thank God Meredith was slow enough that I caught him and it was no problem. That's how we maintained a lead of 34-27 and won the game, which allowed us to go to Super Bowl I. I think Vince was very, very happy with those two victories, because it proved his point to Tom Landry.

It was true euphoria when I got to Green Bay in 1963. I'd been moving around in a lot of positions after the All-Star game, defensive end, offensive end, and then finally linebacker. When I got there, he felt obligated to tell me what the problem was. He said, "You'd be a great linebacker. We won in 1961 and 1962. Our goal is to win three consecutive World Championships. No one has done this since play was initiated. I don't want any distractions. You'll be the first black starting linebacker in the National Football League. I don't want any newspaper articles or anything else. If anyone asks you about this, tell them to see me." I told them to see Vincent and that was it.

In 1967, he won a third consecutive World Championship. How would you feel if your goal in life was to win an Emmy or something for radio and all of a sudden you've got it not once, not twice, but three years in a row? That's how Vince Lombardi felt about winning three consecutive world championships. We were all so close to our coach that if he was happy, we were ecstatic.

College All Star Game
We never thought we stood a chance. We went into the locker room with 10-10 at halftime. You have to remember that Ray Nitschke didn't play at all. They had Urban Henry out there at defensive end, and he was kind of weak. Urban Henry was not the greatest defensive end in the world.

On top of that, Otto Graham did some things most coaches never do. We went for it on fourth down on our own 30-yard line and stuff like that; crazy moves like that. See, everybody expected him to lose. Otto Graham just made ridiculous calls. We were lucky enough that they worked.

Everything had to fall in place for the All-Stars to win. Later, Vince told me, "If I could have got that All-Star team, the whole team as it was and kept them together, I could win a Championship in three years." Back in 1967, I knew that Vince Lombardi would have kept that team. It was a great team. Guys on that team started all over the league, both in the AFL and NFL. If he could have got them together and trained them, I think he could have won a championship with that team.

Comparison Of Football In 1960s and Today
One thing you've got to remember is that there were only 12 teams in the league. It went to 14 teams later on. They only took the draft choices and the top 20 guys, so they only had 36 people on a team. My rookie year it went to 38. There were only 38 men per team, on 14 teams. You could take the cream of the crop and get them into the league.

Now you have 32 teams with 53 men per team. The problem is, you don't get ball players who are well rounded like Herb Adderley, who played four sports. I think he could have done it all, play running back or defense or anything. Thank God he was my corner. I loved that.

Ballplayers are hard to come by now because there are so many specialists. These guys specialize in high school and they only know one part of the game.

In college, we had to learn both positions, offense and defense. College kids today play offense or defense. Some can switch over, but when they do they have to learn all over again. It was a whole different time, a whole different era. I think when I played it really was the golden age of football. I'm just happy to have played during that time.

When I came up, I was the fourth linebacker, the swingman, until Ray Nitschke broke his arm. Like I always told Nitschke, "Bad break for you, good break for me." That's when I started.

When I was in college, there was an article in Sports Illustrated by Dan Currie about how to key in pro football. I read it, and I didn't really understand what keying was in college. I went to Penn State, a great school, but they hadn't really taught me the keys. I took that article and I carried it with me for six to eight weeks. I idolized Dan Currie. I walked on the field the first day, and who's the starting left linebacker for the Green Bay Packers I'm trying to win a position with? Dan Currie. That team was so good, so many good ballplayers, that when you came in as a rookie you knew you had to be able to do everything.

One last point, I was going along fine during my rookie year. I was the number one draft choice. My wife was home pregnant with twins. I was laughing one day about how Jerry Kramer was kicking off and couldn't get the ball past the 20-yard line. Someone told Vince Lombardi that I'd kicked off at Penn State. He came to me and put his arm on my shoulder and said, "I hear you kicked off at Penn State." I said, "Yes, sir." He said, "Why aren't you kicking off here?" I said, "Well coach, I'm playing the new position of linebacker and I want to practice so hard and study my book, and I want to be the best linebacker in the National Football League." He said, "Well son, your best chance to make this team is as a kicker."

I kicked off because Paul Hornung was gone, so we didn't have a kickoff man. I kicked until I got hurt. That's how it was. There were great men at every position. If you weren't multifaceted, if you didn't have more than one talent, you weren't going to make the Green Bay Packers.

First Black Outside Starting Linebacker In NFL

Now Bobby Bell and I came in the same year. He went to the other league, the AFL. The AFL was a funny league. The AFL brought more black ball players in. I don't know if this is necessarily true but the NFL had sucked up just about all the good white ballplayers in the country. The only white ballplayers that were getting into the AFL were guys who were played out and their career was over. Guys who were cut by an NFL team, they would raid off the cut list.

The AFL needed ballplayers badly. They went down to the black colleges and got that. They were really pioneers in fully integrating the game of football. But there were none in the NFL. I was a first-round draft choice. Herb Adderley was the first black man to be drafted in the first round by the Green Bay Packers, ever, and I was the second. That shows how things have changed. Now, everything is so different.

Racial Climate In Green Bay In 1960s

My roommate had come from Utah State. At Utah State he started dating a Mormon girl who happened to be white of course. All Mormons were white in those days. They were dating and they wanted to get married, her parents were going to disinherit her and everything else.

Word got out that they wanted to get married. Word got back to Vince Lombardi that he was bringing this white woman to Green Bay and cohabitating with her. Vince called him in and said, "What are your intentions?" He said, "I'd like to marry her. I don't want to get blackballed." Vince told him, "You marry her and make an honest woman of her. Let me take care of all that."

Pete Rozelle came all the way to Green Bay to tell Vince, "Do not let this happen." There were no white and black marriages, he thought, in the league. Vince told Pete Rozelle, "You run the NFL and I run the Green Bay Packers."

Nobody who was married to a white woman, no matter what the team, brought his wife to camp. You have to understand, we're talking about pre-civil rights. The Civil Rights Act was in 1964. People denied you rooms in Green Bay. That was perfectly legal. That was their right. People denied you service in a restaurant. It was their right. They were not breaking the law.

Vince Lombardi would not take any kind of guff. Vince would react the same way if you had a white wife or with anybody else. He had a zero tolerance for racism and he felt as though any type of discrimination was wrong. Now Pete Rozelle, it was none of his business as to whom anybody was going to marry. To me, it was like a racism thing for him to come in and try to stop something like that. At the same time, Rozelle knew that there was racism going on in NFL that he did nothing about.

Cookie Gilchrist was a great running back, but he was dating a white girl or married to her, I'm not sure which. He was blackballed out of the league. He had to go to Canada where he played his best football. In his later years when he came back with the Buffalo Bills he was still good enough to make the all-AFL team.

When Vince got to Green Bay in 1959, there were only two African-Americans on the team and they were banned from going to certain bars and restaurants in the city of Green Bay. The story I heard was that the owners of all those bars were invited into Vince's office and they sat down and they pleaded their case. We don't mind this, but our customers don't want to do it, blah, blah, blah, blah, blah. Vince was opposed to this and said, "Listen, you bought, worked, and earned those places. They're your places. You can serve or not serve anybody you want to. That's the American way. I'll go to war to defend your right to deny service to anybody you want to, and you have my word that as of this day, no black Green Bay Packers will go in any of your establishments. As a matter of fact, even white players won't be there because you're off limits." I heard the guy said, "You can't do that. You'll kill us if we can't have any ballplayers in our establishments. You can't do it." Vince said, "I just did." What happened next, as the story goes, was that the whole town instantly became integrated. This was before Herb Adderley got there. They instantly started allowing the black ballplayers to go wherever they wanted in Green Bay restaurants, bars, and anywhere else. The thing I admire the most about Vince Lombardi, there was no big paper, no big band, no NAACP had to come in and march, no Jesse Jackson or

Al Sharpton came in with great speeches. One man, very quietly, in a room with seven or eight bar or restaurant owners integrated the whole city of Green Bay in a matter of minutes.

That is why he was a great football coach, a better than average football player, but his influence on that city, his influence on the National Football League and consequently, his influence on America is far more than anybody realizes. I think the world of Vince Lombardi, I really do.

I grew up in Mt. Laurel Township in Burlington County, where NFL Films is today. The difference between Green Bay and where I grew up is, to use an old term, night and day. The first time my wife came up with me to Green Bay we rented a two-bedroom house. It had two bedrooms, a living room, kitchen, and a bathroom, that's it. That was what we had. My landlord told me, "I know it's not much of a house, but it's probably a lot better than what you have to live in back in New Jersey."

That's when I realized, people in Wisconsin didn't understand. They thought that every black person in America, Philadelphia, New Jersey, and the East Coast, lived in roach infested, ghettos. I told him, "You know what, neither me nor my friends in New Jersey would live in your house." He was offended by it until my wife took out pictures and showed where we lived and our neighborhood.

I wouldn't say the people were biased, I think that they were uninformed. They truly felt, because of the news reports and the lack of black TV shows, that every black person in the East lived in some form of the ghetto. As you know, it wasn't right. I have no ill will toward the people. I know that they were uninformed, but that was what it was.

I got a house one year because the lady had an argument with the next-door neighbor. She said, "I'll get even with you. I'll rent to blacks."

Elijah Pitts brought his wife in during the preseason, and she was the only African-American woman in town except for a couple of people who came in, go-go dancers primarily. She couldn't take it; so she went back to Arkansas to student teach.

The next year, I tried to explain to my wife that none of the black wives were there, and she should just stay in New Jersey and I'd go to Green Bay. Her mother told her "A woman's place is with her husband." I had to go along with that, and she went with me. Once Pitts saw that my wife had moved in, he brought Ruth up. Ruth and Elaine, my wife, were really the first black Packers wives in the city of Green Bay. What they went through was horrendous.

First of all, they were attractive young ladies. Every young black lady in Green Bay at that time, besides them, were usually go-go dancers or prostitutes or something of that sort. They were approached every time they went downtown by the farmers coming into the city for the first time. Some of the things they said … it almost wasn't what they said but the way they said it. Even the way they said hello. They didn't think they were talking to a Packer wife or someone of stature. They thought there were talking to a low-life go-go dancer or prostitute. Many days, Ruth and Elaine came home upset with what was going on downtown. We were recognized downtown, but our wives were a different story.

The thing I regret the most is that my wife passed away five years ago, and she won't be standing there beside me when I get inducted into the Pro Football Hall Of Fame. She is the one who, in my opinion, was the real Hall of Famer for what she did, put up with, and the way she held our family together. I can't say enough about her.

Mike Ditka

I played against Mike Ditka at Penn State when Pitt was our archrival. I went to Penn State for one reason. I wanted to get an education and my mother couldn't afford to send me to school. I only played football in college because that's the way I got a scholarship. That's why I think Herb Adderely went there. We just wanted to get an education. I'm appalled now when kids are coming out of high school talking about what they are going to do with their bonus money when they sign in the National Football League. I never dreamed of playing in the National Football League. I just never had the desire to. I just want to get my degree and get out of school.

In my sophomore year, Mike Ditka was All-American. In the Pitt-Penn State game, I went up against Mike and had a decent game. I didn't crush Mike, but Mike didn't crush me either. The next year, Mike was NFL Rookie of the Year. I said to myself, if he is the best in the NFL, then I could play with those guys.

Not until the end of my junior year, did I even think about playing in the National Football League. I only thought about going there because I wanted to get married and I needed some money. I thought I would go in and play five years, get vested, and come out. The rest is all history.

George Preston Marshall

George Preston Marshall was a defined racist. He admitted to being a racist. He's the one who said that there's not a black man in America good enough to play on his team in 1961. That's why when they boycotted the Redskins at Washington Stadium, he finally succumbed and went out and drafted Ernie Davis. He then traded Ernie Davis to Cleveland for Bobby Mitchell, who was the first black to play on their team.

Also, the rumor until the day he died was there was a meeting in 1932 where George Preston Marshall told all the owners, "White people will not pay to see black people make money playing football." If you check the records, there were black players in 1932, but in 1933, there was not a black player on any team in the National Football League. They all deny that therewas this agreement.

There were no more blacks until 1946 when the Cleveland Browns and the Los Angeles Rams integrated. This was two years before Jackie Robinson integrated baseball. There was black, then there was the white era from '33 to '46, and then there was the modern era. When it came back around, all of those different things about what black guys could do and couldn't do came around because our buddy once said that black guys could run. It can be real but they didn't have the heart to play defense.

You got guys like Jim Parker, the greatest offensive lineman the world ever saw, and they said he couldn't play defense. Willie Wood was a quarterback, a great quarterback at USC, but there was no question when he came to the NFL, he was going to play defense.

Pro Football Hall Of Fame Induction

My first experience with the Hall of Fame was in 1963, its first year. I used to have little quiet conversations with Vince Lombardi, and Vince Lombardi would tell me how much it meant to go there. We were one of the first teams to play in the Hall Of Fame Game. I loved this man. I started watching and I tell you, I can't even put into words what it would mean to me as a person, as a professional football player to be in the Hall of Fame.

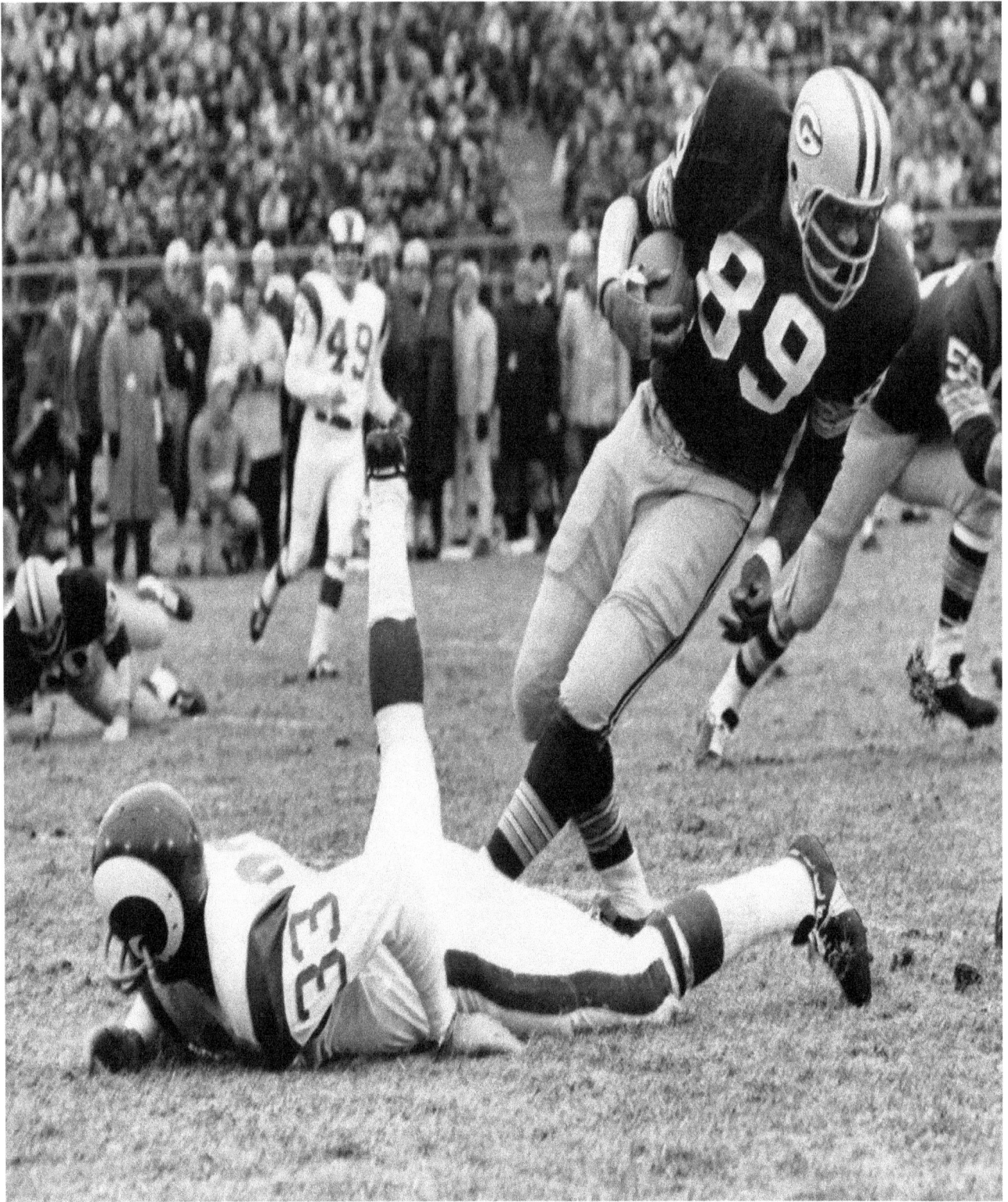

Photograph courtesy Associated Press

Chapter 46

Chris Hanburger

College:
North Carolina

Career History:
Washington Redskins (1965-1978)

2011 Inductee Pro Football Hall of Fame

College Choice
I was in the Army right out of high school. The University of North Carolina stayed in touch with me while I was in the service. They even talked to me about getting out of the service early. I had signed up under a two-year program. It was referred to as a Federal Reserve program. It was two years of active duty and four years of reserve duty. They stayed in touch with me while I was in the military and of course, I didn't get out early. I told them, "Look, I agreed to two years of active duty. That's what I'm going to do. If you guys are still interested in me when my time's up, I'll look into it with you." That's what I did.

Of course, I had to go to summer camp for four years after I got out of the Army. I could file for educational interference while I was in college where I didn't have to attend monthly meetings and things like that. I just had to go to summer camp for two weeks. So it worked out pretty good. That's how I ended up at the University of North Carolina.

Favorite Team
It didn't make any difference. You played both ways then and the way they had it set up, on offense I was a center and we'd flip over on defense and I played linebacker. It didn't make much difference. You didn't get off the field very often, especially when we were all on special teams.

North Carolina
I enjoyed it. I looked at it just like I looked at pro football, a means to an end. I ended up getting a full scholarship. It paid for my education. I struggled since I'm not the brightest guy in the world. I ended up majoring in American History, which I've always been fascinated by. All my courses were from about the year 1700 up to the current times. I'm one of those nuts that drive down the road and when I see a historical marker, I'm going to pull over and read it.

It was a chance to get a college degree, which I had to struggle to do. I had to take courses that were related in some way or another so when I was studying for one, I was actually studying for two or three of them at the same time. It just made it a lot easier for me. In fact, when I was there I don't know of any athlete who got special treatment at all, none whatsoever.

I've never, even today, been a big football fan. People are probably bothered by me saying that, but when I was in college I knew about professional football, I just never watched it.

Draft
When the Redskins drafted me, I think I was away from college. I think it was over a weekend. When I came back some of the guys said, "Do you know you got drafted by the Redskins?" I said, "You've got to be kidding me?"

I didn't do anything and about it. Five days later I go a call from the Redskins go to D.C. to see about signing a contract. They were playing at home and gave me two tickets. My wife and I went looking to sign a contract. I didn't even go to the game. I think I gave the two tickets to a bellhop after I signed the contract. We jumped into the car and headed back down to Chapel Hill.

"The Hangman" Nickname
I don't know how I got the nickname, "The Hangman". It's just one of those weird things. I guess mainly because I tackled high most of my career until they ruled that you couldn't do that anymore. I always remember when I went to my first Pro Bowl. Kansas City had a cornerback called "The Hammer". He got his bell rung real early in the game. I thought man, nicknames sure aren't good to have.

First Training Camp
I just figured I'd go to training camp and do the best that I could. If it didn't work out, I thought I'd enjoy it and try to hook up with another club. Things happened to work out in my favor. You live in the dark when you're in training camp. You don't know what the heck's going on. I remember the equipment manager came to me after we had been in training camp for a while and he said, "Would you like to have the number you had in college?" That number was 55. I said, "If it's available, that's fine."

I guess it was about a day later Sam Huff came up to me and he said, "Look, you keep working hard on special-teams, I think you've got a good chance to make the club." That was the first time that I felt a little relaxed about everything. I just didn't let any of the guys there intimidate me. I was just going to do the best that I could, study, and just try to excel all the time.

Sam Huff and I ended up rooming together for a couple of years during training camp and on the road. I've always told Sam, "The only reason you got to play a couple extra years is because I took care of you. I had to babysit you."

Vince Lombardi
I don't think any of us knew what to expect from him. I had heard stories about him and I think we were all in awe of the fact that he was getting back into coaching. I remember in training camp he mentioned we needed to go around the practice field at least three times before practice started. I'm walking around the practice field and he pulls up in a little golf cart. I don't think he knew my name, but he said, "Mister, he called everybody Mister, how come you're walking around the field? All the other guys are jogging." I said, "Coach in the meeting all you said we had to go around the field. You didn't say how we had to go around." He put his head down and

shook it back and forth and said, "My God, I have mellowed." I thought it was kind of neat and I said,

"Coach, I'll tell you what. I'll jog around this field three times from now on." That's what I started doing. Vince Lombardi worked you real hard, he really did.

Otto Graham was a fantastic player. He really was, but a head coach is only as good as the players he has and as good as his assistants are. It was a much more lax atmosphere with Otto Graham then it was with Coach Lombardi.

If I recall, I think he had gotten sick. He was in Georgetown hospital. I believe we were on strike at that time. Most of us who lived in the area would go to the Georgetown Athletic Field and practice on our own. Edward Bennett Williams was the owner of the club at that time and of course, he got chauffeured everywhere he went. All of a sudden we're on the field and a limousine pulls up with Coach Lombardi in it. He gets out and you could tell he was very weak.

We were just starting to get warmed up for practice and doing his famous, what he called, "ups and downs". He talked to us for a few minutes and you could just tell he was worn out. I think he wanted to stay and visit and talk some more, but he just got back in the car and left and that was the last time I ever saw him.

I think it affected everybody. We all had so much respect for him; we were all just hoping that he could pull through what he was fighting. It just didn't work out.

He had this crazy thing called "up and downs" where you had to jog in place and he would say, "Down, and you just collapsed on the ground." You know more than hit the ground, and he'd say, "Up, and you got to jump up and start running." He'd have you do 50, 60 of those crazy things. People would get sick, throwing up. Then he'd make you run toward one end of one of the field, and then he'd make you run all the way down the other end and around the goal post and back to where you had started.

I'll never forget one day we finished one of those things and he announced that would be the last day of it. He told Sonny Jurgensen, "Sonny, lead them down around the goal post." Sonny said, "I'll try coach. I'll try."

George Allen
It was really nice to have a head coach that was very defense-oriented and it was a wonderful system to operate under. We had a ton of defenses. We called all the defenses on the field. We didn't have to worry about watching the sidelines for signals or anything like that. The preparation was very extensive. Prior to him getting there, I know from my standpoint, there wasn't a whole lot of emphasis on defense. There wasn't a whole lot of emphasis on special teams either. He brought all that to the Redskins.

Of course, I think the defense got a little special treatment compared to the offense. When he came on board, Edward Bennett Williams always joked. He said, "I gave him an unlimited budget and he already exceeded it when he built Redskin Park." It was kind of funny. We started off in the initial building and we would meet there as a team. The defense got to stay in that main room and the offense guys had to break down into some of the real small offices that the offense coaches had.

All the offense guys started complaining. Next thing you know, Coach Allen is giving the offense the defense room and then he's having another addition put onto the building just for the defense. We couldn't even wear shoes in it. It had this real nice carpet in there. It was a great big old room, a real nice facility. Coach Allen really took care of the players. His preparation was just unbelievable as far as getting the club ready.

Deacon Jones

Deacon was a character. I remember going out to LA to play a game. I don't remember if it was an exhibition game or regular season game. Anyway, we get out there and Coach Allen appoints Deacon as one of the honorary captains for the game. We're in the locker room and Deacon gets up and gives a speech.

He says, "Follow me." He doesn't realize that we're in the visitor's locker room. He leads us down some hall that doesn't even go to the field. Now we finally get regrouped and get out and get introduced. They introduce Deacon and he runs out on the field. He gets to the sideline and he sits right down and hooks up to the oxygen tank.

Redskins Cowboys Rivalry

I think Coach Tom Landry and Coach George Allen had a tremendous amount of respect for each other. I don't think either one of them trusted each other at all. I think they were both paranoid about people spying on them. The press caused a lot of it. I'm sure Coach Allen put Diron Talbert up to saying things about Roger Staubach in the press and things like that. It's kind of funny. I never got caught up in all that. I think it was because I was fortunate enough to go to quite a few of the Pro Bowls. The Cowboys would always have a lot of players on the Pro Bowl squad, and I got to know a lot of them. It was just another game to me. I just never get caught up in all hoopla.

Super Bowl VII

As far as I was concerned it was just another game. You still played as hard as you could and you wanted to win. I know when we went to the Super Bowl in 1972, we weren't expected to go anywhere in the playoffs. We get to California and different manufacturers for shoes and apparel and stuff come by the hotel we're staying in to give us things. The stuff they wanted to give us was in Cowboy colors.

Everybody thought the Cowboys were going to go to the Super Bowl. The Super Bowl was just another game. We played Miami. That's the year they went undefeated. They had a heck of a football team. That was so long ago.

If I remember, the goal post hadn't been moved to the end of the end zone at that point. We had a couple of chances to offensively put some points on the board and just couldn't do it. The score probably should have been worse than it was. I think it ended up being 14-7. The only points we got were on a mishandled field-goal attempt, I think by the Dolphins. It just didn't work out in our favor.

Calling Signals

When Jack Pardee retired, it just became a natural thing for me to start calling plays and I didn't have any problem with it. Coach Allen had always been one to tell us we must take the film home, watch it, and study it. I had been doing that even before calling signals. When I started calling signals, everything just seemed to fit in. It was a lot of fun to control the game right there on the field.

We always had a defensive game plan with the defenses we wanted to use. If necessary, we could make the adjustments right away. We didn't have to wait until halftime or go to the sidelines. We could automatically audible if we saw something out there. If I saw something and felt pretty good about it, I could just audiblize real quick. I think we had close to 150 different audibles. It's just made it a lot of fun.

Pro Football Hall of Fame Induction

Well, I never even thought about it, to be very truthful with you, and I mean that sincerely. I played, and I enjoyed it. I've been out for like 33 years, and what's happened is just wonderful. I look back, and I've always thought there were a lot of great players that played before I did, that I played with and against, and guys that are playing now that will never get nominated, let alone get elected into the Hall of Fame. It's unfortunate. I guess I've been lucky all my life, and I feel like I've just been real lucky with what's happened.

I somebody asked me, "What was your reaction when you got the news that you'd been elected?" I say, "Well, truthfully I thought, here goes my normal routine. I've got to go get packed to go to Dallas to the Super Bowl."

It was kind of funny. When I was nominated, I just happened to be watching the news on TV that morning, and all of a sudden up on the TV screen, we've got one of those crazy systems where the ID caller thing flashes up there, and it had "HOF" and a number. I'm thinking what in the devil is that, so I answered the phone and of course it was the Hall of Fame. I hung up, and not five minutes later my son calls, and he said, "Dad, are you aware that you just got" ... and I said, "What are you talking about?" Of course I knew. He said, "I'm getting emails and phone calls from all over the country." I said, "Well, then you better start getting your speech ready."

I just decided that I wasn't going to say a whole lot. I wasn't going to pre-plan anything. I was just going to speak from the hip, keep it short and concise, and get the heck out of there. That's what I tried to do. In fact, the Hall of Fame called me and they wanted to know if I had written a speech. I said, "No." They said, "It's very intimidating to be up there", and I said, "I'm not worried about it. I'm not writing a speech." I said, "Some of these people get up there and talk a half hour, 45 minutes. That isn't me and it isn't going to happen." I didn't write anything down for the speech. I just got up there and talked. I think I was up there between seven and nine minutes at the most, and that was probably five minutes too many.

Greatest Asset

Ironically, it may have been my quickness and speed. I certainly didn't have a lot of size. I'd go to training camp maybe weighing 215 to 218, and toward the end of the season, I would be down to a couple of hundred pounds. We always had weigh-in one day a week. I didn't have an assigned weight, but I would put on a heavy sweatshirt, tape some two and a half pound weights around my waist, and jump up on the scale. They always thought I was a lot bigger than I was.

John Hannah Said You Were the Smartest Player He Ever Played Against

I've heard that and I appreciate him saying that. It's very nice of him to make a comment like that. I don't know why he would say something like that. We hardly ever played against them, but it was a nice compliment.

Conrad Dobler

I think he got a bad rap. He was just a very aggressive player. He probably made a few hits after the whistle blew, but that's football. As long as they were legal, that's part of the game. He was going to go 100% all the time no matter what, but I think he got a bad rap as being a dirty football player. I never thought of it that way.

Favorite Coach

Coach George Allen was my favorite coach, no question about it. He could be a pain in the tail at times, but he was a great coach to work with.

There were times during timeouts, whether we called them or the offensive team called them, I'd go over and see what he was thinking. He used to take and lick his thumb all the time. You'd say, "Coach, what have you got in mind?" He'd say, "Well I don't know," and he'd be licking that thumb. So, I'd just jog back into the huddle and call a defense.

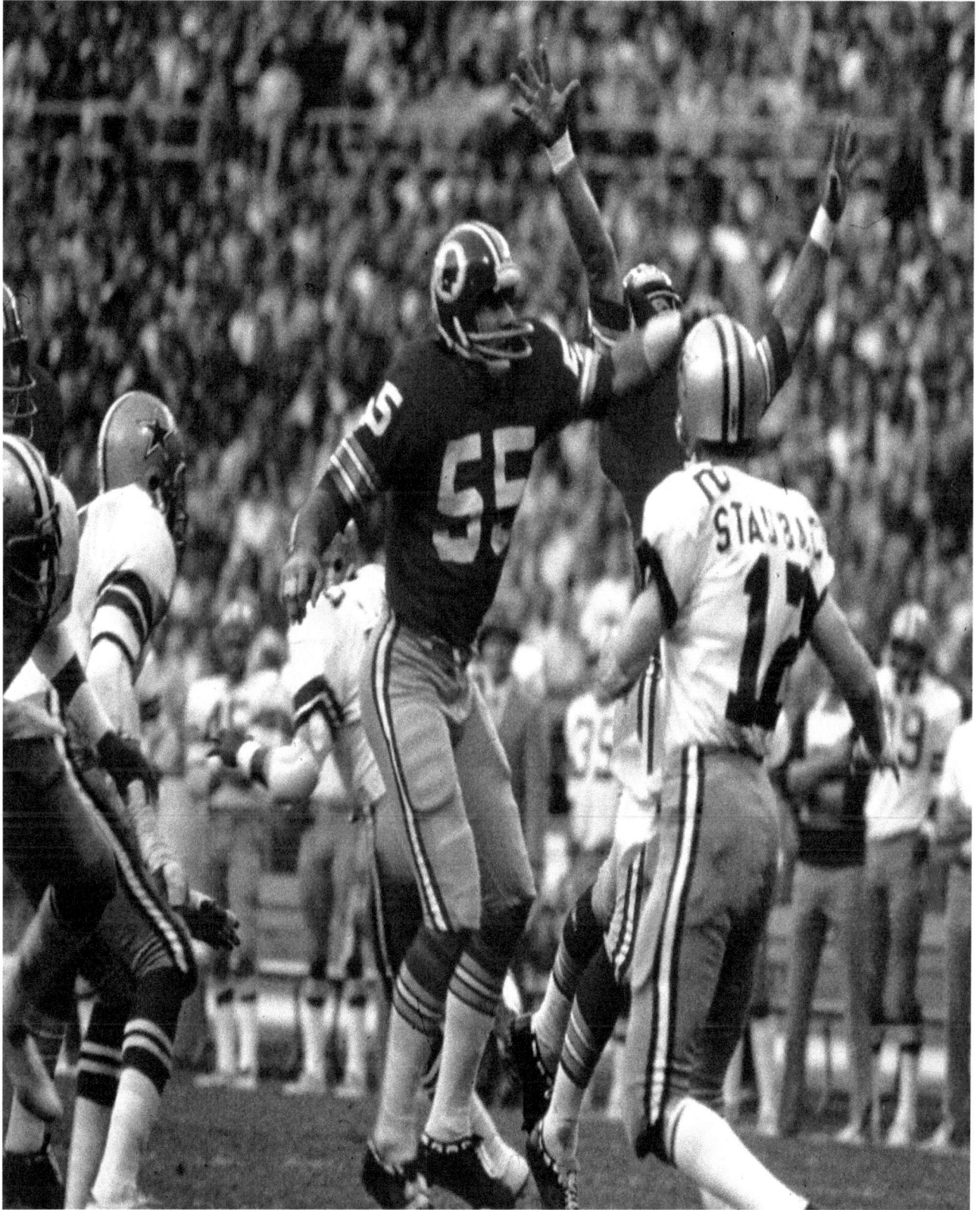

Washington Redskin Chris Hanburger pressures Dallas Cowboy Roger Staubach. Photograph copyright Associated Press

Chapter 47

Charley Taylor

College:
Arizona State

Career History:
Washington Redskins (1964–1977)

1984 Inductee Pro Football Hall of Fame

College Choice

I really wanted to go to Prairie View, a black school down in Houston, but didn't get in there. I ended up going to USC. After two weeks and one day I went into the teams' office. I was like the 16th running back.

I immediately called Frank Kush at Arizona State and asked, "Is that deal still good?" He said yes, I thanked him, and that's how I ended up there.

Arizona State

Arizona State was great, Dear old Frank. Frank hadn't gone crazy yet. He was not that crazy. He was just a tough guy. He had that Lombardi thing going, and we all knew it wasn't him because after practice he would talk to you in a different voice.

On the field if you fumbled the ball you had to do laps. He would take the whole day to get through practice and meet and discuss. He was a character.

Frank would never give you a hard time if you did your job, took care of business, and played ball. That's all you had to do.

We practiced at night because it was so hot during the day. We had training camp in Basin, Arizona, up in the mountains. It was freezing up there. There were days we had to wear jackets to practice, because it was so cold. We had drinks all over the place, and the food was great.

NFL Draft

I thought I was definitely going to be a Cowboy, because Dallas was the only team that really showed interest in me. My roommate woke me up and said, "Hey man, come on get up, get up, you've been drafted by the Redskins." I knew absolutely nothing about the Redskins so I said, "Who?" He said, "The Redskins," and then Gil Brandt called me right after that. What happened was Dallas and the Redskins had the same record. They tied. They flipped a coin and Dallas lost. That's how I ended up going to Washington.

Switch From Running Back To Wide Receiver
After I got Washington, I was a running back for two years. When I was switched to receiver, having Bobby Mitchell as a teammate helped. I would ask him, "How do you do this? When do you do that?" It was a learning experience. It worked out, thank God.

We had two running backs Steve Thurlow and Joe Don Looney. Coach Otto Graham wanted to go with the big bull guys. He told me, "We're going to put you outside because we got the two guys in here." I understood that, not that they did any better, but he was happy.

Otto Graham coached me in the College All-Star Game and then two years later, he was my coach in Washington. He called me lazy before the College All-Star Game. I was the first one at practice, and I would leave first.

For him to tell the papers that I was lazy and I was the first one to leave practice was crazy. I was in Chicago. Who did I know in Chicago? Nobody.

Where was I going if I was leaving? I road the bus to practice. It was wild. Frank Kush wrote him a letter about it. Then two years later he's my coach in Washington. How about that?

I probably wouldn't have even been playing had the other running back not got hurt, and they needed a back. So he sent me in.

Vince Lombardi
I can see how those guys in Green Bay kind of loved him and hated him a little bit. He was tough, but he was also fair. He knew what he was doing; he knew how to win. He put together practice so you could win.

Playing Baseball At Arizona State
I played a little third base. I was there with Reggie Jackson. Frank Howard hit a ball off my knee and Frank Kush took me off the team. He said, "No more baseball for you sir." I played three games and that was it.

Sonny Jurgensen
It was a miracle man. Sonny was ahead of his time. The man could throw a ball with a hand behind his back. He was a great guy to work with.

George Allen
Vince Lombardi covered how to win. Then George Allen came in and gave us that little momentum to win. We cared about each other and we looked out for each other. That's what George did.

Billy Kilmer
He threw two spirals in his entire career. I couldn't believe it. I'm going down the sideline, I look back, and the ball is taking off. I go, "Whoa, I've got to go get this thing." He actually threw two spiral balls over thirty yards.

Jerry Smith

We had a tight end, a poor kid named Jerry Smith who also played with me in college. When they would double-team Bobby Mitchell, Roy Jefferson or me, then Jerry would kill them. He would score four or five times. So that took a little pressure off of me. They had to cover him a little bit.

Jerry was great. You know we lost him, but he was a heck of a friend. He was a little light for a tight end because he only weighed 217, but he was smart and we'd let him get the ball.

Was There Racial Tension?

No, not really. I didn't realize Washington had a problem with it until I got there because all our pre-season games were in Florida and places like that. In Virginia before a game, I went to Bobby Mitchell and he explained what was taking place. I had no idea.

Jack Kent Cooke

When Mr. Cooke took over, it was a whole different ballgame. He wanted to win. He was the right guy because he was at his best when we were losing games. He'd come in and half joke, "What are you on? You need something? We got it."

He was not afraid to spend money, but he'd spend it wisely. He'd always consult with the personnel people or the assistant coach. He would discuss it with everybody.

Deacon Jones

Deacon was unreal. You're talking about a guy who loved what he was doing. He was just unreal, a fast but big guy. I don't think we've seen anybody play the game as well as Deacon.

Joe Theisman

I played two years with Joe. Joe was just an athlete. He would go out there be it snowing, raining, whatever, and the ball never slipped out of his hand. He threw a tight spiral. He was just a great player. He just talked too much. He threw a strong ball.

Sam Huff

Sam taught me how to play the game. Sam taught me from the running back spot how the linebackers would take shots at you going across. He didn't tell me he was covering me until he knocked me out, then I had to knock him out. He was a tough guy, God bless him.

Coaching Art Monk, Gary Clark, Charlie Brown

Those guys made it easy. They were easy to work with. Their job was to just catch the ball. All I asked them to do was just catch the ball. We'll work on the rest of it; we could direct the rest of it. The only guy I had a little problem with was Desmond Howard. It took him a couple years to learn how to look at stuff up higher and reach. Good for him, he went to Green Bay and he was named MVP of the Super Bowl. You just have to be truthful with your players, and that's what I did. I would tell them you did it right or you did it wrong, one of the two. We corrected it if you did it wrong and kept on moving.

Doug Williams In Super Bowl

Doug is a tough guy because he had been in the hospital the night before. He came back and played the next day. Outstanding.

Pro Football Hall Of Fame Induction

I couldn't believe it. Of all the people who could call me, Bobby Mitchell was the guy to callme. I said, "You got to be kidding me." I knew I did fairly well, but I had no idea I had made that step being inducted into the hall. I thought I had to be pretty good to be with theseguys.

Washington Redskin Charley Taylor left with Billy Kilmer right Photograph courtesy Associated Press

Chapter 48

Bob Brown

College:
Nebraska

Career History:
Philadelphia Eagles (1964–1968)
Los Angeles Rams (1969–1970)
Oakland Raiders (1971–1973)

2004 Inductee Pro Football Hall of Fame

"Boomer" Nickname
When I was playing for the Eagles a defensive back friend of mine, Joe Scarpati, started calling me "Boomer" our rookie year. I was very, very attack oriented. It just stuck.

College Choice
It's a very interesting story. I wasn't really recruited by Ohio State. I talked to Nebraska and I just liked how they talked to me in terms of an opportunity to play. I didn't come from a great high school program in Cleveland, Cleveland East Tech. It just was a real good fit for me. I felt comfortable after talking with the freshman coach out there and so I took a shot.

Bob Devaney
Bob Devaney was just a wonderful, wonderful man. People who are too young don't remember the '60s. A lot of people forget about the '60s, and the transition that the country was going through. I couldn't have had a better coach, a guy whose door was always open. There were a lot of social issues going on, as you know in the country. He was just a top coach and maybe even a better human being. He was just a wonderful, wonderful man.

NFL Draft
I think I was talking to Charlie Taylor, and he said, "You know the 1964 class was quite aclass," and I told him, "You're absolutely right." There were a lot of very talented guys who came out. It was a fabulous, fabulous class of guys.

I think I was the second guy picked in the National Football League, and I think I was the first guy picked in the AFL. I took the NFL because, at that time, I thought it was the best football in the world. I didn't want to be my age now, 70, and look back and think, "Did I go in the AFL because I didn't think I could dance at the big dance?"

As far as not being a Cleveland Brown, it was a lot of fun playing in Cleveland when I was with the Eagles. I would look up in the stands, because I'd have a lot of friends sitting in the bleachers, yelling at me. These were people that I played against in high school and some people I went to high school with, and they were actually there watching me. I thought that was really a big thing for a young guy.

Joining Philadelphia Eagles
Both teams I played with treated me great. Of course, Philadelphia fans are unique in the sense that they not only love their football, they know the game. I played five years in Philadelphia and was never booed. I don't think many guys can say that. The fans were knowledgeable. They could be critical, but if you gave them what they expected to see when they paid their money, they were great fans.

Racial Tension In Philadelphia
I played on teams with guys who had played in the Southeast and Southwest Conferences. I'm sure at no time during their careers that these young guys had ever played with or against any athletes of color. There were things said that would be considered inappropriate. It was not a great time to play on any NFL team, especially one that was integrated. You had some fellows who had never played in an integrated environment.

Jim Ringo
I don't know how many years he played with Green Bay, but he was a very steady influence. He made the offensive calls as the center. He was not a big guy, if you remember, but he had great technique and was extremely quick. He was a great teammate, a great center, and a great Hall of Famer.

Weight Lifting
Nebraska was always a very innovative place. We had a weight room. Not a large one, but we did have weights. There were guys who were into lifting, so I started lifting out there. As a matter of fact, I just finished my weight program for today. I do it to this day. It's one of those things. It's a part of my DNA now. I knew that it made a difference. I felt that a lot of guys around the National Football League weren't lifting, and so it was putting me one up on them. It did not affect my quickness and my speed, and I think that's been proven more, and more today. Most programs, probably all the programs, have weight-lifting programs. I was lucky. I was not an innovator but I was a guy who got onboard and stayed onboard.

Timmy Brown
Timmy was quite exceptional, a turn the corner type of halfback. We use to run a play in Philadelphia called the 21 flip. I like to think that he liked for me to lead it. I know that I liked for him to be behind me. It was a great play and we got a lot of mileage out of it. I did, however, have an opportunity to play with Timmy in a couple of Pro Bowls that I went to.

Joining Los Angeles Rams
It was different in the sense that, back in those days, everyone thought that the best football in the world was in the old bumps and bruises division, the Western Division of the NFL. Without getting into a long story about why I ended up being traded to the Rams on the other side of the world, to me it was all football. It didn't matter, of course. The great part about it is that I had an opportunity to work every day against the best defensive end ever, David Deacon Jones, and to

work against guys like Merlin Olsen, Roger Brown, and Lamar Lundy. It only helped to put me in a situation where I was working against the very best linemen anywhere. We use to have some battles in practice. That was when one-on-one practice was a part of the daily routine. It was always a challenge, and it was always a good street fight.

George Allen
George would, with his first line guys, let us occasionally mix it up a bit. Basically George was a defensive genius. I believe he could design a defense to stop anything they're running today. George had a leaning toward the defensive guys. If there was water on the field he made sure that they quenched their thirst first. The rest of us had to push our way to the front of the line.

Pass And Run Blocking
I like to say I could do both well. I've always felt like, anything that was born from a woman, I can block. Short of being a transformer, I didn't care. It didn't matter if you called a 34-buck or a pass. I didn't have a preference. I was there to work. I was going to punch in and I was going to go to work.

Deacon Jones Claim He Was Best Defensive End Ever
I couldn't dispute it. I played during an era when I saw Carl Eller, Deacon Jones, Claude Humphrey, and L.C. Greenwood week in and week out. There was always a lot of talent out there.

Bob Lilly was like a cat. He was playing defensive tackle more then defensive end, so I didn't have that many experiences blocking Bob out. His record speaks for itself, but he was not playing defensive end when I was around.

Kenny Stabler
The thing that made Kenny so great is that he never complained. If someone brushed him, or touched him, or was in his face, he never said a word. I never believed that I needed a quarterback to be a leader. We were all out there getting paid. We were all professionals. Kenny never complained. If somebody touched him he never said, "Hey man, get these guys off me." He said, "Don't worry about it. We're going to win it."

Raiders Offensive Line
I played on a line alongside, Art Shell, a Hall of Famer, Gene Upshaw, a Hall of Famer, Jim Otto, a Hall of Famer, and George Buehler, a great guard. I don't know how many guys can say they played on a line that had four Hall of Famers at the same time. I don't know if that's ever happened.

Al Davis
I think the one great thing about Al is that you always knew where you stood with him. If he liked you I honestly believe he would go to the wall for you. If you didn't necessarily have a relationship with him, then that's just how that was too.

John Madden
The best experience I've had as a pro football player. He's everything he appears to be. He's nice, honorable, and funny. He knows when to get serious, too. He has great expectations of his players. He's the kind of a guy you want to give your best for, not only because you're being paid to, but because he's just a really, nice man.

The John you see on TV is pretty close to the John I know. He's just a funny guy. In Philadelphia, of course, I had great admiration and respect for Joe Kuharich, because he was my first coach. George Allen was the Ram experience, a different sort of experience. I would have to say that my Raider experience with John Madden was great. He made it a great experience, along with the guys on the team. The Raider guys were at one time, and maybe even today, a bunch of wild and crazy guys. It was a lot of fun in the locker room. We expected a lot from each other and we tried to truly be a band of brothers.

Ron Mix
Ron's a great weightlifter and a great tackle. He has great technique. We worked out together. The Raiders did not have the expensive weight room that they have now. When I started in Nebraska, weight lifting was not even in its infancy. We were probably one of the few schools doing it. The Raiders did not have an exceptional weight facility at all. I've always had Olympic weights at my house.

Pro Football Hall Of Fame Introduction
The Hall Of Famers always have a bet to see who will be the first guy to cry at the induction. You've got to think about income tax, biting your lip, or something bad. I had to, at least, because it was such a touching moment for me. To be honest, I thought that I would have been in the Hall of Fame sooner. I'm being very honest. You know, it wouldn't have been nearly as sweet as it was had my son as an adult introduced me.

This was the pinnacle of everything that happened in my past, from Cleveland East Tech, to the University of Nebraska, the Eagles, the Rams, and the Raiders. What else could I ask for? This was everything.

In all honesty, my Hall of Fame was every game I played, every player I played against. I just wanted to be able to do it in a way, so when it was over, that I felt I worked hard enough and did enough to be in. I wanted them to say, "Man, Bob Brown's getting robbed." At the end of the day, that's what it was all about for me.

Willie Davis
I'll never forget, I was a high school student and I was at Garfield Park. I was just watching some of the Browns work out before the season. Willie Davis called me over and we were talking about Grambling. He said, "Let me show you some things."

I think that was a fabulous turning point for me. When I had the opportunity to play against Willie in Green Bay, and had a chance to talk to him before the game, that was very exciting for me. I was able to see someone who was kind to me, nice to me, and trying to introduce me to some techniques. Later during the course of the game, he said, "I didn't teach you that." I said, "Well, I picked up a few things along the way." That was a great moment for me.

Comparing Todays Players With His Generation

We didn't make a lot of money, but that's not to say that these guys today don't play as hard, and don't deserve the piece of the pie that they're getting. I don't want to be one of those old guys who say, "Oh, it was better when I was doing it." It's a great game. We've passed the baton on to some great young players. They might not be quite like us because the environment that they're dealing with isn't like it was when I was a young guy coming up. It's still a great game. I think that we handed it off to some great young guys.

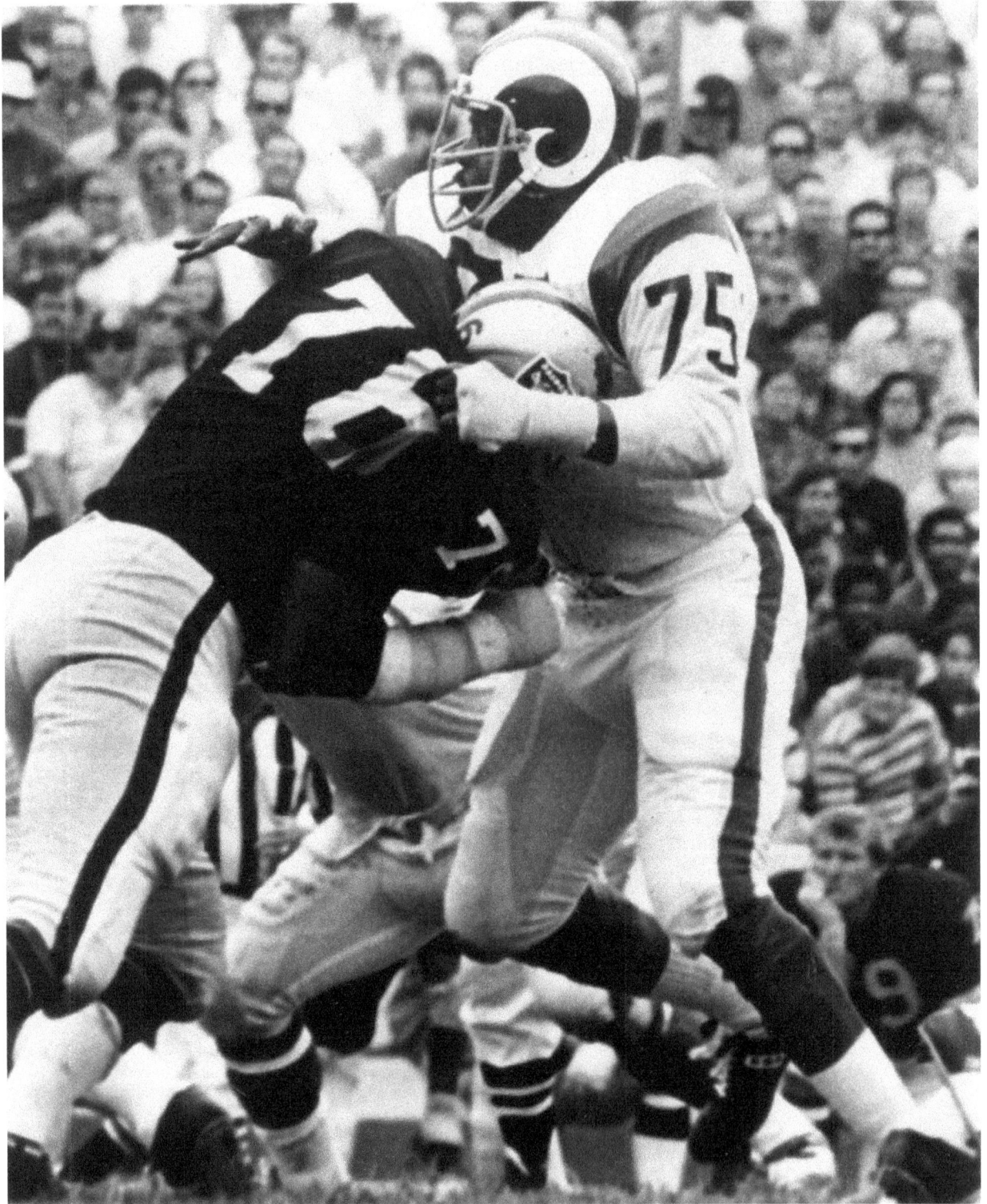

Oakland Raider Bob Brown takes on Los Angeles Ram Deacon Jones Photograph courtesy
Associated Press

Chapter 49

Mel Renfro

College:
Oregon

Career History
Dallas Cowboys (1964-1977)

1996 Inductee Pro Football Hall of Fame

College Choice
I was very versatile in high school. I played almost every position. My senior year, I played quarterback. It just came easy for me.

I was two weeks away from going to Oregon State. I had planned to go to Oregon State but two weeks before it was time to report, my parents sat me down and said, "You're not going to Oregon State. You're going to Oregon." I suppose Bill Bowerman, the Oregon track and field coach and future founder of Nike, got to my parents and convinced them that I should go to Oregon. I did what my parent's wished, so I ended up at Oregon.

Shoe Deal
Adidas came after me. They came to the Cowboys training camp and handed out a lot of free Adidas equipment. I wore a lot of those shoes and what not in my playing career. That's a little payback to Nike for not doing more for me when they had an opportunity.

Len Casanova
Len Casanova had an excellent group of coaches. Max Coley was my coach and Len was the boss, but Max taught us the ropes and told us what to do. He pretty much took care of us. Len was a teacher and he was tough. He wanted you to do your job and do your job right. If you made a mistake and did something wrong, he'd come down on you no matter if you were one of the best or just a mediocre player. He didn't have any favorites. Len was a very fair guy and well liked as a coach.

1964 Olympics
The 1964 Olympics were on the table. As a matter of fact, I was training for the Decathlon, playing football, going to school, and raising a family. It was a little too much for me for me to handle at that time. I chose a pro contract in the National Football League rather than stay and train for the Olympics.

First Encounter With Racial Discrimination While Playing At Texas
It was the first time that I noticed and encountered racial discrimination. It was a situation where we were told what we could and couldn't do and where we could go. Len Casanova tried to keep

everybody together as a team. We were very cautious about how we moved around as an entire team. It worked out okay. We had an outstanding game against the Texas Long Horns right up until late in the 3rd quarter, when I think we ran out of gas. We weren't used to that Texas heat. I think it was in the 90s at night. We were used to playing in 50- or 60-degree weather. We were leading, but we made some critical errors late in the 3rd quarter. They were rated number one in the nation that year. We had a good opportunity to beat them, but we let it slip away.

Ohio State
We played against Ohio State twice, my junior and senior year. When we got there and went into that stadium, there were 87,000 screaming Ohio fans. It was a hard challenge for us. We battled as hard as we could. I think I ended up with 15 unassisted tackles and 23 or 25 tackles all together. I planned free safety. I just remembered that big fullback coming up the middle. The first thing I saw were his knees coming at my head. It was a quite an experience but we had two great games against them. We battled them, but they were tough. We battled, and we gave it our all. We gave everything we had on the field.

Rice
The 1962 Rice game was very, very emotional for me. Being born in Houston and coming back and playing in an all white stadium was just remarkable. I had so much adrenaline. I was so pumped up. I probably had one of my best games ever. I think some of the news reports read, "Renfro Runs Rice Ragged." It was great to see. I can't remember how many of my relatives were there but I know my grandfather was there.

I didn't get to talk to him but I went over as close as I could get to the stands and waved to him. I think I probably teared up because of the special game I had. It was special to have relatives there that I hadn't seen in such a long time, watch me have such a great game. It was just a wonderful experience; something I'll never forget.

Oregon Teammates
We had great quarterbacks in Bob Berry and Doug Post. I was playing wide receiver, running back, and safety. I had my hands full back in those days. You didn't play just offense or defense; you played both. It was tough to do, but you stayed on the field the whole time. I was a punt returner, a kick-off returner, and played offense and defense without ever leaving the field. Sometimes, you were running an 80-yard touchdown, then you were out on the kick-off team, and then you end up on defense. That's the way it was. We had to do it; we had some great teams.

Draft
I thought maybe the Redskins or the 49ers were where I might go. I was passed over in the first round, because of the rumor that my hand was cut off or something. Dallas was the one that held up the draft for 8 or 10 hours. They passed over me and drafted Scott Appleton. Then, they traded him away before the draft was over. They immediately took me in the second round. I don't know what their theory was; maybe there was some deception. They ended up with a first round quality player in the second round.

Position Change In NFL

I came in as a running back and wide receiver, but they had a host of running backs and wide receivers. Tom Landry didn't feel like I would be able to start in my rookie year. He said, "I'm going to put you on defense and see what you do." Immediately, the defense improved tremendously. I was also returning punts and kick-offs. Actually, my first two years, I gained more yards returning kicks than the running backs gained. My first year I was at free safety, and my second year I was strong safety. I had such success returning kicks; Tom decided to move me to offense in my third year.

I started my third year at running back but was injured in the first league game. I broke a bone in my foot, so I didn't play for about 4 or 5 games. When I came back the foot wasn't right, I just couldn't make a cut. Tom decided to put me back on defense and put me back in at free safety. I played the rest of the year at free safety and still went to the Pro Bowl. The next year, they put me at cornerback and that's where I played for the next 10 years.

If I had stayed at free safety, I probably would have intercepted a hundred passes. I love the challenge at cornerback in man-to-man coverage. I was so good at it that in 1971, 1972, and 1973, I had almost no passes thrown in my direction. We'd play a game and they'd grade the film. They were only able to grade me on pursuit because the other team always threw the ball in the other direction. As a consequence, I didn't get the interceptions. After my 10th year, I wasn't able to earn Pro Bowl status because there was no just action over there. Not that I wasn't the same good cornerback. It's just that if you get no action, you get no statistics, and you're not going to end up in the Pro Bowl. Ten years was a good run and I appreciated that.

Bob Hayes

I had a technique where I was a reader. I would read the quarterback's steps, I knew the patterns, and I knew Bob Hayes' moves. I would just get back about 15 yards, wait for him to make his final moves, and then I'd go after him. One thing about me, I had tremendous quickness. I was running against Bob but between 60 and 80 yards, he'd go by me very easily. I really had a tough time covering him in practice and the opponents had a difficult time covering him anytime.

You line up 15 yards deep and when you back up you try to read the quarterbacks drop. You just go for it. It helps to get some deep help.

Dallas Cowboys Defense

Bob Lilly was the number one player for us but the leader was Lee Roy Jordan. He was the team captain, the play caller, and was tough as nails in that huddle. I tell you, he growled and said, "Man, we're not letting them in the zone." He'd say that a hundred times a game. Before every play, we came up with a purpose to stop them, not let them score. Lee Roy was pretty much the trooper who got us going with that.

Favorite Punt Return

I would not say I had a favorite, but I had a one in the fourth quarter of the Pro Bowl in 1971. I ran back two punts for touchdowns. They named me Offensive Player of the Game, Offensive MVP as the Defensive Back. The first punt was a short kick but it started bouncing down around our 12- or 13-yard line. The other team kind of relaxed and I scooped it up. I went right up the middle 83 yards for a touchdown. Just a few minutes later on a short punt, I fielded it on our 44-yard line, cut left, then cut back right, and went 56 yards for another touchdown. That was interesting to be able to score twice on punt returns in one quarter.

Favorite Super Bowl
I have to say that my favorite would be Super Bowl VI, because we shut down Paul Warfield, Jim Kiick, Larry Csonka, Bob Griese, and everybody. Bob Lilly was all over Bob Griese. We had a reputation for not being able to win the big game. We finally won the big game and got the monkey off our backs. That was by far the most exciting, but Super Bowl XII was my last game. I had a bad knee that year and didn't play very much. As a matter of fact, I didn't play the last 6 or 7 games of the season. In the first quarter of that Super Bowl, I think Benny Barnes went down. Mark Washington was the back up and Mark was over rubbing his knee, like he couldn't go. He said, "Fro", he called me his brother, Fro. He said, "Fro, can you go?" I went in early in the 2nd quarter and played three quarters of the game. We ended up winning. I was very thankful that I was able to play in that game because it was my last game. To win a World Championship in your last game and retire, it just doesn't get any better than that.

I kind of felt like it was my last game because my knee was totally gone. I had the cartilage removed, I think in April, just before training camp. I really wasn't supposed to play much and just wore out during the season. I felt like I couldn't play anymore unless they moved me inside to safety. They weren't going to do that because of Cliff Harris and Charlie Waters. Those guys were permanent fixtures there. Their number one draft choice was a cornerback and they wanted him to play. I felt like I was on my way out anyway.

Tom Landry
Tom Landry was a tough, smart coach. He left no stone unturned. He was a very strict, tough taskmaster, but he was fair. He was a great teacher. He taught us all how to play our positions as good as we could. Not only that, he taught us to be good football players and to work together. He also taught us to be better people, better men.

After we retired, most of us realized the influence he had on our lives. We give Tom Landry a lot of credit for the way that we turned out as men after retiring. He strengthened us in faith and consistency. He was just a great man and a great individual. We all loved him dearly.

One time during practice he was demonstrating a linebacker move, and he tripped and fell. He got up and said, "Gosh, darn." Everybody just broke up. The closest he came to a curse was, Gosh, darn.

Although he came up as a defensive back and was a defensive coach, he concentrated on the offense, in multiple sets, multiple posts, and all the movements. Dick Nolan was a great defensive back coach who did a great job. Tom kept an eye on the defense to make sure that everything was in order.

Toughest Receiver
Paul Warfield was good. I learned Paul's routes, his tendencies, and I was able to cover him well. Roy Jefferson was good when he was with Pittsburgh, then the Redskins. Cliff Branch

could flat out fly. I bet he could even run as fast as Bob Hayes. Guys who could run really fast gave me problems. I didn't have too much difficulty in covering them.

Favorite Quarterback To Compete Against
I loved to go up against Sonny Jurgensen. The guy could throw the ball extremely well. I think in my rookie year, I picked him off twice. In the first game that we played, I ran it in for a touchdown. Then in the Pro Bowl at the end of the year, I picked him off and again ran in for a touchdown. He was a great passer, easy to key, but he could throw the ball extremely accurate. He loved to pass.

I played against Joe Namath one time. I thought he was a very good passer. He was at the end of his career when I played against him, but I thought he was excellent quarterback in his heyday. I loved Johnny Unitas. I grew up watching him and fortunately, my rookie year, I intercepted a couple of passes against him in Baltimore. I will always remember Johnny U. as being one of the greatest. I just admired him. Of course being able to play against him was just kind of a dream come true.

1970 Dallas Cowboys vs. St. Louis Cardinals
It was probably the worst experience we ever had. The Vikings beat us in the preseason like, 53 to 14, but we came back that year and did extremely well. The Cardinal game was a nightmare. I think it was on national TV, but we didn't lose a game after that.

We all had different attitudes toward practice and meetings. Coach Landry kind of loosened up a little bit, telling us to relax. I think we were like 4 and 3 at the time. To him, that was like the season's about over. He relaxed and we never lost another game, we went right on to the Super Bowl.

Jim Brown
I think Jim Brown is the greatest running back who ever played the game. I tried to tackle him. I hit him as hard as I could and he ran right over the top of me. A guy that big … nobody ever ran him down from behind in his career, except me. One time in the Cotton Bowl, I chased him 73 yards and he said, "Mel, you're the only guy after I broke loose that has ever run me down." I appreciated that compliment coming from the guy who I thought was the greatest running back who ever played a game.

I grew up watching him. It was a highlight for me to be able to play against him and then to play with him in two Pro Bowls. Spending quality time with him at the Pro Bowl was really exciting for me.

You would hit him, hold on, and pray for help. That's what I did many times when I hit him and he was running over me. I know one time I grabbed his leg and held it until two or three of my teammates came to help me take him down.

Pro Football Hall Of Fame Induction
I think what excited me the most was the thousand cameras out there glaring at me. When you are there, you know that everybody in the world is looking at you. You had become one of the

greatest players that ever played a game. You're in a fraternity with Jim Brown, Lenny Moore, and Paul Hornung. It's an elite group. The whole world's looking at you, your family's looking at you, even your fifth grade school teacher's looking at you. It's just a wonderful feeling knowing that you have accomplished something. It's just a great honor and probably the highlight of my life.

America's Team
We were America's team not only because we were winners and successful, but Gil Brandt and Tex Schramm did a great job of promoting the Cowboys. They promoted the cheerleaders. Their scouting program entailed going to all the colleges, becoming friends with the coaches, and giving them the cheerleader calendars, pins, and frequent visits. It wasn't by chance that we became America's team; it was by design.

Photograph courtesy Associated Press

Chapter 50

Paul Krause

> College:
> Iowa
>
> Career History
> Washington Redskins (1964-1967)
> Minnesota Vikings (1968-1979)
>
> 1998 Inductee Pro Football Hall of Fame

Playing Both Ways
We played both ways in my time. I think we were one of the last classes in the NCAA that played both ways. We played both ways in high school and both ways in college. All of a sudden when I went to Pro Football, there was only one way. I was a defensive back and that was easy because I didn't get tired or anything. It was a strange feel for me only to play on one side of the football.

College Choice
I'm from Flint, Michigan. It's 45 miles to East Lansing and it's 45 miles to Ann Arbor. I almost went to Ann Arbor and the University of Michigan, but I didn't even consider going to Michigan State. I don't know why, but I never had a desire to go to Michigan State.

Transition To NFL
I started as a wide receiver in college, and then I was a safety. I never did play cornerback. It really didn't matter to me because I had played both in college, so it wasn't a strange position. The Washington Redskins drafted me and told me I was their free safety, so I said, "Okay".

The first time I played in an exhibition game was against the Bears, and I intercepted a pass from Billy Wade. The first play I got into the game, I intercepted a pass. Then the first league game I ever played, I intercepted two passes. I acted like a wide receiver back there and it really didn't make any difference.

During the regular season I played against the Cleveland Browns. They had Paul Warfield and Frank Ryan. Frank Ryan threw to Paul Warfield twice and I picked both of them off.

Interceptions
I had seven games with an interception as a rookie and it was, I even hate to say I thought it, a pretty easy game. By the next year they stopped throwing in my direction. I think the second year I had six, which was still a great year. Then I went down to two I think, and they never threw anywhere near me.

I played one more year in Washington and the defensive coach didn't like the way I was playing I guess, and they traded me. I went to the Minnesota Vikings and right away I had, I don't know, eight, nine, or ten, something like that. It was a new life for me. I really wasn't interested in getting traded by the Redskins, but the backfield coach and I just didn't get along. So I accepted the trade and went to the Vikings. It was all history from there. In 10 out of the 12 years I played with the Vikings, we won the Central Division Championship and played in four Super Bowls. It was a good thing. I enjoyed my years with the Vikings. Even though we didn't win a Super Bowl, we played in four of them and that's more than a lot of people played in.

Washington Redskins
Off the Redskins we had a lot of guys go into the Hall of Fame. With the Redskins we just couldn't win, but we had some great players. My old roommate with the Redskins, Chris Hanburger, went into the Hall. So, both roommates went in to the Hall of Fame.

Bud Grant
Bud Grant was probably one of the nicest guys you'd ever meet. He was a great coach. If you didn't play the way he wanted you to play, you were gone. Everybody realized that he was a good coach. He had his own ways of doing things and if you didn't do his way, you were adios. After the records that we started to put together, everybody realized, this guy is good and he knows how to treat people. He's just a great guy and a great coach.

Favorite Teams To Play Against
There were teams that I liked to play against back then. I loved to play against the Bears, the Lions, and the Packers. They were in our division, we played them twice a year, and we knew each other real well, but I still liked playing against them. I probably had more interceptions against the Detroit football team than anybody else. It was always great to play against our Central Division rivals because we knew that we were in for tough games. We had tremendous respect for them.

Difference In Game Now
I think if I played right now I'd have twice as many interceptions because they throw it twice as much. They throw 50, 60 times a game sometimes. Plus, I don't think the quarterbacks are as good as the guys I played against.

When I played, the quarterbacks were calling their own plays. They knew the receivers. They knew the game itself. I personally do not think that the coaches that are calling the plays today are as good as the quarterbacks that we're calling them back in the '60s. Some of the guys that are calling the plays today have never played the game. They have not been in certain situations. All they do is go by the book, or history, or whatever. I don't know how they're calling them, but they've never played the game. How in the world do they know what would be the best way to attack the different players or different offenses? Then it gets into a whole different aspect of the game. I could spend a lot of time on that because I look at the tackling, I look at the blocking, and all of that. I just I don't think the players of today are being taught the way to block, tackle, run pass patterns, and everything. I don't want to get into all that, but it's a whole different game. It's not like it was in the '60s and '70s.

Watching Film

I used to watch a lot of film. I studied the quarterbacks and everything. I'm just going to come right out and say it; I had a God given ability. I watch coaches today and think, how in the world, if they never played, are they going to tell a guy how to play as a defensive back in certain situations?

It's pretty hard for them tell they guys what to do if they've never been out on the field against a guy who can run like Bob Hayes, Paul Warfield, or Randy Moss. They're just throwing paint on the wall and saying, "I hope you can do this. This is the way I want it done." If you've never been there, never been scored upon, or if you've never been run over by Jimmy Brown, then you don't know what it's like. Doggone it; I know what it's like. I've been there. A lot of the old defensive backs sit around at the Hall of Fame and we say, "Geez, I watch this or watch that I know what they're supposed to do and they don't do it."

Jim Brown

I think I made tackles on Jim Brown but you just hung on and yelled for help. He was the best running back I've ever seen in my life, or ever played against in my life. Right now I would say Adrian Peterson is the closest thing I've ever seen to Jimmy Brown.

Quarterbacks

I loved quarterbacks that threw the football. I just loved them because I had a great defensive line, and I had a better than average group of linebackers in front of me. If they were going to throw the football against us, or speaking of the Minnesota Vikings, they we're in a lot of trouble. Well, the Minnesota Vikings defensive line was probably the best group of guys for me to play behind. When we had the quarterbacks in throwing mode, they were playing right to our strength because they had about less than four seconds to throw the ball or they were sacked. It made the defensive backfield's job a lot easier.

I probably felt there was something that we had to prove all the time; that teams could not throw the ball on us. They could run the ball up and down the football field on us, but when they got inside the 20 they had a very, very tough time scoring against the Vikings.

As for the best quarterback, I wouldn't even single out any quarterback. I think Sonny Jurgensen was the best passer I ever played against. I mean pure passer. Then you come to Johnny Unitas, Bart Starr, and of course Jurgensen, Billy Wade, and all those guys. These guys were great quarterbacks. There weren't as many teams back then, so every team had a good quarterback. The thing I hated was when an offensive team started running the ball on us, and we couldn't stop the dang the run. That's what we hated because all of a sudden our defensive backs were making too many tackles.

Four Super Bowl Appearances

I think that we should have won a couple of those Super Bowls. I think we could have won the first one. I think we should have won the Oakland game. There was some reason why we couldn't win and I have no idea.

81 Interceptions

I was so happy to get 81 interceptions. I remember the first one, the one that I tied the record with, and the one I broke the record with. I caught a pass in front of Gene Washington, which was great. I'm going to say it was a great interception because it was a diving interception and I caught it right in front of him, knee-high. Then I got two against LA in LA to break the record. I remember those.

I don't really remember a whole lot of other ones. I remember getting one off Sonny Jurgensen and Johnny Unitas. I remember some of them, but, gee, I never really thought at the time I was playing, that I was going to get 81 interceptions. There's just no way. You don't go into the league thinking, "Oh, I'm going to break a record, or I'm going to go into the Hall of Fame, and all of that." Hey, that's a gift from God I think.

It just happened that Emlen Tunnell and I were both from Iowa. I talked with Emlen Tunnell quite a few times before he passed away. I rode on the airplane from Chicago to California with him. We talked a lot about football, a lot about defensive back play, and things like that. He was a great man, a great football player. You know something; he never said one thing about me getting close to his record or anything like that. It was just never mentioned.

I watch to see if somebody's trying to catch me, and I also think that the league would like somebody to break that record. I think they want a player who is playing or modern day player to break it. As of right now, I don't think anybody is really close. If it happens it's going to take somebody who's going to be in the Hall of Fame to do it because it's a record that I'm very proud of.

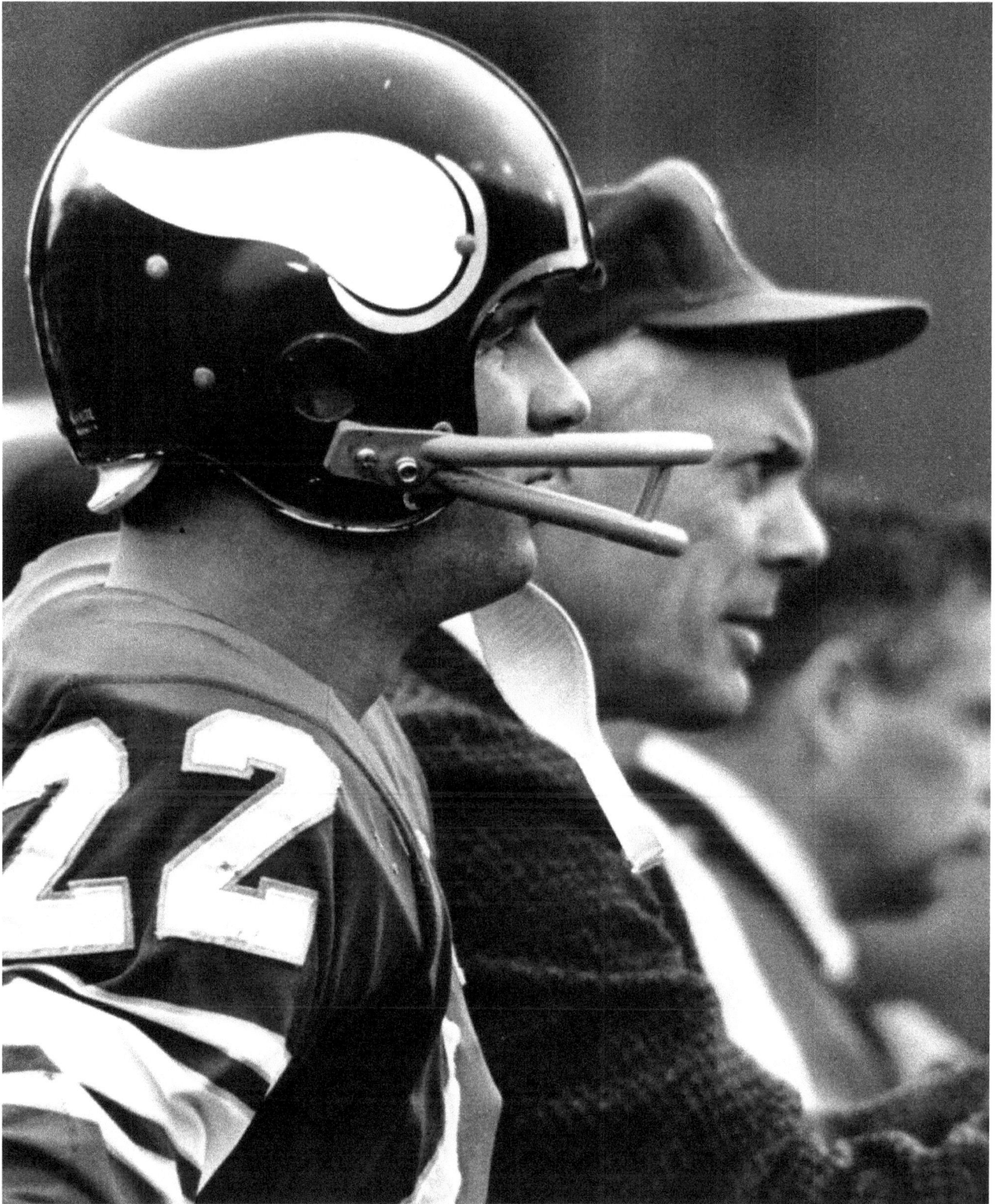

Minnesota Viking Paul Krause next to Head Coach Bud Grant
Photograph courtesy Associated Press

Chapter 51

Carl Eller

College: Minnesota Career History: Minnesota Vikings (1964-1978) Seattle Seahawks (1979) 2004 Inductee Pro Football Hall of Fame

Bobby Bell
Bobby was a great player and those were great University of Minnesota years. We go back and we're talking many years. I'm not even going to mention a number because it goes back to the days of the Great North Woods being discovered up here but those were great years. Bobby was a great teammate. They were National Champions one year and Big Ten Champions the next year. This year, our leader Sandy Stephens who was a pioneer quarterback, one of the first African American quarterbacks, and an All-American at quarterback, is going into the College Football Hall Of Fame. That's a big honor and we're all happy about that. Those were great teams. We never went to Michigan. Timing is everything. I was in the right place at the right time.

Minnesota Vikings Defense
Buddy Ryan was our coach part of the time. We had Jack Patera there too for a number of those years. They kind of combined there for a number of years but we started out with somebody totally different there. Again, it was the timing. We had great talent. We had Alan Page, Jim Marshall, and Gary Larsen. I just think that it was a combination. It was good chemistry. We all really cared and supported each other and just took great pride in being there. That was the kind of players we were and part of the team that we were part of.

Best Running Back Played Against
Well, it's very difficult. I played against some of the great ones, Jim Brown, Gale Sayers, O.J. Simpson, and Walter Payton. All of those guys are different. I won't say that he's my favorite, but I think that Gale Sayers was the biggest threat because he could score from anywhere on the field at any point. Any time he had the ball in his hands, he was liable to end up putting six points on the board. He was extremely quick for a defensive lineman to tackle. You watch these guys and they take a long time to get up to the line today and they can pick the holes. Gale Sayers would be at the line as soon as you made contact with the interior lineman and if you didn't stop him there he was gone.

Super Bowl Losses

Well, we were very close and very competitive. We played some great teams, one of the really great all-time teams in Kansas City, a team that was loaded. We played the Steelers team, which might have been the best Steelers team ever with Franco Harris, Lynn Swann, Terry Bradshaw, Joe Greene, and all of those guys. They just had a great, great, great team that was well balanced. That might have been one of the better teams. Then, we played Miami who was undefeated with Larry Csonka, Jim Kick, Bob Griese, and all those guys. We played great teams including the Oakland team. I thought that we were closer and had a real chance to beat Oakland. I think of the four teams that we played in the Super Bowl; we certainly had a chance to beat Oakland. I don't think that was our best Super Bowl team. Our best Super Bowl team was probably between the teams that played Pittsburgh and Miami in the Super Bowl.

Toughest Offensive Lineman

When I'm asked that question I generally refer to a guy, Bob Brown, who actually went into the Hall of Fame the same time as I did. Bob must have been put on this earth to just really be my nemesis. He was at Nebraska when I was at the University of Minnesota. We were actually the same age and in the same graduating class. I never could shake him and I could never get rid of him. When his teams showed up on our schedule I spent extra time in the locker room and the training room getting ready for him. He was great. The thing that was great about Bob was that he had a different philosophy. He wasn't just satisfied with protecting the quarterback, he wanted to annihilate the defensive end; so you had to be on guard all of the time.

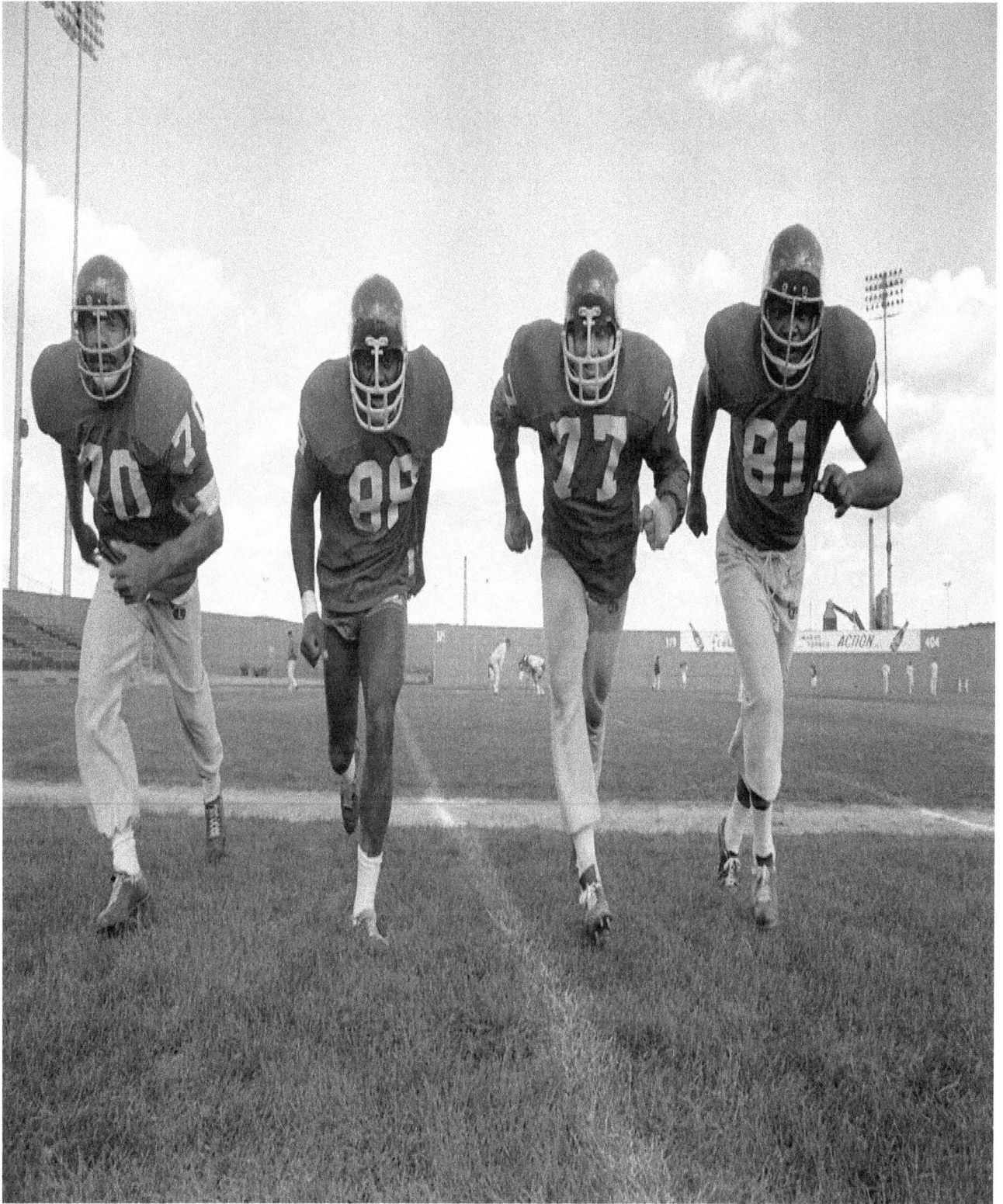

Left to right Jim Marshall, Alan Page, Gary Larson, Carl Eller Photograph courtesy Associated Press

Chapter 52

Floyd Little

> College:
> Syracuse
>
> Career History:
> 1967-1969 AFL Denver Broncos
> 1970-1975 NFL Denver Broncos
>
> 2010 Inductee Pro Football Hall of Fame

College Choice
I had 47 scholarship offers. I was recruited by General MacArthur in New York City with all of the famous Yankees, Elston Howard, Roy Campanella, and some of the other great players I got a chance to meet a great general in his room in New York City at the Waldorf. He gave me an opportunity to get into the Army and got me an appointment by Senator Humphries before he became Vice President. He told me I would be the first African-American general in the United States Army. That means I would have been Colin Powell's boss, General Petraeus' boss, and Norman Schwarzkopf's boss. I would have been a real top level general during that time, if I had gone into the Army.

A guy named Ernie Davis, who won the Heisman trophy that year, came to my house and sat with my sisters, my mom, and me. We went out to dinner and I told him that I would go to Syracuse, because I wanted to eat my steak and lobster, which was getting cold. Three months later he died. I had given him my word, and I don't have anything more valuable than that. When I give my word, that is the only thing of value that I own. When Ernie Davis passed away, I never even knew that he was sick. I called the coach and told him I was coming to Syracuse because I had given Ernie Davis my word. That is how I got to Syracuse.

Syracuse Football
I played with Jim Nance and Larry Csonka. I had two good fullbacks to play with. Jim Brown recruited Ernie Davis, and Ernie Davis recruited me. That is the trilogy. That is the three number 44s. Of course we had some other ones after us, like Rob Conrad, who played for the Miami Dolphins, who was number 44 here, as well as Michael Owens, Billy Owens' brother. We have had some other 44s after me, but Jim Brown, Ernie, and me are the real 44s.

They retired number 44 on Thanksgiving Day 2005. Since then, they have retired Csonka's number, as well as John Mackey's number. They could not retire theirs until they retired ours, so they retired number 44.

My Broncos number is retired, my high school number is retired, and my military number is retired. All of the numbers that I have ever worn have been retired.

Jim Brown

Jim Brown is an icon in the game. He was way before his time. He did some things as a player that nobody had done. That is the reason why his numbers are so high, playing in a 12-game schedule. It took players a long time to carry the ball twice as many times and play in almost twice as many games just to catch him. He is a great player, he's a good friend of mine, and he truly deserves to be a Hall of Famer. He's the best football player that has ever played. No question in my mind.

Nickname "The Franchise"

I saved the franchise. The Broncos were on the verge of being moved to Chicago or Birmingham, because they had never signed a number 1 draft pick. They drafted Dick Butkus and other future stars, but they went to the NFL, not the AFL. The NFL and AFL merged and the Broncos signed me. The Broncos decided to stay and built a new stadium, so I saved the franchise from moving to Chicago or Birmingham. That is how I got the name "The Franchise."

Pro Football Hall Of Fame Induction

Being a Hall of Famer with so many guys whom I've watched and admired over the years, and now I am one of them … I was just thrilled. And, going in with Emmitt Smith, Jerry Rice, John Randle, Rickey Jackson, Russ Grimm, and all of the other guys that went in with me … I think that's just fantastic. That was the highlight of my sports career.

I think a Sports Illustrated article really let people know who I am and where I have been. There are a lot more people today who recognize me since I am a Hall of Famer. I think there are a lot more people who recognize me because of the speech that I gave in Canton. They think that was the best speech ever. In fact, Walter Payton's mother said to me at a function, "I have never heard a greater speech in my life." I think the speech has helped me become more recognizable.

My son and I celebrate his life. He was injured in college and lost his leg and we celebrate his life every year. It took us about an hour, around the pool, for me to write it, he edited it, I re-wrote it, he edited it again, and we put it all together. We only had six to eight minutes to give a speech. I got to talk about my whole life as an athlete and a person, and I had eight minutes to do it. So we had to put in all of the things we needed to make it really effective.

My son went to USC. He was on campus and he went to the local store to get some lunchmeat and some bread, and two guys tried to rob him. They asked for $100 and all he had was $2. They said they needed $100 or they were going to shoot him. He said, "I guess you will have to shoot me." So they shot him at close range with a shotgun. On the way to the hospital, he flat-lined twice and they brought him back.

That is why it was so special for me to have him at my induction, celebrating the highest award in my life as an athlete. It was very special.

The thing about football is, when you are told as a child and a young adult, that you are not big enough, strong enough, smart enough, or fast enough, I think you build resentment in you that allows you to rise above. When you're given challenges all of your life, I think it helps you become a better person, because you know yourself that you are the only person who can say when you have had enough. Nobody can tap you out. You have to tap out yourself. No one can tell you what you can do.

Our problem is, too many of us allow someone else's opinion, or label of us, to become our reality. When people are told enough times that they can't, they start believing it. Me, I didn't believe it. I believed, let me fail me. Don't you fail me before I get an opportunity to fail. I want to be able to fail myself, and you are telling me I can't do stuff without me even trying. Not fair. I am not going to stand for it. I am not going to put up with it. I am going to try it and then I can actually say I couldn't do it, but let me say that. Don't say it for me."

Football has taught me a lot. Not believing what people think of you and you going out there and establishing who you are, what you are and rising to levels nobody thinks you can rise to. That is a part of what football has taught me about life. No one can tell me the level of success that I can reach. That is my call and I am not going to let you take that away from me.

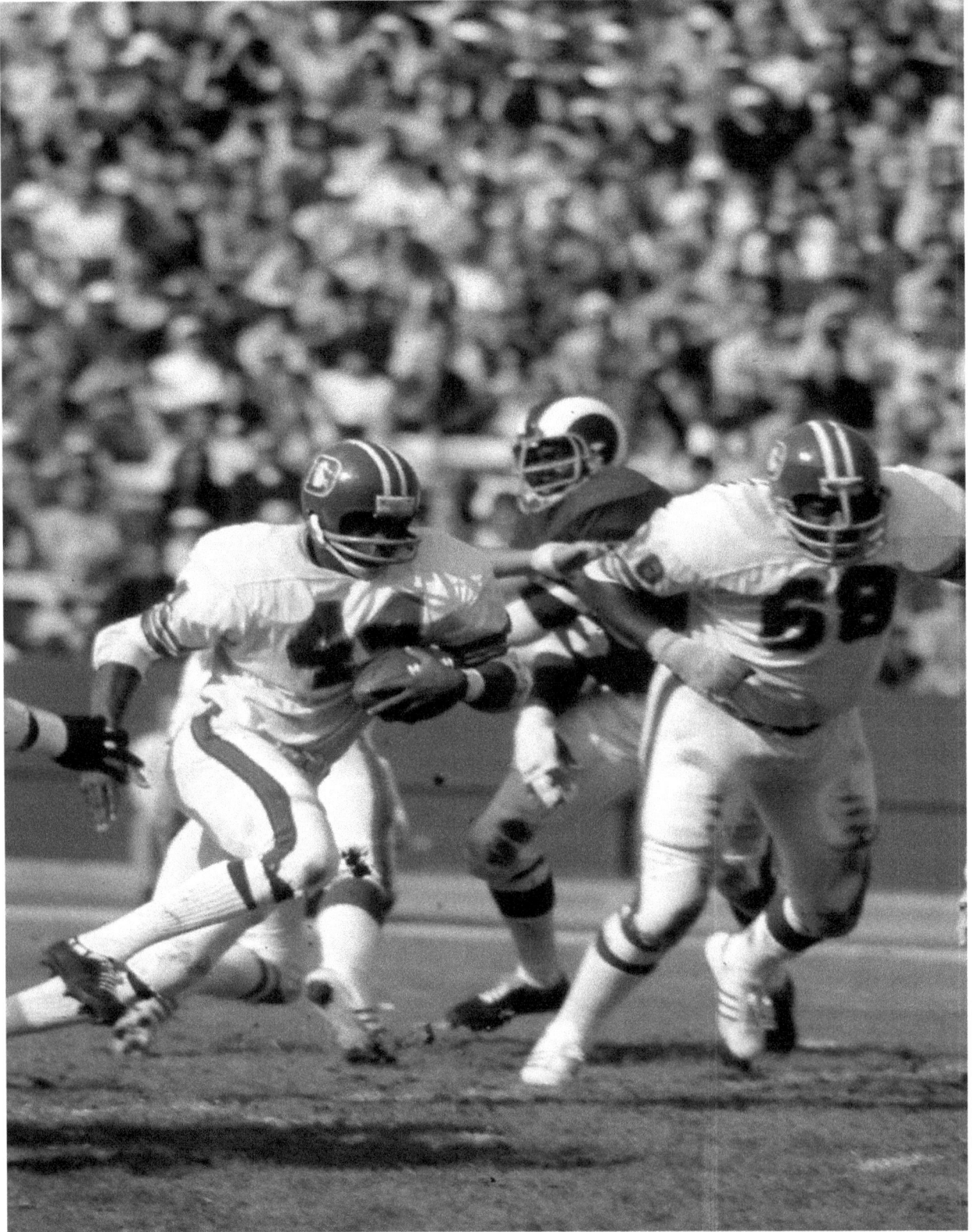

Photograph courtesy Associated Press

Chapter 53

Dave Wilcox

College: Oregon (& Boise JC) Career History: San Francisco 49ers (1964–1974) 2000 Inductee Pro Football Hall of Fame

College Choice

I went to Boise Junior College, which is now Boise State. Boise is about 75 miles from my hometown in Eastern Oregon. Then I went to the University of Oregon. I had an older brother who did exactly the same thing. Growing up in a small community, it was probably six gradual steps instead of leaping into the big city.

Len Casanova was a wonderful man. Actually there was a connection between him and my old coach at Boise Junior College, Lyle Smith. They served in the Navy together during World War II. I think my recruitment, part of whatever that was, included both Lyle and Len Casanova. Len was the most honorable and wonderful person.

There was a guy named Mel Renfro who played at Jefferson High in Portland. He went to Oregon. Even though we never played against each other in high school, I knew about him. He was the player of the state. It was sure wonderful to be able to go and play on the same team with Mel at the University of Oregon.

When we played, you played everything. You ran down on kickoffs, did punt returns, played defense, and played offense. You weren't just a defensive guy or an offensive guy. The only guy that didn't play defense was the quarterback. That was probably good.

Oregon

I was a great tight end. I was a tight end in high school, at the junior college, and during my first year at Oregon. Right before spring practice during my junior year going into my senior year, the coaches asked me if I would move to play guard. We had a whole bunch of tight ends but we had no guards. I said I'd do that on offensive as long as I didn't have to do that on defense. I was a defensive end. I was a multi-talented position guy I guess.

In high school we probably threw the ball three or four times a game because we played a single wing. In junior college, I think we threw the ball maybe eight or nine times a game. Then when I got to Oregon, they threw it probably ten or fifteen times a game. About fourteen of those throws were to try to get the ball to Mel Renfro and the rest of us would get out of his way and leave him alone.

I never had one favorite moment. They were all favorite moments. Going to the University of Oregon there was no Pac-10 or Pac-8 or Pac anything; it was independent. My junior year, we opened with Texas in Austin. I don't know if it was the same year that we played Indiana. We played Ohio State, West Virginia, and Rice. We played all over the place, playing against all those teams.

I remember going to Ohio State and going out to warm up on the field. We had to go down to the corner of the end zone because Ohio State had so many players they took up the whole field. I think we got beat 17-14. They had a guy on their team named Paul Warfield.

I remember going back to West Virginia. We took two days to get there because it wasn't a direct flight. I don't remember the flight, but I do remember we were on a prop plane. I think we stopped a couple of times to get gas and that was good.

I remember going to Morgantown. We were getting ready to check into the hotel and we had a bunch of Hawaiian and a few black guys on our team. The hotel said that they had to come in through the kitchen. Len Casanova said, "No they won't. They'll come in through the front door." The guy said, "No they can't." We stayed somewhere else. The next day we beat West Virginia 46-2 with some of our players they wouldn't let walk into the hotel. We were in the middle of all that back in the '60s.

1963 Sun Bowl
We played SMU in the Sun Bowl. I was just talking about it with some of my old buddies. It just seems like it was yesterday. I think that two major colleges, SMU and Oregon were the first major colleges to play in the Sun Bowl. Before that teams like West Texas State, Texas Western, and New Mexico State were the schools that played in that. We did that and it was a wonderful experience.

Terry Baker
Terry Baker went to high school with Mel Renfro. He's a year older than Mel and me. He was a great athlete. I played against him our junior year in high school. He was a heck of a basketball player at Oregon State. I think they went into something similar to what the Final Four is now. He was a pitcher on the baseball team. Us in state guys followed him. He was the first Heisman Trophy winner out West.

I do know that he was such a great athlete. When people play Pro football, basketball, baseball, or something else, they have to have one skill that's pretty darn good. He was such a great athlete; he covered everything. Just because you're the Heisman Trophy winner in college, doesn't mean you're going to be a success in the Pros.

Draft
Len Casanova knew the owners of the 49ers. There was a guy named Franklin Mieuli who owned part of the 49ers. He graduated from the University of Oregon in the late '40s or early '50s. He talked to Len Casanova. Casanova had taught high school in Redwood City at Sequoia High School. The 49ers workout place was not in San Francisco, it was in Redwood City. Anyhow, that was the connection.

At that time, Houston drafted me in the AFL and then San Francisco in the NFL. Len Casanova told Mel Renfro and I to come see him when the draft was over. I went in the next day to see Len and he said, "You probably need to sign with San Francisco." I said, "You're my agent, so thank you." So that's what I did.

The draft was held in December 1963. That was the year we were getting ready to play Oregon State in our last game of the regular season. That's when John Kennedy was shot. They delayed all the games for a week. Mel cut his wrist sticking his arm through a window somehow or something happened. I don't remember the details, but there was a question about whether his arm would be ok. That's the reason he was taken in the second round.

Mel and I were at the Eugene Hotel for a while during that draft. A guy named Gil Brandt, who was the main connection to this area for the Cowboys, really wanted Mel. So, the Cowboys took Mel. I sure wish he came with me to San Francisco. He was a heck of a player.

Transition To NFL

In college we did everything. When I got to San Francisco they wanted me to be a defensive end, which would be a down lineman. I did that for about two days. Then they needed a linebacker and I did a little bit of that in training camp. When I played in the College All-Star Game in Chicago, I played as a linebacker. I'm not sure I knew what I was doing. Then I went from there.

Ed Pine, who was the linebacker ahead of me, got a bad line burn. They put the wrong chalk on the field at Kezar, and he got a burn. He was in pretty tough shape there for a while. His replacement, a guy named Bill Cooper, hurt his knee during the first game he played. Then all of a sudden, it's the second or third game of the season, and I've got to start. I went from there.

Gale Sayers

We played in San Francisco and Gale Sayers scored four touchdowns in Kezar Stadium. We played the Bears later in the year in Wrigley Field, in the mud and the rain. He scored six touchdowns. I remember somebody three or four years ago, talking about what a great running back he was because he scored 20 touchdowns in a season. I started laughing. You've got to be kidding me. In two games against us, and we weren't very good, Gale Sayers scored ten touchdowns. I honestly think Gale Sayers was the best back we played against in the NFL.

A year or two later, we were playing in Wrigley Field and Gale ran a sweep. The guard was blocking for him. Our defensive back went and knocked the guard down and Gale was right behind him. The back hit Gale on the knee. I know the guy who did that and he felt awful. That's not something you try to do, hurt the guy. You might hit them and knock them down, but you didn't want to ruin their career. From then on it was tough for Gale. Up until that time he was a very special player.

Mike Ditka

Mike Ditka was one of the most tenacious guys to play against. You better be ready to play the whole game. He wasn't going to just play a few plays, that's for sure. Mike Ditka was the mentality of the Bears. You better take a lunch with you because you'd be there all day. It didn't make any difference if they were ahead or behind. You better pay attention to what was going on. You better focus on Mike Ditka.

Exhibition Game During Watts Riots
The exhibition game was always in the Coliseum. We stayed at the Sheridan West Hotel. You'd leave the hotel and go down to Vermont Street and that would take you to the Coliseum. Here we are on the bus at five o'clock in the evening going to the stadium for a seven o'clock game. We're driving down the middle of Watts with smoke coming out of the buildings. Guys with machine guns are on the buildings and I'm thinking, should we really be down here playing an exhibition game? I didn't know about that one.

Dick Nolan
Dick Nolan was a defense guy; I know that. He loved defense. That's what changed the makeup of the 49ers. When he became our Head Coach, it was so he could spend time with the defense. He let the offense guys go, but defense is where his level of specialty was.

When he was in Dallas, Tom Landry and Nolan put together the Dallas defense, which they called the "Flex" defense. It was a little bit different than what anybody else was doing. He brought that to San Francisco. Nolan was one of the most wonderful people. He brought a winning attitude to the 49ers.

Decision To Retire
I got clipped in an exhibition game in Miami prior to the 1970 season. I had torn cartilage in my knee, but I played the whole year. Oh God, that was awful. I missed one game. I couldn't take it. I had to rest. My knee would swell up all the time. After the season I had it operated on in Oregon. They fixed it up. You go in the morning; you're home in the afternoon, and playing again on Tuesday. I was in the hospital for a week for a cartilage operation. I played after that, it was really good for a couple years.

Then it bothered me once again and I had to go in and do again. In May, there was some stuff that started floating around and they had to operate. After that season I played a little better but it bothered me quite a bit. I went in to see the doctor; I was 32 I think, at the time. I talked to the doctors about my knee and stuff. Our team, the 49ers were going through some major changes. Brodie and a bunch of guys retired. I decided that I probably wanted to be able to walk around the rest of my life. The doctors showed me, this is what it looks like. This is what it should look like. This is probably what it will look like if you keep playing. It was a pretty easy choice.

I'd been a member of the team for almost 20 years. Your buddies and the camaraderie and all that, that's what you miss. That's what I missed.

Pro Football Hall of Fame Induction
I really hadn't thought too much about the Hall of Fame until the late '90s. My old coach Mike Giddings had been to the Hall of Fame induction. He called me and said, "You should be in the Hall of Fame." I said, "Well I guess. Whatever I did if it was good enough I think I should be there, if it wasn't then I shouldn't." I got the call in 2000. I'm very fortunate to be included with this group of people.

Bob St. Clair

When you went to training camp as a rookie back then, you'd have your first meal in the lunchroom. You'd all go sit in the corner somewhere away from the veterans. We didn't want to mess up things. We weren't sure what we were doing quite frankly.

After my rookie year, I anticipated this every year. Bob St. Clair would get a piece of raw liver and put it on his plate. He would come over and sit down right in the middle of the rookies and start eating it, letting blood run down his chin. The rookies would throw up and get up wondering what in the hell have I gotten into here with this Pro Football stuff?

Bob is one of the most wonderful guys. We'd have a lot of laughs about that. He did that on purpose. I know that.

A couple years ago in Canton, I'm sitting at this table with Franco Harris on one side and Bob St. Clair's on the other. They brought us our meal and Franco happened to look over. Bob had a raw steak with ice on top of it. Franco looked at the steak, and then he looked at me. I said, "Yes, he'll eat it." I thought Franco might lose his dinner right there. He'd never been around anything like that.

Bob is about 82 years old. That's probably the reason he's so healthy now.

San Francisco 49er Dave Wilcox stops Los Angeles Ram
Jim Bertelsen. Photograph courtesy Associated Press

Chapter 54

Jan Stenerud

College:
Montana State

Career History:
Kansas City Chiefs (1967-1979)
Green Bay Packers (1980-1983)
Minnesota Vikings (1984-1985)

1991 Inductee Pro Football Hall of Fame

College Choice
Nowadays, you don't have ski jumping in the NCAA. In 1962 when I got to Montana State, between 45 and 50 schools in the United States had ski teams, and ski jumping was my specialty. I had to do two things, so I did cross-country skiing as well, but jumping is what I enjoyed.

I think they discontinued ski jumping in the NCAA in the early '70s. I heard some talk it might be coming back, but there aren't enough facilities.

I finished sixth in the junior nationals in ski jumping in Norway in 1962. A guy at Montana State who was already there on a ski scholarship, had a newspaper clipping of this, and he showed it to the ski coach. The next thing I know, I get a letter in the mail offering me a full ride ski scholarship. I thought it'd be a neat experience to come to the greatest place on earth. My plan was to go for one year and see how I liked it.

I also played soccer. That was my summer sport. I played on teams since I was eight years old, and I was a pretty decent soccer player. I would always take the corner kick and the free kick because I could kick the ball pretty hard. For some reason, that doesn't necessarily make you a great soccer player.

I didn't kick any kind of ball for two or three years at Montana State. As a skier, we ran the stadium steps every single day. One day, Dale Jackson who was a backup kicker on the football team and a safety, hurt his shoulder. So, I went down and kicked a few footballs for them. It lasted for my junior year.

I kicked with my toe like everybody else did in those days, and after a few attempts, I asked the coach, "Can you kick with the side of your foot like you take a corner kick in soccer?"

He said, "Yes, you can. There's a guy from the Buffalo Bills named Pete Gogolak who kicks with the side of his foot." Of course, I'd never seen him. I wasn't interested in football. But, I started kicking a few, and I did that once a week or so.

One day, the basketball coach, Roger Craft, was walking across the football field on the way to his office when he saw me. He took a second look and ran over to the football coach, Jim Sweeney. Sweeney later won 200 games at Fresno State, but he was the coach at Montana State at the time. Coach Sweeney finally took a look at me, and he made me try out for spring practice.

My senior year in college, they changed my scholarship from skiing to football. I did both sports my senior year. At the end of that year, the Kansas City Chiefs drafted me. It happened in the third round of what they called the AFL Red Shirt Draft.

After about 13 attempts, three of them being over 60 yards, I was drafted. That probably wouldn't happen these days.

Draft
I was drafted after the '65 season because that was my senior year. There were 25 guys drafted in the AFL Future Draft, or the Red Shirt Draft. We were on the quarter system at Montana State then, so I decided to keep seven credits. I didn't graduate the next spring, so I went to be on the football team in 1966. I graduated at Christmastime after that season. The NFL had a special draft of the 25 or so AFL Future Draft choices from the year before. Atlanta was the first one to have a pick of those 25 AFL Future Draft choices. I was the first one to bepicked.

There was a choice to make between the Atlanta Falcons of the NFL and the Kansas City Chiefs of the AFL. Atlanta had been in the league for one year. People called the AFL the Mickey Mouse League. This was before Super Bowl I, when I had to decide. Bobby Beathard, who later became the GM for the Redskins and San Diego, was a scout in Kansas City. I really liked him. Tommy O'Boyle, the Head Talent Scout for Kansas City, and Hank Stram, were very convincing. I chose Kansas City and was a rookie there in 1967.

Super Bowl IV
The year before I joined them, the Chiefs played Super Bowl I against the Packers and lost 35-10, although it was 14-10 at halftime. The Packers won pretty convincingly again in Super Bowl II against the Raiders. Super Bowl III, is one of the most famous of all time. That's when the Jets of the AFL beat Baltimore 16-7. Our Super Bowl game, Super Bowl IV, was the last game played between the two leagues before the merger. The Vikings were 13- or 14-point underdogs, and we ended up winning 23-7. It was a huge deal for us.

I get asked, "Was the Super Bowl a big deal?" Forty-three years ago we thought it was. It's not like it is now, but still, at that time, it was becoming the biggest sporting event in America. We thought it was huge. It was a really big deal then, too.

During that season, our great quarterback, Lennie Dawson, was hurt in the first or second game. Our back up was Jacky Lee. He got hurt after a few series and our third string quarterback, Mike Livingston, came in. We won six games in a row with him as the quarterback.

The game has changed a little bit. It doesn't seem like you can win now if you only run the football. We mainly ran the ball and had a great defensive team. We won a lot of low-scoring games. Jerrel Wilson was a great, great punter for us, and I was known as a pretty good kicker in those days. We won six games without our number one or two quarterback.

The only thing I thought about the Super Bowl, was please, let us win. I don't care how I do personally, as long as we win. There's nothing worse than to lose the Super Bowl.

There was a guy on the sideline who was a friend of Hank Stram. This guy kept asking me if he had my warm-up jacket. It was a cold, blustery day in New Orleans. It's hard to believe, but I had mud cleats on for that game because the tarp had leaked in several places. This is the Super Bowl. It had rained the night before. Anyway, this guy on the sidelines kept telling me to get my warm-up jacket. Finally, I realized he was Pat O'Brien. I said, "You've got to wait until the game is over. Don't disturb me in case I have to go in and do something again."

Were You Isolated From Team
I've been asked that so many times. Of course, keep in mind that forty-six years ago, we only had one practice field. There was no other field to go and kick. Jerrel Wilson and I would kick the ball across the end zone, back and forth at the beginning of practice. Then we'd go over and watch practice, and hold the bags and help out anyway we could. We even filled in on the punt team if they needed somebody to run or whatever. I tried to get involved as much as I could, although obviously, I could not play football at a professional level.

They had such a veteran team in Kansas City. I was accepted really well, I felt at the time. I didn't have any problems at all. They talk about how nobody speaks to the kicker. The veterans in Kansas City, I think, appreciated my talent when I got there. They made me feel welcome and appreciated from day one, so I had a good feeling the whole time I was there.

Longest Game In NFL History Christmas 1971
At the time, I was bitterly, bitterly disappointed because I let the team down, and I still feel that way. If I had a decent day, we would have won that game.

The strange thing is, those thoughts do not get better over the years. I see a young kid now miss an important kick in a big game—playoff game, Super Bowl. He doesn't know it yet, but he's going to take that to the grave with him. It really stays with you. Although I kicked I don't know how many field goals and game-winning kicks, the one that sticks out is the one that you miss. That is the one that bothers me a lot. I did not realize at the time that it would stay with me my whole life. It says with you because you are accountable, professional, and you're supposed to make kicks like that.

Arrowhead Stadium
The first five years that I was in Kansas City, we kicked in the old Municipal Stadium. In Arrowhead, the wind comes in and goes in every direction. It's certainly not like indoors, by any means. What they have improved on now, it seems like they take better care of the turf versus 30 or 40 years ago. When you see film from way back, there's a lot of mud. There wasn't much grass on the field. Today they do a lot better job with that. As far as the wind is concerned, on a windy day, Arrowhead can be tricky.

Green Bay Packers

I had my best years probably, during my early years and my late years. In Green Bay, I kicked over 90% one year, and it was difficult. You had to adjust, because the footing was bad, it was windy and cold, and the balls were lying on the sidelines in bags for three hours. At the end of the game, the balls didn't go very far. Now they have warm up mats and you warm the ball up and you do certain things. It was difficult, but I had good luck up there. Of course, the kicking has become so much better. In my years at Green Bay, I think I kicked over 80% the four seasons I was there. I wasn't even as talented as I was 15 years earlier.

They started to get special teams coaches. The most important thing, we got reps, a few reps in during the week. They started breaking in the punter as a holder. We didn't have a snapper yet, but I got more reps. That was the big thing for me.

Jersey Number Choice With Packers

Tony Canadeo, a great running back with the Packers in the '30s and '40s, used to wear number 3, but it was retired. I had to pick another number, and that was number 10. It seemed to be an okay number. Not having number 3 didn't bother me. I just respected that the number was retired on Tony Canadeo. Now my number in Kansas City is retired.

Bart Starr was fired after an eight and eight season. The new coach, Forrest Gregg, traded me to Minnesota, and number three was available there. So, I had number three for the last two years of my career.

Favorite Stadium

There's no question, about it. If you kick indoors where it's 68 degrees with no wind and perfect footing, every indoor stadium is the best place to kick.

Centers

In the early days, the best center was usually the one who was the backup center in training camp. He would be the last cut before the season, and I'd get told about a new center four or five days before the first game. That happened so many times while I was in the league. For a while, I had Bobby Bell as a center, and Bobby Bell could do anything. He is a Hall of Fame linebacker, he won the Outland Trophy at Minnesota University, and he was a quarterback in high school in Shelby, North Carolina. He was a good snapper.

Lenny Dawson was a great holder. Keep in mind he didn't really practice it. I broke in Bucky Scribner, Ray Stachowicz, and Greg Coleman, who were all punters.

I just underhanded the ball to the punters, over and over again, so they could practice catching the ball, spinning it if they needed to, and putting it down. They became very good, but Lenny with very little practice, had great hands, and he did that extremely well.

Coaches

I just loved Hank Stram. He gave me a lot of confidence. He came to the practice field and was kneeling down, holding the ball for me. He did this a couple of times a week there for a month before training camp. He wanted to find out if he could see something that he could help me with. He was just terrific, plus he was such an optimistic, positive person. I enjoyed him a lot.

Of course, I had a lot of good coaches. Bart Starr—there's no better person that Bart Starr. He was fired in Green Bay, but you don't fire a person like Bart Starr. He had a pretty good season and did a pretty good job coaching up there. We went to the playoffs in the strike-shortened season in 1982. We were eight and eight in '83. If he had one more year to get the defense shored up a little bit, I think he could have done really well.

I did not play for Forrest Gregg. He's the one that traded me to Minnesota. Les Steckel was there the first year, and Les was ridiculed a lot. They found a way to make fun out of him a lot, but Les was okay.

Bud Grant was the most amazing coach. He didn't tolerate mistakes. He didn't say much, but when he spoke up everybody listened, I guarantee you that. He was an outstanding coach as well. I was very fortunate I had all good coaches.

They're all pretty darn good at that level. I think the coaches are, frankly, fairly equal on that level, and so are the players. It seems that some are better than others, but most of them do the same things. Most teams do the same things, so the difference between a bad and a good coach and a bad and a good player in the league is not very much.

Avoiding Injury

I remember early on they would send a guy right after you, because we kicked from the 40-yard line in our first few years. I would kick the ball out of the end zone most of the time. There were some times that somebody would come right after you, but I could run pretty fast. I was pretty quick on my feet, so I avoided that.

I did get hurt one time in Cleveland when I broke my sternum. It was on the kickoff after a safety. Our punter was hurt, so we had to kick off on the 20-yard line, and somebody had to hold the ball. Emmitt Thomas held the ball for me and I think it was Greg Pruitt who ran it back. Somehow I was able to hang on till they could tackle him at midfield. That was the only time I really got hurt. I never had a pulled muscle. I obviously had the flu, colds, and things like that from time to time, but I never missed a game, so I'm fortunate that way.

Pro Football Hall Of Fame Induction

When I got to Montana State, I said, "You mean, you can get a scholarship for kicking the football?" Then they were talking about the pros. You're kicking the ball further than the people that you see on television. They told me you could actually get paid for kicking the football. I thought that was amazing. Then I got into the league, and they said, "You can get a pension if you play for five years."

When I got nominated in 1991, it was two or three weeks before the Super Bowl and I had been out of the league for five years. I got a registered letter from the Hall of Fame, and it said, "You're one of the 15 finalists. Let us know where you're going to be at such-and-such time the day before the Super Bowl." As far as I knew, no kicker ever, or a person that couldn't do anything else but kick, had ever been a finalist, so I didn't know what to think of it.

I was surprised because that wasn't something that had really come up. I had heard television announcers saying during my 17th, 18th, and 19th years, future Hall of Famer. I thought, well, that's stretching it a little bit.

Anyway, I got in the first year. Nobody had been in that position before, so I didn't give it that much thought. I really didn't. It was a very exciting, very pleasant, surprise. I feel as lucky as anybody can be.

I know that Ray Guy has been a finalist many times. Let's face it, there aren't going to be too many kickers in the Hall of Fame. You can see that now. I could have guessed that, years ago. I guess I'm the only kicker in the Hall of Fame, but I thought that Morten Andersen would get in this year. When I got in, I had the most field goals in history of the league. I think I was All-Pro from various papers or whatever seven times. Morten has the same credentials, except he is also the leading scorer all time. I was the second leading scorer. I never caught George Blanda. The amount of Pro Bowls we made is similar. I know he is disappointed not getting in. I think he will get in. I think he deserves to get in.

You feel like you don't deserve to be there when you see all the names and all the people you read about. Other Hall of Famers will even tell you that they don't feel like they belong there. You feel very humble and very appreciative, but you wonder if it's really true.

I didn't go back for 10 years. I didn't really see the point in going but then they had a 10th reunion. It's almost like you go there to get applause. I enjoyed the 10th reunion very much. Now, they try to bring most people back every year. It's very special.

Looking back to 1991, when I was nominated, I thought a lot about my career and the people involved. My professional teammates, my teammates in college, and my coach in college, Jim Sweeney, all gave me the opportunity.

It's a fairy tale story in some ways, and it's funny how it works out at times. I'm very appreciative of the way it worked out for me.

Photograph courtesy Associated Press

Chapter 55

Paul Warfield

> College:
> Ohio State
>
> Career History:
> Cleveland Browns (1964–1969)
> Miami Dolphins (1970–1974)
> Memphis Southmen WFL (1975)
> Cleveland Browns (1976–1977)
>
> 1983 Inductee Pro Football Hall of Fame

College Choice

I was recruited on a national scale as a youngster coming out of Warren, Ohio. Coming out of high school, as far as I was concerned, Ohio State was what I was looking for. The Buckeyes had tremendous interest in me, but there were a number of other schools in the Big Ten that were vying for me, as well as other schools from around the country. I narrowed it down to two schools in Big Ten Conference, the University of Iowa and Ohio State.

The University of Michigan had a representative that talked to me via telephone, as did Michigan State. I probably had a little bit greater interest in Michigan State than the University of Michigan, because of Clarence Peaks, a former star player I saw on television. He immediately caught my eye on a Saturday afternoon ballgame that was nationally televised. It seemed like Michigan State was a school that generated a tremendous amount of excitement. Ohio State and Iowa were the two schools in the Big Ten that were of greatest interest to me.

Style Of Football In Early '60s

The style of football that was played in those years was a little bit different. Run-oriented offenses were very tight and compact with no wide receiver spread out. As a matter of fact, the position was called end, e-n-d, instead of wide receiver in those years. It was really part of the old, what one would call, smash-mouth football tradition.

There was no substitution in the era I played. It's really kind of interesting because colleges and universities during that period were more interested in the collegiate football program being a part of the educational process. I don't mean to demean colleges and universities today. It was a point of focus that there were limited substitution rules which meant that everyone played with the exception maybe of two players. Usually those players were the quarterback and maybe one other player when the ball exchanged hands. Everyone had to play both offense and defense. If you're an offensive player, you were automatically a defensive player at the same position pretty much. It was considered part of the educational experience. The biggest difference in college football in those days was you would find several different offensive philosophies within a conference or around the conferences.

Some teams played what they called T formation football where you had four backs in the backfield—quarterback, fullback, left, and right halfback. That was what was utilized at Ohio State. The University of Iowa had an offensive philosophy that was called the Wing-T. There would only be two backs in a line behind quarterback and another back called a wingback would be set off to a side right outside the in position, which would be the equivalent of a tight end position today. Then there was an option football running attack. You had all these varied styles of play. Today when one looks at college football, it resembles the professionals for the most part with the exception of maybe one or two adaptations. Everyone in college football is throwing the football as they do in the NFL. In those days, it was quite the opposite.

From the collegiate standpoint, it was not necessary that their game looked exactly like the professional game. They were more interested in the educational experience of learning how to really play football both offensively and defensively, learning how to tackle, learning how to block, and learning how to incorporate these. Collegiate football was considered to be a part of the educational experience. Today, it appears that collegiate football is a breeding ground, to an extent, for the National Football League.

In the years that I was in school from 1960 to 1964, athletic eligibility did not start for student athletes until their sophomore year. Freshmen athletes were ineligible to play their first year because major colleges and universities wanted youngsters to feel a level of confidence in transitioning from high school to college, and academics were placed ahead of that.

I was a defensive back and was considered to be a quarterback, as a matter of fact, when the Cleveland Browns first drafted me. They drafted me with the thought that I was going to be a quarterback instead of a wide receiver.

Position Change To Wide Receiver In NFL
Thankfully, after seeing me do a few things at the first minicamp as both a defensive back and a wide receiver, Coach Blanton Collier changed his mind and said, "We're going to make you a wide receiver instead of a defensive back." Originally, I was drafted as a quarterback.

Woody Hayes
Woody Hayes was one of the great football coaches in college. He was a man who was very, very insistent that Ohio State have teams that were so highly disciplined, that they would not make errors in any given situation. This would tend to allow players to operate at maximum efficiency and make few errors. He was a disciplinarian who demanded a lot of his players. All of us revered and respected him because we understood that he would do any and everything for his players and gave his great support as far as academics were concerned. We all revered the late Coach Hayes.

Draft
I hoped that I would be drafted as high as possible and close to the first round. It's kind of an interesting story because I came out during a period in which there were two separate leagues.

The AFL was a rival of the NFL. The Buffalo Bills, of the American Football League, approached me the summer before I returned to Ohio State for my final year of playing football there and my final year in school. Their general manager had spoken to me and told me to complete my final season of football at Ohio State. He said the Buffalo Bills wanted to draft me in the first round, but were concerned because they understood that I was interested in the possibility of playing professional baseball. They were trying to ascertain as early as the summer of 1963, if I was going to play football professionally or baseball because they did not want to, as I was told, waste a first round draft choice on me.

Jim Brown

Jim Brown is the greatest running back who ever played in the National Football League. Yes, I had the experience of playing with Jim Brown for two seasons, my rookie year in 1964, and in 1965. Although I didn't play much my second year because of injury, I was still in all of the meetings and was in his presence certainly during the 1965 season. I was finally able to play late in the year. I played in the NFL championship game against the Green Bay Packers that year.

Rookie Year With Cleveland Browns

I was very fortunate to lead them in receptions my rookie year. I played on the other side of another receiver by the name of Gary Collins. I've said this time and time again, and I'll say it here and now, in my mind, he is the best red zone receiver that I have ever seen. He was phenomenal inside the 20-yard line, a phenomenal receiver and a big receiver. He was one of the first big receivers at 6'4", and 225. Inside the red zone area, he was just unbelievable in terms of his capacity to score. He beat some of the top defensive backs time and time again, including guys who are in the Pro Football Hall of Fame. That combined with playing with pro football's greatest runner, Jim Brown, it was a great opportunity for me coming in to find some area of success. When you have that kind of supporting cast, people don't pay a great deal of attention to the newly arrived player.

Additionally, I want to add that once the Cleveland Browns made the decision that I was going to be a pass receiver, they really did a wonderful thing for me. They asked Ray Renfro, a former player of theirs who had just retired, to come in and be my private tutor. During four weeks of training camp, he worked solely with me on a daily basis. I benefited from Ray Renfro's instructions because he shared his twelve years of experience with me. We walked through them step-by-step. He taught me pattern execution.

As a first year player, I executed like an experienced veteran because of the expertise passed on to me. It helped me out immensely. My transition was smooth thanks to the coach, the Browns staff, working with veteran passer Frank, and my coming in and playing with other talented players. Frank Ryan understood the offense philosophy of the Browns.

Cleveland Browns Offense

I played with a team that emphasized running the football for the most part. When you have Jim Brown in the backfield, you're not going to be throwing the ball all over the lot. With the kind of ability that he had, he's going to be the main emphasis of the offensive strategy and rightfully so. After Jim Brown's departure, Leroy Kelly, who was drafted along with me, became one of the top backs in pro football along with Gale Sayers. The emphasis was still on running the football.

After being traded down to the Miami Dolphins, I was playing with a team that emphasized the run even more. As Napoleon said, "Ability is of little account without opportunity."

Trade To Miami Dolphins

The trade to the Miami Dolphins was a nice surprise. I was in my sixth year in the NFL and things were going well. It was something that was unexpected. When I received a telephone call from the owner, Art Modell, informing me that the team had made the decision to trade me for the Miami Dolphins' number one pick which was the third pick overall in the 1970 draft, I was disappointed. I was leaving an organization that was a perennial title contender and now Super Bowl contender. The Super Bowl was just in its third year. The Browns were eliminated in 1968 and 1969, by teams that represented the NFL in the Super Bowl. One team was the Baltimore Colts and the other was the Minnesota Vikings. Had we won those ballgames, we would have been in the Super Bowl. I was leaving an established title contending team to go to an expansion team out of the old American Football League. That team had never won more than five games in any season in its four years of existence.

First of all, I didn't want to be traded because I'm a native of Ohio. I grew up in a small town about 50 miles east of Cleveland. The Cleveland Browns were the team that I supported as a youngster. In my wildest dreams, I never thought I'd be with them, but if I was going to play pro football, that's the team I wanted to be with. It was one of pro football's elite teams. Even though they were a run-oriented team for the most part, I relished my role in which I could make a contribution here and there. I loved every facet of playing with the Browns. It just so happened that I got traded. Players didn't decide where they were going to play in those days. You couldn't demand to be traded to a team. Perhaps I could dream or wish that, but I had no control over that. Things worked out well in Miami for me. As I've always said about that trade, I didn't necessarily want to go, and I didn't know it was coming, but in the end, it turned out very well. Things changed overnight in Miami with Don Shula's emphasis, his input, and the willingness of those young players to want to be better. We went on to have as great a success as anybody has ever had in a few short years.

Don Shula

Don Shula came along 10 days after I was traded. I think it was a surprise when he resigned his position. It was his decision. As the story goes, he was approached by the Miami Dolphins, and given permission by Baltimore to talk to Miami. He subsequently signed a contract to coach the Dolphins.

Once he came onboard, I began to feel a little better. I knew of his excellence in the National Football League. Don Shula got the Baltimore Colts to the 1969 Super Bowl against the Jets.

Unfortunately, it didn't work out when they were upset by the Jets and Joe Namath.

Look at it from this perspective. He was going to a team that had never won more than five games in any of the four years that they had been in existence. They were an expansion team out of the old America Football League. Expansion teams were usually put together with castoffs or players who were considered to be on the downside of their careers from existing teams. The America Football League was not on par with the National Football League at that point. There were a couple of teams that you might say were, but basically as a league, it was considered tobe slightly inferior to the National Football League. The makeup of the team, except for a few individuals, was basically players who weren't considered to be on par with the stronger league the National Football League. Don was coming into a situation in which, yes, there was a nucleus to build a winner, but the entire thing had to be built. There was no tradition of winning.

Sports Illustrated would do their yearly analysis of pro football teams just before the teams went to training camp. It's 1969, and I'm reading about all of the National Football League teams that I'm familiar with. Since I knew the leagues were going to merge the following year, I looked at the section on the AFL. I'm thumbing through to see what I can read about the AFL, and I come across, ironically, the Miami Dolphins. The headline of that section said, "The Worst Team In Pro Football." I didn't want to read that. I read about the Chiefs, Raiders, and Chargers who were good. Little did I know that seven to nine months later, I would be on "The Worst Team In Pro Football." Don Shula was taking on an enormous challenge going down there.

Monte Clark

Monte Clark, who was on Don Shula's staff, did a tremendous job. Monte Clark was my teammate in Cleveland in 1969. He retired and was looking for a coaching job. Don Shula brings in Monte Clark, who was highly recommended by Blanton Collier, a great coach who coached Monte and me in Cleveland. Monte Clark transformed Jim Langer, Bob Kuechenberg, and Wayne Moore. He also helped develop Larry Little and Norm Evans. He made them one of the finest offensive lines in pro football.

Football Philosophy

I sincerely believe this: football is a team game, and the objective is to have monumental success and win. In Miami, we had a tremendous amount of success in a very short period of time. We had that because of the willingness of players who wanted to be better and the coming of a great young coach who fulfilled his destiny there. It was an organization that won with a philosophical concept which was a run-oriented, time-consuming, offensive attack that took tremendous amounts of time off the clock and with a defense that proved itself over and over again to be one of the best defenses during those championship years. It was a team effort, and we all benefited from it. We were all a part of the championship play whether you were the high guy on the totem pole or the low guy on the totem pole. In that short period of time, we accomplished something that no other team in the history of the game has done up until now, which is to go through an entire season undefeated, untied, and won a championship. Team play is what I learned from scholastic football to intercollegiate football and certainly in professional football. Play for great teams with great coaches and you win as a team. Individual accomplishments are something that you can be proud of, but basically the real thing you want to do is win championships and that's the most important thing.

Key To Success As Wide Receiver

Whether you're talking about today's game or yesterday's game, I think the ability of pass receivers to create separation for themselves from the individual who is defending them at breaking point, is in essence one asset that pass receivers must have. You can do it with quickness, explosiveness, speed, or if you're fortunate, you have all of those traits, or you can do it with a combination of things. The ability to separate at the instant when the ball is in the air, to create space between the receiver and the defender, is the pure essence of pass pattern running. From a philosophical standpoint, you can do it with technique. There are a number of techniques that I learned from the late Ray Renfro, but again, I must hone in on the fact that the ability to execute your pattern, to create space against the defender, is the key to getting open.

Toughest Cornerback
Early in my career, there was a little defender named Brady Keys, who played for the Pittsburgh Steelers. I thought he did a pretty good job on me. He created some problems for me whenever we played the Steelers. Later in my career, defenders began to get bigger and taller.

Mel Blount of the Steelers was 6'4". That's four inches taller than me. He had a long wingspan in terms of arm length, the ability, and the speed to run with me. Rarely, in the early years that I played, would you find a defender who had the height, the foot quickness, or the flexible hips that Mel Blount had. The same was true of Mike Haynes, who I faced in my final year or two. He was just coming in as a young cornerback and was approximately the same size as Mel Blount. He had the ability to turn, rotate his hips, and run with speed. They made it a little difficult, but at that point, I was trending down and going out of the league. Fortunately, I didn't have to face them on a game-by-game basis when I was in my prime.

Running Style
The uniqueness of my running style was that it appeared I was not exerting a lot of effort, but I was. It probably helped me deceive my defenders who were trying to determine exactly how fast I was going. It appeared to them that I was not running as fast as I was. It was more of a long gliding stride instead of quick acceleration. It was part of my style and deceptiveness, and it came naturally for me.

1972 Miami Dolphins Perfect Season
A few years ago, the Patriots almost had a perfect season. There were just one or two plays in the Giants game that kept them from equaling the mark. First of all, a lot has been made of when the mark will be broken. Teams play two more games now. The feat itself is undefeated, and so we were undefeated. You're going to have to say that the new team is the new and latest undefeated team, but they really don't break that mark. It was a wonderful season as I recall. The season happened primarily because, as I saw it, we were not trying to accomplish perfection.

Pro Football Hall Of Fame Induction
It's something that I never thought would happen as far as I was concerned. My objective in playing football was to play Sunday-in and Sunday-out to the very best of my ability, to have a great experience in doing so, and help my team win football games.

I grew up as a youngster in Northeast Ohio watching Otto Graham and Marion Motley, who played alongside him, in the Cleveland backfield. The two of them are in the Pro Football Hall of Fame. You think of other great players like Jim Brown, who I've had the honor of playing with, or Johnny Unitas who played and was so brilliant.

I watched the 1958 Championship Game between the Giants & Colts in which the two-minute offense was invented. The events of that game were mindboggling. It was the first time sudden death was ever played. Maybe it's not akin to the first time that man walked on the moon, but it had never happened before because football games ended in a tie during that period. It's taken for granted today, but to see the mastery of Johnny Unitas in that game was unbelievable.

Then there was the million-dollar backfield with the San Francisco 49ers, Y. A. Tittle, Joe Perry, Hugh McElhenny, and John Henry Johnson. They were great, great players.

I never thought what I accomplished in pro football would lead me to be in that special place with the greatest players who have ever played. I was overwhelmed. When you are inducted, certain things come to mind. You think about how it happened, and take into consideration your support system. The people who helped you get a spot in the Pro Football Hall of Fame are your family, your coaches, and great teammates that you played with through the years. I think most of us want to acknowledge the great, great respect we have for those who helped us achieve our success and get there.

Years ago, I had the privilege of being with Brooks Robinson, the great third baseman for the Baltimore Orioles who is in the Baseball Hall Of Fame. We happened to have a conversation about the hall of fame. He agreed with me, saying that he just tried to be the best player he could be every time he stepped on a baseball field. We just try to play up to our expectations and our ability. We are overwhelmed. I think about the individuals who said I belong there with the greats who have played this game. I also remember the gentlemen who preceded me in the National Football League. I certainly was a great, great fan of those guys. I've had opportunities to be with Chuck Bednarik, who's a veteran of World War II and was a hero during the war. It's always an honor to be in his presence not only because of what he accomplished in the NFL, but also because of his service to the country during World War II. That was a period when there were a lot greater things at stake in terms of the freedoms of individuals and our nation along with its allies. I was just born right around that time. Things could have been vastly different if the United States and its allies had not been successful.

Hugh McElhenny was as fine as a runner as this league has ever seen. I remember him and his electrifying running skill when he was with the San Francisco 49ers. I was just a youngster. I had the pleasure of meeting him.

I had the pleasure of meeting Don Hutson at a past Hall of Fame session. In my opinion, he is certainly at the top of the list when you start talking about great receivers of an era. The things that he was able to accomplish in his era—it's just incredible.

Richard Nixon Calling Don Shula Before Super Bowl VI With A Play For Paul Warfield
President Nixon contacted Coach Shula and asked him call a quick slant pass to me. I've been a Democrat all of my life and he was a Republican president. It certainly makes one feel special when the President of the United States takes notice of what you do and sends a special note to your coach saying that you gotta do this.

Football Philosophy
I see a lot of things that are happening today. You know, I am an old school guy who obviously comes from another era. I just believe that you respect your opponents. You respect them for

their toughness, for what they've accomplished, and you give them the ultimate respect when you're playing on the field. I wanted to beat them as bad as the next guy and my whole focus and concentration was on doing that. I just don't think you do it on the sidelines with all this verbiage about what you're going to do and so forth. After all, you know you're talking about football and it is a team-oriented sport. I may personally feel that I am capable of doing a whole lot of things, but I've got to have people to help me accomplish those things. If you're playing an individual sport like tennis, golf, or something like that and you want to engage in a lot of verbiage, then you can back that up yourself. You can't account for the rest of your teammates. But, I believe in respect and competitiveness, and that's a part of all sports.

Photograph courtesy Associated Press

Chapter 56

Fred Biletnikoff

College:
Florida State

Career History:

As Player:
Oakland Raiders (1965–1978)
Montreal Alouettes (CFL) (1980)

As Coach:
Montreal Alouettes (1980)
Orange Glen High School (1982)
Palomar College (1983)
Diablo Valley College (1984)
Oakland Invaders (1985)
Arizona Wranglers (1986)
Calgary Stampeders (1987–88)
L.A./Oakland Raiders (1989–2006)

1988 Inductee Pro Football Hall of Fame

College Choice
Joe Paterno always told me he missed out on me. Ken Meyer, who was coaching at Florida State at that time, was from Erie, Pennsylvania. He had an aunt and uncle that lived in Erie, Pennsylvania. One of the coaches on my high school team, Ray Dombrowski was a good friend with Ken. Ray recommended me to Ken. Ken came out and watched me workout and that's how I went to Florida State.

Bobby Bowden
I always tell Bobby Bowden, he would never have become famous if he weren't my receiver coach. Bill Peterson was our Head Coach. We had a pretty good coaching staff at that time with a lot of pass-oriented type of guys in terms of philosophy. Those guys were used to throwing the football. They built up a pretty good core of guys to bring down there to play and do what they wanted to do as far as passing.

Bill was a good friend of Sid Gillman. Bill spent a lot of time in San Diego at training camp with Sid to get the passing game that he wanted. That's kind of how everything fell into place there.

Florida State

My first two years at Florida State, if you were a receiver away from the call, you lined up like a tight end. We ran a tight formation with one wide receiver split out wide and the other wide receiver lined up tight all the time. Those were pretty interesting camps that I had to go through because I had to do all the blocking drills, along with the wide receiver drills. I got beat up pretty good. It made me a lot tougher, though.

Draft

When I made the move from Erie down to Tallahassee, at that time, it was a big move for somebody to go that far away to school. At the end of my four years at Florida State, I was drafted by Detroit and the Raiders. I really hadn't made up my mind that I was going out to Oakland to play for Al Davis. It was a really hard decision for me. I wanted to get away from the cold and snow and go out to California, which I had the opportunity to do. I just figured I'd take a shot and sign with Oakland and go out there. The AFL was going to throw the ball a lot, which was right down my alley. My last two years at Florida State we threw the ball quite a bit. That's the thing that really put it over the top for me as far as signing with the Raiders, and of course, Al Davis's influence, too. That's basically how I made up my mind. There wasn't any hesitation on my part.

Al Davis just gave you a contract and the money was already on there. He had already signed it so he just expected you to put your name on it.

At that time Joe Namath had gotten a big contract. Harry Schuh, who was drafted ahead of me in the first round by the Raiders, also made pretty good money.

I got a decent contract at that time. It was a good enough contract that when I got to camp, all the veterans on the Raiders were mad at Harry Schuh and me because we were making so much money. We still had to go get our offseason jobs. It wasn't that much but we went through that period of time, even in 1965, where we were making a lot of money. It really made a lot of veterans mad.

There was no negotiation. At that time, everybody was given a two- or three-year contract guaranteeing the first two years and the bonus money that ran for each year of the contract. In my third year, I had bonus money but no contract. It worked out well for me.

Oakland Raiders Quarterbacks

I started with Tom Flores, Cotton Davidson, and Dick Wood who would later play for the Jets, as the quarterbacks. Cotton actually played on the Baltimore Colts with Johnny Unitas and Raymond Berry for a brief period of time. Flores was the starter. In later seasons, Al Davis brought in Daryle Lamonica, George Blanda, and Ken Stabler.

I had a chance to play with all four of them. Obviously Lamonica, Blanda, and Stabler were the main guys I played with. I played with Flores for a couple of years. All four of those guys could really throw the football, along with Cotton Davidson and Dick Wood.

With Flores, I was just a young kid and I didn't really help him out. It was hit and miss with me when Tom threw me the ball. Everything turned around for me when they brought Lamonica in and we were throwing the ball more down the field, along with Blanda. Blanda had come from Houston, where they threw the ball 40 to 50 times a game. I had a good rapport with Lamonica, Blanda, and Kenny because we spent a lot of time on the field throwing passes, running routes, and that type of thing.

The quarterbacks were used to seeing what all the receivers did because everybody worked together. You weren't just working with Lamonica; you were working with Blanda too. Later on when Kenny came and Lamonica left, it was Blanda and Kenny. You spent so much time working with those guys on the field in practice, training camp, and during the season that the quarterbacks knew how all the receivers ran routes and what they did. It was a comfortable situation with all of the quarterbacks that I played with.

Adjusting To NFL
When I was a rookie in my very first preseason game I was playing behind Art Powell and Bo Roberson at that time, two outstanding receivers. In the preseason, I wasn't doing very well and was dropping balls. Al Davis probably wondered why he drafted me. I struggled during my first year. Then he traded Bo Roberson away allowing me to be the starter across from Art Powell. The following season, I torn my knee up, so that wasn't very good as far as Al was concerned.

When Al let Claude Gibson go that opened up number 25 for me, so I was able to get my college number. Previously Dick Romanski, our equipment guy, gave me the number 14 and it was probably the worst jinx number I've ever had in my life. When I got the number 25 everything started going better for me.

Super Bowl XI
Super Bowl XI, for me, was something that we had been, to use the term "knocking on the door," every year. In previous years we were losing close championship games where we had an opportunity to get to Super Bowls.

It was almost like we were jinxed. Something always happened, like in Pittsburgh or wherever it may be, that just prevented us from getting to the Super Bowl. When we finally got there, we were a well-seasoned team. We were all veterans at the time. A lot of us were basically at the end or toward the end of our careers. The whole group that we had at that time grew together for a good period of time. We had a lot of veterans that had a lot of experience.

We were always a pretty confident team as far as knowing what we could do with the players that we had because we had a tremendous amount of great players on the offense, defense, and special teams. It was an unbelievable roster that we had at that time.

Super Bowl XI was played in Pasadena and we had over 100,000 spectators. We beat Minnesota. It was pretty awesome. It was really good.

I had a lot of sentiment after we beat Minnesota. I thought about all those guys that I played with when I was young who were playing football in the AFL. I thought about the guys who didn't have the opportunity to go to and win a Super Bowl.

That crossed my mind a lot because I had a lot of close ties with those guys. They brought me up with very good guidance as far as being able to play tough, being a tough guy out there, having a good work ethic, seeing what those guys did and how they worked, and what it took to be a professional football player. We had a lot of veterans on the team when I was a young kid first coming to the Raiders.

Jack Tatum & George Atkinson
I figured I'd have it easy the rest of my career if I could deal with Jack Tatum, George Atkinson, and Willie Brown in practice. We went through a lot of live practices and got hit by those guys. We were able to avoid them at times too. That whole group of guys was a big plus for us. Those guys have always been looked at as the best defensive backs that played in professional football.

Turning Point In NFL Career
After I came back from an injury early in my career, things started to fall into place. I learned that this is a game where if you get hurt and can't make it back on the field, you weren't going to play. You had to have that type of attitude.

After the injury, I really understood that basically football was a business now, not like the football that I had played as a kid in my backyard in Erie, Pennsylvania. I enjoyed playing it there but now I was in a business that if I wanted to survive, I really had to go at it, work at it, and be professional at it.

It was probably in my third year with the Raiders that I finally started coming around as a receiver. I felt that I could compete with the guys we had on our team at the receiver position and against the guys we were going to play to against.

John Madden
John Madden was pretty active, a great coach, and a great motivator. The one great thing about John is that he knew each player individually. He knew how to handle them individually. Even though he had a whole slew of players that he had to handle, he knew everything about the players on his team. He handled you accordingly. If you needed to be reprimanded about something he did it.

There were times when he was not easy on you because he wanted to make sure you were competing. John was really unique in being able to handle that many guys in that manner and really, really understand what he had as a team and what he had to do as a head coach.

John was a tough guy to play for but he was a fair guy to play for. You went out there, practiced hard, played hard in games, and spent time working on whatever position you were playing. John appreciated that. John had the greatest appreciation for the work every individual on the team did as far as the position they were playing. John was a terrific guy to play for.

Toughest Defensive Backs

Herb Adderley was tough because we didn't play against him very often, and he was a really aggressive guy. Jimmy Johnson over at San Francisco was a very good player because he was tall and rangy. During that time, there were basically no rules. Those guys came up and played bump and run on you.

You were getting hit all the time. It was a physical game and you had to learn how to be physical. You also had to learn how to handle the different styles of the guys that you were playing against because they were all different sizes, had different speeds, and had different quickness levels. You had to understand whom you were playing against.

Jimmy Marsalis was a tough guy in Kansas City. Bobby Howard was a good player down in San Diego. There were a lot of good players in the league that you played against when they played bump and run. It was just a physical game. You just had to learn that you just couldn't let somebody get out there and dominate you. You just had to keep fighting.

Al Davis

Willie Brown and I were both fortunate because we spent our entire coaching careers with the Raiders. It was fortunate for us because we didn't have to move all over getting jobs with other teams, like a lot of coaches did. Al Davis had a philosophy about how he liked his receivers to play. I knew what he wanted and what needed to be done with the receivers.

Al had a philosophy about defensive backs, how they should play, and Willie was the example, like I was the example with the receivers. Al wanted to keep that consistency because defensive backs and wide receivers were a big priority on our team. He wanted consistency so he kept Willie and I as coaches, fortunately for us, all of those years.

Pro Football Hall Of Fame Induction

You really didn't know how you got there and what the procedure was for getting in. The writers in your area were basically the ones that promoted you to the rest of the committee to be inducted into the Hall of Fame. You had to depend on the writers in your area promoting you. When that happened with me, I was like, "Oh, wow!"

When you finally go there for the ceremony, it's a whole different perspective, a whole different outlook, and a whole different feeling than when you first found out you're going into the Hall of Fame. When you're actually there with all of the guys already in the Hall of Fame, guys who played for Cleveland, the Eagles, and Pittsburgh years ago when I was a kid, and have the chance to be around them in person and be in the Hall of Fame with them, it seemed unbelievable.

It's not a very big group but that's the great thing about it, being part of a small, unique group of guys. I've always felt that the recognition you get from being in the Hall of Fame is not enough. After being in the Hall of Fame for a number of years and getting to see a lot of the things going on, being in the Hall of Fame isn't recognized enough for what that group means to professional football.

Tommy McDonald

I followed Tommy McDonald of the Eagles. He was my guy. Tommy McDonald still doesn't believe me. I told him, "When I went to Florida State, I got number 25 because you were my hero. I loved watching you play. That's why I got number 25." He didn't believe me. He still hasn't sent me a signed jersey either.

Chuck Bednarik

I'll tell you why Chuck Bednarik was my all-time guy. I call him an all-time guy; I'm one of them now, because those guys have a history of toughness when they played in the league years ago. They played during a time when it was physical and tough. You were getting hit and all type of stuff but man, those guys played tough. That was a rough and tumble group of guys. They were tough.

Favorite Play

We played Miami in a playoff game in Oakland. I had one catch down in the corner of the end zone, right by the goal line, against Tim Foley. To me, that was a pretty good catch. I don't say that too often about myself, but when I see that video every once in a while or see a picture of it, that's a hell of a catch.

Football Philosophy

When you have to pay bills and child support you find ways to get down the field pretty quick. Deception is a word everybody else uses. I've always thought, hey, I'm fighting for my life out here. I better get going right now. There were times you look at yourself on film and see yourself moving a little faster than you think you could move and I think it's just the fact of you having that competitor's spirit. Every athlete has a gift; some of us just don't have all the gifts. At times we're able do something exciting or something good, and we can definitely be proud of ourselves. Playing football all those years, there were times when I looked at film, and I thought, "Oh, I'm not that slow." Other times I looked at myself and said, "Oh, you are slow." It juggled back and forth quite a bit during my career.

Fred Biletnikoff, left, and quarterback Ken Stabler
Photograph courtesy Associated Press

Chapter 57

Gale Sayers

College:
Kansas
Career History:
Chicago Bears (1965–1971)
1977 Inductee Pro Football Hall of Fame

College Choice

In my senior year at Omaha Central High School, my football coach wanted me to go to the University of Iowa. He graduated from the University of Iowa and came back to Omaha Central High as a high school coach. I believed in everything he said. If he said go to Iowa, I was going.

I went on a three-day visit to the University of Iowa. Jerry Burns was the coach at that time. He was looking for a kid named Henry Carr who was a world-class sprinter. The only bad thing about that was he didn't have the grades to get into the University of Iowa.

I was there for three days and Jerry Burns didn't see me one time because he was after Henry Carr. So I thought, there isn't any way I'm going here if Jerry can't at least take time and say how are you doing and shake my hand. If he would have just shook my hand, I was going there. It was automatic since my high school coach told me to go there.

I went to the University of Kansas and talked to the coach, Jack Mitchell, who I liked. He was a great coach and he told me, "Gale, I want you to see a man in Kansas City." So we drove down to Kansas City and saw a man named Ray Evans. He was a good football coach, and was an All-American. He said, "Gale, if you get your degree, I can promise you that we can get you a job after you get your degree."

No other person ever said anything about me getting a degree. I got my degree and didn't have to go to see Ray anymore because I was playing football. That really made me like the University of Kansas, because they were concerned about me after football, not just playing it for them.

Dick Butkus

The first time I ever met Dick Butkus we were both at an All-American game in New York. We talked about the Bears, and I told him, "I think I'm going to sign with the Chicago Bears." He said, "Well, Buffalo is looking at me out of the AFL. I'm going to take little bit more time and see what they've got to offer. Finally he came to the Bears.

I had never heard of Dick Butkus in my life. He had gone to the University of Illinois, but after a half an hour I knew why the Bears drafted him. He was a killer. He was hitting me as hard in scrimmage as anybody had in a game. He came to play the game. I came to play the game too. It didn't make any difference whether he hit me hard or not; I was still going to go get him. He was a great, great football player in the NFL.

Brian Piccolo

Brian always had a joke. He just was a guy who laughed all the time and a good football player. When he came out of Wake Forest, people thought that he wasn't big enough or fast enough and the Bears took a chance on him. He became one hell of a football player. He was fun guy to be around. After about two and a half years, he came down with a cough, and he went in to see what was going on and they found he had cancer. It was just one of those things that happened. It's too bad because he was a good football player.

The movie was 100% accurate. Joy Piccolo and I spent about two months with James Caan and Billy Dee Williams going over mannerisms of Brian and me and they did an outstanding job. Jack Warden was in the movie too. It was a great time doing it. Before they put it on TV they had all the players, their wives, and coaches' wives come to Halas Hall and watch the movie. We saw the movie before anybody else saw the movie. There wasn't a dry eye in the house.

The players enjoyed Billy Dee and the other film people coming out to training camp to film the movie. They did a real good job.

Billy Dee was a nice guy. I really liked him. The only bad thing was we had to put a lot of padding around Billy Dee to make him look bigger, because he weighed about 145 pounds. He was a small individual. He did a nice job.

Barry Sanders

I think Barry Sanders was the only person who could run like me. He had the moves, like I had the moves, and he did all that playing for the Detroit Lions. Now he's in the Hall of Fame. He was a great, great football player. He had a chance to break the rushing record but he decided to quit. He wasn't injured. I asked him several times, "Barry, why are you quitting?" He said, "I don't want to play football anymore." He wasn't concerned about the records or anything. If he played two more years, he would have set all kinds of records.

NFL Career

When I played the game, I ran back punt returns, kickoff returns, and played running back. Many times when we'd go out there for the start of the first quarter after I had run back a kickoff return for maybe 30 yards or so, I'd come back into the huddle and carry the ball for the first four plays. I had to be in shape. No question about it. I had to be in shape. I did it in high school and I did it in college. It didn't bother me if I was going to run a punt return back or a kickoff back at the beginning of the game. I knew I had to be in shape and I got myself in shape.

I think Jim Brown's the best. O.J. Simpson is in that category too, among the best. Me playing in only 68 games, I'm happy to be a part of the top 10.

Jim Brown's Advice

I did not have a TV growing up. Very seldom did I watch the pros play on TV. I had a chance to meet Jim Brown one time when I was a senior at Kansas and he said, "Gale, I heard you are a pretty good football player. Make sure when you come to training camp, you come in shape. That's where you are going to make the team, in training camp. You're not going to make it playing exhibition games. They want to see what you do in training camp blocking, catching balls, and things like that."

I took that advice and it probably made me a better football player.

College All-Star Game

I got injured playing in the College All-Star Game. Otto Graham was the coach of the college all-stars at that time and I told him I hurt my knee. He said, "I don't think you hurt your knee. I'm going to sit you out and I'm not going to let you play in this ballgame because I don't think you hurt your knee." I said, "Okay, fine."

After the ballgame, I got in my car and drove down to Wesleyan, Indiana, and I went in to talk to Coach Halas. Coach Halas said, "Gale, I know you had some problems with Coach Graham. I'm going to judge you by what you do today at the game and that's it. I'm not even going to talk to you about what happened to you at the All-Star game. I'm going to just judge you by what you do on the field."

Rookie Year

We had some decent running backs, but none of them were as quick as I was, as fast as I was; couldn't catch the ball like I could catch it, and couldn't make moves like I could. I knew that if George Halas gave me a shot, I would be a starting running back. I knew it. I felt it. I could see in practice there's no way these people can beat me running and things like that.

George Halas would always go out onto the field before the game. He would come back into the locker room, and name the names of who was going to play. The third ballgame of the season up in Green Bay, he calls out the names of the tackles and guards and I was the last one to be called. "Sayers, you are going to start today." I was nervous but it worked out okay. They beat us but I scored on a 65-yard touchdown run and caught a couple of passes. When Green Bay came back to Chicago, we beat them.

Photograph courtesy Associated Press

Chapter 58

Tom Mack

College:
Michigan

Career History
Los Angeles Rams (1966-1978)

1999 Inductee Pro Football Hall of Fame

Michigan
In the early '60s we went from last place to winning the Big Ten and going to the Rose Bowl during my junior year. We won the Rose Bowl beating Oregon State.

Back in my day, we had a very strong and consistent running game. Although I played tackle, I was probably as fast as any lineman around there. Over the years, Michigan seemed to be able to recruit good linemen who were big but also very agile, and I would attribute most of that to the running game. Certainly Bo Schembechler, after Bump Elliott, had a very strong running game too.

Bump Elliott
Probably one of the classiest people both on and off the field I have ever run into. He was really a true gentleman, as was his brother, who ended up being the director of the Pro Football Hall of Fame in later years. The two of them had played at Michigan in the late '40s on championship teams. They were just really, really classy people.

College Choice
I guess it's sufficed to say that I wasn't exactly a star high school athlete. Interestingly enough, probably my best sport was swimming, not football. I had a chance to go to a number of schools on a swimming scholarship.

My swim coach had been to Michigan a lot and he got hold of some local alumni recruiters. He really helped sell Michigan on the idea that I was going to mature later in life rather than earlier in life. Between the time I went to college and I ended up getting out of school, I gained about 50 pounds of real good weight and I still had all the speed. So, they were right about me maturing late so to speak.

Rose Bowl
At that time when you grew up in the Midwest the family kind of sat around on New Year's Day and there were three or four games you watched. The biggest of them all was the Rose Bowl. I can remember watching Minnesota, Wisconsin, and different teams. When I got to play in the Rose Bowl it turned out to be a bigger deal than I probably realized.

Maybe the most interesting thing is I met a girl on a blind date in Pasadena while we were there. Forty-seven years later she is still my wife. So it was pretty eventful.

She was a young lady who had gone to Cal, was transferring to UCLA, and was putting herself through junior college at Pasadena City College at that time. I honestly met her on a blind date.

Draft
The last year there were two leagues in the AFL and NFL was 1966. They actually competed vigorously against each other. In fact, Miami, which was a new team in the AFL, actually went to my parents' house and tried to convince them to get me to sign with the AFL instead of the NFL.

I had a bunch of people following me around trying to get me to go with them. It was pretty obvious that I was going to get drafted fairly high.

The Los Angeles Rams, partly because of the fact that I had this girlfriend in California, turned out to be the perfect team for me. It was coincidental that the Rams were in last placed in the NFL at that point, so they had the first pick. I was obviously pretty lucky to be in that position. I think the most interesting thing was I was not an All-American. I made the second team, All-American. That was as close as I got to any kind of notoriety, so it really was a big surprise when people heard my name. They were all looking around "Who the hell is he?"

That year Mike Garrett won the Heisman Trophy, the first in a long line of USC backs who have won the Heisman. I have a headline in an old scrapbook. It says Rams draft Mike Garrett and in the second round, a guy named Mack and then it goes "Who" with a question mark. That's an interesting article because nobody knows who the hell I am and it says he better turn out to be good. So, I am glad it turned out both for them and for me.

First Training Camp
It was fairly brutal. Coincidentally, George Allen became the Head Coach after I got drafted but before training camp. He publicly made it clear that he wasn't going to put up with a lot of rookies and he went out and started acquiring veterans. Bill George, a linebacker for the Chicago Bears and Coach Allen talked to him into coming to the Rams. It was just absolutely fascinating. He had all kinds of old players. At the beginning of the year, even though we had probably 10 or 12 guys who had been draft choices and all of us had gotten some kind of guaranteed money, only four of us started the season on the actual roster. By the end of the season I was the only rookie who was actually still on the team and playing.

Well, timing is everything. You've got to be in the right place at the right time. It was interesting because a group of Rams offensive linemen kind of begrudgingly adopted me about a third of the way through the season. I ended up playing with three of those guys for another nine years or so. We became a pretty close group of guys, the four of us.

Fearsome Foursome
Rosey Grier was the guy I practiced against on a daily basis, so that was interesting by itself. Deacon Jones would be on the other side with Merlin Olsen. Lamar Lundy was the defensive end

next to Rosey Grier, who played tackle. That was the original fearsome foursome. That kind of got supplemented over the next few years.

Rosey retired after he tore his Achilles tendon and Roger Brown played for a couple of years. Then Coach Allen started to move people around and it changed the complexion a little bit. The whole time I played, we had very, very good defensive lines.

Head Slap

Nobody tells you exactly how to protect yourself against the head slap. I got slapped more than a few times. When I asked the coach how to protect myself, he told me to put my arm up with my hand high at kind of an angle. He said, "When Deacon tries to slap you, it will slip up over the top of your helmet." So, I tried that. In practice one day, I put my right hand up and sure enough Deacon did not slap me on that side, he slapped on the other side of the head. So I tried putting both hands up and then he used a whip maneuver and came up underneath my arm and took me up into the air and we ran in and jumped on the quarterback. That didn't work very well. Over the years you find out that the best way to prevent a head slap, when it was legal, was to let the guy slap you in the head and while he is slapping you in the head, he is wide open to a hell of a punch in the ribs if you know what you are doing. So you just punched him in the rib as hard as you can and pretty soon he will stop slapping you in the head.

George Allen

George Allen really did serve us well in terms of going out and get a veteran player that could help us. He picked up Maxie Baughan, Myron Pottios from the Steelers, Richie Petitbon from the Bears, Irv Cross from Philadelphia, and got Jack Pardee to come out of retirement. He was an amazing guy. What he did was find veteran players who were playing on bad teams but were still intense people. He would get them to come to the Rams, employ them in our mix, and develop good teams. He is an interesting guy. He was hard to work for because he was primarily interested in defense.

He really did not care what the offense did as long as we did not turn over the ball, which sounds kind of silly. The offense had two jobs, one was to hang on to the ball and not turn it over and the second was that we were supposed to use forty minutes out of the clock in any game playing keep-away from the other team. The reason being that if they didn't have the ball, they couldn't score. As long as we had the ball, whether we scored or not, we were keeping it away from them. He would depend on one or two big plays. Either we would get an interception or we get a touchdown after we worked our way down the field. He was an interesting guy.

One of the George's grandkids is named after Deacon Jones. George was very good with Deacon and Deacon responded by becoming not just a good player, but a great player. Deacon was very much a key leader on the team and that was extremely important. Without George I don't think Deacon ever would have been the great player that he ended up becoming.

Defensive Lineman

To be a good defensive lineman, you have to believe in yourself and Deacon Jones certainly believed in himself. I played against great defensive tackles. Of course, our own Merlin Olsen was a great defensive tackle. I played against people like Bob Lilly and Alan Page, guys who in my mind were the greatest players that I experienced. I always felt it was harder to become a great player on the inside than on the outside.

We were playing the Bears in Chicago and the tackle next to me was having a good game against Doug Atkins. Doug was kind of taking it easy, not really coming all that hard. We ran a play that was supposed to look a little bit like a sweep but it was more of a cross block thing and I came up under Atkins and I cut him and knocked him down. He said a few nasty things to me and called me some names and rookie and blah, blah, blah. So I told him where I thought he ought to go. I walked right to the huddle and the offensive tackle jumps all over me and says, "What the hell are you doing? I am having a good game because that guy is kind of asleep. I want you to go up down next play. After the play, apologize to him." I said, "You've got to be kidding." He said, "No. If we wake that guy up, you know we've got a problem.

I've got a problem, you've got a problem; we've all got a problem." So after the next play, I went over, and said, "I am sorry Mr. Atkins, I didn't mean to cut you." He said, "That's okay kid." He kind of went back to being a sleeping giant again. I just kept away from him and the tackle had a good game the whole game.

I saw him when he was down in New Orleans playing at the end of his career. He was still a fearsome competitor when he wanted to be. He was just really an intimidating player.

Biggest Rivals
You would think the San Francisco 49ers would have been our biggest rivals. We played them, including exhibition games, 38 times and lost about six games. Interestingly, we just seemed to have a whammy on them; we really dominated them.

I played in four championship games and we lost them all. We lost two to the Cowboys and two the Vikings. It was bitter frustration and disappointment but they were great teams.

Favorite Moment In NFL
Well, it is hard to say, probably when we beat the Cowboys in key games and the playoffs. When I played the Cowboys and the Vikings I always had my hands full because I was playing either Bob Lilly or Randy White or I was playing Alan Page. All three of those guys are in the Hall of Fame with me and they were great defensive tackles. Any game we beat one of those teams was the kind of game you remembered.

Pro Football Hall Of Fame Induction
I felt a little overwhelmed by the fact that I was inducted. Back in the day, announcers didn't talk much about offensive linemen at all. You listen to announcers now and they are picking kids in their second and third year in the league and say that guy is a sure Hall of Famer. As a lineman, you've got to be good enough and consistent enough for a long enough period of time. You have to be the dominant player at that particular position for about a decade, and have people remember all that to get in the hall.

I was a finalist to get into Hall of Fame 11 times and I did not get in. After a while I got to the point where I became a little bit cynical about it. When I got nominated, as far as I was concerned, that was as good as the first time.

Career

It helps to be on good teams and it helps to play with other good players. You have to keep from getting hurt. I ended up playing every game for 13 years. It is not that I am tough. I'm probably more of a monumental tribute to stupidity, because you play hurt a lot but I was able to do it.

I played against Dick Butkus in college and then I played against him when he was with the Bears. Dick was a tough guy. I don't think he ever missed a game.

We might have lost one game to the Bears in 1966, and didn't lose again to the Bears until we were trying to play Joe Namath as our quarterback. Joe could not physically play anymore. His legs were no longer good and his arm wasn't any good that year. He was pretty well done. We kept changing quarterbacks, and honestly that probably hurt us more than helped us.

Los Angeles Ram Tom Mack blocks Dallas Cowboy Bob Lilly. Photograph courtesy Associated Press

Chapter 59

Claude Humphrey

> College:
> Tennessee State
>
> Career History:
> Atlanta Falcons (1968–1974, 1976–1978)
> Philadelphia Eagles (1979–1981)
>
> 2014 Inductee Pro Football Hall of Fame

College Choice

I visited quite a few schools before deciding where I was going to college. I narrowed it down to Tennessee State and a little school up in Kentucky called Moreland. Tennessee State appeared to be the best deal for me. Everybody has things that they like. I visited Grambling, Texas Southern, Jackson State, and a few other schools in the Southwest. I liked Tennessee State because it was close to my hometown. That was really a factor for me in choosing a university.

Southern schools shied away from the black athletes. I had one school tell me they would enroll me, but a couple of teams in their conference probably wouldn't allow me to play against them. I was told that, so going to the bigger southern schools was eliminated at that point.

Eddie Robinson

Eddie Robinson almost had me, had he not brought me in to visit there. It had nothing to do with the school. Not that being from Memphis made me a real city person, but I wasn't quite as country as you needed to be to be able to live in Grambling. Grambling's a small place. You had to go so far to do anything other than the activities on the campus. If he had not done that, he may have had a better chance to get me.

Tennessee State was the best decision that I could have ever made for my education.

College

My Head Coach at Tennessee State was John Merritt. The assistants were Joe Gilliam, Alvin Colman, J. C. Coffee, Shannon Little, and Samuel Whitman.

We played San Diego State my senior year. Of course, they beat us, but we beat them physically. We beat them down. I think they scored on a punt return, and something else. They were one of the four losses that I had in my four years at Tennessee State.

At that time I had no interest in playing professional football. I was just there to try to get an education and just play football.

Joe Gilliam

I really didn't realize how great a player he was. He was such a great athlete. I learned that by taking stunts and tumbling from him. He could do stuff that some of us seventeen and eighteen-year-olds couldn't do. He was a great athlete.

Being Drafted By Atlanta Falcons

John Merritt was my coach and agent. He was pretty well informed. That was the one thing about him; he knew what was going on. Maybe a month before the draft, I knew that the Falcons, if they had a chance, were going to take me.

The Falcons were drafting second, but third overall, because that year Minnesota had a bonus pick and picked Ron Yary. Cincinnati picked Bob Johnson, a center from Tennessee. Then it was the Falcons' choice and they picked me.

First Training Camp

It was a killer! It was a rude awakening to professional football. At Tennessee State we practiced really hard. We practiced three times a day. We had two regular practices, and a special team practice, so we were practicing three times a day. I guess, because I was so relaxed practicing at Tennessee State, it went pretty good there.

When I went to the Falcons in Johnson City, Tennessee, it was so hot it was ridiculous. They made no allowances for the heat. We could have practiced earlier in the morning, or later in the afternoon. We went out there in the hot part of the day to practice, and we beat each other down. It was tough. It was nothing like college. Even though in college we practiced three times a day and we were only practicing two times a day in Johnson City, Johnson City was hot.

Norm Van Brocklin

I had Norm Van Brocklin as Head Coach in the College All-Star game. He was tough, but he seemed like a nice guy. Coaches have to be disciplinarians. He disciplined us pretty well at the College All-Star Game. Three games into the season; they fired Norb Hecker and brought Norm Van Brocklin in as Head Coach. Wow! What a difference with Norm. Norm Van Brocklin worked us like crazy. Not only did he work us physically, he worked us mentally, too. It was tough.

He expected everybody to play as well as he did, and better. It didn't take him long to tell you that. He got right down to it. Norm didn't beat around the bush. If there was something that needed to be said, he said it. He disregarded your feelings. You were a professional, and you were going to be treated that way.

Everybody got treated the same, which is really one of the good things about him. When he got on me, he got on everybody else the same way. That's one of the things that I respected most about him. He was pretty tough on us.

College All-Star Game

I was up against the great Forrest Gregg. Forrest gave me a lesson in how to play in the NFL. I thought I was ready. I was up there, practicing, working against Ron Yary, John Williams, and those guys. I thought I was pretty good. I found out that I had a lot to learn and a short time to learn it in. Forrest Gregg gave me a lesson in how to be kept away from the quarterback.

Toughest Offensive Lineman Faced
I caught Forrest Gregg at the end of his professional career, so I can't quite rate him up there with some guys like Bob Brown, Ron Yary, and Rayfield Wright. The time that I faced Forrest Gregg, even though I knew his greatness, I didn't get a chance to experience it, because he was at the end of his career. I understand he was a terror when he was younger.

Early Years With Falcons
Don't remind me of the '60s. We got a little bit better in the '70s when we started to get some good players, like George Kunz and Steve Bartkowski. Prior to that, we weren't very good. Teams knew it, and they took advantage of it.

Larry Csonka
It was a Monday night game and Larry Csonka just ran right up my chest. He used his shoulder and used that form of his. I wasn't ready for him the way you normally get ready for a running back. He showed me that you have to be ready all the time. It never happened again. That was real abuse, having to tackle him. He was a great fullback. He played great for a long time.

Career
I enjoyed the whole game. There was no part of it that I enjoyed more than others. At that time, a sack was just a tackle. Nobody really counted sacks. The most fun was batting balls. I felt like that was one of my strong suits. I got a chance to bat down a whole lot of balls. I probably batted down more balls than some of the defensive backs did for a season, until they stopped throwing my way. They used to try to throw a lot of quick outs on me my rookie year, and I got a chance to bat down a lot of balls.

I was happy about the hurries that I got. It wasn't roughing the quarterback like it is now. We got a chance to tee off on the quarterback. Those were good things that I remember.

Philadelphia Eagles
When I went to the Eagles, I played for Marion Campbell, whom I played for in Atlanta. We became real good friends. When I got to the Eagles, I was playing the same defense that I played in Atlanta.

The only thing is, the offense was better, so it made me play better. I wasn't getting beat up. I wasn't out on the field all the time. In Atlanta we spent most of the time, defensively, out on the field, because our offense didn't do very much.

The offense was very good with Wilbert Montgomery, Harold Carmichael, Ron Jaworski, and Jerry Sisemore. When you'd come off the field, you wouldn't be as tired. When you'd go back in, you could play harder, because the game had progressed so much. I enjoyed playing with a good offensive team.

Super Bowl

It was kind of a lowlight for me. Nothing seemed to go right for me for that game. During the season we had played the Oakland Raiders, and we had beat them. I had three sacks in the game. When we got to the Super Bowl, I didn't get a chance to start. I was standing over on the sideline, getting angry about not getting in the game. When I finally did get in there and roughed the quarterback, they threw a flag. It was just a disaster for me. The Raiders beat us. It wasn't a good week.

I was really pissed, because the referee threw the flag at me, instead of throwing it on the ground. I got offended. I guess he was pissed, too, because he threw the flag right at me. I picked it up and threw it at him. If I had the chance to do it all over again, I wouldn't do it. At the moment, it was the way things were. It was the passion of the game, and the way the game was going. Jim Plunkett had completed a pass to Ken King down the sideline. Ken King was still running. All that stuff just created a furnace inside me. Then he threw the flag at me. That was just too much.

Reason For Having To Wait 28 Years To Get Into Hall Of Fame

I had to wait probably because of my win-loss record with the Falcons. Also probably from the misinterpretation of the reason I left the Falcons. I think that may have had something to do with it. We didn't win a lot of games. I wasn't on a winning team. We didn't go to the Super Bowl. You notice that most of the guys that go into the Hall of Fame are guys who played in the Super Bowl three, four times, like that.

Not to say it, but there seem like there are some rules and regulations that govern you getting into the Hall of Fame. My career just didn't meet that criteria based on the years that I spent in Atlanta and Philadelphia. I think that probably had a lot to do with it. The Philadelphia years may have helped more than the years that I spent in Atlanta, because we were winning.

The good thing about waiting is, it makes it so much better. I don't know what I would have done if I had gotten in my first year of eligibility. I might have been beside myself. It gave me a chance to gain some validity and respect for the game.

Decision To Retire

I wanted to give up after a while. It was tough. It was tough, because it wasn't like the Atlanta Falcons are today under Arthur Blank and Thomas Dimitroff. Those guys really work to put a good program on the field. I don't think they did that back in the day. They were more satisfied that we were filling the stadium every Sunday rather than the caliber of players that they were putting out on the field.

Pro Football Hall Of Fame Induction

In the past, when you were a finalist for the Pro Football Hall of Fame, you had to stay by the phone and wait for the phone call. They would tell you, "If you don't get the phone call, you didn't make it." You had to wait to see who made it on the TV. That was a couple of hours after. You were waiting all that time for the phone call. The phone call never comes. Then, all of a sudden, on TV you see the guys who made it, and your name isn't up there.

This time they did it a little different. They brought all seventeen finalists for the Hall of Fame to New York and put us up at a hotel. They told us that they would call our room. I'm in the room with my daughter, Claudia. I turned to Claudia after twenty minutes, and I said, "Looks like we're in trouble." After twenty-five minutes, I said, "Well, you might as well call everybody and tell them that we didn't make it." Just as I got that out of my mouth, the phone rang, and they said, "Congratulations, you're a member of the Pro Football Hall of Fame." I almost passed out. The blood rushed to my head, and everything. It was amazing! I sat there waiting since I was a first round draft choice for the Atlanta Falcons.

My wife was my biggest supporter, and, of course, my biggest PR person. All those years I was up for the Hall of Fame she worked diligently trying to do what she could to get me in. We really didn't know what it was that she was supposed to be doing. She tried to get in touch with the voters. She wrote letters, and she had people write letters. She just worked. When I didn't make it, we cried together about it. To make it now, and not have her here to enjoy, is kind of bittersweet. But life goes on.

You know what? I felt her presence. We were in the orientation meeting after the voting. I was just sitting there, and I was thinking about her. All of a sudden, I just felt good. I think she's proud of the fact that I finally got in.

Atlanta Falcon Claude Humphrey puts pressure on Los Angeles Ram Pat Haden. Photograph courtesy Associated Press

Chapter 60

Ken Houston

> College:
> Prairie View A&M
>
> Career History
> Houston Oilers (1967–1972)
> Washington Redskins (1973–1980)
>
> 1986 Inductee Pro Football Hall of Fame

Transition From Small College To NFL

At that time, it was prior to integration, so all the guys had to go to Grambling, Southern, Texas Southern and schools like that. We called it the Black SWAC, the Black Southwest Athletic Conference. We knew we could play. We always wanted to play other schools. As a matter of fact, Texas A&M was down the street from us, Texas up in Austin, and we tried to get games with those schools, but for a lot of reasons it didn't happen. I had the mindset when I got to pro ball that I was as good as anybody in America. Most of the guys had that mindset. We just knew that we could play.

Once we got to camp, it was just talent against talent. I think that the first Oilers team that I played on probably had 15 to 17 guys from small colleges. Then when you played Kansas City, they may have had 20. I think if there was only one league that would have existed at that time, a lot of college guys would not have gotten the chance to play pro ball.

I look at the guys who were on my college team. I played with Otis Taylor, Jim Kearney, Seth Cartwright, Bivian Lee, Alvin Reed, and all those guys. As a matter of fact, Charley Taylor came to Prairie View and he couldn't make the team, so he went to Arizona State. He became a number one receiver. At Prairie View, they had so much talent I ended up playing offensive center. I played safety in the pros. Alvin Reed was a defensive end in college and ended up playing tight end in the pros. They had so many players, you just had to go there and find a spot that was open.

Practice In AFL

Practice back then was a little different. We scrimmaged once a week, which was extreme considering we were playing on Sundays. If you can go into a game with a partial injury, you can't play at your full capabilities. During that time, you worked with pads three days a week and one of those days would be a scrimmage.

Becoming A Returner

It was a little bit different back then. I didn't start off being a kick returner. As a matter of fact, we were having a practice in the dome at that time, preparing to play the Chicago Bears. Both teams were working out at the dome and I ran back a punt because I loved to do it. The Chicago coach mentioned to our coach, "He'd make a good return person," and he actually put me back on punts probably two weeks later. I didn't do it full-time because I was a full-time player on defense. You were more exposed to injuries, which is why the coach didn't do it.

I did run back kicks also. My son and I were sitting there watching TV and it came on that he had broken my record of touchdown returns. It was like 35 years the record was there, and mine was an interception return that set the record. I had nine touchdowns by interceptions, I had one punt return touchdown and I had two fumble returns for a touchdown. My son looked at me and said, "Don't worry, Dad, I'm going to break his record. Tell Devin he's got somebody on his trail."

Favorite Quarterback To Compete Against
I really enjoyed Joe Namath, for two reasons. First of all he was a great quarterback. He always brought notoriety with him. You knew that he was going to throw the ball. The Jets probably threw the ball more back then than anyone else, so you were going to have a chance at least to get an interception or make a big play.

We played Kansas City. They had the moving pocket with Len Dawson and they had John Hadl out in San Diego. My favorite people to play against were the people who threw the ball the most.

Daryle Lamonica
As a matter of fact, we gave Daryle Lamonica his nickname, the Mad Bomber. We played the Raiders and they beat us like 50- something in one of the championship games. He got the name the Mad Bomber after that.

Houston Oilers vs. Oakland Raiders Rivalry
Something about the Raiders made them everybody's rival. They were the tough guys. Warren Wells and Willie Brown of the Raiders were from the Southwest Conference where I played in college, so we had a conference thing going on there too. A lot of guys had played in that same conference in college, especially with Houston and the Raiders, so it was a carryover from college.

Toughest Receivers
If you could cover Otis Taylor, you could cover anybody. A name that really struck fear in my heart was Lance Alworth. This guy was very quiet, not a violent receiver, but he could run and jump. He did it very quietly, until he had the respect of all the players. You had guys like Fred Biletnikoff with the Raiders, who was really, really good. He had all the moves. You had Paul Warfield. You have all these Hall of Fame guys who I played against back then, and you know how good they were because they ended up in the Hall of Fame. You could go to any team and find a great receiver. One receiver who is not mentioned much but gave me fits was the tight end for Cincinnati, Bob Trumpy. He was a long guy who ran out in the middle of the field, had good speed, and was a good tight end.

Trade To Washington Redskins

Being traded to the Washington Redskins was frightening for me, because I was an AFL player my entire career up until that point, and I knew how the NFL teams felt about the AFL. They thought we were just a junk league. For them to lose that amount of players for me, and for me to go up there again having to prove myself was really, really interesting. The Redskins had two good safeties, Roosevelt Taylor and Brig Owens, when I got there. They were starters.

I remember being there about three or four weeks and I wasn't starting. I started to question myself. As fate would have it, Roosevelt Taylor broke his arm. They moved Brig Owens over to free safety and moved me to strong safety. About a week later when the season started, I had an opportunity to tackle Walt Garrison on the one-yard line. Thank God I did that, because it changed the whole existence of me as a Redskin. That was just almost instant feedback, and from that point on, I had a tremendous career there.

George Allen was coach, and it was a great time to play for the Redskins. We were called the "Over The Hill Gang." Washington really, really supported that team. It was a good time to be in football period, especially with the Redskins or the Cowboys. They were two of the major teams back then.

The Redskins had an owner back then by the name of Edward Bennett Williams, who was a famous trial lawyer in the Washington area. You had George Allen, Billy Kilmer, Sonny Jurgensen, and Charley Taylor. A lot of those guys ended up being in the Hall of Fame. That was just a good time to play football.

Photograph courtesy Associated Press

393

Chapter 61

Bob Griese

College:
Purdue
Career History:
Miami Dolphins (1967–1980)
1990 Inductee Pro Football Hall of Fame

College Choice
I was not a highly recruited athlete coming out of high school. I was probably a better baseball and basketball player than I was a football player. I went to a new Catholic high school when I was a freshman, and the program wasn't really developed. The coach wasn't that knowledgeable. We didn't throw the ball a lot. The only reason I was the quarterback on the team was because he knew that I was a pretty good baseball pitcher, had a strong arm, and had thrown some no-hitters. He figured that would be a good guy to have at quarterback.

The head coach was a defensive lineman in college and didn't know a lot about throwing the football. We had three passes; one to the right called Rex, one to the left called Lavender, and one over the middle called Milton.

I was not highly recruited by colleges for football. I could have gone to a couple places for basketball. I also had an opportunity to sign with the Baltimore Orioles as a baseball pitcher. I wanted to go to Purdue to get an education.

Purdue
Bob DeMoss was my offensive coordinator at Purdue and Jack Mollenkopf was the head coach. They kind of straightened me out by showing me how to throw the ball. One of the highlights while I was at school was when we went to the Rose Bowl my senior year. It was the first time that Purdue had ever gone to the Rose Bowl, and we beat Southern California in the game. I give Bob DeMoss a lot of credit for showing me how to throw the football properly.

Purdue had quite a few quarterbacks who were very successful and it's basically because of Bob DeMoss being the coach. The system, the way they threw the ball around, and the good coaching that they got were because of Coach DeMoss. We've had some good quarterbacks at Purdue.

Miami Dolphins
We knew we weren't going to get very far until Coach Don Shula came. I got there in '67, the second year of the Dolphins franchise. Coach Shula came in 1970, which was the fourth year. I think in '69 we were like 3-10 and 1. We only played 14 games back then.

In 1970, we completely turned around and were 10 and 4. The next year we were in the playoffs then we were in three Super Bowls in a row. We won the last two. One of those Super Bowls was during the undefeated season, which nobody had done before or after. I would say Shula made a big impact. The first four years of Coach Shula we were in the Super Bowl three times.

Monte Clark

Monte Clark was pretty good. Monte had just gotten out of the league after playing himself. The main thing that he did aside from coaching these guys up real well was that he brought in guys who weren't drafted. Jim Langer, our center, was a practice squad player with the Cleveland Browns. Monte knew about him and he brought Jim Langer in as a free agent. Jim Langer ended up playing for 10 or 12 years and is now in the Hall of Fame. He also brought in Bob Kuechenberg who was also a free agent and played 14 or 15 years. He brought in Wayne Moore from San Francisco. Then Larry Little was brought in. Four of those five guys on the offensive line were free agents. Most of them Monte Clark knew about. We had a really good offensive line.

Paul Warfield

Today's game is a passing game. Back then it was not that much of a passing game; it was more of a running game. The other thing is the rules have changed. Now you can jam a guy. Within five yards of the line of scrimmage you can jam a wide receiver. Then you can't touch him down the field. Back in the day when Warfield was playing you could throw a cross body block on the receiver coming off the line of scrimmage. You could hit him if he was down 15, 20 yards down field as long as he was in front of the defensive back. The defensive back could jam him and knock him off his feet as long as the ball wasn't in the play.

The rules back when Warfield played were a heck of a lot different than when Jerry Rice played and the guys today are playing under. If Jerry Rice played back when Warfield played, he wouldn't have caught nearly as many balls as he caught during his career. I guarantee you.

Favorite Moment In NFL

I'd have to say winning Super Bowls. The first one we lost to Dallas in New Orleans. The second one we were 16 and 0 and ready to go undefeated. We played in the Super Bowl against the Washington Redskins and we were the underdogs. Here we were 16 and 0 and hadn't lost a game. We were the underdogs and we beat them. If Garo Yepremian made a field goal at the end of the game we would have beat them 17 to nothing. Garo kicks the ball and gets it blocked and they run it back for a touchdown. We won the game only 14 to 7.

The following year we go back and validate that win by winning the Super Bowl again. This time, we won against the Minnesota Vikings.

The highlights of my career: in college it was winning the Rose Bowl and in the Pros it was winning two Super Bowls.

Pro Football Hall of Fame Induction

I never expected that I was going to be inducted into the Pro Football Hall of Fame. The last couple years of my career I wore glasses when I played. I had a vision problem. When I retired, they put my glasses in the Hall of Fame because no quarterback had ever worn glasses while he played.

My son Brian, he must have been a teenager at the time, looked at me one time and said, "That's as close as you'll ever come to being in the Hall of Fame; your glasses being in there."

In 1990 when I was inducted into the Hall of Fame my kids were there in the front row and Brian was right there. The first thing I said was, "This is the Hall of Fame, huh?" I looked down at Brian and I said, "In your face Brian." We like to kid each other back and forth. I think that was the best one that I've ever got on him.

Photograph courtesy Associated Press

Chapter 62

Alan Page

College:
Notre Dame

Career History:
Minnesota Vikings (1967-1978)
Chicago Bears (1978-1981)

1988 Inductee Pro Football Hall of Fame

College Choice
At the time I had a choice of a number of schools. Notre Dame just seemed to be the one that provided the greatest opportunity beyond the football field.

It was a transition for any young person. You are leaving home for the first time and going off to a place where you really don't know anybody, but I managed to make that transition. In retrospect I think it was a very good decision.

Ara Parseghian
Ara Parseghian was great coach. He was very driven, very determined, very much focused on doing things, and putting things in place that would allow a team to be successful.

1966 National Championship Game
My approach to the game, whether it was a national championship game or just another game, was pretty much the same. The goal was to go out and perform as well as I could and hopefully come away successful.

1966 Notre Dame vs. Michigan State 10-10 Tie
I was tired, beat up, and just worn out. It was a tough, hard-fought game. I had a feeling of exhaustion, and was more or less glad that it was over.

You go out, you play, and you do the best you can. You hope you do all those things to give you the best chance to win. The fact is, that day we didn't win. As it turns out, we didn't lose either.

There was a lot of tension and a lot of pressure, but from my perspective I approached it as just another game. There was a lot of attention, both local and national. If you're going to be good at what you do, if you're going to be successful, you have to approach, at least for me, each game as though it was the important one. It couldn't possibly be any more important than the situation you were in the week before. The week we played Michigan State, was the important one. To me, it was no more important than the team we played the week before. You can't do anything about past games and you can't do anything about future games, but you can do something about the game you are currently playing. That was always the critical game for me.

Draft
I was excited about the opportunity to play professional football. It was a chance to continue doing something that I enjoyed, and I was going to get paid for it. I was happy to be drafted. It didn't really matter in what place.

Transition to Professional Football
It was learning to play with new people, learning variations in the game, and in my case, learning a new position. I was a defensive end at Notre Dame. When I got to Minnesota, they had Jim Marshall and Carl Eller as defensive ends. Quite frankly, both of them were exceptional. It wasn't likely that I was going to be as good as either one of them. Somebody saw something in me and switched me to defensive tackle. Once I started down that road, it all came pretty naturally.

Bud Grant
Stoic, as he has been projected to be, but also very focused on creating the team atmosphere that allowed the players to minimize their mistakes and increase their chances of success.

MVP of the NFL
It was pretty exciting. It's not something that happens to you every day, and certainly not something that I had anticipated or would have ever thought would happen. I was pretty pleased.

Buddy Ryan
Buddy was always very feisty. He was a great coach. He understood the game both offensively and defensively. Again, he was one of those people who put you in the position that allowed you to be successful. I loved working with Buddy. If I had to pick my favorite coach, it was probably Buddy Ryan. He was a coach who had high expectations of his players. He expected you to not waste time and energy on things that weren't particularly relevant to getting the job done.

Purple People Eaters
We were a group and had a lot of fun playing and working together. As names go, you don't have much control over it and so "Purple People Eaters" was what we got named. I loved being a part of not only great and talented football players, but also a group of goodpeople.

Four Super Bowl Losses
It was about the game in front of you. You go out and try to win. You do everything you can, whether it's the Super Bowl or a game like the 1966 game against Michigan State, or a preseason game. The object is to go out, play well, and do the best that you can. Did I like losing those games? No. I didn't like losing any game. It was hard; it wasn't particularly that much harder than losing any of the other games that I played in. Over the years, while the teams that I was on fared better than they statistically should have, the ones that we did lose I wasn't particularly amused.

The fact is nobody wins all the time. Some people never seem to be able to be successful. For me, the journey was more important than the destination. It is how you did, what you did along the way, which was important in terms of playing. As for the rest of it, it was just a game.

Being an NFL Player Representative

Football back in the '50s, '60s, '70s, and even before that, players didn't have many rights in terms of where they played and the other terms and conditions of their employment. I got involved in the Players Association early on to try to improve those terms and conditions. While our success was modest while I was playing, I think it paved the way for the working relationship, a very good working relationship that players and owners have today.

His Perpendicular Pinky

I had multiple dislocations that ended up with the ligaments on the inside of the finger being destroyed and the ligaments on the outside of the finger pulling the finger out. It's been this way for quite a few years. The first time I injured it was in the middle of a game. I don't even remember what game. It was early on in my career with the Vikings. Jim Marshall, who played next to me, found me holding my finger as the other team was coming up to run the next play. He grabbed it, put it back into place, and away we went.

Going from the Minnesota Vikings to the Chicago Bears

It came to a point in my career where I had probably been playing in Minnesota too long. Going to the Bears reunited me with Jim Finks, Neil Armstrong, and Buddy Ryan. The people of Chicago welcomed me and welcomed my family. It turned out to be a really positive experience. My wife, my children, and I had a great time in Chicago. Those were the good days.

Being From Canton, Ohio

In Northeastern Ohio, particularly Canton, Massillon, Alliance, and Warren, football is very, very important. It's a part of those communities in ways that you don't find in many places. There's a little of that same thing in Northwestern Pennsylvania. Football is just very important and that draws out the best talent in those communities. There has been a lot of good talent.

Pro Football Hall Of Fame Induction

First of all, it was hot. It's always hot in Canton; it's hot and humid. It was kind of neat to be recognized and appreciated by the people in your hometown, people who knew you when. That was nice. It was obviously exciting and fun to be recognized for my football. It gave me the opportunity, on a larger platform, to talk about some of the things that I think are important, particularly the importance of education.

Minnesota Viking Alan Page gets double teamed by Oakland Raider Jim Otto (00) and George Buehler (64). Photograph courtesy Associated Press

Chapter 63

Willie Lanier

College:
Morgan State

Career History:
AFL Kansas City Chiefs (1967-1969)
NFL Kansas City Chiefs (1970-1977)

1986 Inductee Pro Football Hall of Fame

College Choice
A lot of historically black colleges were recruiting me at that time. The traditionally major white colleges in the South were not recruiting African-Americans at all. Some of the schools to the north and west would recruit, but more at the skilled positions, running back and receiver. Very few were recruiting linebackers, especially inside linebackers at that time. I had interest from some of the other historically black colleges in the Virginia and Maryland area, and decided that I was going to go to Virginia State initially. I felt it was too close to Richmond and too close to the Deep South, not as though Maryland was a great distance away, but being a little bit further north was something I thought was important. I reached out to the coach and that's how I ended up going to school there.

It wasn't as though I was this very well known, great high school football player. My skills were developing and starting to present themselves, but my size didn't start to flower until I finished my senior year of high school and was getting ready to go to college. It wasn't as if I was this very well known recruit across the country.

Morgan State
Morgan State had a very good team at that time. They were constantly winning in one of the bowl games. Leroy Kelly attended Morgan and was there my first year. They had a number of players who would go to the pros—Raymond Chester with the Raiders, Mark Washington with the Cowboys, George Nock with the Jets, and John Fuqua with the Giants. There were a number of fellows whose skills happened to be showing. I ended up playing in three bowl games in the four years I was there. They had a 34-game winning streak. Morgan State had a lot going for it, and its notoriety was pronounced.

Draft
I think the reality was that the position of middle linebacker was not being manned by African-Americans, so it wasn't one that teams in the old, quote, National Football League, were interested in. The position had not been played full time by someone who was African-American. The American Football League had become a haven of opportunity for players from historically black colleges.

First Training Camp

When I was drafted as a middle linebacker, Jim Lynch was the other second-round draft choice, and he was also drafted for the position. They were looking to replace Sherrill Headrick, who was a veteran middle linebacker. He was aging and didn't have a big physical stature.

That first year we were both competing to be in the middle. We were both drafted as middle linebackers, which we played in college, and the competition was going to be playing for that position. That's just the way it turned out. The team was not viewing us for any position other than that one. I ended up being injured the last four games of my rookie year. I think Jim was playing but not starting at that time. He ended up stepping into the starting lineup as the middle linebacker the last few games of our rookie year.

We did the competition again the next year, going at it as far as who was going to be the starter at middle linebacker. I was acknowledged as the starter and they shifted Jim to the outside.

Being The First Black Starting Middle Linebacker

Games kept coming too fast, and performance was required. I had a whole lot of work to do. I knew the significance of being the first black starting middle linebacker, but playing in football is performance based. You're trying to win games, you're trying to have others look to you for leadership, and so you're trying to show that you can play. It was just good that it worked out in Kansas City.

I think the Kansas City Chiefs team coming off of having lost to Green Bay in the Super Bowl, were interested in winning. Whichever one of us could help them win quickest was the one that they were going to probably react to. Jim and I became great friends. I was in Kansas City only a week ago, and we had lunch together. We've known each other for years and are very close. He was a realist in that I was a more physical player than he was, so the odds of that position being awarded to him was probably not going to be in his favor.

Realization I Could Play In The NFL

It wasn't anything about getting to Kansas City and really playing the game with all of the players. I was 6'1", 245 pounds, quick, and had upper body strength. The Washington Redskins recruited one of my college classmates. He went to the Redskins for a visit and I went with them. They weren't recruiting me; they were recruiting him. After we left the field, in the bowels of the stadium, I ended up meeting Sam Huff. I saw Sam and shook his hand, but he didn't realize who I was. I was a college student. He was this well-known middle linebacker in pro football. As I shook Sam's hand and I told him a story, I looked at his height. He was a little taller than me. I looked at his build. He was not as broad in the shoulders as me and didn't appear as physical as I felt I was. I had this very clear view—and this is a positive about Sam and not a negative in any way—if he could play, and now I'm standing in front of a guy who's a middle linebacker in the National Football League, there should not be any reason why I can't play.

I had some scouts saying they thought I might be too short and all these different kind of comments. I said wait a minute, I'm looking at a guy who is very well known, a starting middle linebacker, a pro football player. That was sort of a marker for me in terms of confidence and then having the opportunity.

Hank Stram

Hank Stram was very innovative and very competitive as you can see on NFL Films. He was one who had a reach of excellence that was important to him. He always strived for trying to create an environment that you could excel in and hopefully show the talents that God had gifted you.

Super Bowl IV

Super Bowl IV was like any other game, because the game was one week after the Championship Game. All of the games had run one week after another. There was no gap of two weeks from the Championship Game to the Super Bowl like there is now. It was another game that occurred in a round robin elimination at the end of the season. We had played the Jets in New York one week, went out to Oakland the next week and played them in the championship, and the following week we were in New Orleans for the Super Bowl.

This thing had a very fast East Coast, West Coast, and Gulf Coast run in that you found yourself constantly in preparation for the next game that had to be played in a string. The whole idea was to be the last one standing. It moved very quickly, but I think with it moving quickly it didn't give you a chance to focus on it being more than what it was.

The reality was that the two teams that were there at that moment were the Kansas City Chiefs and the Minnesota Vikings. For many of us who were not there for the first Super Bowl they lost, it didn't really mean anything that they lost. We didn't feel it when we went there. We weren't a part of it. The players who had come after that season were all in their moment and their opportunity to play out whatever the reality would be that day, as it had been all season. It was of the opportunity at the moment.

Speech To Teammates Before Goal Line Stand Against New York Jets In Divisional Playoff Game

There was an interference penalty on Emmitt Thomas of our team in the end zone so the Jets had first and goal at the one-yard line. I told the team in the huddle, "It becomes one of opportunity and action and being accountable." I was trying to get the guys to lift their heads, not feel it being a concession, and trying to get them to perform at a little bit higher level. In doing that I realized very quickly that words without action don't mean anything. My thought was that the Jets were going to have to go on a shorter count because of the risk of being offside in motion is a 500% penalty. They go from the one to the five. If I'm offside they only go to the half-yard line, so that's 50%. The odds are completely in my favor, even if I'm offside.

I decided that on whatever play, if they didn't go on the first count he had to go on the second. All I would do is turn sideways and step in between the guard and the center and try to disrupt, and that's what happened. After that occurred everyone else was more livid and viewed the opportunity as being more clear. Then everybody really came to life. We were able to stop them and that made a difference in the game.

Nicknames

Jerry Mays started calling me "Contact" the first year I came to Kansas City because I was improperly tackling people. I'll say it like that. I was tackling with the crown of my head and trying to crush people. After that, about the next year, I was nicknamed "Honey Bear" because I was wrapping people up. I put that "Contact" thing to rest because I wouldn't have survived three years in the league if I continued to try to play like that.

Pro Football Hall Of Fame Induction

I didn't play each game, each season with a long-term view of the Pro Football Hall of Fame. I was near-term in trying to win the game, trying to win a division title, and trying to win or get to the playoffs. If I was fortunate, I played well enough to get to the Pro Bowl. The Hall of Fame was not something that ever entered my mind during the time I was playing. I was not playing for that, I was playing for all these other purposes. The call came during my third year of eligibility. It's an overwhelming, "Thank you, God," because I had been granted the opportunity to play long enough … because you need longevity, with a quality team that had some success and very few injuries. It's a very special moment and one that you never forget because of the clarity of it.

Trade To Baltimore Colts

Retiring was my decision because toward end of my career, I had moved to the East Coast and started working for a tobacco company. I was trying to leave the game two years before the trade to the Colts. I was between the thought of whether I would play or not play. My heart was not in it, so I decided not to go forward and play for the Colts. Again, it had nothing to do with Kansas City.

Favorite Moment In Career

The one I think of, which had nothing to do with winning the game but was the essence of the game, was when the Chiefs opened Arrowhead Stadium in 1972. The Baltimore Colts played in the first preseason game at Arrowhead Stadium. I knew the Colts players because some of them lived in Baltimore. Some of them would come by Morgan State to talk to us about our expectations if we were going to make it to the pros. Sometimes they would just come by to watch games. I knew many of them, like Tony Lorick, Willie Richardson, Jim Parker, Tom Matte, and Johnny Unitas. We all knew them.

In that preseason game there was a swing pass from Unitas to Tom Matte, over the middle. Matte came over the middle, reached up for the ball, and I hit him with a tremendous tackle in his ribs. I knew him and was not trying to hurt him. I'm trying to make a great play, which I thought I did. He hit the ground on his back, I'm on top of him, and he says, "I caught the ball." I'm saying, "No, you didn't, because I felt I hit him with this great tackle." Then he shows me the ball and you can hear me laughing.

The game is one that should be played for the joy of the game. It has nothing to do with anger. It has nothing to do with harm. It has to do with the quality and the joy of the contest. If individuals play it that way, they come away from it with a different view and I think a different approach to the way the game should be played.

I enjoyed the game most of the time. As long as I stayed away from coaches who had a different view and ideas. Unfortunately, that would create conflicts at times. I'm saying the game should be played for joy and not anger, but you have a lot of people who don't quite grasp that. Think of how this all conflicts.

There's more to life even when the game is played, when the game is over, it's always a game. I heard Urban Meyer, a new coach at Ohio State, made a comment last year that he liked his players to be angry when they played. I thought, "That's an odd view of the game. My view is somewhat different."

Kansas City Chief Willie Lanier leaps on top off Baltimore Colt Don McCauley after McCauley fumble. Photograph courtesy Associated Press

Chapter 64

Rayfield Wright

College:
Fort Valley State

Career History:
Dallas Cowboys (1967–1980)

2006 Inductee Pro Football Hall of Fame

College Choice

I went to Fort Valley for the simple reason that I had a cousin who was captain of the football team. I couldn't make the high school football team, but I went to Fort Valley on a basketball scholarship. When I left high school I wanted to play basketball so bad because I didn't make the high school football team. I was a pretty good basketball player at the time. Loyola in Chicago also wanted me to come and play basketball for them but we didn't have the financial resources for me to go there, nor any other school. Fort Valley was a state school, and I got a pretty good scholarship and that's why I went to Fort Valley.

There were a couple of schools out of Atlanta that wanted me but I chose Fort Valley because they had a new coach, Stan Lomax. Coach Lomax, my college coach, was the gentleman who introduced me at the Hall of Fame.

Not Making High School Football Team

I'm from a tall family. I have a brother who's 7 feet tall, my dad was 7 feet, and I was 6'7". We just played basketball. When I went out for football, I didn't make the team because I was a tall, lanky guy. My high school coach thought I would get hurt playing football, so I started playing basketball. I was 6'7", and I only weighed 200 lbs. when I left high school.

Turning Down Loyola Chicago

We didn't have the financial resources because it was just my mother and grandmother raising four kids. If you think about the south back in the '60s, you can understand what I'm talking about.

Playing Football When On Basketball Scholarship

Back in those days you went to college on what was called an athletic scholarship, instead of just a football scholarship or just a basketball scholarship. It meant that I had to play two sports. That's when I started playing football. I chose football because I wanted to play football and I wanted to play wide receiver because I was a pretty fast guy, I thought, running a 4.8 forty.

The first position I played in football was free safety. I played defensive end, tight end, and I was a punter. When basketball season started I started playing basketball.

<u>NFL Draft</u>

I didn't want to play professional football. I wanted to play basketball. The Cincinnati Royals wanted me to play basketball for them. I decided that I couldn't because it was my junior year in college. When I received my scholarship, I had made a commitment in high school with a guy who was in the Air Force. I told him that I wouldn't drop out of school until I received my college degree. Since I made that commitment, I did not go to, or even try out for the Royals.

Then my senior year, the Dallas Cowboys drafted me. The Cowboys were only six years old at that time. I had a football scholarship and training camp started in July. I had a basketball offer with the Royals and practice started in August. I had two opportunities, one in football and one in basketball. I told my mother and grandmother that I had two opportunities. I didn't know what God really wanted me to do, so since football camp started first, I went to the Cowboys training camp. I ended up making the football team with the Cowboys. Back in those days, we had 137 rookies in training camp. That was when they were just signing free agents. I ended up making the team as a tight end. Coach Landry had a system and he knew that his system would work if he could find the right athletes to play in his system. It didn't matter whether you playedfootball, basketball, ran track, or whatever. He was looking for athletes. He didn't build his systemaround a player. He built his system around athletes. That's what really made him very successful and made the team very successful.

When Roger Staubach joined the team in 1969 after having to serve four years in the service, Coach Landry called me in his office and said, "Rayfield I'm going to move you to offensive tackle." I thought he was crazy because I had never played offensive tackle before in my life. Ralph Neely was playing right tackle at the time. He had an ankle injury and couldn't play, so Coach Landry told me that I was starting. That was about halfway during the season, so I had to come in and start playing a position that I had never played before.

The first player that I had a chance to block in the National Football League, God bless him, was David Deacon Jones. That was my first start. I was blocking the Secretary of Defense, the most feared defensive lineman that ever played in the National Football League. My first start was against Deacon Jones.

I never will forget the first play of the ball game. I got down in my stance and I was looking at Deacon squarely in his eyes. He was kicking his back leg like a bull. When a bull starts kicking his leg you know what's going to happen. He's coming. There isn't anything you can do about it. He's going to come and that's exactly what Mr. Jones did. When Staubach made the call, the ball was going to be snapped on two when he said hut and then between the different huts from a quarterback's call, there's a little pause in that call. I hear a statement because an offensive lineman is dedicated to hear only one voice and that's your quarterback voice because he can call a number or color. We call it an audible and he could change the original play that was called in the huddle. I'm listening and in between that first and second hut, in this pause I hear a voice and the voice wasn't Roger's voice, it was Deacon Jones' voice. He asked me a question, which really blew me away because he asked me if my mother knew that I was out on the field. When Staubach called the second play, I was still in my stance and everybody was running their assignment out. He came across that line of scrimmage and hit me with that head slap and knocked me all the way on my back. I rolled over, looked to the sideline to see if Coach Landry was going to take me out of the game, and he turned his back on me. By that time Deacon Jones reached his big arms down to help me up off my back and said, "Hey rookie, welcome to the NFL." I wasn't a rookie; I'm in my third year. He called me rookie, but I was a rookie as far playing offensive tackle. I ended up getting the game ball and I was MVP of the game because Mr. Jones never touched Roger again. That's what started my career at offensive tackle. I played offensive tackle for 10 years.

Playing Offensive Line

The offensive line, as I look at it, is like an engine in an automobile. If you take that engine out of the automobile, no matter how beautiful the car looks, the car is not going anywhere. You put that engine in the automobile then it is going to move. Well, the offensive line is like that. If you don't have an engine, or your engine isn't running properly, then your offense is not going anywhere. You must have everything that the engine needs for the offensive line to move. We were one unit and all of the guys on the offensive line worked with each other. We had a great offensive line coach, Jim Myers, who really taught us how to play that position, based on our athletic ability.

The center is like a quarterback. Your center calls signals like a quarterback. The center calls the blocking assignments for the offensive line based on the defense scheme. The offensive lineman may have a certain blocking assignment, but if the center calls a signal then we know that we going to have to block a different way then the play normally is called.

Turning Down Opportunity To Play In NBA With Cincinnati

I would have been teammates with Oscar Robertson and Jerry Lucas. I was the first professional athlete to come out of Griffin, Georgia and the first one to end up playing professional football. It was a tough decision to make because I wanted to play basketball, but at the same time I had two opportunities. When you receive an opportunity you just don't let it go when it's something that you want to do. I wanted to play professional sports because I knew I had the ability to do so. I just didn't know that the Dallas Cowboys were going to draft me.

Living In Dallas After Being Drafted

I was drafted right after John F. Kennedy was assassinated in Dallas. I'm saying to myself, do I really want to go to Dallas? Things really hadn't straightened out and in some areas, even today, things have not straightened out as far as color is concerned. I decided that I would just go to Dallas. It was an interesting situation. I didn't get a chance to really have a roommate and I can't answer the question why not. Maybe it was because segregation was still out there and our rooms had roommates of the same race. If there was an extra roommate that would cause black and white to be together, then back in those days, they would get two rooms. One player would have his own room and the other player would have his own room.

Bob Lilly & Randy White

Bob Lilly was still playing. Bob was the first player who was ever drafted by the Cowboys in 1960. He came out of Texas Christian University, and was a tremendous athlete. He had a lot of quickness and he moved pretty fast on that defensive line. Of course, Randy White came from Maryland. He came in as a linebacker. Randy made the adjustment to the defensive line because he was an athlete. He was just as quick as Lilly. That's what Coach Landry was looking for in his defense. We had Jethro Pugh, a tremendous defensive tackle on the other side of Bob Lilly, also on the side of Randy White. Jethro put a lot of pressure on the quarterback himself. I don't think that Jethro has gotten the credit that he deserves because no one really talks about him that much. Jethro was a great player.

Playing In Five Super Bowls

In 1970, we played in our first Super Bowl and that was the most important one. I played 13 years and we were in the playoffs 12 of those 13 years that I played. Prior to going to the Super Bowls, we were named as the team that couldn't win the big game.

The first Super Bowl that we had was against the Baltimore Colts. I was blocking Bubba Smith in that game. He was a big, tall, strong guy. I held my own against him, but we lost the game by a field goal that was kicked by O'Brien. That's the game they said that Mel Renfro tipped the ball and John Mackey caught the ball and ran it in for a touchdown. After seeing the film, Mel Renfro didn't touch the ball. O'Brien kicked a field goal and the Colts won that game.

The next year we beat Miami 24-3 for our first Super Bowl win. We picked Coach Landry up and put him on our shoulders and carried him off the field. The Super Bowl was something that we really strived to get to because we knew we could win it. That was a great game for us.

Cowboys Running Backs Blocked For

We had a series of great running backs. I thought Walt Garrison was one of the top fullbacks in the league. Then Robert Newhouse came in as a fullback and the halfbacks were Calvin Hill and Duane Thomas. Calvin and Duane both were excellent running backs. They had their own different styles of running.

Duane Thomas was like a glider. He was fast as well. Calvin was a more powerful running back and he liked to jump a lot over his blocks. That made those two guys a little different. I loved blocking for Duane Thomas because he set up your blocks really well, but he wasn't a straight runner.

Tony Dorsett came in after Duane was traded and Calvin was playing in Washington. Dorsett came in from the University of Pittsburgh. Tony was a power runner even though he wasn't as big as Calvin was and a little bit smaller than Duane. He had the quickness and he could read the plays and the blocks. One of the things that made him a great running back was that he knew the plays and could make adjustments based on the blocking of the offensive line.

Star Defensive Lineman Played Against

We start out with Deacon Jones, Bubba Smith, Carl Eller, Claude Humphrey, Jack Youngblood, and L.C. Greenwood. Each of those guys was awesome. All the guys that I blocked against are in the Pro Football Hall of Fame, except L.C. Greenwood and Bubba Smith.

Dallas Cowboys Being Named America's Team

We didn't give ourselves that name. The fans and the media had a lot to do with it. Since we had become successful in the game, they started calling us America's team. It was because we had a lot of fans in different stadiums or cities that we played in around the country. Everyone knew our names, even the offensive linemen's names, in the different cities in which we played. I think that was one of the main reasons why the team became America's team. It wasn't because it was something that we did or said.

More Popular Cowboys Or Cowgirls
As far as the players were concerned we were. I took my youngest son to a game and I wanted him to take pictures of some of the players. When the game was over and I got the films developed, the only things on the film were cheerleaders. I thought he was taking pictures of his favorite players. He had his priorities in the right place, but we didn't because we couldn't focus on any cheerleaders. We couldn't even focus on the fans because we had to pay attention and keep our focus on the plays that were called.

Hail Mary Pass
Drew Pearson caught the Hail Mary pass from Roger Staubach and went in for a score. I was blocking the Vikings' Carl Eller on that particular play and one of the reporters came up and asked me if I saw the play. I said, "No, I didn't see it." He said, "Well you were on the field." I said, "Well I know I was on the field, but I was doing my job. If I had not been doing my job, I would have seen the play. You do your job and watch everything from the game when we watch game films."

Pro Football Hall of Fame Induction
Well it's very difficult to remain composed because when I was inducted in 2006, my mother was there. My brothers, sister, my niece, and nephews were there. My mother had never flown on a plane before and she didn't fly to Canton. I rented a private bus to take my family to the Hall of Fame because my mother would not fly, period. The nervousness I had of looking at my mom and remembering everything that she had done in raising me, brought a lot of tears to my eyes. At certain times it was a little bit tough to maintain my composure, but the rest of the fans that were in the audience were cheering all of the players that were inducted. That kind of warms your heart a lot. It meant a lot to me because we played, not just as a team, but for the fans too.

The Pro Football Hall of Fame selects the best players who played the game, as well as the best players who helped their team win ballgames. Those are two major factors that really bring a player out for a vote in the Hall of Fame. Even though I knew I was a great football player, I had no idea that I would be a Hall of Famer. I felt overwhelmed to be amongst the greatest players that had ever played the game. We have a little under 300 players in the Hall. I was number 245 placed in the Hall of Fame.

I was overwhelmed. It was exciting. I was just honored and happy to be a part of the Hall of Fame and to be a Hall of Famer who played for the Cowboys, because we didn't have many at that time.

Players Patterned Himself After
You look at a lot of players and you kind of pattern yourself after some of them. Since it was hard for me to make the adjustment to tackle, I went to my offensive line coach and got films of the best offensive tackles that played the game up to that point. St. Louis had two guys, Ernie McMillan and Bob Reynolds, and Green Bay had a guy named Forrest Gregg. Those were players I looked at on film. I tried to pattern myself after those players and I couldn't do it. Bob

Lilly and those guys would pick me up and throw me around and I got tired of that. I stayed up all night watching films and one day it came to me. I'm thinking, "Well, what are you trying to do Rayfield? Well I'm trying to keep guys from the quarterback, so I'm pass blocking, right? The way that you do that is something that I had while playing basketball, quick feet. I had to stay in front of the player. I used my quickness that I had developed playingbasketball.

Uniform Number 70
I was given number 70 by the coaches and the equipment manager because no one had number 70 at that time. I think it was a great number because seven is a good number and it's Biblical. I thought 70 was a good number because it's a number that really stood out among other numbers, like 67 or 52, on the offensive line. It was a great number and I loved it.

Tom Landry
He was awesome. He was one of the greatest coaches that ever coached the game. The thing is that Coach Landry was a player in New York prior to being hired as Head Coach here in Dallas, so he understood and knew players. We became one team. We all respected each other and played together as a unit. He was a coach who really respected the players and a coach who taught us more than just football. He taught us about life itself. He taught us how to deal with people and respect those who are teaching you. A lot of players don't do that. A lot of players feel like they are the ones that are most important and they can forget about everybody else who's on the team. No one player wins a ball game. Coach Landry said, "We win as a team, we lose as a team." One thing he said to me when I first started playing tackle was, "Rayfield, I'm going to tell you something." I said, "What's that Coach?" He said, "Remember that the player you're playing against is a professional just like you." So you respect not only your teammates, you respect your opponents because they are professionals just like you.

Physical Effects Of Playing Football
Fans are just there to watch the game. They don't really know what a player goes through mentally to prepare himself to play a game. There are a lot of hits. I looked it up one day. Players average 60 plays a game offensively. We have 16 games a season. You take 60 plays a game, multiplied by the 16 games played a year, times the 13 years that I played, and I came pretty close to sustaining 3,000 hits. Every time that ball snaps, you're going to hit somebody or someone's going to hit you. That's a lot of hits.

Change In Game
We didn't have all the protection or the equipment the players have today and we couldn't block like players block today. You couldn't reach out and grab a guy and hold him. That was a penalty. That was a 15-yard penalty for us, but today the offensive line, they can just reach out and grab a guy and then it becomes a wrestling match, to me. You don't see the quickness in players today like you did back in my day. The thing that gets to me is that a lot of teams and coaches look for guys that are 300 pounds and run a 4.6, 40-yard dash. That doesn't really impress me because an offensive lineman moves about 10 yards a play. My point is how quick can you get from point A to point B being 10 yards? I don't see any offensive lineman running 40 yards. If they did, they'd be on the sideline sucking up oxygen. The 4.6s, 4.7s, and even 4.5s, that doesn't mean much to me because offensive linemen don't get a chance to run 40 yards. The game is about quickness.

Decision To Retire
You get a feeling and knowledge that based on what you have gone through for so many years the body is only prepared and developed to take a certain amount of hits. Every time you hit someone and they hit you upside your head everyone says, "The man got his bell rung." That could develop into a concussion because it knocks him out or things like that.

When I retired, I thought my body had gone through enough. Once you feel that you can't compete like you should, then you know it's time to get out of the game. You don't just hang around the game just to make money.

Injuries
Don Meredith used to get his nose broken every game. You look at situations like that and there were times when Roger really got his bell rung. Sometimes when your head hits the ground, the ground is not soft. When I played the game we played on regular grass, which I loved playing on instead of Astroturf. Under the Astroturf it's almost like a bed, you got a cushion under the bed. You sleep on that cushion on the bed for a long time and that cushion kind of shrinks, it kind of goes down. Astroturf, to me does the same thing. Under the Astroturf, below the padding is cement. It's a very difficult thing for me to even continue playing on it even though I did.

First Coach My Mom
She was my toughest coach. She used to tell me things like, "Son I know you want to be successful, but you can't become successful by yourself. It take's other people around you to become successful." I don't know anyone who has been successful just by himself. Whether you're the owner of a team, the head coach, or the general manager, you have to have the right people around you.

Financial Help From Others While In School
There was a guy when I graduated from high school and went to Fort Valley for college. A man came to my high school coach and said that he wanted to help a student who didn't have the financial resources but was trying to get an education. My high school principal selected me. This gentleman sent me $50 a month until I graduated from college. I told my principal, "Mr. Daniels, I can't pay him back until I graduate and get a job." He said, "Well, he doesn't want to be paid back." I said, "Well what does he want?" He said, "If you ever got in a position to help another student to do it." That's why I started my foundation. The other thing is that I never knew the gentleman's name. I never cast an eye on him. I knew nothing about him, or anything of that nature. He didn't put it in the newspaper or go on TV to talk about what he had done. That's what I do with my foundation. We try to generate funds to help kids go to college whether they are athletes or not. Very few of them are athletes. We've had several kids who we sent to college, graduate.

Career Perspective
When you go into the National Football League or any other professional sport, you don't go there for the All Pro honors, Pro Bowl honors, or Hall of Fame honors. I never looked for those. I just wanted to perform and do my job to help the team win ball games. That's what players did. We didn't make the kind of money that these guys are making today. Most of the players, had to

have second jobs to sustain their families and those who they loved and were trying to help. It's an interesting life that we lived.

Dallas Cowboy Rayfield Wright carries Coach Tom Landry off the field. Photograph courtesy Associated Press

Chapter 65

Lem Barney

College:
Jackson State

Career History
Detroit Lions (1967-1977)

1992 Inductee Pro Football Hall of Fame

College Choice
I had offers from most of the Southwestern Athletic Conference schools, which included Texas Southern, Prairie View, Grambling, Southern University, and Alcorn State University. None of the bigger schools offered me a scholarship. It wasn't that wide open at the time. I think it was because of guys like Walter Payton and me that the Big Ten schools and other universities started looking down on that coastal area for great ballplayers. In addition to me, Jackson State had Walter Payton, his brother Eddie; Willie Richardson, who later played with the Baltimore Colts; Gloster Richardson, who later played for Kansas City; and Thomas Richardson, who was my roommate at Jackson State and played with the Boston Patriots. A lot of players at the small African-American high schools weren't getting offers at that time, but their eyes were open later on, particularly after Walter came out of a small school in Mississippi.

Eddie Robinson
Eddie Robinson was a great guy. As I look back on my college career at Jackson State, the only school we didn't have a winning record against was Grambling. Grambling beat us four years in a row, twice down in Grambling and then twice at Jackson State. Eddie Robinson was just a phenomenal head coach and a great communicator. He was a father figure. In fact, a lot of people don't know the ins and outs about Eddie. Eddie was a guy who was a one-man show at Grambling. He would tape ankles, do curfew checks every night, make sure the guys were eating right, and going to class. He was just a tremendous guy and he had a great friend over at Alabama, Papa Bear Bryant. It was just amazing, particularly because of the racial tension, which was high in the early '60s. Eddie and the late great Bear Bryant were dynamic friends. They worked together at camps during the off-season. He was just a tremendously great coach.

Eddie Robinson had to give a lot of his ballplayers away to a lot of the Texas colleges like Texas Southern University, Prairie View, and some other smaller schools since he didn't have enough room on the team. Eddie was just a dynamic recruiter. Guys from Detroit and across the country wanted to play at Grambling.

Jackson State

I went to Jackson State as a quarterback. A lot of people never knew that. John Merritt from Tennessee State recruited me during my senior year and said, "Boy, you're going to have a chance to play." He had a great quarterback by the name of Roy Curry, who ended up playing for the Chicago Bears. They didn't give Roy an opportunity to play quarterback in the NFL. They put him on at wide receiver. He was a big quarterback about 6'4" and weighed about 225. He threw a ball to Willie Richardson, who would have been a Hall of Famer if he'd had the opportunity to play in Miami like he did at Jackson State. Willie Richardson was one of the Richardson brothers. There were three of them that ended up playing at Jackson State.

We had Leslie Duncan, who played with the San Diego Chargers, Verlon Biggs, who played with the New York Jets, and Frank Molden, who played with the Pittsburgh Steelers and with Philadelphia. We just had a bevy of great guys. There was just an abundant amount of talent at those African-American schools in the '60s.

Draft

When I was drafted, I said to my college coach, "Wow, I'm going to Detroit." My college coach said, "Just continue to do the things that you were doing to get you there. Keep doing what you've been doing and you'll be fine."

Joe Schmidt

I played my first seven years under the great Joe Schmidt with Detroit. Ironically, as I look at my career, I ended up playing under five head coaches in 11 years. I played my first seven years with the great Hall of Famer and middle linebacker, Joe Schmidt, as my coach. Then, I played for Don McCafferty, whose nickname was Easy Rider. He came from the Baltimore Colts where he was the coach. Don was a great coach. He died the second year in Detroit during training camp. Then Rick Forzano from Navy, who coached the great Roger Staubauch at Navy, took over. After Forzano, it was Tommy Hudspeth and then Monte Clark, who played for Cleveland.

I had five head coaches in the span of 11 years, but had a great time with all the coaches. I always respected the coaches.

Key To Success

Training was the key to my success from middle school, through high school, college, and through the league. My sophomore year in college, I found out that I was going to be a defensive back and not quarterback, so I started running backward for training. I would run down to the beach and I'd run a mile and a half forward and then I'd run two and a half miles backward in the sand. People thought I was crazy. For a long time I thought I was crazy as well.

You find that great sprinters, like Bob Hayes and Dave Sime, practice getting out of the blocks as low as they can, as fast as they can for 15 to 20 yards, then they'll start rising up. To become a good defensive back, I started training running backward in the sand. It was tough. A lot of good athletes could never buy into that theory, but it was my key to being a successful defensive back.

I played in high school, college, and then in the league for 11 years. It was always a joy because you had to learn and teach and train those muscles going backward. As a defensive back, I do realize you're employing yourself in a backpedaling position for over 93% to 95% of the time. You would stop and come forward to help make a tackle, but most of your activity is moving backward, so the more you can train and adapter your muscles to moving backward, the better you'll be. I did that for my entire career.

Jim David
Jimmy David, "The Hatchet", as they called him, was just a tremendously great teacher. He was a great defensive back and he was a great coach. He should be in the Hall of Fame. He went to six Pro Bowls. He should be in the hall with his former teammates who are already in the Hall of Fame.

He wasn't one of those coaches like you see today. Most guys today that are defensive coordinators or defensive back coaches get hired because the head coach was a friend of theirs in college, cronies in college, or something of that nature. Even though Coach Schmidt and Jimmy played together, Coach Schmidt new that Jimmy David could coach because he played the game with that same type of intensity.

I had a couple of people who I thought about being my presenter for my Hall Of Fame Induction. I chose Jimmy David because of the training, confidence, and courage that Jimmy gave me to play that game. It was just unbelievable. We had a relationship that will never end. I still call his wife and speak with her from time to time and his kids. Jimmy was just a tremendously great asset for me and to me as a Detroit Lion Pro Football Hall of Famer. He was just so great. Joe Schmidt, who played the game, could coach the game. Jimmy, who played the game, could coach the game. It was almost like the Lord had Angels on me from my middle school years all through my professional years and I will always be appreciative of that.

Playing Philosophy
My high school coach told me if I wanted to play defensive back, quarterback, or wide receiver, I could do it and do it with a bit of ease.

I discovered nothing was easy about it. It was always a dire, hard, work effort. I was never a guy who would loaf during practice or during training. You see a lot of guys who kick it around during the course of practice. They'll do the same thing in a game. Your body just adapts to what you do for it. So I always played with intensity. In fact, I remember Coach Joe Schmidt telling me on offensive days, "Lem, let the guys catch the ball. This is offensive practice." I'd say, "Coach, if you want them to catch it, you need to put somebody else over here. I'm not letting them catch it." He said, "You're right about it, Lem. If you slow up in practice, your body will take the initiative to slow up during the course of the game."

It was always, right full rudder, full speed ahead for me, and Jimmy David agreed with it. He would sit down and tell me, "They call me the hatchet because I was whacking in practice."

I really enjoyed practice. I was a gentleman who really enjoyed the practice sessions. The particular reason for that is because my training before going into practice was always there.

One of the things that I loved was being able to study film. We really didn't have film in college. We didn't have the means for it. We would see film but they wouldn't break it down like in the pros. We watched everything the opposition did. If we were playing the Chicago Bears, I would have the opportunity to get the last five games the Bears played on film. How you break down film is a tedious job. It's hard work. A player is going to do the same thing in the game against me that he did in a previous game. So, learning how to break down film was a great asset for me. The late, great Jimmy David taught me how to do it; he trained me. He was a great guy.

Marvin Gaye
Mel Farr and I sang on the *What's Going On* album with Marvin Gaye. I think Mel and I might be the only two NFL stars to have a gold record. Marvin was one of my favorites singers when I was in high school. He had to be everybody's favorite. When I found out I was being drafted by the Detroit Lions, I said, "Motown!" The first thing that came to my mind was Motown. Motown was at its pinnacle in the mid '60s with Marvin Gaye, The Temptations, The Miracles, The Four Tops, and The Supremes.

When I was in training camp, I said I wanted to go by and meet Marvin Gaye. One day after practice I found out where he played golf, which was a public golf course named Palmer Park. After the morning practice, I missed lunch and I drove to Palmer Park to look for Marvin Gaye. Everybody said, "No, he's not out here now, but he doesn't live that far." They told me where he lived, and I drove around. I go over, and I see a big brown Brougham Cadillac. That was the marker for me. He drove a big brown Brougham Cadillac. I pulled into the driveway, went up, rang the bell, and I stepped back. The bell had a chime to it, a little musical chime. About 25 seconds later, I was getting ready to hit it again, and the door opened. Who stood in the door? Marvin Gaye.

He said, "Yeah man, what's going on? I said, "Look Marvin, my name is Lem Barney with the Detroit Lions. I just wanted to come by and tell you what a great musician I think you are." He said, "Who'd you say you were?" I said, "Lem Barney." He said, "Not the guy that played with the Detroit Lions?" I said, "Yes sir." He said, "Man, you're too small to be that guy!" I said, "Do you want to see my driver's license?" He said, "No man, come on in, man, I was having lunch."

I go in, and he is in the kitchen having lunch. I said, "No, I'm okay. I'm going to go back to the training camp and have lunch before the second practice. Well, I just wanted to come by and just meet you and tell you how much I appreciate your singing and everything, man." We started kibitzing and I looked at my watch, and I said, "Oh, man, I got about 30 minutes before I have to be on the field, man." It was about 25 miles from where he was to training camp. I was driving, and I mean I was driving like Mario Andretti. I was just hoping the cops wouldn't find me and they didn't. I got back to training camp. I had just enough time to put on my uniform, and nobody knew it because I would've gotten fined for it. I didn't get my ankles taped that day for the second practice because I was a little late, and everybody was gone, but it started a dynamic relationship between Marvin and me.

I told Mel Farr about it, and he said, "Oh man, that's wonderful, man. We have to go back by and see him again." We started visiting Marvin after that. We were getting tickets for him and Smokey Robinson at Tiger Stadium for the Lions games. The players had a special place they would go eat after a home game at Tiger Stadium, and Marvin and Smokey started coming by. Everybody quite naturally was going to love these guys. They would eat with us and have fun. They'd take the piano over. They would do sing-a-longs. Not the sing-a-long with Mitch, but a sing-a-long with Marvin and Smokey, and the bond began from there. They were just wonderful guys. I still stay in contact with Smokey. He's just a great guy.

We'd always go by the studio and listen to Marvin record. One day, he took Mel and me to the studio and sat us in the music room with him. He said, "Lem, you take this part. Mel, now you take this part." The next time you are listening to "What's Going On", you can hear a voice that comes on and says, "Say brother, what's happening?" I said, "Yeah brother, like solid, right on! Wee-doodle-dwee, wee-oodle-dwee, ooh, ooh, mother, mother." As a result, it ended up being a gold record. Berry Gordy, the big guy for Motown, gave us gold records for singing background with Marvin on "What's Going On." It's been a joy. Marvin was a great guy.

I would pay Motown to have a gold record, man. There were no residuals coming, but it was a just a joy to sing with a guy who you fell in love with and became great friends with; and what a dynamic guy he was. A lot of people didn't really know the ins and outs about Marvin. He would give you the coat off of his back, and wouldn't ask you for a receipt or a dollar for it. He just had a compassionate, loving heart. He always wanted to be an athlete. He just didn't have it.

I got Marvin a shot with the Detroit Lions as a walk-on. He went on The Shirley Eder show, The Jack Parr Show, and a lot of shows in the Detroit area on radio and TV. He kept saying, "I'm going to be a Detroit Lion." Coach Joe Schmidt said, "What's this about your man Marvin saying he's going to be a Detroit Lion? Doesn't he know he has to train with us?"

I said, "Coach, I keep telling him that he can't just, you know, walk on. Even if he is a walk-on, he has to get permission from the team." Coach Schmidt set up a meeting where Marvin would come and talk with him. He knew Marvin would be over at the restaurant where all the coaches, players, and the wives would be Sunday night after a game at Tiger Stadium. Coach Schmidt said, "Marvin, do you have any film from when you played in high school?" Marvin sort of held his head down and said, "Well coach, I never played in high school." He said, "That's okay. What about college? Do you have any film on you from when you played in college?" He held his head down again and said, "Coach, I never played in college." Coach said, "Well Marvin, what makes you think you can walk on as a professional without having played in high school?" He said, "Coach, I just believe in my heart. That first time I touched a pass, I score a touchdown, you know, every time I try, I just believe that in my heart." Coach said, "Marvin, I love your attitude and everything, but let me think about that. I'll get back with Lem, and I'll let you know." Coach called me back that evening and said, "Man, I would, but this guy would go out there and get his leg broke or something, and I couldn't live with myself if he did. Let me think about it and I'll get back with you."

Coach had a three-day workout in shorts and a helmet in Flint, and he invited Marvin to come out and practice. Marvin tried out at running back, tight end, and wide receiver. He had the heart for it, but he didn't have the skills or the talent for it, but he was appreciative that coach gavehim an opportunity to work out with the guys.

Chuck Hughes

I think the entire squad, the organization, the town, and the state were pretty much balled out after Chuck Hughes died on the field. A lot of people thought Dick Butkus had hit Chuck Hughes. We were playing the Chicago Bears at Tiger Stadium. A lot of people don't know the ins and outs of this. A week before playing the Bears, we were playing the New England Patriots in Foxboro. Chuck ran a few patterns, came back, and sat on the bench. He had a PVC, a premature ventricular contraction that just shook his heart so bad, it knocked him off the bench backward about 5 yards. When he came back from New England, he started going to the hospital with his doctors. They were checking him out every day, two and three times a day, and thought he had, what looked like, a PVC. They saw no scars or anything, and they thought he was okay.

The next week, we are playing the Chicago Bears at Tiger Stadium. Chuck came in on a 1st and ten down and ran a pass route, and the ball wasn't thrown to him. As he was coming back to the huddle, he gets another pass call, and he runs another route, and the ball wasn't thrown to him. On his way back, as he is passing the Chicago Bears' huddle to get back where the Lions were huddling, he fell between where the ball was and where the Detroit Lions were huddling. He started foaming at the mouth. It was just a horrible site. Butkus started waving because during those years at Tiger Stadium, both the teams were on the same side of the field. Butkus was waving for some of his physicians to come by. People thought Butkus was taunting Chuck because they thought he'd slipped and hurt himself. When the doctors got out there, they saw how his color had changed, and they rushed him off the field and to the hospital. He made his transition to death before they even took him off the field. It was that strong of a PVC this time.

The whole team flew down to Austin, Texas, where Joe Schmidt had the funeral for him. I always had great respect for Dick Butkus, but I fell in love with him when he called the Lions and asked if he could go down on the flight with us to the funeral. I have always admired Dick for that. I have a great relationship with him.

Paper Lion

I love George Plimpton and Alan Alda. My first role as an actor was in *The Paper Lion*, which was written by George Plimpton, a great writer. George always wanted to get a shot at playing professional ball. George was a tall guy and wanted to play wide receiver. In fact, he got the Lions and coach Joe Schmidt to give him an opportunity to play in a pre-season game at University of Michigan. From that, he wrote the book, *The Paper Lion*, about a writer trying out with the Lions, which became a best seller.

Then they made a movie about the book and cast a big guy from *Mash*, Alan Alda, to play the role of George Plimpton. It was just so much fun doing the movie. We filmed it down in Florida at a Boca Raton private boarding school. It turned out being a great film. Mike Weger and I did a lot of singing in the movie. The movie detailed what a rookie has to end up doing during the course of indoctrination as a professional ball player during their rookie year. It was a lot of fun.

The Black Six

The guy who did the Linda Lovelace movie, *Deep Throat*, contacted Carl Eller from the Vikings, Joe Greene from the Steelers, Willie Lanier from the Chiefs, Mercury Morris from the Dolphins, Gene Washington from the 49ers, and me, about doing a motorcycle movie called *The Black Six*.

In the movie we were all Vietnam War Veterans, and while we were in Vietnam, the six of us had a pact that if we survived the Vietnam War, we would come back to the states and buy motorcycles and just ride all across the country, enjoying life. Our motto was, "We will show love and peace; no hassle." That was our motto, but everywhere we went, we ended up running into dangerous troubles across the country.

Dick "Night Train" Lane

The Train. What a great guy. May his soul rest in peace. Train helped to scout me during my junior and senior years down at Jackson State. I thought it was an honor to have him to come down.

As modernized as the game is now with all the defenses, he still has an all-time league-leading record as a rookie with 14 interceptions. They were only playing 12 league games at the time; it's four more games now. He played the left side, and he was left-handed. When a sweep would occur, the cornerback's responsibility is to come up and go on the outside shoulder of the pulling lineman to turn everything back in for the pursuit, to make the tackle. Train, for whatever reason, the coach couldn't figure it out either, would not turn it in. He would go inside and turn it out. Night Train was left-handed, and Night Train would hit you with that meat hook. He would hit you around the neck. It was like a clothesline tackle around your neck. A guy running the ball would think he was outside of Night Train's grasp. When they woke him up, the official would be over him, and he would say, "What happened?" The official would said, "The Train got you, baby, the Train got you."

Interceptions

I could almost describe all of them. I still remember them fondly. The first one was so special. Maybe because of the fact that I had great admiration for Bart Starr, and I still do. Bart and I became very good friends. Again, I had a tremendous respect for Bart because I wanted to be a Bart Starr. Bart was a quarterback at Alabama and ended up going to the Packers. I watched Bart's techniques and fundamentals of the game in passing. He had a great mind as well. After being drafted by the Lions, I found out that I was in the Central Division and I was going to be playing against this guy a couple of times a year.

We go up to Green Bay. They are the defending Super Bowl champions. Coach Vince Lombardi, as well as Bart, used to always test and pick on rookies. The second offensive play of the game, it's 2nd and 7 and Bart takes a 3-step drop. He tries to throw a quick out to All-Pro Boyd Dowler. As Bart sees me closing, he is in the motion to throw it, so he throws the ball like a good fastball pitcher to a good fastball hitter. He throws it low and away. I dive in front of the receiver about 3-1/2-yards, I stretch out, intercept the ball, and do a fall with a shoulder roll. I get up, and I run it into the end zone about 22 yards for a touchdown. As I slam the ball when I get into the end zone, I watched the ball go skyward. I put my hands on my hips, and I said, "Lord, this is going to be easy." First play in the league, first pass, second play of the game, lines up 7 nothing.

Pro Football Hall Of Fame Induction

I'm still feeling that feeling. It's one of the greatest feelings. I'll always remember it, because it's a feeling like you never had before. I don't think playing in four or five Super Bowls would've have given me that type of feeling. First of all, it was something that was totally unexpected. The first year I was on the finalist list, I didn't think I was going to have a chance to go in. Then the next year, I was on the finalist list again. It happened that second time around, and it was news across the country.

Al Davis from the Raiders, John Mackey from the Baltimore Colts, and number 44 from the Washington Redskins, John Riggins, and I were inducted. It was just so unbelievable because, again, coming out of Jackson State, Mississippi, playing with the Lions, I'm thinking that you had to be a two-time Super Bowl MVP and things of that nature to get in. I guess the second time around it was good enough for the writers and the voters. It was just one of those things that I was so appreciative of. I got Jimmy David, my professional football coach, who had signed me, as my presenter at the hall. I had coaches from high school, coaches from college, friends, and teammates, that I could have asked, but it was Jimmy David that I had asked to do it.

The day of the parade, before the enshrinement, I was asking my driver, "Has anybody ever sang at the Hall of Fame enshrinement?" He said, "Oh yeah, they sing the national anthem and things like that." I said, "Oh, no, no. My daughter's going to do that." I said, "What about any of the enshrinees? Have they ever sung before?" He said, "Enshrinees? No enshrinee has ever sung before. Why? Are you thinking about singing?" I said, "Well, if I can muster up to it, yeah. I'm thinking about it." He said, "What are you going to sing?" I said, "No, I can't tell you that now. I'm just going to let everybody know if I sing."

When Jimmy enshrined me and made his last remarks about me, he said, "Lem Barney, if there was ever a greater defensive back than him that played in the National League, I've yet to see it. Here he is, Lem Barney." Everybody started applauding. I walk up and I give a little sigh and I look out and I sang, "For once in a lifetime, a man knows the moment. One wonderful moment when fate takes his hand and this is my moment." It was the greatest moment of my life in football, so I had to sing about it or shout about it or I was going to cry, one of the three or four. I ended up singing. It came off good. I didn't get any music offers or anything of that nature, but it was something I really wanted to do.

Toughest Receiver To Cover
It could've been a fat lady in front of me and I was going to respect her because if she was in front of me, she had the abilities and the talents to beat me. There were some small receivers that had speed and could run smooth patterns, like Paul Warfield, for instance. Charlie Taylor had speed, quickness, and moves. You have guys like Cliff Branch and Bob Hayes who had great speed. Paul Warfield and Isaac Curtis would run good routes and had great speed. Otis Taylor had great speed and was a fine route runner.

Detroit Lion Lem Barney grabs Larry Brown of the Washington Redskin by the leg to bring him down. Photograph courtesy Associated Press

Chapter 66

Larry Little

```
College:
Bethune-Cookman

Career History:
San Diego Chargers (1967–1968)
Miami Dolphins (1969–1980)

1993 Inductee Pro Football Hall of Fame
```

College Choice

When I came out of high school, it was during the time of segregation so I didn't have a chance to go to a major college. I only had two scholarships coming out of high school, Bethune-Cookman and Saint Augustine College in Raleigh, North Carolina. All of my good friends, classmates, and teammates were going to Saint Augustine, so I decided to stay closer to home and went to Bethune-Cookman in Daytona Beach. Ironically, my senior year, Saint Augustine dropped football. So, I made a big choice that was very important to where I am today.

Draft

Before the draft I got a call from Houston and the Rams, who told me they were going to draft me. In the dormitory where I was living, my room was right next to the telephone booth. I wouldn't let anybody use the phone all day since I was expecting a phone call. I stood by the phone. I couldn't eat or sleep. I was waiting on a phone call that never came. The next day I got a call from the Baltimore coach who said they wanted to sign me as a free agent. I asked him how much bonus money I was going to get, and he told me they weren't giving any bonuses to free agents.

So then I got a call from a guy in Daytona Beach by the name of Bud Asher who was scouting for the Chargers at the time. He said they'd give me $750 for a bonus and I jumped at it. The next day, Joe Thomas of the Miami Dolphins called me and said "Larry how'd you like to play at home in Miami?" I said, "Well I would've loved to come to Miami to play but I'm going to sign with San Diego." He asked, "How much money did they give you? I asked him, "How much bonus money are you going to give me?" He told me, "$500." I told him "San Diego gave me $750 so I'm going to San Diego."

Trade To Miami Dolphins

Joe Thomas made a trade for me to come to Miami for my high school teammate, Mack Lamb. Sid Gillman who was my coach in San Diego at the time called it a nothing-for-nothing deal. I don't know if two high school teammates had been ever traded for each other.

Well I really didn't want to play for Miami because they were an expansion team. San Diego wasn't winning championships, but we were winning. We had a lot of talent in San Diego, guys like Lance Alworth, John Hadl, the quarterback, and Paul Lowe, a great running back. I played for one year under George Wilson in Miami. Then they fired George and brought in Don Shula in 1970.

Position Change With Dolphins

Early in my college career, you had to play both ways. It was not until my senior year that I had the choice to play offense or defense. I was accustomed to playing both offense and defense, so it didn't matter what side of the ball I played with the Dolphins. The only thing I wanted was an opportunity to prove myself.

When I got to Miami, Sid Gillman had all the guys in shorts and shoulder pads. I ran a 4.9 forty in pads.

I picked up the San Diego Union newspaper and read that Sid Gillman brought a lot of free agents to training camp before the drafted rookies got to camp, and maybe one or two free agents stick around when the drafted rookies got to training camp. I felt kind of insulted and that upset me because I thought I would have a chance to compete with all the rookies not just the free agent rookies.

So what happened was, I made it through that first week. I was glad it happened that way because I was able to be a week up on the rookies who were coming in. The first four games I was on the taxi squad. After the fourth game I was activated to the regular roster.

I wasn't worried that they had me on special teams. I was a pretty good special teams guy because of my size and speed. They had me at fullback for two days before I moved to guard. They said I could be the next Jim Nance, but I thought they moved me there because they were getting ready to cut me. Then I was told they wanted to try me out on the offensive side of the ball, and I guess you could say the rest is history.

Don Shula

You could tell it would be a whole different atmosphere with Don Shula than it was with George Wilson. On a hot summer day during our two-a-day practices, George Wilson would tell us, "Oh it's too damn hot to practice. Go jump in the pool." No way Don Shula would ever do that. We'd practice through any kind of heat and we'd practice very, very hard. We were probably the hardest practicing team in football. I don't think anybody worked as hard as we did.

Dolphins Offensive Line

One thing we did have was a lot of pride on the offensive line. We liked to call ourselves the best in the business. We always took that attitude on the field with us. We knew we could play the game.

Chicken Little
We were training in Escondido, California and the first night out we were going to the city of San Diego, to a fried chicken place owned by a former Pittsburgh Steeler. I ate a whole chicken, drank a fifth of Ripple wine, and I got the name "Chicken Little."

It followed me all the way down to Miami. I'm still called "Chicken" by a lot of my teammates. I do love the bird though.

Playing Weight
When Don Shula first met me at his press conference when he became the head coach, I was leaning towards 285 pounds in weight. That's what I played at my first in Miami for George Wilson. So I went up to Coach Shula and said, "Coach my name is Larry Little and I'm one of your guards." The first thing he asked me was, "How much do you weigh?" I said, "Oh, 285." He said, "All right. That's all right," and walked off just like that. When I got the letter to report to training camp, the report said, "I want your weight to be 265 pounds." I hadn't been that small in I don't know how long. I knew it was something I had to do and it made me a better football player. I realized that. When I played, it made me faster and more agile. So he knew what was best for me and I accepted it.

Paul Warfield
Paul Warfield was the consummate trophy. Paul did what he could to help the football team win and you couldn't have had a better teammate than him. Paul was also a great down field blocker. He was great for our team.

Marv Fleming
We got veteran leadership from people like Paul Warfield and Marv Fleming when he came to Miami. They had been on winning teams. To this day I still say Marv Fleming was the best blocking tight end to ever play the game. Marv made my job very easy of pulling for sweeps because I knew he would cave and run down and I could get to the corner much easier. He was a great teammate.

Super Bowl VI
Super Bowl VI was an awesome experience. Just two years before that, we were 3-10-1. Two years later we were in the Super Bowl. It was an experience. A lot of things needed to happen for us to be there. We were happy to be there, we were expecting to win but we were just beaten by a better football team I guess, the Dallas Cowboys.

Bob Griese
Bob Griese was another unselfish player. Bob called his own plays. We had a great wide receiver in Paul Warfield, but Paul knew our offense was based on the offensive line and our running backs. He knew that if we did our jobs, which we did very well, we'd be in a position to win football games. Keep the other team from getting the football.

1972 Miami Dolphins Undefeated Season
When we lost to Dallas in the Super Bowl, our main goal was to make sure to get back to the Super Bowl and win it. That was our whole attitude in training camp. We saw the film of the

Dallas game and Coach Shula stood up in front of the team and said, "You see how you feel now and how you felt then. You don't want to have that feeling again, so we've got to go back to the Super Bowl to win the Super Bowl." That was our attitude, to go back and win it. We weren't talking about going undefeated, it just kept happening. We played a lot of close games that year too but we always found a way to win.

Toughest Defensive Lineman
It was probably Joe Greene. We had some great battles against each other. Joe intimidated a lot of offensive line guards. The strongest guy to play the game was Curley Culp. All around Joe was quick, strong, and nasty. He whipped my ass up.

Mercury Morris
When Mercury Morris came to Miami, I saw this guy walking and running his mouth. He was wearing red pants with the buckle in the back. I was like, who's this guy? We didn't get along when we first met because he was from the North and I was from the South, and he probably had more sense than me. Now we are best friends forever. He's a talker.

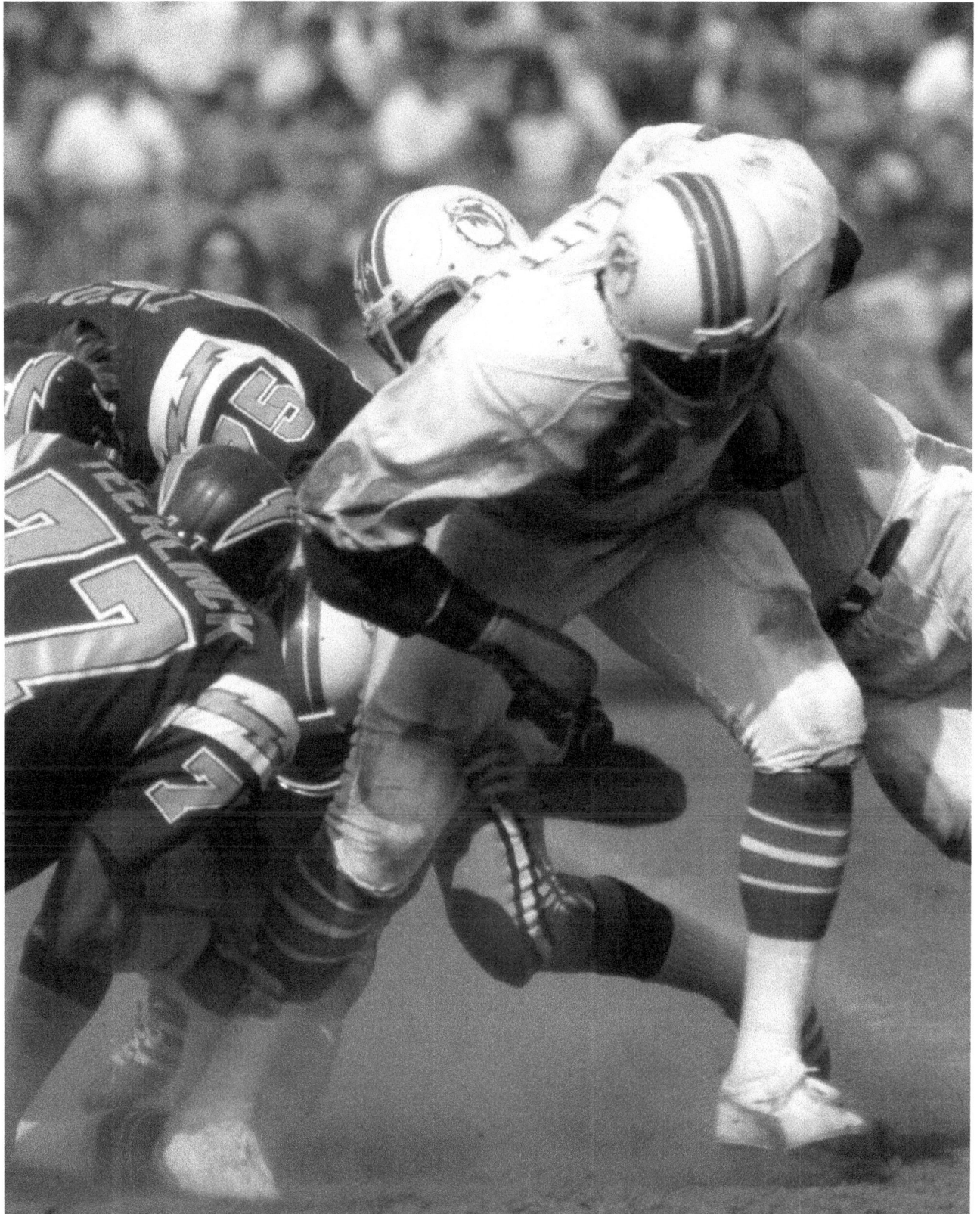

Photograph courtesy Associated Press

Chapter 67

Elvin Bethea

College:
North Carolina A&T

Career History:
Houston Oilers (1968-1983)

2003 Inductee Pro Football Hall of Fame

College Choice

North Carolina A&T was not my choice; my mother made that choice for me. At that time, I had probably about 18-20 scholarships and I really wanted to go to Villanova. My mother went to school with a gentleman who was a football coach at North Carolina A&T, and that was the end of it. I didn't have a say-so in it.

I'm glad I went. I went to a small college and they say if you can make it a small black college, you can make it anywhere in the world. That is the motto.

It was quite a culture shock. I went from a high school, which was very integrated and multicultural to a college, which was predominantly black. It was an adjustment but I enjoyed it. One thing that really shocked me was that the facilities were worse than I had in high school. I adjusted and everything worked out for me. I always tell people that if I had to do it again I would do it the same way.

Houston Oilers Training Camp

I left North Carolina and went southwest. We're talking about real culture shock. My first stop over was in Kerrville, Texas. I would highly recommend doing that for anyone from up north. You'll learn a lot about cactuses.

It was a little west from the middle of nowhere. It was about 80 miles west of San Antonio. Nothing was there. You didn't have a Walmart or Kmart or any real restaurants to go to. It was just a little country. Our training camp location was at a Shriner Institute. It was just a boarding school, and the best facilities at that time were your sleeping quarters. Everything else was back in the 1940s I think.

This was Bud Adams' choice. It was cheap and it was an institute that was small and private. The sleeping facilities were in dormitories but as far as the practice facilities, it was second to none and I mean none. There was no air conditioning unit in the gym. The only thing that was green in that whole area was the football field. Seriously. The temperature at 2 or 3 o'clock in the afternoon was always at least 95-100 degrees, and that's the way we trained.

We trained there and that's what you were there to do. We had six to seven weeks before going to training camp and there was nothing to do. Zero. All you did was drank beer on the weekends. You had a scrimmage on Saturday morning and were off from Saturday afternoon until Sunday and then back to work on Monday. Being there was strictly for training and it was good. It got you away from your family and other obstacles that might tend to bend your ear the wrong way.

We didn't have a winning season because of the type of players they had chosen. Quite a few guys made it by leaving there and going to other teams. Everybody enjoyed it for what little money they were making. We were there for six weeks and we were making $50 a preseason game, before taxes. After taxes you got $46.24.

Adjustment To Professional Football
When you get to the pros you think that you're the hottest stuff showing up, but after you get there, you find a lot of players are above and beyond your talent level and everybody is good at that point. There are people who can help the team and hope to make the team. In my case, I had a lot of competition back then and I just wanted to make the team. As far as the money, I earned $15,000 my first year. All I wanted to do was just have that emblem and logo on my helmet, jacket, or where ever. That's what it was.

You came in with 100 players and only 40 of them were going to stay. For me, I was lucky enough to stay. I worked my tail off because I wanted to be a Houston Oiler. I had no idea what the hell I was doing, but I enjoyed football. Sixteen later I was still there.

Stats
After I realized that there were stats, I would build on my previous year. Every year I wanted to have one or two more than the last year, such as tackles. So, that was my goal. I was always trying to reach a higher goal and set those numbers for myself, but this happened later in my career. When I first started out, all I wanted to do was play. There were no goals except making the Pro Bowl. That was the incentive. I really tried to make. I never thought that I would be in the Pro Bowl for eight years. The incentive if you made the Pro Bowl was you got $1,500 extra. So, that was the incentive. It wasn't like it is now. If you go to the Pro Bowl, the winning and losing teams each get seven figure paydays. We would kill each other for the extra $250 or whatever it was the winning players got. I was just glad to be there.

Experts estimate I had 105 sacks, I still don't agree with it. The NFL didn't keep any records of sacks when I played. I still think I would have been close to the record of 200 sacks that Bruce Smith has. Who knows, life goes on.

When I got chosen for the Hall of Fame, the guy who really helped me was Mark Adams. He kept every stat on me from the day I started. I never followed stats. I just went out and played the game. After I saw the stats, I was impressed with myself. I said, "Boy, I must have been really good."

Earl Campbell
In 1978 when Earl Campbell came, we would have the second team go against the first team in training camp. The offensive first team would go against the second team defense. The first

team defense would go against the second team offense. We really never met up in practice. Bum wanted to make sure that nobody got hurt. Bum wanted to make sure that he took care of his players and Bum was a player's coach.

Bum Phillips

Bum Phillips took good care of us. Bum was a player's coach. He understood every player. That was amazing. I sat there and watched him for years. He knew each player on that team; what button to push as far as getting him motivated. That was a crazy thing because we had players who were from other teams. We were basically misfitting characters. We picked up anybody and everybody who was on the trading block.

The thing is, Bum knew how to push each players button to get them motivated. He is the type of guy who would pull you to the side and say, "Hey, you either get in line or get out of line because I will trade you." You knew right from the start where he was coming from. He was trying to build a team by having them build themselves. It was the greatest thing. If we had a problem with one guy, he would keep pestering him and ask us to take care of the problem. We'd take care of our own house. That was the greatest thing about him. He would let you play the game and make sure that you were fit and that you were prepared. After every game there was a party that he would set up for us. It was a great time for me, especially in the later years.

Bum Phillips Use Of Earl Campbell

Bum would run Earl right, Earl left, Earl up the middle. I think Earl Campbell wanted to run the ball. He was the man. I think that he proved he was the man. That's football. If you have something that's going for you, a play or a player that's bringing you your wins, you go with it. It's sad that Earl only played maybe seven years. I think it was, but now he can barely walk, but that was football. You play the best. I'm sure that Earl didn't want to be sitting on the bench at any time. You go out there, not knowing the effects of playing until after you leave the game. Earl could have backed off if he wanted to, but that was Earl and that's the way Bum saw these things. He knew every button for each guy—what to push and how hard to push it.

Pro Football Hall Of Fame Induction

It got to a point, I think in my 17th or 18th year after retiring, people would say, "Oh, you're going; you're going to the Hall." I would say, "If I haven't gone by now, I'm not worried and not concerned about it." The craziest thing, the day I got the call, I was working for Anheuser Busch and I was heading to a meeting in St. Louis. A guy called and said, "You're in the Hall of Fame. Your name was called." I said, "You know what, until someone calls me and tells me I won't believe it." There was a time that I never thought it would happen to me. It never dawned on me. I thought that my memories were enough. I played on a very bad team. The Pro Bowls I went to helped me get in. How many winning seasons did the teams that I played on have? I didn't expect it. I didn't even follow the Hall of Fame, honestly. I'm just a simple person. It's a very humbling feeling to say that and every time I look at my jacket or look at a picture of myself in the Hall, I'm saying this is it. I've told people that one vote could've gone the wrong way for me and it could've been another 20 years. I'm very happy that I'm there and I wear the jacket very proudly. I go back every year. They have a parade that's better than the Macy's parade, with over 250,000 people every year. Each and every year that I've gone there, we have a parade on Saturday. It's about two hours long and it's just amazing how people come out to see us and just to wave at us. There's one thing they always say is thank you for coming back. That's what really makes me feel that I've accomplished all my goals and I'm finally getting a little accolade for what I did.

There was one kid standing on the side my second year in the Hall. He had a cut off of cardboard and written on it was, "You coming back to Canton, priceless." That sold me. I will be there every year.

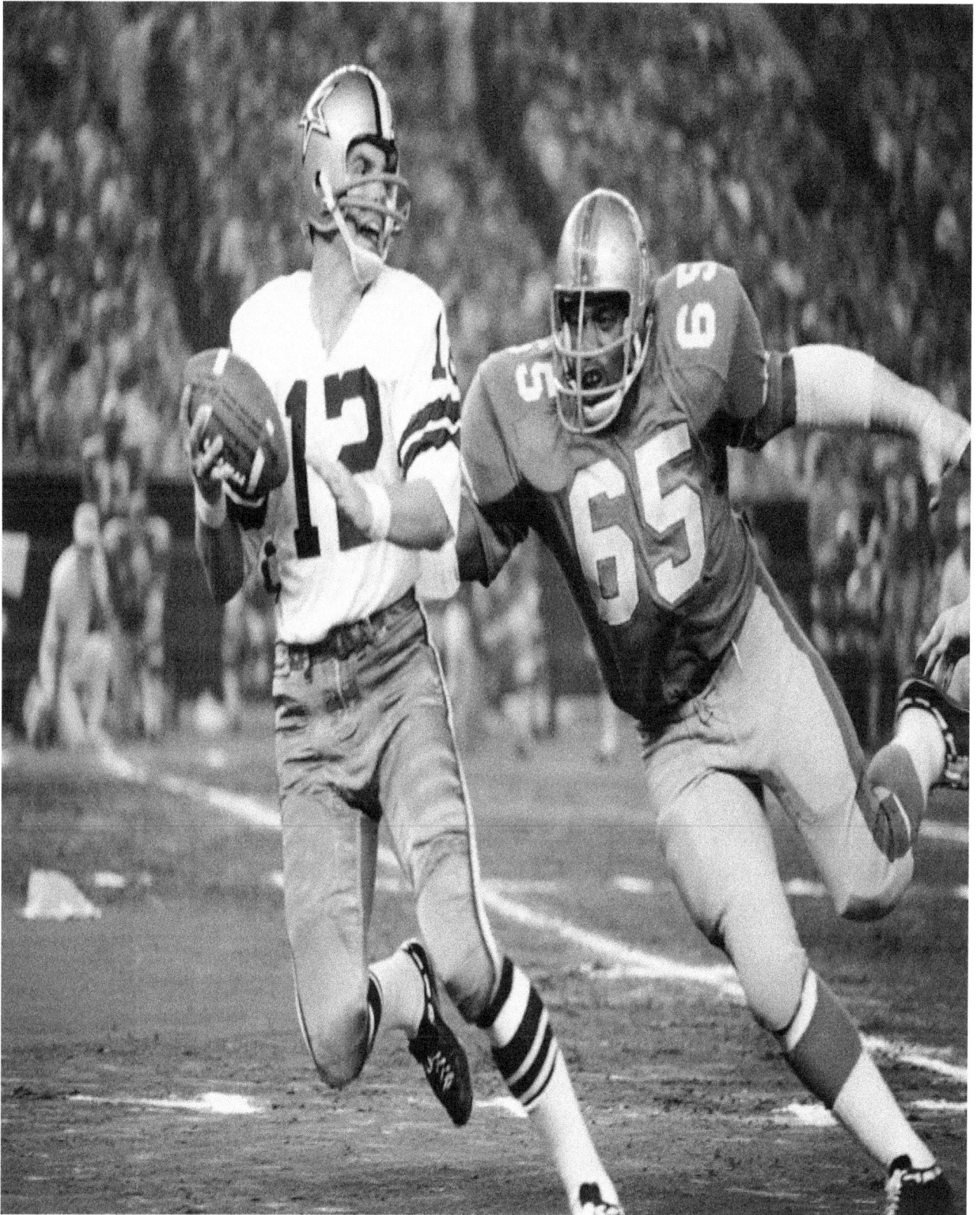

Houston Oiler Elvin Bethea puts the pressure on Dallas Cowboy Roger Staubach. Photograph courtesy Associated Press

Chapter 68

Curley Culp

College:
Arizona State

Career History:
Kansas City Chiefs (1968-1974)
Houston Oilers (1974-1980)
Detroit Lions (1980-1981)

2013 Inductee Pro Football Hall of Fame

College Choice
I had an opportunity to go to UCLA on a wrestling scholarship. The only catch was that if you made the team you would have a scholarship. I won the state championship a couple of years in a row at Yuma High School. At Arizona State, it gave me an opportunity to do two things: one, to play football and second, to wrestle which was really dear to me at that time.

I enjoyed wrestling and football in my hometown, Yuma, Arizona. We had some decent years, but I think my wrestling success was probably overshadowed by my football endeavors.

Frank Kush was the Head Coach at that time. A gentleman by the name of Jack Stovall at Arizona State pursued me heavily through the support of my high school coach at the time, Frank Thomas.

Frank Kush
Frank Kush was a super coach. He brought in a lot of individuals and gave them opportunities in pro football and to get an education at Arizona State University. I think his style of coaching probably wouldn't fit in college today, but he had great success at Arizona State University. He got things done and was a winning coach.

There were a lot of good athletes at Arizona State University, like Charlie Taylor, Mike Haynes, Randall McDaniel, and me. Reggie Jackson started out at football and didn't play much, and then he switched over to play baseball.

Name Curley
I have a twin sister and her name is Shirley. She was born about 15 minutes before me. My sister Lucille told me that she came up with the rhyme between Shirley and Curley.

I had to live with that. A lot of people think that Curley is a nickname. A lot of people have Curley as a nickname, but that's my given name. No middle name just Curley.

Reggie Jackson

Reggie Jackson was a running back. I had an opportunity to block for him as an offensive guard when I was at Arizona State during my freshmen year.

I think there was a situation at Arizona State University where Reggie had to go through the hamburger drill. I think the hamburger drill was what made up his mind which sport he wanted to pursue at the time.

College Wrestling

My junior year I won the Gregorian Award. That was quite an accomplishment. I had a Head Coach by the name of Ted Bredehoft for wrestling. I must say that I was in the best shape I had ever been in my life going into the nationals.

In the first round, I wrestled this gentleman from Lehigh and I beat him 15-5. I took the rest of my opponents to the mat and pinned them all.

In the championship round, I pinned a guy from Adams State in 51 seconds. It was really a great feat for me to be a part of the team. I think that's the first time Arizona State University ranked so highly in the nationals, so it was a big deal. I think it was probably more pure strength than anything. Although we had a weight program at Arizona State, it wasn't really extensive. It wasn't the kind of weight training that they have now in colleges and universities.

I won the nationals during my senior year. Since in my junior year, I had an opportunity to compete for the Olympics. In fact, I made the Olympic squad. I was the number two heavyweight in the country at that time. Larry Kristoff was number one and I was number two.

I went to the trials, I believe in Lincoln, Nebraska. They said you needed to win two out of the three matches. You had the opportunity to pick which way you wanted to wrestle, freestyle or Greco.

Freestyle wrestling is where you use your legs and your upper body. That was my choice. The powers that be wanted me to go with Greco. I wrestled this guy in the first round and I thought I pinned him. A couple of judges said he was pinned and I relaxed a bit, he rolled me a couple of times. The outcome of the match was different than I thought it should have been. I decided to pursue football instead of wrestling at that time.

I guess because I won nationals, everybody kind of knew who I was. They had a picture of me on a little jar that you put money in. Whoever, end up collecting the most money would get the award for "The Boy With the Best Smile," so I won the award.

I think a lot of my teammates came in and dropped a nickel or dime every now to get me the award. It was a great thing that the student body gave me that kind of recognition.

College Draft

I was drafted by Denver and was their first pick. The college scouts in the pros felt that I was a better student for offense. They just felt that I was too short to play D-line I guess mainly because of my stature, my size—my height.

I had an opportunity to participate in the College All-Star Game in Chicago. I was a little late getting into training camp in Denver.

Lou Saban was the Head Coach. Like the college scouts, he wanted me to participate on offense, and I did. I didn't like it, but I did it because that's what he wanted me to do. He gave me an opportunity to do both offense and defense. It just didn't work out there.

I had one game in the preseason and I thought I graded out. I did grade out better than everybody else on the D-line, but the following week, I was out of there. He traded me to Kansas City.

Hank Stram had come to Arizona State for an athletic event and he spoke to the athletes at the event. Afterward he told me if he ever had an opportunity to pick me up, he would. He didn't draft me, but he had an opportunity to pick me up from Denver when Lou Saban decided to let me go.

Chiefs training camp was structured a little differently. The organization was different in the sense that you had veteran ball players there, so things were done differently.

They had a weight-training program. Everybody lifted weights regardless of what position they played. When we moved over to Arrowhead in 1972, we had a big Jacuzzi for the players.

In that building, they had a racquetball court. Everybody was kind of fascinated by racquetball. I start playing racquetball for the first time. I truly enjoyed it because I think the quickness in playing the game allowed me to hone some of the things that might be productive on the football field.

Kansas City Chiefs Defense

It was a great bunch of men. You had Jerry Mays on one side and Aaron Brown on the other side as ends. Then you had Buck Buchanan and me in the middle. Willie Lanier, Bobby Bell, and Jim Lynch were the linebackers. Johnny Robinson and Emmitt Thomas were in the secondary. We had a great bunch of guys.

Jim Marsalis was the guy I roomed with a lot. I think we started rooming together the first year I was there. It was a great fit with the blend between young ballplayers and veteran ballplayers. It was one of those teams that you wanted to be on because it was a good chemistry and Hank Stram was such a great coach. He was an innovator on a lot of things he tried to do as well.

Tom Pratt was the defensive line coach. Most of the time, my interactions were with Tom Pratt. If there was a situation with the team that Tom Pratt thought Hank Stram should become involved with, he would do that.

Hank Stram held two roles. He was a head coach and he dealt with contracts. I thought that was kind of a conflict of interest, but he did that.

Move To Houston Oilers
I played with Kansas City for six and a half years, and six and a half years with Houston. I was in my sixth year of my contract with Kansas City that's when the World Football League started out. I was having some difficulty getting things ironed out with Hank Stram. I decided to move on and pursued playing in the World Football League by signing a contract with the California Suns.

During the 1974 NFL Season, I was basically playing out that year with all expectations of playing with the World Football League the following year. During the middle of the season, Hank Stram and me had a little disagreement of some sort, so Hank Stram decided to let me go.

The World Football Leagues first year was in 1974 and it just dissolved. I worked things out with Houston and stayed in Houston from the middle of 1974 to 1980. In 1981 I finished up in Detroit.

Bum Phillips
Bum Phillips was quite different than Hank Stram of course and even Tom Pratt. I think Bum was with Sid Gillman in San Diego.

Bum came over to Houston when Sid came in as head coach. Bum was a player's coach in a lot of respects. He was a great guy. He was really hands-on and let people do their own thing, so-to-speak.

Bum was the defensive line coach. The following year he became the head coach and Eddie Biles became the defensive coordinator.

I believe his son; Wade Phillips became the defensive line coach if I'm not mistaken.

3-4 Defense
In Kansas City, we had the "Triple Stack". We had two defenses primarily the "Triple Stack" and "Under". The "Triple Stack" was the one in which the defensive line would slide to disturb the formation. The "Under" defense, we would slide away from this vent.

In the Super Bowl, I don't know if I was assigned to the center all the time or if it just so happened. I think it was more situational than anything else.

In this matchup between the D-line against an offensive center the main responsibility of the center is to hide the ball. He has to hide the ball before he does anything else.

I'm engaging him probably at the same time he's hiking the ball. It's an advantage to the defensive line in those kinds of circumstances, although you could have a situation where you have the guards coming down on you too. It's interesting to say the least.

Transition To Oilers
In Kansas City, there were occasions I would get on the nose because it shifted the formation. Then when I go down to Houston, I'm stuck right there with the center. You don't have much movement, you're just right there kind of an apex of action. You can't relax. You're always involved in what's going on, on the football field.

Elvin Bethea
Elvin Bethea was a great one out there playing the right end position. We had Teddy Washington too. Robert Brazile came in 1976 and he helped out. The other guy inside was Gregg Bingham.

We had a good bunch of individuals, not the same talent that was in Kansas City, but we played well. We had good chemistry.

Defensive Touchdown Scored
Against the Chargers in San Diego I picked up the ball and I was just rumbling down the field. Elvin Bethea yelled, "You're going the wrong way." I turned around, and squabbled into the end zone. That was the first one and the last one I had in fourteen years in professional football, is quite neat to say the least. When you're down and you're eating all that grass and you pop-up, man, you just start running.

Toughest Offensive Linemen Faced
There were a lot of tough offensive linemen in the league during that era. I took pride in trying to keep myself physically fit to play the game. With Kansas City, we had the weight training.

Then when I shifted to Houston, James Young and me worked out extensively during the off-season trying to stay strong. We knew that was helpful when you're dealing with offensive linemen.

Favorite Coach
There were so many great coaches. Lou Saban was a good coach. We just didn't get along, but he was a great coach. Hank Stram was a super coach. Bum Phillips was a great coach. They were all good coaches. They just did things a little differently.

The greatest coach that I've been involved with was probably Hank Stram because of the fact that the team went to two Super Bowls, –the first and fourth Super Bowls. Even with Bum, we got to the championship game and played Pittsburgh two years in a row. They were both accomplished, so I guess, we're right there together.

Kansas City's Curley Culp pressures Dallas Craig Morton.
Photograph courtesy Associated Press

Chapter 69

Ron Yary

College:
Southern California
Career History:
Minnesota Vikings (1968–1981)
Los Angeles Rams (1982)
2001 Inductee Pro Football Hall of Fame

Move To Offensive Line At USC

What happened was all of our offensive line members were seniors my sophomore year. They lost everyone, so they moved me to strong side offensive tackle. Then they flipped lines, the left and right played both sides with the "I" formation. They told me after my junior year, that my senior year that they were going to play me both ways, which really got me excited but they never did. We were having a really good year so they thought it wasn't necessary. I was really disappointed they didn't call me to play both sides of the ball.

Playing fullback in high school was enough for me. I realized those guys get beat up. I was sorer after a game as a fullback than I ever was as an offensive lineman. You've got nine guys coming at you. I couldn't run away from guys and I wasn't that nifty. It was either I run over them or through them, that's the type of fullback I was. I was more of a blocking fullback. They let me lead on plays to block the defense end, or block the outside linebacker. They used me more as a blocking fullback than a running back.

College Choice

Nobody recruited me except the coaches. No former players came out or called me. I was, I think, maybe a borderline guy who they wanted. I went to Cerritos College for a semester. I got good grades in high school. I took all college prep courses. For me, I needed to go to a junior college first. I was too immature with study habits, discipline, and areas that are required for you to succeed in college. I just wasn't ready for it.

USC offered me a scholarship; I didn't qualify to get in. I think USC shipped me off to a junior college with the expectation that I would turn out to be ok, but if I didn't they'd have an out. That's what happened.

O.J. Simpson

You never appreciated having O.J. Simpson until you played against him. To me, he was just another running back. He was a very nice guy in college. He was very personable and engaging with people. Everybody liked him. He never hung out with any of the players on the team. I don't know where he was. It was the same with Mike Garrett. You never knew where they were.

They were probably in Hollywood or something, hanging out with all the celebrities. The guys that had to work stayed in the dorms.

John McKay Offense
John McKay liked to run at people. You run at them and if it works, it works. USC didn't have the quarterbacks that they have today. They didn't have the 6'3" or 6'5" quarterbacks to throw 50 yards. It was old time football.

You weren't any good unless you could run the ball. I was raised in a generation where that was your mental approach. If you were to throw the football, it was an insult to the offensive line. It was like, the reason we're throwing the ball is because we can't run the ball. The reason we can't run the ball is because we're not good enough. It was a big insult to you. That was the way that USC approached it back then. I'm sure that a lot of other colleges did as well. We were focused on run blocking and it turned out well.

Mike Holmgren
Mike Holmgren was a very smart guy. We had some smart players on the team, excluding me. Our two offensive guards became orthopedic surgeons. Another guard got his Master of Education.

One of our centers became a dentist. We had a lot of smart guys on those teams.

Mike was one of them. Mike was a throwing quarterback. They never gave him an opportunity to throw the ball. He had a heck of an arm. He could throw. He was a freshman or a sophomore my senior year.

He was a funny guy. Everybody loved Mike because he had a great sense of humor. He could take the worst situation and make it into something you could really laugh about and enjoy. You always need guys on teams like that, and Mike had that great quality. The quality came through when he was a coach. He was able to get players to play up to their abilities because of that. He was really a player's coach; I'm certain of that.

First Offensive Lineman To Be First Pick In The NFL Draft
I think if you're going to take a player and you're going to evaluate him to determine the outcome of his career, what kind a player he's going to be, it's easier to assess an offensive lineman more than any other position on the field. I think it's a safe investment to make when you pick an offensive lineman because of that.

Teams have had a lot of bad experiences drafting quarterbacks high in the draft. I know that they've had a lot of disappointments. I think there are maybe only one or two offensive linemen that they've been disappointed with in the draft.

You don't know how determined a guy is to play the game. A lot of guys don't have that hunger once they graduate from college, to make a career out of it. Chuck Arrobio, our left tackle, was a dentist as well. He was very smart. He went to the Vikings for a couple years and decided it was not worth it and became a dentist. He has had a great life as a dentist. Most of the other guys have done the same thing. They found alternatives or vocations that meant more than football.

Key To Minnesota Viking Success
What makes a great football team is how they handle adversity. We didn't like to lose. I knew that if we lost, the practices the following week would be worse than the game. Everybody would be angry with himself. Not angry at one another, but angry ourselves for losing the game. We were mad at ourselves for letting the game slip away. Once the team developed that quality, it was a tough thing to overcome for other teams. Once we lost that quality, the team began to lose.

We weren't replacing that type of a guy with the same type of a guy. You can't be happy losing.

Vikings Expectations Of Him
I didn't care about what the Vikings expectation were. I was going to do what I was going to do and that was it. I was going to live in my world, not theirs. I wasn't concerned with what their expectations were, or what they wanted me to do, I was going to do what I was going to do. I knew what I could do. I knew my limits. I knew how good I could be and I played the game.

The other thing is, I loved the game. I loved playing football. I would not have done anything other than football. It's the only thing in my life that I have done that I felt that way toward. Now, being a Dad is another. Up until this point, it was all me, everything. I loved going to work in the morning. I loved going to practice. I enjoyed hanging around that type of person. It was a simple life; it wasn't complex. You knew your outcome. You knew whether you'd succeed or fail immediately in your work assignment.

It's not like other occupations where you could go for six months and not know whether or not you're going to succeed. Your reward is known immediately. You can correct issues immediately as well. You can't find a better way to make a living in America than sports; it's ideal.

When you hear these guys talk about all the pressures involved, that's not true. To me I hear that and I don't understand it. You go to work every day, and you set your own goals. You reach your goals. You make a lot of money. You meet a lot of girls. If you're not

Married, you have a lot of opportunities to meet a lot of girls. What more can you ask for in life in your early twenties?

I've seen a lot of tragedies in marriages because of things that went on like that. I was married at 24, divorced at 26; perfect example of that. I was a bad husband; I was not a good husband. I had a great wife. I didn't get married again until I was 51, because I knew that failure ruined me for a long time. There may be reasons for that, but that's not what I'm here to talk about.

Bud Grant
Fran Tarkenton once said that if you can't play football for Bud Grant, you couldn't play for anyone. We all agreed on that. Bud had his ways that you may not have liked, but you could live

with them. There wasn't anything he asked of you in terms of regimen or discipline that was something that you could not accept. He made it clear what he expected of you as a player. What was a good performance or what was a bad one. He never embarrassed you either. He never insulted you in front of your teammates.

He had the ability to stand up in front of the team and speak to you. He had that skill that all great orators have when they talk. It's like you're having a personal conversation with them. That was one of his great qualities. He left the coaching to the assistant coaches. He let our assistant coaches make decisions on the field. It made them feel like I they had a part in the success of the team. He was a great coach to play for.

The only thing that bothered me was that they sat me on the bench my first year. To this day, I can't accept it and I'm angry about it when I think back. I felt that I should have started from day one.

If that had been today, I would not have accepted that. I would have told him either get rid of me or put me on the field. I'm not going to sit on the sideline.

Bud Grant had the same offensive that Norm Van Brocklin had, except he changed the plays by moving the odd numbers to the right and the even numbers to the left. Under Van Brocklin's system, even was the right and odd was to the left. When I played in the College All-Star Game and Van Brocklin was the coach, every play that we learned was exactly the same as Bud had, except they were reversed.

When I joined the Vikings, I was backing up Doug Davis and Grady Alderman, a third tackle in training camp. When they'd run a play I would be thinking seven is to the right, but when you're tired it's hard to work through. I made a couple mistakes and I think it was because of that. I can't think of any other reason. Today I would probably quit the team and walk off. I would go somewhere where they needed a tackle, don't put me on the bench.

I really didn't like sitting on the bench. I'm still angry about my first year. You think about the past, that's one thing that always didn't sit well with me. That's my sole complaint in my life as a football player. That's pretty good.

Vikings Reacquiring Fran Tarkenton
Reacquiring Fran Tarkenton helped our team. It was a big benefit to our team because he could scramble. We were able to capitalize on his talent.

Being an offensive right tackle, I didn't like him scrambling because he liked to scramble to the right. He liked to drift to the right. If you look at the end zone films of Francis when he was playing, he would drift to the right and throw behind the right guard, even when he set up on a pass. I changed my style of play once I found that out. I think it was maybe two or three years after Francis came to the team they put an end zone camera in. I noticed he was drifting to the right when he set up.

I stopped using the normal drop back technique and started taking on guys who were on the line of scrimmage, sooner. I became a short pass blocker, rather than the regular drop back technique type guy. I had to be more aggressive with the defensive end. I couldn't let him get up field because he would be in the face of the quarterback because he was throwing behind the right guard.

That little nuance changed the way I played, which I didn't care. He always drifted right and I didn't have eyes in the back of my head. I couldn't see where he was moving. If I knew where he was, I wouldn't care. Then I could do something about it. When you begin to move and your quarterback is moving and that's not how you practice it or you're not aware of where he's going to be; it makes it more difficult. That's the problem with the scrambler. If there was some way you could determine where he's going to run that would be great.

Vikings Super Bowls
I thought our best one was against the Raiders. I thought that our first one with Kansas City was good as well. You go in thinking you can win them all. I thought we had the best opportunity to beat the Raiders. We never did very well in those games. The team that was better deserved to win. What more can you say? I'm happy for them.

Toughest Defensive Lineman Faced
In the beginning I didn't think anybody was any good. At the end of my career, everybody was great. You're tired of having to prove yourself every year. It's more the regimen that defeats you than the person telling you the truth. I'd have to say, if I picked out the lineman, Jack Youngblood, was good. Vern Den Herder played tough against me. I didn't know that he was from Minnesota when he was playing. I couldn't figure out why he came so hard against me.

Vikings Defensive Line Coaches
Buddy Ryan was our defensive line coach. Jack Patera built the defensive line. Jack left and went to Seattle where he was the head coach. Jack was the one that picked all those guys and he had a lot to do with developing them in the beginning. We were already into the peak of our careers when Buddy took over.

Chuck Foreman
Chuck Foreman made it a lot easier. He hit the hole so quick and he was so fast down the field that he made blocking a lot easier for everybody. That's what great running backs do. They turn an average block into a pretty block. Chuck could hit a hole as fast as any guy I've ever seen.

I remember the first time he came in. The first play we ever ran with Chuck, he was through that hole so fast that he was five yards down the field. I was amazed. I said, "My God, he's going to help our team." He did, Chuck had great speed. Also, he had a great roll when he came to the Vikings. They'd hit him and he'd roll out of it, do a 360 roll and move down the field. He was very good.

Pro Football Hall Of Fame Induction
It's a very humbling experience that is a great culmination to your life and a career that you loved. If you love football and you go in the Hall of Fame, it's a big deal. If you really loved the

game, wanted to play your whole life, and then you get recognized at what 50-some years old, it really is; it's like getting the Nobel Prize in Science to a football player.

Canton does such a great job. It's a great place to have the event. The whole town gets involved for that event. Nobody can give more than what the people in Canton, Ohio do. They make it worth the whole four days you're there. It's a big tribute and a great one.

When I'd go to a banquet, I'd sit out in the audience. Now, I sit at the head table and they introduce me. That's the difference when you make the Hall of Fame. They think that you have some insight about the game that nobody else has, which is not true. Actually, you have less insight probably than most people. That's how they are; you've become a big deal in life I guess.

Les Richter

I met Les Richter one time. He came to our market when I was 8 years old. I was overwhelmed with him. When I saw him, he made me want to play football.

The reason was he had cuts all over his hands and over his forehead. His eyes were all scarred over, he had nicks all over his arms and his face and I thought that was the greatest thing I'd ever seen. I said, "That's exactly what I want to be like. Just like him." I bet he left there and he never knew. I tried to meet him many years later, after I got into the Hall of Fame, to say hello to him. He got in the Hall of Fame in 2011. He's one that who overlooked.

He really loved kids. I could tell when he was there at the market that he really likes kids. He told me to go play football and made a big deal over me when I was a young boy. I couldn't talk to him because I was taken aback by his presence. I was tongue-tied. That was my introduction to football. It was more due to his appearance. He was in a suit, a coat and tie. I'll never forget it. I can see him as clearly today as I did as a young man. He influenced me.

Photograph copyright Associated Press

Chapter 70

Charlie Sanders

College:
Minnesota

Career History
Detroit Lions (1968-1977)

2007 Inductee Pro Football Hall of Fame

College Choice

I can't say so much a pipeline as much as it was a realization, that the black athletes down South really weren't afforded the opportunity to go to the major schools. They were confined to the smaller black schools.

If you want to give Minnesota and a lot of the other Big Ten schools some credit, it was their realization that the great athletes were left down South. If they [the athletes] were afforded an opportunity, they could not only benefit themselves, but more importantly, they would benefit the university and their football program.

The University of Minnesota was able to go down and recruit those black athletes. It really opened up the opportunity for the black athletes to not only participate at Big Ten schools, but also at the larger schools down South.

When I went to the University of Minnesota, there wasn't any snow on the ground. At least they were smart enough to know that if they were going to bring you up, they should show you the campus in the spring when it was beautiful. Then all of a sudden, you saw this snow falling and it kept falling for about four months, and you realize, "What have I gotten myself into?"

All in all, I wouldn't change a thing. It was a great experience for me, especially coming from the South, to not only get out of the South and the way of thinking that was going on at that time in my life, but to go North and see the difference in the way people thought and the way people were treated. So for me personally, being a black athlete, it was an experience that really opened my eyes as to what life is all about. It really gave me a different approach in terms of dealing with mankind.

Change In Blocking For Tight Ends

The defensive side of the ball has changed. Basically years before, you'd line up in your base 4-3 with your defensive end over your tackle. Now, they've gone to defenses where they put the defensive end over the tight end for that particular reason, and generally, the fact that most tight ends can't block a defensive end.

Schematically, from a defensive standpoint, they'd move people around to make it difficult for your running game as well as to aid the defense in the passing game. Most tight ends are not going to hold up against a good defensive end. That's a fact. If you can find a guy that can do both, then you've got yourself a jewel.

Memorable Game

I'm always going to be a little partial to the 1970 game against the Raiders when we made the playoffs. That was a team that started to develop late in the season. We had won our last five games, and four of those five games were against divisional leaders. We were able to do that and go on into the playoffs. Unfortunately, we lost to Dallas, but if you take some glory in it all, Dallas went on to win the Super Bowl. So we lost to the Super Bowl champs.

Dick Butkus

He was my favorite ball player. He was the one that every time I think about football and every time I take a step back, I know that he had something to do with it. He gouged the eyes. He did that.

Deacon Jones

I was a rookie and thought I could stand up to him, and luckily, the whistle blew before he got to my quarterback because I didn't lay a hand on him.

Best Player in NFL History

I had a chance to play against and see Walter Payton. I didn't have a chance to play with Jim Brown. I had a chance to see, coach, and be around Barry Sanders, and if he wasn't the best, he was a year away from that. So I'd have to say Barry was the best I've ever seen.

Coaching

I coached for 10 years, and I think I enjoyed coaching more than I did playing. As far as taking that next step from being an assistant to a head coach, I never aspired to do that. I was just wrapped up in what I was doing and in the glory of watching guys develop and perform out on the field.

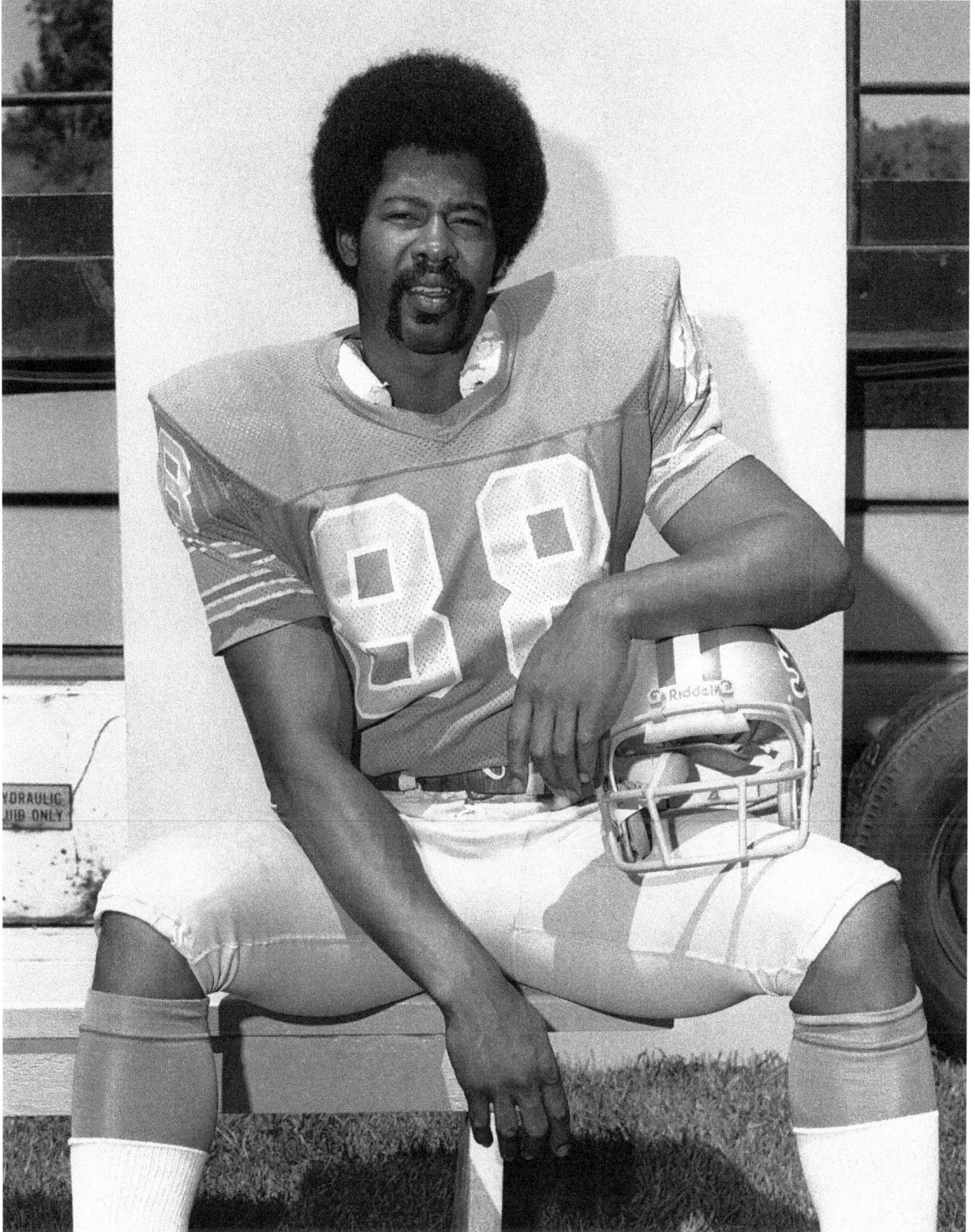

Photograph copyright Associated Press

Chapter 71

Joe Greene

College:
North Texas

Career History:
Pittsburgh Steelers (1969–1981)

1987 Inductee Pro Football Hall of Fame

Adjustment To NFL
I had pretty good coaching there at North Texas. I was a big fan of Deacon Jones and I wore that number and I was a big fan of Bob Lilly of the Dallas Cowboys. I watched those guys play and I tried to emulate those guys. The defense we were playing at North Texas allowed me a little bit of latitude and I could do some of those things.

Fortunately for me when I came to Pittsburgh, we were doing some of the same things. It wasn't that big of a transition in terms of the things that I was doing, but obviously the people I played against were a great deal different.

Goal
My main goal was to win; it wasn't about sacks to tell you the truth. If the sacks were a part of winning then so be it. If I got a sack, the only way you would know I got a sack, is because you saw it. You definitely wouldn't see me dancing.

Steelers Key To Success
Why, over the years, have the Steelers been competitive, had a chance to get in the playoffs, and had a chance to go to the Super Bowl and win? It's because of the stability and the coaches who run the football operation. The bosses up on top, Dan Rooney, Art Rooney III, and before them obviously, Art Sr., understand the hierarchy. They understand the chain of command. They hire people to do a job and let them do it.

When someone has his own self-interest and his ego gets in the way, and that person wants to take control of the team's success, and when anything gets in the way of the team goal, then you have a problem. Again I say that's why the Steelers have had an opportunity each and every year to be competitive. They have seven or eight scouts and everybody has their own input. No one gets lambasted for having an opinion and everybody's opinion counts. They know that the final decision is going to come from the head coach and the ownership. I collect information and give it to them and they make the decisions and that's the way it should be. They've done a good job over the years. I'm just amazed. I'm really amazed that I've been able to be there and be in such a good situation after I have been in some pretty poor ones at times.

Rollie Dotsch

Rollie Dotsch was the offensive line coach back in the mid-70s. Rollie got the offensive line going. He was just a tremendous coach. He believed in technique, in developing those techniques, and hard work. A lot of times you see those big guys grazing as we call it. When Rollie was there, the offensive line guys didn't graze, they worked harder than the defensive line, I would say.

Now the first guy who was there did a great job for us. Then Rollie came in and just kept it going. We missed him when he left. He was one of the guys that incorporated the punch and the tight fitting jerseys. We had smaller offensive lineman who could move, pass protect, run, pull, get out and block on screens, and they could trap. That was the Pittsburgh Steelers way and Rollie was a big, big part of that.

Toughest Opponents

We faced Earl Campbell, the Juice (O.J. Simpson), Do It Pruitt (Greg Pruitt & Mike Pruitt) in Cleveland, and we faced Kenny Stabler. It was always those guys who could hurt you with the ball. There were some great offensive linemen, no doubt about it. Some gave you more difficult times than the others, but in my mind they were incidental. Now I got my butt kicked a lot, but they were incidental because they couldn't score. My thought process was to stop the people who could score—running backs. In my day, teams ran a lot and the quarterbacks threw the football. If you get to the quarterback, usually the team is going to have a difficult time.

Larry Little was an offensive lineman for the Miami Dolphins in those days. He was an outstanding player and I did have some struggles with him. So there Larry I said it, okay.

Miami Dolphins In The '70s

During the '70s, especially the early and mid '70s, the Dolphins were a machine. They didn't make mistakes. They had a very, very good offense, with Bob Griese as the quarterback. By today's standards he didn't have the rifle arm, but he had great touch, great timing, and great leadership. He had just enough maneuverability in the pocket to make you miss and get the ball downfield. They had an outstanding offensive line. They had three running backs, Larry Csonka, Mercury Morris, and Jim Kiick along with Paul Warfield at wide receiver; not too shabby. They were a good football team.

NFL Offenses

Being on the defensive side of the ball my entire playing and coaching career, I just learned to hate those guys on offense. They would make us stay up late at night trying to figure out ways to stop them. As soon as we figured a way to stop them, they would go to the commissioner and have the rules changed on us. Then we had to start all over again. So, I hated those guys and still do.

Best Defensive Line Of All Time

I grew up watching the Fearsome Foursome; the group in New York, the Doomsday Defense, and the Purple People Eaters. Anybody can lay claim to a title, but you have to win to have it. My argument for my group is that we won four Super Bowls. When you start talking about defensive lines, you have to talk about the Steel Curtain, but you also have to talk about the

Fearsome Foursome and the Purple People Eaters. That's my take and because I played, I know how difficult it is. I know what we go through and I would never ever say that we were better than someone else if we didn't have an opportunity to play those guys. I'm not going to say that. Me saying it would be a disservice to them and I just haven't been that kind of guy.

Pittsburgh Steelers Players Off The Field Success
I coached on Chuck Noll's staff in the mid-80s and what Chuck and the scouting department wanted to have on their football team was first quality people. They started from there. They didn't always achieve that, but that was the goal. In my adult life in terms of someone who impacted my life, that guy is Chuck. In all of these years I've never met another guy who was as solid, as honest, as sincere, and as smart as Chuck Noll.

Favorite Season
Our first Super Bowl season was very, very rocky. We lost to the Oakland Raiders the second or third ball game of the year at Three Rivers Stadium, shutting us out 17 to nothing. We had a quarterback controversy with Joe Gilliam and Terry Bradshaw. We lost a division game to the Oilers in Pittsburgh, probably the 12th game of a 14 game schedule. It was very rocky. We got it together in the playoffs and we beat the Raiders for the AFC Championship. That would be maybe the best season, because of the ups and downs we had and how we came through it. There was a mystery in that first one though, for sure. That would probably be my favorite season.

In 1976, we lost four of the first five ball games. Then we went undefeated the next seven games, only giving up 28 points. That was a fantastic year also, although it wasn't a championship year. We fell short, but it was a great year for me. We had a lot of good years, but probably my favorite season was the 1974 season. When you talk about Super Bowls, I don't have a favorite, they were all good.

Pittsburgh Steeler Joe Greene in pursuit of Dallas Cowboy Walt Garrison. Photograph copyright Associated Press

Chapter 72

Larry Csonka

College:
Syracuse

Career History:
Miami Dolphins (1968–1974)
Memphis Southmen (WFL) (1975)
New York Giants (1976–1978)
Miami Dolphins (1979)

1987 Inductee Pro Football Hall of Fame

1972 Miami Dolphins Undefeated Season

If you look at our team during the undefeated season, if you went player by player and you staked us against the teams that were in the playoffs in those years, the Kansas City Chiefs who went to the Super Bowl, the Pittsburgh Steelers who would later go to Super Bowls the next couple of years, the Redskins, the Minnesota Vikings … we probably wouldn't have won those match ups individual to individual. The intangible is what they call the will to win. That makes people like Howard Twilley, our wide receiver from Tulsa, Oklahoma, a kind of guy that got open even in the old bump and run. He would manage to get open somehow, someway. You can't measure that. That's what we had a team full of back in 1972.

Don Shula's Role in Perfect Season

Don Shula was the primary ingredient in the perfect season; make no bones about it. I don't care what anyone else on the undefeated team says, or the media for that matter. I know what the key factor was that season. I was there and it absolutely was Don Shula. He was, for lack of a better description, possessed after he came to us from losing that Super Bowl with Baltimore. He came down to Miami and twisted, prodded, screamed, hollered, and insisted on tremendous attention to detail. I don't think he could coach that way in the NFL today. I don't think the players today would respond to him, but back then they did. We did and got into that first Super Bowl when we lost at the hands of Dallas in Super Bowl VI.

I think his finest moment in coaching was right after that loss because that's what lead to the undefeated season. He pulled us together through defeat, even stronger than we were prior to that happening.

Don Shula Becoming Coach Of Miami Dolphins

I thought he was pleasantly surprised by how much talent had been amassed by a fellow there named Joe Thomas. He was the Personnel Director who put the Minnesota team together prior to coming to Miami. After Miami, he put several other teams together including the 49ers, before he retired from the league. There was quite a litany for his success in the NFL. I think the

Dolphins' nucleus of players was certainly there. I think he was somewhat surprised by how Joe Thomas put together a power running game and ball control game. Coach Shula had never had that in Baltimore. He suffered at the hands of Green Bay when he was a head coach at Baltimore, when Green Bay perfected that with Jim Taylor, Paul Hornung, and their great offensive line.

When Coach discovered he had that here, then we were set to go. He knew how to utilize it because he had suffered at the hands of it at Green Bay when he was with Baltimore.

Paul Warfield
Paul Warfield got open in the old bump and run. The strong safety and weak safety could come across and literary take your head off. He was tough enough to get open even when getting knocked, bumped, and jammed all the way down the field. Think about taking a time machine and putting Paul Warfield in today's game where you can only bump him in the first five yards, and the give him an equal opportunity to the ball downfield. How well do you think he would do today?

I think he qualified for the Olympics or came close to it in the low hurdles and he also ran the high hurdles. There's a guy who had to have a fluid motion. Anyone under Olympic consideration in the hurdles definitely has strong self-discipline and a smooth gait. He was perfect in that capacity and then moved it over to football. If you remember, he played for Woody Hayes. He was a halfback at Ohio State. Paul Brown saw the possibilities with Warfield and brought him to the Cleveland Browns.

College Choice
I attributed most of my success in the pros to Don Shula. I attribute my success in college to having the right coach in Ben Schwartzwalder, a fellow who believed in me enough to let me run the ball. It was questionable at the start. A lot of people, including Woody Hayes, had me pretty much set to be a middle linebacker. I wanted to run the ball. Ben Schwartzwalder was a guy who had a history of having a strong offensive line, not throwing the ball much, and the history of great large running backs. If I was going to have my shot at running the ball, it certainly would be with Ben. That's why I went to Syracuse.

Woody Hayes got us in a room and said we owed it to our state to go to Ohio State. I was about 16 years old and didn't figure I owed anybody anything, so I went to Syracuse.

Best Team Of All Time
When you say best team of all time, first you've got to set the parameters. You know you can't make a statement like that. I just alluded to the fact that Paul Warfield would be a wide receiver in today's game.

The rules today mostly enhance the offensive play a great deal and detract from the defensive play. You've got to look for a team that was a great championship team and had a great defense. You also have to look what rules they played under. There are a lot of prerequisites before you can make an assumption like the greatest team ever. In my era, I think the team that was the most powerful and came the closest to doing what we did was the Chicago Bears in 1985, under Ditka. They seemed so much more powerful than every other team they played in the NFL that year.

Their greatness ran deep. They had great backups as we did in 1972, people who could step in and take over. That's what the Bears had that year.

Best Running Back Combinations On A Team

Again, you've got to look at the different decades. At the time, Jim Kick, Mercury Morris, and I were together, other teams had some great running backs too. The Steelers had Franco Harris with Rocky Bleier. The backfield is only as great as the offensive line can substantiate. When you talk about groups of running for different teams that's all predicated on the ability of the offensive linemen. It's maybe less important today than it was in past decades because the rules changed, but it still plays a major part.

You have to look at the quality of the offensive line. Also, whether they had a great blocking tight end and whether or not the wide receivers could block. Things like that made a tremendous difference in the running game.

Early Years With Miami Dolphins

My first couple of years with the Dolphins was also the first few years of their existence. The team logo and mascot was Flipper, not exactly the most macho thing. When you are out of college, you think a team with a macho mascot like the Cowboys, Bears, or Lions will draft you. The Dolphins drafted me. Our logo was Flipper. Our team colors were orange and aqua, for crying out loud. It was kind of a setback. We were absolutely the doormats of the league. The first two years of my career, things were tough.

Then Coach Don Shula came. He hired Monte Clark and the rest of the assistance coaches. Through trades and signings, the team put some people together. We got Jim Langer, Bob Kuechenberg, Larry Little, Wayne Moore, and Norm Evans. All of the sudden my headaches went away and we started to be a force to be reckoned with.

It was a great transitional period. You can really relate to winning if you've been losing for a while. I think that helps to make a stronger champion.

Hardest Hit Received

The hardest I've ever been hit in the NFL is by a guy named Roy Winston from Minnesota. He was backup linebacker for the Minnesota Vikings. It was a relief pass from a passing receiver on a play when we played Minnesota in 1972. I went out for a pass and was standing there. There was nowhere else to throw the ball. We had Mercury Morris, Jim Kiick, Paul Warfield, and Howard Twilley. Jim Kiick managed to throw the ball to me. I didn't have much chance of getting relief out of the pitch. That hit from Roy Winston on me just about retired me. I think of Roy every once in a while, on cold days when I get up. I think of several people when get out of bed on a cold morning in Alaska and I walk across the floor and my left ankle starts up. I think about Bill Bergey, and then I take another step and think of Joe Greene. I put my pants on and I think about Roy Winston. Then I think to myself, I wonder if any of them are thinking about me?

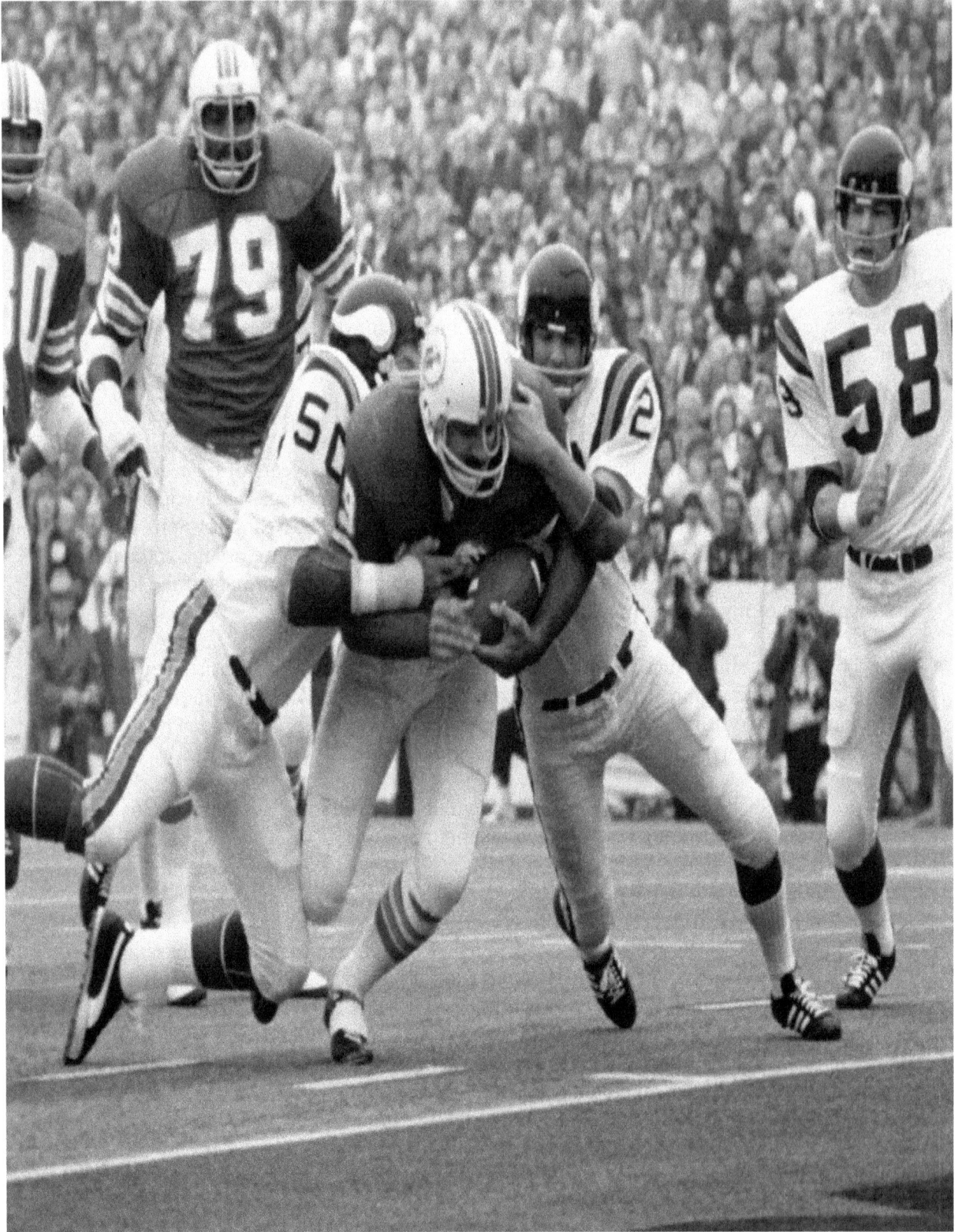

Miami Dolphin Larry Csonka drives between Minnesota Viking Jeff Siemon and Paul Krause.
Photograph copyright Associated Press

Chapter 73

Charlie Joiner

College:
Grambling State

Career History:
AFL Houston Oilers (1969)
NFL Houston Oilers (1970-1972)
NFL Cincinnati Bengals (1972-1975)
NFL San Diego Chargers (1976-1986)

1996 Inductee Pro Football Hall of Fame

College Choice
Eddie Robinson didn't recruit me. I was recruited by my high school coaches to play for Grambling, because both of them played for Eddie Robinson.

That's the way it was in Louisiana back then in those days. When he was going really good, he had been at Grambling for maybe 25-30 years. He was pretty well established within the city because almost everybody went to Grambling for college down in Louisiana. At the black high schools, Eddie Robinson would get most of the best athletes because the coach, the principal, or the athletic director went to Grambling as student athletes, or as students.

It was a joy to play for him. He was tough. He had very long practices, but I think he really taught you how to compete. He taught, don't let anybody get on top of you. You've got to be on top all the time. He was a great coach. His tactics may be a little outdated now, but back then I think he was good for the kind of people we had.

The only time I went to switch from one side of the ball to the other was when I was freshman. We had to have a loop team for the first team. I was a freshman so I was on a loop team. I was moved to the back on the loop team and I played offensive wide receiver for the defense, not offense. When I actually started playing, which was during my sophomore year, I only played one spot.

That was a tough transition for me because I was a small guy. I weighed about 185 pounds. Then I went to Grambling, which had some enormous, massive people. I'm saying to myself, "What am I doing here? I'm just too small. I won't survive." It was just the size of the guys that got me down because Grambling had big people. They had 300 pounders before the 300 pounders became popular.

We were a running offense. When we got James Harris, we started throwing the ball just a little more. Basically Grambling was a rushing offensive team. We ran the Wing-T. We didn't have a split out wide receiver.

1968 Grambling/Morgan State Game

That was a pretty good experience for us. We were a bunch of small college guys from Louisiana. The farthest state we'd been to was Tennessee, and we had to go there by bus. We got the chance to play this game in New York. They couldn't drive the bus that far, so we had to get on an airplane. That was a new experience for us. Plus, we were playing somebody we had never played before, which was another new experience for us. We enjoyed that and we relished the opportunity to be the first ones to do it. It was a big event for us.

Draft

Most of the professionals that used to train us and be with us at Grambling were in the AFL. Willie Brown, who played for the Denver Broncos and the Oakland Raiders, is a Grambling Knight. He would always come back and coach us during spring training. I think the only guy who went to the NFL who trained us was Henry Dyer. He went to the Rams.

Going to the AFL, was kind of a treat for me. I wasn't expecting to get picked high in the draft. I knew I was going to get picked, but being the second pick in the fourth round, surprised me. The reason why is a friend of mine had just become a scout for the Houston Oilers. Tom Williams of the Oilers drafted me that high. From this day on, God bless his heart and soul, I always thank him for drafting me that high. It was a miracle being drafted higher than I was expecting. It got me just a couple dollars more so I could help my parents out.

James Harris A Black Quarterback at Grambling

He just came along at the wrong time, that's all. Just born too soon. He was a drop back passer. He was not a runner though. He wasn't a moving around guy like the guys they have today, but he was a classic drop back passer with a great arm and great accuracy, a very good player.

Houston Oilers Offensive

Back then the coach of the Houston Oilers team was a basic run the ball first coach. He ran the ball to set up the pass. At the time I was with him, I was drafted as a defensive back too. I didn't play wide receiver fulltime until about my third year there.

Floyd Little & Tom Jackson

Floyd Little and Tom Jackson were the only two people that ever knocked me out of a game. Both were damn good football players. One is in the Hall of Fame and the other one should be in the Hall of Fame, as good as he was. Floyd Little knocking me out got me to be a full-time wide receiver.

Paul Brown

He was very stern and ran that ship with an iron fist. The way he'd talk to you was very intimidating, but he's one of the most knowledgeable men I've been around. He knew how to pick talent. Paul Brown had some great coaches behind him. He was good for the league. He was good at discipline because he always scared the hell out of me.

He was our head coach, but I think Bill Walsh, Bill Johnson, and Jack Donaldson, his assistant coaches, did the most coaching. The defensive coach was Chuck Weber. I don't know what kind of coach he was. Bill Johnson was the offensive coordinator. Bill Walsh and Jack Donaldson did almost everything else on offense. Paul Brown was not an active coach. He was the head coach in name only.

Cincinnati Bengals

Isaac Curtis, Chip Myers, and I were the wide receivers. Bob Trumpy was the tight end. Bob Trumpy was one the fastest tight ends I have ever seen. He wasn't one of the bigger tight ends, but he was really fast and was more of a receiver than he was a blocker.

We had a really good passing game. Ken Anderson was an extremely accurate passer. He should be in that Hall of Fame also. I think the completion percentages were high every year I was there.

Bill Walsh

Bill Walsh was a kind of a jovial guy. He liked to laugh and joke with the players sometimes. He got real serious when the time for football came, but other than that he was a real joker. He wasn't the type who you would think was going to be one of the greatest coaches of all time. You just didn't think that with Cincinnati, but hey he had the mind and he put it to work. I bet his personality in San Francisco did not change from when he was in Cincinnati.

Trade To San Diego Chargers

San Diego had a wealth of former first and second round picks. They had Louie Kelcher, Gary "Big Hands" Johnson, and Woodrow Lowe. They had a bunch of talent there and all they needed was somebody to put it all together. Coach Tommy Protho was the coach there and from what I heard, he was a very, very smart man. What really sold me on going to San Diego was the fact that they hired Bill Walsh to be the offensive coordinator in San Diego the same year I got traded there. With Walsh going there, I knew that was the place I wanted to go too. Walsh came in for one year as coordinator, and then he left to be Head Coach at Stanford University. From Stanford he went on to the San Francisco 49ers.

Don Coryell

Coryell did an excellent job of getting some very skilled players. I think we had the best players in the league at the six skilled positions. I was out there catching balls. Whether I was an average player, a great player, or a very good player, I was just having fun going out there on the football field. Coryell excited people before a game. It was fun playing for him. It was really fun. It was more fun than anything else. It wasn't drudgery. It was like you wanted to go out there and participate. It was hard work, but it was fun and we loved looking at Coryell on the sideline every Sunday.

AFC Title Games

One of the AFC title games was against the Oakland Raiders. Oakland came in, and they just ran the football, keeping the ball away from our offense. The offense couldn't do anything because Oakland just came and ran the ball. Then we went to Cincinnati to play in the Cold Bowl. Unfortunately it never rains in San Diego, but it rained that Sunday. It shut down our passing game because it made us feel real slow.

The other AFC Championship Game we went to was in Cincinnati. The wind chill factor was 60 below zero. We just caught some bad weather. They really put a bite on us. It was unbelievable up there. I still say that game should not have been played. That game should have been moved to a central site somewhere. We could have had a better AFC Championship Game.

The football was like picking up a concrete brick. We had to try to throw it because we got behind pretty quick. We were trying to throw the football. There is just no way you can throw that ball, no way. They should have cancelled that game.

Don Coryell Not Being in Pro Football Hall of Fame

Don Coryell was probably the greatest offensive innovator around. I cannot understand why he's not in the Hall of Fame. It's strictly up to the writers and the voters. I think I'll just leave it at that because I think I've done as much as I possibly can. I've talked about it as much as I possibly can. I've written about it as much as I possibly can. It's just up to the writers and the voters now, but I just don't understand why he's not in the Hall of Fame.

Comparing San Diego Chargers Offense Of Late '70s & Early '80s With Buffalo Bills Teams Of '90s

The only difference between what we did when I was a receiver for the Chargers and receiver coach for the Buffalo Bills, is Jim Kelly actually called the plays. Dan Fouts did not call very many plays. He got the signals from the sideline and that's the way he liked it. He liked for the coordinator to have the pressure of calling the plays or having the luxury of calling the plays, and he would execute them on the field. If there was a play the coordinator called that Fouts didn't like, he would definitely change it, but he was more receptive to being told the play from the sideline. Kelly, in a huddle fashion, called every play. He and the coordinator did a great job of setting their game plans every week. Both offenses were very similar. They both had three wide receivers in the game most of the time, and they both had one great tight end that could catch and also block. They both had great quarterbacks. Basically that offense was almost the same, the teams just got to it in a different way.

Toughest Cornerbacks Faced

I always thought Willie Brown was the best bumper at cornerback I ever faced because he was a little bigger and a little stronger than me. I always thought Mel Blount of Pittsburgh was the best cover-two cornerback that ever played. Those two guys gave me fits because they were so big. They were a little bigger and a little stronger than receivers were back in those days.

I don't know if they could handle a receiver today. The wide receivers today are just a little bigger than we are, but they could handle the wide receivers back in my era. Those two guys gave me fits because they were bigger and it was just hard to get around them.

San Diego Charger Charlie Joiner makes a leaping catch between Denver Bronco Steve Foley (43) and Bernard Jackson (29). **Photograph copyright Associated Press**

Chapter 74

Roger Wehrli

> College:
> Missouri
>
> Career History:
> St. Louis Cardinals (1969-1982)
>
> 2007 Inductee Pro Football Hall of Fame

Missouri

I think Coach Clay Cooper, who was the defensive back coach at Missouri, and the Head Coach, looked at me from the start as a defensive back at Missouri. My sophomore year, they decided to use me on punts a few times. I played quarterback and some safety in college. All three years of my college career, I returned punts. Back then you didn't play as a freshman; you could only play on the freshman team. They didn't allow freshmen to play on the varsity back then. We only had three years of varsity in college.

Johnny Roland was a senior when I was a freshman. They gave me the same number that Johnny had my sophomore year. Obviously I was very thrilled with that because he'd had such a great career at Missouri. Then I was drafted by the Cardinals, and obviously would have like to have had 23, but Johnny was already on the Cardinals and he had 23. They gave me the next number down, which was 22.

Dan Devine

I think Dan Devine's degree was in psychology. He was very exacting. The two best coaches I ever had were Coach Devine in my college years, and Coach Don Coryell when I was with the Cardinals. They couldn't have been more different.

Coach Devine was more the type of coach that was up on a pedestal looking down over everything and letting individual coaches do most of the on field coaching, as far as technique and things like that. Coach Devine would take the team over on Friday and start getting us ready for the game. I always had a great mental frame of mind going into every game, no matter whom we played.

Coach Coryell with the Cardinals was just the opposite. He was a fiery type of coach. He would get right in your face or be your best friend. He was very much into the offensive side of the game. He didn't coach the defense much. He was an offensive innovator and had his hands on every little bit of the offense that we had in the mid '70s when he was our coach with the Cardinals.

Beating Alabama In The Gator Bowl

We always had great seasons at Missouri. The most games we ever lost in a season was three, but never won the conference championship. We would have had a shot at it, but Kansas beat us the last game of my senior year. Obviously getting an invitation to the Gator Bowl was a big deal at that point because we wanted to redeem ourselves after that loss. To go down there and beat Alabama in the Gator Bowl by a pretty good margin was a great way to end my college career and a great thrill for all the players.

Mel Gray

Mel Gray came in as a junior college transfer. The first time I didn't know who he was. I guess it was training camp before my senior year. We were just running patterns one on one against each other, the defensive backs against the receivers. I came up in line against him. He reached to the outside and got about a step on me. We went down the field about 40 yards and he still had a step on me. I went back to the hurdle and I said, "Who is that guy I can't even catch him?"

One of the other defensive backs told me who he was and how he was a junior college transfer who won the Junior College 50-yard Dash before he came to Missouri. After that, I remembered who he was. He was a great receiver. I played with him that one year at Missouri and then the Cardinals drafted him a couple years after me.

We had Johnny Roland, Mel, and me all on the Cardinals there for a while.

Jim Hart

I've never seen a better pinpoint passer who had an arm like Jim Hart. He could break open defenses. When Don Coryell came to the Cardinals in 1973, he had the offense that he needed. Hart threw pinpoint passes and quick passes to the backs out of the backfield. Basically, it was the west coast offense that Coryell brought which was kind of ahead of its time. Hart was the perfect quarterback for that. He had a great career with the Cardinals and is one of my better friends.

NFL Draft

It's amazing the way the draft is today. It's on television; they have tryouts and do timings on the players, strength testing with weights, the vertical jump, the long jump, and all of those things that they test the players so extensively on now. I hadn't really even talked to any of the Cardinals. I had letters from different teams … San Francisco, Dallas, and a lot of different teams, but none from the Cardinals.

As it turned out, apparently one of the Cardinals' scouts, I found out later, was in Hawaii at the Hula Bowl. He was the one who asked me to run the 40-yard dash for him at the Hula Bowl after practice, which I did. A few years later he told me that when I ran the 40 there, they decided to draft me because I was actually faster than they thought I was going to be. I guess they thought I could play cornerback. That was what resulted in me being drafted in the first round by the Cardinals.

Jimmy Marsalis and I played in a couple of all-star games together. He was drafted, I think, two picks later by the Kansas City Chiefs.

I think the fastest I ever ran was a 4.4 on Astroturf. Back then you didn't prepare for the draft like they do now. The first time I ever ran the 40 was when we were out in Hawaii. I ran that 4.5 on grass.

I just had a helmet, shoulder pads, and shorts on when I ran it, just like we worked out at the Hula Bowl.

Transition To NFL

It's always a tough transition. You're going up against the best players in the world. The best players on every team are the best players out of college. In college it's just not that way. I was really fortunate when I came to the Cardinals to have two guys playing safety there—Larry Wilson and Jerry Stovall. They were veterans and excellent ball players. When I first came in, they mentored me a little bit; Larry was calling the defenses and alerting us to team tendencies. That was something I really appreciated. It helped me a lot early in my career for sure.

It's a big transition no matter what and I got my jock handed to me a few times in my rookie season. You just have to go through that, learn from your mistakes, and work to get better. That's what I tried to do all during my rookie year with St. Louis.

Roger Staubach Called Roger Wehrli Best Cornerback He Played Against

Roger Staubach was such a great athlete. We played in the same division so we had to play against each other twice a year. The '70s was a big decade for him. Early in the '70s, he went to the Super Bowl a couple of times. In the mid '70s, we hit our stride and won the division a few times. During the mid '70s, it was always a challenge to beat Dallas because they had such a great team. They were an innovative team and had a lot of good receivers, Drew Pearson and those guys.

Obviously with Staubach at quarterback, as a defensive back it was a nightmare. You knew you had to cover the receiver not only the first four or five seconds of the play, but if nobody was open he had the ability to scramble. Then he was just looking for whoever was open, so we had to chase the guys all over the field. Playing his team was a struggle. To get those praises from him really meant a lot to me. I think it probably meant a lot to help me get into the Hall of Fame.

Beating Cowboys 38-0 On First Season Of Monday Night Football in 1970

It was wonderful. It was the first year of Monday Night Football. It was the first time that we had ever played on Monday Night Football, and I'm sure it was probably the first time for Dallas too. Don Meredith was in the booth with Howard Cosell. Don had just retired from Dallas and was obviously very partial to the Dallas Cowboys. We played in Dallas and had a great game. I had a couple of interceptions and a couple knockdowns on passes to Bob Hayes, deep down the field. We just pretty much dominating them.

Roger Staubach did not played in that game, and not played very much with the Cowboys at that point. He was just back from his service duties. I think that game spurred the coach to put him in more during upcoming games. They started alternating quarterbacks after that.

That was the last regular season game they lost that year. They ran the table, ended up beating us out for the division title by a game, and then went on to lose to Pittsburgh in the Super Bowl. I think the turning point for them was when Staubach started playing more and they started winning more after that game.

Toughest Receiver To Cover
That's tough to say. I think when I first came in, I look at Charley Taylor as a guy who was as tough as anybody to cover. Throughout our careers, we were in the same division so we had to play against each other twice a year. He came to the NFL as a running back. He was great receiver, had all the moves, he was tough, a great blocker, and a great pattern runner.

Bob Hayes with Dallas had speed, so he was a great receiver. Drew Pearson, on the other side down in Dallas, was a great pattern receiver.

Quarterback Who Had Most Interceptions Against
I had my most interceptions against Roger Staubach. Even though he was probably the best quarterback I played against, I had more opportunities against him. I think he was more stubborn than the rest of them and kept throwing the ball at me. I think I had six interceptions off of him. That's the most that I had off of any one quarterback.

I played against Billy Kilmer and Sonny Jurgensen; they didn't look very athletic back there at the quarterback position. I swear they could fling that ball in there. Many times I thought, "How did that guy get the ball to that player". They just were wily veterans and were able to get it done.

Jackie Smith
Jackie Smith was something else. Jackie was a competitor. Even in practice, he hated to get the ball knocked down from him if you were covering him or whatever. Once he caught the ball, he was something to see. I can still remember one of the greatest plays I've ever seen is when we were playing Dallas in St. Louis in the mid '70s. He took a ball across the middle about 10 yards, and broke five tackles from two linebackers, a corner, and a couple of safeties, and scored on the play. We were standing on the sidelines and just couldn't believe what we saw. I think it's one of those highlights that they always show when they're talking about Jackie Smith.

Favorite Moment In NFL
My favorite moment, other than the day that I got elected into the Hall of Fame, was early in my career, that Monday Night Football game in Dallas, when we beat them. That was such a great thrill.

Then in the mid '70s, when we won the division and had good teams. We were nicknamed The Cardiac Cardinals. We won the division a couple of times, and made it to the playoffs after falling short the first five or six years in my career. That was the most fun time to play with Don Coryell as our coach. He was such a great coach, a great offensive innovator, and a great coach to play for. The players just loved him. We had a lot of fun in the mid '70s, playing football in St. Louis. We had the town behind us. I think it was the most fun I ever had playing football.

Firing Of Don Coryell & Hiring Of Bud Wilkinson

We had such a great team and Coryell wanted to a draft a big defensive player. Instead we drafted a quarterback when we didn't need one because we had Jim Hart. Coryell basically blew up and went to the press. He ended up getting himself fired. That's when management hired Bud Wilkinson. It was tough for him because the players loved Coryell and we had winning seasons under him. Obviously the Cardinals hadn't really drafted the people that were needed. It was a tough situation for Bud for to come into. He was a great individual, a great man, and a great motivator. He was more the Devine type of coach. He left the nuts and bolts to the assistant coaches. He came in and was more of a motivator. Some of the stories that he told about his experiences kept you on the edge of your seat as a player. He was well respected in the sport as well as respected outside of football. It was kind of an odd time. It was a thrill to interact with him because he was kind of a legend at the time. Still, the football situation was not that good in St. Louis. He was only here a year and a half, and we didn't win that many games during that time. We weren't able to continue the good times that we had under Coryell. Bud came into a very tough situation because a very popular coach had been fired.

Pro Football Hall Of Fame Induction

Just basically a dream come true. I had been out of football for a good number of years. They put, I think, 100 people on the ballot, and then they vote it down to 50, then down to 25, and then down to that final 15 that they actually do the voting on. I had made those other lists numerous times and had been down to the final 15 one other time. I knew that it was a possibility that I could be voted in, but I think I had pretty much made up my mind that they'd probably pass me up. I probably wouldn't make the Hall of Fame unless I made it through the senior legends category.

Then I made the final 15 and was on edge again. When I got the call it was just an amazing time. I was so happy to be included with the players that I had played against and played with all those years. It's been a thrill to go back every year and be a part of that and be a part of everything that being in the Hall of Fame means.

Scoring Touchdown On Fake Field Goal

It was very satisfying because it was actually the last home game that I played. When I first came to the Cardinals, Jim Bakken was the place kicker and Larry Wilson was his holder. In my fourth year after Larry retired, I started holding on field goals for Bakken and then the other kickers that we had throughout my career.

I'd already announced that I was going to retire at the end of the season right before our last home game. We had a ceremony before the game. We were playing the New York Giants and needed to win the game to make the playoffs. That was the strike-shortened season. It was a very important touchdown that put us ahead. We had seen in the films during the week that there would be an opportunity for a fake field goal if they lined up in a certain way.

The coach put the play on and the alignment was right, so we tried it. I obviously got into the end zone, which is a big thrill any time, but especially during your last home game. It was really a special treat.

Photograph copyright Associated Press

Chapter 75

Mel Blount

College: Southern

Career History:
Pittsburgh Steelers (1970–1983)

1989 Inductee Pro Football Hall Of Fame

College Choice
I grew up during segregation and when I came out of high school in 1966, the University of Georgia, Georgia Tech, Alabama and all of those types of schools weren't recruiting black athletes. I had an opportunity to go to schools like Savannah State, Albany State, Fort Valley State, and Southern University. Southern University just happened to hear about me and came recruiting me. That's why I decided to go there.

Southern University is in Baton Rouge, Louisiana. I was in Georgia, but there was an official who officiated one of my games my senior year in high school. He knew some people at Southern University. Well, the night that he officiated my high school game, I scored five touchdowns.

I was a kickoff returner, wide receiver, and defensive end. I was able to get into the end zone five times, so I obviously made an impression on the official. The official knew some people at Southern University and told them about me. They came and offered me a scholarship.

Head Coach Eddie Robinson Of Grambling
Believe it or not, Southern University was more popular than Grambling. Southern was a bigger, historically black, college than Grambling. Eddie Robinson did get some great players and so did Southern. Southern didn't have the stability at the coaching position that Grambling had because even when I was there we had a turnover at a head coach. Eddie Robinson was at Grambling for a long period of time and was able to build a tremendous program.

NFL Draft
I had never really heard of anybody on the Steelers. I did see the Steelers play the New Orleans Saints when I was still in college in 1969. When the Steelers drafted me, I had no idea who they had on their team. I had never heard of Joe Greene, who had been drafted in 1969. I didn't know the Steelers were going to draft me. I was somewhat disappointed when they did.

I wanted to play for the New Orleans Saints obviously because I was in Louisiana. I just thought that would have been a great team to play for, but little did I know that God had different plans for me. I was a third round pick and I felt like most players do after being drafted, that I should have gone higher in the draft. But it all worked out.

Chuck Noll

Chuck Noll came to the Pittsburgh Steelers with a plan that he was going to build his team through the draft and it was going to take some time. My rookie year, Terry Bradshaw was the Steelers first round pick in the NFL draft. Ron Shanklin, a wide receiver from North Texas State, the same school Joe Greene went to, was the Steelers second round pick. I was the Steelers third round pick. We all came in and we made contributions to the organization. In fact, I think all of us at some point were All-Pros.

Chuck started acquiring players, through the draft, to build a championship team. Certainly there were expectations. The Steelers were at the bottom of the barrel in the NFL. They really were the doormat of the National Football League, so there was only one direction that they could go, and that was up.

Chuck was a fair coach. He was tough and demanding, but I thought he was fair and very detail oriented. He was just a great coach. I think he was the reason that so many of us were not only All-Pros, but wound up in the Pro Football Hall Of Fame. He made you want to be the best you could be.

Chuck wanted his players to be professionals on the field, family men off the field, and good community leaders. He was a tremendous leader and had a tremendous amount of influence on my life. I think any player you talk to that played for Chuck would tell you the same thing. He didn't get the kind of notoriety that Vince Lombardi got, but he was right there in that same class.

Pittsburgh Steelers Players Mentality

There's a thing called accountability. I think every player wanted to be held accountable and wanted to make sure that they didn't disappoint their teammates. It was a tremendous thing to be a part of. So much respect and love grew out of that because when you're out on the football field, you have to believe in the guy that you're lined up next to. I think that was the thing that really separated us in the '70s from the rest of the teams. Every guy wanted to make sure that he didn't disappoint the next guy.

Leader Of Pittsburgh Steelers Defense

The Pittsburgh Steelers whole defense was built around Joe Greene. When you talk about leaders, a leader to me is whoever will go out there and make a play for you. I think in the sense of being recognized by the public, the fans, or the front office, Joe Greene was the leader without a doubt. That was his team. That was his defense.

Joe Greene

To me, Joe Greene looked like he played angry all the time. Joe wants to make people believe that he didn't deserve the name Mean Joe Greene, but Joe Greene was something man. He was just a tremendous player. He was also a guy that didn't mind getting into fights or getting in your grill. I'm not just talking about the guys that he played with. I'm talking about the opponents, too. On the banquet circuit, everybody's got a Joe Greene story.

Playing Cornerback In NFL
Chuck Noll put me where he thought I could help the team the most, and that was playing 14 years at the cornerback position. I led the league in 1975 with 11 interceptions. I became the Pittsburgh Steelers all time interception leader, so I can't complain about the position I played. I just wanted to be a great player whether it was at safety, cornerback, or wherever they put me on special teams. I just wanted to be out there making a contribution.

Being successful starts with attitude. It starts with just wanting to be the best. You must have a willingness to work and do the things that will help you get better. I've always said, there's no substitute for hard work. I don't care how talented you are. I enjoyed the game. I enjoyed the preparation. I enjoyed working during the off-season and getting ready for training camp … the whole process.

"Mel Blount Rule" Established By NFL In 1977 A Receiver Can Only Be Bumped By Defender Within Five Yards Of the Line Of Scrimmage.
When the NFL passed the rule change, it just made me raise my game to prove that I could do more than bump and run. We went on to win two more Super Bowls after that. After the rule change, I still played the bump and run within five yards. It's a compliment any time a player can have an impact on the game that they start legislating the game to slow you down, or to takeaway what they would call your aggressiveness.

I also think the Steelers were so dominant, the NFL decided to take away the head slap and all those other things that Joe Greene, L.C. Greenwood, and those guys were doing on the defensive line. We were just talented people.

Paul Brown was on the competition committee and he was going against us twice a year as Owner of the Cincinnati Bengals. He had seen enough. So he wanted to see what he could do to change the rules and help free up Isaac Curtis. But after all that, we still performed at a high level.

Toughest Wide Receiver
All the wide receivers I faced were tough. When you get into the National Football League, there is no cakewalk. I think one of the things that helped us, and I'm talking about myself and the guys who played in the secondary with me, was that we played against the best every day in practice. So we when got up against a Charlie Joiner or Paul Warfield, you know those kind of guys, we knew how to play and we knew what we needed to do. Well they all were tough. We were prepared because we were going against the best every day in practice in John Stallworth and Lynn Swann.

Pittsburgh Steelers Practices
I think what separated us from a lot of teams is that our starting defense practiced against our starting offense. I think that's why we were dominant and won four Super Bowl championships. Nobody was above anybody on our team. I don't care if you were a special teams player or if you were Mel Blount or Joe Greene. We all went out there to work and to get better. The only way you can get better is to go out against the best. So, the first team defense always went

against the first team offense. That might have been one of the secrets to the Steelers, and the way they operated.

Super Bowl IX Pittsburgh Steelers vs. Minnesota Vikings First Steelers Super Bowl
For me our first Super Bowl was a tremendous experience. It was also a confirmation of what kind of team we had. A lot of people said we shouldn't have been there and that we weren't going to win because we were playing the "Purple People Eaters." They said we got lucky against the Oakland Raiders. I think our winning that Super Bowl was not only a confirmation, but it was an eye opener to the rest of the league about who the Pittsburgh Steelers were and where we were going.

Favorite Super Bowl
My favorite team to play against in the Super Bowl was the Cowboys. There was so much motivation because they were being promoted as America's team. It was what they call bulletin board material against the opponents. So, I think they were my favorite.

I think our toughest Super Bowl was against the Los Angeles Rams. The Rams were the team we went in trailing to at halftime. Our offense with John Stallworth, Lynn Swann, and Terry Bradshaw kind of opened things up in the second half and we were able to get out of there with a victory. They played a good game against us.

Intercepting Roger Staubach In Super Bowl XIII
My interception of Roger Staubach in Super Bowl XIII was a big play. It was a big play right before halftime since the Cowboys were driving. Any time you can stop a drive it's a big play. Every time I see Roger, he relives that play. He asks me what I saw on that play.

When you have that many great athletes on the field, a lot of things happen. I was fortunate enough to be able to read the play and jump in and get the interception. That really stopped their momentum. It allowed us to go into halftime with the lead.

Decision To Retire
I decided to retire because I had just gotten tired mentally and I wasn't enjoying the game anymore. It's interesting because I had another year on my contract that would have paid me more money than I had made all of my years, but I just wasn't there. I have never been the kind of guy that hung around just to hang on. I had my own standards. I didn't need anybody to tell me just to come back and be a part. My standards are my standards and I don't lower them for anybody. It was time and I knew it from a mental standpoint. Physically, my body was fine. I was just tired mentally.

Pro Football Hall Of Fame Induction
Being inducted into the Pro Football Hall Of Fame was really something that I never thought about. When it happened, it took awhile for it to sink in about what it really meant. I'm grateful for the guys I played with, because you don't get there by yourself. We are all standing on somebody's shoulders. It was a tremendous thing. I don't know if anybody can ever explain the feeling to you.

When I came to the Pittsburgh Steelers, even when I retired, I never thought about the Hall Of Fame, let alone being selected in my first year of eligibility. It's just something that you didn't think about in those days because they didn't talk about it on television like they do now. Now everybody is a future Hall Of Famer, if you listen to the commentators. I'm sure guys who retire now think about it. When I played, it wasn't even mentioned.

Being Called Greatest Cornerback Of All-Time
I don't know if I'm the greatest; I haven't heard that too much. I think Gil Brandt just did a list and listed me as being the sixth best cornerback in the history of the game. So everybody has his or her own opinion. The only thing I know is that I played the best I could play. I was part of four world championships and made the Pro Bowl numerous times.

I don't have a real problem when somebody says, "Hey, so-and-so was better than you," or "They list you as number six or number four or whatever …" I think what's important is that you played the best you could play. You left the game and went on to do something to help people become better. Helping people who are less fortunate, that's what it's all about. Just trying to make the world a better place than what you found it.

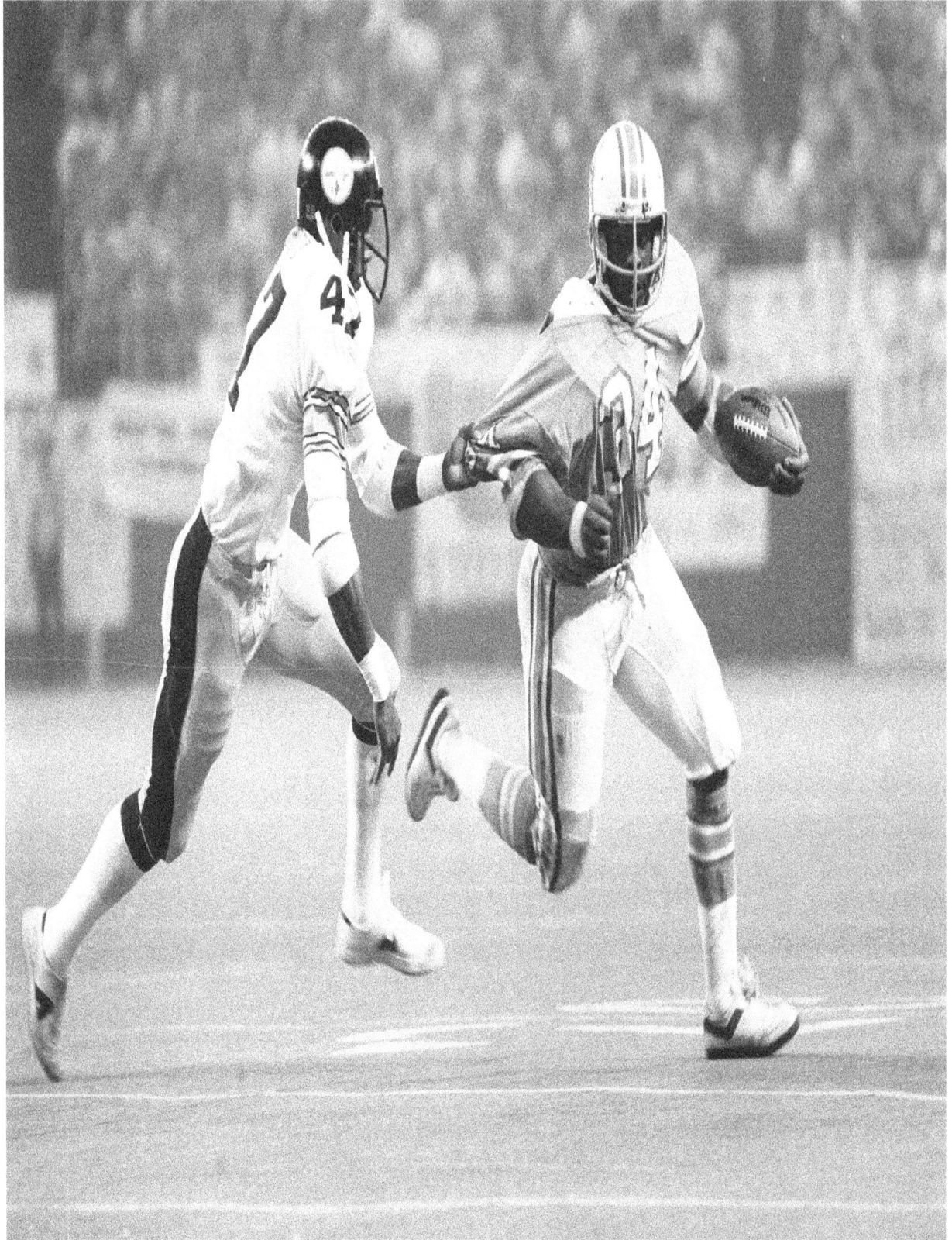

Pittsburgh Steelers Mel Blount hauls in Houston Oiler running back Earl Campbell for no gain. Photograph copyright Associated Press

Chapter 76

Jim Langer

College: South Dakota State Career History: Miami Dolphins (1970–1979) Minnesota Vikings (1980–1981) 1987 Inductee Pro Football Hall of Fame

College Choice

I played high school football in a town of 500 people. If you ran an out pattern in the end zone, you ran into the Platte River. A lot of the end zones I played in were partial cornfields. I don't think I was ever recruited. My high school baseball coach had been a quarterback at South Dakota State. I played baseball, football, and basketball. Those were the three sports we had in high school. I was actually a pretty good pitcher.

My high school coach said, "Jim why don't you come out to South Dakota State with me? We'll go visit the campus. You can play two sports out there." South Dakota State was Division II at that time in the North Central Conference with North Dakota State, North Dakota, and those schools. That's where I went to school. I never heard from the Gophers.

When I went out to South Dakota State, I ended up playing on the offensive line and I did play some linebacker. I didn't carry the football at all. I played offensive tackle and some offensive guard. I played a couple of years at linebacker.

Cleveland Browns

I actually went to Cleveland as a free agent. My baseball coach knew a scout from the Cleveland Browns named Bob Nussbaumer. He signed me as a free agent in 1970.

I was intimidated. I had been a commissioned second lieutenant. I was supposed to report for active duty in October 1970. I went to the summer training camp just for the experience. In fact, I talked to a good friend of mine, Gale Gillingham, a great guard for the Green Bay Packers at that time who was from Little Falls, a town near where I grew up. I was hoping he would help me talk myself out of going. He said, "There's going to be a strike this year. You aren't going to embarrass yourself. Go out there. The veterans aren't going to come to camp. You'll get a good look and if you can't play with the Browns, maybe somebody else will see you. Just take it a day at a time and do the best you can. What the hell do you got to lose?" It was the best advice I ever got.

I went over there and the Browns had drafted Mike Phipps, Craig Wycinski from Michigan State, who was my roommate, and Bill Yanchar from Purdue, a defensive tackle. These were all guys I had been watching on Saturday afternoons on TV. It was pretty humbling. Nobody knew who the hell I was. I really didn't have to prove anything to anybody. So I just took it a day at a time and went at it as hard as I could.

It got down to the last preseason game and I was still on the roster. Blanton Collier called me in and said, "We think you can play. We're going to put you on our taxi squad. We're going to pay you $500 a week." I went to Cleveland with $50 so I was pretty elated. I called my wife and told her what was going to happen. He said, "Now, we're going to put you on waivers tonight. For 24 hours any team can pick you up.

The next morning I get a call, go into his office again and find out the Dolphins had picked me up off of waivers. So I flew down to Miami. Quite honestly, I didn't even know Miami had a football team. I landed there and we played the Atlanta Falcons that night. The rest worked out pretty well.

Rookie Year With Miami Dolphins
The Dolphins were staying out at Doral, at the country club. That's where they stayed the night before the games. I got picked up at the airport and went to my room at Doral. Wayne Moore, who they had just picked up from the 49ers and became our great left offensive tackle, was my roommate. We had no idea what the hell was going on. You just take it a day at a time. You go where you're supposed to be. At that time, I didn't know Don Shula from any other coach. We were practicing four times a day.

Coach Shula was the most intense man I had ever seen. We had 22 rookies on the team that year. I was on the taxi squad for about three weeks, and then I got moved onto the roster, and started playing center.

Monte Clark was my line coach. Monte became a great friend. He was the key that got to me to Miami. I didn't know that for quite a few years. He played for the Browns for 11 years and had just retired. He became a coach for Don Shula. It was his first year as offensive line coach. About two weeks before I got picked up off of waivers, he talked to a couple of his old buddies that were still playing for the Browns on the offensive line. He said, "You guys got anybody up there you think can play? I'm looking for a couple more linemen." They told him that I was a possible prospect that had some upside and that's how I got down there. It turned out just how old Gale Gillingham said it would.

It was quite a whirlwind. I remember the first game. My wife was going to drop me off at the stadium; that's when the Orange Bowl was still there. We stopped at a minor-league baseball park I thought was the Orange Bowl. It looked like there was a game going on. There was no GPS or cell phones or anything like that at that time. We stopped at a gas station and said, "Where the hell is the Orange Bowl?" It was quite a time and Miami was one step from being out of the league. After being with the team for several years, I started finding out the history of the team and how all this went together.

That team was literally one year from being insolvent. Joe Robbie picked up Shula and Paul Warfield, put this team together, and they started winning. By the time I got there, it was the last preseason game. There were 80,010 in the Orange Bowl and they were going nuts. They hadn't lost a game yet in the preseason.

It just all came together. It's one of those things. I don't know if you can duplicate that by some formula. Don is still, obviously a dear friend. That was one of the most incredible bunch of people who ever got put together. Whether it was just a stroke of genius, by accident, or whatever the hell happened, it was the damnest group of players I had ever been around in terms of how hard they worked and how they approached the game.

The coaches were incredibly dedicated people. It became a very cohesive well-oiled machine. We accomplished a lot in the world of football. We broke our team up even though we probably could have gone a couple more years. That was the way things were back then. It's an interesting period of time because my first contract I signed was $14,000. The year we went undefeated was the first year I started. I played every play that season, 17 games and my salary that year was $26,000. To win the Super Bowl was another $15,000; that was a big deal. Now these guys spend that much on dinner at night from what I've heard.

Pro Bowl
I went to six Pro Bowls. The winner's share was $2,500 and the loser's share was $1,500. That was a big deal to win that damn thing because another $2,500 that was a lot of money to me.

Bob Griese
As great as Bob Griese was and he truly was, he wasn't a physical player like Peyton Manning or Tom Brady. If you look at Bob in his playing days and saw him with his helmet on and glasses underneath, you'd swear he it was an accountant playing football. He was a student of the game. He was an analyst on the field. Of course, the rules were different. Out of 70 to 75 plays around 40 of them were running plays.

The offensive line was very methodical and very well schooled. The plays that we ran were executed with a lot of precision and consistency, much like Green Bay had done. You knew Green Bay was going to run the sweep, but you couldn't stop that damn thing.

The Dolphins were a very well oiled machine and weren't that fancy. The offense was very effective because it was executed; the perfection of the execution was the goal.

First Game Starting
My first game starting was the first game ever played in Arrowhead Stadium against Curley Culp, Buck Buchanan, Willie Lanier, and those guys. That's the year we beat the Redskins in that Super Bowl. The next year we went back and beat the Vikings in the Super Bowl.

I'll never forget my first game because it was 110 degrees on the field and was the first game of the season. Buck Buchanan was a pretty imposing figure. I'm probably 6'2" and he was 6'8". I got to know a lot of the Chiefs. Curley Culp and I became good friends. Curley Culp was the best damn nose guard that ever played the game. He was something, and he was an NCAA heavyweight wrestler.

Dick Butkus

I remember the first time I lined up against the Chicago Bears and Dick Butkus was out there. This is a guy I watched as a kid and as a college player. I had a hard time believing I was looking at this guy.

I always had a white towel tucked in my pants in the back. Bob Griese had a fear of lining up behind a guard. He was very attuned to looking down the field, looking at coverages, and looking at secondary. He wanted the towel so when he'd break the huddle, he would automatically have a visual as to whom the center was. As silly as that sounds, that was a very good thing to do.

Butkus pulled that towel out of my butt every play and laughed. He was a great player. There were some great players back then. They played every down. They didn't come out on nickel and dime packages. I was looking at Dick Butkus the whole game. I'm talking about Ray Nitschke and all those great players; it was quite the time.

Monte Clark

Next to Don Shula, Monte Clark was probably the most intense guy I've ever known. Monte was a master of attention to detail and the psychological part of the game. He taught us to visualize the game and to play the game over and over in your head before you actually played.

Other teams had cut our whole offensive line. Bob Kuechenberg was drafted by the Eagles then got cut. Then he played for the Chicago Owls, an amateur team, before joining the Dolphins. Larry Little and Wayne Moore had been cut. Monte wanted us to make the right step, get in the right position, and get our head on the right point. Through our effort and execution, we became one line that could execute as well as any I've seen since. It was a great bunch of guys.

We started to play as a unit. We started to know each other as a unit. It became a really close bunch of guys. That whole team, those guys are like brothers to you. We paid our dues. It was a hard-working team. We put in a lot of time working on that field and working on execution. I look back and see it was quite a journey.

Don Shula's Concept

Don Shula's concept was if somebody got hurt, somebody came in. The year we went undefeated, about the fifth game of the season, Bob broke his ankle. Earl Morrall, at 35 years old, replaced Bob. Earl ran the 40-yard dash in about eight flat and couldn't throw the ball maybe 40 yards. Earl took us all the way to the AFC championship game in Pittsburgh. By the way, we were undefeated at the time. We got to go on the road and play Pittsburgh at their place, to win the AFC Championship; because that's the way the rules were then.

Earl takes us all the way. We didn't think anything of it other than Bob was hurt and Earl's our quarterback. Earl, of course, had the respect of everybody. He could run our offense. Everybody respected him and everybody picked up the pace. The defense played harder, probably subconsciously. The offensive line knew that we had to get an older guy behind us, not as mobile; we had to do better. Our running game, of course, was still there. We went undefeated with our backup quarterback.

Garo Yepremian

For the first few years, I didn't really think too much about the kicker because I was just worried about my job and worried about what I was supposed to do. Gary Yepremian talked funny, but he could kick the ball pretty well. I think the closest Garo came to death, was when we played the Chiefs in the Super Bowl out in Los Angeles. We were dominating the game, but were not ahead by much. I think the game ended up 14-7. He tried to kick the field goal, but the kick was blocked. He caught the ball and tried to throw a pass. The Redskins ran it back for a touchdown, which at the time put them back in the game. There was still some time left on the clock. It got a bit hairy. Even though we pretty much had our way with the Redskins that day, they were back in the ball game.

Garo's a great guy. I always felt kickers were an important part of our team. They certainly didn't take the abuse that the front line players took, but when the game's on the line, they're carrying a lot of the load on their shoulders. I always felt Garo was a good teammate. We were a very close bunch.

NFL Coaches

Don Shula is an amazing man. There have been great coaches in the past, and there will be great coaches in the future. All of these guys knew how to push players to a point they didn't think they could go. It's a hard thing to describe. Coach Shula worked as hard as we did. The coaching staff lived and slept the game just like we did. During the football season, I never got away from football. You didn't take off for the birth of your child. I had two sons born while I was playing football. One son was born the night we played Oakland in a playoff game. There was no thought of leaving while my wife was in labor. That might offend some people, but that thought didn't exist. The number one thing you did was take care of the team. You take care of the team; they'll take care of your family.

I think it was my second year of training camp and we were playing a scrimmage against the Saints. Coach Shula walked in before the game, called me in a little office and said, "Jim I'm going to tell you now. I just got a call and your father died. After the scrimmage, we'll get you on a plane and we'll fly you back home."

Comparing Bud Grant To Don Shula

It was a 180-degree difference; both were successful. Don Shula was very much hands-on, in your face, and dominated the meetings. He was in charge of the offensive meetings game film. Bud Grant sat in the back, ate granola bars, and Jerry Burns did the critiquing and film study. Bud would always say, "There's more important things than football." He was very philosophical about the game. Don was more we're going to win or I'll kill you.

Minnesota Vikings

When I got to Minnesota, I had a good time here. The Vikings were great to me. It's a great organization. It was just a different philosophy. I remember the first game. I wasn't starting then,

I was playing a backup role. We got beat. We weren't a dominant team by any means in 1980 and 1981. I was struck by the fact that after a loss, the team went in the locker room, and the music was on. Everyone showered, cleaned up, and was ready to get back on the bus and fly back home.

I remember talking to Ron Yary one day. He's a Hall of Fame tackle, a great guy, and a good friend of mine. I said, "I can't believe this." He said, "What's the matter?" I said, "We just lost a football game." I wouldn't smile for three days after that. It would just eat the shit out of me. He said, "It's no big deal. It's just a game." I said, "I guess I'm from a culture that didn't look at it that way."

It was a different way of looking at the same occupation. It just wasn't something you carried with you outside the locker room in Minnesota. In Miami, I didn't turn that switch off until after the season.

Miami Dolphins Perfect Season
I have always said somebody will break it. I thought the 1985 Bears were a team capable of breaking it. The Patriots came within an absolutely astonishing play of doing it. I think someday it will happen. People say the Patriots played two more games than you did. I say, "Yes, but you've got to remember, back in my day we played six preseason games the first four or five years of my career. I played every game in the preseason, which would be six games plus every game of the regular season, which would be 14. We didn't look at preseason games like they do today.

We didn't set out to go undefeated. I remember sitting in a hotel room with Bob Kuechenberg prior to playing the Giants, in the last game ever played at Yankee Stadium. Kuech says, "I don't know how to say this. I'm not so sure it's a good thing we win every game in the regular season." I said, "What are you talking about?" He said, "Well, it's an odd thing. Sooner or later it's going to bite us."

Yet once the game starts, you don't think about that. You go out and you execute the game plan. You play as hard as you can and you hope you win the game. You hope everything turns out. Your defense, your offense, special-teams, you hope everybody comes together and you end up winning the game. We had several games that year we could have lost quite easily. Minnesota should have beaten us. The Bills should have beaten us.

There's a record nobody talks about, by the way. I think the Dolphins beating the Bills for 20 consecutive games is still the longest winning streak against a team in the history of the NFL. I never lost to the Buffalo Bills.

I still give Joe DeLamielleure a hard time about that. They had a couple of games when O.J. Simpson was running wild. If they would have kept trying to build up his running yardage, they could have won a football game. I think we beat the Buffalo Bills 20 times in 10 years.

Preseason Games For Miami Dolphins

Preseason games were a big deal with Don Shula. There was none of this, we won't play the veterans for the first two weeks, and we sure as hell won't play them the last week. The first team played every game, not necessarily four quarters. When the backup quarterback came in, I would usually play because they wanted to make sure the offensive line was intact to give that guy the best opportunity. I might sit out in the preseason after my fourth or fifth year of starting in the league. I might not play the fourth quarter, but I played three quarters for ten years.

Miami Dolphins & Minnesota Vikings Practices

I would like to say that the practice habits of the Dolphins were very hard. The guys worked hard. We didn't practice very long. I remember going to the Pro Bowl and I had John Madden as head coach two or three times. John would always come up to me and say, "You guys execute better than any team I've ever seen. How long do you practice?" I said, "An hour and 45 minutes." He'd say, "You're shitting me." I'd say, "No. You've got to understand that's preceded by an hour and 45 minutes of meetings."

Don Shula was very precise in practice. There was absolutely no standing around. In an hour and 45 minutes you never stopped moving. The plays he wanted to run were absolutely choreographed, scripted. He knew exactly what he wanted to run. He knew exactly what he wanted to get accomplished. If you didn't do it right, you still got it done in an hour and 45 minutes, you just had another practice that day. He could not get over that.

When I got to Minnesota, we'd practice for two hours, two and a half hours, or three hours. I would notice that when you got one of these marathon practices going, if the players didn't know exactly how long they were going to be on the field, they would save themselves. In Minnesota our practices went boom, boom, boom. You went from this drill to this drill to this drill, team drill, individual, team passing, team defense, and practice was over. I think that was a very critical part of our organization.

Pro Football Hall Of Fame Induction

I was totally overwhelmed to be amongst those great players. To be considered part of that—it's hard to describe. It's just an overwhelming feeling. They're tremendous people.

You listen to Hall Of Famers talk about their day and how they played for $3,500. It leaves you with a sense of what you are actually a part of.

I'm not so sure today in the high-tech world we live in, that we're not losing that. I think it's easy to lose that. I think those guys are incredible with what they went through. They formed the game. I go back and watch Monday night football every once in a while. We played St. Louis with Conrad Dobler and those guys, and it's like watching a home movie compared to today.

The graphics were ridiculous. There were no TV timeouts, one or two camera angles, and no slow-mos. It's pretty remarkable what it's like now. It's just hard to believe where this game has gone and what a big production it is.

I remember the first couple Super Bowls I played in, the halftime entertainment was a high school marching band. Now, God knows what you see at halftime now.

How Teams Deal With Injuries

I think every team had its own way of dealing with medical situations. We had a team physician around. You'd have a hip pointer so bad you couldn't squat down. If you wanted to get a shot, you could get a shot.

We played the Steelers one Monday night. We got done with a play in the first quarter and Bob Kuechenberg couldn't get up. He said, "I think I broke my ankle." They got him off the field. He came back in the second quarter and played the rest of the game. He had broken his ankle in six places; six bones were broke.

You couldn't say I can't go. That wasn't in the gene pool at that time. We didn't think if I go out there and play I might shorten my career. It never crossed my mind.

I broke my ankle when we were playing the Packers. I was blocking back on a trap play inside. Anyway, the opposing player falls on my right leg and I know something's broken. I went down. I hadn't been injured before other than torn cartilage and stuff. I'd always get surgery in the off-season.

I know something's broke. I get off the field. They do an x-ray which shows the top of my tibia was broke off. We had six games left until the playoffs. I said, "What do we have to do so I can get out there and play?" He said, "I don't know." Then he said, "I've got an idea here. I'll meet you at the hospital tomorrow. I think I can screw that piece back on there." I said, "Let's do it." After surgery I wait five weeks and take the cast off. I work out a little bit, go back out and practice for a week. Then I realize it wasn't going to work.

I go back in for x-rays, and find out the screws had come out. They popped out about an eighth of an inch. He says, "You're done. We've got two choices. We can go back in and tighten the screws up with a screwdriver, or I've never done this before, but I think I can fix it externally." I said, "What have you got in mind?" He said, "We'll take a piece of wood and we'll just pound them back in."

So I go to University Hospital down in Miami. I get on the operating table and he brings in the x-ray so he can see exactly where the screws are. There is a 2 x 2 piece of oak, about 6 inches long and with a ball-peen hammer he pounds the wood which puts the screws back in. He pounded them so hard that it broke the incision open from five weeks earlier. I still have that block of wood.

Then I said, "Here's the deal. I can't play anymore this season. Make sure you put the cast on so I can drive my pickup back to Minnesota in the off-season." He made the cast so when I sat on the seat, it was at the right angle for my accelerator. What we did would cause today's players to pass out. They'd freaking pass out.

Mercury Morris

Mercury Morris, in his heart, was a great player and was a great asset to us. He was a little difficult maybe, but never to the point of being a problem. That was with our whole team. We didn't have any emotional issues. The team would deal with that. If Mercury started getting a little too cocky, we would deal with that. The coaches didn't have to; Mercury and Larry Csonka knew their places. Larry Csonka knew his place. We all knew our place. We were one part of the machine and one part wasn't bigger than the machine. I don't think any of us ever felt that, including Mercury.

Snapping For Punts & Kicks

I had never snapped in my life for punts and field goals. The first time I ever did it was at my first Pro Bowl. There was nobody on the roster that knew how to snap.

The first Pro Bowl I played in was in Kansas City. I think John Madden was my first Pro Bowl coach. He came to me and said, "You're going to have to snap." I said, "I've never done it." He said, "You're going to learn." Jan Stenerud comes over and he says, "Jim look, it's no big deal, you can do this. We'll work with it this week. You can do it."

I'm left-handed and I snapped to the quarterback right-handed. He said, "You snap the ball left-handed, don't use your right hand like you do to snap to center. He said, "Pretend you're throwing a pass. Bend over and you can do it. He said, "Don't think about it. Throw it back there. They'll catch it."

He kicked five field goals that game and I snapped for every one of them. I don't know how they got there. Some of them might have gone end over end I suppose. Anyway, I came back to training camp and Monte said, "You snapped for extra points and field goals." I said, "Yes." He said, "We're going to start working on that. I was never that good at it." I practiced. My wife would catch snaps in the backyard. I snapped to everybody.

Miami Dolphin Jim Langer blocks for Bob Griese.
Photograph copyright Associated Press

Chapter 77

Jack Ham

> College:
> Penn State
>
> Career History:
> Pittsburgh Steelers (1971–1982)
>
> 1988 Inductee Pro Football Hall of Fame

College Choice
I was not a five-star recruit coming out of high school. One of my teammates, a guy by the name of Steve Smear, was already at Penn State. He recommended me to Joe Paterno and the Penn State coaching staff. At that time, I was in a military school in Virginia. I was going to go to Virginia Military Institute but the more I got involved in a military life, the less I enjoyed it. I ended up getting a scholarship from Penn State. I was very fortunate that they gave me an opportunity. I only had a scholarship offer from Penn State.

Penn State
Penn State was very strict; there was no question about that. Education was always paramount. Joe Paterno felt that only a few people would get the opportunity to play pro football and even if you play pro football, your chance of getting hurt is pretty high. So education was very, very important to him. Plus it was during the Vietnam War era, and if you didn't stay in school, you ended up being drafted. You'd be surprised how hard guys worked in school when there was that kind of incentive to continue with your college deferment time.

John Ebersole and Mike Reid went to Altoona High School and continued to Penn State together, joining Steve Smear and me. John Ebersole played for the New York Jets for a number of years as a linebacker, but he played defensive line for us. Those three guys along with a guy by the name of Gary Hull played defensive line. So we had a front four that could really get after it. At that time, freshman could not play. Most of the time you were fodder for the varsity.

I found out that I was good enough to play, and in spring practice I became a first team linebacker on defense. We had the guys already mentioned, as well as Dennis Onkotz, Jim Kates, and Neal Smith. We had a big time defense coming back. It wasn't where there were nine or ten spots opening up because of graduation, this was a veteran team coming back. I played with that group for a couple of years.

Franco Harris and Lydell Mitchell ran the football for us. Everything was predicated on the running game on the offensive side. We had gifted running backs and a solid offensive line. We won a lot of games 17-7, 14-3, scores like that.

Our defense was about as good as you're going to get. That front four was a critical part for us on the defensive side of the ball. That was the way you played the game back then, solid defense, run the football offensively, don't make mistakes, don't turn the football over, and you had a chance to win a lot of football games.

Freshman Year At Penn State

I played outside linebacker my freshman year. We played a cover two defense back then with our linebacker coach, Dan Radakovich. The key was you're never going to let the tight end inside release and get up the field because it was always stretched to two safeties downfield. So the first play of the first practice a tight end goes in, gives me a move, goes inside, and gets up to field. The tight end was Ted Kwalick, who was not some shabby tight end. He ended up being a two time All-American and played for the 49ers. My linebacker coach took the clipboard and his whistle and threw it at me. That was my first indoctrination into how to play defense and be disciplined out there.

I learned so much about how to play. If I could play against him, I could do a pretty good job against anybody I played against on a Saturday afternoon.

Penn State & Pittsburgh Steelers Defensive Lines

I played with Mike Reid, Steve Smear, and John Ebersole up front on defense in college football. In pro football, I had LC Greenwood, Joe Greene, Ernie Holmes, and Dwight White up front. When you are a linebacker, you are as good as the people up front, and I was fortunate in my college and pro careers to have that kind of talent up front. Those defensive front fours set the tone for us.

NFL Draft

I'm normally not a very gullible guy. The day before the draft, the Giants and San Diego both called and told me they were going to draft me in the first round and I actually believed them. The next day, I didn't get drafted until the beginning of the second round. Pittsburgh took Frank Lewis, a really gifted wide receiver out of Grambling, and I was drafted by Pittsburgh in second round.

I grew up in Johnstown, Pennsylvania, and then I went to Penn State. I thought pro football would give me an opportunity to live and experience a different part of the country. It was not meant to be. I really wasn't all that happy about being drafted by Pittsburgh. Pittsburgh was not a very good football team. So it wasn't this euphoric day for me. I thought that I was going to go somewhere else and get drafted a round earlier so it was actually more disappointing, in a sense, for me. In retrospect, it could not have turned out any better for me in my career.

No one from Pittsburgh even called me prior to the draft to ask me any questions or conduct any kind of interview. So I never expected to get drafted by the Steelers.

There was a debate between Chuck Noll and other members of the Steelers. Coach Noll wanted to take me in the first round and others thought get Frank Lewis first and then you can get Ham in the second round. It turned out fine for me. I have no complaints about it at all. I was going forward.

Chicago Bears

I was late coming into my first training camp. I actually scrimmaged against the Chicago Bears when I was a member of the College All-Stars. We ended up beating the Bears in the scrimmage.

Our first regular season game was against Chicago. Back then, Chicago was not a very good football team. We were winning 15-3 in the fourth quarter. Butkus hit one of our running backs, who fumbles the ball, and Chicago runs it in for a touchdown. The next series, he does the same thing again to another running back and we lose the game 17-15. We lost to a bad Chicago Bear football team and I'm thinking, "Is this what it's going to be? My career is going to be just like this? Oh God, this is going to be a terrible, terrible situation here."

We kind of plotted along my rookie year, and then in 1972, we drafted Franco Harris in the first round. All of the sudden, things turned around. I think we were eleven and three that year. We went to the playoffs and Super Bowls from there.

Chuck Noll

I think we bought into Chuck Noll's style. He was a very business-like kind of a guy. We knew he was a real smart guy. He was more of a renaissance guy as a head coach. He was a wine connoisseur and flew his own plane. I think we all felt we have Chuck Noll, so we have a little bit of an advantage over everybody else because we have him on our side of the field. He was a stickler for detail and treated the first to the 50th player the same way. If you weren't good enough, you knew you weren't going to be on our football team.

The best thing he ever did was after we won our first Super Bowl. The first day in training camp the following year he told us, "You can put your Super Bowl rings up on the shelf because there's not a damn thing you did last year that's going to win you a job on the team this year." We bought into that. He said, "Each game you're going to play this year after winning that championship, every team is going to be gunning for you." We took that as a challenge and we bought into all of it. I'm proud that we were able to win back-to-back Super Bowls twice. I hold that in very high regard.

We had great players, but you don't win and have the chemistry needed unless you get it from the top. I don't think we would have won our four Super Bowls if we didn't have Chuck Noll.

Andy Russell 93-Yard Touchdown

Andy Russell was playing with a pulled groin muscle. I came to Pittsburgh and Andy had already been playing for about five or six years on the team. He was a smart guy, anticipated well, prepared, and knew how to watch tape. I was smart enough to realize I could learn a lot from this guy who was on the other side playing right linebacker. I was like a sponge with him. In meetings and out on the field, we would talk about different techniques. I learned a lot about playing the game from Andy Russell. I don't know what his 40-yard dash time was, but he was All-Pro for seven or eight years. If we didn't win all those Super Bowls, I think he would probably be in the Hall of Fame right now. He has the credentials to be there. All of us get inand Andy Russell is the one guy who hasn't. I learned more from him on how to play and how to be professional than from anybody else in my career. It was great to be able to learn from him on the job.

Super Bowls
We won our Super Bowl against Minnesota. Two weeks before that, we beat the Raiders out in Oakland, to go to the Super Bowl. The games against the Raiders were the most fun. I don't know if I made one or two tackles in the Super Bowl against Minnesota. Minnesota tried to run the football right at Joe Greene and Ernie Holmes. To this day, I don't know why you would try to do that. That was the strength of our defense. After that game, not that I wasn't thrilled that we won the game, but when we played the Raiders, those were epic games for us.

My favorite Super Bowl was probably the first one because it finally gave Art Rooney an opportunity to win a championship and get him the Lombardi Trophy. I think to any man in that locker room, that was probably the most important thing for us.

Franco Harris Immaculate Reception
All I knew was that the crowd was going crazy, but at that time, I had to make sure they weren't going to call the play back. I didn't really see the play, but it was amazing. I think that stadium held about 50,000 people. I probably met about a hundred thousand people who said they were there that day for the game. I think the stories get embellished as they go along. I did not have a good view of that play. The Franco Harris run was just an amazing thing. It is one of the most exciting plays in NFL history.

Terry Bradshaw
A lot of people don't realize Terry Bradshaw called his own plays out there. Back then, that's what quarterbacks did. The thing I admire most about Terry is the fact that in our first two Super Bowls, we ran the football and played great defense. Normally, quarterbacks want to throw the football 35 times a game and throw touchdown passes. He was very content handing off to Franco Harris and winning low-scoring games. When we needed him to throw the ball, we probably weren't as good defensively in the last two Super Bowls. He was never a quarterback who complained and bitched about not being able to throw the football enough. All he cared about was winning football games. The team's personnel evolved where we had to throw the football. Obviously he had that talent. He was able to put together incredible years passing. That's what I admired about him. All he cared about was winning, and whatever way that was, he was happy with that.

Toughest Running Back
I think for me, it was Earl Campbell because I had a misfortune of playing against him twice a year since we were in Earl's division. Then we would play against him again in the playoffs. O.J. Simpson was illusive, but Earl Campbell had such power, you could not get underneath him. He was about 5' 10" and 240 pounds. If the Oilers had an average offensive line, he would've racked up some numbers that would've just been incredible. He was, by far, the toughest running back that I had ever had to fill up against. I wish he was not in my division.

We played in the AFC Championship Game in Pittsburgh. It was cold and rainy. It almost turned to snow in the second half. This was kind of the worst weather in the world for the Oilers. We're winning the game 34-5, with two minutes left in the game, and we know we're going to the Super Bowl. You want to make sure you don't get hurt in the last two minutes of the game. The next play Earl Campbell is running away from me. I'm thinking "Okay, I'll just kind of jog along here so I don't have to make the tackle over there on that side of the field." Then he bent the play all the way back toward me, and we have a collision. He shattered the facemask right off my helmet. I could have lost an eye. I'd never had that happen before. The facemask was in pieces and I was on the ground. I said, "Earl, it's 34-5." He said, "You know Jack, I'm going to go a hundred miles an hour on every play. I don't care what part of the game it is or whatever."

That's the kind of running back he was. Fortunately, I got to play with him in a couple of Pro Bowls and finally got him on my side. What a class guy and a great, great competitor. That's the way he played on every play.

Defensive Philosophy
Well, you know, as a linebacker even in college, I always enjoyed the passing game. I always felt that if you're a linebacker and you can't cover, or you can't react in zone defenses, then you have become a live dummy. That's why they take a lot of these guys out on third-down situations now. I was always very good at ball reacting and zone coverage. I took a lot of pride in man-to-man coverage out in the backfield, or on tight ends or whatever. I wasn't rushing off the edge a lot and bluffing. I was more in coverage. It gives you time. You know the quarterback doesn't have the luxury of pump faking because we've got a darn good front four just going to collapse the pocket, and we anticipated that in that secondary. So it gives you a chance to anticipate jump routes and react on your own coverage.

Joe Greene
Joe Greene got into the Hall of Fame the year before I did. He was the cornerstone of our football team and the true team leader out there. I knew how intense he was when we'd lose a football game. We lost that Chicago Bear game my rookie year and he threw his helmet against the doorpost and shattered it. He was so mad after that game. I know people talk about not wanting to lose, but he took it to a whole new level there at that game and I knew how intensive a player he was going to be.

I think that Coke commercial he was in goes down as one of the best commercials of all time. He did a fabulous job. It was a great, great commercial.

Pro Football Hall Of Fame Induction
When the Hall of Fame committee called me I was ecstatic. Joe Greene got in the year before me. When I got in, it said so much about our football team and about all the guys that are in the Hall of Fame now from the Steelers. We had a great collection of guys. When you get into the Hall of Fame, I think it reflects more on your football team. I think because we won championships, people look at that football team in a different light and that's why we ended up getting so many guys in.

Two Defensive Touchdowns
The one I just fell on the ball. I forgot what team it was but they were on the one-yard line and the quarterback fumbled the snap from center. I fell on it for a touchdown. How much credit can I take for that? It probably was the most embarrassing touchdown, to tell you the truth.

At that time, Jim Plunkett was playing with New England. He threw an interception that I couldn't, even if I had the worst hands in the world, I could not have missed that one. I don't know what he was thinking on that play, but I ran some 30 yards for a touchdown.

Photograph copyright Associated Press

Chapter 78

Marv Levy

College:
Coe
Harvard

Organizations:
Buffalo Bills General Manager (2006-2007) Coach
1969 Philadelphia Eagles (Kicking)
1970 Los Angeles Rams (Special Teams)
1971-1972 Washington Redskins (Special Teams)
1973-1977 Montreal Alouettes (Head Coach)
1978-1982 Kansas City Chiefs (Head Coach)
1984 Chicago Blitz (Head Coach)
1986-1997 Buffalo Bills (Head Coach)

2001 Inductee Pro Football Hall of Fame

Early Years In Coaching
I graduated high school during World War II. Twenty-one of my classmates and I enlisted in the Army Air Corps. Three years later when the war was over, I returned home. Then, I was recruited to play football at the University of Wyoming. I went to Wyoming, but at that time, they didn't give you a minute to study. There wasn't a free moment, and I was feeling bad about it. I had a high school teammate, Dudley Simpson, a highly decorated Marine during World War II, who was at Coe. At that point of time I had never heard of Coe.

Dudley said, "Marv come here. You can participate in sports and get a great education." I did, and he was right. I entered undergraduate school with the idea of going to law school. I was a very dedicated student, and I got good grades. School was important to me. I enrolled in Harvard Law School. When I left college my football coach at Coe, Dick Clausen, called me aside and said, "Marv if you ever want to coach, you've got a job here."

I entered law school, but about three weeks into it, I realized my heart was out on the athletic field. They allowed me to transfer to the graduate school of arts and sciences, and I got a Masters degree. Then I went to a prep school in St. Louis for a couple of years to teach and coach. While at the prep school there was an opening at Coe and Dick Clausen hired me. I was back there coaching football. I haven't regretted the change for a moment.

I was in graduate school at Harvard University and the headmaster was a man named Robert Cunningham. I still remember him and revere him as a great educator. He was looking for a teacher of English and History. He liked my credentials and called me in.
I said, "Mr. Cunningham, I'd love to teach, but I also want to be a coach." He said, "You can be the head basketball coach and assistant football coach." I took the job.

My wife-to-be asked how much they were going to pay me and I said, "I never asked him that." I took a job at Country Day, and was there for a couple of years before going back to Coe.

We had very successful seasons at Coe. Actually, Dick Clausen was picked as the Division III College Football Coach Of the Year. I think we were undefeated two years in a row. He went to New Mexico as head coach and I went along as a member of his staff. Two years later, Dick left to become athletic director at the University of Arizona, and they promoted me to head coach. At that time, I was the youngest major college head coach in the country. Forty some years later, I was tied with George Halas for the oldest coach in the history of the NFL. Don't question my durability. You can question some of my coaching decisions, but my durability is there.

Why I Went Into Coaching

I loved coaching. I loved the game. I loved the competition. I liked the camaraderie. I liked the excitement. I've said many times, as a coach you put in long, long hours. Certainly we did, seven days a week during the season for seven months, but I never worked a day in my life. It was pure joy and it just appealed to me. My father had been an outstanding athlete, too. I think he was named the outstanding prep basketball player in the city of Chicago back in 1915 and 1916. He encouraged me in sports.

When I was coaching in the NFL, I'd get letters from young guys who were going into the coaching field asking me to tell them how to become a NFL coach. I told them if that's the only way you're going to be happy, you don't want to be a coach. The odds are long that you will be fortunate enough to move there. Do the greatest job you can. I've known some coaches who coached for 45 years at one high school and just adored it, loved it, and are renowned for the job they did. You should coach because you love coaching, not just because you want to coach in the NFL. That won't occur in many cases.

Assistant Coaches Hired

I'm going to do some bragging now. After New Mexico, we had a couple of very good seasons. I was called to the University of California. I took over the head-coaching job during a time of tremendous student unrest. There were no affirmative action programs. We had to struggle.

I hired a coach out of high school, Bill Walsh. I hired a guy that was an intern at Cal at the time, Mike White, who later went on to coach in the pros and at the University of Illinois. I hired Bobby Ross, who went into the pros. I'm bragging now because that's some pretty darn good coaches. Dick Stanfel, who later became a tremendous line coach for the world champion Chicago Bears, was a member of my staff at Cal. I was one step away from hiring Dick Vermeil out of high school, when we all got fired because we couldn't win under the circumstances that were there at Cal. I am proud that I was able to identify those men.

I've had some other tremendous assistant coaches during the years that I worked. I worked with some great coaches. When Ralph Wilson (former owner of the Buffalo Bills) was interviewing me for the Bills job, I remember telling him, "Mr. Wilson, it isn't just a good coach you need." You need a good coaching staff. That's so important. There are times when the head coach doesn't know as much in certain areas of the game as some of his assistants. Yes, there were some coaches I hired that maybe were mistakes, but not many, very few. There were one or two over the years that I could look back on and say no, this guy wasn't really what I had in mind. For the most part, I was very fortunate to work with some of the greats.

I was fortunate enough to work for a man who wasn't just the best general manager in the National Football League; I think he was the best general manager ever. That was Bill Polian. Bill and I worked together. We may have had strong opinions, sometimes even disagreed, but never in mean terms. We selected only people of high character for our team and for our coaching staff. I didn't want to mix up high character with personalities. Some might be very extroverted. Some might be more self-contained. Look at the difference in personalities between Vince Lombardi and Tom Landry. Both were great coaches. Then there was Bill Cowher and Tony Dungy. Both guys experienced great success. I never felt I was being stabbed in the back, so to speak, by any of the coaches. I was blessed with a very loyal staff. Maybe there was one coach who I fired and I felt was detrimental to what we were trying to achieve, but that was all.

Transition to Being a NFL Assistant Coach
I coached at William and Mary for five very memorable years. The guys down there were some of the greatest overachievers you can imagine, fantastic students, and very dedicated. I still remain close to them, but the move to pros, it's different. I anticipated it would be different. You have to make adjustments. "If you don't change with the times, the times are going to change you." I heard George Allen once say that, and he was so right. It was a change, but it was something you anticipate and you have to learn to make that adjustment. I was fortunate to joina good coaching staff headed by Jerry Williams. One year later I was with George Allen out in LA. He offered me, back then, a massive raise of $1,500.

Los Angeles Rams
There were some great players on the Rams, like Deacon Jones and Merlin Olsen. Roman Gabriel was the quarterback. We had a very good season, but George Allen and the owner did not get along at all, so he was fired at the end of that first season. Our whole staff went with him to the Washington Redskins the next year. We had a couple of very good seasons. The second season we went to the Super Bowl and played the undefeated Dolphins. We came close, but not close enough and lost 14-7. It was a wonderful experience for me to work for George Allen and with the coaches on his staff, like Ted Marchibroda, Tom Catlin, Boyd Dowler, and LaVern Torgeson, and Mike McCormack. I could keep going.

Super Bowl VII
That year we blocked 11 kicks. I say that proudly because I was the special teams coach. Going into the fourth quarter with about five minutes to go, the Dolphins were beating us 14-0. They were trying a field goal. The kick was blocked. Garo picked it up and saw one of his teammates open in the end zone, but when he let the pass go, it semi-slipped out of his hands, and Mike Bass picked it up and went 75 yards for a touchdown. We were back in the game. It was 14-7, but that's the way it ended.

CFL
When I was an assistant with the Washington Redskins, I was offered the head job with the Montréal Alouettes. Being a head football coach in the pros sounded very interesting to me. It wasn't an easy decision, but I decided to take the opportunity. I had seen other coaches come out

of Canada after great success there and succeed in the NFL, like Bud Grant. That wasn't the reason I went. I went because it was an opportunity to be a head coach on the pro level.

Certainly it is different; the strategies are different. I was very careful at selecting my staff. I found men who had experience in the CFL. It was very important that I hired several of them. You study the game, but when it comes down to it the exact same things that win in the NFL win in Canada. If you run, throw, block, tackle, catch, and kick better than your opponent, you're going to win. Sure there are different rules, but the fundamentals of the game are very much the same.

J.I. Albrecht, the general manager, said when he interviewed me, "Marv when you come up here, you can use 12 men on offense." I said, "Wow that sounds great."

I walked into his office one day after our first game and said, "You didn't tell me the other team's good, too J.I."

Our owner was a man named Sam Berger, a wonderful, renowned gentlemen and a lawyer. He had been a general in the Canadian Army during World War II. He was just a wonderful man. He went out and paid the biggest contract ever for Johnny Rogers, a Heisman Trophy Winner, and brought him to Canada. Johnny was a fantastically, talented athlete, but he had a lot of personal problems that finally made us let him go after a couple of years. He has since resolved those problems. I understand he's back at the University of Nebraska as an advisor to the students there and is very well thought of there. So I'm so pleased to hear that the pendulum did swing back in the right direction for Johnny.

When I went to Canada, good things happened there. The five years I was there, we went to the Grey Cup Championship three times, and won it twice. My final year there, we had a 41-6 victory in front of the biggest crowd in the history of the CFL. At that time, we played in Montréal's Olympic Stadium. Things were going very well. I had three NFL teams approach me about being a head coach. One of them, I felt, was a team that was getting very old. They had been near the top for a while, but they looked they were about to descend. The Chiefs also approached me and even though they had experienced some tough times, I thought they had a chance to ascend and get better. There wasn't much doubt in my mind that I wanted to take a head job in the NFL if offered. It came and that's when I made that move.

Kansas City Chiefs

When I went to Kansas City, they had just completed two or three consecutive seasons of being 2-14. I knew it was going to be a little bit an uphill battle. The first year we improved. We doubled our wins; we won four games. We kept improving a little bit incrementally. We won four the next year and then I think six the next. The following year, seven, and then nine. Then the strike year hit and things didn't go well for us. It was my demise. I got fired, but a couple of years later, Lamar Hunt, the owner of the Chiefs who I have a great regard for told me, "Marv, I think we made a mistake in letting you go." I told that very same story to Mr. Wilson of the Buffalo Bills during my interview with him and was hired there.

After the 1982 season, I was let go. I did a lot of broadcasting and television work in '83. The USF Chicago Blitz hired me in '84. It was great to come back to my hometown, but then the league went out of business after '84. I was back doing radio and TV in '85. In '86, I came back to Montréal as Director of Football Operations and halfway through the season, I got a call from Bill Polian and Ralph Wilson in Buffalo inviting me down and the rest is history.

Joe Delaney

Joe Delaney, a young lad from Northeast Louisiana, was our running back with the Chiefs. I think he was a second round draft choice of ours. He wasn't very big as running backs go. I think he only weighed about 180 pounds. That's comparable to about 190 or 195 today, but Joe was unbelievable. He was a tremendously talented player and a wonderful family guy. After his second year, he was at home with his family and some little children fell in a sinkhole or a pond. Joe couldn't swim, but tried to save them. He saved one, but Joe and the other young person didn't make it. What a tragedy.

Buffalo Weather

This may come as a surprise. The average temperature in Chicago during the winter is about a degree or two colder than Buffalo. However, the snowfall in Buffalo is three times the amount you get in Chicago. That's because they're on the east side of the lake. The weather pattern comes across the lake, picks up snow and dumps it all on the city.

Our fans reveled in it and late in the season, it was always a big help to us. We used to have a mantra, one I learned from my father, the old Marine: "When it's too tough for them, it's just right for us." That was the way we used to treat the weather.

Buffalo Bills Organization

Bill Polian once said, "It's amazing what you can accomplish if no one cares who gets the credit." This is one of the most team-oriented organizations you could ever imagine. Everybody was important. For example, during the four Super Bowl games we went to, Ralph Wilson took every single person in the organization from the ladies that cleaned up at night, the switchboard operator, the security personnel to those games. He flew them down, paid for their hotel, meals, tickets, and they were part of it. He wanted it known, Bill Polian wanted it known, I wanted it known, and all our players did that everybody in that organization was fine. That's what led to the resilience it took for our guys to keep coming back from the crushing disappointment of losing those games and still finding our way back after what proved to be the impossible dream.

Scott Norwood Missed Field Goal In Super Bowl

Forty-seven yards off of grass, fewer than 50% of those are made, but nevertheless it went wide by a foot or two. I feel so much for Scott Norwood, a quiet, unassuming young man, another high character guy, and a good family guy. Our players and fans rallied around him when we flew back into Buffalo. We were taken downtown to Lafayette Square and we came out on the balcony of City Hall. There were 30,000 people below chanting Scott's name. He was moved to tears and said, "You're the reason we'll be back next year." He was right."

Team Playing in Four Straight Super Bowls
I have to admit it's quite an accomplishment. I think it's even harder, to go back to four in a row after you've lost the previous one because many people would say what's the use after the second time and give up and throw in the towel. I remember on a call-in show after our second Super Bowl loss, one of our fans called in and said, "Coach, please don't go back next year. I can't take it. I can't stand the agony. I can't go to work on the Monday after." I said, "Sir, I understand your anguish. I share it, but I'm glad you're not on my team."

Motivating Players
The answer to motivating players is simple. Select only intrinsically, motivated players. Select guys who are hungering for instruction, who want to get better. Select guys who, if you do say something that's meaningful, they respond to it. That was the way we selected them. I used to say to them, "Don't tell me you have the will to win. Do you have the will to prepare? If you lack the will to prepare, you don't have the will to win," and our guys had it. There was great internal leadership on that team. We had Jim Kelly, Darryl Talley, Kent Hull, Steve Tasker; I could go on and on. I always hesitate to name three or four or five guys because I think I'll leave out so many more who deserve to be acknowledged that way.

Origin of Buffalo Bills No Huddle Offense
During the 1989 playoffs we were playing the Cleveland Browns before they moved to Baltimore. Going into the fourth quarter, we were losing by 18 points. In those days, there was no two-point conversion; it was only a single point. Eighteen points down going into the fourth quarter, we were not going to piddle-paddle. We said let's go to our two-minute drill right now and we did and marched down the field, scoring a touchdown. Now we're down by 11. Somehow we got the ball back, marched down again and scored a touchdown with about three minutes to play. Now we're down by four. We stopped them, got the ball again with about a minute and a half to go. All of this occurred while in the two-minute drill. The whole fourth quarter was a two-minute drill, fast tempo, and fast pace.

We marched down the field and got down deep in their territory. One of our great running backs who was a great receiver, Ronnie Harmon, looked down at his feet to keep them in bounds in the end zone and dropped what would have been the winning touchdown pass. We lost the game, but as we're walking off the field after the game, Ted Marchibroda, our offensive coordinator and a former fine quarterback and Tom Bresnahan, our offensive line coach said, "Marv, how about making that our offense next year?" I said, "How come you guys are thinking the same thing I am?" So that was our style of offense, the no huddle, go quick offense.

The whole idea was that the opponent would not have time to substitute players. They won't have time to signal their calls in and we would wear their players out. Those were the advantages. One of the things you have to be willing to do is to pare your playbook down to less than half of what it would normally be, so the players can master it and get it quickly. You have to simplify the offense. Also, you're off the field very quickly so our defensive coaches weren't in love with the two-minute drill. In almost every close game it was a 20-minute time of possession for us and 40-minute time of possession for the opponents.

If we had a good comfortable lead, we would come out of the quick pace, no huddle. Say we had a 17-point lead early in the fourth, we'd slow it down and run the clock and so on. We might have a greater time of possession in games where we won by a comfortable margin.

Buffalo Bills Players

What great players we had. That again was the work of Bill Polian, and our Director of Player Personnel, John Butler, who later became general manager when Bill moved on, and so many of our scouting staff. We had great personnel. We stuck with guys for a while and developed them. We had some low round draft choices, guys like Andre Reed a fourth rounder, who was so great. Steve Tasker, who was put on waivers by the then Houston Oilers, the greatest special-team player ever. We had guys like Jim Kelly, Thurman Thomas, Bruce Smith, linebackers like Cornelius Bennett, Shane Conlin and Darryl Talley. What a group of guys. I remember them so.

I used to kid them a little bit. I said, "You guys have character and I've got to tell you there are a bunch of characters on this team." Again, it's not just the coach. It's not just the players. It's the owner and everybody else. After the greatest comeback game in the history of the NFL when we defeated the Houston Oilers in the playoffs after being down 35-3 in the second half, in the locker room after the game when all of the celebrating finally calmed down, I said to our players. "Hey guys, I want you to know that I just coached the greatest comeback in the history of the NFL, and I want you to know that I couldn't have done it without you." We had some great players.

The Comeback Against the Houston Oilers In Playoffs

That was one of the most memorable, playoffs. We played the game without three of our star players. Jim Kelly was injured. Cornelius Bennett was out injured, who was our great linebacker who didn't get the credit I think he deserved even now. Thurman Thomas was out injured. Still we came back from that tremendous deficit. It was an unbelievable experience.
Frank Reich led the greatest comeback in collegiate football history, and he led the greatest one in pro football history. That's amazing. There's another high character, talented guy. I never had a problem with him and Jim. They were very close in fact.

Pro Football Hall of Fame Induction

First of all, you wonder, am I really here? I never dreamed that this would occur when I first started the game. I wasn't a Pro Football Hall of Fame playing talent, but when I started coaching, it never even occurred to me that someday I might be up there with guys like Vince Lombardi and so many other guys. I still think about it. My initial expectancies couldn't have been very high by anyone who was predicting. I looked out at the audience at some of the great ones that were out there, from Chuck Bednarik and so many more. I saw them out there and the looks on their faces. 'Wow am I here?' That's the feeling you have. The Pro Football Hall of Fame is a very uplifting place to be. It was magnificently run by the previous executive directors, and now by the current one, Steve Perry. It's always just a delight to go back and share memories and maybe a few exaggerations too, with some of the guys there.

Job of a Coach

Getting a team to play as a team and not as individual talents is a huge part of the coach's job. It starts with the type of players he brings on board. We were so aware that weren't going to bring a guy on board who had an attitude problem, who had a history of drug abuse, who was a distraction, or who was selfish. Now don't mix that up with personality. We had some guys that were bubbling extroverts and some that were more laid back, but they team oriented. They showed up for practice every day and they didn't place blame on their teammates. We tried to make sure they walked off the field every single day a little bit better off from what they learned in practice. Those were the kind of guys we were after.

Players
Most of the players are a lot smarter than you might think to tell you the truth. I just tried to be myself. Everybody should coach within himself. I didn't try to impress them by being too intellectual. Once in a while they'd laugh because they thought I used a word that maybe was not en vogue or not used very often. That's why jokingly, at one of my induction speeches at the Hall of Fame where a lot of our players were, I used a big word and said, "Look it up Thurman." He was sitting in the audience because he used to once in a while raise his eyebrows if I said something that sounded a little bit high blown but I communicated in my fieldwell.

Best Coach He Coached Against
Don Shula was the best, but there were so many others. I think we competed as an assistant against Vince Lombardi, against Tom Landry. I can go on and on. There were many good ones. Bill Parcells we competed against, Marty Schottenheimer. I can go through a litany of names. There are a lot of good ones. There are none of them I don't respect. There are none of them that I dislike.

Coaching Philosophy
I told our players, "You don't get paid for Sunday, that's fun. Getting ready for Sunday, that's the work."

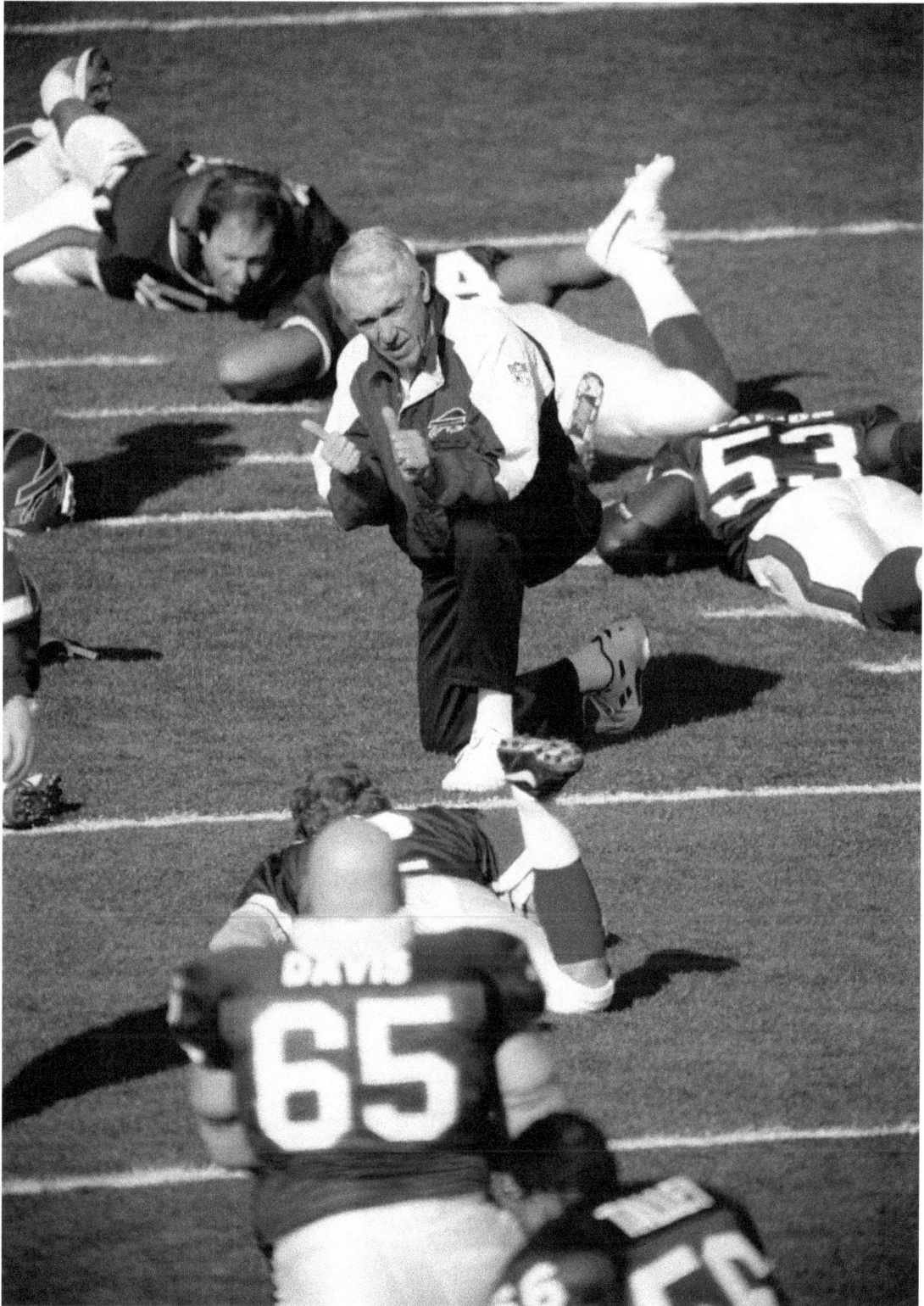

Buffalo Bills Head Coach Marv Levy prior to Super Bowl XXVII, Sunday, Jan. 31, 1993.
Photograph copyright Associated Press

Chapter 79

Bobby Beathard

College:
California Polytechnic State University

As Scout:
Kansas City Chiefs (1963, 1966-1967)
Atlanta Falcons (1968-1971)

As Executive:
Miami Dolphins (1972-1977)
Washington Redskins (1978-1988)
San Diego Chargers (1990-2000)

2018 Inductee Pro Football Hall Of Fame

Hiring By Kansas City Chiefs
The Kansas City Chiefs had an employee back then by the name of Don Klosterman. He knew how much I was involved with football and liked football. He knew that I played in high school and college. He wanted to know if I would be interested in scouting for him on the West Coast, in around 13 states. I said, "Sure, I'd love it."

Then, the Chiefs expanded my area. Later the Chiefs asked me to go to all around the country, just looking at the top prospects everywhere. It was something I was really excited about. It was kind of a natural thing for me.

Chiefs Owner Lamar Hunt was one of the nicest people I've ever known. It was a wonderful place to work.

Scouting In the (American Football League) AFL
Scouting in the AFL was kind of fun. We did things that they don't do now. The AFL and NFL were competing against each other. We were hiding players out where the NFL couldn't find them. The NFL was hiding players out where we couldn't find them. If you couldn't find a player and see him personally, you wouldn't draft him. There were a lot of things going on like that, that don't go on anymore. It was a lot of fun. Looking back on it, it was a real exciting time in the league.

Kansas City Chiefs Winning AFL Championship
I don't know how to describe the Kansas City Chiefs winning the AFL Championship, but it was terrific. The three players from the team that come to mind right away are Curley Culp, Mike Garrett, and Jan Stenerud. It was great. The AFL was always the little brother league. It was something that wasn't at the level of the NFL. To be able to go up against the NFL and do

well, that was a big step for that league.

Time With Atlanta Falcons
Tom Braatz was down in Atlanta with the Falcons and he brought me down there. We were friends. It was really a good thing for me to see how different organizations did things. I brought some things from the Chiefs that the Falcons wanted to know about. I learned things from the Falcons. It was fun. I was lucky. I tell my wife now that I got through life without a real job. I got to do something that I loved to do every day.

Working For Don Shula With Miami Dolphins
Working for Don Shula with the Miami Dolphins was great. I probably learned more working for Don than anybody. He said, "Okay, you're down here to get us players." He turned it over to me to do that and let me hire a scouting staff. I was never second-guessed or anything. He was the best. I'll tell you, the guy was just great. I really enjoyed my time there. I learned so much under Don that it really set me up for how to do things the rest of my career.

Don knew every aspect of the organization, to do with football. He could coach any position on the football team, offensively or defensively. He was a very demanding guy with the players. They all responded to the way he did it. He was just one of those guys that could get the best out of anybody.

When I look at some of the guys we had when we had the perfect season and when we won Super Bowls, I don't know if there's any other coach that could have done that with that group of players. I mean, they were good, but when I look at some of the later teams, I think maybe they weren't as good as these guys, man for man, but as a team, they were as good as anybody that had ever played.

On game days, Don told me, "You're not just going to sit in the stands and watch the game. You're going to do something." He had me working with special teams to make sure every special team player was ready to go in when we had to punt, or kickoff, or go for an extra point.

Don would say, "We have one player that no matter what, you always make sure you have his jersey in your hand when we call for special teams because he'll forget to go on the field."

One time, we sent the special teams on the field and I didn't even notice there were only 10 men on the field. Shula yelled and he knew exactly who wasn't on the field. He came over and grabbed me. I thought, "Oh my God!" I never made the mistake again.

Don Shula's Ability To Adapt
Don Shula and Joe Gibbs could adapt to anything. When a key player would go down, some coaches would say, "Oh, no. Now what do we do?" Shula wouldn't bat an eye. He'd say, "Hey, we're going to be fine." Jim Del Gaizo came in at quarterback and won games for the Miami Dolphins. Nothing bothered Don Shula. He'd say, "We're going to go on. We're fine. All our backups are as good as our starters." It was just amazing how he handled it. I've been with teams where somebody got hurt and coaches would show it bothered them. It affects the players, but it never affected Shula. Shula never let it show or affect the players.

Miami Dolphins Offensive Line
The Miami Dolphins had a great offensive line. Those guys would have been great today.

Monte Clark was a great offensive line coach. When you look at Jim Langer, Bob Kuechenberg, and all those guys, they were terrific.

Losing Paul Warfield, Larry Csonka, & Jim Kiick To World Football League (WFL)
It was tough when Paul Warfield, Larry Csonka, and Jim Kiick left the Miami Dolphins for the World Football League (WFL). Thinking of the money the WFL was throwing around, I just didn't think the WFL would make it. Of course, it didn't. It was tough to lose those guys.

Don Shula was amazing in that anything that happened that was bad, he didn't want to address it or talk about it. It was like nothing happened. His viewpoint was "We're just going to go on. We're going to be better now than we ever were". He could get his point across, where everybody felt, "You know, it's not a big deal. We're going to be fine. We have other guys that can do as well." Son of a gun, we would! He was just an amazing guy, that anything bad that happened, you never dwelled on it. It was, look at the good side of things and we'll be better.

1972 Miami Dolphins Perfect Season
It got harder for the Miami Dolphins team as they approached the end of the 1972 season. Every team that the Dolphins played had more incentive to win that game than anything because we hadn't lost a game. There was also a lot more pressure on our team. It was just amazing how that team could go through and do it. I don't think it will ever be done again. I watch the NFL closely every year, looking at all the teams, and I just don't think it's likely.

Earl Morrall Replacing An Injured Bob Griese During 1972 Perfect Season
The most amazing thing during the 1972 Miami Dolphins season was when Bob Griese went down, we won with Earl Morrall. I really think Earl was a great person. I liked Earl and he was a good quarterback. Earl wasn't what Griese was, nor a Marino type or anything like that. Earl wasn't the quarterback that you thought would take you to the Super Bowl.

Don Shula did things a little different with Earl than he would with Griese. Sure enough, we pulled it off. It was just amazing. I think the things that Don did in cases like that were just amazing. I don't know if many coaches could do that.

Decision To Work For Washington Redskins
I decided to leave the Miami Dolphins for the Washington Redskins because I was given more responsibility. It was just a step up, I thought. I talked to Don Shula, about it. Don said, "You know, that's a great opportunity." It was. Maybe he was trying to get rid of me, I don't know. It was one of those things. He encouraged me to go. I didn't want to go. I said, "I don't want to leave here. I've grown up by the beach all my life." He said, "No. You ought to go for the interview. Go and meet them and see what it's like."

I went to Washington and met with Edward Bennett Williams, the Redskins Owner. Edward was such a nice guy. After the interview, he offered me the job. I went back to Don and said, "You know what? I'm going to take the job. It's going to be different, but it will be fun."

Rebuilding the Washington Redskins
With the Redskins I went into a situation where their prior philosophy was completely different from mine. I wanted to build through the draft. During the recently completed George Allen Era, George was keeping all the old veterans and would always trade for old veterans and forget

about the draft. Washington didn't have any draft choices when I went there. George traded them all away for veterans. I had a whole different philosophy to build thru the draft. I've got old letters and hate mail for getting rid of some of the old veterans that had won for George.

The old guys weren't required to do the work that you have to do in football. George had his way of winning. I just had a different philosophy. There was a lot of pressure on me in Washington because of getting rid of all the old guys. The Redskin fans hated me for getting rid of those guys. The players wanted lifetime jobs and to get all that money. Even though they weren't at the level to play in the NFL anymore and win.

When I go back to Redskins reunions every year, I still see a lot of those guys. I always go out with Sonny Jurgensen, Billy Kilmer, and a lot of those guys, and have a lot of fun talking about those days.

I pretty much had a plan in my head, what I had to do. You have to look at what the prospects are in the draft. Is it a strong year for offensive lines? If it just happened to be that, we drafted a lineman.

Plus, you have to have the right coaches. I've been with teams where if you draft a guy in the tenth round, the coach has already got in his mind, "No tenth rounder is going to make our team." We had a coach where it didn't matter if we drafted someone in the tenth or eleventh round, or if a player wasn't even drafted and we signed him as a free agent. My agreement with the coaches was to give all players the same opportunity they would give a first round pick. We had a lot of kids that weren't drafted, or were drafted late, make it and do well.

The best example I can think of is when we took Darrell Green as last pick in the first round. I had scouted him prior to the draft. I called Darrell to tell him we had drafted him. He said, "Bobby why did you take so long to take me?" I said, "Well, that's where we had a pick because we won the Super Bowl. We didn't have a pick that early in the round. Don't blame me. Look at all the other teams that passed you up."

Darrell came in and Richie Petitbon, our secondary coach said, "Bobby, a guy that small can't play in this league." I said, "Well, this guy's different." Darryl played around 18 years in the NFL.

Joe Gibbs
I had a good friend, Ernie Zampese. Ernie and I used to talk a lot. Ernie had coached with Joe Gibbs for a long time. Joe was coaching with Don Coryell. I liked Coryell's style of football. Ernie and I had talked about Joe before. I called Ernie and said, "What do you think? Is Joe ready to be a head coach?" Ernie said, "Joe's ready now." I called Joe and said, "Hey, will you take the job if I get to pick you?" He said, "Yes." I said, "Okay, figure out who you want on your offensive staff and keep our defense staff." He said, "Okay."

Jack Kent Cooke called me in his office and said, "Okay. What are we going to do about head coach?" I said, "Well, I've already got a guy." He said, "What do you mean you got a guy?" I said, "I got a guy to be our coach." He said, "Who you thinking of?" I said, "Well, you don't know him. You haven't heard of him. This guy named Joe Gibbs." He said, "Joe Gibbs! Who in the hell is Joe Gibbs?" He said, "They'll crucify me if I bring a guy in here named Joe Gibbs.

Nobody knows who he is." I said, "I know they don't. That's the good thing about him. Everybody isn't after him. It will be fine."

Mr. Cooke let me hire him. Joe put the offensive staff together and kept the defensive staff. Then, we went on to lose our first three games. I would go out of town, usually on Tuesday mornings to go to different colleges around the country scouting. I would look at the game film on Monday with the coaches, and go out Tuesday scouting and come back Friday night. Mr. Cooke called me and said, "I want you to get out to my house right away." I said, "I can't. I've got to go scouting." He said, "Do you own this team?" I said, "No, sir." He said, "You cancel your plans and get out to my house now." I had to drive all the way out to where he lived. He sat me down and said, "I should fire you and that coach you hired."

After we lost a couple games Mr. Cooke said, "You bring your coach out here with you." I go into the offensive room and say, "Joe you got to go to Mr. Cooke's." He said, "I can't. We're doing game plan." I told him Mr. Cooke was not giving him a choice. Mr. Cooke chewed Joe and I both out and sent us back home. It was awful for the first five games.

Then, we started winning. Later on Mr. Cooke would tell Joe, "You're the coach I always wanted. The first thing I told Bobby was, "You get Joe Gibbs. That's the guy we want." Joe and I still, to this day, laugh about that.

John Riggins
John Riggins had quit football. The funny thing is that when I used to go to colleges scouting, I had met John's sister. She was a secretary at the coach's office at the University of Kansas. I called her and said, "Hey, this is Bobby calling. I want to know if you can set it up so I can come out there and meet with John." I had met John before. I had a decent relationship with him, and he trusted me.

I flew out there and saw his sister. Then she set up the meeting so I could talk to John. I met privately with John and said, "Hey, look it, it's all different. It's not the George Allen thing anymore. This is Joe Gibbs; just give it a try. The best thing I can do is have Joe come over here and to meet you personally, and you'll trust him." I had Joe come over and meet with John. John agreed that he would play for Joe. That was the way we got John to come back to the Redskins.

Decision To Leave Washington Redskins
My mom and dad were getting old and living in California and I missed them. They used to go to Washington for a game each year, but they were getting to an age where they didn't want to travel. I wanted to be near them. We were really close. They were getting way up there in age. That was the reason that I left. That was the only reason.

Mr. Cooke told me to not go to another team for a year. I agreed to sit out a year. Then I got a call from NFL Network to broadcast for them. I was at NFL Network for a year and then joined the San Diego Chargers.

Decision To Retire
The travel, going everywhere in the country looking for players, was starting to get to me. I was never home much. I thought, "Is this what I want to do the rest of my life?" I didn't want to

draft players I hadn't seen personally. If I couldn't travel and see them, and could only see them on tape, I thought it was time for me to do something else and retire. I had kids and I wanted to see them play their Friday night games and all that stuff. A lot of things went into the decision. It was a pretty easy decision.

Most general managers stayed in the office. I was one of the few general managers that went all around the country all football season, looking for players. I don't know many general managers who wanted to do that. I was afraid not to do it because I wanted to see the players in practice and do all the other stuff before we ever drafted them. That's why I made the deal that I'd be the general manager, but I still wanted to go out all season and look at players. I'd come back every weekend for the games.

Dexter Manley
Dexter Manley was a heck of a player. Dexter was a fun guy to be around. He practiced like it was an actual game. It was tough for any offensive tackle to handle him in practice. He was just a screwball. He practiced hard every day. He gave the offensive linemen a real picture of what a game was like. That guy was, he was really something. I would have hated to be an offensive tackle to have to play against Dexter every week.

Photograph copyright Associated Press

Chapter 80

Ron Wolf

> College:
> Maryville College in Tennessee
> University of Oklahoma
>
> As Executive:
> Oakland/Los Angeles Raiders (1963-1974, 1979-1989)
> Tampa Bay Buccaneers (1976-1978)
> New York Jets (1990-1991) Green Bay Packers (1991-2001)
>
> 2015 Inductee Pro Football Hall Of Fame

Early Years With Raiders

I had finished taking my last final at the University of Oklahoma when the phone rang. It was Al Davis. He had just been named head coach and general manager of the Oakland Raiders. He said he was looking for somebody who could work in his talent department and asked if I would be interested in coming out on a trial basis. I said, "Certainly." I went to training camp with the Raiders, and from there I was hired full-time.

It was a wonderful experience for me, because at that time, being in the American Football League, there were eight teams with thirty-three players each for a total of 264 players. Every night Al would sit with his coaching staff, which consisted of four people and two scouts. They would study each position of their opponents in the American Football League. They had the opportunity to watch all the left tackles, and then rate them one through eight. The theory is a picture is worth a thousand words, which in fact it is true. By listening and seeing what a good player was versus a bad player, really enabled me to get a big insight into what it took to play professional football. That was kind of how he did things. He did things by comparison.

After being hired, I was doing pro scouting. Everything was done from a pro perspective, and then we delved into college scouting the next year.

Early Drafts With Raiders

In those days, the draft was in November, so the bulk of your scouting was done in the spring. That's when all the staffs went out, which included the coaches and scouts, and could really get a handle on who the good players were during colleges spring practices. In those days during spring practice, they really practiced. They had scrimmages, and they were a lot looser then, because there were no games coming up. It was about building their football team. You had a lot of information available to you, and it came down to the ability to pick the player. What you would do in the fall is just follow up on injuries and things of that nature.

Importance Of Offensive Linemen

The offensive line is the only position in the game, if you don't have five guys, you can't play. You could lose your receivers, you could lose your tight end, lose your backs, you could lose your defensive linemen, but if you don't have five offensive linemen, you can't play the game. There was an emphasis on that.

Comparison Of AFL vs. NFL

The AFL was a little more wide-open game. No question about it. There was more single coverage in the American Football League then. I know a lot of people in the NFL said at that time, and some still maintain, that the AFL couldn't play defense. The AFL did okay in Super Bowl III and Super Bowl IV playing defense. Then there was the merger of the two leagues. It's no different than the game today. If you have good players, you're going to be a good team, and there's no question about that. The object is to get as many good players as you possibly can. Our whole basis with the Raiders was size and speed.

Recruiting Against NFL

It was very difficult recruiting against the NFL the first couple of years. Then what happened in 1965, was Joe Namath signed with the Jets. Suddenly the whole image of the American Football League changed. It changed because of the money that Joe Namath was paid. It was difficult up to that point, but it became just like college recruiting or recruiting in any sense. The big recruiting tool is dollars. If you had more dollars than the other team, the guy was going to sign with you.

Ken Stabler

Ken Stabler was a pinpoint passer. He was very accurate and very smart. He was a terrific runner in college, but got hurt in college and that was taken away. He got the nickname Snake with how he ran.

We used to have practices where the ball was never on the ground. That's how accurate he was. He was, until Tom Brady did it, the first quarterback ever to take his team to the championship game in the Super Bowl era in five consecutive years. He was calm, cool, and collected, which is a perfect demeanor for a quarterback. He was very, very talented.

Transition From Al Davis To John Madden As Coach

The team got better, so it was a big transformation. We had better players and John Madden was a superb football coach. When you have really good football players, suddenly you're a lot better off. I think that's what happened there. John really had some quality teams and tremendous players. John Madden came and Gene Upshaw and Art Shell followed. Ken Stabler came in 1968 and although he didn't play '68-'69, and hardly played at all in '70, it was a big difference.

Daryle Lamonica & Jim Plunkett

Daryle Lamonica was a tremendous long passer and perfect for what we were trying to do. Jim Plunkett was a tough guy. He won two Super Bowls as a quarterback with the Raiders. I've been told that the problem with Plunkett getting into the Hall of Fame is he didn't win enough games. I don't know. I'm not a big fellow with stats.

Tom Flores Not Being In Pro Football Hall Of Fame

I think it's a shame that Tom Flores is not in the Hall of Fame. He was 6 and 1 against Don Shula, and I think 11 and 4 versus Don Coryell. Don Coryell gets nominated all the time. Tom won two Super Bowls. Coryell never even won a championship. I guess Tom has gotten lost in this whole process, which is a shame, because he was a very, very talented, good coach. He won two Super Bowls as a head coach. That has to speak volumes, but he's overlooked for some reason.

Reason He Went To Work For Tampa Bay Buccaneers

There was an opportunity for an expansion team. I thought that I was ready to leave. I thought I could lead. Once I got there, I discovered that, whoa, I'm not as smart as I thought I was. I'm not as polished as I need to be. Things just didn't work out.

The Buccaneers are the only true expansion team that ever, within four years of starting, played in the championship game. You had Paul Brown, Tex Schramm, and Tom Landry— all those guys and they weren't able to do that. The Buccaneers were able to do that with 15 of the players I had a hand in getting there. I'm very, very proud of that.

Lee Roy Selmon

Lee Roy Selmon is probably still the best player they've ever had with the Tampa Bay Buccaneers. I know this from my 38-year career; he's the best player I ever personally drafted. He was just a fabulous football player, but unfortunately for him, he played in a three-man front in Tampa. If he had been in a four-man front as a defensive end, there's no telling what records he would have broken as a pass rusher. He was a superb football player. They do not come any better than Lee Roy Selmon as a person and as a football player.

Importance Of A Quarterback

I saw how important it was for the Buccaneers. I believe firmly that if you do not have a quarterback, you do not have a chance in the National Football League. When I went to the Packers, I knew what I had to do. I had been through the experience in Tampa, so I knew all about that. I knew what I had to do in order to be successful in Green Bay. The chips kind of fall as they may for me. I was able to hire Mike Holmgren and able to trade for Brett Favre. Those two things turned that whole franchise around.

Brett Favre

The first game I ever went to as Executive Vice President and General Manager of the Green Bay Packers was in Atlanta. We played the Falcons. Ken Herock, whom I worked with at the Raiders for many years, was the person that ran the Falcons football operations. He told me up in the press box that if I wanted to see Brett Favre throw, I'd have to go down before the team came out, because when the team came out, he wouldn't be permitted to take any throws. Right away, I knew I had an opportunity to get this guy. I started working on it at that point, and then finally we got in done sometime in February.

Convincing Players To Play For Green Bay

The addition of Mike Holmgren, coming in from San Francisco, kind of changed that a little bit. Then the emergence of Brett Favre helped. Plus, we started really doing a heck of a job, I thought, of selling Green Bay throughout the league. We showed all the advantages of being a part of the Packers. I started a system where we would have honorary captains. Each game we'd bring an honorary captain back. Think about all the great names in the lore of Green Bay Packers football. It was a thrill to bring back Paul Hornung, Ray Nitschke, Willie Davis, Bart Starr, and others.

We started to win. Everybody likes to be involved in winning. There's no question about that. Plus, we had some great facilities up there. The only thing we ever asked our guys to do was to conduct themselves properly, and be professional football players. That was all the guys were ever asked to do as members of the Green Bay Packers. We didn't have socials they had to go to, like dinners. That was all we ever asked our guys to do, and they bought into it. When I went with the Packers, the Packers had the poorest record in the National Football league. With the advent of free agency, and when I left, the Packers had the best record in the National Football League. I'm very, very proud of that.

Brett Favre was a phenomenal player. They say the old Yankee Stadium was the house that Ruth built, but that new Lambeau Field is obviously the house that Favre built.

Guys were being threatened that they would be traded to Green Bay, or told, "You keep this up, and we'll send you to the Packers." Well, suddenly it became a pretty good place to go play football. We won 25 straight games in Lambeau Field and it worked out very, very well for us. There were a lot of people that made that happen, but it was a great. It was a great thrill to win that title.

Leaders On Packers
It was Brett Favre on offense and LeRoy Butler on defense. Reggie White played an enormous role, don't misunderstand me, but LeRoy Butler was the real leader of the defensive group. LeRoy took control. He could cover, he could tackle, and he could dog, a perfect safety.

Favorite Moment In NFL
My favorite moment in the NFL was when the Green Bay Packers beat the Carolina Panthers for the right to go to the Super Bowl. That's the best moment I ever had, because it happened in Lambeau Field. Everybody said the Packers would never go to the Super Bowl again. When free agency came to pro football, people said teams like Green Bay would die. Well, we won the title in Lambeau Field, and that was a big, big thrill to me.

Pro Football Hall of Fame Induction
It was unbelievable. There are so many people that I'm deeply indebted to for their contribution to the fact that I am in the Hall of Fame. To be recognized with those great names of the people that are legendary figures of the game, it's an awesome responsibility, and an awesome feeling.

Ron Wolf holds the Lombardi trophy as he sits on the team plane next to his wife, Edie, after Super Bowl XXXI. Photograph copyright Associated Press

Chapter 81

Bill Polian

> As executive:
> Montreal Alouettes (scout)
> Kansas City Chiefs (1978– 1982) (pro scout)
> Winnipeg Blue Bombers (personnel director)
> Chicago Blitz (personnel director) (1984)
> Buffalo Bills (1984–1985) (Pro Personnel Director) (1986–1992) (General Manager)
> Carolina Panthers (1995–1997) (General Manager)
> Indianapolis Colts (1997–2009) (General Manager) (1998–2011) (Team President)
>
> 2015 Inductee Pro Football Hall Of Fame

Kansas City Chiefs

I had been scouting for the Montreal Alouettes in the CFL. The head coach and general manager there was Marv Levy. When he took the Kansas City Chiefs head coaching job, he brought me over there as an advanced scout.

The Chiefs were in a rebuild situation. We actually got pretty good. I think we got to 9-7 our fourth year with the team. We had a terrific young back named Joe Delaney, who unfortunately drowned in a tragic accident trying to save a child at a picnic just prior to training camp.

I remember reading about what happened. Joe was at a picnic. He didn't know how to swim. All of a sudden he heard kids were in trouble. He didn't wait; he just jumped in and tried to save the kids. I think he saved one of them.

Joe dying was devastating and on top of that, we had the players' strike, which ate up 8 or 9 games. Because of the way upper management, not Lamar Hunt but people working directly for him approached the players when they came back off the strike, we were badly, badly fractured. Even though we beat the Jets who actually went to the conference championship that year in the last game of the season, it was too little too late. We were fired.

Chicago Blitz

Well, when Marv and I left Kansas City, I went to the Winnipeg Blue Bombers of the CFL. I was the player personnel director there. Marv got hired by the Chicago Blitz of the USFL and called me. He told me to come work for the Blitz, and I did. I was the player personnel director and eventually the acting general manager.

I thought the opportunity was a bit better in the USFL than the CFL. I enjoyed my time in the CFL and had some overtures from folks that were thinking about me as a possible general manager. I just felt like the opportunity to go to Chicago and be in a growing league like the USFL was a better one. Obviously when Marv was with the Blitz, there was a comfort level there that was off the charts.

We had to start from scratch with the Blitz. The previous years team had all gone to play for the

Arizona Rattlers. The only thing we had was the Blitz name and the geographical rights to certain players from Notre Dame and other local schools. That was the situation, but in professional football and really in professional sports, you can't pick your battles. You've got to go where the opportunities are and it was an opportunity. We tried to make the best of it.

We were in training camp in Arizona and Steve Ehrhart, the Deputy Commissioner of the league, came out to see Marv and me to inform us that the doctor who had been the Blitz owner had simply pulled out and wasn't going to put any more money into the team. He returned the franchise back to the league. So we were in essence working for the league office. Steve indicated that Marv and I should carry on in our executive capacities. We were told to keep going, and that the league would get back to us with a budget relatively soon.

The budget obviously was bare bones. Subsequently, it got worse. At the end of the season, we ended up just existing on fumes, really. We are very fortunate in the sense that they were able to sell the team soon after the season ended to Eddie Einhorn, Jerry Reinsdorf, and a wonderful man from Chicago named Gene Fanning.

Despite having no highly paid players, no budget, and basically having to trade things like jerseys and memorabilia for towels for the last game of the season, we ended up winning 5 of our last 7 games. It just goes to show you what kind of a coach Marv was. He kept the guys going and focused in that kind of situation. It was amazing.

Joining Buffalo Bills

Don Lawrence was the defensive coordinator of the Bills and had been one of Marv Levy's assistant coaches in Kansas City. Don and I were good friends. In 1984, the Bills had just hired a Personnel Director. They had not had one prior to that. They hired a gentleman in January, and in the spring he sustained a debilitating spinal injury that didn't allow him to work. Ralph Wilson, the owner of the Bills, had grudgingly funded the position but this gentleman wasn't working. He was on disability. They decided to try to fill the position. Don Lawrence went to Kay Stephenson who was the head coach and said, "Listen, I've got just the guy for you! He's the acting GM of the Chicago Blitz. He's been in Canada and was with us in Kansas City."

Kay asked me to come in for an interview and I did. We hit it off immediately. He called me back and told me he could offer me the job, but it's going to be for a very reduced salary because they didn't really have the funding for it. The amount was even less than I was making in Chicago. I talked about it with my wife and she said, "Listen, it's a chance to go back to the National Football League. You can't pass it up no matter what the circumstances are. We'll figure out a way to handle the finances." We did. Fortunately it worked out okay.

Signing Bruce Smith

Signing Bruce Smith was my first major signing. Terry Bledsoe, the general manager, had suffered a very debilitating heart attack and was out of work for the better part of about six months. Pat McGroder, who was a Senior Executive with the Bills, was in his early eighties. He had been with the Bills and with Ralph Wilson from the inception. Pat told Mr. Wilson we have a guy here who can do this. He's signed guys in the USFL. He understands what the USFL challenges are all about. He can negotiate contracts.

They had me fly over to Detroit, which is where Mr. Wilson lived, and meet with him. He gave me my marching orders and said, "Go ahead, and let's see if we can get him signed." So in conjunction with Mr. Wilson's CFO Dave Olsen, who is as fine a man, as you'll ever have the opportunity to meet, we negotiated with Bruce's representative. We were negotiating against the Baltimore Stars who had his rights in the USFL.

At that point, the USFL was still a growing concern. Donald Trump had not taken it under at that point. The Stars were located very close to where Bruce had grown up, which was in the Tidewater area of Virginia. It was a tough negotiation and a long one. We had to beat both the Stars financial offer and convince Bruce to come to Buffalo, which was coming off a 2 and 14 season. Buffalo had a downtrodden reputation both in professional sports and society in general, because of the weather and the economic downturn that had taken place there. We had to convince Bruce to come and we had to convince him that he was going to be the first step in the road to the ultimate success.

Signing Jim Kelly
I didn't really feel any pressure to sign Jim Kelly. You go to work and you do your job. The following January after we signed Bruce Smith, I was well prepared for the job. I was absolutely unknown outside of a small segment of the pro football industry, but I was well prepared. I'd been an advanced scout in Kansas City and signed players there. I'd done some minor league coaching. I'd signed players in Canada and helped build two championships teams there. I had gone through the experience of the USFL which, to say the least, was unique.

It wasn't any pressure. I knew what I had to do and set about to do it. I had been through situations. The money was a little bit more in the NFL and certainly the exposure was greater, but the job was essentially the same. I've said on numerous occasions when young people ask me how they can get to be a GM in the NFL, or how they can get to be an executive in the NFL, the answer is get as much experience at lower levels as you can, because that's what helps you. That's what prepares you.

I didn't feel any inordinate pressure. It was a situation that we had to take advantage of. We owned Jim's rights. The USFL, thanks to Mr. Trump, was in a position where they were not going to go forward, and as a result we were in a situation where we had a great opportunity to get a player who was going to make a huge difference for us. Mr. Wilson said, "Go do it," and that's what we did.

I explain to Jim what the rights situation was. We held his rights. Jim's agents and Jim said, "What if we force a trade?"

I said, "Well I don't know how you can force a trade other than by going to court, and even that's not probably going to work. Let's assume that you can force a trade. You can't force us to trade him just anywhere. What we'll do is trade him to the last place he wants to go which is probably Green Bay." At that time Ron Wolf had not made Green Bay competitive, so they were maybe football wise a step below the Bills. I said, "You are not going to the Raiders under any circumstances."

It was the Raiders who had contacted them, and the Raiders with whom they had negotiated. I said, "You will not go to the Raiders under any circumstances. This is not the USFL. Al Davis doesn't have the right to decide what players he is going to sign and not sign. We have your rights and you are not going to the Raiders."

I said to Jim, "Here's who we have on this team. We built it with you in mind. This is how we are going to do it going forward. This is not a situation where we want to sign you because we want to sell tickets, or we want to get the newspaper off our back, or anything of that nature. It's because we want you to be a quarterback who takes us to the Super Bowl. That's our vision. That's our drive. That's our dynamic."

We had a long discussion about what things were like and what commitment Mr. Wilson was willing to make. He'd already made a significant commitment by signing Bruce Smith, Andre Reed, Frank Reich, and others. I said, "He's prepared to make an incredible commitment to you and then we are going to go ahead and continue to build the team. If you want to be with a winner, if you want to go to a place that really cares about football, this is the place to be. It will take a leap of faith, I realize, but if you feel that way, we can do it."

For that I am really grateful. The folks, the fans at Buffalo, took a chance on me. The support came pretty quickly.

I've often said there was a black cloud over the franchise but the day Jim Kelly signed, that black cloud lifted and there was nothing but blue skies from there on out. The prodigal son came home. He had finally chosen Buffalo after he had initially rejected it. He was here to lead us to the Promised Land. I realize I'm mixing my biblical metaphors here, but that's the way it was. That's the way it was; not only portrayed, but we lived it.

On the flight to Buffalo after he signed the contract and we were going into the press conference, I said to Jim, "You've never experienced anything like this in your life. You are going to see a reception the likes of which you have never experienced."

As we exited the plane there had to be 15 or 20 media crews there. People from all over western New York, Canada, etc. We took an expressway into the city. We had to hold the press conference at a downtown hotel because the Bills facility could not accommodate the number of people. It was so large! We had to drive down a freeway that had any number of overpasses on it. About every quarter of a mile there was an overpass. From the overpass, people were standing with signs— Welcome Back Jim! Thank God Jim, You're Here! Let's Go Win A SuperBowl! People 4 or 5 deep on the overpass, just waiving at the motorcade.

He was dumbfounded. He couldn't believe it. When we got to the hotel, it was as if it was a Presidential press conference. There had to be at least 250 media people there. They preempted the networks' evening news in Buffalo, nearby Canadian cities, and in Rochester, to carry the press conference live. It was a big, big, big day. People there were simply rejoicing. This great quarterback that the Bills drafted, who had chosen not to come, was there and we were on the right road. That was the catalytic moment where once again everybody said, "Hey. The Buffalo Bills are back!"

Marv Levy's Coaching Prowess
Marv Levy along with Tony Dungy, are the best teachers I've ever been around in this business. Marv has a way of boiling things down so everybody can understand him. He's got a firm grasp of what it takes to win and how to teach players to do that. His greatness was pretty evident in

Montreal, and even more so in Kansas City.

First of all, he's the greatest communicator I've ever been around. Keep in mind that's high praise because I've been around Tony Dungy, Cal Murphy in Canada, and hall of famers. He's incredible in that regards. Secondly, he's a tremendous organizer. Third, he is the greatest teacher I've ever been around. He's able to boil things down and get them across to the players in a way that both instructs and inspires. Finally, he has a vision that is unique in terms of how to prepare a football team, how to treat professionals, and how to create a culture of inclusiveness. He's caring and honest. That's the kind of person he is. In terms of understanding what it took to win and the ability to do that immediately, I had no question that he was the rightman.

Lamar Hunt told Mr. Wilson, who called for a reference, the greatest mistake I've made in my entire football career was letting Marv Levy go. I think that cinched it for Mr. Wilson in terms of making the hire. Marv's everything you want in a football coach. He's the measuring stick I've used from that day on. Everything you want in a coach—vision, strategy, organization, and inspiration—he's got it all.

Scouting Success With Buffalo Bills
We didn't get lucky. Former Texas Coach Darrell Royal said, "Luck is when preparation meets opportunity." That's what occurred there. We knew exactly the kind of player we wanted. Knowing that made it relatively easy to scout. We didn't concern ourselves with outside forces, noise, consensus, or other peoples' opinions. We simply took the players that we felt were the best for our team. We used every avenue we could to try to unearth those players, the college draft, collegiate free agency, USFL, waivers as is the case with Steve Tasker, and trades. Leonard Smith, Kenneth Davis, and Cornelius Bennett all came through trades.

Improving Buffalo Bills Image
When I first took the job in Buffalo, the first person I saw after I got back from the press conference was the ticket manager. He said, "Congratulations we have 12,000 season tickets sold in a 80,000 seat stadium." I was a bit floored by that number. I could understand it given how bad the team had been, not signing Jim Kelly after drafting him, and the loss of Joe Cribbs. It was a snowball rolling in the wrong direction.

Our general manager and I went out and tried to meet with as many groups as we could. A, to try to take their temperature—why were you not supporting the Bills? And B, what can we do to make it better? I would always introduce myself the same way I did at the press conference. I'm a guy whose name nobody knows but here's my background. Strangely people almost all accepted me as a football guy. I was told we trust you; you'll get it done.

I was told here's what you need to do. You need to make tickets more available to us. We need to have better seats and customer service, and by all means we need to have better security at the stadium. At over 200 events I attended, that was an absolute consensus. I guess because my football background was so extensive and my notoriety was so limited, people just assumed this guy's a blue-collar guy who knows football. He'll get the right players.

Marv Levy's Initial Meeting With Buffalo Bills Team
Jim Kelly's arrival was part 1 of the puzzle. Part 2 really was Marv Levy. When Marv came in the morale was really, really bad. Jim was playing, but he didn't have a good relationship with

his position coach or with the head coach. The offensive line guys were really out of sorts. The defensive was not performing well. Everybody was more down in the dumps then when we were 2-14 because the players' expectations were higher. Constant harping and criticism beat down the players.

Marv came in and called the team together. He spoke for about 7 or 8 minutes. One of the things he said was, "What it takes to win is simple, but it isn't easy. We're going to do the following things. We're going to play smart football. We're not going to be dumb, and we're not going to be dirty. We're not going to beat ourselves. We're going to pay attention to detail; the devil was in the detail. We are going to expect adversity, but we are also going to expect to overcome it. No one is preordained as a loser; no franchise is preordained as a loser. Finally, we're not going to have a lot of rules. I want you to be on time, I want you to be a professional inside and outside this building, and I want you to be good citizen. Those are our rules. Now, let's take the first step. Our goal here is very simple. We're going to win the Super Bowl. We take the first step this Sunday against the Pittsburgh Steelers. Let's get ready to go beat the Steelers!"

The players stood up and applauded! Unbelievable. I have never seen it before or since. They simply stood up and applauded! It was though they had said to themselves, "Okay. We finally have the guy who can take us where we want to go." The very first time he stepped up to the podium, he had them in the palm of his hands.

January 3, 1993 Houston Oilers vs. Buffalo Bills ("The Comeback Game")
At halftime I said, "Oh boy. What a way to end. This is awful." You know, given all we'd accomplished.

In those days, I used to sit out on the photo deck, and fans sat directly in front of me, within an arms distance of me. All during the first half, the 5-7 guys in front of me were just furious, yelling, "You guys stink! This is awful! It's terrible!" They got up at halftime and walked out, as did many of the people in the stadium.

By the way, the game was not a sellout. People forget that now. We didn't even televise it in western New York because it wasn't a sellout.

After halftime, we got scored on right away and things were looking even worse. Then bingo, Kenneth Davis ran for a touchdown. Frank Reich through a touchdown pass to Don Beebe. We were still, I think, 3 scores down at that point but it was obvious we were going to onside kick. Marv got the onside kick group together on the sideline. You could see that. I turned to Bob Ferguson, our assistant general manager, and said, "You know what? If we get this onside kick, we're going to win the game."

He said, "You've lost your mind! You have finally gone over the edge." We just kind of laughed, and boom! We get the onside kick. On the very next play, Frank threw a touchdown pass to Andre Reed, and now the route is on. Houston is in a position where they are now saying to themselves, "Uh oh! We've awakened this giant and here they come!" Naturally, the fans went bonkers. Our security director, who was seated next to me, said that people were trying to get back into the stadium. Our policy was to close the gates at halftime after people left and not allow them back into the stadium for obvious reasons. You don't want people coming in without a ticket halfway through the game. He wanted to know what to do. People were trying to climb the fence! I told him to open the gates.

People came flooding back in. We scored again, and then quickly scored again to tie the game. Then here come these guys who were really letting us have it before they left the stadium, come running up, high fiving us, and going, "Wow! What a great team! This is unbelievable!" At halftime, I don't think any of us thought we had a chance except for the players and Marv.

Chances Of Another Team Playing In Four Consecutive Super Bowls

Well it's going to be awfully difficult. I think it's like Joe DiMaggio's 56 game hit streak. There may be people who come close, but it's going to be awfully difficult to match it or beat it. The rules have changed dramatically with the advent of the salary cap. Teams turnover so much, particularly teams that are fortunate enough to make the Super Bowl. They turnover so much, it's hard to have the kind of continuity that you need to go to the Super Bowl consecutively as many times as we did. Also, I think the grind of the season and the grind of going back to the Super Bowl time and time again, is really difficult. It wears on a team after a while.

Not Winning A Super Bowl

I regret it for the fans. For me, that was the most important thing. The fans who had supported us so loyally throughout that whole run, who had made the Bills story number one, 24/7 365 days a year. For us not to win a Super Bowl for them was pretty frustrating. When you are in the business you realize that the Super Bowl is just one game, it's not a 7 game series. A game can turn on luck. It can turn on a break. It can turn on anything that you, in many respects, can't control.

For example, if we had one more time out in Super Bowl XXV, Thurman Thomas probably could have run for another 15 yards, and we could have taken that time out and kicked a field goal. The results I'm sure would have been different but we didn't have that extra time out. That's the way it goes. From the standpoint of the fans, I still feel very sorry that we didn't get it for them.

Interestingly enough, what makes Buffalo so special—when I was with the Indianapolis Colts and we went to our first Super Bowl, I heard from upwards of 75 or so fans, who called or sent messages saying, "We're rooting for you. This is our Super Bowl."

Carolina Panthers Playing In NFC Championship Game In 2nd Year Of Existence

It was a unique situation with the Carolina Panthers. We were able to take advantage of the NFL rules because any veteran contracts that we had inherited through the expansion draft were simply counted dollar for dollar against the cap.

With maybe two or three exceptions, we took the lowest contracts we could in the expansion draft and left ourselves with as much salary cap room as we possible could. The first two years of the franchise's existence, we were able to sign any number of free agents who could really make a difference for us. That first year we had a 7-9 record, which was the best record of any expansion team in any sport.

We had a veteran defense with guys who really could play. Coach Dom Capers had just a phenomenal defensive mind. By the end of the first season, we were able to build a defense that was as good as any in the league.

By adding Kerry Collins, Tim Biakabutuka, and Muhsin Muhammad in the draft along with a darn good offensive line, we were able to grow the offense the second year. In addition, we had another great free agent acquisition in Wesley Walls.

We had gotten Anthony Johnson and Mark Carrier in the expansion draft. We were able to put together an outstanding team quickly. Had we run up against anybody other than Mike Holmgren and the Green Bay Packers, we might have gone to the Super Bowl. We had to go to Green Bay and play against what was a very special Green Bay team with Brett Favre and company. Green Bay went on to win the Super Bowl, but we deserved to be there. It wasn't a fluke by any means.

Joining Indianapolis Colts
Jim Irsay had taken over from his father Bob. Jim and I had worked together on the NFL Management Council. We negotiated and executed the bargaining agreements from 1989 to 1993. We'd gotten to know each other, respected each other, and became friends.

He told me if there is ever a time when I feel like I want to leave Carolina, to let him know. There'd been some changes in the management in Carolina. I just felt like maybe we'd gone as far as we could go there. The players were getting a little old and there wasn't quite the commitment I thought to rebuild the team that I thought was necessary.

Jim Irsay asked me, "How's everything going?" I said, "Well if you are interested in making a change, I might be interested in coming." He went and called Jerry Richardson and they worked out a trade for my rights. When I found out what the price was, I was shocked and chagrined. I was traded for a 3rd round draft pick. That was unbelievable. In any event it worked out and I had 14 great years in Indianapolis.

Reason Didn't Hire Marv Levy As Head Coach Of Indianapolis Colts
Marv was still coaching the Buffalo Bills and I wasn't going to disrupt that. Mr. Wilson had been too good to me and Marv had been too good to me for me to go in there and do that. That wasn't going to happen. We hired Jim Mora and subsequently, Tony Dungy, as head coaches. Tony led us to a Super Bowl victory.

Decision To Hire Tony Dungy As Head Coach Of Indianapolis Colts
It was an amazing situation. Tony Dungy and I knew each other. We'd chaired on the competition committee for 4 or 5 years before the head coaching position opened at Indianapolis. Mr. Irsay had posed a question for me. He asked, "What would happen if Tony Dungy is fired by Buccaneers?" I said, "All bets are off! Call the airport, get the plane ready, and I'll go to Florida and get him done. He's our first and only choice!"

Jim said okay, and low and behold, that's exactly what happened. I flew to Tampa and met with Tony for about six hours. Neither of us, even to this day, can believe that it was that long. Our meeting went so quickly and so swimmingly. He had to leave to fly to Carolina. He had promised Mr. Richardson that he would interview there. I asked Tony a question about how he would prepare the team and what his practice regiment and organization would be doing, going from training camp to the Super Bowl.

About 1/3 of the way through he stopped me and asked, "Have I said something funny?" I said, "No. Why?"

He said, "Well, you are smiling and nodding your head ..." I said, "Oh, I am sorry. I've heard this all before, verbatim from Marv Levy. This is all ... You are channeling him."

Then we had a little side bar discussion. Have you ever crossed paths with Marv? Have you ever been in a situation where you'd been exposed to his teachings?

He said, "No. No, I haven't. I know of him very well." Ironically enough, we tried to sign Tony in Montreal when Marv was there, but he elected to go to the Steelers. He was a quarterback in college and would have been a great Canadian quarterback but he elected to go play defensive back with the Steelers. In any event, he said, "I've never had any real up close exposure to Marv."

I said, "Well, it's just incredibly amazing that you two are so alike philosophically." I knew then and there that this was going to be a match made in heaven. We saw things so alike in terms of how you should build and run a program.

Deciding To Draft Peyton Manning
When I got to Indianapolis, I met with the scouting staff. That was in early January. They were split right down the middle 50/50. Fifty percent wanted Peyton Manning, 50% wanted Ryan Leaf. I said, "Okay. Let's go back to ground zero."

We had our film department put together every pass that both guys had thrown as college players. We had a number of people go through the films—scouts, coaches, even Bill Walsh. I asked them to take a look at it and give their opinion. Of course, I went through it on numerous occasions.

We finally reached a decision around March 1st. I would say the decision was clear among Tom Moore our offensive coordinator, Bruce Arians our quarterback coach, and me. There was aclear consensus that Peyton was the guy for a number of reasons. The conventional wisdom was that Peyton had a week arm, he wasn't very athletic, and he was "a product of the system". To this day, I don't know what that means. The opposite was true in every aspect. Peyton was, by far, the better choice. From a psychological and maturity standpoint, it wasn't even close. It was Peyton hands down.

The No Huddle Offense
It takes a special quarterback to operate it. It is very difficult to defend. It dictates to the defense. But it takes a while to learn and different quarterbacks have different personalities. Jim loved the up tempo part of it. He wanted to go, go, go. That fit his personality perfectly. Fast break football; that was Jim to a T. Jim Kelly, Frank Reich, and Ted Marchibroda had a signal system worked out. They would simply signal at one another, the play would come in, and away you go!

Peyton, when he first started with Tom Moore and Bruce Arians in the no huddle, wanted to go much more slowly because he wanted to make sure that every blitz that could possibly come at us was picked up. That was good because things had changed. Carolina and Pittsburgh came to the floor with the zone blitz. They were the two biggest proponents of it at the time. You better make sure you know who's picked up because if you don't, you are liable to get the quarterback killed. We went at a much slower tempo in the early days in Indianapolis.

When Peyton and our offensive line became comfortable with the blitz pickups, we were able to go at a much higher tempo. Peyton learned to master and control the tempo of a game like an orchestra leader. If he wanted to go fast, he would go fast. If he wanted to go slowly, he would go slowly. When we became a mature team 3 or 4 years in, we all recognized that we could control what the Patriots, among others, did to us in many ways by simply using tempo. We could wear them out. That was true with virtually every 3-4 team we played. Those big guys can't go at that tempo. They aren't conditioned to do it. Tempo became a very important thing for us, although it wasn't at the beginning.

Winning Super Bowl
I've always believed that if you get there, it is a marvelous thing. Unfortunately, the media down plays what a terrific season the Super Bowl losers had. Often the media treats that team as though they were 2-14, when in fact they've had a great season. Obviously it's great to win, but my life wasn't going to end if we didn't win it.

It's only one game and there is a lot that you cannot control or cancel. That particular game was the only foul weather game there has been in the history of the Super Bowl. Rain poured from start to finish, in Miami of all places! Not just a mist, either. It was a pouring hard rain. We were fortunate to come out on top, but that's one game and there's a lot you can't control. Having said that, there is no loss like the Super Bowl. It stays with you forever, really. You can't get it out of your system until you tick it off the next year.

Winning is obviously the opposite. You have to be careful not to let it hang on too long. We came back and had a great season the following year. It's wonderful to win, no question about it. For me, going to the White House was the most special part of it. I wouldn't trade that for anything in the world. As I said, I wasn't going to go out and run in front of traffic if we had lost the game.

Pro Football Hall of Fame Induction
I was dumbfounded. I had written a book and I was in Buffalo, of all places, promoting the book. I had just gotten back to my room. It was around three in the afternoon, when I got a call from David Baker, the president of the Hall of Fame. When the call came in on my cell phone, it was a California number. I almost just let it ring. I don't know anybody in California who would call me other than the media, and I wasn't getting those calls anymore.

I answered it and David said, "It's my honor to tell you that you've been nominated as one of the two candidates in the Senior category." He explained that I still had to be voted in. The nomination would stand alone and it would be an upward bound vote, not in competition with any players or anybody else. I didn't have a response! I was completely dumbfounded. In fact, I think I said, "Holy shit", to be very honest. David said, "There are others in the room here. This is an open line." I apologized and said, "Never in a million years did I ever think that this would come about. Never!"

I had been there for the induction of many players. And, I was fortunate to be with there with Marv for his induction. In fact, I presented Marv when he was inducted, so I knew exactly what was going to take place. It was extremely surreal. It's almost as though it's happening to someone else.

I got into this business hoping to be a small college head coach. That was the extent of my dreams, if you will. I grew up watching Frank Gifford, Charlie Conerly, and Andy Robustelli and the New York Giants. They were always my heroes, but I never thought I'd make it into the league. I mean it's always an ambition you have, but it's something that's way off in the distance. I never thought that I'd become friends with Frank Gifford and talk football with him, or get to know Don Shula or Paul Brown, or any of these giants that I had admired from afar. Many times I just thank the Lord that I've had the opportunities that I have had. It's amazing to be a part of such a good thing. I never envisioned it, that's for sure.

Bill Polian, right, poses with his bust and presenter, Hall of Fame coach Marv Levy, during inductions at the Pro Football Hall of Fame. Photograph copyright Associated Press

Chapter 82

Dan Dierdorf

College:
Michigan

Career History:
St. Louis Cardinals (1971–1983)

1996 Inductee Pro Football Hall of Fame

Hometown Canton, Ohio
I grew up about a mile from the Pro Football Hall of Fame. If you're from Canton, Ohio, your DNA is mixed with the DNA of the Pro Football Hall of Fame. Everyone in Canton is involved, in one way or another, with the Hall of Fame. I'm a little more fortunate than most to actually be a member.

Being One Of Two Hall of Famers From Canton
Alan Page is also from Canton. I went to Glenwood High School, and Alan went to Canton Central Catholic. We are both from Stark County. Canton is the county headquarters. Stark County actually has five members in the Hall of Fame. Lenny Dawson is from Alliance, which is a city that actually touches the city limits of Canton. Paul Brown is from Maslin, Ohio, which is right next door. Marion Motley, a former fullback who played for the Cleveland Browns in the '50s, is also from Stark County. We're well represented.

College Choice
I was an okay player in high school, but never really a great player. I was one of those guys that were a little late to blossom. I wasn't offered a scholarship by Woody Hayes to Ohio State. I like to say that they didn't offer me a scholarship because they offered one to a linebacker on my high school team. I don't have to make excuses to anybody in the state of Ohio as to why I went to Michigan. It was my best offer.

Playing For Bo Schembechler
I was actually recruited by Bump Elliott, the head coach at Michigan at the time. Bo Schembechler came to Michigan my junior year. I started with one coach and then I played my final two years for Bo. It was the best thing that ever happened to me. He was a huge influence in my life and I'm honored to have had that opportunity.

Transition From Coach Elliott to Coach Schembechler
The transition from Coach Elliott to Coach Schembechler was about 180 degrees. Bob was a fatherly figure. He was just a wonderful man. He is still alive, and till this day, he's just a gentleman personified. Bo was like a tornado coming right through. He came in and wanted to change the culture, and boy did he. We had guys quitting left and right. I'd never worked as hard

in my life as I did for Bo Schembechler those two years that I played for him, but he got results. He taught us that we were capable of doing much more than we ever envisioned. We are capable of pushing ourselves farther than we ever though possible. If you've never been exposed to that kind of motivation, that kind of teacher, I feel sorry for you because you learn an awful lot about yourself.

Playing Against Ohio State

When you played Ohio State you were fulfilling your mission in life. There was no other reason to be at Michigan other than to beat Ohio State. It's the same way in Columbus. When you're a part of a rivalry of that magnitude, you realize that the other games are great, but the only game that really matters is Ohio State. It would be interesting to ask a Michigan guy, "Would you rather be 11 and 1 and lose to Ohio State, or be 6 and 5 and beat Ohio State?" You'd be surprised how many guys would settle for 6 and 5. The rivalry was everything. It's fun to be apart of something like that.

Looking back, I've always taken it for granted. It's like my last name. Michigan is part of me. Every now and then I sit down and it dawns on me that, wow, I was really part of something special. Just to be able to say I played in front of all those people in Ann Arbor is special. I know what it's like to run out of that tunnel with over 100,000 people on their feet cheering. It's an experience that I can cherish my entire life.

Playing For St. Louis Cardinals

It was a little bit different culture. I lost more football games my first year in St. Louis than I'd lost in high school and college combined. It was a tough transition. I was thrilled to be in the National Football League. You don't have a say so in where you go. Some guys get drafted by Dallas and some guys don't. I was one of the don'ts. It's funny how your life works out. I've been in St. Louis ever since. It's my home.

It's kind of interesting when you're a professional football player. Somebody calls you and tells you, "You've been drafted by a team." It circles around somebody else's choice.

When I played for the Cardinals my paychecks were from the Chicago Cardinals doing business as the St. Louis Cardinals. We were still an Illinois corporation. My first couple years in the league we had training camp in Lake Forest, Illinois. We didn't go back to St. Louis until after training camp was over, six weeks later. That's how long training camp lasted back then. We were playing football in St. Louis, but in many ways there were a lot of strong Chicago ties.

The Bidwell brothers owned the team. Billy lived in St. Louis, but his older brother Stormy, lived in Winnetka, I believe. For the first twelve or thirteen years after moving to St. Louis, the club continued to have training camp in Lake Forest. Ultimately the Bears took over the training facilities at Lake Forest College and the Bears trained there until they built their own new complex.

When Billy bought out Stormy, he made the decision to no longer go back to Chicago. He kind of severed the Chicago ties, and we starting having training camp in Bloomington Normal at Illinois State.

Jackie Smith

The Cardinals had a lot of talent. I lined up next to a Hall of Famer Jackie Smith. Jimmy Hart was our quarterback. We had Terry Metcalf and Jim Otis in our backfield. We had Mel Gray, who might have been the fastest man in the National Football League, at one of our receiver spots. We had a great offensive line. In fact, we had the best offensive line in football. We were a pretty good offensive football team.

Larry Wilson

Larry Wilson and I were teammates my first two years in the league. Larry stayed with the club and became General Manager. Larry Wilson is a dear friend and has been for a long time. He was the first great free safety.

His defensive coach in St. Louis, Chuck Drulis, was still there when I first joined the club. He was the originator of the safety blitz. That wasn't a staple back then. He realized there was a tough guy in Larry Wilson. He'd bring Larry in on a safety blitz and let me tell you, a lot of quarterbacks were sorry. They weren't used to having the safety come up the middle. A lot of times he had a free run at the quarterback. The league was a little different back then. If you had a free run at the quarterback, you hit him any way, as hard as you wanted to, and just about any time you wanted to.

Cardinals Offensive Line

Conrad Dobler was a lightening rod. It seemed like I was the guy playing next to a tornado all the time. There was yelling and screaming, people cursing and what not. All of this was happening about 18 inches away from me. He was a piece of work.

We led the league in the least number of sacks allowed approximately five years in a row. Jimmy Hart enjoyed great protection and he delivered. A lot of that was to Jim's credit. He was a quick decision maker. He had a quick release and he was a rhythm quarterback. It was nice from an offensive linesman perspective, having a quarterback that you knew wasn't going to move a lot and put you in a bad position. I always liked blocking for a guy who I knew where he was going to be.

Playing Offensive Line

There is a huge difference in the offensive line positions. There is a different skill set involved in the positions. First of all, many times the centers and the guards are interchangeable because they're passing guys off from one to another. In other words, the majority of the time, if you can play one you can play the other. Playing tackle is unique. For the most part, you're out there by yourself. You're dropping and giving more ground than the guards do. It's a completely different skill set playing tackle than either center or guard.

Position Change

I started out playing guard my first couple years in the league because that's where the Cardinals had a need. Both of their starting tackles had been in place for a number of years and they didn't really need a tackle, so I started out at guard and played left and right guard. At the beginning of my third year in the league, they moved me to tackle. That's where I played the majority of my career. I moved to center my last couple of years in the league because of a pretty serious knee injury that I thought had ended my career. I wasn't capable of playing tackle anymore. I didn't have the moves necessary to play tackle the way I wanted to play it so I moved to center where I didn't have to move as much.

Toughest Defensive Lineman Faced

I played against a lot of great players. I broke in playing against guys like Bob Lilly, Deacon Jones, Willie Lanier, and Buck Buchannan—a long list of Hall of Famers. I didn't play them very often, maybe three or four times during my career. One of my really good buddies, Jackie Youngblood, was always a challenge for me. We were teammates in the College All Star Game. He was a smaller guy, and he wanted to run around me. I would have preferred if he tried to run over me, but he never obliged me in that request.

I went two whole seasons without giving up a sack. It's something I was kind of proud of. I never did a lot of pass blocking in college. We were predominately a running team. I was always a better run blocker than a pass blocker, but I worked hard at it and I got to the point where I thought I was pretty good at pass blocking.

Being Elected Into the Pro Football Hall of Fame As A Player and A Broadcaster

Winning the Pete Rozelle Award is a thrill. This award is a real treat for anybody in broadcasting, if you're fortunate enough to be chosen by the Hall. I'm one of the few people, who are in the Hall as either a player or coach and also in the Hall with the Rozelle Award. There are four of us—John Madden, Frank Gifford, Lenny Dawson, and me.

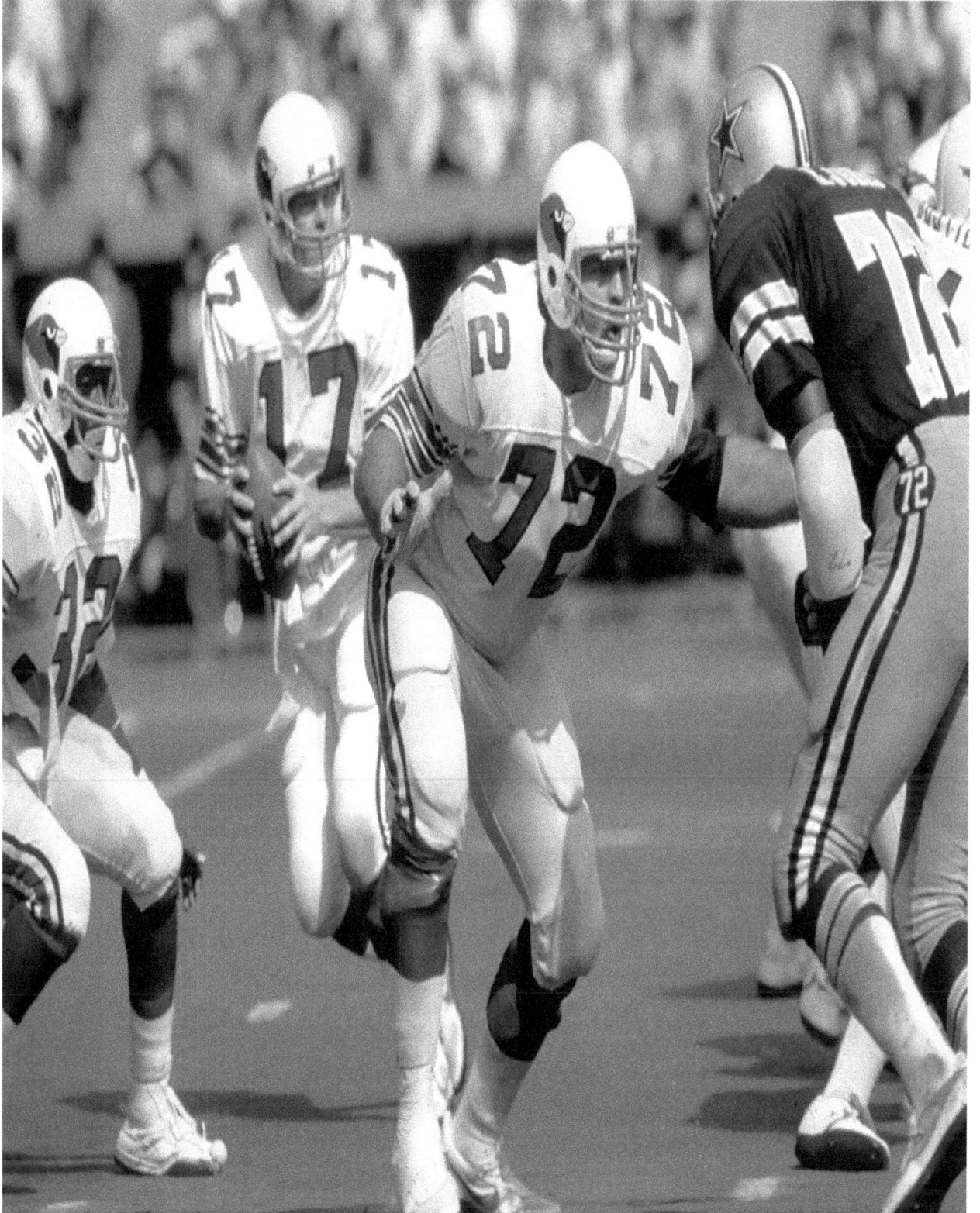

Photograph copyright Associated Press

Chapter 83

Ray Guy

College:
Southern Mississippi

Career History:

Oakland/Los Angeles Raiders (1973-1986)

2014 Inductee Pro Football Hall Of Fame

College Choice

I had an assistant coach that actually played at Southern Mississippi when Thad Vann was the head coach. One day when I was doing visits at different schools, the assistant coach asked me if I would like to visit Southern Miss. I went there one weekend and just fell in love with Southern Miss. I fell in love with the program, the campus and everything about it. It wasn't a hard choice because I'd get to come right in and play freshman football. I was also going to play baseball, so it wasn't a hard choice.

It was kind of a small school at that time, probably 7,000, maybe 8,000 students. They were on a mission you might say, to rebuild and make the school and its program bigger and better. I felt like I could be a part of that. I had no regrets going to Southern. In fact, I'm still here working. I work at the University with the Athletic Department and the Alumni Association, giving back and trying to help increase enrollment and make it bigger and better than it is now. I love every minute of it.

Being Drafted By The Cincinnati Reds

It might sound a little awkward compared to what the younger generation is doing now. Today athletes start at a young age. They kind of train themselves or are being trained to reach that higher level in athletics. Their goal is to one day become professional athletes, which is a very good way to look at things. It gives them something to work for. I wasn't really that way. I enjoyed playing many different sports. I didn't weigh one against the other or compare one to the other. I just took what came and went with it.

When I was in high school, the Reds came to me. They offered me money to play baseball for them in the summer, and pay for me go to school. I had already signed a scholarship with Southern. Once I make a decision and tell somebody I'm going to do something, I do it because that's the way I was raised.

If you tell somebody that you're going to do something, don't back out. You go ahead and fulfill that obligation. I went to Southern and I was fortunate to play baseball and football. I still got drafted in college by major league baseball teams. I made the choice to go with the Raiders because I thought I got a good deal out of it and I've never looked back. I mean, I always think about what it might have been if I'd have chosen the baseball route, but I don't think there'd have been any difference. I'd have given it my all in baseball just like I did in football.

Southern was a small school and they didn't have a big budget. In fact, when they started recruiting, many of the football coaches actually had to pay a lot of expenses out of their own pocket. Coach P.W. Underwood took over the year I came in and organized the Big Goal Club. It's a booster club that raises money to help the coaches go out and recruit players, and then bring them to Southern.

I don't think there were any players that we had strictly on baseball scholarships. If there were, I didn't know about it. It seemed every year Coach Taylor, who was the baseball coach then, would actually have tryouts for players. He'd pick his team from that group of kids. We were a scrappy little bunch, I can tell you that. I don't think there was really anybody on a full scholarship in baseball.

Better Baseball Or Football Player
I could throw the ball. I was averaging 98 miles an hour and had really good control. I knew exactly where the ball was going instead of just roaring back and letting it go. I could position that ball where I wanted to. My key role at Southern in football was starting free safety.

That's what I played. I was able to do all the kicking phases, so I just continued with that. I never set out to be just a punter.

In 1973, the Raiders drafted me strictly as a punter. I knew my job was kicking, but I was still prepared to do other things during the game. I was more involved because I wound up being the third string quarterback with the Raiders. I got involved in practice. I wanted to be involved so I knew what was going on in a game situation. I wanted to know what we were trying to do against certain teams, and being involved in practice kept me in the game.

I think my active participation made me more accepted by the team veterans. I guess they looked at me as more than just a punter. I was an actual player.

I wanted to get my head in the game. That stems from playing defense. Your body's trained. It's hard to break something that you have been doing for so many years. I wouldn't shy away getting in there and busting somebody. Believe me, it made me mad if somebody even got a yard return on me. Hell, I'd do the same thing again if I were young enough. I'd show these young ones how to do something.

Starting Out As Punter and Placekicker
It was just something I did growing up as a young kid, at about 6 years old. I'd go out in the backyard and play with different balls, depending on what sport was in season. I didn't want to stay in the house; I still don't. I'd rather be outside doing something constructive. I'd just go out, a lot of times by myself, and punt in the fields behind the house. I would break windows and do all that good stuff that kids do before getting your butt tore up when your dad got home.

I give all the credit to the good Lord for my ability to do anything and do it well. I guess you'd say I had a natural ability to understand the mechanics behind what I was trying to do. I understood how to take those mechanics and work for me. It's like playing golf. I just picked up a set of golf clubs and started playing. I finally got it down to a scratch but realized I wasn't going to make a living playing golf. I might as well put the clubs away. I had accomplished what I was after.

The good Lord has always been good to me. Even though this old body doesn't move fast anymore and it takes a lot more Bengay at nighttime, it works.

Being Drafted In the First Round
I really don't think any owner beside Al Davis would have drafted me in the first round. I think Al understood the importance of the kicking game.

Looking back, the Raiders always had great special teams. They put a lot of emphasis on that because a game is determined on the amount of field positions you gain during the course of the 60 minutes. Whether it's running the ball back on a kick off or a punt, or the punter making a long directional-type kick to gain some field position back, it all goes hand in hand.

Over the years, I've heard John Madden mention me in interviews. He has said that when the Raiders drafted me, it was the first time he was sitting in a draft where everybody agreed on one thing—to draft me. I think John understood the importance of kicking too.

Once I joined the Raiders in spring training camp and started kicking the ball, John told one of the managers, Bobby Romanski, to get him a stopwatch. Romanski brought him one that was still in the package.

Apparently, they'd never used it before. John opened the package and asked, "How do you work this damn thing?" Maybe that was the first time he used one.

I guess John came to realize, hey look, we've got us a weapon here. We took a lot of pride in playing special teams. I took a lot of pride in it, as did the guys who were protecting me and covering after the ball was punted. That's why we were so successful all those years. We made a lot of playoff games and won a lot of championships and Super Bowls. The special teams of the Raiders were dominating too. It made a big difference.

Being Named MVP Of College All Star Game
To me, everybody is an MVP regardless of their position and the game plan. The kickers and the punters are MVPs too, but they just don't get recognized a lot. I was very proud of being named MVP, but I was also proud of the class of 1973 that came out of that game. We had Burt Jones and John Hannah. I think three quarters of the guys on that all-star team are in the Hall of Fame, if I'm not mistaken. We had a great class that year and we gave the Dolphins fits in the game. The Dolphins only won 6-3. That tells you something about the class of 1973.

Hang Time On Punts

Hang time was natural with the kicks, but with each punt I found ways to make the hang time longer. I knew I could probably get it a little bit higher and maybe a little bit longer. I'd focus on the position of the ball and my foot to make it feel better. That gave me a more solid impact. I learned there was very little I could change with each punt to make it better. The kind of distance and hang time I had at the time was a just natural.

I think one of the things that helped me so much was my flexibility. That flexibility helped me achieve the extension I needed to get my leg far above my head after each punt. I had people wanting to know if I took ballet. Hell, I didn't take ballet. You weren't going to catch me in a tutu. I was just fortunate to be very flexible. It's just one of the gifts that the good Lord gave me.

Hitting Video Screen During 1976 Pro Bowl At Louisiana Superdome

I hadn't even thought about hitting the screen until I walked out on the field. I knew I could hit it. During the game I called whatever play we were going to do; which way I was going to punt it. My ten teammates turned and walked toward the line of scrimmage. I got 15 yards from the line of scrimmage, which happened to be on the 2-yard line, and I stood there waiting. Everybody was set for the snap. I just looked up and thought to myself, I'm at the right angle; I'm going to try to hit the video screen. I didn't even tell the guys. Jim Tunney, the Head of Referees for many years, was the referee. He was standing there and I heard him say, "Ray, you're going to try this aren't you?" I said, "Yup."

Of course, trying and making it happen are two different things. In that situation you've got to have everything just working together. You've got to keep yourself under control with your steps, and you've got to make good solid contact with your foot. When I hit it I knew I hit it good, believe me. The ball released from my foot and took off. I always followed it off my foot up to the height of it. I just kept watching and that ball hadn't even peaked yet, it was still climbing. I said, "Uh oh, here we go." Sure enough the ball hit the top edge of the screen and fell right down so we had to come back and punt again.

I don't think the players were very happy because the majority of the cover team was made up of guys who never played punt coverage. Here's the funny thing, the second punt almost hit the screen again. If I had hit it again, I would have just left the Superdome. I would have gone to the locker room and got dressed.

The Pro Bowl is a fun game. The rules are a little bit different. I had the opportunity to try that without technically getting the ball blocked, because that's one thing they couldn't do. The only time they could really hit me was when I actually fumbled the ball or had a bad snap. I was able to take my time and hit. I said, "Well, let's go for it and see if we can do it."

The first thing people typically ask me is, "Did you hit the roof?" I say, "No, I didn't hit the roof. This isn't a fishing story." You know how fishing stories go, you catch a little bitty minnow and 25 years later it's a whale. Yeah, I hit the thing, but mom said never to play inside a house anyway.

Al Davis

You hear so much about people, but you can't really judge them until you've been around them, conversed with them, and watched them in certain situations. You have to spend time with someone to really know what that person is like on the inside. Al Davis was a businessman. He was a very smart man. He knew exactly what he wanted to do and he knew how to go about doing it. If he didn't, he wouldn't have been so successful all those years.

It's like anybody that starts from scratch and goes on to create a dynasty. Whether it's in sports or in a corporate environment, there are going to be things that you do that technically may not look right, but it usually works out. I'm sure some of the players did not always see eye-to-eye with him. In those days, if you had a gripe with the coaches or the owner or anyone else, it was pretty much behind closed doors. It wasn't out in the open.

When players wanted to renegotiate contracts, nobody else really knew what was going on. We weren't that concerned with each other's salary. All we wanted to do was play. We wanted to go practice, play the game, and win. We all stuck together. There was no inner distinction between the players. We were just like big families. We backed each other up, kind of like brothers. We got into little squabbles like families do, but we got over it. We did what we had to do to work it out, brushed each other off, and went down to the pub for a beer. That's just the way we were.

Reason For So Few Blocked Punts

I credit it to the center and the line up front because you've got to have protection up there. You've got to have guys that are dedicated and really want to block the opposing team because you know they're going to try to block it. The center is 50% of a punt or a kick. I was fortunate enough starting in high school, then in college, and in my career in the pros, to have great centers. I could probably count on one hand all the bad snaps I had. You're going to have bad snaps because people are going to make mistakes. But, you don't want them to happen a lot. I never had to worry about where the ball was going, whether it was going to my right or my left, or wherever it went on the field.

When we practiced the center always asked, "Where do you want it?" I'd tell them where I wanted the ball and very rarely would it be offline. My job was a lot easier because I didn't have to worry about it. What I had to worry about was trying to generate too much power into the ball, which in turn makes the steps that I take a little bit longer than I should take. With that kind of security up front, knowing that the ball is going to be where I want it, I didn't have to rush it. I didn't have to overpower it. I just did my thing and kicked it under 2 seconds. That's fast enough from the time it was snapped to the time it left my foot.

There were times there was a missed block, a missed assignment, or something went wrong up front. I don't hold any grudges against anyone I know. Mistakes happen because we're human. I made a lot of mistakes, but I took the mistakes and analyzed what went wrong and I corrected it, which in turn made me better.

Changing Punting Scheme Toward End Of Career

Toward the end of my career, the return guys were getting faster and the return schemes were getting better so I had to come up with another scheme. I reassessed why I wanted to kick the ball down the middle of the field as far as I could, all of the time. That was only going to hurt me and hurt the team in general. I changed by not punting down the middle of the field anymore. I started punting directionally, whether it was punting out of bounds inside the 20, or punting it out of bounds before the 20. It just depended on where I was on the field. I also hung the ball between the numbers on the sidelines to eliminate a lot of the return area for the return guy.

It got to be a strategy for me and it got to be very important to my team, They knew when I told them where I was going to punt, they didn't have to worry about chasing the ball all over the field once they got down there. They knew the ball was going to be in that position or in the area I told them. It made their job a lot easier. When you've got to change, you've got to change. That's just the way it is. You learn to adapt to the changes in football.

Waiting 22 Years To Be Elected Into Pro Football Hall Of Fame
It was very hard all those years. There are guys out there who have waited longer than I did. You know, some of them need to be into the Hall of Fame. It's tough. After being passed over a few times, you realize that's how it works sometimes, and you learn to accept it. You just wait until the next year and see what happens. Of course, the more you wait and the more it does not happen, the more frustrating it gets. But you have to realize that it's not the end of the world. I would have liked for it to happen the first time around, but who wouldn't? Sometimes those things don't happen.

As the saying goes, good things are worth waiting for. You just hope that you're still around when it does happen. All of the finalists had to be in their hotel room before 5:00 p.m. on the Saturday before the Super Bowl, and wait for the announcement of that year's enshrinees. We were told we would get the announcement call at 5:30 p.m. We were sitting there and it was 5:35 p.m., then 5:40 p.m. I was thinking, well, maybe not this year but at 5:42 p.m., the phone rang.

I almost didn't answer it. The previous September, Joe Boykin of the Veterans Committee for the Hall of Fame said he would be the one calling me if I got in. I put his number in my cell phone, which is a 330 number, the area code for Canton.

I took a deep breath and said, "Well, maybe it's not going to happen this year." I looked down at the phone and the area code was 714, a California area code. Now I'm thinking, it's probably a reporter. After the third ring, I reached down and picked it up.

It was Dave Baker, who is now the president of the Hall of Fame. He said, "Ray? I'm Dave Baker, President of the Hall of Fame. I personally wanted to make this call to you and let you know that you are now a member of the Class of 2014." I said, "Dave, you're kidding me aren't you?" I asked him three times before it hit me. You wait all these years and when the phone call comes and you don't know whether to really accept it or not.

My legs got weak and I just kind of sat back in the chair, trying to let it soak in. It took about a week to a week and a half before it really soaked in. It was after I got back home. Now it's a reality. I'm in there. It's hard to explain how it feels being placed in the Hall of Fame beside all of the other football legends. That's the final game. There are no more records to set. There are no more games, championships, or Super Bowls to win. The Hall of Fame is where we sit forever. I am proud to be part of that.

When I got back to Southern Miss, I spoke to some fans at a Meet and Greet held during halftime of a basketball game. I told them, as I tell everybody I talk to, even though my name will be enshrined in the Hall of Fame, this is for all of you. You are the ones who stood behind me. My supporters and friends kept the push going to get me in. I said, "It's for you, it's technically mine but it's not mine. It's ours."

I'm really proud to be the first one from Southern Miss to go into the Hall Of Fame. I bleed black and gold, black and silver. I'm going to help Southern Miss. It's going to be a great boost to Southern Miss from the standpoint of recognition too.

Brett Favre
I was a player at Southern Miss before Brett Favre played there. I taught Brett everything he needed for three years. I was a volunteer coach at Southern Miss Brett's last years there. I knew then what everybody knows now—how great he was going to be and how much of a competitor he is. But, I would never let him know that. He always wanted to wear my Super Bowl ring and I said, "Well, Brett, what do you want it for? He said, "Well, me and a couple of the guys we're going down to such and such a place." I said, "You're not going with my ring, and you're not taking my 4x4 either."

He was a great kid; still is. I don't see him very often around here. He's kind of like me. He does his thing and stays on the west side of town, and I'm on my south side of town. We run into each other once in a while but I don't bother him. I don't really want to bother him. He's been there, he's done that, and now it's time for him to sit back and relax and enjoy life. That's what I do. I want to do what I want to do. Some of the things that I haven't done I want to do now. I'm just being myself.

Raiders Who Should Be In the Hall Of Fame
One of the objectives now is to start campaigning for Tom Flores and a bunch of other Raiders that need to be in the Hall Of Fame. We've got Cliff Branch, Jim Plunkett, and a ton of deserving Raiders.

Tom Flores is great and he should be in there. He was very intelligent. He was John Madden's offensive coordinator. He had been around a while then he got the opportunity to step forward and be the Head Coach of the Raiders. I knew he was going to be a successful coach. Just the way he was with the players; that was the key to it. He had the player-coach relationship just like John had. There was no changing. We didn't have to change anything. We just kept the same flow going.

He was a brilliant offensive coach and he was a brilliant head coach. He knew how to handle the players without getting upset and screaming. He just talked about the different problems, what we needed to do, and how we needed to handle things. Once we came to an agreement then we just left it alone and went on. We're going to have a big campaign for a lot of those guys.

1984 Game Against Chicago Bears
Jim Plunkett was on injured reserve. Marc Wilson was our starting quarterback and got hurt.
Then we had to bring in Dave Humm, who we drafted years before out of Nebraska. Of course
they had me. That was a very brutal and a bloody game because Jim McMahon got hurt. Shoot,
we were falling on both sides of the ball like flies. It looked like the MASH unit. They were
taking the army cot out there and carrying players off the field. Dave Humm got knocked out.
Marc was already in the locker room because [I think] he had hurt his thumb or something on the
helmet of somebody. Head Coach Tom Flores, already had me get ready. We were discussing
what play to call, and of course, Marc came back out. I had one foot on and one foot off; you
know what I'm saying?

That defense made no difference to me. I'd have given it my best. Heck, I might have got
knocked out too who knows. We had other objectives to worry about then. We were going to roll
that pocket, man, and give me time to throw that ball.

Stickum
It wasn't only Lester Hayes using stickum. Fred Biletnikoff used it too. Mark van Eeghen was
the worst, in my opinion. After running the ball, the ball would still be stuck to his chest it had so
much Stickum on it.

They took lighter fluid and washed the ball down after every play because they had so much pine
tar on it. Every once in a while they would miss a spot and for of my fingers would always touch
that spot when I got ready to release the ball. One day I said, "Mark, would you get away from
me? Go on down to the other end where you belong. That's where the running backs are. Let me
stay up here by myself, man." It's like the wind blowing pollen; that stuff gets blown all over
you.

It didn't bother me that much. That's what they wanted to do, and I let them do it. Lester did
kind of abuse it a little bit, though. It looked like he was having some kind of seizure when it was
dripping out from under his helmet. Freddy used a whole jar of that pine tar stuff before every
game. No wonder they could catch the balls.

Faking A Punt
We always had an audible to fake a punt if the opportunity was there, by the look of the defense.
They would always say on the sideline when we went out, just be alert. What that means is if the
return team had a certain look with a certain player somewhere then the option would be there.
We ran a couple. We ran a couple and threw a couple. You don't want to do it too much because
it becomes too obvious. Teams look at those films and they say wait a minute now, they don't
normally do this but there's a chance there might.

One year, I think it was a Monday night football game against Seattle at the Kingdome; the
Seattle end guy was real quick off the corner. He had just come off the corner and just laid
himself out trying to block the punt.

The ball was somewhere around midfield and Tom Flores said, "Look, if he's sitting out there
and you see that, go ahead and catch the ball, and go through your routine and let him lay out." I

said, "Okay." Man, I was excited. I was ready to go. Sure enough, I look over there pre-snap and he had his weight forward on his down hand, which told me he's coming. The ball was snapped and I took my time a little bit. I took about a step forward, and sure enough he laid out trying to block it and I pulled it back in. Hey, I made 25 yards on that run. I'd have still been running if the edge of the field hadn't got so close to me.

Photograph copyright Associated Press

Chapter 84

Jack Youngblood

College:
Florida

Career History:
Los Angeles Rams (1971–1984)

2001 Inductee Pro Football Hall Of Fame

College Choice:
I had only one opportunity to go and play college football. Florida State was 25 to 28 miles from my backdoor, and they had no interest in me. In fact, Bill Parcells was scouting for Florida State at that time and made a stop at my high school. He told my coach, "That kid will never play college football."

We won the Class B state championship. We were cheering and carrying on, celebrating on the field, when a gentleman grabbed me by the elbow. I turned and looked at him not knowing who in the world he was. He said, "How would you like to play football for the University of Florida?" I said, "Let me think about it. Yes sir." It didn't take me long to figure out that might be my only opportunity to play college football.

I was a center and middle linebacker in high school. During the first game of my senior year, I think I had 45 yards in holding penalties in the first half. That's the last time I touched a football on the offensive side.

Florida State University was in my backyard, so I kind of followed them and knew what was going on. I didn't follow Florida when I was in high school that much. I knew that they had an historic program down there, the oldest program in the state. I was thinking that maybe I would get the opportunity to stay at home and play in Tallahassee for Florida State. Anytime Bill Parcells and I run into each other at social events, he tells the story about not recommending me as a player for Florida State.

Position Change In College
Once I got to Florida they looked at me as this 6'4", 205-pound kid and said, "He's got some room to grow. We got an All-American middle linebacker we just signed in Mike Kelley. Let's see if we can make him into a defensive lineman."

It hurt my feelings at first because I thought that I was going to be the next great middle linebacker for the University of Florida. I loved to play, loved to control the game, and all of the signals. Then you become one of the big and ugly and you've got to put your hand on the ground and get into the real mix of it in the pit. I walked around with a fat lip for about two or three weeks. I realized that if I was going to have the opportunity to play, I needed to make the most of it.

College Coaches
I had Doug Dickey as coach for one year, my senior year. In 1969, we went to the Gator Bowl and beat Tennessee. Doug became our head coach and coach Ray Graves was just the fulltime athletic director at that point.

It was a change that somewhat upset the applecart a little bit for the football team. We didn't quite understand the change because we loved coach Graves. He was like a father to us. I mean we really did love him. Then Doug came in with a different philosophy. At first he was not nearly as personable. It seemed like he didn't want relationships with the players. I don't know why he didn't come in and embrace us, especially the seniors who were going to be the foundation of his football team.

Teammates John Reaves and Carlos Alvarez
They were superstars my junior year. We got to practice against them and you could see that we had some talent there. We had talent at quarterback, wide receiver, and running back, all sophomores.

There were a couple offensive linemen who were pretty good too. We could see that we had some talent to work with.

NFL Draft
I think it seemed as though there was some divine intervention going on. In 1971, the draft wasn't publicized like it is today. I didn't know that I was going to be drafted in the first round. My line coach, Jack Thompson, told me that I might get drafted in the 10th - 12th round. I think there were 16 or 17 rounds back then. He said, "You'll probably have the opportunity to go to summer camp with a team."

Draft day came and I wasn't expecting anything. In fact, I had already been to Georgia and accepted a job at a bank. I was preparing to move on to my next job after graduation in June. Low and behold, the Teletype started going off and I saw Jim Plunkett, Dan Pastorini, John Riggins, and all those boys come off with the first 10 or 12 picks. I was sitting and all of a sudden one of the boys at the newspaper said, "There's a phone call for you." I said, "Who in the world is calling me down here?" He said, "It's the Los Angeles Rams." All I could think was, "What?"

I have a series of pictures of that moment where I have my hand over the receiver. I was asking the people I was with, "Who is the coach?" I had no idea who the man calling me from Los Angeles was on the other line. In 1970, we didn't get to see much Rams football in Gainesville.

Tommy Prothro, the Rams coach said, "Youngblood, we're going to draft you." I was thinking to myself, thank you very much coach. As I was talking to Tommy on the phone, I saw on the Teletype, "First round, 20th pick, University of Florida, Jack Youngblood." The words over the telephone didn't seem real. Seeing it in print, you think oh my goodness. There was a whole different world I was about to step into.

I had no idea what it would be like. I had heard about the Fearsome Foursome, so I started doing some reading about the guys. I saw stuff about Deacon Jones and Merlin Olsen. Rosey Grier and Lamar Lundy had already moved on. Coy Bacon was there along with two or three different right tackles. I thought I was a left defensive end, and I wanted to know who was in that position ahead of me. I discovered it was Deacon Jones. I didn't think I'd make the football team. In fact, I thought it might be a short trip. I kept my contacts with the bank because I did not know how long me I'd be with the Rams. Fortunately, I got there and by the grace of God, both Merlin and Deacon put their arms around me during training camp and said, "Son, you can play. We're going to teach you how to play our style," and they did.

I was playing behind Deacon that first year. He got injured and I had to fill his shoes. Not only did I have to fill the shoes of Deacon, I also had a responsibility to Merlin. I was playing with two of the best that ever played the game, and I had a responsibility to them to play up to that level. Certainly I didn't play up to that level, but I held my own and didn't hurt the football team.

Rams Trade Deacon Jones
During the offseason before my second year, I was in Orlando with my family. We took a trip to Disney World. We were watching the news in our room when we heard that Deacon Jones was traded from the Los Angeles Rams to the San Diego Chargers.

I thought did I just hear that right? I said, "Whoa, wait a minute here. Now what?" I was on the phone for the next couple of days trying to figure out what was going on, and what position I'd be playing. Tommy Prothro tried his best not to let me be the left defensive end. He tried everything. For whatever reason he just did not like me.

Deacon Jones Head Slap
Deacon Jones taught me the head slap. We used it for another four or five years, I think. Everybody thinks that's a malicious act, but it's not. It's not intended to hurt anyone. It's intended to turn the opponents head. It makes his eyes blink so he can't see you. He can't react to you at that moment. You make your move when he's got his head turned, or you made him blink. Actually, you could fake it and get the same effect. The offensive linemen hated it. They would come out almost in a boxing stance so they could block your left hook. It was funny. I got cussed at several times. Offensive linemen did not like that little maneuver.

Acting Career
I tried a little bit of acting. I did some cameos during the off seasons. I was on television a couple of times. When I retired, I got a call from Billy Friedkin. He wanted me to be a character in his TV movies.

I did two movies, one that spring and the other the next spring. I didn't like the undisciplined part of it. They're never on time. I know you have to practice and rehearse like in sports, but the timing of the things took so long. It was never sharp and to the minute. Coach Chuck Knox used to say, "You're on my time. When I say 8:00, I mean 7:55. Don't be late for anything." That's not the nature of show business.

Freddie Dryer and Merlin Olsen were natural at it. I wasn't a natural. Freddie actually went to acting classes during the season. He was looking forward to being an actor, as was Merlin. Merlin was a natural as a commentator for the ballgames, and that turned into acting as Father Murphy and on Little House on the Prairie.

Playing With A Broken Leg
It's not that I don't like the fact I did this, it just seems like people always go back to the fact that I suffered through the pain to compete and contribute to my football team. That's what it was all about. It wasn't because I was this big, ugly, mean, tough character. I wanted to play and if I could, I was going to contribute to the football team. The coaches trusted me enough that I would not go out on that football field and be a detriment to the team. If I couldn't play and I didn't play up to my level, I was probably 20% off. To this day, I still think that maybe if circumstances had been different, we might have won Super Bowl XIV.

Adjustment From 4-3 To 3-4 Defense
I hated it. It was absolutely not one of my skills. I played at 250 pounds. You play the 3-4 straight up the field. You play the 4-3 from an angle. You take advantage of position in the 4-3; you take away the running game and the vertical running game.

In the 3-4 all you're doing is mass on mass. You're pushing an offensive lineman who's trying to push you. You're trying to push him backward and he's trying to push you backward. That's not the philosophy of the 4-3. I couldn't play the 3-4. I felt it was the wrong concept, but I wasn't the coach then.

To this day, every time I see former Rams Head Coach John Robinson I say, "You're the reason I didn't play three more years." I couldn't play the 3-4.

Decision To Retire
I think that after you've had the success that I was fortunate enough to have, deciding to retire is as big of a decision as deciding to get married. You have a relationship with your career and what you've established. The reward is being successful, being good, and being able to work at your craft. The decision to retire was a huge, huge one.

What really drove me was that I knew I had a job. There was no question that I was going to work in the front office. I had blown out L5-S1 in my back in the Tampa Bay game the year before. I had trained the entire offseason to see if I could come back from the injury. I came back and was fine.

In my mind, I question whether I could play at the level that I wanted from a physical perspective, for the full season. I did not want to play and then five games into the season, injure my back and get put on injured reserve. If I was going to play, I was going to play from game one to game sixteen, and then into the playoffs.

I did not want to go into the season thinking that something may go wrong some place along the way, although that's the mindset you start with every year. After 14 seasons, you realistically wonder if you can play the 3-4 defense being 34-years-old, the same way you know that you can play the 4-3. That is why I had to make the decision, and it was a tough one.

Best Players
One of the best players I've ever seen play was my teammate, Nolan Cromwell. He was one of the most athletic players who ever stepped on the field. Unfortunately, he got hurt too. He blew out his knee.

In today's game, Adrian Peterson is a pretty good football player. Some of these big, tall receivers are fantastic athletes. There's no question about that. I enjoy watching them. I enjoy watching not so much what they're doing, but how they do it. Adrian Peterson is so smooth. He's going in one direction, and the next minute he's turned 90 degrees, and going in a different direction.

It was a pleasure sitting on the sideline watching Eric Dickerson play too. He was one of those players that didn't look like he was going as fast as he was. He loved to touch the football. I like to see a player who wants to play, and be on the field, a guy who doesn't want to come off the field.

One time the coach sent somebody out there to replace Eric, and I saw Eric wave him off. He wanted to touch the football. That's the difference with the game today. I believe there are a lot of players who don't have that attitude.

Toughest Offensive Lineman Faced
There are three of them—Dan Dierdorf, Ron Yary, and Rayfield Wright. They're all in the Hall with me. I knew they were going to bring out the best in me because I was playing against the best. Gene Washington is another one I remember. He has not gotten the recognition I believe he should have. He was a nightmare for me. He just wouldn't go away. He was a shadow and he was a big shadow at that.

Waiting To Get Inducted Into Pro Football Hall Of Fame
I was the Susan Lucci of pro football. I kept getting nominated but never elected. I was nominated ten times. There was nothing I could do about it. All I could do was hope that at some point, the voters would recognize that I had a career that qualified for the Pro Football Hall Of Fame.

When I got elected into the Hall Of fame, it was one of those surreal moments. I thought, really, after all this time? Now? The monkey is off my back. It was a shining moment.

Georgia Frontiere
The players all had to sit back for a while and see how much influence Georgia Frontiere was going to have on the management side following her husband's death. We didn't know if she going to try and follow Carroll Rosenbloom's way. Carroll loved us. He was at practice every chance he had. He'd fly his helicopter down and land it on the field.

We didn't know what kind of influence she would have on the team, or if she possessed the same desire he had, to be around us. It would have been difficult to have her in the locker room. We didn't know how that was going to work. We had to wait and see.

She loved us. She did not surround herself with people that really wanted to win. The key to success in any endeavor is having people who are smarter than you, around you.

I wasn't convinced that those who were giving her advice really wanted to win. They wanted to continue to be a valuable franchise but there's a difference in that and really having a drive to win a championship.

University Of Florida & Gatorade

The Florida players were the guinea pigs. The first Gatorade was horrible. One of the inventors, Dr. Robert Cade, used to stir it up in a steel washtub.

We were practicing and it was hot as blue blazes, as it often gets in Gainesville. We came off the field and Mike Kelly, our middle linebacker, reached down and grabbed a can out of the ice. He threw it back and fainted. He just went down.

We were all looking and thinking, "Damn. I'm not drinking one of those." I don't think it was the Gatorade as much as it was the cold. I think the cold got him. We were the guinea pigs for it. It changed the whole concept of training, how to hydrate the body, and what it takes to hydrate the body. There was real science behind it.

In my high school days, it's a wonder half of us didn't die. I mean we were literally taking salt tablets. Then for the discipline part of it, we couldn't have water more than twice during practice. That's how we were conditioned. We adapted, but looking back, it could have been tragic.

Favorite Play

There was one play in Gainesville. We're playing Georgia and the game was close. They were driving the football on us. They were inside our 10-yard line. I literally remember saying we've got to take the football away from them. They ran a running play right at me and a guy got both hands around the ball. I literally reached in and snatched the ball out of his hands. That turned the ballgame around and we beat Georgia. That's one play that stands out.

Another time, I intercepted Jimmy Hart's outlet pass. It happened in the 1975 Divisional Playoff Game. I went 45 yards and scored. I knew I could run that far and I knew that I was not going to get caught by Dan Dierdorf or Jimmy Hart. I would have never lived that down. That was a good moment.

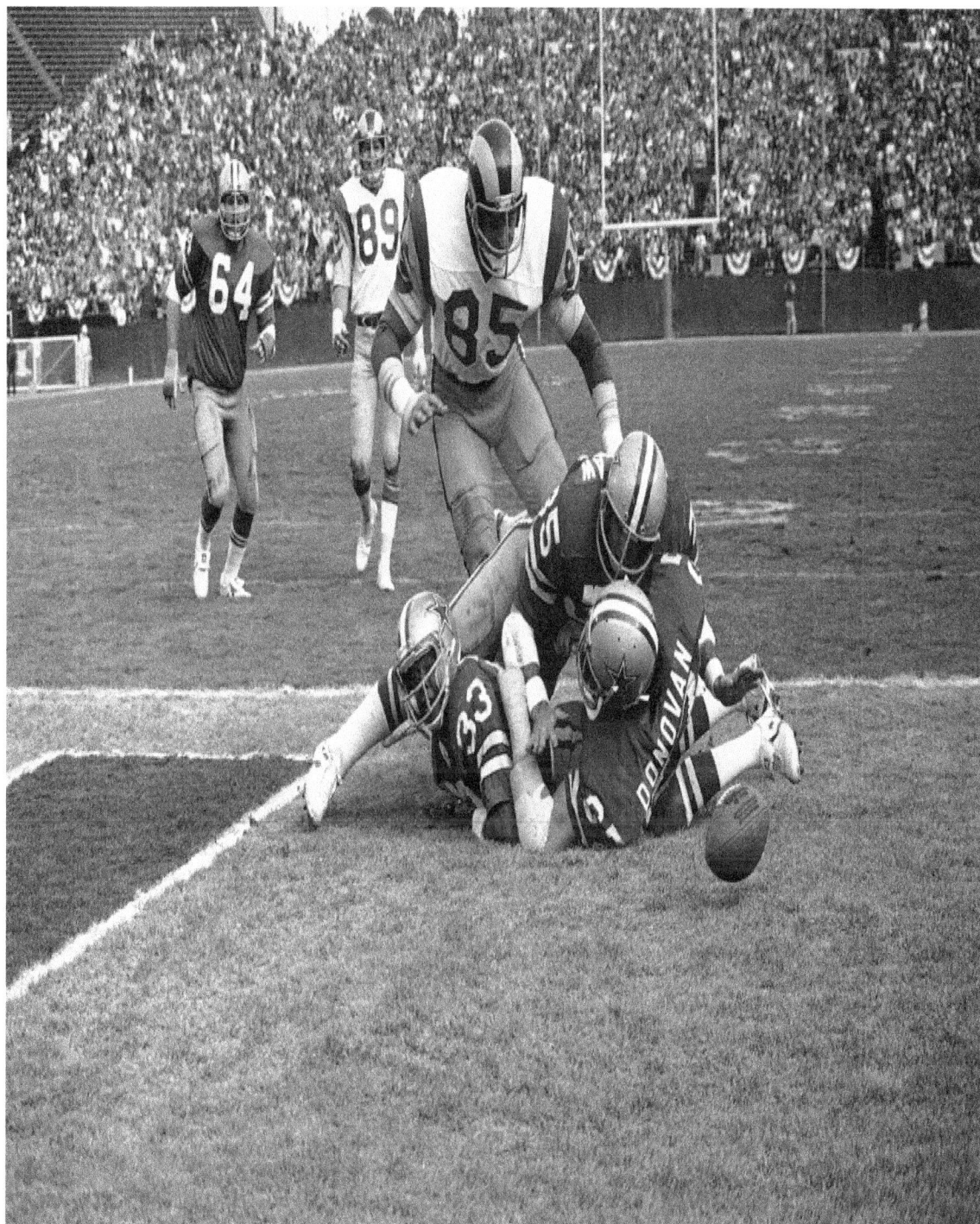

Los Angeles Ram Jack Youngblood recovering the Dallas Cowboys fumble in the NFC championship game in Los Angeles on Sunday, Jan. 7, 1979. Tony Dorsett and Pat Donovan of the Cowboys couldn't get their hands on the loose ball. Photograph copyright Associated Press

Chapter 85

Franco Harris

College: Penn State Career History: Pittsburgh Steelers (1972–1983) Seattle Seahawks (1984) 1990 Inductee Pro Football Hall Of Fame

College Choice

When I was being recruited, I visited ten colleges. I visited Notre Dame, Ohio State, Michigan, Syracuse, Pittsburgh, and Cornell. All of them were good schools, but in the end I had to make a decision. It was a tough decision, and went with my gut. In the end, my gut told me Penn State, and boy did that gut feeling work out well.

A lot of times that's what you have to go by. We really weren't a college family. My mother and father didn't go to college; none of my relatives went to college. There was pressure, but as I mentioned, my gut said Penn State and my gut was right.

Joe Paterno

Joe Paterno was out on that field everyday. If you were on the other side of the field running a play, all of a sudden you would hear from way across the field, "Hey Harris, what are ..." You know what I mean. You wouldn't even think that he'd be watching you. You'd think wow, how did he see that? He was really aware of what was happening on the football field. He went on to build great programs there, and have one of the highest graduation rates for football players in the country. It was just an incredible experience.

Lydell Mitchell

With Lydell Mitchell and me in the backfield at Penn State, there was a great balance. We both had a lot of opportunity to show our talents and to help the team. There really wasn't a competition where I wanted it more than him or he wanted it more than me. We ran in spurts of "Hey, who was doing well?" Our senior year, Lydell had a phenomenal season. I believe he scored 26 touchdowns and set a new NCAA record. I believe he held that record until Barry Sanders broke it.

My sophomore year, I had a great year. We complemented each other very well, because I was in the fullback position and he was in the halfback position. It worked so well that both of us were drafted into the NFL the same year.

Joe Paterno's History Of Wanting Recruits To Change Their Positions Like Tony Dorsett

Joe Paterno didn't ask me to change positions from high school to college. I know you hear many stories about that happening with Joe Paterno. Joe Paterno wanted to make Jim Kellya linebacker. In the end, I like it when things work out well for people. As we know, Tony Dorsett ended up going to University of Pittsburgh and being an All-American, Heisman Trophy winner, and Pro Football Hall of Famer.

Look at Jim Kelly. They wanted to make him a linebacker, now he's in the Pro Football Hall of Fame. I'm glad those guys made the decision to say, "Hey, you know what? I want to stick with my position," and I think that worked out well for both. I have to say there were many times when the Penn State staff would think that a player would be better at a certain position, and they would make that switch. Once again, that player turned out to be an All-American at Penn State in that new position, and went into the NFL in that new position. Sometimes it works and sometimes it doesn't.

Pittsburgh Steelers Drafting You and Not Lydell Mitchell

I was surprised. I definitely had no inclination that I was going to be drafted in the first round or by the Pittsburgh Steelers. As a matter of fact, I had never thought about playing in the NFL. During my senior year in college people were telling me, "Franco you are going to be drafted," and it kind of surprised me. It was a complete shock and a surprise that I was the first running back taken.

Coaches

I had a great high school coach in Bill Gordon. During my journey in football from high school, college, and the pros, I had the right coach at each level. I can't tell you how lucky I was to have great coaches, at each level. Coaches need different talents, different skills, and have to handle players differently at each level. In each level I was at, I had a great coach and great teams.

Pittsburgh Steelers Pro Football Hall Of Famers

The Pittsburgh Steelers have nine Pro Football Hall of Famers and I feel that a couple of guys are on the bubble, like L.C. Greenwood and Donnie Shell. We were so well balanced in every area; it was incredible. When you think about offense, we have a Hall of Fame quarterback, two Hall of Fame receivers, a Hall of Fame lineman, and me at running back. You look and say, "Wow!" That covers everything offensively. You look at our defense and you say, "Wow." We have a Hall of Fame defensive lineman, two Hall of Fame linebackers, and a Hall of Fame defensive back. You look at all those different segments of offense and defense and it just blows your mind. We had Hall of Famers in each segment, which helped us win four SuperBowls.

Mike Webster set the tone for the lineman, but for the offense, it was Terry Bradshaw. He was the quarterback. Mike Webster was an unbelievable guy and a great leader on and off the field with our lineman, and it was great to see because our lineman really jelled. That's what really made things happen for me; it started with the line.

Controlling Players

There were not a lot of people that needed control. You don't win four Super Bowls with things being out of control. When you look at our defense and with our guys playing with the intensity that they had, I guess you would say they'd be out of control sometimes with some things that they would do. When you have two guys like "Mean Joe" Greene and Jack Lambert, phew! Man! You didn't worry about them being out of control. You liked it as a matter of fact.

Steelers Practice
Practice was very physical. The defense wasn't allowed to touch me but believe me, they wanted to. It frustrated a lot of those guys. I just loved frustrating those guys, because then they would take it out on the opponents running back come Sunday.

Favorite Super Bowl
The Super Bowl that's dearest to me is the first one, which was down in New Orleans. It was just so unbelievable realizing that, "Wow! We made it to the Super Bowl, and our location is New Orleans." It's an unbelievable town, and to be there, wow! That first one was pretty incredible. It was so good, we said, "Hey let's do it again. Let's do it again. Let's do it again." We enjoyed going to the Super Bowl. That was a big goal of ours every year.

Immaculate Reception
The Immaculate Reception has gotten bigger, what can I say? When you look at the whole situation, it still seems so unbelievable. The circumstances, the timing, what it meant, all those factors added together it just keeps getting bigger and bigger over the years. It's almost 43 years later, and that play is still considered the number one NFL play of all time. It makes you feel special. It still brings recognition to our team and was the start of our incredible run.

Great Running Back In Football History
I appreciate when people say I'm in the category of great running backs, but to me Jim Brown will always be number one. He was number one since I was in high school. I was always a big Jim Brown fan and of what he accomplished in those days.

How can you not be a Walter Payton fan? That guy was so amazing, incredible, and extremely talented in many ways. You have to rank those guys number one and two as far as I'm concerned. You also have Barry Sanders, Gale Sayers, and Emmitt Smith, all great guys who did unbelievable things.

I was in a system that worked great for me. I was on a team that was great for me. With that, I was able to accomplish some things personally, but beyond that, I was able to be in four Super Bowls. Being in four Super Bowls, is more important than individual rushing accomplishments. When I look at the whole picture, we were balanced offensively, which helped in our greatness along with our defense. The scheme that the Steelers used at that time was perfect for me, and allowed me to show my talent.

Pro Football Hall Of Fame Induction
That was an incredible feeling. I look back on my career, the Super Bowls, Pro Bowls, and individual accomplishments—what could be better than that? When you put that Gold Jacket on, phew! It's like the whole history and the whole universe of football just went inside of you. It's an awesome, awesome feeling.

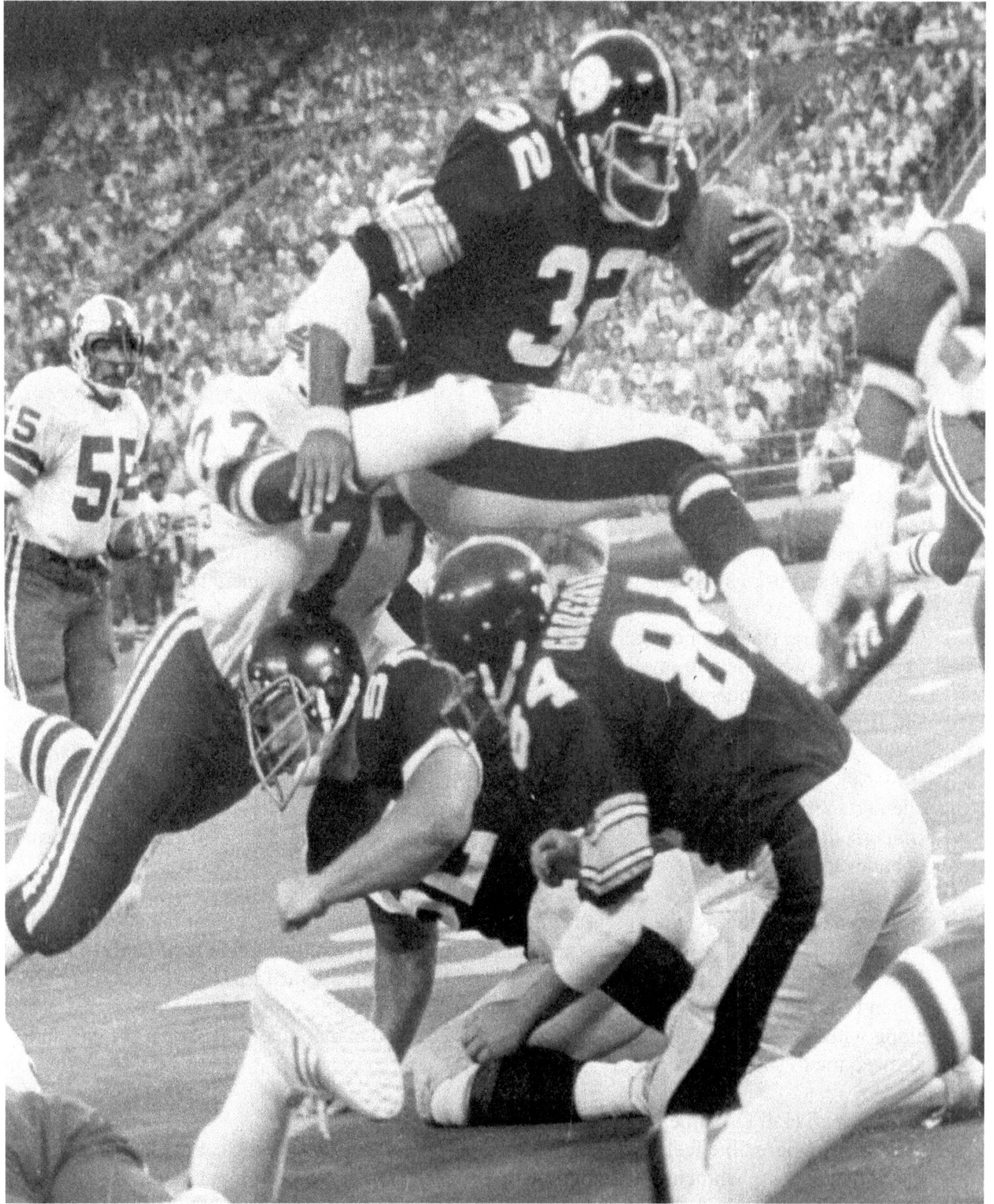

Pittsburgh Steelers running back Franco Harris goes airborne to elude Buffalo Bills left end Ben Williams. Photograph copyright Associated Press

Chapter 86

Joe DeLamielleure

College:
Michigan State

Career History:
Buffalo Bills (1973–1979)
Cleveland Browns (1980–1984)
Buffalo Bills (1985)

2003 Inductee Pro Football Hall Of Fame

College Choice
I'm from Detroit, and I wanted to go to the University Of Michigan. I was Bo Schembechler's first recruit at Michigan. Then I wanted to go to Notre Dame. Notre Dame coach Ara Parseghian's defensive coach was Johnnie Ray, who coached both of my high school coaches. I was going to go there because of Johnnie Ray. I'm the ninth of ten kids, so obviously we were very Catholic. My dad said, "You go to Michigan State because Duffy Daugherty is Catholic and I want you to be coached by a Catholic." That's how I ended up going to Michigan.

My dad said, "That Parseghian guy is a phony. He's not even Catholic and he's coaching at Notre Dame." I said "Alright dad." At that time you did what your parents told you to do, no matter what. I did what he told me and that was a good move for me. I loved it there. I had great friends and attended a great school.

Duffy Daugherty
Duffy Daugherty taught me a lot. He would always tell the guys at the beginning of the year that it takes three bones to play football—a backbone, a wishbone, and the most important bone of all, a funny bone. I lived my life like that; you have to have a backbone, you got to wish for things, and last, but not least, you have to have a good sense of humor. Life can be kind of humorous.

Being Drafted By Buffalo Bills
Paul Seymour, who also grew up in Detroit, and I were both number one draft picks of the Buffalo Bills in 1973. The Bills drafted Reggie McKenzie, who's also from Detroit, the year before us. Jim Ringo, who was our offensive line coach, had played center for the Green Bay Packers when they ran the famous Green Bay sweeps. He said we were going to run the Green Bay sweeps just like he did in Green Bay with Jim Taylor and Paul Hornung. We had Jim Braxton and O.J. Simpson as our running backs, and we did really well. He put the team together to do just that. We had two guards who could really run, Reggie and me. We were pretty quick for that era.

Transition From College Game To NFL

Jim Ringo was a great coach. I played in the Senior Bowl for the Buffalo Bills' coaches. I was comfortable going to Buffalo when they drafted me, because Coach Ringo coached me the week of the Senior Bowl. When I got to Buffalo, the coach said we weren't going to throw the ball a lot. Four out of five of the offensive linemen had played in the Big 10, where all the teams primarily ran the ball. Mike Montler played at Colorado, but he was from Columbus, Ohio. The rest of us all played in the Big 10—Donnie Green, Dave Foley, Reggie McKenzie, and me. Coach Ringo would say he had a great play, and we would just run it over and over. Nobody could stop us.

O.J. Simpson's and My Head Size

O.J. Simpson and I had fat heads. O.J. has a bigger head than I do. I used to tell people, "All the better to block you with," like the Big Bad Wolf. It was a different game back then. You hit with your head. If you didn't put your face on guys and block with your head, you weren't going to be in the league very long. One of the first things they'd say is, "That guy is a wuss. He won't put his face in there."

The next thing you know, that guy was gone. We were the guinea pigs for the current players right now. We had head slaps, now there are no head slaps; we had the wedge, now there's no wedge, and there's no chop block either. We used to practice every day on AstroTurf, which is basically colored concrete.

O.J. was embarrassed about his head size. I heard when they made his bust for the Hall Of Fame the girl that measured his head said, "Oh my God!" and the guy who was making the bust said, "Don't ever say that to him. He is really conscientious about his head size." If you watched him during his trial, he was always moving his head so the camera didn't get a good shot of it.

Favorite Moment

I'm the ninth of ten kids. When I was born my dad was 43-years-old and my mother was 41. No one went to college except me. I thought to myself, my mom and dad are sitting in Detroit watching this game saying, "Holy cow! My son is starting in the NFL." I was thrilled they were able to see me. You see, my parents had the guts to have kids when they were in their 40s. They made us go to school. They sacrificed to send us to Catholic school so we had discipline and learned what to do, and how to treat people. My mother always said, "Treat the President like the janitor, and the janitor like the President, and you'll be successful in life." My biggest thrill was just being able to start in the NFL.

Joe Greene

Nobody wanted to go against Joe Greene. When I flew into Pittsburgh, I would get butterflies thinking about Joe Greene; he was a great player. We did the smart thing, we ran away from him. We'd run sweeps and plays like that. O.J. had over 188 yards rushing in one game against the Steelers. We rushed for 303 yards in a 1975 game against the Steelers. Joe Greene was frustrated a lot in that game because he didn't get to pass rush much.

Photograph copyright Associated Press

Chapter 87

John Hannah

College: Alabama Career History: New England Patriots (1973–1985) 1991 Inductee Pro Football Hall Of Fame

College Choice

My dad grew up pretty rough. He was a sharecropper. My parents met when my dad was in Naval Preflight School. After he got out of the Navy, one of his good Navy friends talked Dad into going to college. Dad said, "Who'd take me?"

His friend was a big Clemson fan so Dad went to Clemson and said, "I got half of a VA scholarship, but if ya'll give me a half football scholarship, give me a bed to sleep in, and three meals a day, I'd love to come play football for ya'll." They said, "Herb, we can give you the half scholarship and we can give you a bed to sleep in, but we only give you two meals a day."

Dad went down to the University of Alabama and there was a guy there who had coached Dad when he was in the Naval Preflight School at Georgia, Hank Crisp. Hank basically agreed to Dad's terms. For the price of one meal Dad went to the University of Alabama. Not only that, my Uncle Bill played there, I played there, my little brother Charlie played there, and my brother David played there. For the price of one meal, they got five Hannahs! While he was at Alabama, Dad continued dating Mom. After graduating, my mother was a teacher and a professor at the University of Georgia.

My dad gave me no choice of which college to attend. My uncle was coaching at Cal State Fullerton and said, "If you get to thinking about some other place beside Alabama, you ought to think about Southern Cal." I said, "Okay." I ended up talking to Dad about it and Dad said, "That's great. You can go to any school you want to, but you just got to worry about where you're going to eat supper when you come home." I guess it was pretty well decided.

Bear Bryant

I had a high school coach who played for Bear Bryant and said it best. He said he wouldn't take a million dollars for the experience, but you couldn't pay him a million dollars to go through it again. Coach Bryant was very tough. He demanded a whole lot from his players. When I was there, he basically ruled by fear.

Bear Bryant Said John Hannah Greatest Lineman He Ever Coached

The last time I talked to Coach Bryant was when I was in college. We were getting ready to play Texas in the Cotton Bowl. It was the first day of meetings. I had been getting a lot of letters from the NFL. I went up to Coach Bryant and said, "I don't want to talk about this now because I don't want you to worry about getting my mind off the game, but the draft is in January. When this game's over, I was hoping I could come and talk to you and you might advise me in hiring an agent." Coach Bryant looked me square in the eye and said, "John, you ain't good enough to need no damn lawyer." I think that's what he really thought of me, not what he said later on!

NFL Draft
I didn't think I'd go where I was drafted. I thought I'd be about a second or third round pick. I am short for a lineman at almost 6'3". Everybody thought I was too short.

Even though I am only 6'3" I have a 37-inch sleeve length, which means I'm probably the only guy who can scratch his ankle without bending over. That abnormality in my physique, allowed me to keep the pass rush away from me, once I finally learned how to use it.

The New England Patriots Head Coach, Chuck Fairbanks, realized that and was willing to take a chance on me. Basically, he took a lot of ridicule for drafting me so high.

Joining Patriots
The Patriots weren't much of an organization. It was like a step down from the University of Alabama. I was used to playing in Birmingham in front of 80,000 people in college. I went to the Patriots and their stadium only held about 50-55,000 people. When we played the Giants at home, there were more New York Giants fans than there were Patriot fans. The facilities were just awful compared to what we had at Alabama. It was really a step down. I was shocked that it was so bad.

Chuck Fairbanks
Chuck Fairbanks was the best coach I ever had. He wasn't intimidated by anybody. He surrounded himself with people who were smarter than him and he listened to them. He didn't have a big ego. He had great organizational skills—probably the best I've ever seen. He just had an eye for talent, not only in players but also in coaches.

He listened to his players. Even if he disagreed with his players, he'd listen to them and take their thoughts into consideration when he made decisions. However, he'd eventually do what he wanted. He liked offense, which was something unusual for me. With Coach Bryant, offense for him was a necessary evil. Coach Fairbanks liked offense. That suited me fine.

Patriots Drafts
The 1973 Patriots draft was a great draft. Sam Cunningham, and Darryl Stingley, and I were first round picks. It was reinforcing to play with both of them. I think that the 1973 and 1976 drafts were probably the best drafts that the Patriots ever really had. In 1976, we drafted Mike Haynes, Tim Fox, and Pete Brock in the first round. That was a pretty good draft, too. We drafted Steve Nelson in 1974, and drafted Steve Grogan in 1975.

Darryl Stingley
Darryl Stingley was a great player. As a matter of fact, he was really just coming into his own when he got hurt. Not only was a great ball player, he was a really good human being. It was a

devastating blow for our team. Coach Fairbanks did what he always does. He went out and traded for Harold Jackson. Harold Jackson came in and filled in pretty good. We had Harold Jackson on one side and Stanley Morgan on the other at the wide receiver position. It was pretty good. Coach Fairbanks had an eye for talent. He knew how to bring it in.

Russ Francis
We had a real good tight end in Russ Francis. When Russ wanted to strap it on, there wasn't a better tight end in the league.

Toughest Defensive Linemen Faced
Joe Klecko and Howie Long were the two toughest all-around ball players I ever played against. There are a few others. Doug English and Mike Reid were really good, too.

Alan Page and Randy White were awfully good pass rushers. Gary "Hands" Johnson wasn't too bad either. He played for San Diego. William "The Fridge" Perry, was like trying to move a side of a warehouse, he was so darn big.

Jim Plunkett
Jim Plunkett was a great guy and a great quarterback. The problem was we were running four- and five-man patterns, which meant that the quarterback needed to get the ball off in 2.8 to 3 seconds. Jim was pretty slow, but he had an arm. He could hit the eye of a needle at 50 yards. So what happened was, he went to the San Francisco 49ers and had the same results. The reason why? They were running four- and five-man patterns.

When he got to the Raiders, they were running three- or four-man patterns, which meant they always had another guy in there to help block. That basically bought him another second. Now you're talking about 3.5 to 4 seconds to get rid of the ball. When Jim found that extra half a second, he tore people up. He was that kind of a quarterback. He fit into that scheme.

His talent finally got displayed. He just didn't fit into that quick release type of offense we had. With our offense you had to get it back, set, and throw. When he could sit back there in that rocking chair with the Raiders, he tore people up.

Steve Grogan
Steve Grogan probably was the best quarterback I've ever played with. He was a great quarterback. It was a travesty the way his career ended. A lot of the coaches and assistant coaches who came in afterward tried to put faith in another quarterback that we had drafted. He probably had great skills, but maybe didn't have the courage that Grogan had. The reason being, maybe they felt the owners had invested so much in the draft pick.

Super Bowl XX Against Chicago Bears
The Chicago Bears had a unique defense because the Bears Defensive Coordinator, Buddy Ryan, realized that you could always send one more guy that an offense can block. It gave everybody a lot of headaches until they started figuring it out. They had great talent. Richard Dent was a great pass rusher and Dan Hampton was a great ball player. Steve McMichael used to be with us, but the dumb coaches had traded him away.

That was a great defense. They had great linebackers. They had great defensive backs. That year the only team that beat them was the Miami Dolphins. The reason they beat them was Miami dropped back and they ran what they called turmoil. The quarterback would drop back, everybody would shoot (that's in the blitz), and then Dan Marino would basically roll away from the blitz. That bought him an extra second, so Mark Duper and Mark Clayton were able to get open.

Buddy Ryan said, "I can cover anybody for two seconds man-on-man, and you ain't going to have but two seconds because I'm going blitz more than you can pick up." Don Shula said, "No you can't, because I'm going to roll my quarterback out and you won't get to him in two seconds." The Dolphins were able to beat the Bears that way.

One thing that hurt us in the middle of the week leading up to the Super Bowl there was an emotional letdown for our team. Rumors spread throughout the offense that Steve Grogan was going to be ready to play. The whole offense got excited about it. We were lifted up that Grogan was going to be back.

The coaches came in after a practice one day and said Grogan is ready, but Tony Eason's got the starting nod. I think a lot of the guys basically were let down because of that. I think that hurt us emotionally.

Plus, there were a lot of things going on. There was an article a *Boston Globe* reporter had written regarding drug issues and things like that. Everybody was thinking about that being inthe newspaper the day after the game. It was just kind of crazy.

We got there, but we weren't all there when the game was actually played. Not that we could have beat them, but I think we could have probably got it a lot closer.

Leon Gray
Leon Gray and I had the closest of bonds. When they traded Leon away, I was madder than a hornet. That was 1979. I loved Leon. I thought the world of him. It was the worst thing they could have done for our team. It was the worst thing they could have done for Leon. I wasn't happy and I let it be known. I was very, very upset. I was very angry when I found out about it.

Almost Being Traded To Los Angeles Raiders
In '83, I was trying to get traded. Robert Irsay, the Colts owner, had talked to the Sullivans, the owners of the Patriots. The Colts were going to trade John Elway to the Patriots for me and possibly another draft choice. The Patriots wouldn't trade me.

My brother Charlie was with the Tampa Bay Buccaneers. He wanted to stay in Tampa, but wanted to make a little more money. One Friday or Saturday night in Alabama, we were going to a catfish place to eat some catfish and hushpuppies, and Charlie was late. Finally he came in. He was all 'hang dog' (his head was bowed). I said, "What's wrong?" He said, "I've been traded." I said, "Where have you been traded?" He said, "The Raiders." I said, "You sorry son-of-a-gun.

You stole my job." He went out to the Raiders. They changed his number to 73, moved him to left guard, and he won the Super Bowl.

Al Davis came up to Charlie and said, "Charlie, you know why we got you, don't you?" Charlie said, "No." He said, "Hell, the Patriots wanted two number one picks for John." He said, "He's good, but he's not worth two number ones. Tampa Bay only wanted a fourth-rounder for you!"

Decision To Retire

I was very good friends with an orthopedic surgeon. In 1977, the Patriots trainer and the doctors basically told me that I had a leg strain. Anyway, it never got better, so when I went to a legitimate orthopedic surgeon, he told me it was actually a tear.

Back then they couldn't do what they could do now. They were going to have to reroute the hamstring to the front of the knee. He said it was only about 50% successful. I went to the orthopedic surgeon and I said, "Here's the deal. If you ever see a situation where you think I could cripple myself for life, I want you to tell me." He said, "All right."

After the Bears game I'd already had both my shoulders operated on. Once that healed up to where I was able to get around a little bit, they decided to work on my knee. I went in for my knee surgery. After I got out, he called me down to his office. He said, "John, you remember what you asked me?" I said, "Yeah." He started telling me about everything and I said, "Well, what does that mean?" He said, "Well, John, I'll tell you. You could play. But if I had another job that I could make a living at, I think I'd do that instead."

So that's what it was. It was my left knee that caused me to end my career. I was hoping I'd get at least three more years in. Because they had lied to me and told me it was a strained ligament instead of a torn one and not let me get it fixed during the season, it cut my career short.

Photograph copyright Associated Press

Chapter 88

Dan Fouts

College:
Oregon

Career History:
San Diego Chargers (1973–1987)

1993 Inductee Pro Football Hall Of Fame

University of Oregon
Oregon was the only major football program that offered me a scholarship. We had a very good football team at St. Ignatius High School. Eleven of the guys from our 1957 Championship Team received college scholarships. There was a lot of attention given to our team. We won the city title and we had a great running attack. A couple of running backs attended USC. My job basically was to hand the ball off. The Oregon coaches were in attendance at a game where I threw a lot and had some success. Two of the coaches, George Seifert and John Robinson, recruited me because they were from the area.

They were outstanding coaches and I think that goes a long way. Our head coach, Jerry Frei, really put together a great staff. We were underdogs a lot because at the time, there was no limit on the amount of football scholarships a school could offer. In those days, it was difficult to compete with the big schools. We competed as well as we could.

Oregon vs. Missouri Game
We had a screen pass go for a long touchdown and the referee said we had a man illegally down the field. When I look at the tapes all these years later, we still didn't have that man down the field. It was a little home cooking there in Columbia, Missouri. I didn't need to keep the tape. That play is in my mind with all the other close controversial plays that happened during my career.

NFL Draft
I hadn't heard a word from any team prior to the draft. In those days, there weren't the combines or the 24/7 NFL news coverage. There had been a lot of teams going around working guys out. When the Chargers drafted me, I was completely surprised.

First Training Camp With Chargers
It was great because Johnny Unitas was there and I learned a lot from him during the short time he was on the team with me. He was such a great guy. I don't know why he took a liking to me, but we hung out a little bit and had a couple of cold beers after practice. For a 22-year-old kid to be able to look across the locker room and see Johnny Unitas, it was pretty awesome.

Johnny Unitas Routine Of Throwing To Raymond Berry After Practice

That's pretty much what you've got to do. That is the secret to success, but I think with Johnny Unitas and Raymond Berry, it was like a science. They were so good and they played together for so long. I eventually developed that type of rapport with Charlie Joiner, and then with Kellen Winslow, John Jefferson, and Wes Chandler. If you want to be good on Sundays, you better be good the other six days of the week.

Don Coryell

When Don Coryell came in as coach, our team was in disarray. We had some pretty good talent on the team, but we just couldn't seem to get it together. Don Coryell basically relaxed us a little bit, gave us some good plays, and put in his system. The rest is history. We had the talent of John Jefferson, Kellen Winslow, and Charlie Joiner—three outstanding individuals. They were All-Pros and the offensive came together.

Chargers Receivers

The receivers were dependable. They were all very tough going over the middle and enjoyed playing the game. We had a good time in practice because we were throwing the ball around and the guys were making catches. It's not drudgery. It's upbeat. That's the way we played on Sundays. I describe the four top receivers I had in all different ways. I just knew where Charlie Joiner was going to go every time he ran down the field. He was so reliable. Kellen Winslow set the standard for tight ends because of his versatility, and he could make the most spectacular catches in a crowd, or with one hand. Wes Chandler was a guy who could run to an inside defense if you got him the ball in the right space. I was just the luckiest guy in the world to have four receivers like that.

San Diego Charger Offense Under Don Coryell

It's hard to describe how enjoyable it was to play in Coach Coryell's offense. We would have such a good day of practice on Wednesday when we would practice the game plan. We couldn't wait to get to Sunday because we knew were going to be successful against certain teams and against certain defensive schemes. Coach Coryell's time, his plan, and the way he coached us, was up-tempo. You hear a lot now about teams and how they practice, but we practiced as fast as we played. I think that really helped.

Our offensive system was based on timing, flooding zones, looking for the two-on-one, and eventually the one-on-none. The receivers all knew that. I was just reading the defense and the receivers were reading at the same time, pretty much every time. If we were on the same page, the defense would dictate to us where the ball would go. It really wasn't a matter of egos or playing favorites. It was really very mature on the part of our receivers knowing that I was not playing favorites. The defense was telling me where to throw the ball.

Toughest Cornerbacks Faced

There were so many good ones in my era. Mike Haynes with Raiders and Louis Wright of the Broncos were great. When I broke into the league, Willie Brown of the Raiders, a Hall of Famer, used to pick me off once a game until I got smart and quit throwing the ball in his direction. Look at the Hall of Famers from that era. Those were the guys I had to face.

Don Coryell's Greatness
I think it was his adaptability, his steadfastness going about things, and his belief that we could win games throwing the ball, and be fearless doing it. The commitment that he had to his system, permeated throughout the team. It gave us all the feeling that we were going to be successful. Any great coach makes sure his team has the confidence to go out and win every Sunday.

Bill Walsh Chargers Offensive Coordinator
I certainly missed Bill Walsh when he left the Chargers. He was in San Diego with me in 1976, Up until that point, I really never had an offense coordinator or quarterback coach of his caliber. He and I had a great rapport. He left after one year because the Chargers decided not to hire him as a head coach. He went up to Stanford and turned that program around and then of course, the 49ers. Walsh meant a lot to my career. He rebuilt my game from the ground up as far as footwork and reading defenses went. Then it all came together two years later when Coryell came to San Diego.

1981 AFC Championship Game
It was windy. I think that was the biggest problem for me. It was cold, but the Bengals played better than we did that day and they handled the weather a little bit better. They deserved to win. We had a rematch the following year in San Diego that we won, but that day they were better than us and you've got to give them credit.

Toughest Defenses Faced
I think teams with great players always gave us problems. Playing against the Raiders was always an adventure. We played Oakland twice a year. Once a team has familiarity with you, it is difficult to come up with new ways to beat them, but the Raiders were great at times. The Steelers obviously, in their hay day, were awesome because of the great players they had.

Decision To Retire
My body told me it was time to retire. You've got to be honest with yourself because you don't want to embarrass yourself. I knew that after 15 years, I had enough and I was anxious to get on with my second career.

Pro Football Hall Of Fame Induction
I was absolutely thrilled. I was with my family when I found out. We were sitting around waiting for the phone to ring. When it did ring, the emotions that I felt … the gratitude of all the people that helped me get where I got … the support from my family and friends, was overwhelming. It's the most humbling experience, even to this day 20 years later, to realize that I am in the Hall of Fame with all these great players. It's an awesome feeling.

It's fun to go back to the Hall Of Fame every year and reminisce with guys about how great we used to be, even if we weren't that great.

Decision To Become A Sportscaster
My dad, Bob Fouts, was the long time voice of the San Francisco 49ers when I was growing up. I spent a lot of time in the broadcast booth with him keeping stats or spotting for him. As a kid, it looked like a really cool way to make a living. Fortunately, when I retired from the Chargers, I

had an audition with CBS and it worked out well. I'm going on my 27th year as a sportscaster. It's a great job.

Photograph copyright Associated Press

Chapter 89

Fred Dean

College: Louisiana Tech Career History: San Diego Chargers (1975–1981) San Francisco 49ers (1981–1985) 2008 Inductee Pro Football Hall Of Fame

College Choice
Louisiana Tech was right in my backyard. My grandmother lived a block from the school, so I was able to watch them play. I'd go watch from the top of the hills at the stadium. That's how close it was. I really enjoyed that.

1st Training Camp With San Diego Chargers
My first training camp was interesting. I had to go out and prove myself. It was an experience like I'd never had before. It was different than high school and college because I was playing with actual men. I had to be able to sustain and go through the necessary pressure that comes with football. It was an interesting time for me.

I think that training camp in San Diego had a lot of advantages, but there were also disadvantages. First of all, I was used to the heat in Louisiana. Whenever we went to play in a climate similar to Louisiana, I always seemed to fair pretty well. The weather is great in San Diego. Here in Louisiana it's hot and humid. That's a big difference. It was an advantage to me in so many ways.

Don Coryell Being Named Head Coach of Chargers
I would say Coach Coryell was mostly committed to the offense, but we had real good defensive coaches. They made a difference overall for us. Coach Coryell was more offensive mined and concerned about putting points on the board. When he came to San Diego, our defense got the opportunity to expand and try different things in order to stop opposing teams' offenses. It was a proven fact to us at that time.

Changing Positions With Chargers
In college, I was a linebacker and defensive tackle. Once I went pro, I was more of a defensive end. I was drafted as a linebacker because of my size. I wanted to play. I wanted to be a down lineman. I guess you could say it panned out for me.

Chargers Defensive Line
We had the defensive linemen in Louie Kelcher, Leroy Jones, Gary "Big Hands" Johnson, even Wilbur Young, and later on Charles Dejurnett. There were a lot of guys who came along that were instrumental in our success. I would say the years that we led the league in sacks, were our more dominant years.

Coach Bill Walsh was in San Diego as an assistant coach for a short time. While he was there, he saw how I put pressure on the quarterback in practice. He liked that. I guess he felt that I could be instrumental to him when he was the head coach with the 49ers.

Practicing Against Dan Fouts
I didn't really go after Dan Fouts. You couldn't hit the quarterback even back then. You would be able to just get close to him and be in his face every now and then. I would make him look at my face and he'd probably get tired of looking at me. The goal for me was to work on my skills. We had great defensive units in San Diego when I first went there. I looked up to the older players because of their skills. I thought maybe I would hone my skills by watching them and practicing with them.

San Diego Chargers Defensive Line With Louie Kelcher & Gary Johnson
We had each other's back and it kind of clicked. The thing is we were very motivated. My thing was always to go after the passer. When you stop the run, you can go after passer at a free pace and normally, you would come out victorious if you were successful.

San Diego Chargers Never Playing In The Super Bowl During His Time
I can't really say why we didn't make it. We had the personnel to have made it there. I know that at the time I was traded, I felt that we had an opportunity. After I got traded to the 49ers, my hope was that we would meet the Chargers in the Super Bowl. We didn't because unfortunately, they had lost to Cincinnati in the playoffs. We had the personnel and game plans to get into the Super Bowl and actually win it, but we weren't able to do that with the Chargers.

Reason For Trade To San Francisco 49ers
It boiled down to a contract dispute; the business aspect of it. I guess that the owner, Mr. Gene Klein, didn't feel that I was deserving of what I was asking for, like John Jefferson wasn't, or the rest of the players he let go. The bottom line is that it panned out pretty good for me.

Trade To 49ers In Mid Season
Coach Walsh had been in San Diego and saw me play. He witnessed me disturb the offense in some shape, form, or fashion. When he brought me to San Francisco, I guess he felt that I was the final link in what he needed to get some things done. I remember the first game I played in was against the Dallas Cowboys. The 49ers hadn't had much success in been beating them.

When I came to the 49ers, Coach Walsh told me that he was concerned about my conditioning and I wouldn't play against the Cowboys that week. I hadn't really played against the Cowboys much prior to joining the 49ers, but I played against the Cowboys that week.

I didn't really have anything to prove. I wanted to advance my skills as far as rushing the quarterback. Being traded was a good thing because Coach Walsh gave me the opportunity to do that.

I left a good quarterback in Dan Fouts. When I first went to the 49ers, Joe Montana and I went to do an autograph session together. We drove together to the session and we had a pretty good chat.

There were a lot of adjustments for me just going to San Francisco. I found that Joe was very cool, and I enjoyed being around him. His humor was really good for me because he made me feel like I was a real part of San Francisco. He was a good guy.

Difference Between Dan Fouts and Joe Montana
Both guys were pretty good quarterbacks. I'll say it like that. When you look at them now, you can see why both of them are in the Hall of Fame. As far as their differences, they were different people with different styles. Joe was much more mobile than Dan. Dan was more of a pocket passer and had great receivers around him. Joe had great receivers, but he was able to get out of the pocket and make things happen. Dan was more of a pocket passer. That was the difference in itself; but they both were good.

Second Game With 49ers Against Rams
I knew that I was a halfway decent. I knew that I could have a big impact in various games. With the guys beside me, Lawrence Pillers, Dwaine Board, Keena Turner, Ronnie Lott, Eric Wright, Dwight Hicks … all those guys made me feel comfortable playing. I had adjusted to the Chargers defensive line, but I just felt at home with those guys. My attitude was to always give other players their due. It was overall a good situation.

Dwight Clark Catch Against Cowboys In NFC Championship Game
It was a great feeling being in San Francisco my first year because that catch caused us to move on deeper into the playoffs. It was an exciting moment for me to see Dwight make that catch. The Dallas defense was doing well and had won a lot of different ways, but the bottom line was the 49ers were destined to be champions. We were sort of the Cinderella team. I think we did things to really surprise people. All along the way, we had something to prove. The great players that we had, Ronnie Lott, Hicks, and all those guys … those DBs set some precedent.

Winning A Super Bowl In First Year With 49ers
It was a place you could very easily fall in love with. It was kind of lonely in the beginning because I didn't know my teammates that well, but they made me feel at home. There was camaraderie among the guys in the locker room. There was a connection there that you really can't describe. People weren't tense like I had witnessed in the past with the Chargers.

In some places the tension is so strong, you could cut it with a knife. We were so relaxed going out to play because we had people like Hacksaw Reynolds, Keena Turner and those guys. They made it about going out and hitting.

We all came together as one. It's kind of difficult to describe because we had leaders across the board. My thing was, I didn't have to say a whole lot. You go out there and you hit them in the mouth and we can be successful. We had guys go through their rituals, their routines. It was a combination of everything. Everybody wanted to win. We did or said whatever it took to get to that next step, that next stage.

Ronnie Lott Cutting Off Part Of His Finger To Continue Playing In A Game

I didn't realize that took place until after the game. For him to do that and to finish the play, spoke volumes about Ronnie, his heart being in the game, and his desire to win. A lot of things like that happened. It makes everybody realize that you've got people beside you that have your back. That's the interesting part of playing the game of football. Some people make mistakes and there's someone there to compensate for that. When we made mistakes there were others who would always compensate. It was an overall team effort.

Offensive Linemen Competed Against

I was smaller than the majority of the offensive linemen I competed against. As far as I'm concerned, the offensive linemen whom I played against were all pretty tough. The linemen who really gave me a good game every time we played against each other, were the Raiders ArtShell, Rams Jackie Slater, and later in my career, Anthony Munoz. These guys were good and it was always a good game. It was always a chess game to play against those guys and try to achieve your next goal against them. Those guys are in the Hall of Fame. They were pretty skilled players and they would give me a hard time. I had my share of success against them, but they did vice versa against me. Those guys were pretty tough. I would say that it all balanced out in the long run.

Pro Football Hall Of Fame Induction

I didn't really picture myself going into the Hall of Fame. I never really thought about it. I just heard of it and knew there were some great players in there. I didn't let it bother me at all because I knew how good I was. I didn't need to get into the Hall of Fame to understand that. I got a stamp of approval when I did get in, though. It's a great pleasure to be among those guys.

Jerry Rice Joining 49ers

When you look at some people and their work ethic, you know that they're going to be successful. When I looked at Jerry, he didn't have that true speed, but he worked at running good routes. He would work on the way that he ran them continuously. I looked at some of the greats when they played. I'm quite sure that Jerry did too, and he was inspired by the greats. I knew that he would be good. I just didn't know how good he would be. You could see that in Ronnie Lott and those guys. You knew that they'd be good and they were, but you couldn't really say this person or that person was going to be that good.

Bill Walsh

Bill Walsh was a great coach. He knew successful plays, to get the job done. That's what he did. He mastered doing those things. Some coaches in the league handle situations better than other coaches. The bottom line is getting the basics down and then going forward with it and he did that. He knew how to keep his players relaxed going into the game. If he wasn't relaxed, he didn't always show it. I guess there were certain things he tried to keep from the players. They would be relaxed, go out and do well, and play for you regardless of the circumstances.

Edward DeBartolo

Mr. D was a top-notch owner. He was the guy who called for Bill Walsh and everyone else to put forth their best effort to get the job done. He was behind you 100%. Mr. D. gave off positive energy for the guys who played for him. He was interested in the players and how they felt about things. He would talk to you on a level that would make you want to play for him and go out and be as successful as you could be.

The success has shown throughout the years. There are going to be times when players have disputes with owners, but the bottom line is, the majority of them didn't really have disputes with him because he did a lot of great things for people.

He was a players' owner. He helped you in every way. He chose smart people to get the job done to be successful. He made the fan base feel comfortable because of the extra things that he did. A lot of times, he was doing things to make it easier for the players to play.

Even though we'd go through periods that were rough, he would always do things that made the players feel comfortable. It shows to this day. I look forward to him going into the Pro Football Hall of Fame one day because people like that deserve to be there. He is a great man. You could see it in his organization—everything he did and how he did it.

Favorite Player Growing Up

I had a variety of them from running backs to linebackers, and every now and then, a quarterback. Growing up, Jim Brown was one of my favorites. Lineman Deacon Jones was another one of my favorites, and then there was Dick Butkus. Those were the ones that I grew up really knowing and understanding. I know they put forth their best effort on the field. Their skills were really impressive.

Being In Hall Of Fame With Players Watched Growing Up

To see them and be around the guys you once idolized was incredible. I never ever thought that I would meet them, but the bottom line is, one day I did. My thing was always to grab some of that success that they had for myself because I wanted to be as good as they were. I wanted to just change the way the game was played in some form or fashion. That's what all of them did. They changed the way the game was played. They were successful at football and made me feel really special whenever I could go out and play at the kind of level that they had played at and be as successful as they were.

If they ask me for a favor and it's in my ability to be able to do it, there's no question in my mind that I won't go out to go out of my way to try and do something for them. I'd do that because they are guys I looked up to. These are the same people that established the game the way they played in the past and are getting rewarded for it. That's something very special.

Just to be in that echelon, makes you feel special because there's a brotherly feeling among those guys. You see all the different personalities, the things they did, and the way they are today. It is just a feeling that I will never forget. I'll always have that feeling until the day I die. It's something that I want to pass on to kids … to let them know that if you work hard, you can change things.

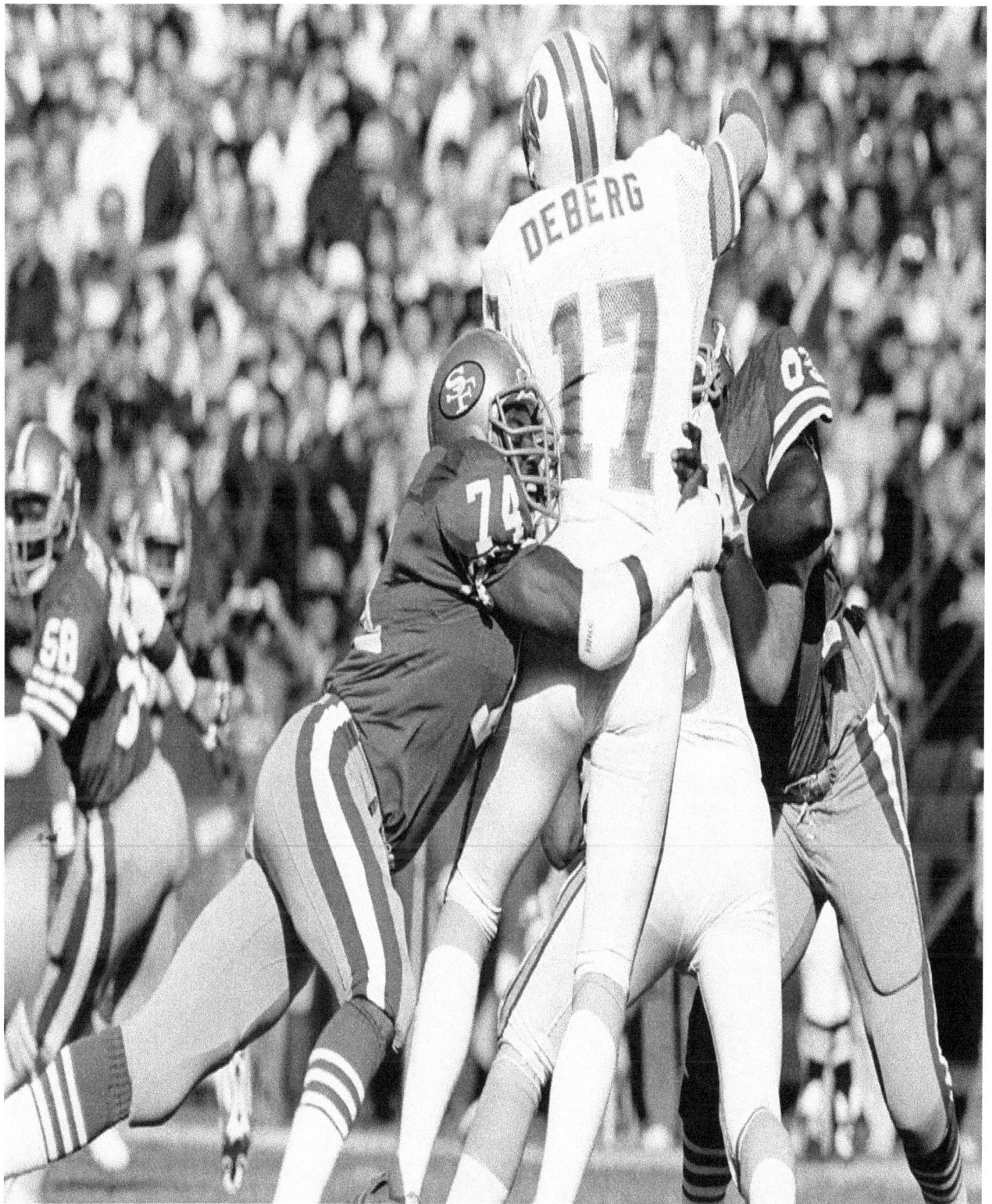

San Francisco 49er Fred Dean brings down Tampa Bay Buccaneers quarterback Steve DeBerg. Photograph copyright Associated Press

Chapter 90

Lynn Swann

College:
Southern California

Career History:
Pittsburgh Steelers (1974–1982)

2001 Inductee Pro Football Hall Of Fame

Marv Levy

I remember when Marv Levy was coaching early on. I was actually working in broadcasting during the offseason when he was named coach. I went down for a press conference and one of the members of the media pointed me out and said, "Hey, maybe you'd like to have a receiver like him." He looked at me and he said, "Well, I don't know if you can play but we may have an open try-out. You're welcome to come." Someone said, "I think he's already played a little bit of football." He responded, "My apologies, I'm sorry." Good guy though, good guy.

Chuck Noll Not Becoming A Media Member After Retiring As A Coach

Chuck Noll was not a guy who was going to be a broadcaster. He was not looking to get into the media. As a matter of fact, if you recall Chuck's demeanor and personality, he gave it all to the players and to everyone else. He didn't have a coach's show or any of those things because he chose not to have a life in the media beyond being the coach of a championship football team.

Ronald Reagan

He began as a sports announcer at Iowa covering football games. His ability to articulate a message that people could understand and grasp was one of his greatest assets as Governor of California, and eventually President of the United States.

He loved football and broadcast football. He had teams come to the White House. He was in Los Angeles in the '90s and was giving a speech at a luncheon. The next day he went over to the stadium and flipped the coin for the USC & Notre Dame football game. I think he understood the value of sports, the life lessons you learn in sports, and what it means to be a part of a strong team. Certainly those things were practical for him in his roles.

Favorite Moments While Playing

I mean payday was a good day. Then of course there were Super Bowls, the day I was drafted, and the day we won the national championship. Some other memorable moments were the day Willie Brown walked into my hotel room and told me I made it to an All American Team my senior year, the first catch I made as a professional, and catching a touchdown in the Rose Bowl. I consider myself beyond lucky. I consider myself to be extraordinarily fortunate to be able to have more than one moment that I can look back on and think it was a great moment.

Will There Be Future Dynasties In Football

I think it's possible, but winning four in six years? You may see teams, like the Patriots, that win championships over a longer period of time without necessarily the same people. The 49ers were multi Super Bowl winners but over a longer period of time. I think there were only five players from that team who had all four Super Bowl rings. I think it is possible, but it's not easy. We may not see four Super Bowls in six years again. I think we'll see teams that are consistently strong and considered dynasties. Look at the Steelers and the success that they're currently having. They didn't win the last Super Bowl, but they got there and they continued to press on to be competitors, to be in a position to win Super Bowls.

More Pressure To Win At USC Or With Steelers

There was pressure to win everywhere. Sometimes it's not really pressure that anybody else puts on you, it's the pressure you put on yourself. Championship caliber players and individuals always want to win and always want the best. When you look at the amount of pressure they put on themselves to make things happen, it's incredible.

Look at the guys at USC now and guys in college. There is pressure on them because they want to win for that school, and the pressure is on them to win because they want to get drafted. They want to be one of those guys who signs a contract and plays for a pro team for a million dollars. I'm not sure if that's not more pressure than the guy who is already on the team and playing professionally experiences.

Terry Bradshaw Becoming A Media Personality

Terry gave no indication that was a direction he wanted to go in when he was a player, but it's something that evolved. It happened for him. He was in the right place at the right time, with the right skills, with the right kind of personality, to make it work. He has done well and continues to do well.

Mister Rogers

Fred Rogers started his broadcast at WPGH I believe, a public broadcasting station. He was phenomenal in terms of his talent and the impact he has had on kids and adults around the country. Being on his show was a lot of fun.

Becoming A Politician

I think essentially it is the fact that I view politics and being an elected official as volunteering. You give your time to help in a big way and a strong way. That's what I was doing. I was never looking to be a professional politician. I was never looking at it as a career. It was always my intent to actually try and win, have an impact in Pennsylvania, and then step back and go back into the private sector.

Running for office is certainly much more difficult than playing football. What's required of you in terms of responsibility and getting things done has more impactful on people. Football is entertainment. Football is a competitive sport. In politics, like being governor of a state, you're in a position to change and alter lives in positive and in negative ways depending on the decisions you make or you don't make.

Big Brothers & Big Sisters

I have work with Big Brothers and Big Sisters for more than 35 years. I'm on the national board. Mentoring has always been important to me. I think everywhere we look around the country, in any job all of us have been helped by people along the way. Sometimes it's important to have that direct mentor who can help us grow from an adolescent into a responsible adult.

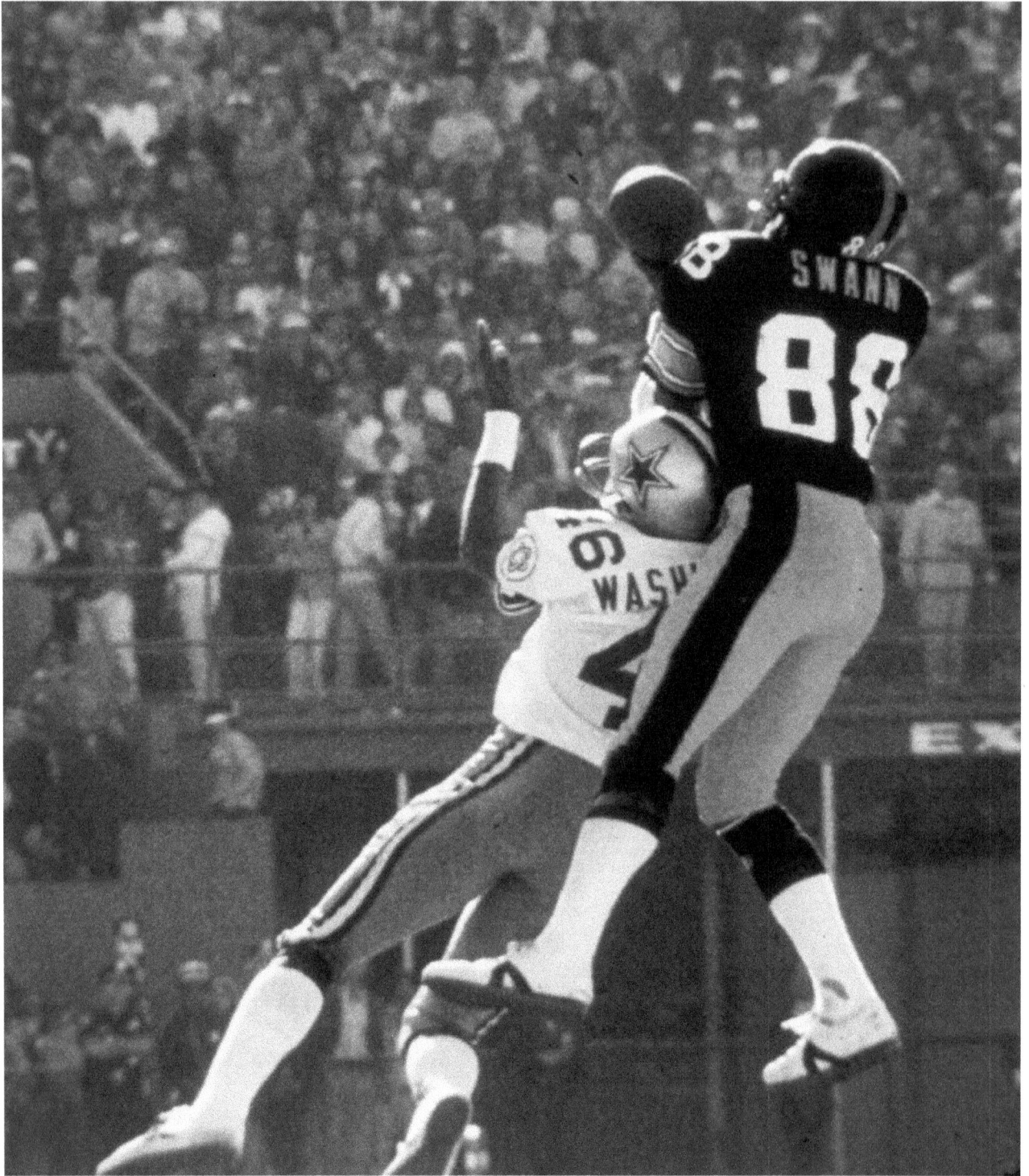

Pittsburgh Steeler Lynn Swann goes up to make a catch over Dallas Cowboys cornerback Mark Washington in the Steelers 21-17 win over the Cowboys in Super Bowl X on January 18, 1976. Photograph copyright Associated Press

Chapter 91

John Stallworth

College: Alabama A&M Career History: Pittsburgh Steelers (1974–1987) 2002 Inductee Pro Football Hall Of Fame

College Choice

It was a different time; it was the early '70s. My last year in high school was 1970 so it was before some changes took place at the university. I actually got one offer to go to college on scholarship and that was at Alabama A&M.

Alabama A&M

It was a great experience for me. Black college football was certainly a different experience. I went to a predominately white high school. Sometimes the approach that we took in high school was different than the approach that was taken at Alabama A&M, but that was good. It was the first time I was in a passing offense. My forte, I've always thought, was catching the football. In high school we didn't have a quarterback that could throw the football. So, I was a tall, skinny, running back. When I got to Alabama A&M, I had an opportunity to do the thing that I thought I was good at. Football was a good experience. The academics at Alabama A&M was good for me too. And, I met my wife at Alabama A&M. A lot of good things happened there.

NFL Draft

Alabama A&M had not experienced a lot of players being drafted. The Pittsburgh Steelers drafted me in the fourth round. At that time, I was the highest draft pick out of Alabama A&M in their history. I felt being drafted by the Steelers was probably going to be my kiss of death. At that time the one thing Pittsburgh did really well was run the football. They had a great running back in Franco Harris who was entering his third year when I joined the Steelers. The Steelers played great defense. The offensive philosophy was three yards and a cloud of dust. They just didn't throw the ball that much.

Change In Steelers Offensive Philosophy

With Terry Bradshaw's development, and Lynn Swann and me coming on, we changed the offensive philosophy a little bit. Rocky Bleier played a crucial role for us in all of our Super Bowl wins.

Lynn and I both liked the big play. We liked coming up with the big play. That gave Terry the opportunity to do that, which went with Bradshaw's style of play. We all came together at the right time. Bradshaw's early years with the Steelers were up and down. Then he started playing with some consistency, and we were there for those years.

Practicing Against Steelers Defense

We never got anything done offensively unless the coaches called them off. We couldn't run the football against the defensive line. With guys like Mel Blount, Donnie Shell, Mike Wagner, and J.T. Thomas, it was kind of hard even to throw the football. Going against those guys at practice everyday was good for us because when we got to the game, it was a lot easier.

Normally the offense comes along a lot slower than the defense. You get to training camp and the defense starts clicking almost right away. The offense, because of the timing of blocks and throwing the ball with the timing of the quarterback back and receiver, takes a little bit longer to develop. The defense knew exactly what we were going to do. There wasn't going to be anything that we were going to do that was going to surprise them. So when you had guys on defense who were as talented as they were and then they knew where you were going, sometimes they'd take the short cut and get there before you.

Catching 75 Yard Touchdown Pass In Super Bowl XIII

It was my best performance in a big game—a playoff game. I think I had other games where I played better catching the football and blocking, but that was probably my best big game performance.

Super Bowl XIV

In that Super Bowl, we were not running the ball very well. Three of our coaches had left right before the season started and were now coaches with the LA Rams. So, the Rams knew what we were going to do. They knew Bradshaw's strong suit and they did a great job of game planning for that. The only thing they left us with were big plays down the field and it worked well for us. Lynn Swann had a big play for a touchdown and then the two that I caught, a 73-yarder for a touchdown and later a 45-yard catch that put us in position for our final score. As a kid you dream about having a great performance in the big game of the year. For professional football, that's the Super Bowl. So I came up with the winning catch and a Super Bowl win. It was a dream come true for me. I have a lot of great memories. For our era of the Pittsburgh Steelers, that was the last Super Bowl we played in, so it was special place for us.

Favorite Super Bowl

My favorite Super Bowl was any that I played well in. The first one against the Minnesota Vikings we played great defense and ran the football. We didn't throw it a whole lot. It was a good game and I was happy with the victory. As a receiver you like to do more and be more of a factor in the outcome of the game.

Chuck Noll

Ultimately, I think Chuck was a great teacher. He cared. He was communicating effectively so you knew not only what you had to do but also why you were doing it. I think that gave us a leg up in understanding what we had to do in the game. I think there's a part of Chuck that most people don't see when they look back. He had a lot of compassion for the guys who played for him, but he thought that a coach couldn't show compassion. So, he didn't show that side of his personality. He definitely cared about the guys who were on his team. He cared about their development not only as football players, but also their development as human beings. There was a lot of truth to what he said about why you do certain things and how you react when certain things happen. Those truths transcended football. They were life lessons we could take to our next job, our life's work, as he would call it. Whatever we were doing, they were applicable.

Rollie Dotsch
Rollie was a good man and an excellent coach. He had a great rapport with all of us. We really hated to lose him when he left our team and went to coach in the USFL for Birmingham. He was such a good person, not just a good coach. He was a good person and a friend.

Rollie actually had a great singing voice. I don't know if anybody has ever said that. You'd catch him in a moment when he was totally relaxed and feeling comfortable and he'd belt something out for you. You'd come away from it amazed.

Terry Bradshaw
Terry Bradshaw is a very approachable guy. He comes across as a real easy, likable guy. With Terry there was always that awkwardness of starting something new. When he came to the Steelers getting adjusted to the game at that level was new to him and it took him a while. When he transitioned into broadcasting, it was awkward. I think the first few years he was doing that, he'd only broadcast games out of New Orleans.

We joked with him about that because at that time, New Orleans wasn't a successful team. So, if you screwed up nobody would know. Terry practiced his craft. He's fully comfortable with that, so I could see him being where he is and being very successful. Nobody knows when you leave the game what you're going to do. Everybody's got something they'd like to be able to do. To what degree that we're going to be successful when we transition, nobody knows. I think all athletes ask themselves, 'What's next?' If you can answer that question, then your transition out of football is easy. You make it and you welcome it. If you can't answer that question, you tend to cling to the life that you've got because that's the only one you know.

Toughest Defensive Backs Faced
I liked playing against the tough defensive backs like Mike Haynes with the New England Patriots and then with the Raiders. Hall of Famer Mike Haynes was an excellent defensive back. There was a guy that played a number of years with the Cleveland Browns named Hanford Dixon. I had some good battles against him. I also liked to play against Ken Riley of the Cincinnati Bengals. There were guys out there that I knew going into the game, were going to be tough to play against.

Pro Football Hall Of Fame Induction
After we settled down and the screaming stopped, I thought deeper about what it meant. You look back over my career and I was never the guy that was going to be in the paper all the time. I saw myself as a hardworking receiver who had some big plays in big games and did well. I wasn't the guy who was going to spike the football or win MVP in the Super Bowl. I felt good about my career. Going into the Hall of Fame, sort of justifies or verifies it. The way I approached the game was to keep my nose down, do a good job, and catch the ball when I was

called to catch it. At the end of the day, people recognize it for having a great value. A lot of times during the course of my career, other things were going on and people on our team were being highlighted for this and that. I thought, well maybe I will change, maybe I will do things a little bit differently, but I didn't. I continued to do what I felt comfortable with. Being voted into the Hall of Fame sort of let me know that I made the right choices.

Leaders On Steelers
On defense you have to look at Joe Greene and Jack Lambert as leaders. Certainly, Lambert was the more vocal of the two. Joe's actions and words made him a leader, but Lambert was a lot more vocal than Joe. We had a group of leaders on the offense. The quarterback has to be one of the guys that stands up and does the job. At times during our heyday, we would call plays by committee because Bradshaw, in his wisdom, would listen to what Swann, Franco, and I wanted to do and what Mike Webster thought the offensive line could do. Terry had a lot of input. He was his own quarterback and he called his own plays. A number of quarterbacks had the philosophy that everyone should just shut up and they'd call the play. That was not our approach in Pittsburgh with Bradshaw. We all had suggestions of what we wanted to do and Bradshaw respected that.

L.C. Greenwood Not Being In The Pro Football Hall Of Fame
No question in my mind that L.C. should be in the Hall of Fame. Look at his performance over the years on the defensive line, the number of sacks he had, and how he influenced major games for us. Just his steadiness over the years should have put him in. Without a doubt I think he has all the credentials to be a Hall of Famer, and I'm hoping it's going to happen.

Joe Greene Nickname (Mean Joe Greene)
He was called that when I got there. He came to the Steelers in 1969 and I came in 1974, so I think those early years are when he was Mean Joe Greene in the truest sense of the word. When I got there, Joe was starting to be more Joe Greene the leader. Joe Greene was the guy who, when you wanted an assessment of where the team was, how we were doing, and how we were going to get through whatever phase we were going through, offered those words up. That was the Joe Greene I knew. I told him that back then. I never knew Mean Joe Greene, I knew Joe Greene the consummate leader. Joe Greene, the guy who by his actions and his words set the path for us. Joe owned the field. As a young guy, you kind of looked at him and thought, "What's Joe going to say? How's Joe going to react to that?" You took your cues from him in that regard. So, to me, I never knew the guy called Mean Joe Greene. I knew Joe Greene the leader.

Biggest Rivals
In the sense that we saw the Dallas Cowboys twice in the Super Bowl, they were our biggest rivals. And, we had a big rivalry with the Oakland Raiders. I had to learn to hate the Oakland Raiders when I got to the Steelers. We played a couple of championship games against them. Then, we had a big rivalry with the Houston Oilers. We had to play them a couple of times in conference championship games. As far as the big games go, our big rival was the Cowboys because there was a big difference in player style. Our player style was smash them on the field. Coach Noll said we had to hit them harder than they hit us if we were going to win the football game. In Dallas, with the flex defense and multiple sets of offense, they were

going to finesse you. That was the difference in playing style. In that era, the smash mouth against the finesse won out most of the time. The Cowboys were America's team and that's how they promoted themselves. We were Pittsburgh's team--Western Pennsylvania's team, and we took a lot of pride in that.

Favorite Player Growing Up

I had a number of favorite players. I liked Raymond Berry. Raymond Berry wasn't the fastest guy, but he ran good rounds and caught the football when it came his way. That resonated with me even as a young football player. Paul Warfield was smooth, steady, and came up with the big play. He just happened to be on an offense that wanted to run the football in Miami with John Kiick, Larry Csonka, and Mercury Morris. When they threw the ball, Paul got it. I really liked to watch him play. I just liked receivers in general. I also liked Otis Taylor with the Kansas City Chiefs. He came from a black college, so I could identify with that. As for a quarterback, Johnny Unitas will always be a hero to me.

Meeting Raymond Berry

My first encounter with Ray Berry was when he was with the Detroit Lions as a receiver coach. That year, the Lion's coaching staff was at the Senior Bowl and I was there as a player. Ray came over to me to me said, "Well, I hear you've got great hands." So, he put me in a drill. Standing in front of me, he put his hands out and had someone throw the ball to me. He was right up close to me, distracting me with his hands. The ball had to go by him to get to me. I was thinking this is Ray Berry doing this, rather than thinking about catching the ball. He didn't have to move his hands; he could have just stood there. I've never told him that.

Detroit obviously didn't draft me. He probably left thinking whatever they say about this guy's hands, is completely false. He can't catch a thing.

I've read stories of what Ray Berry and Johnny Unitas did after practice. Berry would run so many yards and then cut to the outside, and Unitas knew the timing of the route. Unitas released the ball before Berry went into his cut, so when Berry came back, the ball was right there so he could make the catch. That type of work ethic breeds success.

Pittsburgh Steeler Mel Blount, left, and John Stallworth hug each other in the locker room Sunday, Jan. 5, 1976 after the Steelers beat the Oakland Raiders 16-10 for the AFC Championship. Photograph copyright
Associated Press

Chapter 92

Randy White

College:
Maryland

Career History:
Dallas Cowboys (1975–1988)

1994 Inductee Pro Football Hall Of Fame

College Choice
I was born in Pittsburgh, Pennsylvania, and grew up in Delaware. My entire family is from Pennsylvania. Penn State never looked at me in high school. I never had an offer from them. I had three offers. They were from Arizona State, Virginia Tech, and Maryland. Maryland was the closest one to where I grew up, so that's the main reason I ended up going there.

At the time, I hadn't been to a whole lot of places. I went to Arizona State for a visit, and they had me room with Mike Hartenstine. Mike ended up being a Bear. Before that, though, he played for Penn State. I got to room with Mike again during the College All-Star Game.

Maryland Head Coaches
My first year at Maryland, Roy Lester was the head coach. My first visit to Maryland my dad and me sat down with Coach Lester. Coach Lester told me, "I don't know if you can play college football for the University of Maryland, but we're going to give you a scholarship." I said, "Well, that's good. I'm glad you're giving me one." Anyway, he was gone the next year. Jerry Claiborne was the head coach for my sophomore, junior, and senior years.

I didn't realize at the time what kind of a foundation Coach Claiborne was giving me. He gave me the foundation play on the professional level. He was a great coach and a real disciplinarian. I learned a lot about football playing for him.

NFL Draft
If the Cowboys had the opportunity to do the draft over, they probably would have taken Walter Payton instead of me. The way it worked out, I ended up a Dallas Cowboy. The Baltimore Colts had the number one pick in the draft that year. Joe Thomas was the general manager of the Colts and had been down to Maryland. Joe said, "Randy we're taking you with the first pick." Even up until the day before the draft, that's what he was telling me. At the last minute, the Colts traded their number one pick to Atlanta. Atlanta took Steve Bartkowski; Dallas acquired the number two pick by trading Craig Morton to the Giants, and chose me. That's how I ended up being a Cowboy.

The Cowboys not drafting Walter worked out good for Walter and me. Walter was a great player and a great guy. We came out of school the same year. I got to know Walter from playing in the

East West Shrine Game, the College All-Star Game, and then competing against him over the years. He was the best player of all-time.

Playing Middle Linebacker For Cowboys
Lee Roy Jordan was getting ready to retire. Coach Landry was the one who kind of invented the middle linebacker spot with Sam Huff and the Giants. I guess they felt that since I was 6'4", weighed 260 pounds, and could run a 4.6 40, I would be an excellent middle linebacker. That experiment didn't work out, though. The Cowboys flex defense was a little different than playing in a conventional 4-3 defense. The moves that the middle linebacker had to make, the reaction time, and a lot of involvement in pass coverage, just never became natural to me. Most of the time I was a beat off, because I was thinking too much.

Position Change To Defensive Tackle
My third year in the league, Coach Landry told me, "Randy, we're thinking about moving you to defensive tackle. How do you feel about that?" I said, "Coach I just want to play football wherever you think I can help this football team win. That's where I will play." I had moved from middle linebacker to strong side linebacker, to weak side linebacker, and I was running out of spots.

He asked, "You want to play on the defensive line?" I said, "Sure." I was always undersized for the defensive tackle position, but it was a natural position for me. I felt like somebody took the handcuffs off of me and I could play football the way I knew how to play. It was a good moment for me when Coach Landry switched me.

We had an excellent middle linebacker, Bob Breunig. He just stepped right in there. That was his natural position. I went to the right defensive tackle spot and had some success. They started mentioning my name with Bob Lilly and I said, "Whoa wait a minute. If I can do this for 14 years like Bob did, then go ahead and mention my name with him."

Bob Lilly is Mr. Cowboy. As far as I'm concerned he's the greatest Cowboy that ever played along with Roger Staubach. We had a lot of great ones, but Bob is right up there.

Cowboys Defensive Line
We had Larry Cole and Jethro Pugh split time on the left side. After Jethro and Larry retired, we got John Dutton from the Colts, who was an All-Pro defensive end. John moved into that left tackle spot. So, we had a pretty good defensive line back then.

Playing In Super Bowls Early In Career
We had a great group with a lot of talent and we got along. We had a great team. I went to the Super Bowl my rookie year, I went there my third year, and I went there my fourth year. I thought we'd get back to the Super Bowl but we ended up playing in three NFC Championship Games after my fourth year in the league. I played for 14 years and never got another opportunity to play in the Super Bowl after my fourth season. If you get an opportunity to play in a Super Bowl, savor that moment because you never know if it's going to come backaround.

Winning Super Bowl MVP

Winning the Super Bowl MVP was the furthest thing from my mind. I wasn't even thinking about that. Ed Jones had a great game that day, our strong safety, Randy Hughes, intercepted a pass and had two fumble recoveries. Roger Staubach and a lot of guys were the most valuable players in that game. That was a big day for Harvey Martin and me. We were chosen as the MVPs. I remember I was standing on the sidelines at the end of the game and Harvey came over to me and said, "We were chosen as the MVPs in the game." It didn't sink in with me.

The big thing was winning the Super Bowl. I had played against Pittsburgh my rookie year in the Super Bowl, and the most exciting thing I remember about that was the after game party. Willie Nelson, Waylon Jennings, and Jimmy Buffet were there. We got up and sang with them on stage after the game. Having the chance to go back to the Super Bowl, win, and get a Super Bowl ring was a great experience.

As MVP, each of us was given a new car. Harvey and I went to New York and we each got a new Thunderbird. I thought they gave you the car and it was yours. Well, I found out at the end of the year that, you had the use of the car for a year. After that, you had the option to buy it at the end of the year or you could turn it back in. That was a little disappointing.

The Super Bowl definitely turned into something more than what it was. It was great back then, but now it's like the greatest sporting event of all time every year. It was wonderful; it was a great experience playing in the Super Bowls.

Transition From Maryland To Dallas

At that time, going from college to the pros, I was just concerned about having a chance to make the football team. I wasn't thinking about the fans or what it meant to play for the Dallas Cowboys, but over time you start to realize that. My main thing when I first went down there was figuring out what I had to do to stick around there for a while. That's what I wanted to do, make the football team. Playing the middle linebacker spot for the first couple of years was kind of frustrating for me. Finally in my third year, I started being able to play football the way I liked to play it.

Tom Landry

It was obvious that Coach Landry was a great football coach. He did a lot of things to change the game defensively and offensively. As far as a person, he was a great example of a real Christian. He just didn't talk the talk; he walked the walk. A lot of things about him were special and impressive but for me, in the 14 years he was my coach, I never once saw him lose his temper or get out of control. Now he would get angry and he would not be happy, but he didn't do it by yelling and screaming. He had a way of getting his point across by just looking at you. You knew he wasn't happy. He was definitely a special person.

Jerry Jones Firing Tom Landry

It was a tough time for everybody when the ownership changed and Coach Landry was gone. That was a hard transition. Coach Landry used to tell us all the time, "One thing you can be sure of is things will change." Sure enough, they do. When Jerry Jones bought the team, he came in there and the team won three Super Bowls. It was tough when Coach Landry left, but time heals and you pull for the Cowboys. You want them to win.

Jerry is one of the best owners in the league. He really takes care of his players. He does everything he can to put the best football team on the field. It was tough back then.

Super Bowl XIII
The second time we played the Steelers in the Super Bowl, I had a broken thumb. Roy Gerela squib kicked the ball to me. I pick it up, started running with it, and fumbled the ball. Pittsburgh recovered and one play later they scored a touchdown.

Everybody thinks Jackie Smith dropping that pass in the end zone is what what made us lose, but there were a lot of other things that happened in that football game that caused us to lose. Jackie was one of the best of all-time. He was a great player and really helped our football team when he joined us. He is one of the greatest of all-time. He is in the Hall of Fame and deserves to be.

Mike Ditka
Mike Ditka was my special teams coach for two years. He also coached tight ends. I got hands on with Mike for those two years. You're never going to meet a more competitive guy than Mike Ditka. He's hardnosed.

I always liked Mike. I like the way that he coached and I like his attitude. He was an inspiration to all of us. Anybody who was ever around Coach Landry had the kind of respect for him that Mike had for Coach Landry. I've never met anybody who has one bad thing to say about Coach Landry. He was a very special person.

Coach Landry demanded a certain amount of control from his coaching staff I'm sure, but Mike was always Mike. Coach Landry didn't accept anything except 100 percent. He wasn't afraid to express his position on things. If you made a mistake, you knew you were going to hear about it, but that's what made him a great coach. Mike's a special guy too.

Any time we played against the Bears, it was always a dogfight. When Mike Ditka went to coach the Bears, they adopted his personality. You were going to be in a dogfight no matter what happened in that football game.

Toughest Offensive Lineman Faced
Bob Young from the St. Louis Cardinals gave me as hard a time as anyone in the running game. I could pretty much pass rush against the best of them. I played against John Hannah and Mike Webster.

A guy who gave me a hard time that played for the Bears was Noah Jackson. He was a left guard. He had a big belly and they called him Buddha. He was an artist at the flex. He would give me head fakes, cut me, and have me on the ground more than anybody I ever played against. They had Walter Payton running the football, which made it that much harder, but Noah Jackson was a pretty tough guard.

<u>Danny White</u>
Danny White had to follow Roger Staubach. Who can fill those shoes? Roger was Roger. People expected Danny to do the things Roger did, but Danny White wasn't Roger Staubach. Danny was an excellent quarterback, though. We went to the playoffs ever year and three NFC Championship games. The quarterback doesn't win or lose them by himself. It takes a whole team effort. Danny was a great quarterback.

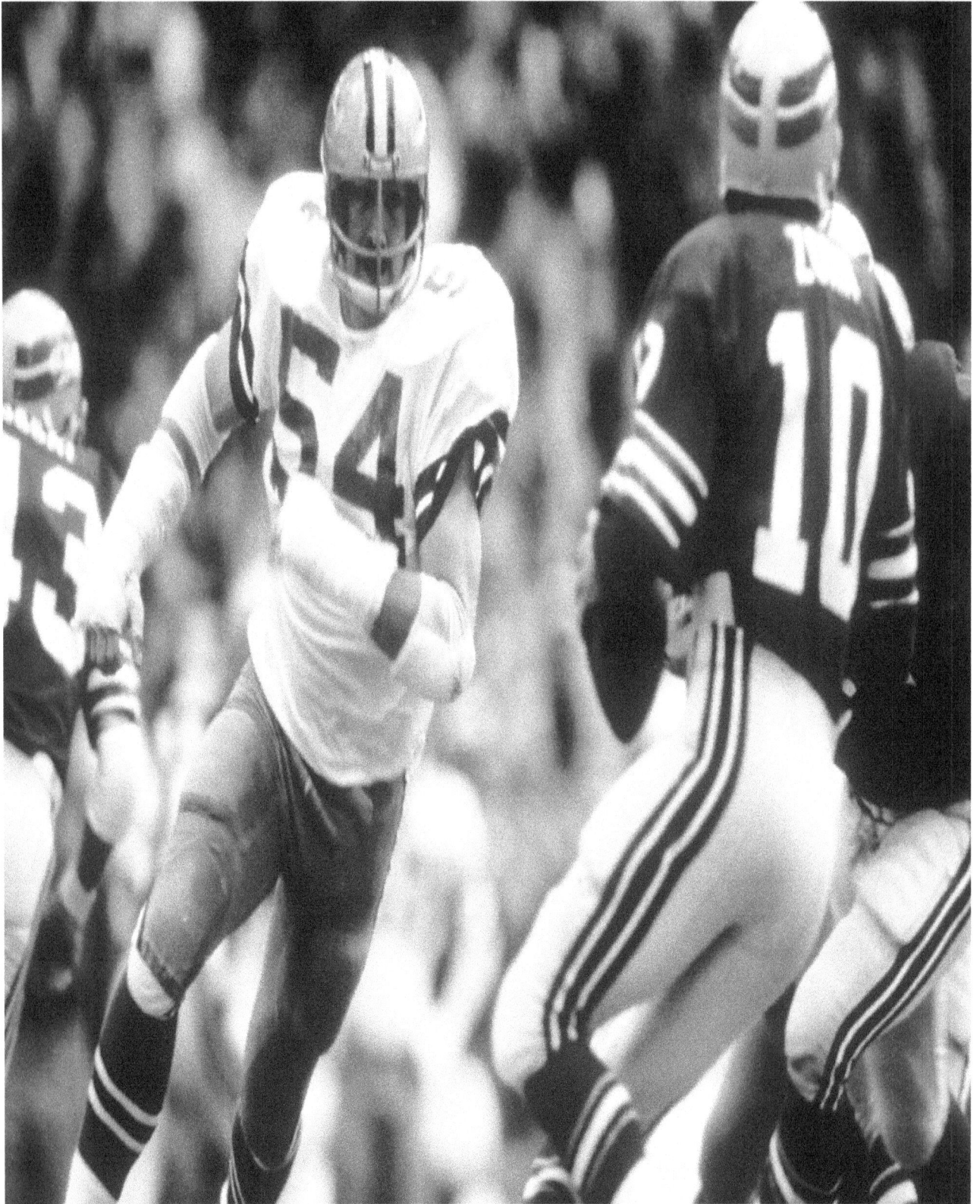

Dallas Cowboy defensive tackle Randy White coming in for the sack on Seattle Seahawks quarterback Jim Zorn. Photograph copyright Associated Press

Chapter 93

Robert Brazile

College: Jackson State

Career History:
Houston Oilers (1975–1984)

2018 Inductee Pro Football Hall Of Fame

College Choice
When I came out of high school, which was back in the '70s, I originally signed with Troy State. Troy State is one of the major colleges in Alabama. Rickey Young was a very good friend of mine. We had grown up together and we wanted to go to the same college. So, we took a bus trip up to Troy State for a visit and we each signed a letter of intent with Troy State. We thought we were going to end up playing there, but my mom and my dad wanted to see the college that I had chosen.

We went up to Troy State at the wrong time of the year, which was spring. All the people were out sun tanning. My momma drove up to the campus and said, "Well, that will tell you one thing." She looked at Rickey, my dad, and me, and said, "Turn the car around. They need to find another school, there's nobody going to school here." So, that ended me going to Troy State. I think there were too many naked people laying around on the campus for my momma.

I had a cousin who played at Jackson State. He had told Jackson State Head Football Coach Bob Hill, that he had a couple of guys that wanted to come visit. So, we went over to visit Bob the following Saturday.

Bob wasn't interested in Robert Brazile; he was interested in Rickey Young. He looked down at Rickey's legs and said, "You play football?" Rickey said, "Yeah." They had a good conversation and Bob signed Rickey. I asked him, "What about me, coach?" He said, "Well, you come on. You've got pretty good confidence." So that's how I ended up at Jackson State.

Jackson State
Playing at Jackson State was a challenge when you look at what we did and what we had to go through during the '70s in the SWAC Conference. The SWAC had a bunch of great athletes from Grambling, Texas Southern, Prairie View, Alcorn, and Mississippi Valley. After my senior year, we had eight guys go to the pros. Before that, Jackson State had four or five guys go pro and even before that, they had two or three. We had talent on the field every day.

Walter Payton
Walter Payton and I roomed a little bit on the road as well as on campus. We had three to a room.

I played against some great athletes coming out of Mobile, and I played against some great running backs during my college career. Walter was an exceptional, different type of athlete.

Walter could do anything he wanted to with a football, a basketball, or anything that involved a ball. Walter could do it. I saw Walter grow up and mature.

People ask me all the time, "What made you such a great pursuer and also a great tackler?" I say, "If I could just get my hands on Walter, I could make a great tackle." Just to get my hands on him. I'm not talking about getting him down, just being able to touch him. When you touch a gifted guy like Walter everyday, it betters your game and your program.

NFL Draft
I thought that the Dallas Cowboys were going to draft me. All I wanted to do was just hit players and prove my ability. I just wanted to be drafted by a team. Rickey Young always want to go to the West Coast. Walter Payton just wanted to play. I think he wanted to be a Chicago Bear. I just wanted to go play professional football.

College All-Star Game
Playing in the College All-Star Game was quite an experience. We trained with the Super Bowl Champion Pittsburgh Steelers. We lined up against these champs and were told we had a good team of players. The College All-Stars all thought, "Hey this our chance to shine." We led the Steelers during the game and Joe Gilliam of the Steelers asked, "What are you guys trying to do?"

The Steelers made a couple of touchdowns in the second half and beat us. I really thought we were going beat the Steelers. It was a great experience for me. I was ready for the Houston Oilers training camp when I got there. I knew what to expect.

Bum Phillips
Bum Phillips is one of the coaches I think should be in the Pro Football Hall Of Fame. Bum was one of the best coaches I play under. I played for some coaches that I admired and respected. My high school coaches were great coaches.

My college coach, Bob Hill, was a drill sergeant. He would work us to death. As a matter of fact, when I got to the pros, I was thinking, "Is this all we're going do?" After a couple of days, I got a chance to build and go on.

You earned Bum's respect when you respected him. It was a total father-like situation. You could go to Bum and ask him anything, and he would give you a truthful answer. It was probably the answer you wanted to hear.

One day I said to him, "Bum, I need to go home. We are having Fathers' Day in Mobile, Alabama." Bum asked, "Can you be back the next day?" I said, "Yes." Bum said, "Then go to your folks." He was one of the most lovable and understanding coaches, a professional would want to play under.

Houston Oilers 3-4 Defense
Bum Phillips knew what he wanted when he put that 3-4 defense together. On one side of me was a Pro Football Hall Of Famer in Elvin Bethea, and next to him was another Pro Football Hall Of Famer in Curley Culp. On the other side there was Tody Smith. A lot of people forget

about my strong side linebacker, Teddy Washington. Teddy Washington was one of the strongest strong side linebackers that I'd ever seen play the game, and that's taking nothing away from anyone else in the NFL. Teddy Washington was great.

We had Teddy holding up everything on his side and Elvin and me on the right side most of the time, coming up on the offense. It's hard to perceive that but it's what we had. Bum drafted the people that he needed for his 3-4 defense. It started with Curley Culp who was the best nose guard. We had Elvin and me on the same side. Gregg Bingham, Steve Kiner, and Teddy Washington played linebacker. That was one great 3-4 defense.

Rivalry Between Houston Oilers & Dallas Cowboys
The rivalry between the Houston Oilers & Dallas Cowboys started before I got to Houston. Bum came to the Oilers and put together a great group of guys. He traded John Matuszak for Curley Culp. He got other players, like me, thru the draft.

We were still under the shadow of a winning organization in the Cowboys. The Cowboys had six future Pro Football Hall Of Famers playing for them all out of the Houston area. Because they were winners, they were America's Team. We had to duel in the state by winning on the field, and that's what we tried to do. We knew that if we could win games, we'd get fans out.

Early Success With Houston Oilers
I was in the right situation. I was learning when I first joined the Houston Oilers. We had two or three All-Pros on defense and one hell of a teacher in Defensive Coordinator, Eddie Biles. They utilized me knowing what I could do for that defense. I could rush, I could pass-coverage, and I could do what they needed from me at my position. I had originally been a middle linebacker at Jackson State. I developed a great sense of leadership at Jackson State and carried that over into the pros.

We played as a team, as one big unit. That's what made us so successful. It wasn't just me. I had some talent, but we had a unit that played together.

Earl Campbell
Earl Campbell and I spent some time on the road as roommates. I joke with people, I slept with the best two running backs in the NFL—Earl Campbell in the pros and Walter Payton in college.

Earl would run over you, run through you, or around you. He was fast. People didn't think Earl was as fast as he was. They were both great running backs and both Pro Football Hall Of Famers.

I was lucky to play with Walter in college, and then come to the pros and play with Earl Campbell. When you practice against those guys every day, you've got to better your game and their game. The more you challenge your talent, the better you get.

Houston Oilers Players Attitude
The Houston Oilers players played hard for 60 minutes. The attitude we had was whatever it takes. We were not the type of guys who would say, "We coulda, shoulda, woulda," after a game. We wanted to win every game. We gave all we could.
I'm really proud of my career and the guys that I played with. I know that if I have to go to war, I'd love to go to war with these guys again.

Toughest Opponent

The toughest opponent for the Houston Oilers was the Pittsburgh Steelers. The challenge for us was that we knew that we needed to beat the Pittsburgh Steelers to get where we wanted to be, which was in the Super Bowl.

I still think we had a great shot in 1980. The referee made a bad call in the 1980 AFC Championship Game against the Steelers. I'll probably take that loss to my grave. I did not get my defense ready after that bad call. Sure, that was a bad call, but we still had to play defense. I feel so bad today, every time I think about that. I could not get my guys back together to play the defense we needed to win and go to the Super Bowl. You've got to get over the adversity, you've got to get over the bad calls, and you've got to play the rest of the game. We never recovered after that. I still feel some personal blame about that because we did not overcome.

Decision To Retire After Wife's Death In Car Accident

After my wife died in a car accident, I left the decision whether I should retire up to my son, who was eight at the time. Right before I went to training camp the decision of whether I should retire was in the back of my mind.

I told my son, "Daddy has to go to training camp." He said, "Dad, maybe let's go to Mobile and live with Grandma." He was referring to my mom.

I came back from training camp after the Oilers released me that year. I think the Oilers did me a favor by releasing me. I knew then what I wanted—to come into the league as an Oiler and then leave as an Oiler. It was kind of rushed, but it made it clean for me.

Photograph copyright Associates Press

Chapter 94

Mike Haynes

College:
Arizona State

Career History:
New England Patriots (1976–1982)
Los Angeles Raiders (1983–1989)

1997 Inductee Pro Football Hall Of Fame

On Attending John Marshall High School In Los Angeles
When I was going to school there, it was more known for academics than sports. We were actually called the Marshall Barristers, after John Marshall. I played football there. Our team didn't win any games my senior year. Since that time, they have played in the CIF championship, so it's different now. The demographics in the whole area have changed over the years.

College
UCLA came after me for track. Back in those days, I think every kid playing football in L.A. wanted to play at USC when John McKay was there. He had a lot of Heisman Trophy winners.

At Arizona State, we had a lot of good guys on our team. Some of the guys went on to have great NFL careers before me and after me. There was Charley Taylor, Hall of Fame wide receiver for the Washington Redskins, Curley Culp, Hall of Fame defensive tackle, J.D. Hill, Art Malone, and Ben Malone, to name a few. Then with me, Danny White, Steve Holden, Woody Green, and Al Harris, who played for the Bears; just a whole bunch of good players. We played in three Fiesta Bowls. My senior year, we were undefeated and beat Nebraska in the Fiesta Bowl.

When I was playing in college, not very many teams went to bowls. Playing in a bowl meant a lot more than it does today. Fortunately, the Fiesta Bowl is still recognized as a great bowl. I still think going to a bowl is pretty exciting for the players.

Playing For Coach Frank Kush At Arizona State
We could beat teams, but for Coach Kush, it mattered how we beat them. We might beat them at halftime 14 to nothing, and he'd come in and rip us like we were doing poorly. So, we'd go back in the second half and score 30 points. He was an interesting guy. I'm glad I had a chance to play for him. My senior year, we only had six seniors. The year before we had more than 20 seniors. He said the team that I was on my senior year was maybe the best team that he'd ever coached.
As of today, it is still the only undefeated team in ASU history. That was back in 1975.

They've had some other teams that have come close, but they lost in a bowl game. Coach Kush was on to something. He knew a little bit about us, and off that team we had several first-round draft picks. Larry Gordon, linebacker, went to the Miami Dolphins, and Al Harris, a defensive lineman, went to the Chicago Bears. Some of the other guys, including me, went in the early rounds of the draft. We were putting up a lot of points in those days and we had an unbelievable defense. They're trying to get back to those days now, but it's not getting any easier.

Getting Drafted By The Patriots
The year I got to the Patriots, in 1976, they were coming off of a terrible season the year before. They had only three wins, but they had quite a few draft choices so they had three first-round picks. They were defensive back Tim Fox out of Ohio State, offensive lineman Pete Brock from University of Colorado, and me. We had other guys on our team from the draft that year that were all big contributors. We turned that season around and only had three losses during the regular season.

Dealing With Brisk New England Temperature
It was culture shock to play in New England and think that was where I was, hopefully, going to be spending the next 10 years of my life playing football, but I adjusted. I can remember the first time it snowed. I'd never really seen snow come down except in the movies. I'd been up to the mountains where it snows in Southern California. One of the great things California is you can drive out to the beach and go surfing, or you can drive up to the mountains and go skiing on the same day. I'd been up to the snow, obviously, but I never really saw it come down.

I'll never forget seeing it snow for the first time. Tim Fox had invited me over to his home for dinner. I went out to my car then I went back inside and called him. I said, "Hey, Tim. It's snowing, man. I can't make it." He started laughing. He laughed so hard. I don't think I'll ever live that down.

Getting Eight Interceptions His Rookie Year
One of the things I loved to do was to have the ball in my hand. I liked to run with it. Being a rookie, every team picked on you. When you are trying to figure out where the weakest area of the defense is, you think, let's go after the young guy. I did make a lot of mental mistakes that year. I probably led the team in mental errors, but I would self-correct in the middle of a play. For instance, if I was lined up outside the receiver, back pedaling on the outside, and then remember, "Oh, wait a minute, if both the backs go away, I'm supposed to switch to the inside."

Because I was on the outside and the quarterback recognized I was on the outside, he thought I was going to stay on the outside. But, I would just seem to switch back to the inside just as he was throwing the ball and consequently, I'd be in great position for an interception. I almost led the league that year in interceptions. I did lead the league in punt return yards. I had a thing back in those days. I never used to fair catch, so my average probably wasn't as high as it could be, but it was one of the higher averages in the league that year. I led the league in total return yards.

Giving The Patriots Their First Punt Return Touchdowns

I thought it was kind of strange they had that record and no one had ever returned a punt for a touchdown. I knew early on that we would break that, because of the commitment that the guys had on special teams. We had a lot of guys who were just really awesome special teams players, like Dickie Conn and Jess Phillips. We also had a lot of starters on our punt return team. It wasn't like taking guys who weren't playing. These were guys who were excellent athletes who wanted to score. I'm kind of lucky to be the guy who was chosen to be the returner. It was a lot of fun. I think people used to love to come see if I was going to fair catch or not. It was just a good time to be back there and a good time to be a Patriot fan.

Ending Up With The Raiders

I was having some contract problems. The way I got there is a long story. I jumped on an airplane, flew out, and signed a contract with the Raiders. Technically the Patriots still owned my rights, so I played out my contract. The league challenged my situation, but in the end everybody decided that it might be the best thing to happen and they let me go to the Raiders. They gave the Patriots a couple of draft choices for me, so I was happy because it got me back home into Los Angeles.

It was pretty difficult. It was October and my wife was pregnant. It was pretty hard to be home wondering if I was going to play that season, but everything worked out in the end. It was one of the better decisions I made in my life.

Playing In The Super Bowl After Playing In Five Regular-Season Games

It doesn't get any better than that. The Raiders had a great team. They had a young corner, a guy named Ted Watts out of Texas Tech, and he was playing great. Just like when I was a rookie, they would pick on him. I think even though the Raiders would still win the game, they felt like they wanted to take that off the table, you might say, for other teams, and brought me in. They didn't pick on me. I wish they had, but they didn't. That helped the defense and we went on to win the AFC Championship, defeat the Seattle Seahawks. Then we went on to the Super Bowl to play the defending champions, the Washington Redskins.

Playing With Lester Hayes

The only difference between the two of us was just the spelling of our names. We both loved playing corner, loved playing man-to-man, and liked getting after people. Lester was a little bit more aggressive in the way that he approached the game than I was. I wouldn't really call anybody out and say, "I'm going to shut you out." I wouldn't say anything like that, because I wouldn't want to say anything that was going to amp up your testosterone. For me, I tried to just keep it low-key, but with Lester that was hard to do. I think as a result though, we would always get the best effort from our opponents. It made us bring out our "A" game more often.

Use Of Stickum

It didn't last for very long. They had to outlaw Stickum, not only because Lester was using it. Other guys in the NFL started using it. Lester led the NFL that year with interceptions. In fact, he was the MVP of our league because of that great year.

When Stickum gets on a football, you can't get it off. You have to take it in the back and use some kind of special chemical to get if off. It ruined a lot of footballs. They were going through too many balls for a game. So, Stickum was outlawed.

A 97-Yard Interception Return For A Touchdown
That was against the Miami Dolphins and I was covering Mark Duper. A quick little three-step-drop type play, and I stepped in front of it. It's really kind of funny. I've seen him a million times since then and never asked what he was doing. You would think that one of them made a mistake. Either Dan Marino made a mistake or Duper made a mistake, because Dan threw the ball and Duper was breaking out. I looked, took a little peek, and saw the ball coming, so I just grabbed it and ran with it. I tried to get to the other end zone before he caught me. That guy was one of the world-class sprinters, a Cliff Branch type. He could really run.

I knew I had six as long as he didn't catch me, and that was my only concern. When I'd caught the ball, I really lost sight of him. I didn't know where he was. I didn't know if he was right behind me, or deep in the end zone. I had no idea, and I didn't want to take a look to my right to find him there, so I just kept looking downfield and kept going.

Going From The Raiders To Working For The NFL
It was a great change, because I became educated with what the league was all about. I think as a player during my era, we didn't really think that the league cared about the players, and didn't care about the game as much as it should. I found out that was totally wrong, and probably the biggest thing that the players and the league needed to do was communicate with each other. If both sides were just able to talk about common issues, they would have come up on the same side of the table every single time. Commissioner Tagliabue, who was Commissioner when I joined the league, was really good at doing that and so was Roger Goodell. Roger, the current Commissioner, is also very good at getting information from all the sides before he takes a position.

It was probably one of the best things that ever happened to me. I know that when it comes to the game, the players and the safety, a lot of times when we think they maybe didn't care, it's that they just didn't know what was going on. Everybody assumed that they did, and I know from being there that wasn't always the case. Today there seems to be a lot of polarization between sides on many topics. There are a lot of safety issues, you have replacement officials and things like that, and it's sort of an organized chaos. You would think an enterprise as big as the NFL, with all of the money involved, could somehow get all their ducks in a row and have things run smoothly.

It does amaze me, but sometimes I don't have all the facts. I'd like to see the referees, the officials, taken care of. They are big contributors to the game. I don't even know, to be honest with you, what their real issues are and why they're not on the same page.

I know that those guys really, really work hard to be the best officials they can be. I worked in the league office and I saw them do their work firsthand during the season and during the off-season. There is a commitment to the head official in football operations and to getting it right. They want the coaches and players to communicate with the league office about different penalties and situations, all with the idea of trying to get everybody on the same page. They want to be sure that they're making the right decisions in the best interest of the game.

As a consequence, things are much better. Safety is extremely important and looked at completely different now than it was when I played, in the '70s and '80s. They're constantly looking at equipment and all kind of other things, which I think is important for the future of the game. For me, because it was my sport, I'd like to see the game played all over the world and continue to grow. When you look at where it started and where it is now, that has a chance of happening during my lifetime. I'm excited about it. It's not perfect. It will probably never be perfect due to the evolution of the game. Overall, it's all been going in the right direction, and a good direction for the growth of the game.

People's Criticism Of Gene Upshaw

For me it was very hard because Gene was also a friend of mine. I never really played with him as a Raider, but I did play with him in Pro Bowl games. I got to know him well. Even when I got the job in management for the Player Development Department with the NFL, I had a lot of interaction with the Players Association and I saw Gene quite a bit. I knew where his heart was and what he was trying to do. I can't say that I always agreed with what he did, but I knew where he was focused. I really didn't understand why he said some of the things that he said. He really upset a lot of the guys. We all had a lot of respect for him, so he put himself in a situation where there was a lot of room for criticism. But, there was also a side of him that was very good and did a lot of good things for players.

The thing I hate is that all of the good things he did will be forgotten. People will remember the things they wish he had done, but I totally understand that. I can't really say that the way a lot of former players are looking at him is wrong, because I understand their point of view. I see what they're seeing, and I wish it wasn't that way. I wish Gene would have done things a little bit differently, but he's not here to tell us why he did them. He was constantly trying to defend himself.

I would see him in different situations and talk to him privately, and he would share a different side of the story that he could not share publicly. I still think people should remember him as one of the great players of all time, and one of the guys who really led change for the Players Association. It's just unfortunate he didn't get things done the way that we all would have loved him to. Hopefully, that'll happen in time. Let's just say he got the ball rolling. He'll be judged by a lot of people, by how his decisions impacted them individually. I think there's a real good reason for criticism from a lot of the pre-'93 guys.

Decision To Retire

I thought I had a couple more years left in me. Once you've been in the league for a while, you can see how guys are being moved around and how they are getting ready to play. I could see that. I wasn't ready to stop playing. I really didn't feel like I got beat out, so that made it a little bit tough to leave. When they asked me to step down and let the other guys play in front of me, it was hard. How do you say, "Sure, great, this is wonderful?"

In hindsight, I wish I had done that. Maybe I would have gotten three more years in and I would have been able to do a lot of things that I wanted to do anyway. My attitude, I guess, with the end of my career and how it was going to end, was ... no one knows this, but I wish I had done things differently. I had a chance to do things differently and I think I may have made the wrong choice, but I'll never know.

Owner Al Davis

I don't think there could possibly be anyone like Al Davis. One, it's just the era that he was a part of, the friends that he made, and the impact that he had on the league. All the great things that he did as the owner have been adopted, really, into the NFL. He did different things that were really special. When word got out that he was doing it, other owners started doing it. I think they probably owe him a lot, but his personality was one where he walked alone a lot. I hope he'll go down in history the way he should go down in history, as one of the greatest owners of all time.

Pro Football Hall Of Fame Induction

The first time in Canton was very tough, because I was being inducted into the Pro Football Hall of Fame. That was my first time there, and it was whirlwind. You're going from one banquet room to the next, celebrating something, either a terrible cause or being introduced as the next guy who's going to be inducted this weekend. It was a blur. You don't really get to enjoy too much time with your friends until after the ceremony. You had your little party, and you got a chance to be with your family and friends. For the most part, before that, it's very difficult to enjoy it. You have to come back and enjoy it the following year.

Involvement In National Prostate Awareness Month

At the Pro Football Hall of Fame, the NFL and the American Neurological Association had partnered up for free screenings for retired players, and they kicked it off at the Hall of Fame. At that time, I was an employee of the NFL. They asked me to go down to where they were doing the screening because they were going to do a Public Service Announcement. While I was there, the ladies that were working there ... I now call them the angels ... convinced me that I should take this simple blood test and told me I might encourage other guys to do it, so I did.

Then the doctor called me in and started asking me about my PSA (Prostate Specific Antigen) and asking what my baseline PSA was. That was the first time I had heard of PSA for blood tests. Anyway, the doctor scared me when he gave me all the statistics about one in six men will be diagnosed with prostate cancer in their lifetime, and when you compare that to one in eight women will be diagnosed with breast cancer in their lifetime.

I was diagnosed with prostate cancer and was successfully treated. It's important for men to know about the PSA test and prostate cancer screening.

Seattle Seahawks wide receiver Steve Largent is covered by Los Angeles Raiders cornerback
Mike Haynes. Photograph copyright Associated Press

Chapter 95

Harry Carson

> College:
> South Carolina State
>
> Career History:
> New York Giants (1976–1988)
>
> 2006 Inductee Pro Football Hall Of Fame

College Choice
I wound up following friends who were attending South Carolina State. I wasn't heavily recruited coming out of high school because I quit the football team during my senior year. I had a little disagreement with my high school coach.

South Carolina State
I knew that I was going to be playing football at South Carolina State. I didn't know what I was in for in college. Even though I played in high school, college was a completely different situation. The competition was more intense than I thought it would be. I had to adjust very quickly to fit in.

As it turned out, I wound up being a starter as a freshman. I was able to sort of adjust to the program. I thought I fit in very well.

We had a pretty good team. During my first year Donnie Shell and Barney Chavous, who played for the Denver Broncos, were on the team. Willie Mays Aikens was primarily a baseball player but he was also my backup on the football team.

I had the opportunity to play with some really talented guys during that era. Outstanding athletes surrounded me. I think Willie Mays Aikens and Gene Richards were one or two in the baseball draft in 1975. There was a lot of talent at South Carolina State.

NFL Draft
I really didn't have a whole lot of expectations about what round I was going to be drafted in. Being chosen to play in the NFL was good. Scouts, GMs, and personnel people had scouted me. Some had projected me to be drafted as early in the second round. Others projected me to go later than the fourth round.

I was drafted and quite frankly, I was a little disappointed when the Giants drafted me. They wanted me to play middle linebacker, but I had never played middle linebacker before. I was comfortable playing right defensive end and being able to get after the quarterback from blindside.

Marty Schottenheimer drafted me and taught me how to play the middle linebacker position. I had to adjust whether it was in high school, college, or on the Pro level as a rookie. I had to learn a new position, middle linebacker. Middle linebacker in the 4-3 defense at the Pro level, is probably the toughest position to learn. It was a challenge but I think that I validated Marty choosing me in the fourth round to be the player to play that position.

The transition was hard and entailed a lot of studying. I used to work out at the University of South Carolina. Carolina gave me the freedom to come to their facility and work out.

Their coach was Jim Carlen. I remember engaging in a conversation with Coach Carlen. He said, "When you're in college, it's about 80% physical and 20% mental. When you get to the pro level, it's the reverse. It's 80% mental and 20% physical."

I heard what he said, but it didn't dawn on me until I got into NFL training camp. The playbook that I got was about 10 times thicker than the playbook that I got when I was with South Carolina State. There's a lot more intellectual work that you have to do, a lot more studying. It's more mental. People look at the NFL game and they see the physical side of it. They have no clue as to the mental aspect of the game you have to be able to deal with once you come into the National Football League.

Sam Huff
Sam Huff had retired years before I got there but I was certainly aware that Sam Huff had played with the Giants. Quite frankly that was the other thing that I liked about the Giants at that time, the rich history and tradition of the players who played before me. It gave me something to shoot for, to basically follow in the footsteps of an iconic player like Sam Huff.

Giants Linebackers
I'm not going to go so far as to say that we had the best linebacking group in NFL history. I like to think that, but I'm not going to say it out loud. The guys who I first played with, Brad Van Pelt and Brian Kelley, were very good players. Then when the Giants chose Lawrence Taylor and we went from a 4-3 defense to a 3-4 defense, we became a very dominant group of defensive players. We couldn't have been as dominant as we were without a strong defensive line.

After Brad and Brian left, Carl Banks and Gary Reasons assumed their roles, so it was Carl, Lawrence, Gary, and me. We wound up being a pretty good quartet of linebackers in the mid-'80s.

Being Named To 1978 Pro Bowl
It was gratifying. It was even more gratifying for me to come in and make the all-rookie team playing a position that I'd never played before. A couple of years later I made the Pro Bowl. It was before Lawrence Taylor got there and I sort of made that on my own merit. I was named NFC Linebacker of the Year twice. Those were tremendous honors.

When Lawrence arrived we got even better. He just elevated our play the way that he played the game. It took some pressure off of the other players, put a lot more pressure on him, and it gave us an opportunity to make plays. We all worked together and it worked out well.

Lawrence Taylor

Lawrence Taylor was an outstanding player. We were good but he was better. You want to focus on the best. He established himself as being the best. Again, we were able to infuse our game with the way that he played and it just elevated our play. There was no jealousy of the attention that Lawrence was getting.

For us, it was just about bottom line … the production that we were able to produce on the football field. That was ultimately the bottom line. Each guy understood his role. I knew that my role wasn't to rush the quarterback. My role was to stop the run so I tried to pursue my role as best as possible. Lawrence did a great job and the other linebackers on the defensive line did their job.

The spotlight is always on the flashy guys. Lawrence was one of the flashy guys. He deserved the attention that he got as a player. If a player has a problem with the media attention then that could be a problem for the team. The player can sort of lash out at any time when it becomes a bit too much for him.

It didn't bother me because I had to deal with the media anyway as a captain. It allowed the other payers to just focus on playing the game and not have to deal with the media. They just flew under the radar and did not have to deal with cameras, microphones, and so forth. In some ways, that can be a plus for your teammates. In other ways it can be a negative for your teammates.

Lawrence Taylor Breaking Joe Theismann's Leg During A Monday Night Football Game

Every Friday the team would sit down and go over our goals as a defensive unit. The one thing that I remember saying during the meeting was, "Don't knock Joe Theismann out of the game." We knew everything about Joe. We wanted him in the game. If we had him in the game, there was a very good chance that we were going to win the game.

The play was a flea flicker. It initially looked like a running play where Joe Theismann handed the ball to John Riggins. Ultimately my responsibility was to stop the run. When I saw Riggins pitch the ball back to Theismann, I was already up into the line, trying stop the run. I was sort of in this no man's land where I didn't know whether I should go back to my pass coverage spot or go ahead and rush the quarterback.

I decided to react as a football player and I rushed the quarterback. Theismann sidestepped me. When he sidestepped me, Lawrence Taylor came in for the kill shot and went down on Joe's leg. If Joe was not as nimble as he was at that time, I would have tackled him. That was probably the most gruesome injury people have seen watching NFL football.

It was a situation that nobody wanted, but it happened and you reacted. As a humanitarian what you do is you stop being competitors and combatants and you take on a more humanitarian role.

Both teams started to talk to Joe because we didn't want him to go into shock. Football just wasn't that important for those minutes that he was down on the ground.

Bill Belichick
Bill Belichick was a very headsy coach. It was about thinking. It was about creating new situations on the defensive side of the ball to disguise coverage. He utilized the strength of different phases of defense. Bill Belichick started us rushing two linemen, which was unheard of.

A lot of times when Bill would write things on the board, just diagramming as a coach does, we'd look and say, "Bill, that won't work." We'd go out on the field and incorporate it into our practice sessions, and it would work. During games we'd do things our opponents hadn't seen before and it would throw them off. We got to a point where we really began to trust Belichick.

We sort of looked at him as this mad scientist who could come up with all kinds of coverage and all kinds of fronts that would help us tremendously if we just bought into it. At that time, we all bought into it full tilt.

Bill Parcells
Bill Parcells came in and tried to coach a certain way. He treated guys like men and gave them a certain amount of freedom and flexibility. It didn't work for him. We had a disastrous season. We had a lot of injuries. His first season as head coach we went 3-12-1 and Bill almost got fired. The next year he decided that he was going to do things his way.

When he did that he let some players, like Brian Kelley and Brad Van Pelt, go. He got players who were younger and had a hunger for playing. He experienced success in '84 and '85. Then in '86, we went to Super Bowl.

After Winning Super Bowl
I was an older player when we won our first Super Bowl. I was going into my 11th year and I could tell that I didn't really have much longer to play. As it turned out, after we won in '86, I played two more years and then that was a wrap for me.

I just wanted to move on with my life I wasn't really thinking about how many Super Bowls we could go to. I just felt very fortunate that we were able to get to at least one. One was better than none. There are a lot of great players who have never gotten to a Super Bowl.

Origin Of Gatorade Shower For Head Coach
It was Jim Burt's idea and started in 1985. Parcells had been riding Burt all week prior to the Redskin game. He was really getting under Burt's skin. We were playing the Redskins and as time was winding down, Burt came over to me and said, "You know that Parcells is a real S.O.B. We should get him." I said, "What do you mean 'we'?"

He said, "If you do something to him he won't say anything, but if I do something to him he will have my ass. You've got to do it with me." I said, "What do you propose?" He said, "Let's get him with the Gatorade." As time was winding down, Parcells took his earphones off and we doused him with the Gatorade. Nobody really saw it.

That was the one instance it occurred, in 1985. The next year, we lost our first game against the Dallas Cowboys. In the second game, we were playing the San Diego Chargers and nobody thought we'd win. As it turned out, we did win. We were all very jubilant about winning the game, so I grabbed the bucket of Gatorade and I doused Parcells.

The next week, we won again. I had to douse him again because if you do something one week and it works, you've got to keep doing it. Parcells is very superstitious and some of us were also very superstitious. So as long as we were winning, we had to get Parcells with the Gatorade. That's how the whole thing started. It perpetuated itself during the '86 season. It's one of those things now that everybody does and after all these years, players are still doing it.

Standing Next To Bill Parcells During National Anthem
It was just one of those things that happened. I remember the first time standing there as captain. I was standing there because I had to get instructions from Parcells as to what to call on the coin flip, or what side of the field we were going to defend. If I wasn't by him when the national anthem was being played, he'd call me and I had to stand to his left.

That's the way it happened and I really didn't think about it at the time. In retrospect, there were people who noticed. There are people who have written about it. He's a very superstitious coach and it's almost funny thinking back as to how superstitious he was.

Pro Football Hall Of Fame Induction
The Hall of Fame was never a goal of mine. I saw what it was doing to people around me more so than me. I was pretty good dealing with it. When people care about you, they want the best for you. I think there were so many people who wanted the best for me, when they held that Hall of Fame voting and I didn't make it, there were people who were upset. They would cry, they'd show anger, and so forth. It was like I was the only one who was taking it in stride.

I remember going to the gym to work out. There were people who would avoid me in the gym because they didn't know what to say. It's like having a death in the family and you don't know what to say to someone who is close to the person who died. You avoid them so you don't have to say anything. Many times people said, "Oh, I'm so sorry. You'll get it next year."

After five years, you get tired of hearing it; they get tired of saying it. And, they start to avoid you. Or, you go to a dinner at the Waldorf Astoria and there's an emcee and he's introducing the athletes or celebrities in the audience. It would always come down to, "This man should be in the Pro Football Hall Of Fame." When you hear that over and over and over, you get tired of hearing it.

I made a decision that I wanted to take my name out of consideration for the Hall so I could live my life and just be a private person. I sat down, wrote a letter, and asked them to remove my name from consideration. It wasn't out of frustration as a lot of people thought. Honors really don't define me. They never have. I wanted to take possession of my life, take it back and just be able to go on and quietly do the things that I wanted to do without any kind of fanfare.

In 2006 when I found out I was being enshrined, it was interesting because I had divorced myself of the whole Hall of Fame situation. Once I wrote the letter and dropped it in the mailbox, I was done with it.

When I was elected, I didn't really have any feeling about it because it didn't mean anything to me. When I make up my mind to do something, my mind is made up. I really didn't feel anything. I had to accept the award. I could've easily have said, "Thanks, but no thanks," but my wife sat me down and told me I couldn't decline the honor because it wasn't about me. It was about my coaches, my family, and my kids. She was right.

Mr. Mara was probably my strongest advocate. He was my big supporter. For me to say, I don't want to deal with this, probably would have been an insult to him. I just decided to move forward and accept the award. During the days leading up to the Hall of Fame ceremony, I didn't really have a speech. I could have just got up and said thank you and then sat down, but I wanted to use that moment as an opportunity to shine the light on the issues of retired players.

Quite frankly, the first thing that I said, and that was probably the only thing that I remember about the speech, is that I implored the NFL and the Player's Association to do a better job in taking care of its own players. Doing that shined a light on the issues of meager pensions for former players.

Being Only Member Of Giants At Midfield For The Super Bowl Coin Toss
That wasn't planned. At least I didn't know anything about it until it happened. Coach Parcells told me to go out there. I started walking out on the field by myself and I felt the Bronco players walking toward me. I was like, oh man, wow, what five, six, seven, eight ... and I was the only player representing the Giants. It was an honor for me. I recognized at that time there were some great players on the team, but I was being singled out to lead the team, represent the Giant organization, and represent all the Giant fans. That was a tremendous honor for me.

New York Giant Harry Carson runs after intercepting Washington Redskin Joe Theismann's pass as Theismann tries to make the tackle. Photograph copyright Associated Press

Chapter 96

Tony Dorsett

College: Pittsburgh Career History: Dallas Cowboys (1977–1987) Denver Broncos (1988) 1994 Inductee Pro Football Hall Of Fame

College Choice

I was a big fan of Lydell Mitchell and Franco Harris who played at Penn State when I was a kid. All I wanted to do was go to Penn State to be like Lydell Mitchell and Franco Harris. That's all I talked about. As a matter of fact, my last game in high school, I had a monster game and in big bold print in the newspaper the next day was Penn State, next stop.

I was what you call the Blue Chip recruit. USC, UCLA, Arizona State, and schools way out west, recruited me. Michigan, Ohio State and all these schools back on the East Coast were recruiting me. I was waiting for Penn State Coach Joe Paterno. I'm like, "Where is he at?" I lost interest in Penn State after a while because I thought that they showed a lack of interest.

Another thing that caused me lose to interest was my Penn State visit was one of the more negative visits that I took. Back then, we had unlimited visitation rights. I was going somewhere almost every weekend. I was also getting frustrated and confused along the way. When I went to Penn State, all of the players I talked to said, "You may come here as a quarterback, but you may leave here as a center."

Penn State had John Cappelletti and he was going into his senior year. He was a contender for the Heisman, which he ended up winning that year. Joe Paterno told me when I finally had my visit, that he wanted me to be a defensive back my first year. He said when John Cappelletti graduated he would put me at running back. The only thing that kept going through my mind was the fact that all the players said, "Come in as a quarterback, you may end up as a center." My training was to be a running back first.

I figured, and don't take it wrong, I had cockiness and everything, but I had a little swag back then. I said to myself, "If Joe wants me to be a defensive back, I'll be a be damn good defensive back. Then, Joe's not going to want to put me back on offense."

When Notre Dame was recruiting me, Tom Pagna, Coach Ara Parseghian's right-hand man, supposedly told Ara that I was just a skinny little kid from Aliquippa, Pennsylvania who would never make it as a major college running back. You could only imagine what my thoughts were during the week of preparation to play the Fighting Irish. That tells it all right there. That's one of the motivating forces that helped get me ready to play against the Fighting Irish. Against Notre Dame as a freshman, I think I went for over 200 yards rushing and then as a junior, 303 yards rushing. I set a record for the most yards against an opponent and that was Notre Dame. They had great defenses back then.

Adjustment To College At Pittsburgh

There was an adjustment to college. I almost left school because I was pretty much a very introverted young man. It was hard for me to make friends. I hid behind my little dark round sunglasses. I could play on the field, but socially, it was hard for me to make the adjustment.

As a matter of fact, my hometown is only about a 30-minute drive from the university so I spent more time back home. My mom was like, "Boy, what are you doing home?" It just took me a while to get acclimated. Once I did, my Mom was saying, "When are you coming home?"

Socially, it was a big adjustment for me. Pitt was rebuilding at that time and it was just a perfect fit. I was glad that the University of Pittsburgh made a coaching change because I probably wouldn't have gone there if they had not.

Pittsburgh Winning National Championship

We went to bowl games every year and won the National Championship my senior year. That was a script made for Hollywood.

We lost our first two starting quarterbacks my senior year. The second or third game of the season we went down to Atlanta. For Robert Haygood, our starting quarterback, it was his hometown. He got hurt tearing his knee up. We lost him for the year.

Then Matt Cavanaugh came in as the starting quarterback. During training camp those two were fighting for the starting position, the outcome could have gone either way. Matt came in and about three or four games later, Matt got hurt. Fortunately for us, it wasn't for the whole year. We were down to our fifth year quarterback who had never taken a snap.

Our offense was pulling for our defense and our defense was pulling for the offense. Our defense won a couple of games for us. They came up big for us during the absence of Matt Cavanaugh. Tommy Yewcic, who is a congressman now, filled in pretty good for Matt while he was out.

Matt came back later in the year. We ended up undefeated. We went to the Sugar Bowl and beat Georgia. We beat the dog and we won the national championship.

NFL Draft

Tampa Bay just hired coach John McKay from USC, who had coached Ricky Bell there. Ricky Bell was "their prototype running back" at 6'3", 230 pounds, whereas I was 5'11", 183 pounds.

John McKay knew all about Ricky Bell because he coached him at USC. He drafted Ricky Bell with the first pick in the draft. Seattle had the second pick. Somehow the Dallas Cowboys bamboozled them for the pick and I ended up in Dallas. Thank God for that because I found it a lot healthier for me to be running behind an established offensive line with Dallas than Seattle, an expansion team in the NFL the year before.

Roger Staubach
I was blessed to have the opportunity to play behind one of the more prolific quarterbacks at that time in the National Football League, Roger Staubach. He was a role model, the ultimate pro, ultimate family man, and a God-fearing man. We had his leadership. You learn from guys like that on how to become a real pro, how to handle yourself both on and off the football field. I was privileged to have that opportunity. I respect him to this day. I have nothing but admiration for Roger Staubach. I always say, if I wanted somebody to be my role model and my mentor, it would be Mr. Staubach.

Not Being Inserted into Starting Lineup Until 10th Game of Rookie Year
Coach Landry and I went at it indirectly through the media. Tom Landry had a way of humbling people. Coach Landry said he saw a young kid coming in who won the national championship and got all this media attention. To keep me grounded he did not start me until the 10th game of my rookie year.

When I finally went in to have a one-on-one with him, he told me, "We expected you to be a starter by now." I said, "Coach, so did I." I guess he realized he was getting the best of me because I was getting a little lackadaisical.

My attitude changed after I told him, "Coach, I've written this year off." I was pretty much going to go to training camp the next year and start up. He told me, "All you need to do is just pick it up a little bit, change your attitude a little bit, and act like it bothers you when you drop a pass or something like that. Then you'll be a starter."

I went out to practice. I started exhibiting a little bit more effort, and he made me the starter. I felt bad because Preston Pearson was the starter. Preston came in from the Pittsburgh Steelers. I had just been in Pittsburgh a year earlier, winning the national championships. He made me the starter coming back from playing the Steelers in Pittsburgh, which was a great feeling for me. From there, I guess you could say the rest was history.

First Player To Win National Championship In College & Super Bowl The Next Year
It was like a set-up, because I didn't have anywhere else to go, but down. I won the national championship one year and the Super Bowl Championship the following year. Fortunately for me, it didn't go down. We didn't win another championship, but we went back to the Super Bowl the following year. We were in three other consecutive conference championship games, but unfortunately we weren't able to get over that final hurdle to win another Super Bowl. I enjoyed it. I had a lot of great teammates. I had a lot of great rivalries going and made a lot of great friends during my career in the National Football League.

It was great winning the Super Bowl. I thought, this is what it's all about right here. We already had a Super Bowl win. I thought it was going to be cool, but it just didn't work out like that. We were always in the thick of it. We had some great teams and great players. I enjoyed every one of my years here in Dallas.

Losing To Steelers In Super Bowl

I was mentally prepared, mentally ready to play against the Steelers. Growing up in Western Pennsylvania, the Steelers are what you're all about. I'm still a big Steelers fan. That's my roots. That's what I'm all about. I watched those guys play when I was a kid. Then all of a sudden, I got the opportunity to play against them in "the ultimate game." I was up and ready to go. I was hyped. Trust me, I was hyped and ready. It was just unfortunate; it was one of the better Super Bowl games. I think it was 35-31.

99 Yard Touchdown Run On Monday Night Football

That's one of the more memorable moments of my career. There are a lot of people who remember that run more so than any other run because of the platform that it took place on, Monday Night Football. It was the only ticket in town. Everybody was watching the NFL. You can only tie that record.

We only had 10 men on the field. It was partly my doing because I came in with the play and you can run that play from the two-back or a single-back set. In the single-back it's going to be me. I told Ron Springs, the other running back, to get out. I said we're going to run a single-back formation.

When Ron went back to the sideline, everybody said, "You're supposed to be on the field." He always said, "There was no way I was running back out on that field." He realized we could never play with ten men on the field. He said, "I wasn't about to get us a penalty, backed up on the one-yard line and have to come back and face Tom Landry." So he stayed on the sideline and I said, "Well, he wouldn't have been able to run that far anyway so it's a good thing he did not come back in."

When I got to about midfield I made a move and I was behind Drew Pearson. There were two defenders ahead of me. I was looking at Drew Pearson's legs from behind. Drew's a little knock-kneed and pigeon-toed. I was looking at his legs and he started tiring and I said you know what, I'm going to make a move right now and see if I can get past Drew and these guys. I actually thought I was going to get pushed out of bounds because I was so close to the sidelines. I was tiring myself. The opponent pushed me, but he didn't shove me hard enough to push me out of bounds. I ended up going all the way for a touchdown.

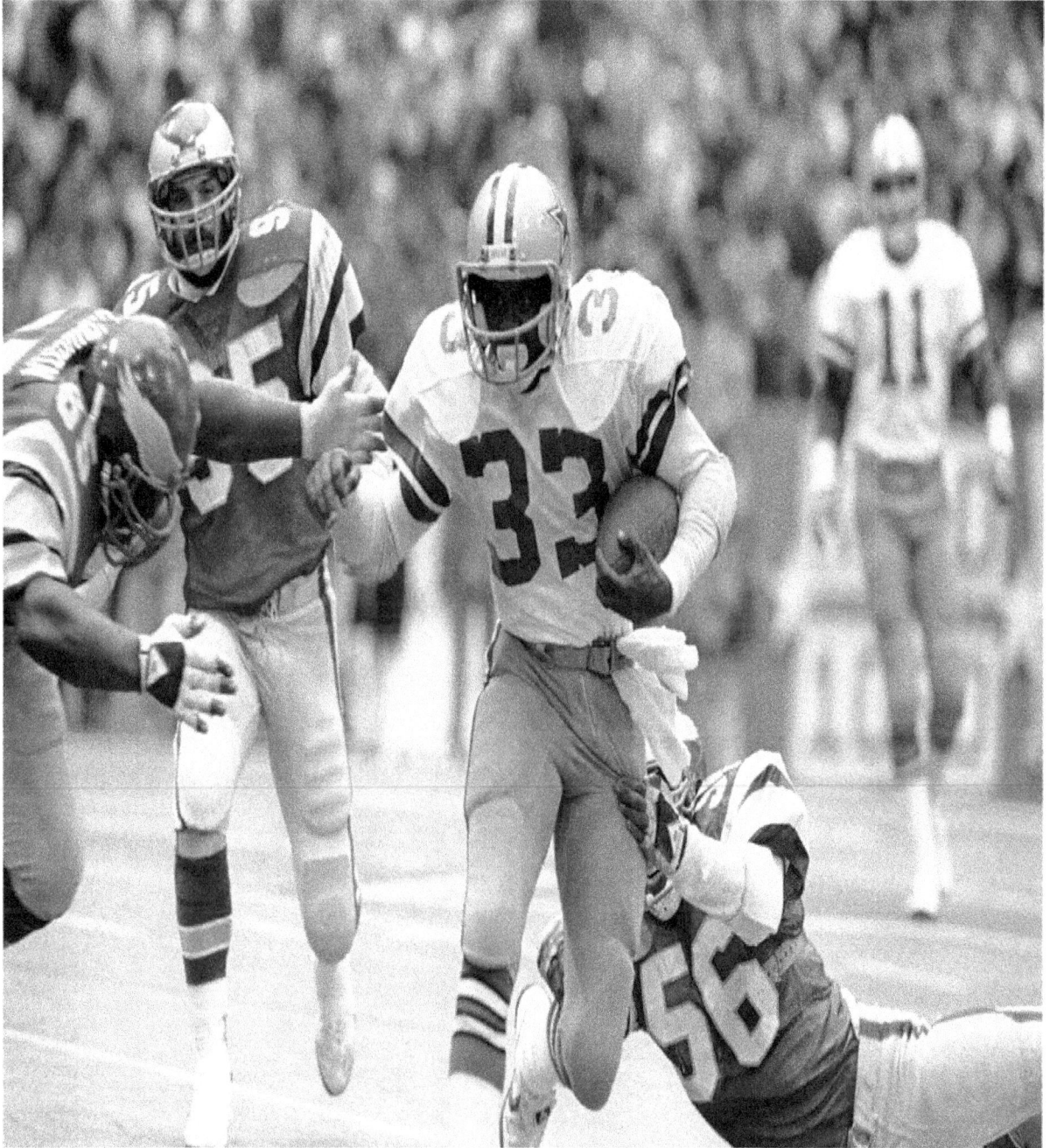

Photograph copyright Associates Press

Chapter 97

Steve Largent

```
College:
Tulsa

Career History:
Houston Oilers (1976)
Seattle Seahawks (1976–1989)

1995 Inductee Pro Football Hall Of Fame
```

College Choice

I would have loved to go to Oklahoma University. The football team there was running the wishbone offense at that time. I was a receiver even in high school. There weren't a lot of opportunities for catching many passes at OU with the wishbone offense. They also signed Tinker Owens that year.

My grandfather was a big influence in my life when I was deciding where I would go to college. He had really encouraged me to consider the University of Tulsa. Then when they ended up offering me a scholarship, it was a done deal.

NFL Draft

I was drafted by the Houston Oilers in the 4th round of the NFL draft in 1976. Bum Phillips told me that I was not good enough to play in the Oilers organization. They released me and I packed my bags and headed home looking for work. The Seahawks called me the same week and said, "Hey we want to give you another chance." It turned out they worked out a trade with the Oilers.

I was not a good rookie player. I didn't really know how to study; I didn't know how to prepare myself for practices or for games. It was a real learning experience for me going through the process that I did after being released from one team and getting a second chance in Seattle. I did everything I could to take advantage of the chance I had.

Joining Seattle Seahawks, An Expansion Team

I knew when I went into the Seattle locker room that it was a different situation. Even the veterans in training camp that year had their names written on tape on their helmets. Nobody knew each other; everybody was vying for a position on the team. The real key for me making the team was the fact that Jerry Rhome had come from the University of Tulsa, my alma mater, that same year to become the quarterback and receiver coach. He was the guy that really convinced the Seahawks to get me after the Oilers released me. When I came to Seattle, we were essentially running the old University of Tulsa playbook. We ran the same plays in Tulsa for three years. I knew the game plan in terms of the passing attack with the Seahawks the first day I stepped on the field. That was a real advantage for me.

Jim Zorn

Jim Zorn and I became fast friends and teammates as well. He is my best friend to this day. There was a connection that we had that is unusual for quarterbacks and receivers to have. Our relationship was one that carried over beyond the playing field and locker room. I think that was extremely instrumental in our development as players with the Seahawks. Jim was vying for a starting job as a quarterback and I was doing the same thing as a receiver. We just kind of connected because we were both guys that like to work hard, stay late practicing after the coaches had blown the whistles, and all the other players headed into the locker room. We would still be out there working on routes, catching balls, and just throwing the ball as much as we could. I think that really worked as an advantage for both of us.

Jack Patera

The first season for the Seahawks was also Jack Patera's first year as a head coach. We didn't win very many games. He was willing to do anything, including running fake field goals, punts, and things like that just to try to keep the ball on offense. Actually, during Jack's first several years as head coach, the one aspect of the team that worked well was the offense. Defensively we had more struggles.

Offensively, most of the time, we put a lot of points on the board. It was fun to play on that team because we had a lot of great veteran players that came from other teams. They would tell us stories about the way they did it in Miami, Cleveland, Dallas, or wherever they came from. There was a good nucleus of players, including Sherman Smith and Dave Brown, with whom you could really bond. You knew they were winners even though we didn't win that often in Seattle.

We were two and twelve that first year. I don't think the Tampa Bay Buccaneers won a game. In fact one of the two wins we had was against Tampa. We were not very good, but we were better than Tampa.

Playing Philosophy

My attitude was always, how do we win? It was not how many passes I caught. I worked just as hard during the offseason after my first season, as I worked before my first season in the NFL. It was never about how good could I get. It was about how could we get better as a team. That was always my focus every year I played.

Seattle Seahawks Progression

We were nine and seven in both the third and fourth seasons. That was pretty incredible back then considering that we were playing in the AFC West with the Oakland Raiders, Denver Broncos, San Diego Chargers, and Kansas City Chiefs, all of which were good teams. We were very competitive and felt like we were right on the cusp of becoming a real playoff contender. Unfortunately, that didn't happen because the wheels kind of fell off after the fourth year.

Transition At Quarterback From Jim Zorn To David Krieg

In the middle of the 1982 season, Jack Patera was fired. In 1983, Jim Zorn's position as our starting quarterback really began to be challenged. During the 1981 or 1982 season, Jim broke his ankle. Jim was never the same after he broke his ankle; he wasn't as mobile as he had been the previous five to seven years. Jim's decreased mobility really hurt us as a team and him as a player. The Seahawks began eyeing other quarterbacks. Dave Krieg came in about 1982 or 1983, and started contending for the starting position, which he eventually took over by the end of 1983.

Chuck Knox

Chuck Knox came in in 1983 as head coach and really turned the team around. He got a few veteran players from other teams and he really inspired the young guys and me. We knew this was a guy that knew how to win and get us into the playoffs. We all thought he was going to take us there. We didn't know it was going to be in his first year. He drafted Curt Warner from Penn State, in the first round. Curt came in and had an outstanding year. He ran the ball great, rushing for twelve or thirteen hundred yards. We played great football. After a couple of dismal years it was fun being a playoff contender that first year under Chuck Knox.

Chuck had experience. I think it's really important for a team to believe in their coach. The fact that Chuck had coached teams that were championship level teams meant he knew what needed to be done. He implemented what needed to be done immediately. Everyone had a lot of confidence in him, his coaching ability, and his coaching staff. That meant a lot to our team and was what we were missing before Chuck got there.

1982 & 1987 NFL Lockouts

The NFL owners locked out the players. My philosophy was that I signed a contract with the Seattle Seahawks not with the players association. My first obligation was to play.

In 1982 I felt obligated to play, but there was no opportunity. In 1987, there was an opportunity to play because there were games with replacement players. I went to play in the first game when they had replacement players and the ownership actually came to me and said, "Steve we don't want you to come in. We want you to stay out and let this process work out because we don't want to disrupt the positive momentum we have as a team right now." I listened to them, and I said, "Okay. I'm not going to do that." Toward the end of the strike, they said there was a deal; then they said there wasn't a deal. The owner said he erected a superficial time-line that if you weren't in by this certain time, you couldn't play in the game the following week. I reported for the last game for the replacement players in 1987. I played that game in Detroit.

I think all of us were frustrated with the deliberations, or lack of resolution, to the situation. In my situation in 1987, that was about my twelfth year in the league. I knew I didn't have many years left; in fact I was playing on borrowed time. The fact that we were under a union that was striking, was penalizing me in the opportunity to play in what I viewed the twilight of my career.

My teammates reported, literally two days after I did. They had come in after the deadline so they couldn't play in the game that Sunday. Since I had reported two days earlier, I was able to play in the game on Sunday. When I played in the Sunday game, the overwhelming majority of the guys didn't hold it against me. There were a few players, including prominent ones, who held it against me. They even continued to hold that grudge against me until a few years ago.

Most Memorable Tackle

In 1988, we were playing the Broncos in Denver and I ran a twelve-yard post route. Dave Krieg hung the ball and Mike Harden got to me just before the ball did. He hit me with a forearm to my head. He bent me over backwards and I was out before I hit the ground. I don't even remember hitting the ground. In fact, the ball came down, hit me on the chest, and rolled off. I think the league fined him $5,000, which was a lot of money back then. Then we played the Broncos in Seattle in December in the next to last game of the year, which was an ESPN game. Harden made an interception in the end zone and came running out of the end zone. I was on the other side of the field. I just drew a beeline right for his chest and I made a great tackle and the rest is history. I will never forget that tackle.

Lester Hayes & Mike Haynes
Lester Hayes and Mike Haynes were both equally good cornerbacks. Mike is in the Hall of Fame and Lester is not. They were both very good. Lester Hayes played linebacker at Texas A&M. He was a big, strong cornerback, but he could run too. They were both very difficult to play against. I played against Lester before Mike. Mike was with the New England Patriots before going to the Raiders.

Lester loved to wear that Stickum. Every time I played against him I would end up being covered in Stickum. He would have it on his hands, wrists, shoes, and socks. They played bump and run coverage and he got it all over you. I would get grass and all that other kinds of stuff sticking to me. It was gross. Lester felt like he could catch the ball better on interceptions if he wore it. Fred Biletnikoff used it, so Lester was going to use it too.

Pro Football Hall Of Fame Induction
Being inducted was like a dream. I had never really thought of myself as a Hall of Fame player. I had never let myself imagine that big of a dream for myself. It was extremely fun, extremely gratifying, and rewarding. I've always looked at it as an honor that I share with my teammates, coaches, and the organization that helped get me there.

Physical Traits As A Wide Receiver
I was average sized and had average speed. They used to say I could play well in a phone booth, meaning I didn't have the breakaway speed of a James Lofton or John Jefferson. If I needed to catch a seven-yard pass or fifteen-yard pass, I could get open and catch the ball if the quarterback got it there. That's kind of the role I played in Seattle. It's really surprising that the passing game is totally different today than it was when I played. I averaged over sixteen yards a catch. At the time, I held the records for the most yards and most catches in a career. The sixteen yards per catch that I had is pretty amazing when you consider that I was known as the too small, too slow guy.

What I found is that the guys who were really, really fast didn't really like going over the middle. I was just one of those guys who wasn't very fast, but didn't mind going over the middle. I didn't love it. Nobody loves getting their brains beat out, but I could make a living there, and I did. There is a place for every style, fashion, and form of a NFL receiver. I had one style and I tried to maximize it.

I say this to young people, including my four kids, all the time: "Don't let other people limit your desire or your ability. Just make the most of what you've got. You'll surprise yourself and surprise a whole heck of a lot of other people as well."

Photograph copyright Associated Press

Chapter 98

Earl Campbell

College: Texas

Career History:
Houston Oilers (1978–1984)
New Orleans Saints (1984– 1985)

1991 Inductee Pro Football Hall Of Fame

College Choice
I felt like Texas, with Darrell Royal as head coach, was the best school for me, not Oklahoma. Those were the two schools that were really dominating everything when I was coming up. So many people were going to Oklahoma. It wasn't that I was afraid of it. I just thought that being from the state of Texas, it was best to have players from the state of Texas there. It worked out.

Darrell Royal had a scout named Ken Dabbs. Ken Dabbs spent more time with me than Darrell Royal, because he was the recruiting coordinator. Once I got a chance to meet Coach Royal, we hit it off right away. Coach Dabbs started coming to my high school during my sophomore year, recruiting guys. He lost those guys, but I believe that I was the first one he recruited to come to UT that he was after. Then Coach Royal and I got involved.

Darrell Royal
He was a great man, no-nonsense. He wanted the best players and wanted to get the best out of you. It was about football, but it was also about being a student and getting you ready for life after sports.

Coach Royal suddenly decided to retire after the 1976 season. It was a shock then. As I got older, I learned that after you've stayed in the game so long and won national championships and all that, there's nothing left to do. I've heard that he couldn't control some of the players and couldn't sign the best players like he previously did. I believe that he decided I came in winning; I'm going out a winner. Nothing's wrong with having another interest in life.

Fred Akers
I was sure Darrell Campbell was going to replace Coach Royal as head coach because he was the defensive coordinator under Coach Royal for many years. He was right under Coach Royal, so I felt as though he was going to take over. During my freshman year, Fred Akers was the running back coach. He had been working for Darrell Royal for twenty some years. When he got the job it just made sense, because we all knew Fred Akers.

Looking back on it, the best thing that happened in my whole career was when Coach Akers came in and changed everything up right away. I believe that's why I was able to win the Heisman Trophy. Even though we lost against Notre Dame in the national championship, we competed. Coach Akers is the coach with the most wins in the history of the university.

All the guys knew him because he was there with Coach Royal. He was a great guy and a dynamic coach. We always used to get on him because he was just very neat all the time. You'd see him at practice and he looked like he was a GQ model. On game days he always had his suit on. He was an unbelievable guy and a very, very good coach.

I will continue to say the best thing that happened to me in my football career was when he came and changed the offense from the wishbone to the single backup. I won the Heisman Trophy and competed for the national championship. As a gentleman told me a few years ago, "Fans weren't wondering how many games Texas was going to win back then. We were wondering how many points we were going to beat them by."

1978 Championship Game Against Notre Dame
It was great. We were just getting into redshirting players. Not to make any excuses, but Notre Dame had been redshirting players for years. We had fourth year guys playing against fifth year guys from Notre Dame. One of the fifth year guys for Notre Dame was Ross Browner. They had a very good football team. Unfortunately we fell short, they won, and life goes on.

Joe Montana
I really didn't realize who Joe Montana was until I got into pro football and he was playing for the San Francisco 49ers. O. J. Simpson was on the 49ers. We were playing the 49ers in the Astrodome and I was concerned about watching O. J. Simpson as a runner. I saw Joe Montana and I said, "Oh, that's the quarterback from Notre Dame, that beat us."

Winning Heisman Trophy
Winning the Heisman Trophy was unbelievable. I never knew what the Heisman Trophy was until a guy named Tony Dorsett won the Heisman. I was working a construction job during the summer before my senior year and a guy on the construction job had a newspaper. He was reading it and talking about Tony Dorsett the Heisman Trophy winner joining the Dallas Cowboys.

That is when I made the decision that I wanted to try and win that trophy. I went and told the Texas trainer, Frank Medina, my decision. He said, "If you want to do that, you come over here and work out." That season our team was on a roll and I won the Heisman Trophy. Dreams can come true.

NFL Draft
I really didn't know I was going to be the first pick in the draft. My roommate was a guy named Alfred Jackson. He played split end on our team, and he went to the Atlanta Falcons in the draft. I was a speech communication major. The day of the draft I had a test. Alfred said, "Hey, what are you doing, Earl?" I said, "I've got tests today. I'm going to school." He said, "Man, are you crazy?" I said, "No, Albert. I've got this test. I'm going to school. I'll be back in a while."

I got over on campus and was messing around with some guys. I didn't make it home until 6:00 p.m. Alfred said, "Man, you've got to be the luckiest guy in the world. This guy named Bum Phillips has been calling you." I said, "What did he want?" He said, "That's gonna be your coach, that guy wearing a cowboy hat down there in Houston, Bum Phillips." That's how I found out I that was the number one draft choice.

Bum Phillips

Bum Phillips never knew my name was Earl Campbell up until this day. He knew me as "EC." Back then, it was popular that you'd get the uniform number you had in college if you were the Heisman Trophy winner or one of the big-time running backs. I wore number 20 in college. He said, "Hey, you want number 20?" I said, "It doesn't matter to me. I don't think a jersey gets you into the end zone." He said, "I don't have number 20, but I'll get it if you want it." I said, "No, it doesn't make any difference."

We were in the Oilers locker room and he reached in a laundry bag, got a jersey, threw it, and hit me in the face. He said, "Have you thought about this number?" I said, "Great with me." That's how I ended up with number 34.

My relationship with Bum was like a marriage from heaven. Bum and I were like father and son.

All I wanted to do was prove that I wasn't going to be a failure as a Heisman Trophy winner. Back then most of the Heisman trophy winners didn't produce in the NFL. The way Tony Dorsett produced in Dallas, I wanted to be like that in Houston. I knew I could play football. I knew God gave me that gift. Bum Phillips was about being part of a family. I think Bum Phillips cut some good guys that didn't want to work as part of the team. He wanted us working as a team. There was no "I" with him, and that was fine. I believe our football team was a team of overachievers because of his belief.

Bum was the total opposite of any coach. He was just a great, great guy. I really miss him. He knew a lot about life, too. He was a cowboy who loved country music and had ranches with cutting horses. Bum and Mel Blount of the Pittsburgh Steelers were really tight because they would compete with those horses. Mel would go to his ranch a lot. Mel was always in our locker room. We would play against each other hard. Everybody loved Bum, because it was more than just about football, it was being a good human being.

Ranching

I used to work on a ranch when I was growing up. It used to be in my mother's family when she was a little girl. I went back and bought it during my rookie year. The owner told my mom he would only sell it to me for this price. I bought it in 1978, and have owned it since.

Work Ethic

I would have to say my mother taught me the work ethic that I have today. Darrell Royal messed with it a little bit, put his blessing on it; Fred Akers put his blessing on it; Bum Phillips put his blessing on it; but the good Lord and my mother taught me how to do all that.

My mother was my toughest critic, as far as making sure I was trying to do the right thing. Of course, I have six brothers and four sisters. As she says, "Earl is just one of my kids, number seven in the family."

Nickname "The Tyler Rose"
Tyler, Texas is known as the Rose Capital of the World. I started working on ranches, hauling hay and all that stuff. That's what I would do as my second job. My first job was working in the rose field. My family owned a rose field business and we worked in the rose fields for other people. One day this guy named Rick Ingraham, who was our left guard for Texas, heard me doing an interview. He said, "Way to go, Tyler Rose." Rick's mother was from there, and that's how he knew. That was my freshman year, and that's how I got that nickname. It stuck with me, "The Tyler Rose."

Competing Against Tony Dorsett
I competed against a guy in Texas named Tony Dorsett. I would get the pilot on the airplane to call Dallas and see how many yards Tony Dorsett gained. I always wanted to outdo him. On Mondays I would try to find out what Eric Dickerson and Walter Payton did. I think in my day, Walter was the top out of all the running backs. Of course, the master was Jim Brown. The more I played, the more people said I was like Jim Brown, but Tony Dorsett and Walter Payton were the two guys I really competed against.

Walter Payton
Walter Payton could kick those legs and put a move on you, and he could run over you as well. He was an all-around running back. My deal was I couldn't catch the football very well. I didn't like that. I wanted to run with it. Different running backs will do different things.

Dallas Cowboys America's Team
The Dallas Cowboys used to play the Washington Redskins every Thanksgiving. The first year Dallas decided to play somebody else, it was the Houston Oilers. During his pep talk before the game, Bum Phillips said, "Hey, let's go play, guys. Hell, let's go play America's team. They may be America's team, but we are Texas' team." We beat them on that Thanksgiving Day.

That was a time in Texas when the Cowboys were hot; the Oilers were hot. Everything was just great: Nolan Ryan was pitching for the Houston Astros; Hakeem Olajuwon was down there in Houston. That was a great time to be in Texas.

Common Opinion Bum Phillips Ran Earl Campbell Into The Ground
I feel if I didn't run the football twenty-five, thirty times a game ... right in the middle of the fourth quarter was when I woke up and really wanted to play football. I needed that football in my hand that many times to do what I had to do. You pay a price for everything. To get something out of life, you pay a price for it. I paid a price for it, but I did it my way.

Toughest Defense
There isn't any doubt; it was Joe Greene, L.C. Greenwood, and the Pittsburgh Steelers. You get through Joe and you had to deal with L.C. You get through L.C., you had to deal with Dwight White. They were just good all-around.

Steve McMichael

We used to call Steve McMichael Bamm-Bamm in college. He had his hair sticking up like Bamm-Bamm on that cartoon. People in Chicago say Steve McMichael to me and I say, "Who?" They say, "Your teammate." I say, "Oh, y'all are talking about Bamm-Bamm." When he tackled me, I would say, "Bamm-Bamm, take it easy."

Decision To Retire

I was playing one Sunday with the Saints in New Orleans, and I noticed I couldn't get in there and fight the opponents like I used to. In preseason, you've only got three to four hours after the game to mess around and go do what you want to. Then one Saturday night during pre-season Ricky Jackson and a bunch of guys were saying to me, "Come on, Earl, come on, go out." I said, "No, man. I can't." When I wanted to go to the restroom, I was crawling on the floor because my feet had swelled up so much and were so banged up. I just said to myself, "Earl, this is enough of this." I called my wife and Bum Phillips and said, "Hey, this is the way I want to go." Bum said, "You've gotta do what you've gotta do," and so I did.

Pro Football Hall Of Fame Induction

I don't know how it feels to be President Obama, but that's the way I would say that it feels getting into the Hall of Fame. That's the highest honor you can get as a pro football player. I am very proud that I played well against the people I played against. I am also proud that my peers thought enough of me and felt like I was good enough to belong in the Hall of Fame.

Earl Campbell Statute Outside Darrell K. Royal-Texas Memorial Stadium

That was a great honor. My mom is no longer here, but I'm so happy she had a chance to be at the ceremony. That's something that represents your life and your accomplishments. Not only the state of Texas, but also the University of Texas, felt like I deserved it. I felt honored to be alongside the Ricky Williams statute.

Photograph copyright Associated Press

Chapter 99

Tony Dungy

College: Minnesota

Career History:
As Player:
Pittsburgh Steelers (1977–1978)
San Francisco 49ers (1979)
New York Giants (1980)

As Coach:
Pittsburgh Steelers (1981–1983) Defensive backs coach
Pittsburgh Steelers (1984–1988) Defensive coordinator
Kansas City Chiefs (1989–1991) Defensive backs coach
Minnesota Vikings (1992–1995) Defensive coordinator
Tampa Bay Buccaneers (1996–2001) Head coach
Indianapolis Colts (2002–2008) Head coach

2016 Inductee Pro Football Hall Of Fame

College Choice
I grew up in the heyday of Michigan State football during which they played to a 10-10 tie with Notre Dame. I always wanted to be a Spartan. During my senior year in high school, Duffy Daugherty retired and that took a little luster off things. Michigan State was looking for a coach and Duffy's number one assistant, Cal Stoll, had recruited some monster players for the Spartans. Coach Stoll got the job with the University of Minnesota. Coach Stoll knew my high school coach and one thing led to another. I took a visit to Minneapolis and loved it. It was a great opportunity for me.

I met Bobby Bell on my recruiting trip up there. They had an African-American quarterback by the name of Sandy Stephens, who led them to the national championship. He was the first African American quarterback to play on a national championship team. Obviously that meant a lot to me and it made a big impression on me. They played some really good football in the early '60s. It had been a while and we kind of set out to rekindle some of that flame. It was a fun, fun time.

NFL Draft
I thought I was going to get drafted. I worked out for a lot of people before the draft, including a lot of NFL quarterback coaches. I felt that I would get a chance to play. Marv Levy was actually the coach of the Montreal Alouettes in the Canadian league at that time. They had my rights there and they wanted me to sign with them before the draft. I said, "No I'm going to wait and just see what my options are." I didn't get drafted and that was a huge disappointment. I just thought my career had really come to an end. I was thinking of taking up Coach Levy on his offer and going to Canada.

I got a call from Tom Moore who was my quarterback coach my first three years in Minnesota. He had taken a job with the Steelers. They wanted to sign me as a free agent and switch me over to defense. That was something I had not even thought about, the option to play another position. When I got that call something just told me I wanted to play with the best and I wanted to see if I could make it in the National Football League. I think it was God's way of kind of delivering me into the coaching profession. I went to Pittsburgh and it was the best thing that happened to me on a number of fronts. I learned a lot about football, I had the opportunity to be around Coach Noll, to be around some great Hall of Fame players, and win a Super Bowl. It was the best of all worlds.

Tom Moore

Tom Moore was tremendous. We ran the exact same offense the Indianapolis Colts ran with Peyton Manning, but we did it 30 years before. It was a no huddle, up-tempo offensive. The quarterback controlled everything at the line of scrimmage. I loved playing for him. We set some Big Ten passing records back in the '70s. It was fun but the big thing for me was having to control things, take things that you learn in the meeting room from watching the video, and put it into practice out on the field. It was a lot of fun. I enjoyed that.

He ended up going to the Steelers to coach their receivers. When I got there, he kind of paved the way for me. I was playing defense but I loved working for Coach Moore. Years later I ended up having him on my staff as our Offensive Coordinator in Indianapolis.

Chuck Noll

Chuck Noll was absolutely the best. He was a teacher. He helped you play better and learn not only about the game, but also about yourself as a person. I remember our first meeting because he said two things that I will remember the rest of my life. The first thing he said was that the National Football League was business; it was a profession, but you couldn't make football your life. For those of you who make football your entire life, you'll leave the game disappointed. You have to be well rounded. He wanted you to look at other things and get prepared for your next career. You can't pour everything into football.

Then the second thing that he said was, champions in this league don't do extraordinary things, champions do the ordinary things better than everyone else. That's what we're going to work on. We're going to be fundamentally sound and we're going to out technique people. We're not going to out think people and fool people. That became my philosophy. It was very successful there, and I put that into practice as a player.

Then, I got a chance to work on his coaching staff for eight years. I learned why he said those things and how to get that message across to people. He was just the best mentor and tutor that a person could have in football.

Coach Noll always talked about preparing yourself for your life after football, away from the job. He taught me that. He had a lot of things that he enjoyed doing. I watched him as a player and then when I was on his staff, the things that he did away from the game.

We used to have seven weeks off in the summer and we would never hear from him. There wouldn't be a call to check in or any of that. He was gone doing different things.

He gave us one week a month off during the off-season and that was a practice that I tried to continue with my coaches as well. Those guys work so hard during the season, when they're in the off-season, they should get away from it and find other things to do. When he decided to retire we knew that we wouldn't see him involved in football again.

Being Named Youngest Assistant Coach & Also Youngest Coordinator In NFL History
It's funny because I played three years in the National Football League and at 24 years old, I was basically done. I had been traded a couple of times and cut once. I wasn't sure what I was going to do. Coach Noll said, "I would love for you to be on our coaching staff. I think you have a good head for the game. You would be an asset to us, and you would benefit." I was 25 years old when I started with him. Three years later, assistant coaches had moved up to the ladder and we lost some coaches to promotions.

Coach Noll said, "You know more about the defense than anybody else in the country. You're going to be the coordinator and you're going to run it." I was 28 years old with not much experience. That was the way Coach Noll did things. He didn't worry about what other people thought. He had faith in his people. I owe him a lot for making that move when I was so young.

Waiting For Chance To Be Named A Head Coach In NFL
I was still very young, so I wasn't worried about it that much. People started talking after Pittsburgh had some success in the late '80s, that maybe I was going to be the first African American head coach in the NFL. I was still 30, 31, 32 years old so I knew I had quite a long time to go. The one time that I did get disappointed, was in 1993. I was the defensive coordinator with the Minnesota Vikings. We had the number one defense in football that year, leading the league in fewest yards allowed and in most takeaways. We played great. There were seven job openings and I didn't even get an interview. That's when I thought man how many times are you going to have the number one defense and have this many openings? If it doesn't happen this year it may never happen.

I was really fortunate the chaplain with the Vikings, Tom Lamphere, a good friend of mine said, "You can't worry about those kind of things. You just have to do your job the best you can and let God control everything else." That kind of took my mind off of it. I thought, let me just do my job and not worry about anything else or about what's going to happen. Two years later I got the job as head coach with the Buccaneers, and it was the perfect timing for me.

John Randle's Trash Talking
I told John Randle, "If you spent as much time on the game plan as you spent on finding out about the other team's offensive guards and their life history, we would be a lot better." John loved trash talking. He was a smart player and felt trash talking would give him an advantage. He worked on our stuff and our game plan inside and out. He would spend hours finding out little details about the opponents that he could just spring on them at the right time. He was a great trash talker.

He tried to tell everyone how to do it, but nobody could spend that much time finding out those little details and nobody was that bold to say some of the things about people's parents, girlfriends, where they went to school, and maybe their transcript or police record. He would research everything on guys.

Being Named Head Coach Of The Tampa Bay Buccaneers

By that time I was 40 years old. I was fired up about being named a head coach. The Bucs had had a losing culture. They had 13 straight losing seasons and everyone told me don't go there, it's not a job you can succeed in. We had some tremendously talented players. It was a challenge for me to change the attitude and get guys to think like winners, and believe as Coach Noll said, "Ordinary things would make a difference." I talked about being on time and being places when we say we are going to be there. If we are scheduled to have an appearance, to be there not on time, but be there ahead of time. I wanted them to represent the team and the city well. We talked about those things constantly. When that got going, our play on the field pickedup.

Key To Buccaneers Success

It was getting guys who could play and had talent. Then getting them to buy into the system, believe in it, and to support each other. So much of it was really, really good fortune and again, I think God's planning and timing. When I was with the Vikings, we had an idea of the type of players we wanted. When I was with the Vikings and John Lynch was coming out of college, I remembered saying, "Boy he would be perfect for us." Tampa Bay beat us to the punch in drafting him. In 1995, my last year with the Vikings, we had a chance to draft Warren Sapp but we didn't. I was disappointed Tampa took him with the very next pick. Now I started focusing on Derrick Brooks and what do we have to do. Maybe we can get him in the second round in 1995. Tampa traded up and got ahead of us, and took him. I said, "Here are two great players and now I'm going to play against them the rest of my life. They will torment meforever."

The next year I was the head coach in Tampa and all of those guys were sitting there waiting for us. I remember having the conversation early on when I first got the job, hey you guys are going to be the key to this defense, the under tackle, weak side linebacker, and strong safety, the three most critical spots. You've got to carry the load; you have to be the leaders for us. We had another middle linebacker, Hardy Nickerson, who had played for me in Pittsburgh. He was there and understood how we did things.

Getting those guys to buy into it, have the determination to be the best, and to support each other was great. We had a lot of communication with our scouting department. What we were looking for in players were guys who didn't need to be the biggest. We liked speed, mental toughness, physical toughness, and explosiveness. If we could get those things in a player, it didn't matter whether you were from a big school or small school. If you were undersized it didn't matter. If you didn't run the 40-yard dash as fast as people thought you should, it didn't matter. If you were productive and tough, we could use you. Then we got Donnie Abraham, Ronde Barber, and a number of players who were under the radar, but were exactly what we needed. That defense became a tremendous unit.

We built our team where we were going to have a strong defense and we could also run the ball. By running the ball we shortened the game.

We played low scoring games and a style that people weren't used to or familiar with, and it was to our advantage. We built our offense around the running game with Mike Alstott and Warrick Dunn. We were able to control the clock and win a lot of those low scoring games. It was a different style. We called it "Buc Ball." It wasn't throwing the ball all over the field and scoring points. It was playing a physical style, and it became our trademark. It was a lot of fun for the guys.

Being Fired By The Buccaneers And Being Hired As Head Coach With Colts

Our owners got a little frustrated when we got close and didn't win it all. We were making the playoffs but weren't winning it all. We lost the NFC Championship game in St. Louis 11-6, and our owners were very frustrated. The owners said, "If we just scored a couple of touchdowns we would have been in the Super Bowl. We want to make changes." We had to get people to buy into it and stay in tune with what we believed. That was a challenge. It was different and wasn't what people were used to. Maybe it wasn't going to sell tickets, but we felt we could win that way.

What happened was we raised the bar and the expectations; however, it wasn't enough to be a winning team. It wasn't enough to go to the playoffs. It was the Super Bowl that everyone was focused on. Jon Gruden came in as Head Coach with his group and they did a great job. They actually changed the offense around and got a little more explosive. They won the year after I was fired. It was difficult seeing a lot of our players and the guys that I coached in the Super Bowl. By that time I was in Indianapolis as head coach, and looking forward to that challenge. We were a little different team in Indianapolis.

Indianapolis had a great offense when I got there. The challenge was to get the defense up to speed. We had more of a challenge because of the salary cap. We had so many high-priced offensive players, we couldn't pay a lot of the defensive players. So, we had to do it with young talent. It was a fun challenge to put that together and get guys who could protect the lead and rush the passer. We played a different style in Indy then we did in Tampa, but we adjusted.

Tom Moore

Tom was with the Colts when I was hired. He had coached me 25 years prior. I knew his style and it was very compatible to what I wanted to do. I knew the offense was in good hands. We had to get the defense up to speed and there was a lot to concentrate on that side of the ball. We got some players in Dwight Freeney and Gary Brackett and got some impact players like Robert Mathis on defense. We got to the point where we were challenging to win championships every year and it was fun. We put together a run of 12 win seasons that was really, really enjoyable. It was exciting football and we finally got that Super Bowl championship over your Bears in 2006.

2006 NFL Playoffs

The first game that we played was against the Chiefs in the playoffs. The Chiefs Head Coach Herm Edwards and I we were on the Hula Bowl team together. We had been friends for years and coached together. Then, I was coaching against him. We were able to beat them and then we came to the Super Bowl against Lovie Smith, the Bears head coach. I know how Super Bowls are, if you win you're the hero and you're going to be highly praised; if you lose everybody is going to point the finger at you. I guess it was better they pointed at Lovie then pointed at me. That part of it wasn't fun.

Tampa 2/Cover 2 Defense

I absolutely did not invent it. I learned it when I went to Pittsburgh in 1977. Bud Carson actually brought it to the NFL in the early '70s. Bud and Coach Noll perfected it. I laugh because I tell people that the playbook I put in Tampa Bay in 1996, was exactly the same as the 1976 playbook in Pittsburgh. It was plagiarism all the way. We didn't change much, and it still worked 20 years later.

Christianity
I am a strong member of Fellowship of Christian Athletes and I wanted my players to see that yes, I was an athlete, I was a coach, but I was always going to be a Christian first. I was going to treat them that way and we could be successful doing it that way. I had some great role models like Coach Noll, Tom Landry, and Joe Gibbs. I was watching them when I was a young coach. They were winning Super Bowls and winning the right ways. It was a tremendous reassurance to me that you could be a man of faith and have that in the forefront, while still doing your job in an excellent way.

Decision To Retire
It was just a matter of what was the right time. I started coaching very young, at 25. By the time we got to 2007 and 2008, even though I was still relatively young at 51 or 52, I had been coaching 25 years already. Most of my married life I had been a coach. My kids grew up around the game, and they loved it. But, I felt like I needed to branch out and do some other things. In 2009, I felt it was the right time and it was. It was perfect timing for me.

No Huddle Offense
The no huddle offense is a great tool, but you have to have faith in your quarterback. You have to have quarterbacks who want to put the time in to learn and they've got to be as well versed as your coaches. If you have a quarterback like Peyton Manning who loves it, who wants the responsibility, it can be a big advantage.

Peyton Manning
He was just so driven. He wanted to not only be the best, but he wanted his team to excel and he put the hard work into it. He's very, very fortunate because in Indianapolis, he played in one system his whole time there. He never had to switch or learn a new system. The scouting was so good that we got players who fit the system. We had Marshall Faulk, Edgerrin James, and Joseph Addai as running backs and receivers like Marvin Harrison, Reggie Wayne, and Dallas Clark who just fit the system so well, and for 6-7 years at a time. It just allowed the timing to grow. It was just a perfect storm of a very, very talented player in Peyton, a lot of other talented players who fit the system, and that system basically staying for 13 years.

Pro Football Hall Of Fame Induction
That was one of those that you don't expect; you don't even think about. As a kid I dreamed about making it to the NFL or about a Super Bowl, but never dreamed of being in the Hall of Fame. That Thursday night before it was announced, there was a reception with all of the finalists. There were 15 other guys in the room and I was thinking, gee I would vote for this guy, I would vote for that guy, I would vote for that guy. You don't see any way people are going to vote for you. I just didn't think it was going to happen and when I got the knock on the door it was quite a surprise.

Indianapolis Colts coach Tony Dungy is hoisted after the Colts defeated the Chicago Bears
29-17 in Super Bowl XLI at Dolphin Stadium in Miami, Sunday, Feb. 4, 2007. Photograph
copyright Associated Press

Chapter 100

Lee Roy Selmon

College:
Oklahoma

Career History:
Tampa Bay Buccaneers (1976–1984)

1995 Inductee Pro Football Hall Of Fame

Playing In College At Oklahoma With Brothers

It was an awful lot of fun. I look back on it and have a greater appreciation for the opportunity to play with my brothers, Lucious and Dewey. Those were some really, really, really good times for that reason. We look back on it and reminisce.

NFL Draft

What was most exciting for me about the draft that year was not the point of being selected where I was, but that my brother Dewey was also selected by Tampa Bay. We got to play six more years together here in Florida. I can say the good Lord knows exactly what you need, because I certainly needed him here. We broke into the league together and I think that's the reason why I was able to hang around for as long as I did. As rookies, you're just glad to have an opportunity for your dream to come true. For us, it was to play in the National Football League.

Joining First Year Expansion Team In Tampa

There was some tough treading along the way, but people realized we were a young team and an expansion program with a lot of young players just like myself, trying to learn how to play in the National Football League. We had no idea the level of competition and all that we needed to do to compete and be successful. The first year and part of the second year was what that was all about. I think that John McKay did an outstanding job of positioning us to where, even though we were losing games, we could still hold a positive outlook, go out and practice hard, and just keep trying to get better.

Best Selmon Football Player

There's never any argument there. I've always said that my brother Lucious was the best, Dewey was second, and I was last. That's in order of age. That started a long time ago and it's still that way.

Rule Changes To Make The Game Safer

I understand the intent of the rules and trying to make it a little bit safer for the players and everything, particularly now that we know what some of the long-term effects are as we get older. With the physical nature of the game, I doubt if there are any rules that are going to change that. It's moving so fast. Even if a player is trying to avoid a helmet-to-helmet hit, or if both players are intent on trying to avoid it, they end up in the same spot anyway. How can you tell if that was intentional or if they were trying to avoid it; it just happened. I think it's tough, but I do like that they are at least looking at it, and trying to determine if there's anything that can be done to maybe reduce that particular risk a little bit. I think that it's worthwhile in the long run.

I think the nature of the game and what's being found out about it, should be a part of the conversation. We certainly need to figure out what we can do to keep the players as healthy as possible. You only get one head and one brain. If you can protect it better, than I think you should.

Evaluating Players Performance Thru Statistics
I think that there are many ways to contribute to teams. This league is so competitive and so tough to where if they want to take you out and make you ineffective in a game, they have ways of double-teaming you, slowing you down, and those types of things. To me, when those things happen, and you get that kind of attention, the players know which guy they have to get out and who they have to stop in order to be successful. So, while that is one part of the statistics on players, I generally like to look at what impact a player had overall for his team when he is on the field playing.

Photograph copyright Associated Press

Chapter 101

James Lofton

College:
Stanford

Career History:
Green Bay Packers (1978–1986)
Los Angeles Raiders (1987–1988)
Buffalo Bills (1989–1992)
Los Angeles Rams (1993)
Philadelphia Eagles (1993)

Coaching History:
San Diego Chargers (2002–2007)
Oakland Raiders (2008)

2003 Inductee Pro Football Hall Of Fame

Bill Walsh
Bill Walsh had been an assistant coach with the San Diego Chargers the year before, being named the head coach at Stanford. Prior to that, he was with the Cincinnati Bengals. You've got to remember, the world was a lot bigger then, and by bigger, I mean you didn't have the Internet or cable television. You weren't able to track people and say, "Okay, we watched a lot of Bengal highlights." On the West Coast, we never saw Bengal highlights. He was an unknown to our city.

The very first meeting he had with the team was in the Maples Pavilion, which is where the basketball team plays. All the guys were sitting around and he started talking to us. He said he wanted us to call him "Bill," that he didn't want us to call him "Coach." He just had this really warm personality, and he started talking about dress codes. He said, "We're not going to have a big dress code when we travel. The only thing … those bib overalls, if you wear those, make sure you wear a shirt under them." Everybody just started cracking up laughing. He just had a great sense of humor.

We learned more about him as the season went along. Everything he accomplished after he left Stanford during his 10 years with the 49ers, just added to his legend. He was Coach of the Year twice and won three Super Bowls with the 49ers. It made those two years that he spent at Stanford even more impactful.

Position Change From High School Quarterback
I got tried at quarterback a little bit at Stanford. Steve Dils, who came to Stanford at the same time as me, was probably in a more sophisticated passing offense in high school than I was. In high school, I threw five to ten times a game. I just rolled out and ran the ball a bunch.

I also played defensive back for a little while at Stanford. George Seifert, who later on was the head coach of the 49ers, was a defensive backs coach at Stanford. I played for him for just about a week, and then I got stuck back on offense. I played a lot of special teams, covering kicks and punts. I had a lot of fun the first few years before I got to be a starter my senior year.

Hall Of Fame Coaches

I had some pretty good coaches who are in the Pro Football Hall Of Fame rub off on me. Jack Christiansen, who played for the Detroit Lions and was one of the greatest punt returners of all time and also a defensive back, was head coach at Stanford. Bill Walsh was another one of my coaches at Stanford. In the NFL, Bart Starr and Forrest Gregg coached me when I was in Green Bay, and Marv Levy coached me in Buffalo. Then there was Art Shell for a quick moment during training camp with the Raiders.

I had a lot of great coaches, who were really influential men. You've also got to throw in there I played a year with Tom Flores, whom a lot of people think should be in the Pro Football Hall of Fame, and also Mike Shanahan. I was really fortunate to play for some good coaches.

NFL Draft

It was so much fun. It was just exciting to get to go to the pros. I didn't start my junior year. Between my junior and senior years, the NFL had reduced the draft from 12 to eight rounds. So going into my senior year I thought, "Man, they cut the draft. I probably won't get drafted. I can make it as a free agent or something like that." It was really surprising that I had what they would now call a "breakout" senior year and was able to move up as much as I did in the draft.

Transition To NFL

It was kind of neat for me because I was going to a team that obviously needed me. The Packers drafted me high with the sixth pick, and I was able to come in and be a starter right away. I didn't have to wait a half a season or a season and a half to work my way into the starting lineup. I was penciled in as a starter from day one and made the Pro Bowl that year. I was the NFC Offensive Rookie of the Year. It was a big transition, but I guess I didn't know any better not to think that I couldn't do it.

Packers Offense

Offenses were pretty much run first and run second all around the NFL at the time. I think the leading receiver before I got to Green Bay had caught 23 passes the prior season. If you look at the numbers they were probably 75% run, 25% pass. Nowadays in the NFL, teams are about 65% pass, and 35% run. So it has really switched around a lot. We were heavily into running the football when I got there.

Bart Starr As Head Coach

I got the opportunity to coach years after I finished playing. There is a tremendous amount you need to learn to manage people. I look at Bart and his coaching career, and obviously, he wishes that he could have had a lot more seasoning, maybe two years more before starting as a head coach. I think because of his leadership capabilities, he was destined to be a head coach.

I heard somebody say about Vince Lombardi, "You either loved him, feared him, respected him, or hated him." Some people said, "He encompasses all four of those." Somebody said, "What about the hate?" He said, "Well, it's such a thin line between love and hate.

There are some days when you love him, and there are some days when you hate him for the way he is yelling at you." But, he had a certain fear about him and a certain respect.

I remember Bart telling us that respect is something that you earn it is not given away. He also said he had to earn our respect just as much as we had to earn his respect. I think that anybody who played for him really loved him and really respected him.

John Jefferson Joining The Packers

It was exciting when John Jefferson joined the Packers. John had such a great start to his career, the first three years that he played with San Diego. With the addition on our team, it really gave us a leg up on throwing the football, and it was a transition period. The Chargers, under Don Coryell, were really throwing the ball unlike a lot of teams had before, and we started to throw the ball a little more once we got John Jefferson. It was certainly exciting. He was a very enthusiastic player and added a lot of spice to the team at the time.

Packers and Bears

There was always a big rivalry between the Bears and the Packers. Players today tend to change teams a lot, and I think some of those rivalries get diluted a little bit. But we had a healthy rivalry against them and a real good respect for the Chicago Bears. I'm pretty sure that Forrest Gregg and Mike Ditka respected each other, too.

Memorable Bears-Packers Games

Probably every one of the Bears-Packers games was memorable. Even the ones played today are fun to watch. I'm looking forward to Jay Cutler going up against Aaron Rodgers, watching Urlacher play, and then watching Clay Matthews play. It hasn't lost any of its appeal over the years.

Raiders Wide Open Offense

Yes, they love the deep passing game. When I got there, we had great running backs in Marcus Allen and later Bo Jackson. Al Davis was always about trying to get the best talent there and get that best mixture so that he could win championships.

Differences In Coaching Between Marv Levy And Bill Walsh

Bill Walsh was kind of a … he was called "The Genius," obviously because of the West Coast Offense that he implemented, so from that standpoint, they were different. Marv Levy had coached for a while, and he said one of the things that he had learned is you hire the people and you let them do their thing. Marv hired Ted Marchibroda, as offensive coordinator, and let Ted do this thing. One of the things that Ted did was have us run the no-huddle offense in Buffalo. It was such a fast pace, that it made it hard for teams to keep up with us. That was really innovative at the time. We won a lot of ball games because of that system, but also because Ted was able to look at the talent that we had and say, "Okay, this is the best way to utilize it."

Playing In Super Bowls
I actually played in three Super Bowls. I played in 25, 26, and 27. I wasn't there when they played in Super Bowl 28. But there was so much winning that goes on in between. There was a stretch where over three years at home, if you add the regular season games, eight of those, we had a couple of playoff games, two more of those, I want to say we were 27 and 3 at home, so that never tires.

We had great players offensively and defensively. It was interesting because we would find unique ways to win, whether it was on offense, defense, or special teams. We had great special teams players, Mark Pike and Steve Tasker. The combination of great players, just getting to win on a regular basis, and going into the game believing you're going to win, helped us win. I think it was the 1990 season and we were playing in the Super Bowl. We were favored in every game that we played that year, whether it was at home or on the road.

Having Jim Kelly As A Quarterback
Jim Kelly was a strong athlete. He was certainly in his prime. He was really confident in his ability, and he would find a way to win ball games, whether it was by big scores or a comeback win. He was extremely competitive with Frank Reich, who was our backup quarterback. He and Jim Kelly had a standing gag bit that Friday's lunch would be bought based on whether or not Jim Kelly completed 100% of his passes in practice, so there was a lot of pressure on the receivers to not drop a pass because $7 worth of lunch was being bet on that practice.

There was one game against the Oilers where the Oilers' fans, and probably a lot of Bills fans too, thought we lost the game, but we hung in there. We had some fortunate things that happened. Our defense played great in the second half, got the ball back for us, and we were able to pull out a win.

A Career That Lasted 16 Seasons
I never thought about how long I was going to play when I first started playing. I didn't understand how physical the game could be or that you could get cut down by an injury and your career could be over. I didn't think about playing 10 years or playing until I was 30. I just got on a path. I really enjoyed working out there in off-season, so that always made it easy for me to come in to training camp in shape. I was just really fortunate to be in the right place at the right time, I think.

Coaching
Coaching gives you the opportunity to see if you can accomplish something, the competitiveness of the game. Coaching at Stanford would have been a great job. It would have been great to get to go back to the place where you went to school. It's like a way of paying them back, saying, "I really enjoyed my time here." That ship has sailed. They've had a great run with Jim Harbaugh lately, and now, Coach David Shaw is doing an outstanding job there. Coaching college football is a big time commitment. I think the coaches earn every penny that they make.

Broadcasting
It was something that I wanted to do. I broadcasted, I think, for eight years after I retired as a player, then I did eight years as a coach. Now I'm back broadcasting. It's been something that I've enjoyed. They say if you can't do it, if you can't coach it, you might as well talk about it.

Analyzing The Players Actions In Today's Games

I think we just want to know, because we have high definition television and you get great shots all over the place, you want to know what's going on, and you want to almost know it instantly. That's what Twitter has done to us. You have athletes who are commenting before the reporters get to them in the locker room. There is a lot of information out there, and I think people just thirst for it.

Being Inducted Into The Pro Football Hall Of Fame

I had been on the ballot, but I didn't think of it as a slam-dunk or anything like that. I was aware of it, and I had been a finalist for a couple of years, so I was very grateful when it finally happened. I think the longer that you're in it, the more the importance grows. You realize you are among a select few, especially when you see guys who don't get in who you look at and go, "Boy, he was really a good player that I played against, and hasn't gotten a chance to get in yet."

Favorite Career Moments

Getting to play for a number of teams was really significant. Getting to be a broadcaster in this league has been a lot of fun. I work with Dial Global Sports, who used to be Westwood One Radio. I also worked at CNN and for NBC before they lost football the first time around. Even doing college football has been fun.

But there are some things that are ironic. I won the first NFL game that I played in. I won the last NFL game that I played in. I won the first NFL game that I coached, and I won the last game that I coached. Every game that I broadcasted has been on the winning side. You could call that too. You can say yes, I like that team so they won.

Photograph copyright Associated Press

Chapter 102

Warren Moon

College:
West Los Angeles Junior College
Washington

Career History:
Edmonton Eskimos (1978–1983)
Houston Oilers (1984–1993)
Minnesota Vikings (1994–1996)
Seattle Seahawks (1997–1998)
Kansas City Chiefs (1999–2000)

2006 Inductee Pro Football Hall Of Fame

College Choice

Major colleges didn't want to recruit me as a quarterback. They wanted me to change positions to wide receiver or defensive back. Schools that ran the option recruited me as a quarterback, but I was a passer and I wanted to go to a school that threw the football. I decided to go to a junior college because I didn't get the type of offers that I wanted coming out of high school. I went there for a year, got a little more exposure, had another really good season, and finally started to get recruited as a quarterback.

I had actually committed to Arizona State whose coach was Frank Kush. All of a sudden they signed the two top high school quarterbacks in the nation that year, Dennis Sproul and Bruce Hardy. Once they signed those two kids they told me they were going to change my position. I decommitted from Arizona State.

After looking at my other options, I decided to go to a junior college. It was mainly because I believed in myself as a quarterback and I believed that I could throw the football with anybody. My high school coach was going to the junior college as the offensive coordinator. I followed him and we just continued what we had done in high school. It was just a matter of somebody giving me that opportunity.

I would have never even considered Washington or any other school if I wasn't going to play quarterback and if I wasn't going to be given the opportunity to play. It was a matter of just going where I thought I had the best chance to play was. That's what I looked for. USC was the team that I had grown up admiring and watching all their players throughout the years. Vince Evans was the USC quarterback at the time and he was going into his senior year. I would've had to redshirt if I went there and I had already went to a junior college for a year, so I didn't want to waste another year redshirting. I decided to go where I had a better opportunity to start during my first year. So I went to the University of Washington.

Transition To University of Washington

The transition to Washington was easy in some ways as far as playing football, but we weren't very good. Don James had just come in as head coach. I was part of his first recruiting class. The team was 2-9 before I got there. I knew it was going to be a rebuilding process.

We had a very tough schedule that year. We didn't get off to the greatest of starts. I got a lot of criticism being the starting quarterback. I was 18 years old and in a new city for the first time. I was also the first African American to ever start at the University of Washington. I endured very tough times early in my career. Things turned out very well once we got the type of talent that we needed and we all grew together.

Washington Offense

Robin Earl was a really big running back, 6'5" and 240-45 pounds. We ran a ball control offense, tried to eat as much time off the clock as we could, and keep our defense off the field. I didn't get to throw the ball as much as I wanted to, but I guess that was our best way of winning because we didn't have a lot of speed on the outside.

Don was more of a ball control type coach who tried to keep the score close. We had a pretty good year. We finished 6 and 5 and we were one win away from going to the Rose Bowl. We were very competitive and it was a good start for the players and the new regime.

Senior Year Playing In Rose Bowl

We beat the Mighty Wolverines in the Rose Bowl. We were rated number three in the country at that time. We were 17-point underdogs in the Rose Bowl. Nobody gave us a chance, but we had tremendous confidence in ourselves. We went into that game and let everything flow. I ended up having a pretty good game and was the MVP of the game. It was one of the great days for me in my sports career. I was able to come back to Pasadena, where I lived, which is right outside of Los Angeles, and be able to play in front of my friends and family in the Rose Bowl. As a kid I had always admired the Rose Bowl, watching it and going to the Rose Parade. I was now getting a chance to play in it as a college senior.

NFL Draft

I had the same problems coming out of college that I had coming out of high school. Everybody wanted to change my position. I knew it was a time when African Americans weren't looked highly upon as quarterbacks. There were a lot of stereotypes about us playing the position and I got caught up in that. I wasn't going to let it deter me. Again I was going to go where I would get the best opportunity. Just like I went to a junior college, I decided to go to Canada because they were going to give me a chance to play quarterback. Even though I wasn't going to be able to fulfill my dream, which as a young kid was to play in the NFL, I never lost sight of that dream even though I had to go a different direction to do it.

African American Quarterbacks In NFL

I don't think there were any black quarterbacks in the league when I came back from Canada. In 1978, the Tampa Bay Buccaneers drafted Doug Williams but that was because the Buccaneers coach, John McKay, had always had African American quarterbacks at USC. He had Jimmy

Jones and a couple other guys play quarterback for him at USC. So, drafting an African American quarterback for him wasn't anything different.

Who knows where Doug Williams would have been picked in the draft if John McKay hadn't drafted him in the first round. Doug Williams and Vince Evans were in the league, but Vince wasn't playing very much. Doug was dong a pretty good job with Tampa. By the time I came into the league in 1984, they were out of league because of problems they were having getting resigned, so they went to the USFL.

Many African American quarterbacks were changed to different positions. Sometimes your athletic ability penalizes you as a quarterback because they want to put you at a more skilled position, whether it's wide receiver or defensive back. I just never felt like I was that good enough of an athlete to play another position. I was a good athlete for quarterback, but I wasn't a great enough athlete to make the transition to wide receiver or defensive back. Maybe other guys were better athletes than I was and were able to make the transition.

Playing For Edmonton Eskimos
I loved it. It was a great opportunity for me. It was a veteran football team. I didn't have to come in there and be a leader or anything. I could go there and just learn. I got a chance to develop my game. We won a lot. We won five championships while I was up there. It was a great environment for playing football. Even though I was in another country, learning another culture, and a long way from home, because we were winning and I was having fun doing something that I love, playing football, it made it bearable. No question about it.

I became friends with guys on the Edmonton Oilers including Wayne Gretzky, Paul Coffey, Kevin Lowe, Jari Kurri, and Grant Fuhr. They had a great hockey team. At one point we won five straight championships in football and then they won four or five Stanley Cups. During that 10-year period there were nine championships in the city, so they kind of renamed Edmonton the "City of Championships". It was a very good sports town and a great fan base. It was a good time to be living in Edmonton, Alberta.

Decision To Sign With Houston Oilers
I had plenty of teams looking at me. There were scouts in our press box all the time. I was always made aware of the teams' scouts that were going to be watching me. I got a lot of exposure when the NFL went on strike in 1982, since our games were televised in the U.S. You knew when you had a chance to play on U.S. television; you wanted to play a little bit better. It was kind of a motivator. It was just a matter of my contract getting to a point where I could get out of it, or it running out. Then was I going to decide whether to go to the NFL or not because I really was enjoying playing in Canada.

My dream was always to play in the NFL. I had accomplished so much in Canada over those first five years that there wasn't a whole lot left for me to do up there. That's when I started saying, "Hey, maybe it's time for me to go to the NFL." I wanted to get the right opportunity in the NFL and see exactly how good I was as a quarterback. I think the only way you can judge yourself is to play against the best, and there's no question the best were in the National Football League.

It came down to the Houston Oilers and Seattle Seahawks, which is where I was living in the off-season. I went to school at the University of Washington, so it was a natural progression for me. Chuck Knox was the Seahawks coach at that time. They had a very good football team. They had gone to the AFC championship game and lost, but Dave Krieg was their quarterback at the time, so the Seahawks were making a big push for me. It kind of puzzled me that they even wanted me as their quarterback because they had a really good football team.

Houston was more of a draw for me, because it was an up and coming franchise. It was a team I could build with as opposed to going to Seattle, a team that was already good. I really liked the challenge of going somewhere and making a bad team good. Also, my head coach from Canada, Hugh Campbell, was named the head coach of Houston. I went to a team that had a coach who was familiar with me and I was familiar with him. I thought maybe we could have some of the same success we had in Edmonton in Houston.

Joining Oilers
The Oilers didn't have great talent when I got there. They were coming off a 2-14 season and we had to rebuild our personnel. We had a very young offensive line, with some really good offensive linemen for the future. Bruce Matthews, Mike Munchak, and Dean Steinkuhler, who was the number two overall pick in the draft, were on the offensive line when I first came in. We were building upfront with young guys. Later on, we got more outside talent with Ernest Givins and guys like that, which really made our passing game start to take off. Once the talent was around me, we could utilize my strength, which was throwing the football. Then we started really making some noise offensively.

Jerry Glanville
Jerry was a very energetic coach. He was known at the Man in Black, or whatever he wanted to call himself. We had some really hard-hitting defenses. The Astrodome became known as the House of Pain on the defensive side of the ball. There was a lot of enthusiasm built into our football team when Jerry took over as coach. We started to run more of the spread offense, more of the four-wide receiver type thing called the Red Gun. Later on we changed it to the Run and Shoot.

He was a very big personality who liked a lot of attention. We'd butt heads sometimes. I think it was because as a quarterback, I got a lot of attention and I'm not sure if he always liked that. I respected him because he was my head coach and he called the shots, but there were a lot of things that he did as a coach that I didn't necessarily agree with.

1992 Oilers vs. Bills Playoff Game "The Comeback"
It wasn't a very good day. It started out to be a very good day. We jumped ahead, something that we wanted to do early to try and get the crowd out of the game and take the momentum away from the Bills, especially being on the road and being in Buffalo. We were able to do that. We had a commanding lead at half time, I think 28-3, and then we jumped ahead 35-3 in the third quarter. Then that's when the dam broke and we gave them the opportunity to get back into the game with two quick scores. Then after an on-side kick, they got the ball back again and the momentum in the ballgame just changed from there. We just didn't put them away when we had them down. We have nobody to blame but ourselves.

Being the quarterback of that football team, I put a lot of blame on myself for not being able to make the plays down the stretch to make the game ours. That's something that I'll always look back on and say, "We let that one get away," because I really thought that team was good enough to make it to the Super Bowl that year.

Being Traded To Minnesota Vikings
I was a little bit surprised, but not after it was explained to me. I had gone to six straight Pro Bowls. We had just come off of a 12-4 season. I was being traded mainly because the salary cap had come into play and our backup quarterback, Cody Carlson, had just been signed to a pretty good deal the year before. They couldn't keep us both because of the salaries, so they looked at me being 38 years old and him a younger guy, they had been developing for the future. They decided to make the change because they didn't know how long I was going to continue to play at that level at that age.

They thought Cody was ready to take over as starter. I understood where they were coming from. I also knew how I felt as a player and where I was physically. I told Floyd Reese, our general manager at that time, "I think you're making a mistake, but you've got to do what you feel is best for the organization."

I went ahead and accepted the trade to the Minnesota Vikings. I thought the Vikings were a team that could be pretty good if they didn't lose some guys on defense to free agency. All they were really lacking was on the offensive side. I went there and we had a couple playoff appearances, but we never were able to really get over the hump.

Favorite Moment In Professional Football
The day that I signed my first NFL contract because I had to take such a long road to get there. My dream was to play in the NFL all the way back to when I was a young kid. No matter what I had to do along the way, whether it was going to high school, junior college, or going to Canada and play after my college career was over, I finally got to the NFL when I was about 28. I think my most memorable day was when I was able to sit down and actually sign that contract as the richest player in the NFL at that particular time, believe it or not. After all I had gone through, that's where I ended up. That was one of the most memorable days for me, being able to sign that first NFL contract.

Opening Opportunities For African American Quarterbacks
I think my success coupled with Doug Williams's success winning the Super Bowl in 1988, and Randall Cunningham's success, helped the next generation of African American quarterbacks get more opportunities to be drafted. We all played at about the same time and we were three African American quarterbacks playing at a very high level. One of us won a Super Bowl, one was an MVP of the league, and I had a very consistent career, playing at a very high level over a long period of time.

Not only did I play a role in it, so did those other two guys that I talked about. That's something I think we'll all be very proud of for a long time. We were able to make a difference in people's minds in the NFL and open up the gates for other young quarterbacks like Donovan McNabb,

Daunte Culpepper, and Michael Vick. They now have an opportunity to play at a very high level and are drafted high in the draft.

Pro Football Hall Of Fame Induction
I knew compared to who was already in the Hall Of Fame, that I had a chance to make it in there one day. I wasn't really sure because it's not in your control. Other people are voting on you. I knew I had a pretty good resume. I knew I didn't have a championship under my belt, but I also knew that there were other quarterbacks in the Hall of Fame that didn't have championships under their belt either. When I got the call in my first year of eligibility that surprised me a little bit, but I took it.

Favorite Receiver
My favorite receiver was probably Cris Carter, who finally made it to the Hall of Fame. I got a chance to play with him for three years in Minnesota. He set an NFL record for most receptions the first year I was there with him. The record was broken the next year by one reception. Over a two-year period, he caught 244 balls from me. We had a very good rapport early on, even though we didn't know each other that well. That was because we both practiced really hard and we gave each other a great picture in practice. Once we got to the game, it was like second nature. It's like we had been playing with each other for years.

Toughest Defense
I would say that maybe the Philadelphia Eagles had the toughest defense. One year when I was with Houston, the Eagles had a very physical defense. Reggie White, Jerome Brown, and Seth Joiner were with the Eagles. They had a really, really physical defense and they got after our Run and Shoot offense pretty well. They intimidated our receivers and knocked them around. They were one team that I had difficulty with in the one game we played against them that year. In our division, Cleveland always gave us a lot of problems in the AFC Central because we played them so much and we knew each other so well.

Buddy Ryan & Kevin Gilbride Fight During Oilers/Jets Game
During the game, Buddy Ryan took a swipe at Kevin Gilbride. Their issues started way back during training camp when Buddy took over as the defensive coordinator. Buddy wasn't a big proponent of our offense. He felt his defense could dominate and stop our offense, so it became a them against us thing in training camp. It probably shouldn't have been. Jack Pardee, the head coach, probably should have nipped it in the bud at some point. Buddy and Kevin competed too hard in practice.

It finally came to a head that game when Kevin called a play and the ball was intercepted. Cody Carlson was our quarterback at that time. Buddy felt that we should have run the football and run the clock out at the end of the first half. Kevin called a pass and it was picked off. Buddy's defense had to go back out on the field, so Buddy was pretty upset about that. That's when they got into the argument and that's when Buddy took a swipe at him.

Playing For Seattle Seahawks Toward End Of Career
Seattle was of the places where I thought I was going to go coming out of Canada. I'm glad I got a chance to at least play up there for a couple of years, even though I was 41 when I got there. I

really enjoyed my couple of years playing there. I led the league in passing my first year there. I was MVP of the Pro Bowl that year, too. It was a fun year for me. I got a chance to play in front of all of those fans that I played in front of in college. I really thought my career was over after playing for Seattle, but I got a call from the Kansas City Chiefs to come play for them. I decided, "Hey, I can still play physically, so maybe there's an opportunity there." So, I went to Kansas City.

Favorite Player Growing Up
Wow, there are too many to name. I was a big Rams fan because I grew1 up in L.A. and Roman Gabriel was one of my favorite quarterbacks. I also loved Roger Staubach because I used to watch the Dallas Cowboys all the time because they were on TV, it seemed, every weekend. I just loved the way he played the game. Believe it or not, O.J. Simpson was one of my favorite players as well when he was in college.

Photograph copyright Associated Press

Chapter 103

Dan Hampton

College:
Arkansas

Career History:
Chicago Bears (1979–1990)

2002 Inductee Pro Football Hall Of Fame

College Choice
Frank Broyles was an iconic figure. This was back when the Arkansas Razorbacks were the only game in town. Anything to do with the Razorbacks was bigger than life. When Frank Broyles showed up at my little modest home, my mom and him sat on the couch. It was a big deal for us. Frank Broyles was bigger than the governor of the state of Arkansas at that time.

I got to play at a time in the late '70s, when Jimmy Johnson was our defensive coordinator under Frank Broyles, and then we got Lou Holtz as head coach. We won the Orange Bowl. It was a great time to be a Razorback football player.

Under Lou Holtz, Monty Kiffin was our defensive coordinator. Obviously, Monty Kiffin has made a name for himself in both college and pro-football over the last 25-30 years. I used to tell people, "If I would have had coaching worth a damn, I could've done something." I was the most fortunate guy in the world. I had Hall of Fame coaches up and down the aisle during my career. I can't say which one meant the most because they were all huge, and in their own special way, they were amazing to play for. Lou Holtz made young people understand that you're not just an 18-year-old kid; you've got your whole life ahead of you. You need to start thinking about bigger things than the team and winning, like building your career and all of those things. Jimmy Johnson taught the little techniques that kept me in the NFL long after I couldn't run and play the way that I once did. Each and every one was special to me.

Lou Holtz
Lou Holtz had all those great one-liners, like the one he used when he was asked how he decided who would start. He said, "I told them that we're playing the number one team in America. They have five All-Americans and everybody that's played them has been beaten 50-0. The last 11 out of the locker room have to play." He said some crazy things. Lou showed up after quitting as head coach of the New York Jets. As a football player, you never quit and you never say die. Here's a guy who had things that didn't work. We knew that he had credentials, though. It didn't take long, after a day or two of being around him, to know that he had a plan. He knew what he wanted and what we were going to doing. From the get go, we were all on board.

When I heard the rumor that he was hired, I wasn't that impressed. I think a lot of people realized that Jimmy Johnson wanted the head job, but Frank Broyles didn't think he was ready. Frank said, "I'm not going to hire you. I don't promote assistants." Jimmy proved that little scenario incorrect. He went on to Oklahoma State, Pittsburgh, University of Miami where he won a National Championship, and then Dallas where he won two Super Bowls. We were all hoping that Jimmy would get the job. Jimmy had played for the Razorbacks 12 to 15 years earlier. He was a hog. Barry Switzer and Jerry Jones were the offensive guards and Jimmy was a nose tackle on the 1963 Arkansas National Championship Team. At first, we were a little reluctant to embrace Lou Holtz, but it didn't take long for him to win us over. He had a hell of a soft stitch.

We came within one play of winning the National Championship. Losing to Texas was the only loss we sustained. We were leading up until the last seconds of the game when Earl Campbell caught a screen pass and went 28 yards. He had never caught a pass before that and didn't after that. We weren't prepared. It was a great treat to play for Lou Holtz.

Steven McMichael reminds me, almost on a daily basis, that we never beat Texas. We won the Southwest Conference twice and beat everybody else, but we never beat Texas. A lot of people want to know why the Chicago Bears defense, the one that Buddy Ryan coached, we built, and a lot of people say was the greatest defense of all time, was so good. In baseball they have the old creed, good up the middle. I was the 1978 Defensive Player of the Year in the Southwest Conference. Steve McMichael was the 1979 Defensive Player of the Year in the Southwest Conference. Mike Singletary was the 1980 Defensive Player of the Year in the Southwest Conference.

We really felt that was the best conference and the best brand of football in America. We were obviously pretty good players in that conference. I think that was instrumental in what we were trying to build in Chicago. For a decade, I think that we were rated the best defense in the NFL.

Brad Shearer was the player of the year the year prior to me. Brad came with a load of knee problems. He had had two or three surgeries in Texas. He had three or four while he was with the Bears. His career was always cut short by October. I always said that Brad never brought a coat to Chicago because by October, he was always back in Austin. I'm making light of it; I hated it. Brad was a great college football player. He was the Outland Trophy winner and the Player of the Year in the Southwest Conference. You can't scowl at that.

Realizing He Could Play In The NFL At A High Level
It was interesting. You never know where you're going to end up. I was one of the last guys recruited at Arkansas, and after a year or so, I figured out that I could play! I'll never forget Jimmy Johnson talking about the pro-scouts coming to see some of the upper classmen, but they wanted to see me, the skinny kid who was a sophomore. It was all predicated on hard work, and I worked really hard. People have told me over the years that Lou Holtz said I worked harder than any kid he ever had. In a way, I had to. My father died when I was in 8th grade. My mom went to work, but it wasn't much. Football was my vehicle to do something and achieve something. So, I worked real hard, had a lot of great teammates, and had a lot of great help and great coaching.

When I went to Chicago, I didn't know anything about the NFL. I didn't realize that the pass rush was the ticket. In college, I was playing the run because everybody ran the ball. I didn't have much in the way of pass rush moves, arsenal, or whatever you want to call it, early on. I'll never forget when Ted Albrecht, our offensive tackle said, "Hey, you need to watch Lee Roy Selmon. He's the best in the business." I watched a film of him before we played the Tampa Bay Buccaneers, and I think I got two or three sacks that Sunday. I was the Defensive Player of the Week in the NFC. It all kind of crystalized right in my head how to rush the passer. At that point I thought I could be pretty good.

In 1982, Pro Football Weekly voted me the Defensive Player of the Year. It was an abbreviated strike year with only nine games. Don Pierson, our beloved football writer in Chicago, didn't vote for me, but everybody else did. By that time I had kind of figured it out. I had a bunch of great players around me like Steve McMichael, Mike Singletary, Mike Hartenstine, Richard Dent, and Otis Wilson. I could make a list.

I really, really felt like I had a chance to be a great player. During my second or third year I was having dinner with Ed O'Bradovich and he said, "Hamp, I played with some Hall of Famers. You can be a Hall of Famer." I kind of laughed and said, "Yeah, yeah, yeah. When that day happens, I will call you and you can induct me." It was kind of a running joke over the years.

I think that from the 1983 season on, I would have to go to the hospital and have knee scopes every off-season. I was under doctors' orders for no lifting and no running for two to five months sometimes. Other times, I would be on crutches for a couple of months. It was one of those deals where there was always an obstacle that I would have to overcome. I'll be the first one to tell you that in 1989, I wasn't the same player I was in 1984 or 1982. With age, I had kind of figured it out. I knew what to do and learned to live on the margins. I wouldn't make a bad step and on any pass rush I wouldn't flop and flounder around like a lot of kids today. There was no wasted motion and I was still pretty effective.

Going into the Hall of Fame, did I ever think that I would? Did I ever think in a definitive way? No. Did I ever hope to? Did I aspire to achieve that? Hell yeah. Like I said, would it have happened in Tampa? Would it have happened in Seattle? I don't know. But in Chicago, I got lucky and I got to play with what people say was the greatest defense of all time.

Reason Don Pierson Didn't Vote For Me As Defensive Player Of the Year
I think he was infatuated with who knows, Lawrence Taylor or somebody. Everybody has his own perception. A defensive tackle player of the year … you know, back 30 years ago, nobody paid much attention to defensive tackles like they do now. All I can tell you is that I'm flattered that people today really have a better understanding of the game. They understand what a dominant, what I used to call a wrecker, a guy that could collapse the pocket, how much their value is in the NFL. To get the answer, you'd have to ask Don. I'll just tell you this, I've seen him many times over the years and I've never really gotten a great answer, so I don't know.

Enduring Legacy Of 1985 Chicago Bears
I've got two businesses in Chicago. A lot of the guys that played on that team have different things that they do, the residuals, the benefit of playing on that team. Nobody really makes a

living by being one of the members of that team, but it is kind of cool. We still have a certain level of notoriety because of our association with the team.

Look at what Mike Ditka has been able to do. I know that he coached in New Orleans for a while, but I ask you to find me a coach that is probably more well known in Asia or Africa than Mike Ditka, and why? Did he coach somebody a year ago or 10 years ago? No. It was what he did with the Chicago Bears organization back in the '80s, and I have to say it was kind of like being validated. You get to be prom king for a long time.

A lot of people in the media want to ridicule it. The media doesn't propel this or basically propagate it. It's the people of Chicago. They just absolutely loved that team at that time. It was a great time to play for the Bears. People say, "That's our team." If I could build a team, that's the kind of team I would build. Nobody is fighting that, but we're just tickled pink that we were able to be a part of it.

Changing Positions

When I went to practice long ago, I was an offensive lineman. Jimmy Johnson said, "No. I want him on defense," and so I moved to defense. I understand the old motto and the old creed, the more you can do to help the team, well, that's the whole thing. I was drafted as a tackle and Al Harris was an end. Al hurt his knee and Tommy Hart, the old defensive end, hurt his knee. I was moved to defensive end, and boom, I did pretty well. They kept saying, as soon as Alan Page retires, we're moving that ass inside. I would shake my head and say "No way, no way. I like it out here because there's a hell of a lot of beatings going on inside. You got people falling around your legs and you're getting double-teamed." I liked being outside with a lot of one-on-ones."

In the light of day, you've got to just say, "I was the logical one to play that position, and so I did." I really fit it and I was a pretty good end. I made the All-Pro and Pro Bowls, but I was a better defensive tackle. I was pretty dominant inside. It was good for our defense. Everybody, in a vicarious way, was able to benefit from it. That was great.

Then, in 1985 they drafted William "The Fridge" Perry. After a while they wanted Fridge to play and McMichael couldn't play end, but I could. I was the logical guy to go back outside, so I went back out to end. Then after a few years, Fridge had knee trouble and got too heavy. By the end of the 1988 season they moved me back inside and that's where I finished my career.

At the end of the day, it was where could I help, and what could I do to help. Most of the guys on the defense all had that same attitude.

Not Being In the Super Bowl Shuffle

Willie Gault came to me and said, "You've got to be in it. You're the only one who can play an instrument." I said, "Don't let that stop you," and it didn't. The shuffle crew was going to the Super Bowl. I didn't mind them saying it, but I couldn't say it because we had never been to the Super Bowl. A lot of those guys were still in their second,
third, and fifth years. I think I was in my seventh or eighth year. I didn't want to jinx it. I'm superstitious. They wrote a part in it for McMichael and he said to me, "Why didn't you take it?" I said, "You idiot, your more superstitious than I am. What do you mean, you're thinking about

it?" He said, "You're right. I ain't doing it." We would mock the guys that did it, but I'm really happy they did. Every time I see Fridge I say, "You're looking at the Fridge, I'm the rookie …I may be …" It was a great source of entertainment for us. We'd tease them and it was amusing to us, but it wasn't right for me and it wasn't right for McMichael.

It had a great little tune. It was catchy with clever little words, and it made some money. Yeah, the guy was a damn thief and took off with the cash … I don't know. All I'm saying is, almost 25 years later we're the only ones that ever had a soundtrack to our season. What's wrong with that?

I will do an appearance at Jewel or a car dealership, and somebody will start singing some of those words. I am telling you, it's an amazing little piece of Americana.

Two weekends ago, my buddy texted me letting me know he was at a wedding in Minnesota, and they were playing the Super Bowl Shuffle. I was like, get out of here. Oh my God, let it go. But, who am I to fight it?

Transition From Neill Armstrong To Mike Ditka As Head Coach
So much of the time, when you're in the middle of it and almost in a selfish way, you don't worry about everybody else. In subsequent years, I've looked back and I felt bad for Neill Armstrong and some of the other guys on the offensive staff. They were good people, but it was just not working. Our offense was in disarray.

One reason that Buddy Ryan and his assistants kept their jobs was there was progress. I think that back then, there were 26 to 28 teams in the league. We started out the season 23rd or 25th, and by the end of the year we were 3rd or 4th. The offense was turning the ball over. I feel bad now, but at the time I was pragmatic. I was like, who gives us a better chance of winning. We're not winning now; these guys aren't doing what they have to do for us to win. It didn't bother me at the time. Like I said, years later I felt bad, but I wanted to win.

I had never won anything and I couldn't live with losing. When I started in high school, the team was horrible. By the time I was a senior, we had gotten into the playoffs. In college, initially we weren't very good but by the end, hell, we were in the top 10 in the nation. I just couldn't stand losing.

When Ditka came in, he made some comments that made an awful lot of sense. He said, "I've been in the Super Bowl as a player. I've been in the Super Bowl as an assistant coach, and I know what is required. We got a lot of guys that give us a chance to be there, but we've got to make some changes. We are going to have to work awful hard." I thought, that's no problem; let's work. I've always been an optimist. I've always been a pragmatist and it just seemed like a natural thing to do. I had been through a change in college and it was for the better. We becamea better team and there was every indication that we would become better. It didn't take long.

I'll tell you this; everybody asks me what I miss about playing. I miss being in the room the Saturday night before a game when Ditka would ask the waitresses to leave and close the door. That's what I loved.

It didn't take long for me to understand. The first two games we got beat in overtime, Ditka went nuts, punched a trunk, and broke his hand. Everybody laughed and mocked it. I loved it. I was like, this guy ... he wants to win. Nobody had ever punched a trunk before. We had lost a hell of a lot of games and nobody .... I'm just saying that I welcomed it because I wanted to win. I couldn't live with losing, and to me Ditka was the better chance to win.

Losing To the Miami Dolphins & Not Going Undefeated In 1985

Over the years, we have all become so sickened by the Miami Dolphins and their nostalgia overload about their perfect season. In a way I'm glad we didn't go undefeated because everybody would really hate us the same way. Have you've seen those movies where the rock stars don't know what town they're in, but they just keep going and they keep on? That was kind of the way it was. We had things that did not work out for us in Miami, but you know the one thing about it is the Dolphins weren't some expansion team. Their quarterback is in the Hall of Fame. They didn't get there by being dumbasses; they knew what they were doing. You know what? We played dumb and did a lot of stupid stuff as far as our preparation, our game plan, and our actual performance. Sometimes you don't deserve it and we didn't deserve to win.

Numerous Surgeries

I think I'm probably the clubhouse leader right now in the amount of surgeries I've had. On each knee and then replacements, I'm at a smooth 15. I have had a bunch of other operations on my fingers and this and that. It's an unfortunate moniker being the surgery king.

I remember about 1985 or 1986, the doctor said, "You need to quit." I looked at him and I could tell he thought I was nuts but I said, "No way. No way. I love it." I loved being on a team and on Saturday night finding out what we were going to do, and the next day going out and doing it. I mean there are a lot of great things in my life today. I have my wife, my kids, and I get to play golf. That place and time, can never be recaptured. It was a great ride.

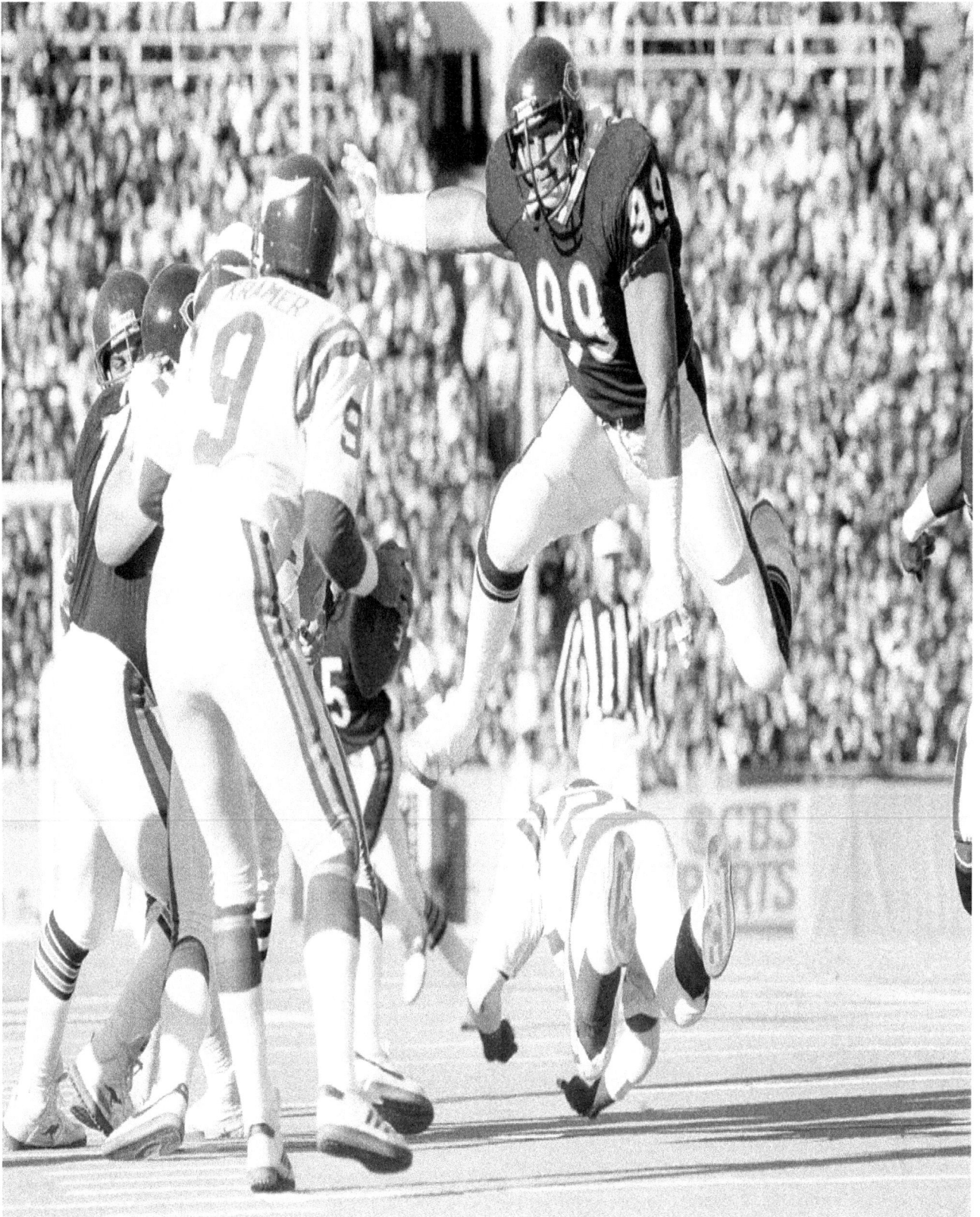

Chicago Bears Dan Hampton leaps over a Minnesota Viking player to corner quarterback Tommy Kramer. Photograph copyright Associated Press

Chapter 104

Kellen Winslow

College:
Missouri

Career History:
San Diego Chargers (1979–1987)

1995 Inductee Pro Football Hall Of Fame

College Choice

I had a job at United Parcel Service working after school during my sophomore and junior years in high school.

One day before the end of my junior year in high school Cornelius Perry, the head football coach, along with Jimmy Lewis, an assistant coach, came to my geometry class. They told me I belonged on the football field. I'm looking at them like, "What?" I still remember being in the hallway standing next to the door of my geometry class. They took me down to the principal's office and he talked to me about the advantages of playing sports. Coach Perry told me I did things in his gym class that he'd been trying to teach other players to do. I just did it. They convinced me to come out for football.

One of the advantages of not playing football until I was in high school was that I saw other things. I came from a different perspective. My original plan was to work after school at UPS, go to a junior college, and then transfer to a four-year school.

I played on a very good high school team that had a lot of college scouts coming in from all over the country to watch us play. Scouts happened to bump into me when they watched film. My high school coaches promoted that they thought I might be okay on a college level.

Missouri, Kansas, Kansas State, and Northwestern were all recruiting me. Missouri just seemed like a good fit. The guys at Missouri did a good job of promoting how close it was to home—one hundred twenty miles away. A lot of guys at Missouri were from the St. Louis area, and it felt like a nice little family to be a part of.

Al Onofrio

Al Onofrio was the head coach when I went to Missouri. Al was a very caring man. He cared for his players and respected them. He expected them to act accordingly and always do what was best. He always said if you could pass the three-prong test in whatever you do then it's okay. The three-prong test is whatever you do reflects on your parents, your school, and the football team.

Playing Tight End At Missouri

My senior year at Missouri I had 29 or 30 catches. During the four years I was there, I had 71 catches.

Favorite Game In College

Our biggest rival was always Kansas. It's a border war—Missouri versus Kansas. Every Saturday in Columbia was special because it was such an event to have a football game. I don't remember ever playing in bad weather at a home game in Columbia. It would snow on a Monday or a Tuesday, but on Saturday just before kickoff, the sun would come out and we always had a beautiful day. We had bad weather in Nebraska and Oklahoma and places like that, but never at home during my four years.

NFL Draft

In 1979, that was the early days of ESPN. You got the information of who drafted you from the radio station or when the team called you. That was how you tracked the draft. The draft wasn't televised with all the analysis going on.

My senior year, my roommate Leo Lewis and I had moved to an area outside of Columbia into a fourplex. The night before the draft we lost phone service. I had to ride down to the local newspaper, The Columbia Tribune, to find out I was drafted.

Don Coryell

The first thing Coach Don Coryell said to me was, "How would you like to play wide receiver?" To me, that was music to my ears because most of the time that I was at Missouri, I worked out with the wide receivers. I had more fun lining up wide and running those routes than I did running in the routes the tight end did at Missouri.

Coach Coryell wasn't afraid to throw the football. He believed in throwing the ball. The goal is to score points, and the quickest way to get there is to throw it down the field. A lot of coaches, especially in the late '70s and early '80s, just feared the middle of the field. He didn't.

Advantage Of Playing Wide Receiver Before Tight End

As a wide receiver you have to get in and out of your breaks. You have to be precise with your routes. It's the person who runs the smoothest and gets in and out of the break the quickest. So, a guy who runs a 4.4, 40-yard dash may not be as good of a route runner as a guy who runs a 4.6 when the 4.6 guy is nice and smooth and precise in his routes, and understands the importance of the timing.

Learning How To Play In NFL

Learning how to play in the NFL was something more organic than taking the very direct route of taking somebody under your wing. Ernie Zampese was the receiver coach and then the offensive coordinator for the team. Al Saunders was our receiver coach. It was always, "Watch the guy." "Watch Charlie Joiner." "Watch John Jefferson." "Watch Wes Chandler." That's how you learn. The older guys taught the younger guys. It was always, "Watch, Watch" and pointing out things that the player was doing.

Dan Fouts

Dan Fouts was looking to the sideline getting the signals when people in the huddle might have been conversing. When Dan stepped in the huddle everything got quiet and all eyes were on Dan.

Depending on which team we were playing, we had a "Check with me" system that would allow Dan to get into a pass play or get into the run play or be able to check off at the line. Dan had a lot of options based on what he saw when he got under center.

Our offense got to a point where Dan learned the receivers tendencies and the receivers learned the quarterback tendencies. Dan knew where to put the ball and expected that receiver to be there. That was the beauty of our offense. It was really like a big, choreographed event for the ballet.

Setting Record For Most Catches By A Tight End In Season With 89 Catches In 1980

When I set the record for most catches in a season for a tight end, I was young and uninformed about what it meant to catch that many balls. I was just too young to understand the significance of it. At the time, all I thinking about was doing my job. The great thing about playing for the Chargers was I was just a piece of the offense. I wasn't the one who had to carry the load. There w/ould be a week where I would catch two or three passes, and a week I would catch five or six passes. It was up to the quarterback to take what the defense gave us. The year I had 89 catches, John Jefferson had 82 catches and Charlie Joiner had 71 catches. That was unheard of at that time. We had running backs that had 24, 26, and 29 catches in Chuck Muncie, Clarence Williams, and Mike Thomas. That was the beauty of the offense.

A coach like Don Coryell understood the personnel and didn't get caught up in certain parameters on players. He was a coach who watched a player and the things the player did during practice and allowed the player to take advantage of those things during games. Coach Coryell put in the tight end option pass because he saw that I would stay out after practice and play catch with the wide receivers. He said, "Let's put this in. Let's use this skill."

The same thing with James Brooks who was probably pound for pound one of the better players in the National Football League at the time.

Tying NFL Record For Most Touchdown Receptions In A Game

The game against the Oakland Raiders was a must win for us. We had started off the season strong and then ran into a mid season rut. We needed the victory against Oakland. Had we lost that game in Oakland, we probably would have been eliminated from the playoffs. We were playing the Raiders up there and we had to win. We got into the game and things just started to flow. The Raiders liked to play man-to-man. They liked to rush four players and thought they could pressure opposing teams. Dan Fouts did a great job of taking advantage of the mismatches.

They could have double-teamed me, but they had to pick their poison. Did they want Wes Chandler or John Jefferson with the ball in the middle of the field running if they double-teamed me? Did they want Charlie Joiner to run a quick route on them and make one of their defensive players miss Charlie and he gets into the end zone? Do they want the ball in the hands of Chuck

Muncie? Did they want that ball in the hands of James Brooks? They figured they would make me [the big, slow guy] beat them.

"The Epic In Miami" 1982 Playoff Game San Diego Chargers vs. Miami Dolphins
It was a hot day in Miami during the 1982 playoff game against the Miami Dolphins. Everybody was playing under the same conditions.

There are so many things that I remember about that game. We were using zoom, zip, slide—all kinds of motion—and I was the motion guy, so that took a toll on me. Then Miami got a little physical with me. Being a playoff game you've got all the injuries and issues that you've dealt with during the year that come into play. I thought I prepared myself properly for the weather conditions including the humidity, but it just all took a toll on me. We realized that we couldn't continue this type of motion on offense. The Chargers coaches took some of the burden off of me and used other players in motion, or in some cases, went away from it.

I think we were 17-0 when I went to the sideline, and Charlie Joiner was sitting on the bench while the whole Chargers team was celebrating. I think it was right after Wes Chandler had scored on a punt return for us. Charlie's sitting there, and he's got this long look on his face. I thought he was hurt so I go over to check on him.

Charlie being the veteran that he was said to me, "We're too high. We're too excited." I said, "What do you mean?" I will never forget what he said.

"You don't come into Miami and do this to a Don Shula football team." He said, "Don is going to pull David Woodley. He's going to put in Don Strock. Don's going to throw the football and we're going to be here all day." The very next series, Coach Shula pulled Woodley, the rookie out of LSU, and put in Don Strock, the veteran gunslinger. We were there the rest of the day. I never will forget that.

I got upset when Charlie told me that because I could not see myself being a part of a team that had that big of a lead and then lost it. So whenever I came out the game, I was trying to get back into the game.

The decision to put me in on special teams was planned. The special team was the do-or-die team. We needed to play to win. We put the best people in on special teams to do the job. It didn't matter what position they played, what their salary was, or what their profile was, because we needed to win the game. So, I was on the do-or-die field goal block team. My job was to try to time the Dolphins field goal kick up, leap over the middle, and block the kick.

I remember getting in the huddle with Leroy Jones, Louie Kelcher, Fred Dean, and Gary Johnson. They were looking at me and I was looking at them. I said, "Okay guys, just give me some penetration and I'm going to get it. I'll get it."

I was just trying to talk it up and really felt that we could block the field goal. It just so happened that we got some penetration and I timed the kick just right and the ball hit my finger. I didn't knock it down. It wasn't manly where I slapped the ball to the ground. The ball just hit my finger, which took a few rotations off the ball and made the kick come up short.

1982 AFC Championship Game San Diego Chargers vs. Cincinnati Bengals

We found out afterward that there was some discussion about whether the 1982 AFC Championship Game should be played or not. Urban legend is that the NFL called a cold weather expert in Chicago and asked if the players would be okay. I'm sure the cold weather expert was sitting in his den next to the fireplace with a blanket over him and a dog lying across his feet as he said, "Oh, yeah, they'll be okay if they just dress properly." That's my version of it.

The wind chill factor was 59 below. The ball was a rock. The field was a rock. Our thigh pads were a rock. Our helmet was a rock. Everything just froze.

They would not cancel that game today. Today they have cold weather equipment. We were making our equipment up. We got our ankles taped, then put on a sock, then put a plastic bag over our foot, then put on another sock, and then put on our shoe. The bag was there to keep the cold air from getting to the sweat on your feet so you wouldn't get frostbite.

I wore two pairs of gloves. One was a pair of baseball batting gloves, and the other pair was a pair of scuba diving gloves that were cut down as small as possible. There was no Under Armour® in those days. We might have been okay with the Under Armour® cold weather body suit. We wore either pantyhose or thermal underwear.

That day we used the same offensive game plan what we had been using all year. We tried to make some adjustments in the passing game by going to a shorter passing game and running the ball. We had Chuck Muncie at running back. But I have to give the Bengals credit. They did a better job adjusting to the weather and were able to put a bunch of points up. I remember the first pass that Dan Fouts threw. The wind just took it and blew it away.

Not Playing In A Super Bowl

We played in two consecutive AFC Championship Games; one was against the Cincinnati Bengals and the year before against the Oakland Raiders. We thought that we had as good a chance as anybody of playing in the Super Bowl. We just came up short twice.

The Raiders got a very fortuitous bounce early in the AFC Championship Game in San Diego. The ball got tipped and went right into Raymond Chester's hands. He ran to the end zone for the touchdown. We ended up losing by seven points.

The next season in the playoffs, after playing in Miami against the Dolphins and winning, we ended up in Cincinnati playing against the Bengals in one of the coldest games in NFL history.

Ability To Line Up In Any Formation

It wasn't like I was so unique in being able to line up in different formations. There were other players in the league who had the same ability—Charlie Sanders in Detroit, John Mackey did similar things in the earlier days of the tight end, and Jackie Smith with the Cardinals was a great athlete.

It was Don Coryell who said, "Let's use Kellen this way." He trusted me with the offense and knowing the different concepts, understanding the concepts, and playing the different roles. Then he just moved me around. He gave me the ability to do that. There were other guys who could have done that before me and during the time I was playing, but a lot of coaches just didn't have the innovation to do it.

Decision To Retire

When the moment of fire is burning and people give you a chance, you want to be out there. There's a fire that burns inside every player. If you're honest with yourself, you know when that fire starts to diminish and it's time to do something else. It was time for me to go do something else. The team had changed. I had gone from being one of the youngest on the team to one of the oldest. Dan Fouts, Charlie Joiner, Wes Chandler, Billy Shields, and Rolf Benirschke were all gone. I think Donnie Macek, Dennis McKnight, and I were the only ones that were left.

Pro Football Hall Of Fame Induction

I still can't believe I am in the Pro Football Hall Of Fame. I go to the Hall and they treat me so well, with so much reverence. I almost didn't play football in high school. One decision changed my entire life. I was very close to deciding to not play football.

Everywhere I played, I was so fortunate. I played on a great high school football team and because of that, schools came around looking for guys and they bumped into me.

I played on a great college football team. We were loaded. I played with James Wilder, Earl Gant, Gerry Ellis, Leo Lewis, and Eric Wright. We were turning out guys who played in the pros on offensive, defensive line, etc. I fit in at the right time.

Then I was picked in the NFL Draft and end up in San Diego. I was the final piece of the puzzle for the offense. It's been a very blessed, very fortunate, situation for me. That's why I'm in the Pro Football Hall Of Fame. If I had played with another team at that time, you wouldn't be talking to me.

Keys To Being Successful In Football & Life

You can't have a low IQ or not understand the concepts and play football well. You just can't. I tell people that all the time.

I played chess in high school. I lettered in chess for three years and football in one. One day I realized that football and chess were a lot alike. I thought, "Oh, I get football now. I know what I do. Better yet, I know why I do it and I know what everybody else does. I know why they do it. Football just made sense to me."

Some people think that because you play in the NFL, that you're not very bright. There are many former players who have gone off and become professionals—doctors, lawyers, very successful people—or become leaders, and football was the basis for that. I just get so upset when I hear those stereotypical type things.

Jim Brown

It's so hard to compare players across decades, eras, world changes, etc. Jim was so much better than everybody else. He was bigger, stronger, and faster. He was playing a position where he had the ball the majority of the time, so his impact was always great.

You have to look at it by era to see who was the superior player during that era, because it changes by era. Jim was a big running back. Now every team has a big running back or two huge running backs. I was one of the bigger tight ends in the League when I played at 6'-5", 245-250 lbs. I'm the H-back in today's game. You've got guys who are 6'-6", 265-270 pounds, playing tight end and running legitimate 4.6 40s. That barroom talk about which guy was the greatest of all time ... I just kind of let it go in one ear and out the other. I really appreciate a player for the way they played and the things that they did when they played. Jim Brown was just so much better than everybody else it was just ridiculous.

Chuck Muncie

Chuck Muncie was so amazing. He was a great basketball player. He could jump out of the gym. He could have been anything he wanted to be. When Chuck came to us in San Diego, we were like, "Oh, wow, he can't be that big. He's just huge."

The coaching staff understood what they had and his ability. When he came to play, there was nobody better.

In one game against the Denver Broncos, I was the basically the fullback and Chuck was the tailback. So you're talking about a 250-pound tight end/fullback, and a 248-pound tailback in Chuck. We would line up in the I formation, which is physically daunting. Then we would go in motion, and run a play based on what Dan Fouts saw and how Denver reacted to the motion. We lost that game.

Two or three weeks later we played Denver again, and we changed the strategy where we lined up in the I formation and snapped the ball. Denver was waiting for us to make the adjustment, and we snapped the ball and caught them off guard. To me that was brilliant coaching.

When Chuck would get the ball and I was leading as the fullback, I wanted to get out of his way. I didn't want Chuck running up behind me or over me, because he would. So I was really moving and finding somebody to put a helmet on. The defensive back or linebacker was looking for you because they didn't want to run up against Chuck. He was so much fun to watch. He could catch the ball coming out of the backfield. He could run over you, run away from you, and make you miss. He had great vision.

San Diego Charger Kellen Winslow is helped off the field by teammates following the Chargers win over the Miami Dolphins on January 2, 1982 in the AFC Divisional Playoff Game. Photograph copyright Associated Press

Chapter 105

Dwight Stephenson

College:
Alabama

Career History:
Miami Dolphins (1980–1987)

1998 Inductee Pro Football Hall Of Fame

Pro Football Hall Of Fame Induction
Being inducted into the Pro Football Hall of Fame is an accomplishment that I never ever considered possible. It is awesome to be in that club with the great guys whom are already in there. I am happy to be in the club.

Being inducted into the Hall of Fame was truly an honor. It was something that I didn't even think was possible. I look at and compare myself to some of the guys already in the Hall of Fame, and I realize some guys had a lot longer career. They deserve to be in the Pro Football Hall of Fame. I am in there even though my career was not 15 years long. I was in the league nine years; eight as a player and one year was on injured reserve. Compared to some guys' careers, my career is not that long. It is one of those honors that I am not going to give up. I am very, very happy to be there. Because I did it only playing for eight years, I am even more proud.

Only Playing For Two Head Coaches In College & NFL
I didn't really realize how fortunate I was at the time. Playing for one coach, Bear Bryant, probably the greatest coach ever in college football. He taught me things that I still carry with me today.

I left there and went to Miami where I played for probably the greatest coach to ever coach in the NFL, Coach Don Shula. I knew I was around some guys that were the best at what they did, but I probably didn't appreciate everything the way I should have. I really enjoyed it. If I had to do it all over again, I think I would probably just appreciate it that much more. I enjoyed playing at the University of Alabama and playing for Coach Bear Bryant. It was a great experience.

College Choice
I had some really great high school teammates, that could have gone anywhere in the country. Scouts from Alabama and a lot of other schools came to our high school, because there were two great football players there: Woodrow Wilson and Simon Gupton.

We all went to grade school and high school together. They had the opportunity to go pretty much anywhere they wanted to go in the country. The University of Alabama came to our high school to recruit those two guys. Coach Mike Smith, my high school coach, who is a great coach in his own right said, "We got Dwight Stephenson here and I think he can play at the University of Alabama." Anyway, they looked at me and said, "Okay, yeah, we'll take him too." I think they really thought they were going to get those other two guys and that I was coming along. Those other two guys had a deal they were going to go to school together. They went to North Carolina State. We all signed on the same day. I decided to go to the University of Alabama. After I had already made my commitment, the other two guys decided to go to North Carolina State.

It worked out well for everybody. I went to the University of Alabama and had a great time. Then they went to NC State, and both of them made All Conference. They did well there. We are still great friends today.

Bear Bryant Said Dwight Stephenson Best Player He Ever Coached
When people say that, I tell them, "No, no he didn't say I was the greatest player or the best player that he ever coached." What he said was, "I was the best Center that he ever coached." That alone means a whole lot to me, right there. There are some great players that played for him at the University of Alabama. Joe Namath, John Hannah, Terry Jones, and Tony Nathan were some great, great football players. I am happy to be mentioned with them.

Importance Of Center Position
The Center is very, very important. It is one of those positions that I think is kind of a natural leadership position. You see how everybody has set himself around you. You are the first one to break the huddle. When you walk to the line, everybody else walks to the line. If you are running to the line, they are running to the line. It is a natural leadership position. Now, at different times, we have a lot of responsibility. We have blocking assignments to make. We need to be sure that we can protect the quarterback or if there is a run play, to make sure that the run play is successful. I enjoyed it. Of all the positions on the football field, that is the position that I wanted to play.

I would have played anywhere, but that position was something I always gravitated toward. When I was coming up there, was a Center with the Minnesota Vikings, Mick Tingelhoff. I never got a chance to meet him, but he was a guy whom I kind of watched. I watched all the great Centers of course … Mike Webster, Jim Langer, and Jim Ringo. I always gravitated toward the Center position.

Bear Bryant
Coach Bryant was probably the right guy for me at that time in my life. I went to the University of Alabama not expecting a whole lot, wondering if I could even play there, and if I even deserved to be there. Coach Bryant got us in training camp and that is where he pretty much broke us all down. He let us know that it was great we were good in high school and it is great to feel good about ourselves, but we were all starting there on an even level. It depended on how hard you worked, what you did, and the decisions that you made as to how good a football player you'd become at the University of Alabama, and what you'd do for the rest of your life. He was the right guy to come into my life at that time. I enjoyed him.

689

Don Shula's Coaching Style Compared to Bear Bryant

They were very similar and also very organized. There was no lollygagging at their practices. Both practices were very, very organized. They would go over game type of situations. They did not leave much to chance. They controlled where we stayed, and everything. Those guys were involved in the details. They knew what was going on.

It was a great experience playing at the University of Alabama, seeing how Coach Bryant was dealing with boys. I mean, pretty much, we were older boys who were trying to be men. He kind of handled us that way, knowing that we need to be molded in the decisions we were going to make, like quitting or those types of things. You can't quit. If you quit once, it is easy to do it the next time. Those were the kind of things we learned at the University of Alabama.

When I went to the Dolphins, Coach Shula was molding men. Some of us had families. We had a lot more responsibility. He treated us that way, but he didn't leave much to chance either. When it came to the football games, he would go over situations. We would overlearn situations. One of his phrases was, "You overlearn it." Both coaches were highly organized, very competitive people, who taught us things we could use for the rest of our lives.

Don Shula Changing His Offensive Philosophy Thru The Years

He recognized the rule changes. You can't keep on doing the same things as, say, 30 years ago. The rules change, and I think Coach Shula changed with the rules. The passing game became more of an opportunity. Then you had Air Marino. No question. It was kind of like a match was made there. We were a good football team and Dan Marino was what we needed. We needed a guy like that. The guy was an awesome leader and competitor. He is just a guy who is tough. A really tough guy, physically as well as mentally. I mean, a very, very tough guy. I enjoyed Dan.

Dan Marino

When we saw Dan, we just saw something different about him. We thought, "This guy can throw the football." Then you watched him in games, and he wasn't afraid. I heard other people say that he wasn't afraid of making a mistake. He would go out there and try something.

If it didn't work he wouldn't necessarily say that he would never do that again. He looked at it like, "I only did this," or "I only did that," and the next time he would go out there and make the correction. He was a guy who was going for it. He wasn't interested in, I feel, almost getting there. He wanted to go for it and that was a great attitude to have.

At times you did want him to do his own thing. Coach Shula would be more open to hearing some of his wide receivers ideas, and let them try things. Dan would call his own plays at times, and stuff like that. Some times in the situation, especially in two-minute drills, you just have to go out there and make adjustments on the field. Dan was the right guy.

Importance Of Offensive Line

Any successful team realizes that the offensive line as a whole, not the individual, is very, very important. That offensive or defensive line decides who wins the game, for the most part. Coach Shula realized they were important, and the offensive line had a real great coach in Monte Clark.

In 1972, the Dolphins undefeated season, they put the emphasis on the offensive line. The offensive line did not necessarily have all #1 draft choices on it either. The guys really put it on the line every time they played. That is what you need to do as an offensive lineman. You have to have a guy who is not necessarily the most talented guy, but the guy who will literally put it all on the line every play and give you all he's got. That is very, very important. The offensive linemen are very important to the success of a football team. They are literally a must on the field, not just because I was a part of it, but they are usually the hardest working group on the field. If they are not on the field, they are in the weight room, studying plays, and trying to coordinate and make sure that they work well together as a unit.

Toughest Defensive Lineman

Joe Klecko is one of the strongest guys I ever played against, and one of the nicest guys. He is not in the Pro Football Hall of Fame, but he should be. He was an athlete who could play the run. He was a smart guy, and just one heck of a football player. He could pretty much do it all.

He could play the run as well as pass. When that defensive line had it going, they were the New York Sack Exchange; they were something. He was a special football player and a great, great guy.

Dan Marino And Isotoner Gloves

Dan Marino actually gave us Isotoner gloves. I think he might have given them to more than just the offensive linemen. He brought some into the locker room and made sure we got some. Dan was always taking care of the guys, like when we would go to dinner and that kind of stuff. He did those things for the team. He was a great guy. He wasn't standoffish. He would hang out with the offensive linemen.

Photograph copyright Associated Press

Chapter 106

Rickey Jackson

```
College:
Pittsburgh

Career History:
New Orleans Saints (1981–1993)
San Francisco 49ers (1994–1995)

2010 Inductee Pro Football Hall Of Fame
```

College
Pittsburgh was on TV all the time, so that was great for me.
Dan Marino got recruited my junior year. He lived with me. We had a lot of great times. He used to come down to Florida and visit with me all the time.

Russ Grimm
Russ Grimm could have played any position, but he settled for playing on the offensive line and he was a load. Opponents could not mess with him. I think he was the best lineman I have ever seen, you know as far as being around or being with.

Hugh Green
Hugh Green was one of the best college players that ever played. For him to come in second for the Heisman Trophy as a defensive player, that was pretty strong.

Jackie Sherrill
Coach Jackie Sherrill was a great guy. Everybody liked him. I cared for him a lot. He was a coach who was for the players. He always tried to keep a good team and keep a lot of good guys together. Nick Saban is just like Jackie. Nick keeps a lot of good guys around him.

Not Winning National Championship At Pittsburgh
It was really hard because two years in a row, we went 11-1. It was something that one game a year got us. We stayed around the top five in the rankings every year. It wasn't bad. You hate to lose and we struggled with losing. Our thing was that at Pitt, we weren't supposed to lose. Every year for two years, that one game did us in. It knocked us out of being where we wanted to be.

North Carolina beat us my junior year, and Florida State my senior year. We should have easily beaten those teams. But, we didn't play that well. We had a lot of turnovers.

Best Game In College
My best game in college was in the Gator Bowl. I had a lot of good games, but in the Gator Bowl, scouts were looking at Hugh Green and George Rogers. I had a chance to show my skills

and my power. I felt that was the game where people noticed me. For the world to get a chance to see me, that was my marquee game.

Being Named MVP Of East/West Shrine Game
I took off from there. Everybody knew then how good I was. Lawrence Taylor always knew that I was real good. We were good friends and stuff, but a lot of people were just waiting to see what would happen when I turned pro. A lot of times when you're in college, you really don't know how a guy's going to turn out. Just like all these guys you see now, you think some of them are going to be superstars, but they end up not panning out in the pros. It's a whole different ballgame when you get to the NFL.

NFL Draft
We had about 13-14 guys get drafted off the 1980 Pittsburgh team when we came out of college that year. A lot of them made the NFL that year. Russ Grimm, my teammate at Pittsburgh, and I went into the Pro Football Hall of Fame together. You don't see stuff like that too often.

A lot of people said I was going to get drafted in the first round or early second round. I was playing basketball when I got drafted. I didn't even know I was drafted. I thought, when they take me, they take me, but I wasn't going to stay home waiting to see where I went.

New Orleans drafted me along with George Rogers, Frank Warren, Jim Wilks, Hoby Brenner, and Hokie Gajon. Johnny Poe also that made the team, and Russ Gary was drafted in second round. We had a lot of good players that were drafted.

Bum Phillips
Bum Phillips was a great guy. You could tell he was a players' coach. He brought Leon Gray, Ken Stabler, and Earl Campbell, all of whom had been with him in Houston with the Oilers. Those were guys with experience. Bum felt like he could use them for a year or two and win with them, so he brought them over.

Rookie Year With New Orleans Saints
We came out ready to play in the NFL after playing at Pittsburgh. You went up against some of the best guys in the country when you were at Pitt. Our running back, Randy McMillan, was a first round pick. He was the twelfth pick in the draft by Baltimore that year. We had a lot of great running backs we went against in practice.

You were going against Russ Grimm, Mark May, and Jimbo Covert. We had a lot of good players to go up against. Those guys were big football players, so if you could beat them, you were going to do well in the pros.

New Orleans Saints Linebackers Best In NFL History
I agree we were the best. The only thing we didn't get to do was win a championship. Everything else we had. We had all the accolades. All four of us went to the Pro Bowl. That will never happen again. Everybody thinks that you aren't great unless you win the Super Bowl. When teams came down to the Superdome to play us, the four of us were somehow going to get you.

You were going to get your bell rung. So I think we had the best group of guys that you could put together. It was Pat Swilling, Sam Mills, Vaughan Johnson, and me.

The Giants linebackers played a different system than us. They played a system where there were four guys up front to do the most damage. We had three guys up front so our linebacker had to fill in and do a lot of stuff. Plus, Bill Parcells had a great coaching staff. They did wellthere. They won the Super Bowl a couple of times.

They had Carl Banks, Lawrence Taylor, and Harry Carson. They got two of them into the Hall of Fame, Lawrence Taylor and Harry Carson, so they had great linebackers too.

The Bears had some pretty good linebackers in Otis Wilson, Wilber Marshall, and Mike Singletary. I think overall we were more physical, faster, and made more plays.

One thing about us, we were cover guys too. We weren't one dimensional, and that was great. I think I was a better player against the run than most guys. We were great pass cover guys too.

136 Career Sacks As A Linebacker
You have to look at the tackles that I had. I had over 1,100 tackles. I look at that more than anything, and playing in over 200 games. I look at that more than the sacks and stuff. People talk about the sacks, but look how many games I played … that meant more to me. Having over 1,100 tackles over a career … you aren't going to find that too often. That's the kind of stuff that counts the most to me.

Best Game In NFL
The best game was probably a game against the Atlanta Falcons. Atlanta was trying to beat us and I had about four sacks that day. The last drive Atlanta was coming down the field, I jumped across and tackled the quarterback. We ended up winning the game. I was always trying to get the Falcons, 49ers, and Rams, in our division games.

Reason Joined San Francisco 49ers
The chance to win a Super Bowl and Eddie DeBartolo was a great owner. He let me know exactly what I could expect. He had always helped older players at the end of their careers and gave them a couple more years. You didn't have to practice a whole lot or do a whole lot. You got the chance to get prepared for the game.

It was just my time was up with New Orleans. They didn't want me anymore. Coach Mora got rid of me along with Vaughan, Sam, and Pat. He wanted to go with younger guys. He didn't want us anymore. We had to go somewhere else, so everybody left.

A lot of older guys went there for the chance to win a Super Bowl. Look at the team we had. Our team that won the Super Bowl should have won it two years in a row. I was playing with Ken Norton, Gary Plummer, Tim McDonald, Eric Davis, Bryant Young, and Dana Stubblefield. We had so many great guys on that team. That was an all-star team. Richard Dent got hurt that year, tearing his knee up.

On offensive, we had Ricky Watters, Jerry Rice, Steve Young, and William Floyd. We had an all-star team. We didn't have to practice against our offense too much. We didn't have to do a whole lot against each other out there as far as beating each other up.

Best Player In NFL History

I would definitely say Jerry Rice is in the top three. I really liked Earl Campbell too. I think Earl Campbell was a load. For the years that he played, I think he earned the ball. There are so many great ones. It's hard to say, but a couple of guys who were really great at their positions were Jerry Rice, Earl, and Walter Peyton. They had some great guys. Then Emmitt Smith came along. All of them are great guys.

Jim Brown, Joe Montana, and Dan Marino were great too. Every time I look at Mean Joe Greene, he looks like he still can play today. There are a whole lot of great guys. I also got the chance to watch Jack Ham, so I've seen a whole lot of great guys. It is hard to say who was the greatest. All of them were great.

Player Modeled Himself After

I saw Jack Ham more than anybody. I studied Jack Ham more. Jack Ham was just that guy. The only difference between Jack Ham and me was I was a pass rusher with everything else.

Pro Football Hall Of Fame Induction

It was late. I should have been picked a lot earlier. When you look at my stats and some of the guys who were in there before me, I know that I should have been in there a long time ago. I was thinking this morning, other people have your fate in their hands and you don't really know how it's going to come out so you just have to thank God for just getting in. Even though I know I deserved to get in and should have been in a long time ago, that's something I didn't have any say in. You don't have a say in that, so you have to go in whenever they let you in.

Toughest Offensive Lineman

The toughest guy I went up against was probably Jackie Slater. He played for 20 something years. He gave me a battle. I knew that if I beat him, I was doing well. I always worked to get ready to try to beat him because I knew he was going to come with a good fight. Willie Roaf was tough too. I'd just go against him in practice. Those were the best two, Jackie Slater and Willie Roaf.

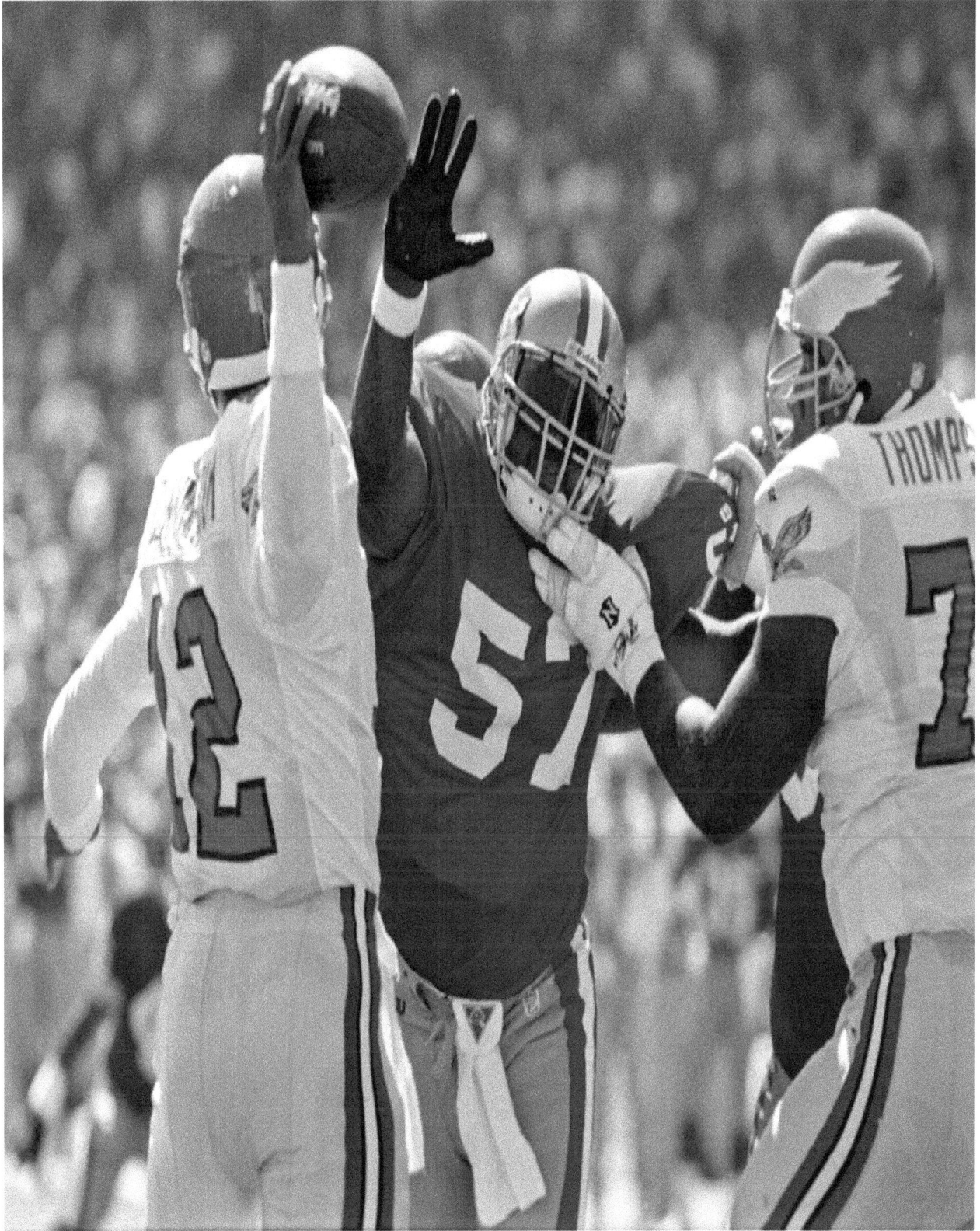

San Francisco 49ers linebacker Rickey Jackson rushes Philadelphia Eagles quarterback Randall Cunningham. Photograph copyright Associated Press

Chapter 107

Anthony Munoz

College:
Southern California

Career History:
Cincinnati Bengals (1980–1992)

1998 Inductee Pro Football Hall Of Fame

College Choice
USC was always the school I wanted to go to. When I first fell in love with USC, I didn't know if it was because of the football tradition or it was Traveler, the big white horse that runs circles around the field every time they score. I was aware of the great offensive linemen that played there, but it was more the tradition and the program.

Growing up 40 miles down the street, I watched USC football every Saturday afternoon. I also remember seeing them in the Rose Bowl all the time, and I wanted to be a part of that. It was about getting the opportunity to go to school and play football because financially, I don't think we would have been able to swing it.

Baseball was my first love growing up as a kid. I always wanted to be a major league baseball player, but I started to get recruited for football. Of course, the selling pitch of most of the schools I talked to was that I could play baseball there. USC had a track record of letting guys do that. I wanted to go there, and the fact that they were going to let me play baseball and football, made it extra special and extra attractive. I was going to play a sport that I loved as a kid in college. Those were the primary reasons that I was excited about going to USC.

Winning A Baseball Championship As USC
I was a member of the team that enabled Rod Dedeaux to win his last College World Series. I was able to make the trip to Omaha and win a national championship in baseball.

I hit pretty well in high school. Then in college, I became a relief pitcher. I was also playing first base and DH a little bit. I was still able to hit some. I'll never forget my first game as a JV player. We were playing Cal Poly Pomona. My first at bat, the pitcher hung me a curve ball and I hit a home run, which was pretty exciting. I hit a couple others in college. I wasn't a great hitter, but I could hit the ball pretty well.

Coach Dedeaux was unbelievable. He had so much baseball knowledge. I'd be on the bench charting pitches during the game or just sitting there watching, and he was constantly up and down the bench asking questions about situations. Even if you were a player on the bench, he made you really stay in tune with the game. And, personality-wise, the guy was just the greatest.

He was unbelievable. I was very fortunate to play for Rod Dedeaux and John Robinson while at USC. I'm thankful.

Transition From College To NFL
Technically, I was well prepared coming out of USC. Experience-wise, was different. When you play one game your senior year, then all of a sudden you're at an NFL camp, you're wondering, "Okay, how's this going to go?" I was very fortunate when I got to Cincinnati. I had a good offensive line coach who started to teach me. I knew it wouldn't be easy.

One of the great things about going to USC, I learned work ethic from the coaches. We had John Robinson, Hudson Houck, and all the guys at USC. That's what it was all about: working hard, and trying to be the best. I knew if I came in with that work ethic and really turned it up a few notches, something good might happen. I didn't think it was going to be easy.

Working Out Against Forrest Gregg Prior To Draft
Having gone through three knee operations in four years at USC, Cincinnati was the only team that sent somebody out to scout me. Cincinnati Head Coach Forrest Gregg, came out and put me through a pretty rigorous two-hour workout. Forrest was still in pretty good shape, a young coach, with a southern drawl and an intimidating look. He was about 6'5", and 260 lbs. He said, "Just relax. I'm going to make some pass rush moves. Just react." My reaction as an offensive lineman, when he faked me out and came in, was to try to get his chest. I hit Forrest right in the chest. He went down, and hit the back of his head. I was like, "Oh my goodness." I extended my hand and apologized. He just looked up at me, smiled and said, "That's all right, Anthony." All I could say was, "Oh." I went from being totally frightened to thinking that maybe it was good that happened. Hopefully that helped out. And it appeared that it did.

After Playing In The Super Bowl
After playing in the Super Bowl, I thought maybe we were going to have a run. I was used to playing in Rose Bowls at USC. I figured, I played in my first Super Bowl during my second year in the NFL and we might put a few together. You quickly become aware of how difficult it is to get to consecutive Super Bowls.

Even though Buffalo didn't win one, it's impressive the Bills got to four straight Super Bowls. It's so hard getting back the following year, after you've been to one.

Sam Wyche
Sam Wyche was unbelievable. I still believe he was one of the greatest offensive minds around. What we did offensively was amazing. He brought in the no huddle offense. He put together a great offensive staff with Bruce Coslet, Jim McNally, and Jim Anderson. It was just amazing.

I enjoyed both Forrest Gregg and Sam Wyche. They had totally different styles of coaching. Forrest Gregg was more the CEO, managing both sides of the football. He had his coordinators on both sides. They ran the show offensively and defensively. He had his plan for the team.

Sam Wyche was more the head coach, offensive minded, and involved with the offensive. Sam was an amazing coach. I still have a great relationship with Sam. He comes to my foundation event every summer. He made football for an offensive player very fun. For an offensive linemen like me to be able to catch some touchdowns, he made it extremely enjoyable.

It was his idea that I thought he was a little crazy at the time having an offensive linemen catch a football. After that first catch, it was like, "This is pretty nice." His rookie year, he started bringing in two extra offensive linemen in to tackle. Then he moved another linemen and me out to the tight end. He just started designing plays. They worked, so we weren't going to argue. The impressive thing was the yards per catch. I think I averaged a little over a yard per catch, which is very impressive.

Blocking For Ken Anderson & Boomer Esiason
Both were extremely smart. People look at the differences between having right-handed or left-handed quarterbacks. Things really don't change as far as formations. Most teams are predominately right-handed; meaning formations are usually strong right side. That didn't change a whole lot. The difference was the whole personality.

Boomer was a lot more outgoing, a lot more verbal. Kenny was more of the silent assassin. The guy was one of the most accurate quarterbacks. He didn't say a whole lot, but when he said something, it was pretty profound. Since I was the left tackle, we rarely had a tight end over on my side with either guy playing quarterback, even though one was right handed and one was left handed. So the adjustment wasn't that different.

Punting
Pat McInally was an excellent punter for us for years. Friday practice was always a light work out, so Pat and I would have punting contests. I got word from up top that they didn't want me punting in those. Paul Brown ended our punting contests pretty quickly. Anytime Paul said something you just ... did it. I enjoyed punting. I actually punted and kicked in high school and enjoyed it.

Playing Against San Francisco 49ers
I kept thinking why do we have to play them in the Super Bowl and regular season. I think I went hitless. I think I was 0 for 5 against them in the two Super Bowls and regular season. When I have nightmares it usually includes Joe Montana, number 16, wearing that 49ers uniform.

Paul Brown
Paul was regimented. It was the same schedule all the time. He was very involved in what was going on. He was around and very connected with the team and the staff. He was very engaging with the players. One thing we could always count on is he would come into the locker room and just kind of interact with us. The thing I loved about it was that the questions led to stories, and we heard a lot of stories.

There was a perception that he was a tightfisted patriarch by one of the radio shows in Cincinnati. He was very innovative in what he brought to the NFL, and that was the impressive. During the ten or eleven years of my career that I was around him, he brought so much to the game, and added so much to it. It was just great being around the guy.

Toughest Defensive Lineman

I never really feared anybody or went into a game saying, "I don't want to play against this guy." One guy who probably wasn't the fastest, Mike Bell from Kansas City, was a guy I could never figure out. He wasn't the quickest, the fastest, the biggest, or the strongest. He just had a way about doing his job.

Durability

I had four years of high school where I played three sports, football, basketball, and baseball. During those four years, I never missed a game.

In college it was just one of those things, where I was at the wrong place at the wrong time. All three injuries in college were kind of these freak accidents.

Of course, my injury history was a concern of many people in the NFL. When you go through injuries like that you want to make sure that you're physically fit, and I took that very seriously. I was a workout fanatic with weight training and conditioning. I really didn't think about the injuries, but I knew that it was part of the game. I can't really say that my durability in the NFL surprised me because of my track record in high school. I was just in the wrong place at the wrong time in college when I got injured.

Acting

You're out there in that crazy place close to Hollywood. USC is known for their TV Department. You've got the George Lucas School of Theater on campus. You get some opportunities. Young guys who don't know a whole lot say, "Oh, let's check that out. It might be fun." You do it, and you think, "Wow, sitting around all day waiting for your scene ... it's not for me." It's fun while you're doing it. I got to meet people like Charles Bronson, Ed Harris, Scott Paulin, and Scott Glenn. It's pretty cool being able to meet individuals like that.

Pro Football Hall Of Fame Induction

It's unbelievable. It's very humbling, thrilling, and exciting. It's one of those things where you think, "Bart Starr, Deacon Jones, Gale Sayers, Merlin Olsen, ... Anthony Munoz? Oh, man. This is pretty exciting." The fun thing for me was, I grew up in Southern California, played at USC, played my entire NFL career in Cincinnati, and then I actually got the word that I was going into the Hall of Fame in San Diego. It was kind of like it went full circle, when I got the actual announcement back in California.

Even now it's still kind of crazy thinking that I'm in the Hall of Fame. I walk around the place, and think, "My goodness, this is crazy." It's still hard for me to believe at times.

Most people don't forget where they come from, including me. I haven't forgotten where I came from. For my acceptance speech, it was easy for me to do a time line of 'thank yous' to the people who made it happen for me. I chuckle even today when I hear about self-made men. This guy is self-made. I haven't met anybody who is self-made. Everybody that is successful has a supporting cast starting from the time they're young. The easy and fun thing for me was selecting those who helped me along my journey. It was fun for me. The tough thing was making sure I didn't forget anybody along the way. That's the one tough thing I was concerned about, because there were so many people in my life that helped me. I had support from family members, coaches, teachers, and friends. Hopefully I didn't leave anybody out. That was the only tough thing about writing the speech.

Halftime Ceremony During Final Game

The one thing that made the halftime experience so great was that just about the entire stadium was filled with Bengals fans, guys and gals that had watched most of my games over my career. While the Hall of Fame experience is the pinnacle of a professional football career, you know that the audience is not all Bengals fan. The fact that I had that experience at the home stadium where I played all 13 years was really extra special. It was in front of my hometown. The Hall of Fame, of course, is very, very special, but it's a different setting. The only difference is that you're in front of fans of all football teams.

Photograph copyright Associated Press

Chapter 108

Mike Singletary

College:
Baylor

Career History:
As Player:
Chicago Bears (1981–1992)

As Coach:
Baltimore Ravens (2003–2004)
Linebackers coach
San Francisco 49ers (2005–2008)
Assistant head coach / linebackers coach
San Francisco 49ers (2008)
Interim head coach
San Francisco 49ers (2009–2010)
Head coach
Minnesota Vikings (2011–2013)
Special assistant to head coach / linebackers coach

1998 Inductee Pro Football Hall Of Fame

College Choice
Texas asked me to play running back. They wanted me to be a blocking fullback for Earl
Campbell. I said, "Can I at least have an opportunity to compete to play middle linebacker?" I
was told, "No. We're looking at you as a blocking fullback." I said, "No, thank you." That was
it.

A couple of things caused me to chose Baylor. Number one was the coach. When I met Grant
Teaff, I was sold. He was a wonderful man who had the ability to make you feel like he really
cared about you and that he had your best interests at heart. I really felt good about that and he
sold my mom. I was going there anyway, but the other
thing is Baylor was the only other school outside of Texas that would let me play linebacker.

Adjustment From High School Football To College Football
In high school you think you're working. You have practice, but at the next level in college, it's
like a job. You're going to school and you have your studies and then after that, you've got to get
ready to go out and compete every day. If you're not competing at a very high level you're not
going to play. Then you're not going to enjoy the game. For me it was just the intensity about
practice. In high school, you go out and do what you have to do and you don't know what you
don't know, but at the collegiate level it's a whole another ball game.

Starting As A Freshman At Baylor
When I left the poor neighborhood that I lived in with all of the broken dreams and everything else that I saw to attend Baylor, I made a commitment. I was going to number one, honor God and honor my family with every decision that I made, and just go full speed with everything I did.

I think that went a long way in really helping me to become a starter. In everything I did, I kept asking the coaches what do I need to be able to do in order to start? At first it was, "We don't really have freshmen come in and start on our team." I said, "Well I'm asking you what do I need to do in order to start?" Once they answered that question, I just went to work on what they told me.

After a while it just became a reality because I wasn't backing down. For me there was no other way. I was going to do what they said I needed to do and then it was up to them to keep their word. That's how it worked.

Process Of Becoming A College All-American
At Baylor I talked to my defense coordinator and I asked him, "What do I need to do in order to be an All-American. What do I need to do to be the best?" He said, "Mike, you know we're at Baylor, we're not at Oklahoma, Alabama, Ohio State, or any of those schools. In order for you to do that you're going to have to go outside of the realm, you're going to have to shatter everything that has ever been done, to even be mentioned in the category of All-American. You have to make every tackle with every opportunity you have."

That's what I did. I tried to make every tackle I possibly could. That really became my standard. Every time the ball was snapped, I wanted to be where the ball was and be responsible for bringing the guy down. That was kind of how that happened.

Breaking Helmets At Baylor
I was beginning to think man, am I just getting a bad deal on these helmets? I was the only one cracking them, so something was up. Once again it was going full speed, giving my full attention and everything in me into every hit. Whether it was in practice, games, or whatever it was, I always putting 100% into it.

Players Modeled Himself After
There were three players that I basically modeled myself after. When I watched the Cowboys the guy that I looked at was Roger Staubach. The thing about Roger Staubach that stuck out to me was he always seemed to find a way to win. He had the will to win. That's what I loved about the Cowboys, and particularly that's what I loved about Roger Staubach. As far as linebackers are concerned, there was Willie Lanier who was with the Chiefs, and Lee Roy Jordan. Those are the three guys that I looked at.

Willie Lanier First African American Starting Middle Linebacker
I studied Willie Lanier's history and how that whole thing came to be. I met him several times and talked with him. I really apprenticed what he stood for and what he brought to the game as a linebacker. He is a very sharp guy.

Winning Two Davey O'Brien Awards In College

I didn't even know what the Davey O'Brien Award was. It is given to the best player in the Southwest. It is a very special honor, so to win it twice was really cool. I am very thankful I was able to do that.

Realization Could Play In NFL

I thought I could play in the NFL when I was in high school and college. The same way I asked my defense coordinator in college what I needed to do in order to be the best, that's what I asked my high school coaches. The thought never crossed my mind that I couldn't do it as long as I was willing to work. A lot of times people say things, but they're not willing to do the work. Well, I was willing to do the work.

NFL Draft

I knew that there was a possibility the Chicago Bears would draft me. There were several teams that talked about drafting me. I think San Diego was one that talked about the possibility of drafting me. So I thought, shoot I'm going to be gone in the first round. I didn't really think about it too much. When the Bears drafted me, that's what I hoped for. I just thought it was going to be in the first round.

Chicago Bears Hiring Mike Ditka As Head Coach

It was a big change, but it was a great change. When I first heard Mike Ditka was hired I knew that he was exactly what we needed. He was a visionary. He was very strong willed and he was very demanding. We needed that. The Bears, at that time, were a team that really did not expect a whole lot, we didn't get a whole lot, and we didn't give a whole lot either. He was a great addition.

Buddy Ryan

There were some special guys that we had on defense. Anybody that was smart and was a good football player, Buddy loved them and respected them. We had Alan Page, someone Buddy had in Minnesota with the Vikings. He loved Alan Page, Dan Hampton, and Gary Fencik. Those guys were our leaders during my rookie year. They thought, hey we need to keep Buddy. Of course, part of me said I don't know about that and the other part of me knew what they were saying was exactly right. I felt the same way. Buddy is just that way. He's the kind of guy that grows on you and if he likes you, you know it, if he doesn't you know it. That's just who he is.

1984 Raiders vs. Bears Game

The Raiders were a physical team and they were coming to our house. We were striving to be a physical team. We wanted to be the team that was the most physical in the league and we wanted everybody to know it. We didn't want to do it in a dirty way. We didn't want to really make a name for ourselves that way. We just wanted to go out, dominate, and be respected that way. I think it worked that way for us. It just worked out.

Origin Of "Samurai" Nickname

I just made a lot of different noises. I was always moving, always making noises and the guys just thought it was funny. Man, we need to name this guy "Samurai" or something like that because he makes so many noises. A very interesting name, but it stuck.

Sustaining Only Loss During 1985 Season To Miami Dolphins

I would never go back and say, man we should have won that game. As a matter of fact, I think the fact that we lost that game gave us a chance to win the Super Bowl because it brought us more into focus. I think it was more of a blessing then it was a curse. I'd think wow, I hate that we lost a game, but when I really think about it we were the youngest team to ever win the Super Bowl up until that time. The fact that we lost to Miami really woke us up and made us realize hey, it doesn't matter how many games we win. If we really want to make something special happen we have to win the big game. That means we have to get better every week and stop drinking the Kool-Aid. Let's go out there and get better each week so we can be ready for the Super Bowl. At the end of the day, that's really what it's about.

46 Defense

The 46 Defense comes down to the personnel. If the personnel are driven, you've got the right personnel to play it. If you don't have the right personnel, you can't play it. It's just as simple as that.

Personnel are the key. We just happened to have the right personnel. We had linebackers who could cover and we had a defensive line that could get off the ball and get to the quarterback. That's the combination you need to have a successful 46 defense.

Vince Tobin Taking Over As Defensive Coordinator When Buddy Ryan Left

We loved Buddy. He was a guy whom we believed in and he believed in us. I think that's a heck of a combination to have. We lost that, so it was an adjustment. It took time to adjust to just playing a regular defense instead of playing a defense that's exhilarating, exciting, ever changing, and always adjusting. It made a difference.

Reason Why Bears Only Won One Super Bowl

The biggest reason we didn't win another Super Bowl is just immaturity. We just took it for granted that we were going to win another Super Bowl because we were the Bears, not realizing that we had to work just as hard.

We were in a city that was so hungry for a Super Bowl. After winning the Super Bowl, it was just one of those things where everybody took advantage of every opportunity that came instead of saying we'll get more opportunities. Someone needed to have the wisdom to say we'll get more opportunities, let's just make sure that we get ourselves ready to repeat and do all the things necessary. All of us needed to be on the same page. We didn't have the foresight to do that.

Best Player Faced

I have to do it in categories. The best offensive linemen I ever played against would be between Dwight Stephenson and John Hannah. Running back would be between Earl Campbell and Eric Dickerson. Receiver is Jerry Rice. Quarterback, I'd have to say Joe Montana.

San Francisco 49ers

The 49ers ran a very, very efficient, disciplined offense. They were better on defense then most people gave them credit for. I really appreciated the execution they had in terms of really understanding the offense and knowing the strengths and weaknesses of the offense. They were able to put the ball into the hands of the playmakers. That's what that offense did.

Pro Football Hall Of Fame Induction
It was great. It was a very special day and a very special honor. Everything about that day was special. My family was there and all of the people that had given so much to me, allowing me to play the game at that level. It was just a really, really wonderful day. It was one of the best days of my life.

Photograph copyright Associated Press

Chapter 109

Kenny Easley

College: UCLA Career History: Seattle Seahawks (1981-1987) 2017 Inductee Pro Football Hall Of Fame

College Choice
My choice of which college to attend came down between Michigan and UCLA. I really liked Michigan when I went there. I was impressed with not only their athletic program, but that they had a 100,000-seat stadium. I could not believe that 100,000 people would attend a football game, week after week after week. That was unbelievable to me. I just liked the way they ran their program there. I mean, they have a long history of success, so I sort of got locked into that opportunity. Michigan was going to give me an opportunity to play for a championship team. The problem was that they wanted me to play quarterback. I played quarterback and free safety in high school. Most of the teams that recruited me were viewing me as a quarterback, with the notable exception of UCLA.

UCLA want me to play free safety, and I wanted to play free safety. When I told Bo Schembechler that I didn't want to play quarterback, he was taken aback. He said, "You have to be kidding me. Why would you want to play free safety when you can play quarterback at the greatest football institution in the nation?" I told him that I really thought I was just a good athlete playing quarterback, but I thought I could really be a fantastic free safety. He just wouldn't buy into that. When he left my house, he was really upset with me and the fact that I didn't have enough sense to take advantage of an opportunity that only a few had a chance at. Conversely, UCLA wanted me as a free safety, so that sort of sealed the deal.

The fact that Michigan quarterbacks traditionally handed the ball off to the running backs for the majority of plays was a consideration. My dad and I talked about that. At that particular time there wasn't a plethora of black quarterbacks in the National Football League. It was sort of just coming into vogue at that particular time in college football. Most black quarterbacks were option quarterbacks not throwing quarterbacks. We thought about all that. I knew that to make it in the NFL, you had to be a throwing quarterback. Being an option quarterback at the University of Michigan or anywhere else was not going to get me to my objective, which was to play in the National Football League.

Terry Donahue
The interesting thing about Terry Donahue, and he'll tell you this himself, is that when I got to UCLA in 1977, that was his first season as head coach. He had to go through a learning process. Because it was his first season, I think he sort of overreacted when it came to disciplining the

players. He'll tell you that today. We really didn't get along famously when I was there because he thought that I was too much of a hothead, or I wasn't coachable, and so forth. We bumped heads a great deal the first couple of years.

I believe it was during my junior year when he kicked me off the team. J.D. Morgan, the athletic director, overrode Terry's decision. J.D. said, "We brought this kid out here 3,000 miles from home, and we're not just going to kick him off the team for what he did." I had hit the quarterback who had a red jersey on. J.D. Morgan came to my defense and said, "You know, the kid is 18. He made a mistake. You just can't kick him off the team for doing something like that."

Coach Donahue had recruited me and signed me to come to UCLA. Luckily cooler heads prevailed and after a couple of days or maybe even a week, Coach Donahue, through the defensive coordinator, told me to come back on the football team.

Terry and I had sort of a rocky relationship. I spoke to him after I found out I made the Pro Football Hall of Fame. That was the first time I had spoken to him since I left UCLA in 1981. He called and we talked passionately. It was good to talk to him and hash out those things that had bothered our relationship 30 years ago.

College
I got an opportunity to play right off the bat at UCLA. When I got there in 1977, a senior free safety named Michael Coulter was number one on the depth chart. A junior by the name of Johnny Lynn was at number two. Then in our freshman class, we had two freshman free safeties, Dave Gomer and me. I had a big mountain to climb. I came to UCLA on a mission because there were so many people in Virginia and from my high school that didn't think that I could do it. So, I was sort of on a mission to show them that they were wrong.

The first game of the season we played the Houston Cougars in the Astrodome, in Houston. The defensive coordinator played Michael Coulter the first two quarters of the first half, and I played the two quarters of the second half. Michael Coulter never started another game. I didn't find it easy. It was hard work. I believe I had seven interceptions and led the conference as defensive freshman player of the year. I was just on my way from there. I just got better. We had a coaching change on defense, and then they brought in Gary Rikeny as the defensive back coach. I learned a great deal from him. By my senior year, they brought in Tom Hays. I also learned a great deal from him. I was very fortunate. I got some good coaching there, but I was also a hard worker.

Playing Basketball At UCLA
Basketball was good conditioning for me. I was discovered playing intramural basketball at UCLA. The UCLA junior varsity basketball coach asked me to come out for the junior varsity team. I was running and getting the benefit of exercising by playing basketball, which is good conditioning for a football player. I had a great time playing basketball at UCLA. I led the junior varsity team in scoring.

Comparing Football To Basketball At UCLA
Basketball was the dominant sport at UCLA, even then. John Wooden had retired the year before I got to UCLA, but basketball was still the cream of the sports there. Terry Donahue was in his first year as head coach during my freshman year. Coach Donahue went on to have some really successful football teams in the '80s with Troy Aikman and all of the other players that came along. Basketball was key.

Best Game Played At UCLA
I don't think I had a best game. I was fairly consistent all the way through college because of the way I played. I went out with the intention of playing every game the best that I could play, because I was uniquely aware that any one of those games could have been my last game. So if any game was going to be my last game, I wanted people to be able to say that the last game I played was my best game. That's the way I played every game. Some players can view a particular game and say, "That was my best game." I can't say that because I played every game as if it was going to be my last game.

NFL Draft
The day before the draft, San Francisco 49ers Head Coach Bill Walsh and his entire defensive staff asked me to meet him and the coaches in Pauley Pavilion. They came down to UCLA and worked me out. After working out I took a shower and came back out to talk to them. Bill and his defensive staff were sitting about 10 rows up in the stands. I sat down and Bill said, "Hey, look, we have the 8th pick in the first round tomorrow. If we select you with the 8th pick, would you be okay with that?" I said, "Absolutely," and we did a little bit more talking.

I asked him if he would play me at free safety and he said he would. I knew that they had Dwight Hicks playing free safety for them.

I remember I first met Dwight Hicks at Michigan, when I went there for a recruitment visit in 1977. I had a great deal of respect for the work that Dwight Hicks had done at Michigan and the work he was doing for the 49ers at free safety. I was concerned about that. I wanted to know, if they drafted me, what they were going to do with me. He said right away, "Yeah, we're going to play you there. We'll figure out what we'll do with Dwight Hicks," so that's where I thought I was going.

I actually called a few people, including my mom, and told them there was a pretty good chance I was going to get drafted by San Francisco the next day. My mom didn't like that because that just drew me further from home.

I told a couple of my buddies that I was going to San Francisco. When Seattle drafted me, I was really upset and thought about telling Leigh Steinberg, my agent, to engineer a trade. When I went to Seattle the day of the draft, I was really taken by the acceptance of the fans. It seemed like the fans were really excited to have me there and have me as a part of the team. So, I decided to forgo any type of trade and go play for the Seattle Seahawk fans.

I absolutely don't regret it because Seattle has the best fans in the National Football League. That was evident some 30 years ago when they wanted me to be a part of their organization.

Jack Patera

Jack Patera was a different guy. First of all, when I got to Seattle in 1981, the organization was only five years old and the team was still trying to find its way. Seattle didn't have a great deal of talent. They had Jim Zorn and Steve Largent on offense. Those two guys were sort of the offensive show. They were still trying to build a defense.

I give Jack Patera a great deal of credit because before I got there, they drafted Manu Tuiasosopo in 1979 as their first round draft pick. Then in 1980, they drafted Jacob Green, a defensive end out of Texas A&M as their first round pick. In 1981, they drafted me as their first round pick and in 1982, they drafted another defensive player, Jeff Bryant, as their first round pick. So, they were really working on building a defense.

Jack was definitely trying to build the defense, but he got fired about two or three years after I got to Seattle. Jack had a tough job because he was the first coach of the Seahawks. It was tough sledding for him.

Chuck Knox

Chuck Knox was named head coach in 1983, and brought in a bunch of veteran players including Reggie Mackenzie, Terry Jackson, Charle Young, and Cullen Bryant. Being a young team those guys came in and basically taught us how to win and how to play pro football.

We started winning right away. Chuck got to Seattle in 1983, and the very first year we went to the AFC Championship Game. We lost to the Raiders, who ended up beating the Washington Redskins in the Super Bowl that year. We had beaten the Raiders twice during the regular season in 1983. We beat them in Los Angeles, and then we beat them in Seattle. Then in 1984, we went 12 and 4 and played the Miami Dolphins again in the first round of the playoffs. We had beaten them the year before. We lost to them that time.

Playing Strong Safety After Being Drafted By Seahawks

Jack Patera took a look at me and probably thought that I was a run stopping defensive back, so he put me at strong safety even though I had played free safety basically all of my life. From the time I was in Pop Warner football, I played free safety. I played free safety in middle school, I played free safety in high school, and I obviously played free safety at UCLA, but when I got to Seattle, they put me at strong safety.

I should have demanded that I play free safety. I think I had the right to do that as a first round draft pick. I grew up in an environment where when you were asked to do something, you learned how to do it and did it. So when they asked me to play strong safety, instead of bucking the system and saying, "I want to play free safety," I just did it. That was the type of environment that I grew up in. Although I regret not telling them I wanted to play free safety, I did what they wanted me to do and tried to make the best of it.

Tom Catlin

In 1983, Seattle hired Tom Catlin as defensive coordinator. He revamped our defense and put me in position to make plays on defense. He took advantage of my athletic ability and designed our defense to take advantage of what I did best, which was run, hit, and make plays.

We went from a two high safety defense to a single free safety. He always put me in a position where I had a chance to affect the offense. So I have to thank Tom Catlin for having the wisdom to take advantage of the things that I did best.

Playing Philosophy
The only way I knew how to play was to just lay it out there every game. If I got hurt, so be it. If I never played again, that's the nature of the beast, but I was going to play. I was going to play as if it was going to be my last game, and in hindsight I don't regret that. I believe that because I played that way, I was looked at again as a Pro Football Hall Of Famer when I was in the Senior Division. I think the voters looked at the way that I played during my seven years of playing, and thought that they had to consider me as a Hall Of Fame player. I was NFL Defensive Player Of the Year, AFC rookie of the year, made Pro Bowls, I was an All Pro, and I was named to the All Decade Team of the '80s. Maybe the way I played was special enough for the voters to have reconsidered me for the Pro Football Hall Of Fame.

1984 Game Against Kansas City Chiefs
Our game against the Kansas City Chiefs in 1984 was a game for the ages. We had six interceptions in that game and returned four of them for touchdowns, setting an NFL record for interceptions for touchdowns in a game. From a player's perspective, it wasn't much of a game because we dominated the game. I believe we beat them 45-0, so it wasn't one of our harder games. It turned into a cakewalk of a game.

Those are the games that you like to play because once you get up by a certain amount of points; the opposing team has to throw on almost every down. When we got up by 30 points, Kansas City threw the football on every play after that. All we had to do as defenders was jump every route. A defender is probably going to make an interception at some point if they're jumping every route. The only reason you would jump every route is if you're 30 points ahead and you know that the opposing team is going to have to throw. It's going to increase your chances of making interceptions.

I've played in better and more interesting games, but certainly when your team gets six interceptions and four of them are returned for interceptions, it's a big joy that you can produce those results.

Seattle Seahawks Defense
Our entire defensive line was the catalyst of our defense. The defensive line consisted of Jacob Green, Jeff Bryant, and Joe Nash. Those guys put a great deal of pressure on the quarterback, which made my job in the secondary a whole lot easier. When a quarterback is being pressured all the time, he's going to throw interceptions. In 1984 we had 38 interceptions and 60 turnovers, finishing second behind the Chicago Bears, who led the league that year in turnovers. The guys who set the table for the rest of the defense were Jacob Green, Joe Nash, and Jeff Bryant.

Practicing Against Steve Largent
I hardly ever practiced against Steve Largent unless it was during the off-season. During the season, our number two defense practiced against our number one offense, and our number two

offense practiced against our number one defense. I hardly ever got a chance to practice against Steve because of the way that our practice was set up.

During the off-season when Steve and I were working against each other, I tried to cover him as many times as I could, as would the rest of the defensive backs. We knew that Steve was going to make us better covering him. In a two-hour workout, I probably got a chance to cover him 8 to 10 times in between the rest of the defensive backs who wanted to coverhim.

We had other good receivers too. Obviously none better than Steve, but they were quality NFL receivers. So if you ended up covering say Paul Johns, Steve Raible, or Ray Butler you were going to get some good work in. There's no question that Steve was the best receiver we had, and when you got a chance to cover him, you knew you were covering the best.

1987 NFL Players Strike
We had a couple of our veteran players on the Seattle Seahawks that crossed the players' picket line. That was really the hardest part of the strike because the players that crossed the picket line were out there playing with the replacement players when the league got up running again with the replacement players. To see our teammates out there playing was really difficult on us. It was a tough time for the NFL and for the players who hung in there, staying out until the strike was resolved. It took some teams longer than others to resolve those types of issues. Those issues were resolved, at least on our team. We got back to playing and being respectful of our teammates.

Discovering I Had A Kidney Ailment In 1988
Discovering I had a kidney ailment was one of the toughest things that I had to deal with, not only during my career, but also in life. I was 28 years old and at the top of my game when I found out that I had a kidney ailment. More importantly, I found out much later, once I sued the Seahawks, that the organization knew about my ailment. The Seahawks were trying to unload me, hoping that the team they traded me to would miss finding out that I had a kidney ailment.

The Arizona Cardinals traded for me and I failed their physical. The media found out that it was a kidney ailment and the Seahawks general manager said, "Whatever ailment caused Kenny to fail his physical, it was non-football related." I just could not believe that he would make a statement like that. At that point it wasn't clear what had caused the problem, but once my lawyers subpoenaed all of my records from 1981 thru 1987, we found out that the organization knew about the kidney ailment and they were going to try to make me someone else's problem.

It was really disheartening that the team I had played for, and played so well for, would do that to me. After that, I sort of divorced myself from the team for well over 15 years. It wasn't until 2002 that I ever talked to anyone in the Seattle organization. That was when they wanted toplace me in the Seattle Ring Of Honor. During the time I was away from the organization, Paul Allen had purchased the team from Ken Behring who had bought the team from the Nordstrom family.

Being Inducted Into the Seattle Seahawks Ring Of Honor
First of all, I felt like I should have been in the Seattle Seahawks Ring Of Honor already. Secondly, I was grateful to Paul Allen and the organization for reaching out to me and bringing

me back into the Seahawks family. I thought that it was long overdue. I had been away from the team for 15 years with no communication. That was when Garry Wright, who was vice president of the team at the time, called me. He told me that Mr. Allen said they couldn't induct anyone else into the Seahawk Ring Of Honor until we induct Kenny Easley.

It made sense for me to drop the animosity and do the right thing after a 15-year absence. Plus, I had young children, my youngest being 6, and they had never seen me play pro football. It made sense at that time to drop the animosity and go in the Ring Of Honor. It gave my children a chance to understand that their dad had played pro football and had done it well.

Pro Football Hall Of Fame Induction
The Pro Football Hall Of Fame voters decided to take a fresh look at my career, thanks to Frank Cooney and Bob Kaupang. Bob was sending articles to the Pro Football Hall Of Fame about my career and the things that I had done. The voters decided to take a fresh look and thought, perhaps we need to get away from the criteria that a guy had to play double digit years to be considered for the Hall Of Fame."

When you look at the Hall Of Fame, you have Gale Sayers who played six years, and my former defensive back coach, Jack Christianson who I believe played eight or nine years. The voters probably thought they needed to take a look at the quality of the years rather than the quantity of the years.

I believe with Terrell Davis and me, getting in with seven years of service each, and you can also include Kurt Warner because I believe he played just eight years in the NFL, hopefully what happened this year will dispel the myth that you have to play double digit years to even be considered a Hall Of Fame type player.

It's going to sound interesting or strange, but it was like Christmas for me when David Baker, President of the Pro Football Hall Of Fame, knocked on my hotel room door and told me I had been selected for the Hall Of Fame. It was like being a little kid again. You go to bed the night before Christmas knowing it's Christmas Eve, knowing that Santa Claus is going to come sometime during the night. That's what it was like having David Baker knock on my door. When David knocked, I was excited to open the door. Then he announced that I was a Hall Of Famer. After that it was like Christmas when you get to play with your toys.

That's how it felt to me, and it may not be an apt description, but that's the only way that I can explain it because when I opened that door and it was David Baker, man, was I excited. My family was excited. I had my wife and children there, and they got to yelling, hugging me, and being excited with tears running down their faces. It's just something that is hard to describe to someone who has not experienced it, that type of joy.

Seattle Seahawk Kenny Easley knocks New York Jet quarterback Richard Todd to the ground. Photograph copyright Associated Press

Chapter 110

Russ Grimm

College:
Pittsburgh

Career History:
As Player:
Washington Redskins (1981-1991)

As Coach:
Washington Redskins (1992-2000)
Pittsburgh Steelers (2001-2006)
Arizona Cardinals (2007-2012)
Tennessee Titans (2016-2017)

2010 Inductee Pro Football Hall Of Fame

College Choice
I actually attended the University of Pittsburgh by default. I wanted to be a linebacker at Penn State. Penn State was recruiting me early on. Once the recruiting period hit, I didn't hear from them for about two or three weeks. They came in late and I had already made up my mind that I was going to stay in the area where I lived and go to Pittsburgh.

College
My first two years at Pittsburgh I was a linebacker. I played on special teams some of my sophomore year. Head Coach Jackie Sherrill called me into his office after my sophomore year, right before spring ball, and said that they had lost a bunch of guys on the offensive line. They thought it was in my best interest if I switched over and played center.

I never had my hand in a three-point stance prior to Coach Sherrill asking me to play center. I was a linebacker and quarterback in high school. Playing center was new to me. I weighed 242 pounds at the time, and spring ball was a little rough because we had an All-American nose tackle in Dave Logan, who went on to play for the Tampa Bay Buccaneers. I came back in the fall weighing 265 pounds and won a starting job. By my senior year, I weighed about 280 pounds.

I think we finished second in the country in both 1979 and 1980. Nobody wanted to play us. Any team ranked number 1 didn't want to play us in a bowl game. We always had to sit and hope somebody lost and they didn't lose. That's the way it goes sometimes. We had some really good football teams.

Joe Moore

Joe Moore, our offensive line coach at Pittsburgh, was great. He's a great motivator and a good teacher. We had a lot of good players. All five guys that I played with on the offensive line during my senior year all went on to play in the NFL. Mark May was our right tackle and Jimbo Covert was our left tackle.

Not Winning A National Championship At Pittsburgh

It was tough not winning a National Championship at Pittsburgh because we felt we had the best team. We lost one game each year. We lost one game to North Carolina 17-7. During my senior year, we lost to Florida State 36-22. We should have run the table.

Dan Marino

It was great playing with Dan Marino at Pittsburgh. The guy was talented. He got the ball out of his hand in a hurry. It was a lot of fun. There were a lot of games that were over by halftime.

NFL Draft

I thought I had a chance to play in the NFL after my junior year.

I was just glad with whoever drafted me. The draft wasn't televised back then. Actually, it was trout season and I was fishing that morning. When I got home, my parents said the Redskins had called. I called them back and they said they'd drafted me. I was off to D.C.

Early Years With Redskins

We started out the 1981 season 0-5. We finished 1981, 8-8. We thought that things had turned for the better. We had a little momentum going. We won the Super Bowl after the 1982 season. In 1983, we went to the Super Bowl again, but we lost to the Raiders. We had some good teams.

1982 & 1983 Washington Redskins

The key to winning Super Bowl XVII against the Miami Dolphins after the 1982 season was Head Coach Joe Gibbs staying with the game plan of running the ball.

In 1982 and 1983, we were solid everywhere including special teams. The 1983 team has a record. We were plus 42 or 43 in turnover ratio. I don't think that will ever be broken. We were just a smart and physical football team. We tried not to beat ourselves.

Prefer Run Blocking Or Pass Blocking

I preferred run blocking. Pass blocking is a little passive. You've got to be under control for a little while. I always say it's like controlled aggression. Run blocking, you can cut loose.

"The Hogs"

Our Offensive Line Coach, Joe Bugel, gave us "The Hogs" nickname. During training camp Coach Bugel said, "Let's just go hogs, time to hit the sleds." One of the reporters picked up on it. The next thing you know, the fans got a hold of it and it took off from there.

The nickname was great. We had our own fan base and things like that. Then again, every Sunday we had to be able to back it up.

Super Bowl XVIII Washington Redskins vs. Los Angeles Raiders

We played the Los Angeles Raiders that year and beat them. It was a tight game and we beat them in the last minute or two of the game. They were a good football team. They were solid and talented.

We made some mistakes during Super Bowl XVIII. Joe Theismann threw an interception on a screen for a Raider touchdown. The Raiders had some big plays on special teams against us. We may have gotten a little complacent too, since we had already beaten them during the year.

Toughest Defensive Lineman Played Against
The toughest defensive lineman I played against my first couple of years in the NFL was Randy White of the Dallas Cowboys. He was quick and strong. He had both those qualities as a defensive lineman. And, he was a good player.

Darryl Grant
I went against usually Darryl Grant in practice. He was physical and quick. We wanted to make each other better. You can't just take plays off and go easy. Nobody gets better then.

Joe Bugel
Joe Bugel was a great teacher of assignments. I think that was his biggest thing. Our offensive linemen went into games knowing exactly whom we were going against and what we needed to do against them. We never went in where the defensive linemen surprised us with something. Coach Bugel was solid in making sure we knew whom we were covering and we knew exactly what to do.

Washington Redskins Winning Three Super Bowls With Three Different Starting Quarterbacks
All three of those teams weren't one-dimensional. We didn't necessarily need the quarterback to carry us. We had a running game. We had a defense. It was a combination of everything.

Washington Redskins Fans
Washington, D.C. is a transient area. As long as the Washington Redskins are playing well, everybody jumps on the bandwagon. As soon as things start to head downhill [for the team] for a week or two, everybody jumps back, and says, "I'm originally from Boston. I'm originally from Pittsburgh. I'm originally from wherever." They jump back to their home team if the Redskins are not playing well. I loved the fans in D.C. They were great.

Head Coach Joe Gibbs
Head Coach Joe Gibbs was a hard worker and consistent. We knew he slept at the office. He put in the time. When he installed the game plan, we could look at it and know that all the 'i's were dotted, the 't's were crossed, and everything was checked off.

Leader Of The Offensive Line
I don't know if the offensive line really had any leaders. It was more making sure everybody was on the same page. The guys that were playing on our offensive line just fit that mold. We were a close-knit group that didn't want to let the other guys down.

Favorite Washington Redskins Team Played On
I would say probably the 1982 team was my favorite Washington Redskins team I played on, because it was my second year in the NFL and my first Super Bowl win. I tell people all the time that the 1983 team may have been the best team that I ever played on. We lost two games that

year, both of them by one point. Then we lost the Super Bowl.

Pro Football Hall Of Fame Induction
When I played, I never thought about being inducted into the Pro Football Hall of Fame. It was never a big thing on my mind. It was never a big goal. I just wanted to win games. When I was done playing, it was something that I looked forward to. When I made it, I couldn't believe I made the Hall of Fame. Then I went to Canton. I was in the same room as and listening to Joe Greene, Franco Harris, and other guys that have been in the Hall Of Fame a long, long time, talking about their experiences. It was a great feeling.

Joe Jacoby
Joe Jacoby deserves to be in the Pro Football Hall Of Fame. It's especially tough for offensive linemen because there really aren't any stats on them. It's not like the defensive linemen, where you can count how many sacks they had or anything like that. One time, I told the Pro Football Hall Of Fame Selectors if they don't induct seven guys a year, then there's going to be a lot of guys not getting in that deserve to be in.

Favorite Players Growing Up
Growing up I always wanting to be the next Dick Butkus. I was also a big Jack Lambert fan, since I grew up in the Pittsburgh area. I just liked to hit people. I wanted to be a linebacker. I started out as a linebacker my first two years at the University of Pittsburgh. Then the coaches switched me over to the offensive line and I had to put my hand in the dirt.

Harry Carson
Harry Carson, with the New York Giants, and I used to have some battles. There would be days that I thought, I got him now; he's going to go out of the game. He wouldn't leave the field, though. He was a tough nut.

Coaching Philosophy
I tell the players I coach, "I'm not going to get up here and try to have you do something that I know can't be done." I think the players all know I've played. I treat them the way I wanted to be treated. They play pretty well.

Comparing Linemen From Different Eras To Today's Linemen
Somebody wanted me to compare myself to Alan Faneca when I was coaching him with the Pittsburgh Steelers. I said, "It's not even close. Alan is 30 pounds heavier than I was. He's quicker than I was. He's stronger than I was."

Everybody thought that we had the biggest offensive line in the league when I played for the Redskins. We had one guy over 300 in Joe Jacoby when we got the nickname "Hogs." We were the biggest line in the league. I can't remember any time in the last 20 years of my coaching, that I had a guy weigh less than 300 pounds.

Favorite Games
I had a lot of favorite games. The runs John Riggins had in the Super Bowl against Miami; the big second quarter we had against the Denver Broncos in the Super Bowl ... There are certain moments here and there. After awhile, it all blends together.

<u>Super Bowl XXII Washington Redskins vs. Denver Broncos</u>
Super Bowl XXII was great. I tell people all the time that Jay Schroeder won 11 games for us that year. Then Jay got hurt and Doug Williams stepped in. Doug was hot. We just stayed with Doug through the playoffs.

George Rogers was our running back all the way to the Super Bowl. Then Coach Gibbs says we're going to start Timmy Smith in the Super Bowl. We're looking around going, what? Timmy runs for 200 some yards; a Super Bowl record back then. You just never know. Those are coach's decisions. Things panned out. I guess that was a good call.

New York Giant Lawrence Taylor tries to evade the Redskins Russ Grimm. Photograph copyright Associated Press

Chapter 111

Ronnie Lott

College:
Southern California

Career History:
San Francisco 49ers (1981–1990)
Los Angeles Raiders (1991–1992)
New York Jets (1993–1994)
Kansas City Chiefs (1995)
San Francisco 49ers (1995)

2000 Inductee Pro Football Hall Of Fame

Career History

I was looking at a lot of schools. I was looking at schools all over California and I was looking at schools throughout the Midwest. John Robinson decided to recruit me, and I thought it would be a great place for me to go. So, I chose to move in the direction of a lot of great Southern California players, and decided to go to USC.

It wasn't a tough sell. The reason it wasn't a tough sell was even though I wanted to go to UCLA, my high school coach said, "Look. If you really want to play football, and it is definitely really what you want to do in your life, you should go to USC. You're going to get a great education and you won't only be a Trojan for four years, you'll be part of the Trojan family for life." I realized right after my coach said that, it was the right thing for me to do.

Possible Position Change At USC

I started off as a defensive back, but when they lost Charlie White, they were looking for a tailback. At the time they had Marcus Allen, Dennis Smith, me, along with a host of other defensive players. They thought, "You know what? We should try one of these guys and see if they can play."

I think they chose the right guy. Marcus Allen was pretty good. Marcus was great on defense. That was the problem, though. He was great at whatever he did.

USC Talent

We had a lot of talent on that team. We had an offensive line that was arguably better than a lot of pro lines. We had phenomenal athletes and guys who loved the game, loved playing it, and worked very hard at it.

Biggest Rival Of USC
Notre Dame was and will always be, for a lot of reasons. Both teams have great athletes. They had a group of guys over the years that I learned to love and hate competing against. When you are competing against the likes of Joe Montana and others, it makes your life really very difficult.

John Robinson
John Robinson was a great coach, and arguably the best coach I ever played for. Bill Walsh was an exceptional coach. I really enjoyed what I learned from Coach Robinson and all the things that he brought in terms of his enthusiasm and his passion for wanting to win.

Difference Between John Robinson & Bill Walsh
The difference was you had one guy who talked about competing, and you had another guy who talked about execution. I think Bill focused more on execution and the way the game was played. John just said, "Look. You've got to out-compete the guys. You've got to find ways to impose your will." I think that attribute was something that resonated with me. I think that was one of the differences that allowed me to be a great football player.

Transition From High School To College
It was very difficult, because there are things that you had to learn that you didn't learn in high school. And, you have to get ready for the size and the speed of college players.

Big Games Played In College
A lot of games were big games. Obviously, playing against Notre Dame was great. Playing against teams like Stanford and Bill Walsh, UCLA, Alabama and Bear Bryant, were just as exciting.

There were a lot of great games that we played at USC and a lot of great teams that we played against. I would say that going on the road and winning on the road were some of the best parts about playing sports.

Charles White
Going up against Charles White in practice was very tough. Charlie was one of the great competitors, one of the most dominating backs in college football.

Jerry Attaway USC Conditioning Coach Convincing Bill Walsh To Draft You
I'll be the first one to tell you, it happens when you have somebody who trained you, worked with you, and helped you. Jerry Attaway was essential to helping me develop as a football player at USC as well as helping me develop as an athlete with the San Francisco 49ers.

NFL Draft
I wasn't confident. I did not know the 49ers were going to draft me. I think they chose three defensive backs in the first three rounds at that time, because they felt like they needed to find ways to shore up their secondary and shore up their defense. I know that the year before, they'd had a lot of challenges with the secondary. They had a lot of injuries. I think they wanted to go young. Thank God they went young. We were all excited to play together and come together. It

turned out that playing with those guys was the best part of my life, because all of them were great guys.

George Seifert

George Seifert, our assistant coach, made sure that we were humbled and we stayed on task every day. I think that the focus was for us to continue to do the things that we were capable of doing. George was the taskmaster and made sure that all we did was focus on the game of football.

I think what happens is you find yourself realizing every day how you've got to get bigger, faster, and stronger. Every day you had a lot to work on.

Playing In Four Super Bowls

Obviously, I think of all the Super Bowls, and about all the things that went on. I think about the one in 1989, when we came back and beat Denver and how that went. The Super Bowl playing Cincinnati was a very close game.

In 1984, we played against Dan Marino. That was a phenomenal, phenomenal game for us, playing in front of a home crowd and playing in front of our fans. That was a lot of fun. You had a chance to stay with your family and friends. You didn't have to go to a hotel that week. There were a lot of things that made that week very, very special. At the same time, it was also one of those weeks where you were nervous, because nobody had ever played in his hometown before. We were able to go out and win convincingly.

The thing that people forget is that team was very, very special, because it didn't lose a lot of games. We found ourselves with a lot of great football players. Some of the football players on that team were some of the best at their positions. What I loved is that we didn't have Jerry Rice on that team. We had "Big Hands" Johnson. We had Louie Kelcher. Those were the best at their position at one time or another.

We had guys who really supplemented, helped, and complemented our team. When we got down to the end, it was really our defense alone in that game that put on a show and allowed us to win. It was just wonderful execution by guys playing great football.

When I think about the first Super Bowl I played in and how it played out, it's unbelievable. The reason I think it was unbelievable is we had so many things that went well that day. It was a phenomenal day. I think the first one's always the best one, because there are so many things that you accomplish that day, and so many things that make you feel really good about it.

When you think about those moments and you think about all the things that you're trying to accomplish, the first one is the hardest one. The reason it's the hardest one ... nobody knows that you can get there. Clearly, we didn't know it. We didn't walk into the season that year saying, "Boy, we're going to the Super Bowl." We walked in that year saying, "Man let's just make sure we can play great football." We ended up playing a lot of great football that year, and it became a phenomenal year.

Having Finger Amputated During Game
In 1985, we played the Cowboys the last game of the season. During that game I may have smashed my finger. I ended up deciding that I was going to play the following game. The doctor said I shouldn't play. I said, "Look. I've got to play."

I ended up playing against the Giants in a playoff game. We ended up losing in New York. That was a tough loss. We went there and gave our best effort, but Joe Morris and the Giants prevailed that day. After that game, everybody was saying, "I can't believe you played in the game." I was, like, "Those are the things that we do in life." The doctor said to me after that game, "You have to amputate the finger." So I ended up amputating the finger during the offseason. I realized that I was going to have to continue my career playing with my finger cut off.

The story is a Paul Bunyan story. A lot of people have said a lot of different things about it, but it was not a part of the '84-'85 season.

Transition From Playing Cornerback To Safety
It wasn't a tough transition. I went to safety in 1985, around the fifth game of the season. The coach said, "Look Lott, we want you off the corner position. We want you out of there. We'd like for you to go back and play the safety position. We think that's better for you. We think that you'll have a better opportunity to have success there."

I went to safety and made the most of it that year. That was the one-year I didn't make the Pro Bowl. So that was a tough year for me, because I lost out. I had to regroup. I came back the following year, and ended up making the Pro Bowl. I had a phenomenal year and played really well. The 1985 season was a very difficult for me, because there were a lot of things that didn't go well, like the transition of going to a new position.

Pro Football Hall Of Fame Induction
Anytime that you feel that you have a shot of making the Pro Football Hall Of Fame, that means that you've worked your tail off and you've given a lot to the game. So many things have to fall in place. The only thing you know is what you did. What you don't know is what other people are going to think about your body of work. You don't know how people will judge it.

Unfortunately for me, I had friends telling me that there was no way that you're going to make it your first year. There were some guys that said, "Hey, you might have a shot." I ended up getting lucky and going in the same year with Joe Montana. I think that the momentum of him and Dave Wilcox carried me in. That's what got me into the Hall of Fame.

Edward DeBartolo
He's one of the best, if not the best, owner ever. He set the tone for how ownership should be; how they should interact, help players, and find ways to enhance their lives. He did an incredible job; he still does. He still continues to help people and finds ways to enhance their lives. He's just a very phenomenal leader and a phenomenal person. I'm forever indebted to him because of all the things that he was able to accomplish.

Favorite Moment Of Career

The favorite moment for me was in 1981. That was the defining moment to me. We learned a lot about what we could do and how we could get better. I think we applied that each and every year. I think that everybody who was associated with that year realized that there was so much more that we could do.

Looking at that year, at the guys, and what we were able to accomplish, I realized that, man, we set a new tone for the game of football. We were guys who constantly believed that we could always be better and we could always accomplish a lot for the game of football, and more importantly, for the San Francisco 49ers.

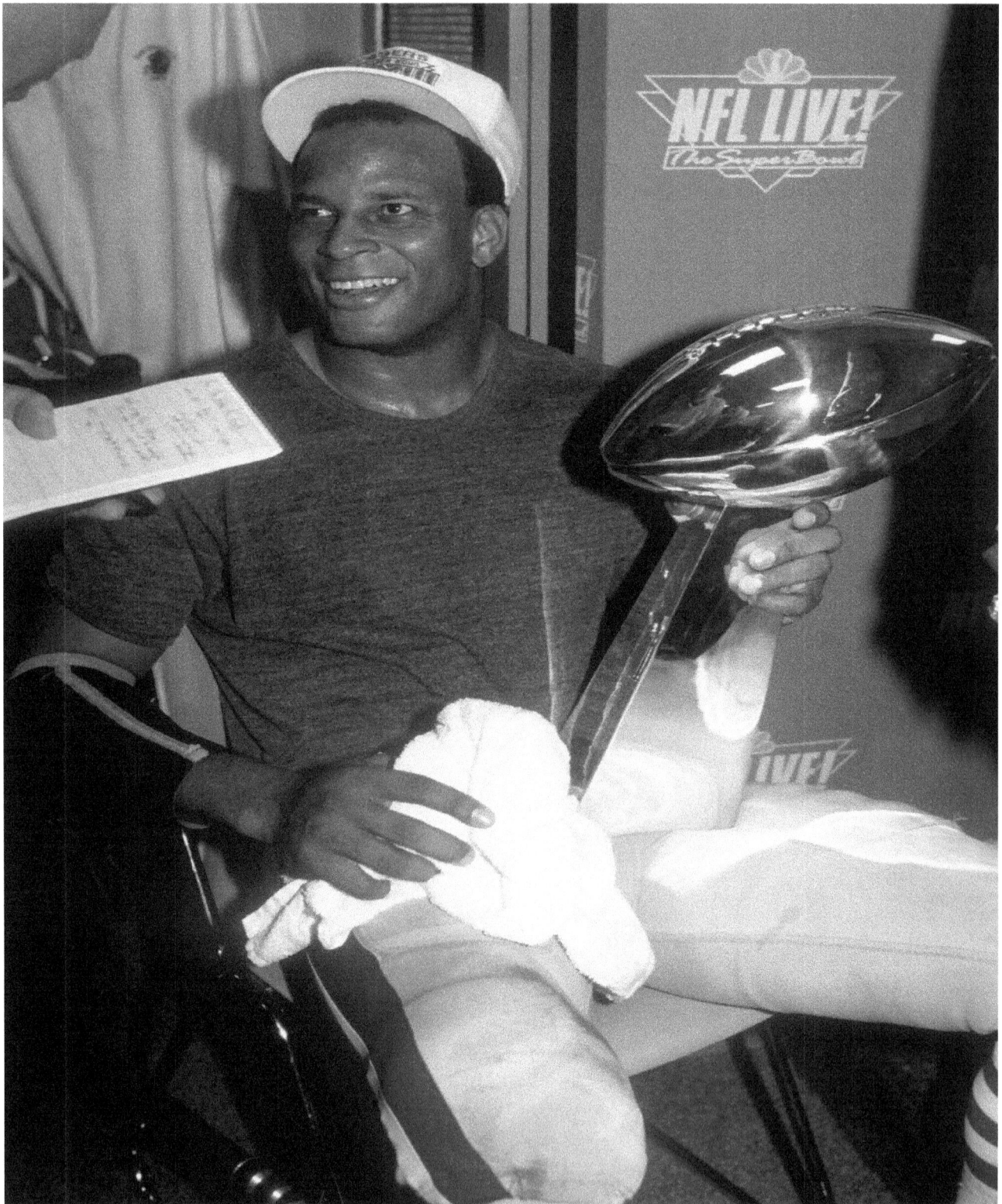

San Francisco 49ers safety Ronnie Lott smiles while holding the Vince Lombardi Trophy during a postgame press conference after winning the Super Bowl XXIII against the Cincinnati Bengals on January 22, 1989 in Miami, Florida. Photograph copyright Associated Press

Chapter 112

Howie Long

College: Villanova Career History: Oakland/Los Angeles Raiders (1981–1993) 2000 Inductee Pro Football Hall Of Fame

College Choice

I was living with my grandmother in Charlestown, Massachusetts. The desegregation busing rides started my freshman year of high school. I missed the majority of my freshman year because of that. At that point, I grew up right under the 'L' tracks in the city and played in the street every day. I played basketball, baseball, and mostly street hockey. I wanted to be Bobby Orr, but I had never played organized sports of any kind.

My Uncle Billy, had grown up in Charlestown and worked for the Boston Housing Authority, the projects in the city, his entire professional career. He had lived a kind of "American dream." He was the first person in the family to graduate from high school. He had moved to Milford, Massachusetts. I went to Milford to live with him at my grandmother's request. He had two kids of his own and two adopted kids and took me in at 13 years old.

The high school football coach saw me walking down the hallway and asked who I was and if I was interested in coming out for the football team. Once I figured out how to put the equipment on, it kind of grew from there. I was a raw, big kid.

By the time I got out of high school, I was 6'5", 225 and had scholarship offers from Boston College and Villanova. My grandmother made a very sage decision that was probably best for me, given the turbulent circumstances of the area that I grew up in, to head down to Pennsylvania to go to Villanova. They were both Catholic schools, and she was very heavily Catholic, an Irish Catholic, from Boston.

Villanova

Villanova was great. It was the perfect place for me. I probably had the opportunity to go to some other schools that were probably smaller, but never really considered or thought about it.

I was 6'5", 225, when I went to summer school down there prior to my freshman year. I had a meal card and was working out for the first time. By the time I got to training camp, I was 6'5", 262, and went from probably playing outside linebacker to nose guard in a three-man front.

I started every game my freshman year and took every snap. It was just the right level for me. We never played on television. We bused to most of our games. We stayed three to a room on the road. They were the best of times.

I made a lot of great friends there. I met my wife, Diane, there. To this day, we have four or five really, really good, close friends and a number of friends that have been kind enough to support causes that are directly associated with the university. They're supporting an older coach who needed some help and the university program. It's been great.

Being Heavyweight Boxing Champion In College
The majority of the time, I would get there and whomever I was supposed to fight would kind of walk away. So, it really wasn't much of a title.

I enjoyed boxing. I boxed in high school. There were four or five of us in high school who would just box regularly in the basement of the high school. Still, through my NFL career, I always had a heavy bag and a speed bag somewhere on whatever property I lifted in.

The only thing that boxing really helped me with regarding football, was conditioning. If you think you're in shape and you think you understand what taking yourself to the limit is, get in a boxing ring and go three minutes.

I was holding out from the Raiders in 1983, and I trained with a trainer by the name of Richie Giachetti. Richie worked with Larry Holmes. As part of a contract ploy, I was kind of dancing with the idea of turning pro as an alternative to laboring for what I considered to be less than consistent wages for services rendered as a football player, but it didn't work out real well.

NFL Draft
If you're at a big school like Oklahoma or Texas, they schedule a Pro Day and every NFL team sends a representative there. Players do their drills, whether it's the 40-yard dash, vertical jump … all that stuff. They do it one time for the scouts. By the end of my senior season, I really wasn't on a lot of people's radar.

I played high school football with a kid by the name of Joe Restic Jr., who ironically went on to Notre Dame and ended up captaining the team at Notre Dame. His dad was a very famous Ivy League coach at Harvard, Joe Restic, Sr. Joe Restic Sr. was on the Blue-Gray All-Star Committee. I think a player got injured or pulled out or something, and they needed someone to step in for that player. Joe Restic Sr., I think, was responsible for getting me selected to the Blue-Gray All-Star game. Ironically the coach of that game was Jimmy Johnson, who was the head coach at Oklahoma State. That was in December of 1980, in Alabama.

I ended up winning the MVP of the Blue-Gray game and then suddenly I was on everyone's radar. Since small schools don't have a Pro Day, I probably ran the Pro Day drills 25 to 30 separate times for different scouts.

A scout knocked on my St. Mary's dorm room door on a Sunday. St. Mary's was the name of the dorm that I lived in. He wanted me to run on the front lawn of my dorm with sneakers on. I ran for everyone. I ran in the rain and in the snow.

Before Villanova changed their facility, if it was snowing or raining, I had to run inside the old Jake Nevin Field House, which was not a big place. If you ran a 40-yard dash, you had to start in the hallway of the facility with the double doors open and run kitty-corner across the gym into the other hallway at the other corner.

I ran at least two or three times on really rainy days for scouts or coaches. Obviously all those scouts or coaches put me through a battery of tests. A Raiders' coach came by, eyed me up, talked to me for a couple minutes, and wasn't particularly friendly. There were a couple of other scouts waiting. He had me get in a stance, take two steps, come off the ball, take two steps,plant, and come inside. Then he left, and I wrote them off. As it turned out, that was the team that ended up drafting me.

Joining Raiders

It was incredible on a lot of levels. I went from Villanova to the Super Bowl Champion Oakland Raiders. It was a team that was larger than life. Walking into that locker room as a 21-year-old was pretty shocking. I went from Villanova where there was a priest on every floor, to the Oakland Raiders locker room, and it was amazing.

Art Shell, Gene Upshaw, Cliff Branch, Jim Plunkett, Ted Hendricks, Lyle Alzado, and Lester Hayes were there. The list goes on. Cedrick Hardman was my roommate my first year. He was Joe Greene's roommate in college at North Texas. He played on the defensive front with the San Francisco 49ers and was a great pass rusher. I think they called the San Francisco defensive line the Gold Rush with Tommy Hart and Cedrick.

I had no idea what greatness looked like before I walked into that locker room. The one thing about the Raiders is if you dare to envision yourself being great, you certainly knew what it looked like because it was all around you. Whether it was the owner, Jim Otto, Fred Biletnikoff, Art Shell, or Gene Upshaw, greatness was all around you. Those are the guys who brought me up.

Practicing Against Raiders Offensive Line

Early on, it was kind of like going to graduate school. Art Shell and Gene Upshaw were just so physically dominant. They took great pride

in, for lack of a better term, breaking a young guy in. Those lessons learned during my first year were really greatly appreciated. The further away I get from it, the greater the appreciation I have for having guys like that. I think it's something that's missing in many cases in today's game because of the salary cap. You can't have that 33, 34-year-old guy around to mentor the younger players telling them, "This is how you play. This is how you act. This is how you handle yourself. This is what it means to be great." I had that all around me, which I was fortunate to have.

734

Al Davis

The Raiders are one of the iconic franchises in NFL history. Al had an impact on the game over many decades, whether it's the AFL or coaching the Raiders in the early part of his tenure there. He hired John Madden, a guy nobody else was considering. John ended up being one of the most iconic presences in the history of football, both as a coach and as a broadcaster. I would like to say Al was the conscience of the NFL, making sure that the game was treated, played, and thought of the right way.

He got so many great players from small schools, like Art Shell from University of Maryland Eastern Shore. The Raiders were kind of the Ellis Island of the NFL. The writing on the Statue of Liberty states, "Bring me your tired …" I'm not sure of the exact quote, but that might as well have been on the front door of the building.

Whether it's Jim Plunkett, Lyle Alzado, or Cedrick Hardman, the list goes on and on of players that he brought in. These were guys who were great contributors and yearning to be great, not just individually, but collectively. And, they wanted to win championships. Championships end up defining your career as a player. I think relationships are built when you win. Those were all great players who performed well. The Raiders have always had a great connection with those players.

Super Bowl XVIII Win Against Redskins

Michael Strahan and I have had this conversation. Michael went to a Super Bowl early on in his career and lost badly. He was fortunate enough to win a Super Bowl in his final season. I won early and thought to myself, "I've got Marcus Allen, Jim Plunkett, Cliff Branch, Ted Hendricks, Rod Martin, Lester Hayes, Mike Haynes, and the list goes on and on and on. Boy, this Super Bowl thing is easy. We'll do this every year."

We had lost to Washington, interestingly enough, earlier that year, and it was kind of a shootout. We had a number of players who were out, including Marcus Allen, Cliff Branch, who pulled a hamstring early in the game, and Vann McElroy who missed the game. It was a really hot day up in Washington, and they ended up beating us. I believe it was a long screen pass to Joe Washington. Joe was just an amazing talent.

Ironically enough, fast forward to the Super Bowl, we had them on the ropes early. Joe Washington came into the game with Washington backed up on second and long. What ended up happening is we substituted Jack Squirek for Matt Millen. His job was to spy Joe Washington. Jack read the play perfectly, intercepted the ball, scored a touchdown, and the game was over. So it was a contrast from the earlier game, particularly defensively. We were dominant.

I have a great deal of respect for that Redskins team, and particularly their offense, because they were very physical, with two and three tight ends. They pounded you with a lot of counters. They were a team that ended up winning three Super Bowls with three different quarterbacks, and could have won more. The Redskin team that we beat that year had set a scoring record that stood from 1983, until that Randy Moss-Chris Carter team in Washington broke it. Can you believe that?

You could still be very physical within five yards of the line of scrimmage, and our corners were. You can look back at that game as a how-to play corner. Mike Haynes was so good, he was boring. When they talk about the great cover corners of all times, you rarely hear Mike Haynes' name, but people inside of football know who Mike Haynes was. Lester was the consummate riverboat gambler. A lot of bump and run; he really rolled the dice a lot, and more often than not came up a winner. That performance those two cornerbacks had in the Super Bowl was amazing, really amazing.

1984 Raiders vs. Bears Game
I think that that Bears defense was, if not the best, one of the best of all time. It was the perfect marriage between talent and scheme. No one knew how to block the 46 defense. Then you couple that with the group they had on defense talent-wise, and it was a prescription for disaster, particularly when you're playing on the road.

During the game we lost two quarterbacks, and the emergency quarterback was either going to be Marcus Allen or Ray Guy. Ray Guy would occasionally quarterback the scout team for us. Ray was a great athlete and could throw the hell out of a ball. Guys were breaking scot-free. David Humm blew his ACL; guys were just beat up.

That was a very physical game. For our offense it was as physical a game as they had ever played, because the Bears brought so much pressure. If you left five in, they brought six or seven. If you left six in, they brought seven or eight. If you left seven in, they brought eight. They always brought more than you had, and you were guaranteed at the very least, a one-on-one matchup if not breaking scot-free, and more often than not, somebody got turned totally free.

Then people figured out the 46 defense. Like the spread read option, where teams really struggled with it for a couple years and it was going to be the new wave in the NFL. Then people figured it out and it went away. It was the same with the 46 defense. Nobody runs that anymore. Really you can't.

Raiders Deserving To Be Enshrined In The Pro Football Hall Of Fame
Jim Plunkett won two Super Bowls. Jim's a great story. When you're the number one pick in the draft, you go to the worst team in football. Jim nearly got killed up in New England, ended up signing on with San Francisco, and got beat up there. Al Davis took a chance on him, and it ended up resulting in two Super Bowls.

Lester Hayes is another guy that should be up for consideration. There are a lot of really good players from those teams. Cliff Branch threw the fear of God in every defense, and look at Cliff Branch's numbers in playoff games and Super Bowls.

I would compare Cliff to Bobby Hayes. Cliff had better hands. Just look at the numbers and compare the two careers. Cliff won three Super Bowls.

Here's the irony of it. Tom Flores won two Super Bowls with a pretty drastic change in personnel across the board. That team that won in 1983 was completely different than the team that won in 1980, for the most part, particularly on defense. Marcus Allen was on the 1983 team. It was just a different group of players.

Pro Football Hall Of Fame Induction
It's kind of a surreal feeling. It's … I don't want to say a confirmation of your career. I mean, I don't know if you necessarily need that. I think when you've given everything you had to the game and your career, you went till you couldn't go anymore, and you rode off into the sunset, I think you're at peace with that.

The process is a very tough process, particularly for guys that have to wait five, 10, 15, sometimes 20 years to get in. Look at the top 10 finalists from last year. Each and every one of them, you could make a case, is definitively a Hall of Famer. It's just a question of when.

At some positions it's more difficult than others. The wide receiver seems to be a position where there's a real conundrum in terms of today's numbers versus the numbers from years ago. When you're playing for the Steelers - Lynn Swann and Jon Stallworth - and they're throwing the ball 22 times a game, you're not going to put up the kind of numbers that teams are putting up now, but they were big time players in big time games.

It's a tough job the voters have. When you get the call that you've been chosen, it's really special.

Toughest Offensive Lineman
Not as much an offensive line as much as maybe a system. With San Francisco, everything was angle blocking, odd blocks, and trap blocks. The passing game was three steps up, five step drop, ball's out, get the ball to the receiver on a slant or quick out, and let the receiver run for yards after the catch. So you play in a game, they put 30 points up.

It's a totally different feeling when you're playing the Redskins. It's the "Hogs". It's two, three tight ends, John Riggins. You know you've been in a football game.

San Francisco was just more surgical. The tackle influences blocks outside, the fullback comes from the inside. Or the tackle influence blocks inside and the fullback comes from the outside and takes your legs out. A lot of high low blocks and things like that. San Francisco was probably the biggest challenge looking back on it, but it was more schematic than it was personnel.

People have to realize that when you're playing against John Elway, you can't go inside on the tackle. Let's say you're rushing the quarterback. You have to stay outside or just bull rush. So your numbers aren't going to be great, and the way you rush the quarterback is not going to be great because you have to account for John. The Broncos with John Elway and his ability to run and extend plays, and help his offensive line out was very difficult.

Talk about an era of great quarterbacks. Jim Kelly, Dan Marino, Warren Moon, John Elway, Joe Montana, and Steve Young … the list goes on and on.

John Elway was as difficult as anyone to deal with. Joe Montana was surgical. It was death by a thousand cuts. With John, when his pocket broke down. John would spin out to his left, reset his feet, and throw the ball 70 yards across the field for a touchdown. That's John.

Whereas Joe would take a three steps drop or five steps drop, and hit whomever in stride, whether it was Jerry Rice or one of their other great receivers, for a touchdown.

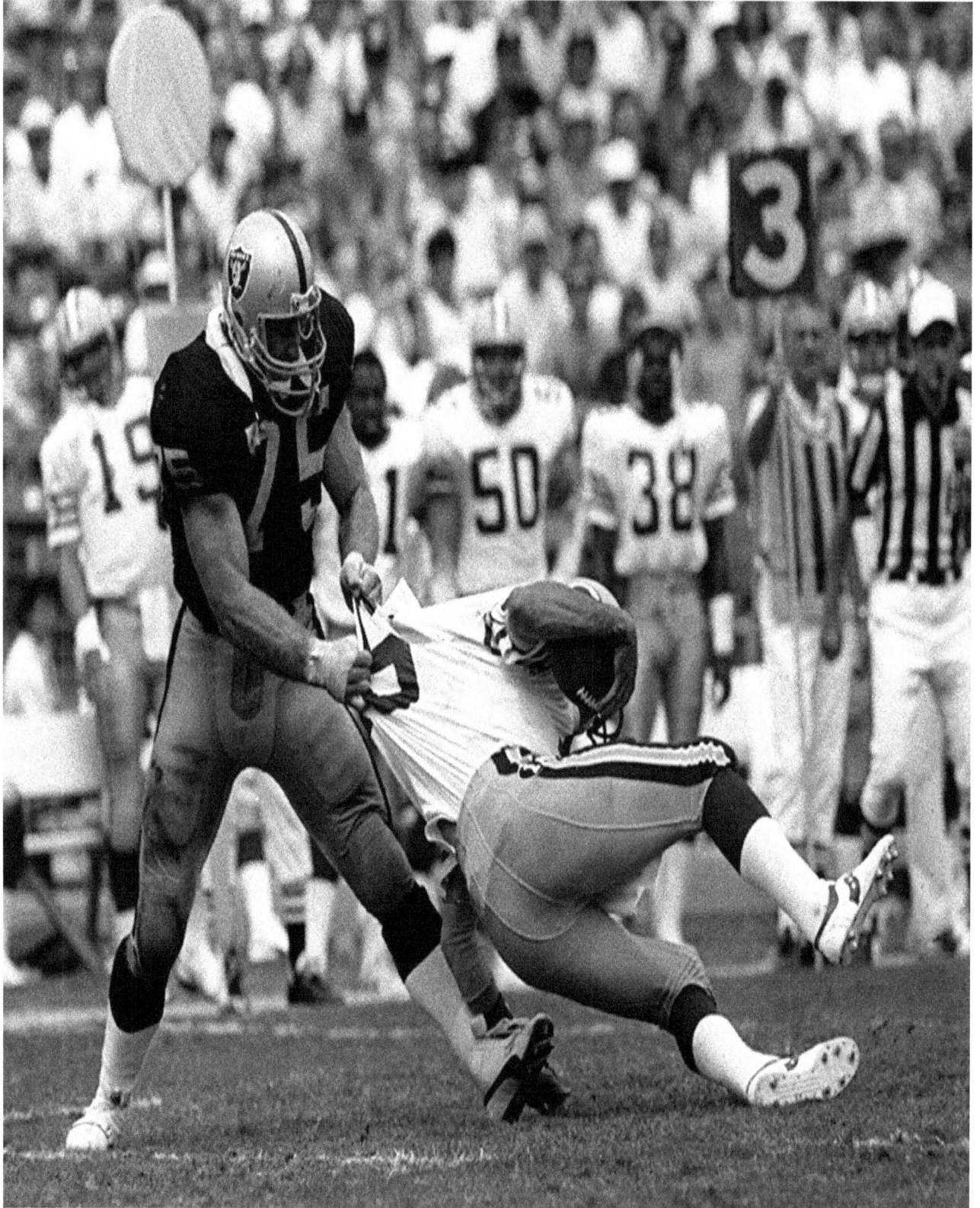

Los Angeles Raiders' Howie Long takes down Green Bay Packers Randy Wright. Photograph copyright Associated Press

Chapter 113

Jim Kelly

College: Miami Career History: Houston Gamblers (1984–1985) Buffalo Bills (1986–1996) 2002 Inductee Pro Football Hall Of Fame

College Choice
Lou Saban was the Miami head football coach back then. I was told they were going to run a pro-style offense and I thought that was what was going to happen.

I wanted to go to Penn State, but at the last minute Joe Paterno told me they wanted me as a linebacker. I was like you've got to be kidding me. I said, "No, thank you." Miami seemed to me to be the best fit. Unfortunately, Lou Saban was there for only one year.

I shouldn't say unfortunately, because what happened was Howard Schnellenberger came on as head coach the following year, and brought in Earl Morrall as the quarterback coach. Earl was a former quarterback with the Dolphins and the Colts. It was a blessing for me that happened. That's when I really got the opportunity to show that I could play quarterback.

I wasn't mad that Joe Paterno wanted me to play linebacker. To be honest with you, I liked playing linebacker because I was able to dish out the hits. I grew up in a family of six boys. We had to fight every day of our lives not only for food, but in anything we did. We used to drive my mother crazy. I'll put it this way, my high school football coach moved me from linebacker to free safety my senior year, because I wanted to make every tackle. I wanted to make sure that whomever I hit remembered what number and what person hit them at the end of the game.

You earn respect that way. I've never been a dirty player. Don't be dumb, don't be dirty, but you want to make sure that when you walk off that football field that those guys know who they played against. My father taught that to me early in life. Play to your ability every play. One of the things he always told me, which is now probably an old cliché, "Every time you walk out this front door son, remember you represent the Kelly name." My five brothers and I always took that to heart and we tried not to tarnish the Kelly name.

I went to football camp my junior and senior year. I thought I showed Joe Paterno enough of me playing quarterback. Anyway, it all worked out pretty good, so I have no complaints.

Howard Schnellenberger

One of the good things, from my point of view, was Howard Schnellenberger was like a drill sergeant. He was a noble guy. He demanded respect. He didn't even need to say it; you knew just by being around him what type of guy he was. He was no nonsense, but he knew how to talk to players. He knew how to get us motivated, especially me. Coming out of high school, some players need that. They need a little kick in the butt, and I'm sure I did at the time. He knew how to get the best out of players.

Of course the old cliché, again, is you're only as good the players around you or the coaching staff around you. Howard brought in a bunch of big guys, some big coaches, and he wound up winning a National Championship at Miami.

As you get older you start learning, you mature, you start thinking that maybe I don't know it all. It's a good time to start listening a little more. I'm sure that works with coaches too. I'm sure looking at some of the guys that have been behind Howard, that I'm sure they learned the same thing. For me, I've been very blessed. From high school to the NFL, I was blessed. I had great head coaches.

Miami Practices

Back in the late '70s and early '80s when you asked for a water break, they said, "What are you crazy. You get one water break. Be happy with it." Nowadays, you have to give kids water. Anytime they want it, you've got to give it to them. Back then we were taking salt pills because you'd sweat so much. In Miami we used to hide water bags underneath the yard markers just so that we could sneak some water.

My teammates would say, "Jim you need to put an ice bag on your shoulder." I'd get ice to put on my shoulder right after team drills, because I knew I wasn't going to practice anymore. Whether I wanted it or not, everybody wanted me to have an ice bag because they were able to bite the tip off of it and everybody was drinking the water out of the ice bag. By the time the practice was over, there wasn't much ice left.

Decision To Sign With Houston Gamblers Of USFL and Not Buffalo Bills Of NFL

The USFL said we need to get top quality players in here. They had already signed a couple Heisman Trophy winners. They said, "Tell me where you want to play; Chicago, Tampa Bay, Houston. Where do you want to play?" I took trips to those cities and I decided that Houston was the place for me with their domed stadium. There would be no wind or rain to deal with. It was exciting to maybe be able to start something that could last forever.

Unfortunately, the USFL only lasted three years. I can't really complain because that's pretty much where I probably learned the passing game. We threw the ball 35-45 times a game.

Mouse Davis

Number one, he's awesome, almost like a father figure. Number two, he definitely helped increase my quickness and worked on my footwork. The offense was more of me sprinting out and throwing on the run. I had to learn that from the beginning because I really wasn't that type of passer. It taught me how to read a defense. I learned a lot from Mouse, there's no doubt about it.

Joining Buffalo Bills

Back then I was just praying that it would work out, and that the owner, Ralph Wilson, would bring players in like he said he was going to. Boy did he ever. Andre Reed was already there. They brought in Thurman Thomas, Kent Hull, Will Wolford, Cornelius Bennett, and James Lofton … I can go on and on naming all the great players. We wound up having a lot of Hall of Fame players. I'm not sure if there's any team that ever had as much fun as we did playing the game of football.

Marv Levy

Marv Levy was a blessing for me. He was the kind of coach that let his players be themselves, but we knew what our guidelines were. We knew the limitations. When we were on the football field during practice, we knew what we were doing. It wasn't like we had two-and-a-half or three-hour practices. We practiced for 100-145 minutes because we knew what we had to get accomplished. We knew that we wanted to be the best.

They were called quality practices not quantity, not having to do it over, and over, and over. We did it right to begin with. Marv allowed us to be ourselves. We knew our limitations. We knew that if we stepped out of line he'd be the first one to get in our face. He wasn't a big rah, rah type of guy. He always said the right things at the right time.

Origin Of Buffalo Bills No Huddle Offense

It was against the Cleveland Browns in a playoff game in 1989. We wound up running the no huddle offense pretty much 95% of the time the next season. That's why we went to four straight Super Bowls. Our offense was clicking. We tired defensive linemen out. We rarely substituted. We had an idea of what type of defense they were going to run.

When Coach Levy allowed me to call my own plays, I knew where to put Andre Reed. I knew where to line Thurman up, knowing he was great against linebackers one-on-one. Andre was a lot better receiver inside than he was outside. It's something I'm very passionate about. It took colleges and the NFL years to really understand that the no huddle will work and give some of these quarterbacks the freedom to go ahead and call the plays.

Playing Professional Football

I would never call it work. I just loved the game. I thank God that they paid players a lot of money when I played and that they still do, to play the game that they enjoy. If the salaries had been a lot less I would have still played. I would have played for whatever they were paying, because I just enjoyed it.

I grew up in a family of six boys. Whether there was snow on the ground or it was pouring down rain, we always had a football in our hands. That's what we did all day. We always wanted to play and we always dreamt about doing that.

For me it was always just a joy to get out there and have fun. At times I would lay out some licks. Unfortunately, well I should say fortunately, I wound up being a quarterback and it's gotten me to where I'm at today. I've been very blessed.

Running No Huddle Offense

Marv Levy knew that I was smart enough to handle the no huddle offense. He put his job security on the line. He knew that if I screwed it up it was his job too. He knew what style quarterback I was. He knew that I thrived on it and knew how to quick pace the offense. That's pretty much the type of person I am. My mother always used to tell me, "Son you need to slow down." I've never been that way. I've always been a guy that was full steam ahead. Let's do it, let's go. I'm not a very patient person. It worked out; I think it worked out pretty good for all of us. We've got a bunch of Hall of Famers in Canton, Ohio.

Playing In Four Consecutive Super Bowls & Not Winning One

I don't care what it is; it's never easy when you lose. The good thing is the resiliency we built up and how we went through it. It would be different if we went to one and then skipped two and then went to another one, skipped one, and played in four Super Bowls over a 10-12 year period. We played in the Super Bowl four years in a row.

The resiliency our team had, the mental toughness that we had to put what we had done in the past behind us and move forward. Even though we didn't win one, I'm so proud to say that I played for the Buffalo Bills.

The more people I talk to, whether it's a reporter or people that didn't pull for us, they look back and say, "Wow. I can't believe you guys were able to accomplish playing in the Super Bowl four years in a row, which will never be done again." When you lose, that lingers on for so long. With a good Head Coach in Marv Levy we were able to focus. The mental toughness and the mental preparation we had before every season and every game was unmatched. I'm just proud to say that I played in that era.

We would have liked to win one or two, but it didn't happen. If you look at my career, Bruce Smith's, Thurman Thomas', or Andre Reed's careers, we all know we were very successful whether we won one or not. Trust me, a lot of guys out there would have loved to be in one Super Bowl let alone going to four. I'm still very proud of our accomplishments. I would never sit there and cry over it. I'll put it that way.

We all knew we wanted to be best. We all wanted to do well. We enjoyed winning even though the last game of the season was a loss as far as when it came to Super Bowls. But the thing is, we were professionals. We knew how we had to get prepared for the following year and try to do it again. I even remember our motto one year was, "Let's piss everybody off. Let's go back to the Super Bowl again. "

I still thank God that for my teammates because I was surrounded with great players, but more than that players with great character.

Toughest Opponent
My brother Pat, when I was in Junior High. Pat was a good kid. I'm serious it was always my brothers. Everybody was tough. When you play professional football as long as I did you get to play with a bunch of great players like Joe Klecko, Howie Long, Andre Tippett, and Neil Smith and Derrick Thomas from the Chiefs. I don't want to start throwing out a bunch of names, but there were so many great players when I played.

I played college football with Fred Marion, whom a lot of people probably have not heard of. He intercepted more passes playing for the Patriots against me, than anyone did. It was always tough but I always enjoyed it. I always enjoyed the task ahead and being able to compete.

Pro Football Hall Of Fame Induction
It was something I had never dreamt about. I dreamt about playing in the NFL, but not the Pro Football Hall of Fame. I thought going into the Pro Football Hall of Fame was reserved for guys like Merlin Olsen, Deacon Jones, Joe Namath, Johnny Unitas, Bart Starr, Bob Griese, and Terry Bradshaw. Then all of a sudden, I'm right alongside them. It's pretty cool, plus my son was there. For me, that was a dream come true and a blessing that my son was able to be there the day I was inducted.

Buffalo Bills quarterback Jim Kelly and Miami Dolphins quarterback Dan Marino talk after play. Photograph copyright Associated Press

Chapter 114

Mike Munchak

```
College:
Penn State

Career History:
Houston Oilers (1982-1993)

Coaching History:
Houston          Oilers          (1994–1996)
(Offensive assistant/quality control coach)
Tennessee    Oilers/Titans    (1997–2010)
(Offensive line coach)
Tennessee        Titans          (2011–2013)
(Head coach)
Pittsburgh      Steelers        (2014–Present)
(Offensive line coach)

2001 Inductee Pro Football Hall Of Fame
```

College Choice

I was probably a middle of the road recruit. People thought Penn State was where I always wanted to go. It really wasn't. I knew of Penn State, obviously. I knew of Coach Joe Paterno and of his great reputation. I didn't know where I wanted to go, or what the future held for me. To be honest, even when I was in high school, I'm one of those guys who just enjoyed the moment.

My junior year I started getting hand-sealed letters of interest from coaches in me playing football for them in college.

I think that's when it hit me [the end of my junior year] that I had an opportunity to maybe get a scholarship to continue in football. I was one of those tweener guys. Because of my height and weight at the time it wasn't an obvious thing, what position I'd be playing in college.

My senior year, I heard from Penn State and some other teams. I took my five or six visits. My sister was going to Penn State at the time. Penn State was only a couple hours away from home. I went for a visit to Penn State. One of the assistant coaches had called me to set up a visit. I went out there in January of my senior year in high school for a visit.

That's when I first met Coach Paterno. It was during a dinner when they had all the recruits in town. There were 15-20 guys there. We were there for the weekend in order to get a feel for what Penn State was like. It's really different than most visits when you would only go for one night.

At the time, there was no football dorm at Penn State. The players were spread around the campus like the regular students. Players were in normal dorm rooms.

At Penn State you stayed in a dorm room as a recruit. You slept on a cot in a room with two Penn State football players. Coach Paterno wanted recruits to experience what they were getting themselves into if they went to Penn State.

That was unique because most schools I visited I stayed in a hotel, which had a nice setup. Whereas at Penn State, it was, "This is what we're all about, here's how we do business, and here's what you can expect." I got a real good taste of college life, for what it was going to be like in the dorms with not just football players.

I thought that was kind of interesting. I actually liked that way of recruiting. I got a chance to spend time with the players and assistant coaches.

On Sunday before I left, I had a chance to sit down with Coach Paterno. That was my first face-to-face meeting with him. Obviously, I was scared to death for that meeting. I was an 18-year-old boy talking to a legend in Pennsylvania. I'll always remember sitting there, talking to him about my opportunity to go to Penn State. That meant a lot to me.

The signing date was coming up in February of my senior year. When I was narrowing down my choices, I had decided that I was probably going to attend a different school.

I called an assistant coach at Penn State to let him know I was probably going to go to a different school. I think that surprised him. He asked me, "Hey, did you sign with anybody?" I said, "Well, no, the signing date is a couple weeks away. No, I haven't done that yet." He said, "Well, hold on a second." He got Coach Paterno on the phone. I was trying to avoid talking to Coach Paterno. I just wanted to talk to the assistant. Coach Paterno got on the phone line and said, "Hey, Mike, why don't you ask your mom and dad if it's okay if I come over to your house tomorrow night. Let me come over and have dinner with you and discuss your decision."

Obviously, who's going to say no to Coach Paterno coming over to your house? My parents were thrilled and excited as heck. The next day Coach Paterno was at the house and had dinner with us. We talked. The conversation was not a whole lot about me. He found common ground with my parents on many levels. Then, Coach Paterno asked for a couple minutes alone with me. We talked about my decision on not going to Penn State. I changed my mind that night. Coach Paterno said that he couldn't guarantee that I ever play a down of football at Penn State, but he guaranteed that I'd have the best experience of my life at Penn State. He said I would come out of Penn State with a business degree, which was what I was working for.

He guaranteed that if I had the talent to play, that they'd bring it out in me, and bring out the best in me. If I was afraid of that challenge, then maybe he shouldn't be sitting here, offering me a scholarship. It was a very motivating and honest talk. When he left, I really gave some thought to what he said. I realized what he said to me was exactly what I wanted. What was most important to me was an education from a good school. I also wanted to be challenged to be the best I could be. I really bought into the fact that if anyone could do that, they could. They could bring that out in me, just like he said. A couple days later, I called the coach and changed my mind, and said I wanted to go to Penn State.

You know what your parents want for you. Mine always guided me. They always let me make my own decisions. That was my biggest decision of my life, to that point, for sure. I think my parents wanted to guide me, but not direct me. I've always appreciated that. I knew in the back of my mind what they probably wanted. But still, the decision was mine. When I said I was thinking of not going to Penn State, they were all behind what I was thinking, what my thoughts were.

Joe Paterno
The best example I'll give of what Coach Paterno was like was the fact that he came to my house, had dinner with my parents, and said the things he said to me in a very positive, but challenging way. That told me everything I was in for. That's how he was when I got to Penn State too, honest and disciplined.

I loved the discipline and the way he ran the program. What he said, he did. He taught you a lot of life's lessons. He always related life to football. The first conversation he had with the team, there were about 100 players there. He made it very clear that the next four years were going to be the last four years of football for a high percentage of us. He said, "The next four years are going to be the best years of your life." He also said, "Your education is your priority. You need to leave with that education no matter what happens."

He instilled that from day one, and not just that first day, but weekly. He always talked about life and life's lessons. I think it was very interesting how he found a way, every week, win or lose, to teach us something. I thought that was very unique. I always thought he was a great speaker within the moment. When you left there, I think you appreciated it more. What he meant to the program, what he meant to us, and what he taught me.
I can meet a Penn State guy anywhere, who played for Coach Paterno in any decade, and we have similar stories and similar feelings. That's a nice bond. It was a nice fraternity to be a part of.

Position Played At Penn State
Coach Paterno was honest with me regarding what position I would play. That day, in my house, he said, "I'm not quite sure if you'll ever play. I'm not sure what position you're even going to play." When I got to Penn State, I thought I was going to be a defensive player. Coach Paterno had me on the offensive side from day one. I moved from tight end after a one-day trial, to defensive line, to offensive line. I move from offensive tackle, to guard, and to center. He moved me around. He did the same thing with a lot of players. He had a knack for finding the right fit for you. It seemed like I never really got what I wanted, but I got what I was supposed to get. I thought I knew what I wanted, but I really didn't. Coach Paterno let the process happen by moving me from position to position.

By the beginning of my sophomore year, I found my home on the offensive line, which I developed into. If you told me I was going to be an offensive lineman coming out of high school, I never would have believed it. I think a lot of guys have similar stories. I think he wanted what

748

was best for you. Coach Paterno and his staff were very well trained to do that. I'm sure most college coaches are, but Coach Paterno had a knack. He wasn't going to tell you something that you wanted to hear. He was going to tell you what he felt was the truth.

Penn State's Biggest Rival
Pittsburgh was Penn State's biggest rival. It was awesome. It was always a Thanksgiving Day game. Obviously, I've heard all the stories. For instance, Tony Dorsett and the tradition they had through the '70s. The time in the early '80s when we were there that was the game you waited for. Win the state battle, east versus west. I thought that was the game. Without a doubt, that was the big game. Would it be at our place on Thanksgiving Day, or at their place? I was just happy that they started the rivalry up again, because a lot of people had forgot how strong that was, and what a big game that was.

Option Of Playing One More Season At Penn State
I had the option of playing one more year at Penn State. I came out a year early. I knew what a good team we had. My freshman year I was mainly on special teams and on the practice squad, so I didn't see the field as an offensive player until my sophomore year. I was a starter at guard my whole sophomore year. Then my junior year I injured my knee in spring training. I had to miss the year and got redshirted.

I came back the next year and started the whole year. I was back to feeling good again. As a young man, I'd never been hurt before like that. The injury spooked me a little bit. The fact was that I was able to graduate in four years and I was able to get healthy. Just about every one of us in my recruiting class was graduating. I just thought the timing was right for me to enter the draft. I had graduated. I had played and had a chance to contribute every year. The timing seemed right.

I think if I were to look back and say, "What if," because who knows what would have happened if I had stayed or didn't stay. I was happy for Penn State when they won the National Championship the next year because, obviously, those guys were all good friends of mine.

Todd Blackledge and Curt Warner did a great job. I was teammates with all those guys. I can't tell you how happy I was for them. My senior year, we were number one for X amount of weeks, and didn't quite get it done that year. I was happy that they were able to do it the next year. I felt like even though I wasn't there, I was a part of it. Any time Penn State has success, I feel like I'm a part of it, one way or another. It was time for me to move on and enter the draft. I was happy for them. I'm not really one who looks back and gets all caught up inthat.

NFL Draft
When I heard that talk from Coach Paterno, it didn't mean I didn't have dreams of someday playing in the NFL. I had thought the same thing Coach Paterno said, and I was going to enjoy my four years at Penn State. I wanted to get the best out of my four years. That's what I bought into, when Coach Paterno was in my house. I was going to hold him to that. I wanted the degree in business.

I wanted to play for Penn State, and that's what I was focused on. I really didn't think about the NFL. I saw my teammates getting drafted and I started thinking, "If this guy can get drafted in the NFL, then heck, I have a shot at this thing." I start realizing that if I continued to develop, continued to play, and continued to work hard; I'd have a chance to play on the next level.

I was developing into an offensive lineman. I had a long way to go between gaining weight, gaining strength, and learning the position. A lot was happening in a short period of time for me. Then, I realized ... I did have an opportunity to play in the NFL. Where I'd go and where I'd get drafted was not something I had any idea of when I became draft eligible.

The draft was on a Tuesday back then. It was 12 rounds, six rounds on Tuesday and six rounds on Wednesday. It started at 7:30 in the morning. It's a lot different than it is now. I think it just started being on TV broadcast live on ESPN around 1980. It was exciting.

I wasn't sure what was going to happen. I played in an All-Star game, which helped me quite a bit in moving up in the draft. That's why I feel those All-Star games are valuable. I played in the Olympia Gold Bowl. I remember Marcus Allen was in it. I thought that helped me quite a bit, in the combine. You never know how it's going to work out, but I was told I'd be drafted in the first round. The day of the draft I thought this could be a long morning.

I went to my girlfriend's apartment the morning of the draft so we could just be by ourselves. The draft started at 7:30 in the morning. It was so different than now. It's become such a big production. My parents were two and a half hours away from me. My dad and mom were working.

A team went up there to draft and I knew they weren't looking for offensive linemen. I remember when Houston came up, I thought, "They have talked about drafting a quarterback or an offensive lineman." Jim McMahon had already been drafted a couple picks earlier. I thought, "Oh, you never know. They could draft me" As my name was being called the phone was ringing. It was the head coach of the Houston Oilers congratulating me. I was hearing my name said live on TV.

It's like you go off on a tangent. "Did this really happen?" You're in a fog. It's the weirdest feeling, to hear your name called and knowing that you just got picked by an NFL team to move on to the NFL level. For a 21-year-old man, it was really, really exciting. It's hard to find the words to describe it. Then, to talk on the phone with the head coach and realize, "Man, I'm going to be blocking for Earl Campbell." That was the first thought that came in my mind. I thought, "This is unbelievable." It was really exciting for my family and me. That was just a great moment for my family. When I spoke to my family they were all screaming and yelling.

It's just a great family moment for someone from Scranton to first go to Penn State, which was a thrill, and then to have an opportunity to play in the NFL. It was a dream come true. There was just a lot of excitement. I'm happy to have had all the people that helped me along the way, including my high school teammates, my high school coach, Coach Paterno, and Dick Anderson, the Penn State line coach. Dick had taught me how to play on the offensive line, which I've always been so grateful for. He's the best line coach I've ever been around. I learned so much from him. I left Penn State with a degree, and an occupation. They trained me to be a football player and a businessman. I can't thank Penn State enough for what they did for me.

Joining Houston Oilers

When I got to Houston they were in the beginning of rebuilding the team. They had battled the Steelers all through the '70s. The Pittsburgh Steelers were building their dynasty at the same time the Oilers were.

Unfortunately, the Oilers kept coming in second to the Steelers. By the time the Oilers hit the early '80s, they were rebuilding. They decided to do it through the offensive line. It was exciting to be part of that. Back then there was no free agency. You knew you were probably going to be on the same team for your entire career unless they decided to trade you. Bruce Matthews and Dean Steinkuhler were drafted by the Oilers and were part of the rebuilding process.

I came into the league and there was a strike, so I only played in nine games. The second year was my first full year. We were two and 14. That's what rebuilding brought.

Warren Moon was a free agent out of Canada. When we got him in 1984 he was the biggest piece of the puzzle. Before he came we were building the offensive line. Obviously, the quarterback is always the most important piece of the puzzle. The Oilers were building through the offensive line and to be able to protect someone like Warren, I think that's what made it come together.

Bruce, Dean, and I learned so much during those years, when we weren't winning. We were playing and growing as players. We knew we were going to be together for a long time. We were hopeful that we were developing something so that we'd be able to win games for a lot of years. It's hard to play, in seasons like that. I think because we were so young and so excited about what we were doing, that made us better players. It's fun to watch them continue to build the team year in, year out, and through draft. That was the main way of building it. There were trades here and there. It was fun to be part of something from the ground level, and watch us build it up to a playoff team for seven years in a row.

It's weird, when you go from college to the pros and you're playing with players you watched on TV, who are years older than you. In high school and in college, you don't have that difference in age. When you go to the NFL, the age difference is unique. All of a sudden, you're teammates with guys you've watched play that are household names. All of a sudden, you are lining up and blocking for them or blocking with them. That's cool. I think that helped us overcome not winning. Obviously, the goal is to win. We knew we were building something, so patience had to be there. I think as they put the pieces of the puzzle together, like they did, it was exciting to know we were part of that, so we appreciated it much more when we started winning.

Earl Campbell

It was exciting to join the Houston Oilers knowing what kind of team I was going to be part of. For offensive linemen, you just had to get the hell out of Earl Campbell's way because he'd run you over like he did the defensive players. He was a downhill north and south runner. He was faster than people thought. To be a lineman in that type of offense was pretty much a dream come true.

He was a great guy. He took guys under his wing and made them feel comfortable. He was so laid back and full of life. He was a big country guy who would sing Willie Nelson songs on the airplane over the intercom. He was very unique. Me being in Houston, Texas, a guy from Pennsylvania, and being a part of that and knowing even though we weren't winning yet, we were building something special.

Elvin Bethea
One of my first memories with the Houston Oilers was of Elvin Bethea. Elvin was in his 16th year in the NFL when I was in my first year. I'm thinking, "Man, look at this old guy." I'm pass blocking and he's playing defensive end. I had a chance to go against him one-on-one. I figured I was this big rookie who was going to jump all over him. I found out real quickly why he had been around for 16 years. His quickness allowed him to arm-over me so fast as I was trying to kill him.

Veterans On Houston Oilers My Rookie Year
When I came into the league, I saw the way Dave Casper played the game and his work ethic. To experience that as a young player and to see those types of guys early in my career really made a difference in me. I saw how these great players prepared. They didn't take it for granted. That's why they were special. Every year was a new challenge in the NFL.

Archie Manning was our quarterback. So I'm around Archie Manning, who I watched for years playing for the New Orleans Saints. I'm sitting there looking through the Oilers program and seeing all these guys listed. I thought "You're part of this team now. They're expecting you to help them win."

Warren Moon
Warren went to Canada and played in the Canadian Football League because he wanted to play quarterback. At that time, things were a little bit different in the NFL. NFL teams weren't buying into the fact that quarterback was his best position.

Warren stuck to his guns, what he believed in, and what he felt he was capable of being. Obviously, he proved it. He had a great career in Canada, which allowed him to be one of the first true free agents in the NFL. When left the CFL he was being courted by a lot of teams. We were lucky to get him in Houston.

When he first came in, I saw his size, strength, commitment to the game, and how hard he worked. I knew we had something special.

Bruce Matthews, Dean Steinkuhler, Harvey Salem, and I had been together for a while playing on the offensive line. I remember how excited we were in thinking, "This guy has a chance to be really special. If he's special, he'll make us and finally turn us into a winning football team." There was a lot of excitement in Houston the day the Oilers got Warren and it proved out.

Run and Shoot Offense

Warren Moon adapted to and ran the Run and Shoot offense. Many people don't realize he was doing what Peyton Manning did years later. Warren was calling all the plays and running the system. Warren and Coach Kevin Gilbride worked really well together. Watching the Run and Shoot grow in the late '80s and early '90s was special.

It took a while to adjust to the Run and Shoot. It was totally different. It was really out of the offensive linemen's comfort zone. The hardest part was figuring out where the quarterback was throwing the ball from. We were so used to the quarterback always being seven yards deep right behind the center.

All of a sudden, we went to an offense where Warren was going to be in a lot of different spots. Sometimes, he was going to be in the conventional seven-yard drop spot. Then other times, he might be a little bit over the left guard, or a little bit over the right guard, or rolling out. It made the defense have to work a little bit. The defense had trouble designing blitzes and line stunts to attack the quarterback. There were some positives to it, but the fact was you had to realize where Warren was.

The Run and Shoot took a while to figure out. You think you're blocking your guy and the next thing you know, your guy is reaching over and grabbing the quarterback. I would be thinking that the quarterback was in a different location. It took time for the offensive linemen to get used to that and also knowing that we were going to throw the ball quite a bit.

Defensive linemen and fans, want offenses to throw the ball. Defensive linemen want the opportunity to rush the passer. It was a whole different mindset for the offensive linemen.

We still had 1,000-yard rushers in Mike Rozier and Allen Pinkett. We still had Alonzo Highsmith running the football. We had some good years. Obviously, the pass set up the run, rather than the run set up the pass.

It put a lot of pressure on Warren. Warren really had to be on his game week in and week out, because so much of what we were doing was on him. The other thing was it was hard to prepare for games for the offense. We went to the Run and Shoot first then Detroit went to the same system. There was very little film on teams defending the Run and Shoot. So when you were going to play against a team, you had no idea how they were going to play you. If we were going to play the Steelers, Browns, or the Bengals, the teams in our division at the time, we had no idea how they were going to play against our offense. We couldn't watch film of teams playing the Run and Shoot because nobody was using it.

It was hard. You were adjusting during the game, after you saw how the defense was going to play against your team, which was using four wide receivers. This offense was new to the league and not too many teams were doing it at the level we were. We had an idea of what teams were going to do, but until we played a lot of teams more than one time, we really didn't know what to expect from them.

That added another element of uncomfortableness for offensive players, especially offensive linemen. Routes are routes, but for offensive linemen, what we had to do and deal with, there was a lot more to it. It grew us as players. I think it helped Bruce Matthews and me. It may have helped our careers. It helped us learn how to adapt to things, learn how to communicate, and to change our technique. It was a learning process, but I think it helped us become better players.

Toughest Defensive Lineman
When I came into the league, the toughest defensive lineman was probably Randy White. We had a big game with the Dallas Cowboys every year. Back then the preseason was more of a big deal than it is now. The fourth preseason game was like the first game of the season. We had a big showdown with Dallas every year. It was a nationally televised game. John Madden was broadcasting it. Randy White was on the back end of his career, but still one of the best in the league. He was another example of a guy I watched win Super Bowls, and play well with Ed "Too Tall" Jones, and that whole group of guys they had. Playing against a guy like Randy White, as physical, quick, and strong as he was, is something I had never really experienced in college.

One of my first starts in the NFL was during a preseason game my rookie year against the Cowboys. After going against Randy I thought, "Whoa, this is the level of play that I'm going to be dealing with every Sunday." That was my first taste of greatness of going against someone like him. He's the guy that stood out for me because when you're young, and playing against a guy that ends up being a Hall of Famer, is something you always remember.

Bruce Matthews
I always tell Bruce Matthews if it weren't for me, he wouldn't have made the Pro Football Hall Of Fame. His last seven years in the NFL I got a chance to coach him, so I always try to take credit for him. Obviously, I had nothing to do with his greatness. He played 19 years in the NFL. I saw every play he ever played, which is hard for anyone else to say.

What a relationship. He introduced me into the Pro Football Hall Of Fame, and I introduced him into the Pro Football Hall Of Fame. We were each other's presenters.

My daughters are like daughters to him. With his kids, I feel like I'm the same thing to them—part of the family. We have a very unique relationship. That's rare. We were blessed to be good friends and good teammates for a long time.

Coaching him was interesting. I think it made me a better coach, coaching someone like him. You learn to coach the good ones, the special guys, the regular guys, and all the other different types of players you deal with.

I thought Bruce handled it very professionally. It's not easy to coach guys who were once your teammates. It doesn't happen very often, but it does happen. It was a great time in my life having him in it, and then coaching with him for a while was unique, too. We've had a great NFL relationship. We're obviously best friends. He's been very helpful to me, not only during my playing career, but also during my coaching career. It was great.

We'd be in a meeting, and I'd say, "I'm trying to coach up this great technique." Usually, I'd go overboard with trying to teach it. I'd look at him, and he'd say, "Man, you can't do that." He'd bring me back to reality that something I was trying to teach was a little more difficult than I thought it was. He'd give me that look like, "No, man, that's not happening." He kept me grounded. He didn't let me get too carried away with my coaching, especially as I was learning the trade. He helped me adjust as a coach, too. He gave me great feedback. He was very helpful to me getting started as a coach. I kept adjusting my teaching style in what I said, didn't say, or maybe my routine, by a lot of the input he gave me. It was a big advantage to me being able to coach him.

"The Comeback" Houston Oilers vs. Buffalo Bills In 1993 Playoffs
At halftime we thought we had the 1993 playoff game against the Buffalo Bills won. I'm not going to lie. We played about as good a first half as a team could play, on the road, against the Bills. The Bills had a great defense with Bruce Smith and Darryl Talley. They had a who's who on defense. We went up there and scored 28 points in the first half. The first four times we had the ball on offense, we scored touchdowns. I try to block out some of the bad memories from that game. What I remember was we were going up and down the field. Everything we did, worked. Warren couldn't have thrown the ball any better. We were blocking and we ran the ball when we wanted to. It was 28-3 at halftime. At halftime, we thought, "We're playing at the level we're supposed to play at." The run and shoot was clicking as good as it could be clicking.

We knew that we had to play a whole second half, but obviously we felt very strong about our position. Then, the second half happened and unfortunately it was the total opposite for us from onside kicks to balls bouncing the wrong way.

The Bills drove down and scored, then they kicked an onside kick and got the ball and scored again. Warren threw one ball, it got tipped, and it turned into an interception. The Bills scored14 points before we got the ball at one point. The Bills scored 28 points in the third quarter. Then we knew it was going to be a game. When that happened, game on. At the end of the fourth quarter we were tied. There still was overtime, and I thought we'd overcome everything. We thought we were still going to win the football game, and we didn't.

The worst part was not going through it one time, but you have to live it the rest of your life. Every time the playoffs are about to start, networks are still playing that game over again on TV. It's one of those things where it's a memory I really don't want to have to relive. I'm thinking, "Wasn't that long enough ago? Why do they keep playing that game?" Unfortunately, it seems like some people still say, "Oh yeah, I saw you in the game."

It's not a great memory but credit goes to the Bills. They were a great football team. They went to four Super Bowls in a row at that time. Jim Kelly wasn't even playing in that game so we had no excuse. It wasn't like we could say, "Oh, Jim, man, Jim." Frank Wright led the charge. He did a great job, as the Bills quarterback that day. As good as we were in the first half was as bad as the Bills were. The first half was amazing. In the second half we flipped roles. The Bills somehow made enough plays to beat us.

That's why I was so happy when I went into coaching with the Tennessee Titans and the "Music City Miracle" was against the Bills and we won. So that was my settling grace, that day. We were the Titans at the time, which obviously were the former Oilers. My payback as a player and a coach was that I returned the favor in a very memorable way.

Pro Football Hall Of Fame Induction

I'll remember the day I found out I was selected for the Pro Football Hall Of Fame forever. I was at home in Nashville, Tennessee. I was a coach for the Tennessee Titans. I knew I was one of the 15 finalists.

I had talked to John McClain who was the reporter that represented me before the voters. Every finalist has a representative from their NFL city that is reminding voters of the player's achievements. We had talked and he said, "You've got a shot." That was about it.

He said, "We'll probably be making the announcement by 11:00 a.m. on Saturday. I'll call you as soon as I know something, either way." My daughter was playing basketball in the YMCA League on that Saturday. I thought the basketball game would keep me busy, and keep the Hall Of Fame decision off my mind. I decided I'm not going to make a big production out of this. Both of my daughters were young at the time, so I didn't want to get everyone all caught up in it. I just played it low key.

We were getting ready to go to the basketball game, and I saw the clock and thought, "Man, I didn't hear anything." I thought that meant I didn't make it. I wasn't giving much thought to it, but I decided to turn the on TV and see who made it. I turned the on TV and I found ESPN. The sportscaster said, "They've been delayed. The team hasn't been announced yet. They'll be announcing the decision in the next few minutes."

I hadn't heard from John yet, so I figured, "Well, I'm going to wait and see who made it." I sat down. My daughters were getting ready for the game. I was in the room by myself. The director of the Hall Of Fame came out and started announcing the names. The director said, "This is in random order." The third or fourth name was mine. Just to hear it—wow. I couldn't believe I heard it. At the same time, just like when I got drafted by the Oilers, the phone was ringing. It was John, screaming into the phone about how happy he was about me getting into the Hall Of Fame. My family came in the room. My wife was jumping around. It was a great family moment. Almost like when I came into the league and got drafted. What do you say about something like that? It was an unbelievable experience. Then the phone rang off the hook for the next 24 hours.

What I like about the induction it's a celebration. All of the people that were a part of your career and have been a part of your experience have an opportunity to go to Canton to be a part of the celebration with you. What a great way to do it. That's why that weekend is so special; it's not just about you. It's about everybody, your immediate family, your football family, your high school, and your college family.

Photograph copyright Associated Press

Chapter 115

Morten Anderson

College:
Michigan State

Career History:
New Orleans Saints (1982–1994)
Atlanta Falcons (1995–2000)
New York Giants (2001)
Kansas City Chiefs (2002–2003)
Minnesota Vikings (2004)
Atlanta Falcons (2006–2007)

2017 Inductee Pro Football Hall Of Fame

College Choice
Purdue University, Albion College, Delaware, and some smaller schools recruited me. In 1977, I was an exchange student from Copenhagen Denmark. We had a really good team that year. We had a lot of good players who were recruited by colleges and I happened to be one of them. A couple months into the season I was recruited by Michigan State. It happened fairly quickly.

A guy named Bob Baker, the offensive coordinator at Michigan State, came down to recruit me. He had been in the CFL for a many years. Hans Nielsen, another Danish kicker who was at Michigan State, also came down to recruit me. He convinced me that if he could do it I could probably do it, too. That was a big factor in me ending up as a Spartan.

I just picked up kicking when I came to the United States. I barely spoke the language when I came to the United States. It was a little bit of a culture shock, but I actually picked it up pretty fast. I landed in the United States on my 17th birthday, and two days later I was kicking field goals for the high school team. It all happened very fast.

Biggest Rivalry In College
Our biggest rival was Michigan, for sure. We beat them my freshman year 24-15.

I had a lot of respect for Bo Schembechler and his teams. Playing in the Big House in Ann Arbor was pretty cool, obviously. Spartan Stadium was equally as fun, but being in front of 105,000 people against Michigan was pretty mind-blowing.

We won the Big Ten my very first year at Michigan State. We had great players in Eddie Smith, Kirk Gibson, and Mark Brammer along with other really good players. When we beat Michigan my freshman year I thought, "Oh, let's do that every year." But, that was the only time in four years we beat them.

We would have played in the Rose Bowl my freshman year, but we were on probation because of the previous head coach, Denny Stolz. Since we were on probation, we were banned from postseason play. I never played in a bowl game.

Being on probation was a bad deal, but it was really none of our doing. It happened because of the previous administration. I really don't know what the reason was for us going on probation because it happened before I got there. We inherited that problem.

Kirk Gibson
Kirk Gibson was great. He was just a great athlete. He led by example and was a true leader on the field. He was an All-American in baseball and in football. He probably would have been drafted in the first round of the NFL Draft if he had decided to play wide receiver in the NFL.

63-Yard Field Goal Against Ohio State
The 63-yard field goal that I made against Ohio State is the longest I've ever kicked in a game. Unfortunately, it wasn't big in the context of the outcome of the game because we got our ass kicked by Ohio State. The kick was before halftime. It was a big moment in my history and a big moment in Spartan history, but unfortunately, it didn't help us win the game.

The kick was at Ohio State in the Horseshoe. I had a little bit of wind behind me, but it was a big kick. I hit it well.

NFL Draft
I had no idea the Saints were going to draft me. I had no communication with them at all. It was a big surprise to me that they took me in the fourth round.

I suppose there were big expectations from New Orleans for me. New Orleans first round draft choice a couple years earlier had been Russell Erxleben, a punter and placekicker from the University of Texas. He had not worked out very well for New Orleans. Obviously they hoped picking me would work out better. Thank God it did. I was just trying to make the football team. I didn't really think about any of the expectations on me, or the history of New Orleans kickers, or the ramifications. I was just trying to make kicks and get onto the football team.

1982 NFL Players Strike
I was recovering from an injury during the NFL Players Strike. I got hurt on the very first play of my NFL career, the opening kickoff of the season. I was out for eight weeks. The strike actually worked in my favor. It gave me a chance to rehab and get healthy again so when the strike was over, I could continue playing. If the strike hadn't come then I would have missed a ton of games.

Bum Phillips
I loved Bum Phillips. He was like a dad to everybody. Everything was a family atmosphere with the New Orleans Saints. We played for each other. We won some games. We would have liked to have won a few more and gotten into the playoffs with Bum as our head coach, but it didn't happen. We had a lot of big moments together. I just loved the man. He was just a great mentor and a great father figure to me.

Jim Mora

Jim Mora was the polar opposite of Bum Phillips. He was completely different than Bum. In defense of Jim and his policy, Bum's way hadn't worked in that we hadn't gone to the next level. We had won with Bum but we really hadn't won consistently and hadn't gone to the playoffs. So that was the mandate that Jim Mora had been given by Jim Finks and Tom Benson, the new owner.

There were a lot of changes made in the front office of the Saints organization and Mora was obviously given the responsibility of turning the team around. He felt the way he had to do it was with more discipline and more structure. With that in mind he assembled the type of team that he wanted and we won a lot of games with Mora.

New Orleans Saints Team With Jim Mora As Head Coach

We had a great defense. Our defensive line consisted of Jim Wilks and Frank Warren. Both guys were great players along with our linebackers.

We kicked a lot of field goals. We had ball control in that we didn't turn the ball over. We ran the ball effectively. Bobby Hebert was a great quarterback for us. Our offense possessed the ball, moved the chains, and scored in the red zone. A lot of our scores would be 15-12 or we would win by a lot of field goals. That's really what we did.

Being A Kicker In the NFL

I felt like I was an integral part of the game. I was busy and that kept me in the game. I loved that. I just felt like, "Hey, they're using me. They feel like I can be an offensive weapon, and let me embrace it." That's what I tried to do.

I always felt like I was part of the teams that I played for. I never felt like I was a separate entity or anything. I know my skill was unique and specific, but I always felt like I was a part of the team. I respected my teammates and they had respect for me.

60-Yard Field Goal Against Chicago Bears

On the 60-yard field goal against the Chicago Bears, that ball was hit really well. That could have been good from 70 yards. In retrospect, it would have been nice breaking the record.

Kicking In A Dome

I never gave that much credence to whether kicking in a dome helped me make the Pro Football Hall Of Fame. My numbers were just as good outside in the elements as they were inside. I feel like I could be, and I was effective. I had big years kicking outside for Kansas City and New York. For me, that was the hand I was dealt. I played for two teams for twenty-one years (the Falcons and the Saints) that happened to play inside. Had they played outside I would have been fine.

Biggest Kick In NFL

I hate to pick one kick out as the biggest, but certainly the one in overtime in the NFC Championship Game against the Minnesota Vikings was big because it sent us to the Super Bowl. A lot of good things happened before that kick as well. That was a big kick, a big moment, but all kicks have the same value so I'd like to think they're all important in their own way. That one was the last play of the game in overtime to go to the Super Bowl, so I would probably say that had the biggest impact.

It felt great to get to the Super Bowl, but it felt equally as bad not winning the game. I was grateful that I did make the Super Bowl, but very disappointed we didn't win the game. Again, it is one of those things. It wasn't meant to be for me.

Key To Successfully Kicking For 25 Seasons In NFL
The key to my success was just hard work; persistence, will, stubbornness, and having great people around me that did their job really well at a high level. Also, having great communication between all of us is what we needed to play at a high level. I think that's probably the key for me.

Evolution Of Kicking Style As Grew Older
I managed my behavior better as I grew older. I kicked less, but I had more quality kicks. I really dialed in and honed in on my skill. I knew mentally exactly what I needed to do, and I understood my workbench where that ball is put down. I really understood my job and defined my job, and I was able to execute what I needed to do. I think in the beginning of my career I was probably winging it more. I think as I matured I probably became a little more methodical, a little more thought out, if you will.

Long Snappers & Holders
Whoever my long snapper was, I was going to make sure that I communicated to him what I needed from him, which was his very best. I didn't accept it if a holder thought he could just put the ball down randomly. That was unacceptable. I also didn't accept it if a long snapper thought he could just snap it randomly. I demanded from those guys, at those two positions, that they knew exactly what they were doing. And, I demanded that they could do it consistently again and again, because that's what was expected out of me. I felt like the three of us worked like fingers in a glove. It was very important that we were on the same page, that they told me what they needed, and I told them what I needed from them. Then there was a trust where we didn't overthink it. When that was clearly laid out, we worked on the skill and we trusted it when we played.

My Best Holder & Long Snapper
Dan Stryzinski was my best holder. He had the best hands. He understood exactly what to do with different snaps if they came in weird. Kendall Gammon was my best long snapper by far in Kansas City. He was an artist. He knew exactly what to do with the ball and he put it in the right place. I was very lucky to have those two guys in Kansas City for two years.

Becoming All-Time Leading Scorer In NFL History
When I became the all-time leading scorer it was special. It felt like a culmination of a long journey. It wasn't a "me" award; it was more of a "we" award again because so many people had helped me along the way. It was very gratifying when the game was stopped briefly and I was able to hand the jersey to my oldest son and get the game ball. It was certainly a nice moment.

Not Playing During the 2005 Season

After the 2004 season I was out for 20 months. During that time I practiced in a public park. I felt very strongly that I would be back. I didn't know it was going to take 20 months until I got a phone call and had an opportunity to come back, but that's what happened.

I thank God I was ready because it could have gone terribly wrong had I not been prepared. In 2006 when the call came to try out and win the job, I was ready to go and got plugged in.

I had a good year and was able to break the scoring record. I played again in 2007. So it was just a matter of having the stubbornness and the will to continue even though most people might have said, "You're probably done."

Not Having the Opportunity To Break George Blanda's Record For Being Oldest Player In NFL History

I tried to come back in 2008, but there were no takers. When I realized that it was probably going to be over, I retired on the day after I would have been the oldest player in NFL history had I played. It was more of a nod towards George Blanda and what he accomplished.

I don't know why no teams signed me in 2008. That's a question you would have to ask all of the different player personnel guys working in 2008. At that time I wasn't kicking off anymore, and I think my range had diminished. I was pretty good from 50 yards in, but everybody goes younger and cheaper. I'm sure that's what happened.

Pro Football Hall Of Fame Selection

When I found out I was selected for the Pro Football Hall Of Fame I experienced a lot of emotions. Relief was one of them. I no longer had to justify, "I did this, this, and this." Now it was an even playing field and I became a part of an exclusive brotherhood. I thought that was unique. It was a unique feeling. The history of excellence among those 310 players who are in the Pro Football Hall Of Fame is incredible. I have tremendous pride and gratitude towards everyone who helped me along the way.

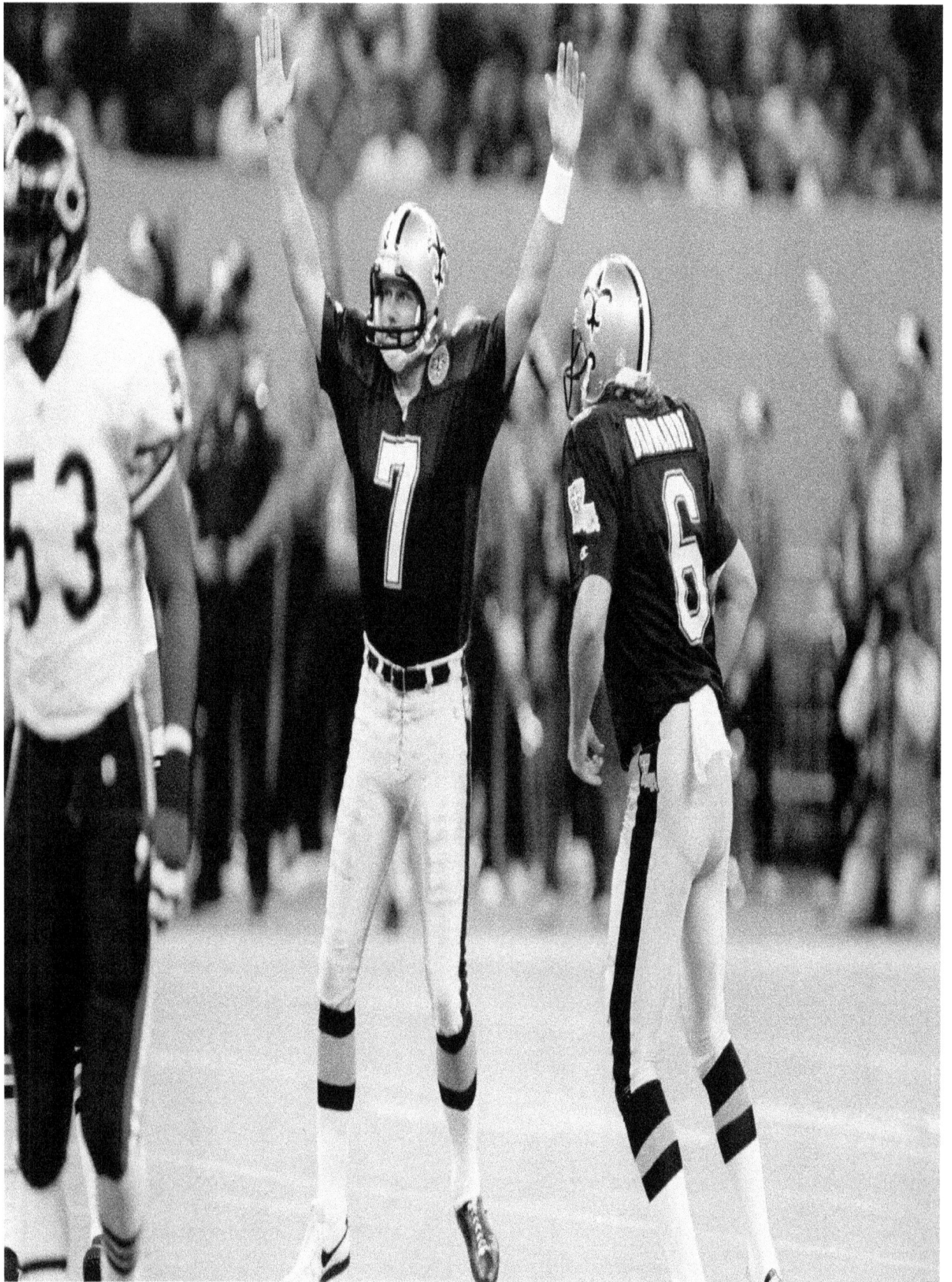

Photograph copyright Associated Press

Chapter 116

Eric Dickerson

```
College:
SMU

Career History:
Los Angeles Rams (1983–1987)
Indianapolis Colts (1987–1991)
Los Angeles Raiders (1992)
Atlanta Falcons (1993)

1999 Inductee Pro Football Hall Of Fame
```

College Choice
I think I was in the ninth grade and a guy said to me, "You're one of the best athletes we've ever seen in these parts in the last 25 years." I didn't get it. I'm like, "Really?" He said, "Yeah. You can really do things." I didn't know what he was talking about.

I started playing sports at an early age. I played football and ran track from seventh grade on. Ron Meyer recruited me. He came to my hometown of Sealy several times. He came to watch me play when I played in the State Championship game. Yeah, that's how I ended up going there because he recruited me so heavily.

College
We were not a passing football team. We were mostly a running football team. I think a lot of people looked at "The Pony Express", and thought that was the main part of our team. We had such great defenses. We really did. We had great guys on defense. I always say that our defense was so underrated and they were so good. I think just because of the notoriety that the "Pony Express" had back in those days people overlooked the defense.

Ron Meyer As SMU Head Coach
Ron Meyer was a very good coach. I think Ron was an even better recruiter than he was a coach. He knew how to get a talent. Ron pretty much could sell your mom, your grandmother, and the whole family on the school and you were going definitely. If you didn't think about SMU before he came to visit, it was at the top of the list for sure after he left the house.

"Pony Express" (Eric Dickerson & Craig James)
Craig James and I weren't in the backfield together that often. As a matter of fact, because SMU was in the offset on offense, we would alternate. My fullback was Charles Drayton and his was Mark Crites. Sometimes they would just switch the fullbacks out. Really, Craig and I alternated. He'd take a series and I'd take a series. You'd run your series and if your series scored a touchdown, you'd stay in that whole time. That's how we did it. It worked for us.

I think Russ Potts came up with the "Pony Express" name. He was the Athletic Director. When we got there it was "Mustang Mania". Then all of a sudden, they switched it up and started calling it the "Pony Express".

NFL Draft

I knew the Rams were trying to get me and they made a trade. I think the trade took place with Houston and Seattle. The Rams called me the night before and told me that I had a ticket at the airport for me to take a flight out to LA. They were going to draft me the next morning. I actually heard that I got drafted when I was in the car on my way to the airport.

When I got drafted I asked my mother and my grandmother, "Which one do you think I should go to, the Los Angeles Express of the USFL or the Rams in the NFL?" I won't forget my mother's reply. She said, "Which one has been around longer?" I said, "The NFL." She said, "That's where you should go."

John Robinson

I liked John Robinson. John was a coach who knew how to run the football. He was a player's coach, and knew how to talk to the players. He was just a really good coach.

John recruited me to Southern Cal, where he was the coach, while I was in high school. When the Rams drafted me he walked up to me and said, "I finally got you."

There was a little bit of a temptation to go to Southern Cal, but Southern Cal is so far from Texas. I was born and raised in Texas. I am a Texas boy from a small town, and Southern California is a long ways away. I took my first official visit to USC, but I didn't end up going there.

Los Angeles Rams Offensive Line

It was never all you as a running back. You got to have the help up front. We had a great offensive line; Jackie Slater, Kent Hill, Doug Smith, Dennis Harrah, David Hill, and Bill Bain. We had a lot of great guys on that line. We had an outstanding offensive line.

The running back has to have help. We had a coach who knew how to run the football. His scheme was to put the other guys and me, in good situations.

When I was younger, I always felt like anytime I got my hands on the ball, that I had a chance to take it all the way. That's what I was. I was a long run hitter, like a home run hitter in baseball. Football is different. I always went for the long run. I didn't look for five or six yards because I had the speed to outrun most guys.

Joining Los Angeles Rams

When I first got to the Rams, we had a two back set. We played the Redskins in the preseason. I'll never forget, they beat us to death in the second pre-season game. We came back the next day and John Robinson said, "Forget everything you learned. We're going to go to the one back set like the Redskins. Eric is my running back." That's when I got a chance to start.

Reason Wore Goggles
I am blind. I can't see. I have to wear glasses. That's where the goggles came from. I still wear glasses to this day. Without the goggles I couldn't have done anything.

A running back goes by feel a lot of times. Stuff happens in a flash, real fast out there. Everything is not done just by vision.

Field Preference
I didn't really care, grass or turf, it didn't make a difference to me. I could run on either one. At that time, the turf fields were not great. They make you feel faster. It was good to have a mix. I think if I had my preference to play on one for a full season, I'd take grass like most players.

Some of the turf was like painted concrete. The field in New England at the time was a terrible field. The Astrodome had a bad field. A lot of fields were not really good fields.

Trade To Indianapolis Colts
It was business. I didn't really want to leave LA, but I had to leave for the money. I felt like the Rams underpaid me, for sure. I was only making about $250,000. A lot of guys were making triple my salary and they weren't even playing up to my level.

A lot of teams, not just the Rams, were big on messing up the players by underpaying them. They thought it was a game, but it wasn't a game to us. That's what they did to you. There was no free agency. You couldn't go anywhere. You were just stuck and you could take it or leave it. That was their motto.

I know there were a couple of teams that wanted me. One was the Redskins. I really wanted to go there because my cousin played for the Redskins. He was the one who called me and told me that the Redskins were after me, but I knew the Rams weren't going to let that happen. They were not going to trade me to a NFC team at that time.

Ron Meyer As Indianapolis Colts Head Coach
Ron Meyer was the Colt's coach. Ron's a good friend of mine. He took care of me in college. He is just a good man. I can say I really love Ron. When he recruited me coming out of high school, he told my mother, "I'll treat him like he's my own son." He kept his word.

Favorite Moment Playing In The NFL
I had so many. One of my favorite moments was when I got drafted. The year that I rushed for over 2,000 yards was another favorite moment. When I made my first Pro Bowl, I was really excited about that. I had so many moments. I can't say one particular moment was my favorite. I never got a chance to play in the Super Bowl, but I have so many great memories and moments in the league.

Playing On Monday Night Football
Playing on Monday night was special for every guy at that time. Every player would look forward to playing on Monday night. When the schedule came out you wanted to see how many Monday night games you had. There weren't all these other stations like ESPN, ESPN1, ESPN2,

NBC, ABC, or CBS televising games on days other than Sunday. Monday night was it. All your peers got a chance to watch you play. The whole world got a chance to watch you play that one game. I think playing on Monday night was a very special night for all players back in those days. Now, I think players take it for granted.

Opportunity To Break Walter Payton's Record For Most Career Rushing Yards
If I would have stayed with the Rams my entire career I think I would have broken it. It just didn't work out like that. Walter Payton, Lawrence Taylor, and I were doing an episode of "Coach" and Walter said to me, "I want to thank you for something." I said, "What?" "I want to thank you for getting traded. You would have broken all the records." We laughed about it.

I thought I had a chance at the record, but honestly when I played, I didn't think about that kind of stuff. I just liked playing football and that was it. I enjoyed the sport and I played it. There comes a point where you figure out the business and the ugly side of it, but it is what it is.

Top Running Backs Of All Time
Most definitely I have got to put O.J. Simpson and Jim Brown in there for sure. Barry Sanders has got to be in there. Walter Payton has to be in there. It just depends on which player you like; that's what it comes down to.

Eric Dickerson NFL Single Season Rushing Record
Someone might break it one day. I hope it lasts for another 25-30 years. Maybe I'll be dead and gone by then. I have a little son who is one-and-a-half. Maybe he'll come along and play football and break my record. You want your records to last as long as they can. There's nothing selfish about that. I'm honest about it. If a guy gets close, that's great, but honestly no guy wants his records broken. I don't care if you have a jump rope record in high school, you don't want your record broken.

Pro Football Hall Of Fame Induction
I didn't know I was going to be elected to the Hall Of Fame my first year of eligibility. I had the numbers. For me, that is what it should be about, the numbers.

I didn't even know what the Hall of Fame was my first two years. After my second year in the league, after I ran over 2,000 yards, I was at the Pro Bowl. Rickey Jackson said to me, "You're going to go into the Hall of Fame if you keep playing like you're playing." I was waiting for him to elaborate what the Hall of Fame was because I didn't know what it was. Finally, he stopped talking and I said, "Listen, I got a question to ask you. What's the Hall of Fame?" He said, "Eric, you don't know what the Hall of Fame is?" I said, "I have no idea." He explained it to me and I said, "Oh. Okay."

I didn't know I was going in. When the moment came and I was chosen to go in, it was a proud moment for me. It kind of solidifies your career as a player saying that you were one of the greatest that ever played that position. I always wanted to be a great player no matter what I did, whether it was running track, playing football, or playing baseball. I wanted to be great at it. I didn't just want to be good; I wanted to be great. I thank God for my talent because that's where it came from, God. I just dealt with the talent he gave me. I worked with it.

Keys To Success For A Running Back
To play running back you can't just be fast. You've got to know your position and work with what you have. You have to know how to slow it down, speed it up, and hit it when the time is right.

The greatest thing for a back is when you get an open field. I didn't look over my shoulder. I didn't look back. If you caught me, you caught me, but I didn't believe in looking back.

When I was in high school a coach told me, "Hey, don't look back. The goal line is that way." I never looked back again after that.

Toughest Defense
The toughest defense, for me was the New England Patriots. They always gave me fits. People would think it was the Chicago Bears. Year in and year out, I don't care if it was with the Rams or Colts, the New England Patriots always seemed to give me fits. When we played in the NFC Championship Game against the Bears they were a tough defense that day. On average, I always played well against the Bears. We didn't fear them and we played well against them. As far as for my career, the team that gave me the blues would have to be the New England Patriots.

Uniform Numbers
I wore number 19 in college. The Rams had numbers 32, 34, 29, 45, and 25 available. I couldn't choose number 19 since running backs weren't allowed numbers in the teens. So I took number 25. When I got drafted I was holding number 25. When I got back to Dallas that night my best friend said, "So, what number did you choose?" I said, "I chose 25." He said, "Why did you take 25? That's a slow number."

I told him the numbers again, he said, "Why didn't you take 29? I'm like, "Okay." I called back the next day and talked to Todd Hewitt, the equipment guy, and I said, "Mr. Hewitt I want to switch my number." He said we already got you in the paper as 25, I don't think we can change that number." I said, "Well, if you all don't change it I'm not coming." He said, "Well, I think we can change that number." That's how I became 29.

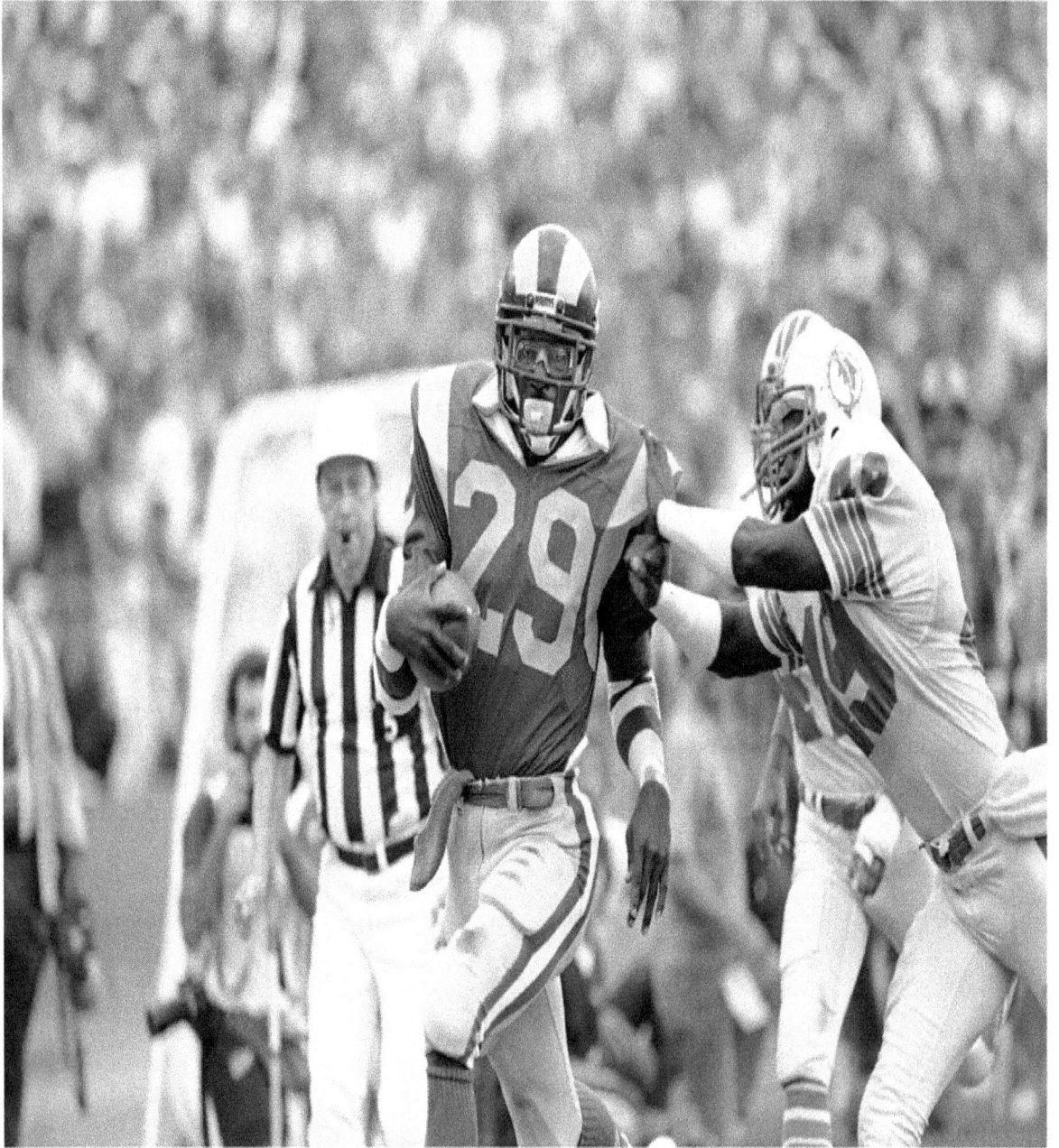

Photograph copyright Associated Press

Chapter 117

Richard Dent

College:
Tennessee State

Career History:
Chicago Bears (1983–1993)
San Francisco 49ers (1994)
Chicago Bears (1995)
Indianapolis Colts (1996)
Philadelphia Eagles (1997)

2011Inductee Pro Football Hall Of Fame

College Choice
I didn't get recruited much in football. I found out later that I had an opportunity to play basketball at Alcorn State, but my high school coach, William Lester, never told me about it. I probably would have played basketball there. I have to be happy with the road that William Lester put me on.

I really didn't start to play football until I got in the 11th or 12th grade. One of my buddies lived a couple doors away from me; he knew I loved the game and he sacrificed himself to play the game to get me out there. I was working and taking care of my own business. My buddy told me, "You know Richard, you can work the rest of your life. Why don't you try your dream one time?" That statement put me where I am today.

Tennessee State
What happened was I noticed that I probably wouldn't be playing any time soon as an offensive lineman at Tennessee State. I did a head count of the number of offensive linemen and doing the math, I figured it would probably be my senior year before I played.

I looked at the defense and saw Joe Gilliam coaching over there. If a guy was performing, Joe was going to play you regardless if you were a rookie, a senior, or whatever. I came there to play ball. I didn't go there to sit around and watch.

I decided to make the transition to defense. During that time when I was practicing on the offense side, I took that time to start preparing myself to be a defensive ball player. I started screwing up offensive plays and making the offense run them over and eventually, I guess, the offensive coaches got tired of me and told me to go over to defense. After spending a full season and spring practice on offense that summer, I was told, "Okay, you're going to defense." Maybe they thought I was going to go away after the season.

I really wanted to play tight end but they wouldn't go for that. I went another route and eventually got pushed over to the defensive side of the football.

1983 Chicago Bears Draft (Jimbo Covert, Willie Gault, Mike Richardson, Dave Dueron, Tom Thayer, Mark Bortz)

That was an amazing draft. Dennis McKinnon was a free agent signee that year. It was one of the top draft years for a team of all time.

When I came to the Chicago Bears, I wasn't used to losing. At Tennessee State I lost five games in five years. With the Bears from 1984-1988 we only lost ten games. We only won one Super Bowl. I was disappointed with that, but outside of that we had a great run.

I had a great time and played with a lot of great guys. Initially my teammates didn't know much about me and I didn't know much about them. You have to show people what you're about and either they'll catch on or you'll catch on to them or whatever. The main goal is all about going out winning, competing and being the best that you can be.

Going into the draft a lot of people were saying I was small. I just wanted to get an opportunity to play in the NFL. Kids today bitch and whine about how they lost money when they don't get drafted as high as they think they should have. It's not about where you should get drafted, it's what you accomplish after you get drafted.

1984 Los Angeles Raiders vs. Chicago Bears Game

I can remember the 49ers, Cowboys, and Raiders players were all calling me saying we're going to get you. That Raiders game was a coming out game. The Raiders had just won a Super Bowl. That day I saw Al Davis walking on the field. I said, "Al, you know you're getting an ass whooped today." He looked at me real crazy. He got whupped. Whupped to gum. That was a 4½ sack day for me. I should have had five, six, or seven on that particular day.

First Training Camp With Bears

Everybody has butterflies. You go through things and you have to build up to that moment. I can remember looking at Keith Van Horne who is about 6'7", and I'm like, "Oh God. Maybe I'm in the wrong league." As soon as I put my hand down to play, your memory comes back that you can play. It's not about the size or anything. You put your hand down and you forget about everything. It's getting to the target; what I'm trying to hit, what I'm trying to protect and play. You have those thoughts while you're standing there. The next thing you know, you get the equipment on and you get out there. You forget about those things. It was probably in the spring or summer we did some stuff, but there wasn't any contact. I was getting off the ball so fast the guys could hardly even touch me. I was running by them.

Some of the older guys were teaching me. They said, "You've got to use your hands." I'm like, "Dude nobody can put their hands on me." Eventually they caught up to me.

Then we got into training camp and I was going up against Jimbo Covert. I got about two or three sacks on him. He was the starter. He joined the Bears just like me in 1983. I knew I was beating him.

I got hurt after the first preseason game in practice. I tore my hamstring and rolled up on my ankle really bad. It was really rough for about a week and a half. Week to week just taking baby steps, it was tough. The last game of the preseason I started to strap it up. I wasn't ready to go; I wasn't 100% as far as running and doing some of the stuff I was expected to do on the special teams.

By the end of the season, my legs came back. The next year the Bears finally started me about game six. That's when things took off.

Competing Against Al Harris For Starting Position
It was Al Harris and I going at it for the starting position. You ask for opportunities for success. You see the team had an investment in Al Harris. It's evident to the team and me that the team's got money in this guy. They want to see this guy come about. I can understand it. He was a first round pick, a couple years before me. Here I am, a guy the Bears paid hardly anything for. I was performing way better than him.

As a businessman, I understood the Bears had money in this guy and wanted to see this guy come around. So they gave him a lot of chances.

It's not a player's fault, but sometimes players don't understand those situations. You have to understand all of what's around you, who's going to support you, what you are supporting so you can understand this is a business. A sports industry is a 600 billion dollar industry. You only make 30% of the 600 billion. That's a lot of jobs in sports.

I basically asked for an opportunity and eventually got the opportunity. My first year I was basically just playing pass rushing downs. I probably wasn't ready at that time. The next year I was pretty much ready. I could have stayed on Buddy Ryan's sideline. After game six I played the last ten games. I didn't have one sack after 6 games, but I end up leading the league with seventeen and a half sacks. In ten games I came up with 17½ sacks. We went to the NFC Championship.

The next year I did the same thing again. I had 17 sacks. We won the Super Bowl. After that they didn't renew Al's contract. They offered him more money but I guess it wasn't what he wanted. That's up to the player. Management and coaching staff eventually made a decision, and decided to go with me. It took them a minute. I can understand that but sometimes athletes don't know what they're really getting into.

Winning Super Bowl MVP
It was a great feeling but it also was a lonely feeling too, in a way, if you can believe that. I don't know how they went about choosing the Super Bowl MVP. I thought it was over all the playoff games. When I thought about that and I sold myself on that conclusion, I said, "Well hell, I've had two hell of a games." First game I had about three sacks, the next game I had a two. I had four forced fumbles and eight or nine sacks in three playoff games.

My Super Bowl performance, I thought, was my worst performance compared to the first two playoff games. I look back and see that my forced fumble there turned the tide. The Patriots had gone up three points on us. I forced the Patriots to fumble and we got the ball. The offense went 13 yards and scored.

I had that thought the night before. I told my roommate Tyrone Keys, that I was going to be on ESPN. I started to say, "I see myself winning the Super Bowl MVP." I thought, I won't be that cocky. I've never been that type of guy. I'm cocky about what I do and how I do it but I don't have to talk about it; actions show it.

Super Bowl Shuffle
Doing something different was cool. We did the Super Bowl Shuffle right after our first loss so it was probably a good time. We were licking our wounds. Before the taping of the video, I was like, "Why am I here? I thought you are doing this for the charities, raising money, and those things." That made the situation a little bit more fun. We got back in town at 3:00 a.m. after losing to Miami. At 2:00 p.m. the next day, I was at the studio filming the Super Bowl Shuffle video. The lyrics were all ready. It was fun.

I've got two grown girls and they crack up about it now. It's funny to them. No one ever did something like that, and I think that's the special thing there.

To put something like that out three or four months before the Super Bowl, was pretty cocky. We talked about doing the video and were able to do it. We committed ourselves to it. We lost a major game the day before the video shoot. In the video, we said we were going to come back and win everything hands down. We said we
were going to come back and kick everybody's tail and bring home the Super Bowl.

1985 Chicago Bears vs. Miami Dolphins Game (Bears Only Loss Of Season)
Mike Ditka wanted to throw the ball to win the game. Miami was 27th in stopping the rush. Obviously, you run the ball since Miami was near last in stopping the run. We had Walter Payton, who had seven consecutive 100-yard rushing games in a row, entering that game. Walter finally got 100 by the end of the game. I think Mike got tied up trying to be like Don Shula. He wanted to do as good as or better than Shula, who liked to throw the ball everywhere at that time.

Buddy Ryan was telling Ditka to run the ball, and Ditka was telling Buddy to stop blitzing. They were going back and forth like that. What do you do as a player? Sometimes we had to take over the game ourselves because the sideline was out of whack. When you're out of whack you say, "We'll talk to them on Monday. Right now, let's go out here and win this game."

They had every ghost on the sideline out there, I was tripping over stuff that wasn't even there. It was one of those games. We realized that there was an opportunity for us to possibly go undefeated. At that point, it looked like they were the last team that we would be playing that could maybe stop us.

We wanted to go to Miami earlier in the week and practice, and get ready for the game. Some of the guys asked Buddy to ask Mike if we could go to Miami earlier. If Buddy came up with a idea and Mike didn't, Mike wasn't going to do it. So we didn't go. There was a lot of bitching here and there, it was crazy.

Miami was the first team to spread us out. Dan Marino would do a half roll from me. He would make a little roll away from the side I was on, and get rid of the ball. The idea there was, let's match up. They made Gary Fencik come up from his usual position, and the matchup was a go to Nat Moore. Then Nat Moore was going against Wilber Marshall or Gary Fencik in the slot. Dan hit Nat in the slot quick, and made us tackle Nat. That's what you can do against the 46 Defense.

When you're losing or the game is not in your hands, the opposing team has more of a repertoire to reach out to see what they might want to do with you.

Favorite Coach
I enjoyed John Merritt and I enjoyed my high school coach. I appreciated what Joe Gilliam, Sr. did, which was prepare me not for just the game, but for life in general. To me it's not about the university where I send my kids to school. If he's going to school, he's going to school. It's the teachers and the university itself. When they're going to play sports, those coaches become the second fathers, you would hope. Kids need to be pushed to a limit that they don't know they have.

Once you've been pushed to that limit, your mind opens up and you appreciate what you have been pushed to, and what you accomplished at that moment. Now your vision comes in play. Now you start to visualize all you can do. You just took a big leap and put yourself in a spot that you thought you never could get to. You get there, and now your vision comes in place even stronger to see whatever else you might want to do, and how you want to do what you're doing. How much farther can I take this? What level can I take this to?

When you know what's about to happen, you can be moving at 60 to 70% and look like you're running at 120%. You can do this because you know what's going on and you know what's about to take place.

Not Winning More Than One Super Bowl
That's the killer. That's why I think that our so-called leaders, the head coach, management, or general manager; they all played a part in us not winning more than one Super Bowl. You should know what makes people go, what makes them tick. Mike Ditka tried a different way to try to make me tick. He didn't need to work on me to make me tick.

I met a man that taught me about life through football, and that was Joe Gilliam. He was the best ever. I never slept in his meetings. His vocabulary, his education, was so strong. He is a person who will always be a memory in my mind along with all that he had given me to accomplish.

The Bears did not have a quarterback for the length of time we needed. Jim McMahon was a great quarterback. He was injury prone, but he had something great between his ears. He could make it happen. When McMahon went down, that's when the team tried to get another All-American white kid in Doug Flutie. Mike Ditka was thinking that he could win with a quarterback he just put on the team, with about five weeks left in season, and go to the playoffs. Ditka was saying the defense could do anything.

The defense knew that we couldn't give up more than 10 to 13 points. That was our model. Our kicker could kick the field goals, but we knew it was going to be hard for the offense to get into the end zone. The defense knew that we could get turnovers, which would lead to field goals. We knew Kevin Butler was good for three or four field goals. Thirteen was a tough number. We couldn't score more than 13 points.

The point was we had two guys. Why didn't Ditka just give Mike Tomczak a chance to start instead of Flutie? The same thing with Steve Fuller; give him a chance. They didn't want to make someone big and have to deal with that situation. It's a brewing storm. You don't want to be in it.

Favorite Moment In NFL
My mother couldn't get to the Super Bowl. She met me at the Pro Bowl after the Super Bowl. That was a great moment. We played the Jets on my 25th birthday. That was pretty cool.

In 1984, right after I visited my mother for her birthday, we played the Redskins. That was a good old fashioned, hard-hitting game. There was something about that stadium and playing in Washington that was always great.

Joining San Francisco 49ers
I went to the 49ers to win and pick up some Super Bowls. I thought that we missed out on some opportunities with the Chicago Bears. The 49ers organization was different from the Bears. They took that extra step.

With the 49ers, you would check into a hotel and there was a fruit basket and Gatorade there. They would pay for all the meals. If we were flying over two or three hours for a game, the team would leave the night before to get ready for the jet lag. The 49ers were more sophisticated.

When I went to the 49ers, I thought that I probably could play there at least three years, maybe four. It was possible I could have played until about 2000. That was very possible with how the 49ers went about things. It wouldn't have been that brutal on me. I could have started there for two or three more years, and then went to a third down role.

Pro Football Hall Of Fame Induction
It was a great feeling. I was happy that I could thank some people who were a part of and helped my journey. My high school coach was an important part of my career. I went into the Georgia Hall of Fame with him, and I was able to say thanks to him before he passed away.

Coach Gilliam treated everybody the same. He had a love for human beings and was able to help one to overcome. Here's a guy who sent over 140 guys to the pros, including Claude Humphrey, Ed "Too Tall" Jones, Cleveland Elam and his own son, Joe Gilliam, Jr. Here's a guy that in 1948, was a quarterback at the University of Indiana and part of the first black backfield. You just don't run across that kind of guy very often. To have him on stage with me for my Hall of Fame induction … I appreciated that more than the induction.

People had been giving me love and appreciation for what I had done. It's nice to see that award take place because it was the first award for my career. We won the Super Bowl and I got the MVP of the game. That's a onetime event; that's not your career. That's not your season. To get the first award for your career or anything related to your career and it's the Hall of Fame, was pretty cool. I guess it's best to say, if you stay on track you're going to be all right. I've always said, "Stars always shine. It may be cloudy, but I'm always going to have some shine."

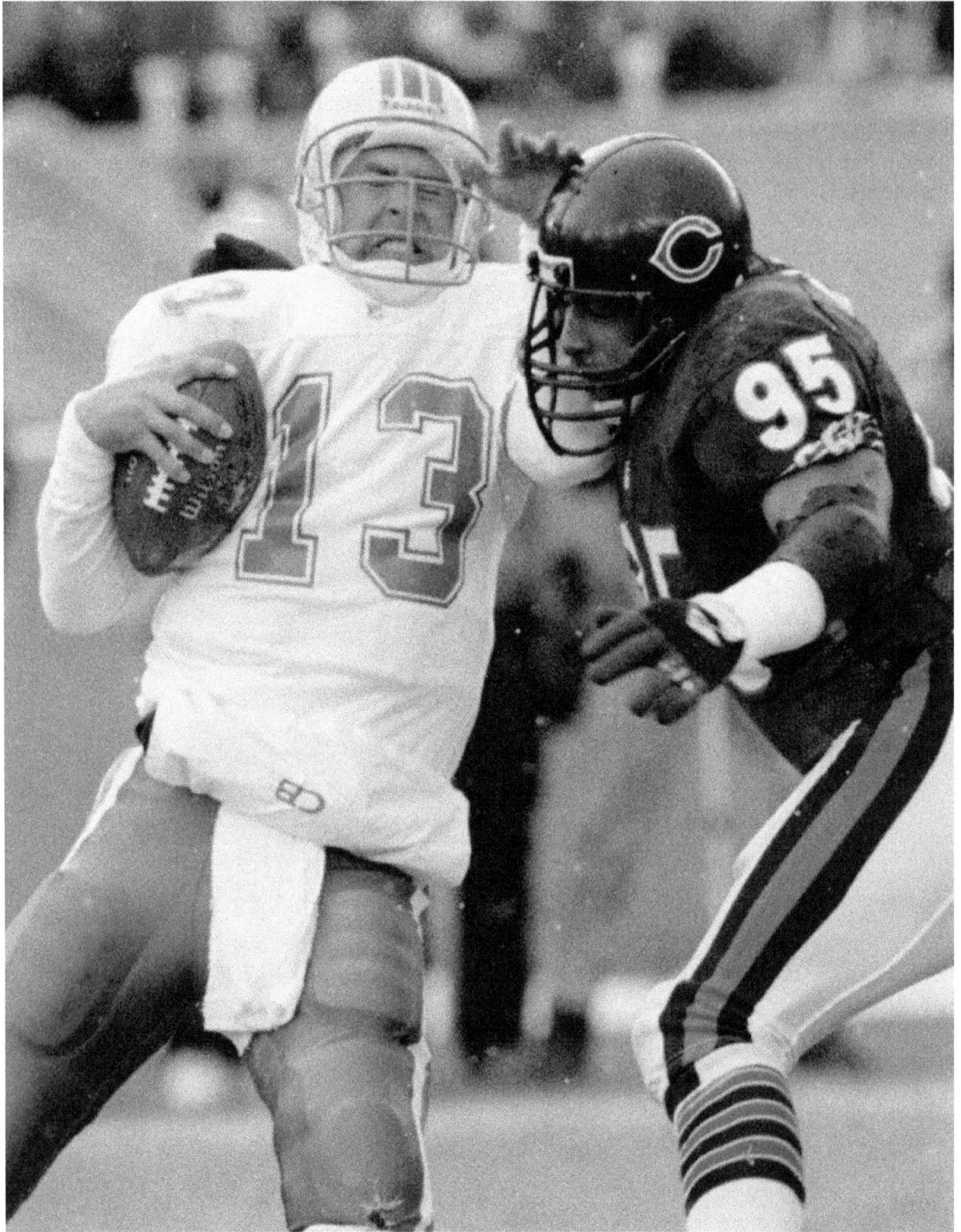

Chicago Bears' defensive end Richard Dent puts pressure on Miami Dolphin quarterback
Dan Marino. Photograph copyright Associated Press

Chapter 118

Bruce Matthews

College:
USC

Career History:
Houston / Tennessee Oilers / Titans (1983–2001)

2007 Inductee Pro Football Hall Of Fame

College Choice
The primary reason I went to USC was that my brother Clay went there and had a great experience. I became a huge fan of USC.

I was getting recruited heavily. My intention was that if USC offered me a scholarship, that's where I wanted to go. They were the defending national champions in football. USC was a half-hour from where I grew up. I went to all of Clay's home games and became a huge USC fan.

Head Coach John Robinson
To this day, I have a great deal of respect for Coach John Robinson and the type of head coach that he was. As an 18-year-old kid going to USC, Coach Robinson really made a big impact on my life. Not to say that other coaches are different, but I think at that time of my life, Coach Robinson just emphasized no individual is bigger than the team.

We had some huge individuals. We had Charles White, Marcus Allen, Ronnie Lott, and Anthony Munoz. As a young player it was apparent to me that all of those guys had completely bought into the way Coach Robinson did business. I just had great respect for him, and to this day I still have great respect for him.

USC Offensive Line
My freshman year, we had six future NFL first round draft picks just on the offensive line. They were Anthony Munoz, Brad Budde, Keith Van Horne, Roy Foster, Don Mosebar, and me. All those guys taught me about what it really meant to practice hard and to play hard. You tend to get a higher opinion of yourself than reality dictates. Being around those guys and seeing their professionalism at such a young age really had a huge impact on my career.

USC Talent
Going into USC, I remember thinking, "Man, these guys are pretty good." We were good not only on the offensive line, but at every position group.

My first year at USC we were blowing teams out and I was playing the better part of the second half in most of the games. Unfortunately, we tied Stanford my freshman year. We were up 21-0 against Stanford and they came back to tie the game. I thought at some point we'd definitely win a championship, but it didn't work out that way.

John Elway played against us in the Stanford game, but it was Turk Schonert who did the lion's share of the quarterbacking. As I recall, Elway didn't have that great of a game. It was one of many comebacks I've been involved in. Fortunately, or unfortunately, it ended up in a tie.

I am hard pressed to think of anybody who would have beaten us my freshman year. I think Alabama won the National Championship that year. I'm biased of course, but I think we'd have beat up on Alabama if we played them that year. In fact, the year before, USC went down to Birmingham to play and crushed Alabama.

NFL Draft
The Houston Oilers had expressed interest in me prior to the draft. Bill Parcells was the new Giants Head Coach in 1983. At the Tampa combine that year, Bill came up to me and introduced himself. Bill said if I was available at number ten, the Giants were drafting me. It was a thrill. I have always been a Bill Parcells fan as a result of this. The Oilers made a couple deals that year, and moved back to pick nine and took me. I wasn't surprised they took me, but I wasn't banking on it either.

Rookie Year With Houston Oilers
As a rookie, everything was so new and cool. I was walking around on cloud nine. Like man, they actually pay me to play football. I don't know that any coach would have had a different impact on my first year because it was just such a thrill to be there.

Earl Campbell
One of the highlights of my career was playing with Earl Campbell. I played a year-and-a-half with him. He rushed for like 1,300 or 1,400 yards my rookie year. I missed a bunch of time my rookie year due to injury. As a kid who grew up in complete awe of the NFL experience, to get to know Earl a little bit, to see he was a legit guy, experience his whole country boy persona, and see he was genuine, was the best. It really was an honor to play with him. It's something I'm really proud of.

Jerry Glanville As Houston Oilers Head Coach
There were pluses and minuses with Jerry Glanville as Houston Oilers Head Coach, obviously. I think the biggest plus was Jerry did a great job of taking a team that had talent and making us believe. We played hard under Jerry.

An opposing team is going to give you their best shot. You don't ever want to empower the enemy. You don't want to give the opponent anything that may be bulletin board material, or something along those lines. Jerry inflamed some of our opponents, or most, I should say. But to his credit, he took a team that was a sleeping giant and woke us up. He was a huge part of getting us on that big playoff run in the late '80s thru early '90s.

Building Houston Oilers Offensive Line Thru Using High Draft Choices On Offensive Lineman
There have been teams that have tried to use the model of building a strong offensive line thru using high draft picks on offensive lineman. Some of those high number ones didn't hit for teams. It's been cool to see the current Dallas Cowboys basically use that model. It's paid huge dividends for the Cowboys with Zack Martin, Travis Frederick, and Tyron Smith.
It reminds me of our Oilers team because our offensive line played a solid nine or ten years together. It's a luxury that you don't appreciate until you don't have it. In a lot of ways, it's taken for granted when you have quality offensive line play because so much of the credit goes to the quarterback, receivers, and running back, and rightfully so. Then all of the sudden, when you have those holes in the offensive line, the good old days are definitely missed.

Run and Shoot/Red Gun Offense
June Jones was kind of the architect of the Run and Shoot Offense. I think the Run and Shoot was an offshoot of the talent that we had.

Warren Moon was such a special talent. We gave him time to throw the ball and had receivers. That being said, we still ran the ball well. The Run and Shoot Offense definitely put more pressure on the offensive line and on the offense in terms of situations where you're trying to run the clock out, or just trying to grind it out, whether it's short yardage or goal line.

During June Jones first years with the team, we ran a conventional offense, two-one-two, multiple tight end sets, and then we would go to the Red Gun. The Red Gun was playing four wide receivers with one running back. Over the years we went more and more exclusively to the Run and Shoot Offense. When Jack Pardee came in we ran the Run and Shoot full time. It definitely did add challenges to us as linemen, but you always looked at it as a challenge and said, "We're going to make this work."

Warren Moon
I think we all struggled early on. Warren Moon came to the Houston Oilers my second year in the NFL. We were a young and talented team and we were emerging. You could see why the Oilers management went out and got Warren. He would make the throws. June Jones came in and really started to utilize Warren's talents. Warren was a special guy. The thing I think that gets overlooked most about Warren is his durability. He did a great job of preparing himself for the season by being in the best shape he could be, including the mental side of it. He was a pro about it.

Through the years, you see quarterbacks that can stay healthy, whether it's Brett Favre, Tom Brady, or guys like Warren Moon. That is a gift they have. It's the little things that are taken for granted that you don't appreciate until they're gone.

"The Comeback" Houston Oilers vs. Buffalo Bills 1993 Playoff Game
The loss to the Buffalo Bills in the 1993 playoffs was hard. I'll be honest; I couldn't stand it anytime we lost. The part that wasn't as painful as it probably could have been was the fact that it was such a freakish deal. You have teams come back and make plays and maybe get a rally, but you somehow find a way to right the ship and you close the deal. Obviously that wasn't the case against Buffalo, and it was almost like, man, this is bigger than us. This is one of those once

in a lifetime deals. The funny thing was, we had to drive the ball late in the game and kick a field goal to send it into overtime. I thought that the fact that we persevered and found a way to make plays in spite of all the points that they scored and all the momentum being in their favor, I felt like, man, we're going to win this thing.

We won the coin toss in overtime, and Warren Moon threw an interception. Buffalo kicked a field goal and won. That was that.

Super Bowl XXXIV St. Louis Rams vs. Tennessee Titans
The St. Louis Rams completely dominated us in the first two-and-a-half quarters of the game. Then in tightened fashion, we kind of bludgeon them. Steve McNair made some amazing plays and kept plays alive with his legs. We finally got in position to score, and sent it to overtime. The Rams were done.

I usually don't watch videos of games. Come playoff time, stations always play Super Bowl XXXIV on either the NFL network or other networks. Or, they play the Buffalo playoff game. During those games, there's a part of me that has a certainty within myself that we're going to win this game, even though I know the facts; I know the history.

In my opinion, it was a foregone conclusion that had we gone to overtime, we were going to win, because defensively they were toast. Unfortunately, we were one yard short. It was a great experience to finally get to the Super Bowl. Even the game itself was the culmination of a lot of stuff that the team had gone through, because of our move from Houston. It easily could have gone the other way. It's still frustrating I guess, to sum it up.

Setting Record For Most Games Played By Non Kicker Or Punter
With the added perspective of time being out of the game and coaching in the league for five years, I see guys injured or tweaked or whatever, and rightfully so, they're sitting out games. I look back on my career and I felt a high responsibility to be out there every game. I really didn't play in a game where I shouldn't have. There were times I didn't feel 100%. I knew once I got warmed up that I wasn't a detriment to the team; that I was playing at a level that I would be satisfied with how I was playing.

I look back on it and I did all the workouts. I was very diligent in that regard. When I look back, it's a very humbling thing. I think the good Lord just blessed me with a body that could take the pounding. He gave me a tolerance for pain. I don't feel like there ever was a game that I went into where I thought, "Oh my gosh, my leg, or my knee, or my back, or whatever the case might be, I shouldn't be out here."

I felt good when I got out there. Now, the warming up process or getting into it might have taken some effort or some extra special preparation, but I always felt good about it. I look at it as God blessed me, and I'm thankful for that. It's a humbling thing, especially when I got on the coaching side, and saw how many times freak injuries occurred or just weird stuff a guy got hurt on, got tweaked, and had to miss time. I was just blessed. I can't think of how many piles there were, where I got rolled up or the pile fell into my leg, and I was able to get up and walk away.

Father Clay Matthews, Sr.

My dad taught me how to approach a game in terms of attitude and having the right perspective. Early on, he taught our whole family that if you go out there, you don't quit. You go full speed at everything and you're the first guy in line. If the coach asks for a volunteer, raise your hand and make them tell you to stop volunteering or whatever the case may be. That really stuck with me. He instilled in us the mindset to go out and do our best. It really was huge.

Toughest Defensive Lineman

It's hard for me to say who the toughest lineman I ever faced was. I feel bad sometimes singling a guy out. There have been so many great players. When it was game week and we were prepping for them, there was added anxiety having to play them that week. There always was anxiety for me in terms of my opponents and preparing for them. There definitely were some real special ones like Bruce Smith, Howie Long, and John Randle. There are so many good ones.

The cool thing about the NFL is that you're tested every week. You may not have heard about a guy, or what college he went to, but in some way (it may be in the run game, it may be in the pass game, it may be backside cutting off whatever the case may be), he's got some unique skill or talent that if you lower your guard, relax, or get complacent, you're going to be embarrassed.

The thrill of the NFL is knowing you've got to stay on edge the whole game every week, every position, every guy, first and second string. It's been kind of cool to go through that again with my sons, and having those conversations, especially with Jake playing left tackle. There are so many special players that you have to bring it every play.

One of the biggest, if not the most important, traits for an offensive lineman is playing consistent. You can't be one of those guys that has eight great plays and then two busts. You've got to bring it every play. Consistency is more important than those flash plays where you go and put some guy on his back. That's great, but I would rather have you be consistent ten plays than have those eight and two, or nine and one play series.

Trash Talking

Some of the stuff guys said would make me laugh. You're out on the football field trying to keep this edge of almost hatred toward your opponent, because you don't want to give them anything. All of a sudden they're making these chirps out there and it's like, hey, that was pretty clever. The funny thing was, the guys who do the trash talking, most of them make you think, "What are you, an idiot?" It was the quiet ones that you had to worry about. John Randle and Warren Sapp actually had some good humor. It's such an odd place to appreciate humor. You can appreciate it the next day, but while you're out there in the heat of battle, it's something you never really think about.

Pro Football Hall Of Fame Induction

I was a huge fan of the NFL growing up. Although my dad played before I was born, I was very proud of that fact. I never hesitated to share it with buddies at school or something along those lines. I was so proud of my brother Clay when went into the league five years before me. Naturally I was a huge Browns fan because of Clay. I grew up in awe of the league. Playing in the league for 19 seasons, making the Pro Bowl and all that type stuff to me was like, man, I can't believe I'm actually doing this. I think in a lot of ways, in terms of my faith and how I viewed God's relationship to this whole thing, I became so much more humble about it. I realized God blessed me to be able to go out and play this great game. This was nothing that I did on my own. God gave me the body, desire, mindset, and intellect to play the game. The whole process humbled me.

Then, being named to the Hall of Fame was the culmination of all these things. It was like, thank you Lord, for blessing me. I see so much of how this is such a group effort, from my parents and the example that they set, to the opportunity to grow up with a big brother like Clay. I was so blessed. It was a very humbling experience. I was very apprehensive about the Hall of Fame weekend and activities because the spotlight's on you for four full days.

I remember thinking I just can't wait until this is over, because I don't want to be in the spotlight anymore. I'm very appreciative, but this amazing thing happened during that weekend. I got up there and initially started feeling anxious about it. Then I saw how much all my friends and family were enjoying the moment, and it really became a special kind of opportunity to see them enjoying the process and the weekend. All of a sudden, it was no longer about me. I was able to enjoy their responses. It was really cool.

Again, it was just another lesson in humility. It was all about my anxiety and me. I didn't want to be the center of attention. The minute I didn't make it about me, I enjoyed myself.

Photograph copyright Associated Press

Chapter 119

Chris Doleman

College:
Pittsburgh

Career History:
Minnesota Vikings (1985–1993)
Atlanta Falcons (1994–1995)
San Francisco 49ers (1996–1998)
Minnesota Vikings (1999)

2012 Inductee Pro Football Hall Of Fame

University Of Pittsburgh's Success

Pittsburgh was an independent. We played against some tough, tough teams. You've got to be on your game every week. It seemed like somewhere along the road there would be a bump and we just couldn't recover.

I have fond memories of playing football at Pittsburgh. My first three years in school, the team was 33 and 3, which is pretty impressive.

I know one loss was to Penn State. In 1981, we played Georgia and beat them. If they had won, they would have won the national championship. I think we lost to Florida State one year. When you're an independent, you're playing the best teams that are out there at the time. I look back on those years often. I made a lot of friends and memories. Those were just wonderful times.

College Choice

Penn State recruited me. I was just never a Penn State guy, even though I grew up in a Penn State environment. I looked at Penn State almost like a cult. You just didn't have the freedom. Penn State is a great school, but I see their uniforms matching their personalities.

There was nothing that stood out. Everybody was programmed, they did what they were supposed to do, and had success. They didn't want to deviate from that plan.

I grew up probably 100 miles from Penn State. The coaches were never warm and fuzzy. I don't remember their coaches coming in and spending time with me. Everybody recruited me. I might have got a letter from Penn State but that was about it. I don't know if they expected kids to run to Penn State and ask, "Hey are you going to recruit me?" Sometimes if you live too close to a school, they know too much about you and they're just not turned on by you.

Teammates At Pittsburgh

When I got a chance to go to the University of Pittsburgh, I played with some great guys like Bill Maas, Tim Lewis, and Bill Fralic, who played in the National Football League. Pittsburgh just had that family fun environment that you think a college should have.

We had so many great players, it wasn't even funny. We had Dan Marino, Carlton Williamson, Lynn Thomas, Pappy Thomas, and Tim Lewis. The Pittsburgh class of 1980 had 12 or 13 guys drafted by the NFL. We were practicing against some of the best players in the country. We expected to win, give great performances, and all the stuff that our players tended to show once they got into the pros and really developed and refined their skill set.

Herschel Walker

We played against Herschel Walker and Georgia in the 1982 Sugar Bowl. We played those guys in New Orleans and we beat them. On our closing drive, Dan Marino threw a pass to James Brown. He caught it, scored, and the game was over.

NFL Draft

First of all, the pressure is on the team. It's not on the player because the team drafted the player, the player didn't draft the team. You have a situation where the team felt that you were good enough to play at the NFL level. I think as a player, you owe them the respect to do everything you can to meet their expectations. If you can't meet their expectations, you just can't. You can't get water from a rock. If a guy can play, he can play; but if he can't, you can't hold that against him. He might have maxed out in college and he'll never become the guy you thought he should have been. That has happened.

The NFL spends millions and millions of dollars scouting guys. It's a situation where the teams might need to adjust because there may be too many opinions. They're missing on too many players right now.

I could have very easily been the second pick in the draft. Buffalo chose Bruce Smith with the first pick. Minnesota had the second pick, and Atlanta had the fourth pick. Atlanta and Minnesota traded picks. So Bill Fralic went to Atlanta with the second pick. Then, Ray Childress went to the Houston Oilers with the third pick. I went to Minnesota with the number four pick. There could have been Hall of Famers drafted with the first and second picks.

Position Change From Linebacker To Defensive End

Basically my first two years in the NFL, I played linebacker. We were making a run for the playoffs late in my second season. We had two or three games left to play in the regular season and our defensive line was pretty beat up. The coach said, "Hey if you could step up there and rush the passer on fourth down, it will help us out a great deal." I said, "Thank God." It got me back to doing what I did in college. It was somewhat difficult. In 13 years, I amassed 150 and a half sacks, I was on a roll. I wonder what would have happened if I'd been playing for the 49ers my entire career, or if I'd been a defensive end from the time I came into the league.

Minnesota Vikings Defensive Line

Man we were a talented group. We were a talented group in the sense that we were so good, John Randle couldn't even get on the field. He was playing behind Keith Millard. When you look at that and realize how great the players and the coaches we had were, we knew we had something special. That has been the backbone of Minnesota for a long time. Everybody's team is built differently. Some teams feature a strong quarterback, some do a great job with the running back, and then there are teams that do a great job with defensive line. Minnesota's definitely one of those teams.

Carrying A Briefcase Into The Locker Room

I felt that they were paying players like executives so players had to act and conduct themselves like executives. Even though I had my hands in the dirt and it was blue-collar work, I always had a thing, I wanted to look good, feel good, and play good. I always respected that. That was how I approached my craft. That was probably what motivated me to carry a briefcase. I grew out of the gym bag stage. I was no larger carrying my wrinkled notes in a gym bag. I was beyond the gym bag stage and needed to act like that. I wore pants now.

Best Coach

I would probably say Bud Grant because Bud didn't talk a lot, but I remember every conversation I had with him. I remember there was a guy on our team who was getting a lot of penalties on the kickoff and special teams. He told this guy, "You're going to play yourself off this team." That stuck with me. He didn't tolerate a lot of nonsense. It was about business. It was about being a professional.

Toughest Offensive Lineman

That would be Gary Zimmerman. We played together for seven years and we played against each other for about three. That was tough.

He knew how to do everything. Gary was a great. He is a Hall of Famer and was a great player. When I was inducted into the Hall of Fame, I credited him for me being in the Hall of Fame just as he credited me when he went in the Hall. This was the right side of the line on defense and the left side of the line on offense. On offense, the tackle was Gary Zimmerman and the guard was Randall McDaniel. On the defensive side of the ball on the right side were Keith Millard, John Randle, and I. Out of the guys I named, four of us are in the Hall of Fame.

If Keith would have been able to play longer, there's no question in my mind that he would have been a Hall of Famer.

Minnesota Vikings Trade For Herschel Walker

The Vikings gave up way too many good players when they traded for Herschel Walker. No player is worth 11 guys.

I had known Herschel since college and there was no way in the world that Herschel could meet all their expectations. He would have had to score three touchdowns in every game. There was just no way that he could be as good as they thought he could be. I don't think it would have even mattered if it were a quarterback. I don't think they could have survived that scrutiny.

Only Missing Two Games During A 15-Year Career
I only missed two games during my 15-year career through, the grace of God. God blessed me with a strong body to go out and play week in and week out. If it were a cold or the flu, you better keep guys away from me because I would get sick in a heartbeat. But physically breaking down, breaking bones, tearing ligaments, tendons, and all that other stuff, wasn't an issue. I could catch a cold in a heartbeat, though.

Pro Football Hall Of Fame Induction
When I found out I was selected for the Pro Football Hall of Fame I thought, "Is this real?" Was my body of work that good that they would consider me one of the best that ever played the game? Was I really good enough for this award? Do I really deserve this award? It's very humbling. It's hard to believe that your bust is going to be in Canton forever, and it's hard to believe that you are part of a very small group of guys who have made the game great.

Having my son as my presenter at the Hall was amazing. I played while he was growing up. He didn't see my whole career but he got a chance to see just how good I was; how much of a professional I was. He was just totally blown away by it because to him, I'm just dad. Now, I'm part of NFL history and it's a little more than just dad, but he still treats me like just dad. There are no perks out of the deal.

I've made not only my parents and my family proud, but I made the Minnesota Vikings, the University of Pittsburgh, and the people that followed me and supported me along the way proud. I'm happy and appreciative of that.

Minnesota Vikings Hall of Fame defensive end Chris Doleman pressures Chicago Bears quarterback Jim McMahon. Photograph copyright Associated Press

Chapter 120

Gary Zimmerman

> College:
> Oregon
>
> Career History:
> Los Angeles Express (1984–1985)
> Minnesota Vikings (1986–1992)
> Denver Broncos (1993–1997)
>
> 2008 Inductee Pro Football Hall Of Fame

College Choice

In high school, I played both ways. Back in those days you always did that. I was recruited by almost everybody in the Pac-10 except USC at that time, and they wanted me to play offensive line, but I wanted to play middle linebacker. I was also recruited by Harvard, Utah State, and Hawaii. I picked Oregon because I thought I was going to play middle linebacker. But, looking back at it, I guess they did me a favor.

When I got there my uniform number was 75. I said, "That's kind of a funny number for a middle linebacker." After the first practice they said, "Well, we're going to move you over to the offensive line." I made lemonade out of lemons there. A lot of kids would have quit, but I stuck it out and worked my way through it. It was actually a benefit for me in that I had to fight through adversity. As it turned out, I met my wife at Oregon.

College

Oregon was rough. It's not like Oregon nowadays. They were just building a program back then. Things were different. It was right after the Vietnam War. We were told not to wear our athletic stuff around campus because people were mad we went to school for free. It was a totally different era. The athletic department couldn't give you anything. They'd pick up our old shoes and throw them in the dumpster. They couldn't give them to us. We got nothing, as far as handouts, like they do today. It was a good experience because I was really focused on football and school, because there wasn't anything else to do there. There were no cell phones or computers around then. So you went to school, you worked, and you worked out. That was basically all you did back then.

Biggest College Rivalry

I'd have to say it was Oregon State. The Civil War is kind of a big thing in Oregon, but every game was a big game to us cause we were underdogs every game. Oregon State was kind of our bowl game, cause we'd been on probation. So it was always the Civil War, the pride of Oregon. The big rivalry back then was with Oregon State.

Draft

I was over in Hawaii for the Hula Bowl, and my dad called me. The Los Angeles Express wanted me to stop by on the way back to Oregon, because I flew back thru Los Angeles. I stopped by, and they kind of threw me out of the office. I thought it was over then, but they ended up drafting me. I knew they wanted to draft me, but I thought I made them mad when I was there that they wouldn't. It didn't work out that way.

Los Angeles Express

I think the idea was for the USFL to try to build a league to compete with the NFL. So, they were trying to snag all the big names. That was their plan.

The USFL was probably the most important period of my career because coming out of college; I was a center and guard. During the first game, Mark Adickes, the left tackle, blew out his knee. That's when I became a left tackle. I spent two years learning how to play left tackle in the USFL. I think those were the two most important years of my career learning how to play the left tackle position.

With the L.A. Express, the first year we went pretty hard in practice. The difference between the USFL and NFL was there were some players in USFL that wouldn't have made it in the NFL. You had lesser quality players, and you didn't have the high quality players at every position. So, I would say that was a little easier. But, the first year was tough back then. They had 8mm tape, and they'd film the practice session. You had to wait for the tape to get developed.

The second year, the team had some money issues. The team ran out of money, so they had no film. We'd come in and practice, then be done and out of there by noon. The first year was just like the NFL, but the quality of the players was not quite the level of an NFL team.

The Express owner had financial issues and the L.A. Express went broke. They told us, "This is our last game Sunday. We ran out of money." After the game, we took our belongings home. Then they called everyone up on Wednesday and said, "Hey, we found some more money." The rest of the league kind of floated us. The league hated us because they were paying our salaries too. I guess they needed us because we were in the L.A. market. A lot of the players went and cashed their checks quickly. I got my money up front so I didn't have that issue. I didn't have to worry about that.

Steve Young and all the older guys kind of knew that the odds of something going bad were pretty high. I think some of the guys who could demand that kind of contract, got it. But if you were a guy just looking for work, you couldn't get that kind of deal.

Sid Gillman

Sid Gillman was the greatest. My flight was late my first day with the Express. When I arrived, the team was in a meeting. The room was dark and Sid was running tape. I heard him say, "Who's that number 63 or something?" Someone in the room said, "Rogers" or whatever his name was. Sid said, "Good job. Rogers." Then a couple of plays later he said, "Who's that number 72?" Somebody said, "Alex" or whatever. Sid said, "I want you out of here tomorrow.

You're horrible." It was an eye-opener seeing him cut someone right in front of everybody, right there in the meeting. So that was kind of awesome. That kind of got my head in the right place.

Another story about Sid that sticks with me is in the USFL, there were always guys wanting to tryout. Someone was coming in for a tryout. Sid was going to time him in the 40-yard dash. The kid started running, and about 20 yards into the 40, Sid just walked off the field and said, "Hell with him."

Those are the things that stuck with me. Sid was kind of a no-nonsense guy. If he liked you and you worked hard, you got along good. If you didn't work hard and didn't do your job, you were gone. That was the kind of mentality back then, and it stuck with me for my whole career.

John Hadl was the head coach, so we had quite a tandem. My line coach was Sam Gruneisen, who played with the Chargers for 10 or 15 years. Jeff Hart was playing on the offensive line. He had played in the NFL. So we had a lot of NFL guys there. We had a lot of NFL experience there.

I was making the transition from center to tackle, so I really wasn't examining the offense that much. But just learning the tackle position and having Steve Young sure helped out. The first two years I had a left-handed quarterback in Steve Young, so he didn't have to rely on my blindside so much. It was a great time in my career. Those two years were some of the most fun and some of the craziest I've ever had.

Joining The Minnesota Vikings
It was different. I was nervous. The first day I walked into the facility, I was walking down the hall with all of my stuff and Jerry Burns came down the hall. I went up to Jerry Burns and he said, "What's your name?" I told him and he said, "Awe hell, you're too little to play in this league." I was 284 pounds.

The Vikings' practice was harder than the game. It was brutal. It took a lot of years off my career because we pretty much hit everyday. Going against Chris Doleman and John Randle everyday was tough in Minnesota.

Difference Between Minnesota Vikings & Denver Broncos
Position by position the Vikings were probably the best team I ever played on. One year we had 22 guys go to the Pro Bowl. I mean it was ridiculous. We could never win the big game because we were so worn out by the end of the season. Back then we really didn't have a game plan. We just had a playbook and they ran it.

When I went to Denver, they game planned everything. The Vikings put the whole playbook out there and called the plays that we ran. The games weren't really game planned. The Vikings' defense was number one in the league for a bunch of years. Our offensive line was also well thought of. The offensive line was Randall McDaniel, Kirt Lowdermilk, Todd Kalis, Tim Irwin, and me. We had one of the better lines back then. We were … maybe a quarterback away from winning the whole thing.

Toughest Defensive Lineman

Derrick Thomas was hard because he was so quick off the ball. Richard Dent was tough. Bruce Smith was a handful. I always said the toughest guy is the guy you play every Sunday, because there are no slouches in the NFL. Every week you're playing against the best guy. I thought they were all great, and that's the way I approached it. I approached it as it's going to be an uphill fight for me just to hold my own. That's the way I approached it.

If you get where you're behind, you have to go to a passing situation. That's a bitch. If you can run the ball, you can play your game. So it's just kind of situational. You don't want to get in certain situations with certain guys. They were all great. Every guy in the NFL is a great guy. And there's not much difference between a great guy and a good guy. Everybody is pretty talented, but there are a few guys that just stand out. Thomas was so quick off the ball. When you couldn't hear, if you were half a second late, it was over. I played with a lot of great players over the years. For me it's hard to pick one guy, because they all gave me trouble.

I've always said that Chris Doleman put me in the Hall of Fame. Going against him everyday ... neither one of us liked to lose, so I'd come up with something to beat him and he'd counter that and come up with something to beat me. We went back and forth. I think it just made us both evolve. We got better and better, because we were constantly trying to outdo each other.

Trash Talking

Back then, there were a few guys like Tim Harris and John Randle who trash talked. Those are the only guys that I can really think of who did it. I think it was different back then. You had mutual respect and you didn't really do that kind of stuff. I don't know, I guess the times have changed and the mentality has changed. I don't think it was really that common when I played.

Jerry Burns

Jerry Burns was different. I don't think he knew anybody's name on the team. All the linemen were "Big Boy". He would say, "Run that play where you run behind Big Boy. Run that play where you throw the ball to A.C." He was an old-school coach. He hammered the hell out of us all week. A lot of the time we were in the playoffs, but we never went very far. I think we were just worn-out from beating the hell out of each other for 20 weeks or whatever it was. We had tough training camps. He just wore us out. That's my take on Jerry.

Dennis Green

Dennis Green and I didn't get along, because I could tell right away that he was phony. He could talk a good game, but he couldn't coach a good game. He could rile you up with good talk, but when you look at his staff and some of the stuff that happened there with the Vikings ... I only played for him for one year. One of the reasons that I ended up out of there was because we didn't get along.

Joining Denver Broncos

I was retired for six months; so going to the Broncos gave me a new life. It's like a dog that goes to the dog pound, and then someone adopts you. After that you have total loyalty to them. That's the way I feel. When I went to the Broncos, it was the first time I had ever met a team owner. I was with the Vikings for seven years, and I was never in the same room with the team owner. Pat

Bowlen, the Broncos owner, would be down in the locker room everyday, coming out to practice everyday, and he'd talk to you. From the top-down, Mr. Bowlen just ran one hell of a program. It was unbelievable. I wish I played my whole career there.

Smaller Offensive Linemen
Back in the day, when I first got into the NFL the linemen weren't that big. It was Dallas that started the "slobblocker", where you get the guy who's just so big that nobody could get around him. At Minnesota, we were kind of a technique team. We worked on technique everyday and prided ourselves on having good technique. Dallas brought in huge guys who didn't have that good of a technique, but they had the size. So, we prided ourselves on being technicians.

After I went to Denver and Alex Gibbs got there, it was like heaven. He was a technician type guy too. He believed in mobile guys, and I just fell into what he wanted. If he wanted a big guy, I wasn't the guy. It just happened to work out. That was his philosophy—having athletic mobile guys.

Wade Phillips
I thought Wade Phillips was a great coach. I think his downfall was that he was too nice. I think what happened was people took advantage of him too much. I think people could get away with things you couldn't get away with, with other coaches. I loved playing for Wade. I think his mentality of being so nice kind of bit him in the butt. He treated us as men. He always said, "I want to treat you guys as men." Of course there's some guys that will always push the limit, and that's what happened. Players realized that they wouldn't get in too much trouble with Wade. I think that kind of got him. I loved playing for him, because he was a great coach. There were guys in the NFL just to get a paycheck. Then there are guys there who want to win. It depends on what kind of guy you are, whether you liked him or not. Some people took advantage of him.

Super Bowl Denver vs. Packers
Nobody gave us a chance. Green Bay had these great big guys who people thought we wouldn't be able to handle. The Green Bay players were going to eat our lunch. It kind of stuck in our gut, all of the offensive line. I wish we were allowed to bet on games back then, because I knew a week out that we were going to win that game. Our team was an older team, and everyone understood how hard it was to get to the Super Bowl. I had played 12 years and had never been to one. There were a lot of guys on the Broncos that were older and had never been to one. We realized this could be our only shot at it. I think we just took it a little more seriously than Green Bay. Green Bay thought they were coming in to pick up the trophy, I guess.

It was both exciting and frustrating, because everything was so different. It was like when you get into a routine where you do everything at a certain time. Then the day of the Super Bowl, we couldn't go to the stadium early because we had to have a police escort over there. They wouldn't allow us in if we had come earlier, by cab. Our timetables were changed up. After all the hoopla the week before, I didn't like that. My whole football career I had never won a championship, and there it was. It was my one shot at it. I was in the playoffs so many times, that people don't realize how hard it is just to get to the Super Bowl, let alone win it.

I just think we were focused for the Packers. Nobody gave us a chance. All the things were in our favor, yet nobody gave us a chance. So, we were kind of proving to the world that we could do it. It was a great game to end your career on.

Mike Shanahan

I always say that's when I learned how to win. In the past, we'd have our meetings and the coach would always say, "Our goal is to win the conference and the division, then work our way to the Super Bowl." When Mike Shanahan came in he said, "Our goal is to win the Super Bowl. Anything less is a failure." Right there, he set the tone. To me, that makes a huge difference in what they expect. Mike carried a book, and in that book you could see every hour where we were going to be the whole season. It was unbelievable. He had every practice with laid out times. Every meeting time was laid out.

I'm a structure guy, so it really fit me well in that he was so structured. I heard other guys didn't like it because it was too structured. I think it was good, because we had meetings at 10 o'clock at night at training camp. All the guys hemmed and hawed, because they couldn't go out drinking. He kept a tight reign on the team and I liked it. Our goal was to win the Super Bowl and I think that permeated and everybody knew what the goal was.

Decision To Retire After Super Bowl Win Versus Packers

I wanted to come back so bad. I told Mr. Bowlen, "If I came back I'd just be taking your money." My shoulders were so shot, I was getting injections before every game. My wife was mad I was doing that. My body just couldn't take it. Then I thought what if I lose a shoulder and I can't play with my kids the rest of my life? I've got one ring. What good are two rings going to do? They'll just both be in the safe deposit together.

Honestly I wanted to come back, but I knew better than to do that. I knew something could have happened. So I wanted to come back, but I didn't.

Pro Football Hall Of Fame Induction

It was a shock, because so many times I was a finalist and it didn't happen. It's the greatest single individual honor I've received. Never in my whole life have I ever dreamed of being in the Pro Football Hall of Fame. It just never entered my mind that I would enter the hall. To get in there and meet the guys I watched growing up was just unbelievable. I go back every year now. To see those guys is like a renewal every time I go back. I get to talk to those guys; it's amazing how many thoughts everybody has. People tell stories and I can say, "Hey, I feel the same exact way." It's kind of weird. Everybody has a common thought process.

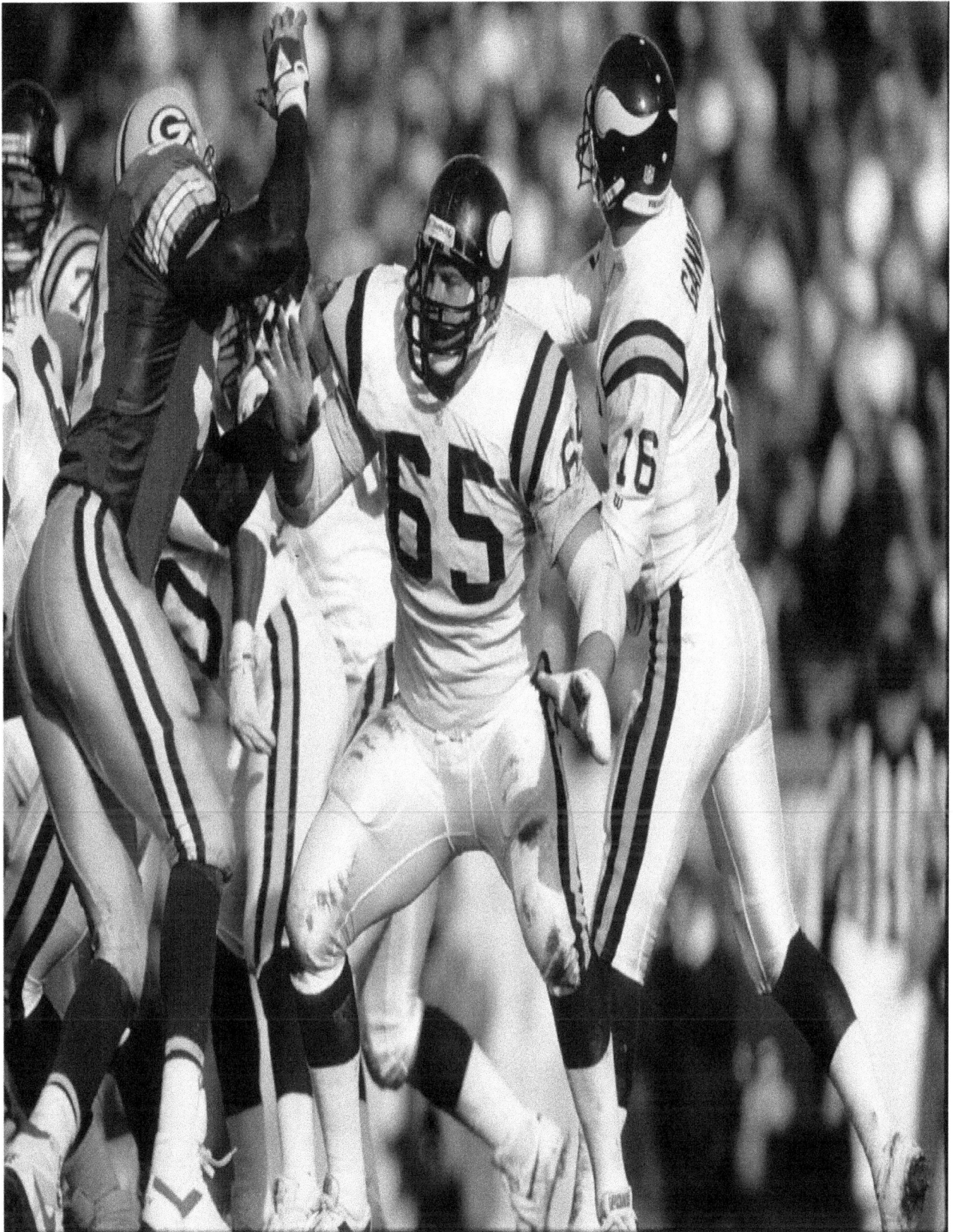

Photograph copyright Associated Press

Chapter 121

Kevin Greene

College:
Auburn

Career History:
As Player:
Los Angeles Rams (1985–1992)
Pittsburgh Steelers (1993–1995)
Carolina Panthers (1996)
San Francisco 49ers (1997)
Carolina Panthers (1998–1999)

As Coach:
Green Bay Packers (2009–2013) (OLB)

2016 Inductee Pro Football Hall Of Fame

College Choice
My mom and dad were from Choccolocco, Alabama, and they grew up Auburn fans. When you're born in Alabama, you're born either into an Auburn household or University of Alabama household. My mom and dad were in the military. Because of that, my older brother Keith and I were born on the road. Since we were born into an Auburn household when it came time for college, there was no question where we were going. We were going to Auburn.

I went to high school in Granite City, Illinois, which is considerably north of Auburn, and Auburn didn't really recruit in that area. Plus, that high school was really known for its soccer team. We were soccer state champions four years in a row. Anyway, the football team wasn't really well known. We were average, but competitive. I sent my films down to Auburn, and they replied with a letter. They said, "We've filled the spots for linebackers. We'd like you to come down and walk on." Essentially, that's what I did.

Auburn Running Backs
We had great running backs during my years at Auburn. We had Bo Jackson, Lionel James, Brent Fullwood, Tommie Agee, and Tim Jessie. It was like Running Back University. It was hard, and I learned a lot.

Bo Jackson got me a number of times. But, I wasn't the only one he was running over, so I felt good about that. I was trying to lay leather on Bo. He was a special cat. I knew that practicing against him at Auburn was going to make me better. I just knew he was special. You could see it from the way he moved and how fast and how hard he hit you. It made you a better player.

That's the way you've got to look at it. You're going to improve as long as you go against people that are better than you. You won't get better if you go against people that you can beat up on all the time, if you think about it. It was really cool playing against Bo and Lionel James, another fine back that played multiple years in the NFL, in practice. It was great.

Auburn's Biggest Rival
There'll never be a bigger opponent than Alabama. Auburn-Alabama is such a huge rivalry that it dates back freaking centuries. I'm sure it goes back to the caveman days. So of course, it's Alabama.

Charles Barkley
I remember Charles Barkley being such a good dude. Charles didn't really know me from Adam, since I was a walk-on at Auburn. I wasn't really known. I was not a scholarship guy. Charles was just as kind and nice to me as if I was a big time famous college player like he was. Charles had such a great heart. He was just a fine person.

Bo was as good as Charles was. He didn't have an ego and he didn't have an attitude. They were just great, classy individuals. They were just both great, special young men.

Auburn
I never earned a scholarship. I did not start until the starting outside linebacker went down. His name was Joe Robinson, and he was a fine player. He would go on to be a first round draft choice with the Minnesota Vikings. He went down about three-quarters of the way through my senior year. Then Coach Pat Dye put me in as a starter. I started making things happen and I ended up leading the SEC in sacks my senior year, 1984, and was Defensive Player of the Year. That's when I really started to step up my play at Auburn. So it was just a blessing. You don't want to wish injuries on anybody, but in that case, it really opened the door for me at that time.

Why would Pat Dye spend a scholarship on a walk-on who was basically just playing for two years? It just didn't make sense, and I understood that. That didn't take anything away from my experience playing for Auburn. I totally understood. My mom and dad could afford to put me in Auburn and keep me in Auburn, so that wasn't a deal breaker by any means. I mean, good God, I had a chance to play for Auburn. It was a phenomenal opportunity. I'm just blessed that Coach Pat Dye recognized something in me, got me in the mix, and got me on the field. I did some good things for them. So that's the way I look at it.

Draft
I was just hoping to get drafted. I really didn't know if I would. I was already a second lieutenant in the Army Reserves, so I was tracking a military career as my folks did. I remember during the season ending interview Coach Dye had with the seniors in 1984, I asked Coach Dye point blank, "Coach, do you think that I can play at the next level?" He told me, "Yes, Kevin. Absolutely. I think there's a place for you somewhere in the NFL."

That's really all I needed. Now I started thinking, I'm going to start running more and training harder. I am going to be ready to potentially walk on somewhere if I get a chance as a free agent in the NFL. I'm going to give it my best shot. We've only got one life to live, and I said, "I'm going to give it my best shot."

I was the first player picked in the fifth round by the Rams. I thought, "Oh my gosh. I've actually got my foot in the door." It was just unbelievable for me as a former walk-on to get drafted. Un freaking real. It was crazy.

The Birmingham Stallions had drafted me in their territorial draft. It was a backup game plan for me. When Coach Dye told me, "Yes, absolutely, I think there's a place for you somewhere in the NFL," that's really what my focus started to hone in on. Being drafted by the Birmingham Stallions was a blessing, too. I had a chance with them, but Coach Dye told me I really had a chance to run on the same field with the big boys; the big guys. So that was really where my focus was.

Earning Playing Time With Rams
Coach John Robinson had me at linebacker with the Rams. I was an outside linebacker at Auburn. We ran a three-four defense at Auburn and we ran a three-four with the Rams. So I just slid into the three-four outside backer position. Coach Robinson had me running down on kickoff team cracking noggins, the kickoff return team, punt team, and punt return team. I paid my dues my first three years playing on all the special teams. Then during my fourth year, I got my first start. I responded with 16½ sacks that season.

With the Rams, we had the same defensive coordinator. His name was Fritz Shurmur, and he was just a fine individual. I really loved Fritz. I think Fritz and John Robinson said, "We've got to find a way to get Kevin Greene on the field 'cuz he's running down on the kickoff team and he's crushing people." The first three years they started getting me in on third down and long to rush the passer. They wanted to see if I had any pass rush skills and stuff like that and I responded.

My second year in the league I had seven sacks as a part-time, third down pass rusher. I was a special teams guy primarily. My third year, I had 6½ sacks in a strike-shortened season. I think we only played nine or ten games that year. So they came up with an idea to get me on the field, and that idea was what they called the Eagle Defense. That put me in a position to rush the passer. They figured out a way to get me on the field.

1986 Los Angeles Rams vs. Chicago Bears NFC Championship Game
The Chicago Bears were tough, no doubt. It was a chilly game, but I felt pretty good. Our quarterback was Dieter Brock. He had played in the Canadian Football League, and he played really well for us that year.

We had Eric Dickerson at running back. I knew Eric Dickerson was special. I figured we had a chance to go into Soldier Field and win.

Chicago was rolling with their 46 defense. The Bears got ahead and then the crowd got into it. The wind started whipping off the water, it started snowing, and it was just brutal. It was a tail thumping. It is what it is. It was really cool to go to the championship game my rookie year.

Los Angeles Rams Change In Defensive Coordinators

Coach Robinson brought in a new defensive staff. Fritz Shurmur was let go, and they brought in Jeff Fisher to coordinate the defense. Jeff really didn't know how to play me. He played me for six games at right defensive end, four games at left defensive end, and six games at outside linebacker. My previous years, in '88, '89 and '90, I had 46 sacks. I was killing people. We didn't have a good year team-wise in 1990, and I think that prompted Coach Robinson to let Fritz and the staff go. Individually, I had a good, productive year in 1990, with 13 sacks. So I struggled and was I only able to get three sacks in 1991.

In 1992, the entire staff was let go. So the Rams brought in Chuck Knox as head coach and George Dyer as defensive coordinator. George put me as an outside linebacker in a four-three defense. I had more coverage responsibilities and less pass rush opportunities. I led the team in tackles and sacks as a part-time pass rusher on third down. He let me rush the passer. I knew I really couldn't have an impact in games as a four-three outside linebacker. I really needed to be attacking to have a direct impact in a game.

Signing With Pittsburg Steelers

Then in 1993, the first year of free agency, I signed with the Pittsburgh Steelers. They put me back as a three-four outside backer. So I was just really blessed. The Lord works in mysterious ways and he orchestrated my steps. I flew into Pittsburgh. Their starting left outside linebacker, Gerald Williams, wanted out of Pittsburgh. Gerald went and signed a free agent contract with the San Diego Chargers. Steelers Head Coach Bill Cowher, really needed a left outside linebacker in Defensive Coordinator Dom Capers' three-four pressure blitz-on package. It was just a perfect fit for me. It was what I basically played those three years that I was highly productive with the Rams from 1988-1990.

Bill Cowher said, "Hey. We're going to put you back at your old position and let you do what you do." I said, "Cool. I'm all about it." I just loved playing for the Steeler Nation. With Greg Lloyd on the other side of me, he was slobbering as much as I was slobbering. He's freaking out as much as I'm going gonzo. We hunted together extremely well. The Steelers had a fine defense and fine offense. Those three years at Pittsburgh really defined my career.

Signing With Carolina Panthers

It was tough to leave Pittsburgh. I wasn't ready to ride the pine after the 1995 season. We lost the Super Bowl against Dallas. I was going into my 12th year, and Coach Cowher clearly wanted to play a young fellow named Jason Gildon. Coach Cowher wanted me to take Jason under my wing and teach him tricks of the trade and show him how to watch film. I just wasn't ready to be a backup to anybody.

So, I left and I signed with Carolina in 1996, which was my 12th year in the league. It just so happened Dom Capers' was the head coach. He said, "Hey, Kevin. I'm going to put you back where you belong, at outside linebacker. Just do what you do, and help teach the three-four pressure to the rest of the brothers on defense." I said, "Okay. Let's do it." I led the league in sacks again. I was a First Team All Pro and Linebacker of the Year again. I really wanted to stay a Steeler, but I wasn't ready to really ride the pine at that point in my career. I knew I had some more football left in me, some high level stuff left in me. So I had to leave.

Edward DeBartolo

Eddie was great. Eddie was wonderful. That was probably my 13th year in the league when I was a 49er. He was a great owner and it was a great organization. I really enjoyed my time during that one year in San Francisco. I think Eddie did a good job of bringing together a lot of talent to make a run at the Super Bowl. We just fell a little bit short. We actually played the championship game there in 1997, against the Green Bay Packers. Favre beat us, and I think they went on to lose the Super Bowl. We had Steve Young, Jerry Rice, Chris Doleman, and Rod Woodson there. We had Hall of Famers on that team. Brett Favre was in the peak of his career and they came into Candlestick and beat us.

I had just a wonderful time in San Francisco. It was essentially a blip on the radar as far as my career was concerned, just one year, then I was back in Carolina. It was great playing for Mr. DeBartolo and that organization for a year.

Favorite Game

It was just a blessing. Good Lord, one weekend I was looking into the eyes of Joe Montana, the next weekend Dan Marino, the next weekend John Elway, Troy Aikman, Brett Favre, and then Steve Young. The list of great quarterbacks just went on and on and on. I knew they were Hall of Famers. I knew they were special when I was lining up on the other side of the ball from them, looking at them. I knew. My job, of course, was to hunt their tail. They didn't even have to pay me to do it. I just knew I was living a dream. I was totally in touch with reality at that time, and I knew that they were special, special cats. My job was to hunt them down and crush them and I did. It was just an unbelievable dream come true.

Sacking Joe Montana 4 ½ Times In A Game

I sacked him 5½ times in the last game of 1988. One of my fellow defenders, I'm not going to mention his name, got called for holding on one play and one of my sacks was nullified. So I ended up with 4½ sacks on Joe Montana in the last game of 1988, to help get the L.A. Rams into the playoffs. That was a surreal game. Obviously that was a big game for me.

I had a lot of big games. I was just blessed to play with a lot of great players that helped me along the way; great coaches and great players. I mentioned, some of those great players that helped me along the way.

Referees

I always thought that I would have more sacks if the referees would make more holding calls. Very few offensive tackles blocked me within the rules and regulations of the game. I've got this saying. It's what I taught my kids in Green Bay as a coach there for five years. "If they can't hold you, they can't block you." So I always thought I'd have had more sacks if the refs would have specifically looked at me and whoever was in front of me, trying to block me each and every play. They couldn't do that. Plus, they want to let the big boys' play. They want to let them play and they know the fans at home don't want to see a lot of holding calls, yada, yada, yada. So that's the way football goes.

Waiting To Get Inducted Into The Pro Football Hall Of Fame
It was confusing more than anything. I just didn't understand the criteria for induction in the Hall of Fame, that's the bottom line. I just didn't understand what qualifies a man to be inducted. They were clearly putting in people that did not play as long as I did, and essentially we played the same position. They didn't have anywhere near the same production, statistical numbers, and impact I had on four different teams. So I was just scratching my noggin. More than anything, I was confused about the process. I wasn't going to get stressed about it. I was patient about it.

I just kept praying about it and trusting in the Lord that my time would come in God's time. Not when I want it, but it's going to happen in His time. It happened in His time and it was the right time in my family. It was definitely the right time in my life for it to transpire. It really doesn't matter now. I'm in and I'm part of an elite fraternity. So it doesn't matter. It doesn't faze me now.

Winning A Super Bowl As A Coach With Green Bay Packers
It was extremely fulfilling. I always wanted a Super Bowl ring. It's something that I fought tooth and nail for during my 15 years as a player and I came up short for 15 years. I went to six championship games as a player and lost five of them. The one championship game we won, we lost the Super Bowl. It's just so hard to go to the Super Bowl, much less win the thing. So as a coach my second year up in Green Bay, to win a Super Bowl was just unbelievable, but bittersweet because we beat the Pittsburgh Steelers. So it was bittersweet to beat the old team that I owe so much to in the big show.

I am grateful to Coach Mike McCarthy for giving me an opportunity up in Green Bay to coach for him and his staff and get a Super Bowl ring. I'm just really grateful to Coach McCarthy and that entire organization.

Favorite Coach
I have been blessed to be surrounded by a lot of good coaches. It started at Auburn. I had a great coach in Coach Pat Dye. What a fine coach he was; a hard, physical coach. I just loved playing for him. My position coach there was Joe Whitt, another good coach.

Then I went into the NFL with the Rams, and John Robinson was the head coach. Fritz Shurmur was a great defensive coordinator who actually created a defense to get me on the field. My position coach there, Fred Whittingham, played in the NFL for a number of years at linebacker. He was just a great position coach. Then I go to Pittsburgh with Coach Bill Cowher. Of course, we all know about him. Dom Capers was there as the defensive coordinator, and my position coach at Pittsburgh was Marvin Lewis. I mean, good Lord. Dick LeBeau was on that staff. Then I go to Carolina and Coach Dom Capers is the head coach there. Billy Davis was my position coach there. Billy Davis has been a long-time defensive coordinator in the NFL.

It just went on and on and on. Wonderful coaches and great players surrounded me. I was just blessed all along the way. I truly was.

NFL Team Most Identify With

There's a part of me that bleeds a lot of different colors. During my eight years with the Rams I was a good player, a Pro Bowl player. Part of me bleeds blue and gold. It surely does. When I went to Pittsburgh, they really put me on the stage and my career really took off there opposite of Greg Lloyd. I was working with Rod Woodson. So, I bleed black and gold. Then I went to Carolina, and was with Lamar Lathon, Sam Mills, and all those guys. I bleed a little bit of that teal blue and black. So I bleed a lot of different colors.

If you look back at my career, there's no question I stepped up on stage there in Pittsburgh. It was a whole other level that we played at as a defense, and what we were able to do as a defensive unit. So I bleed a lot of colors, but it was great to be a part of the Steeler Nation.

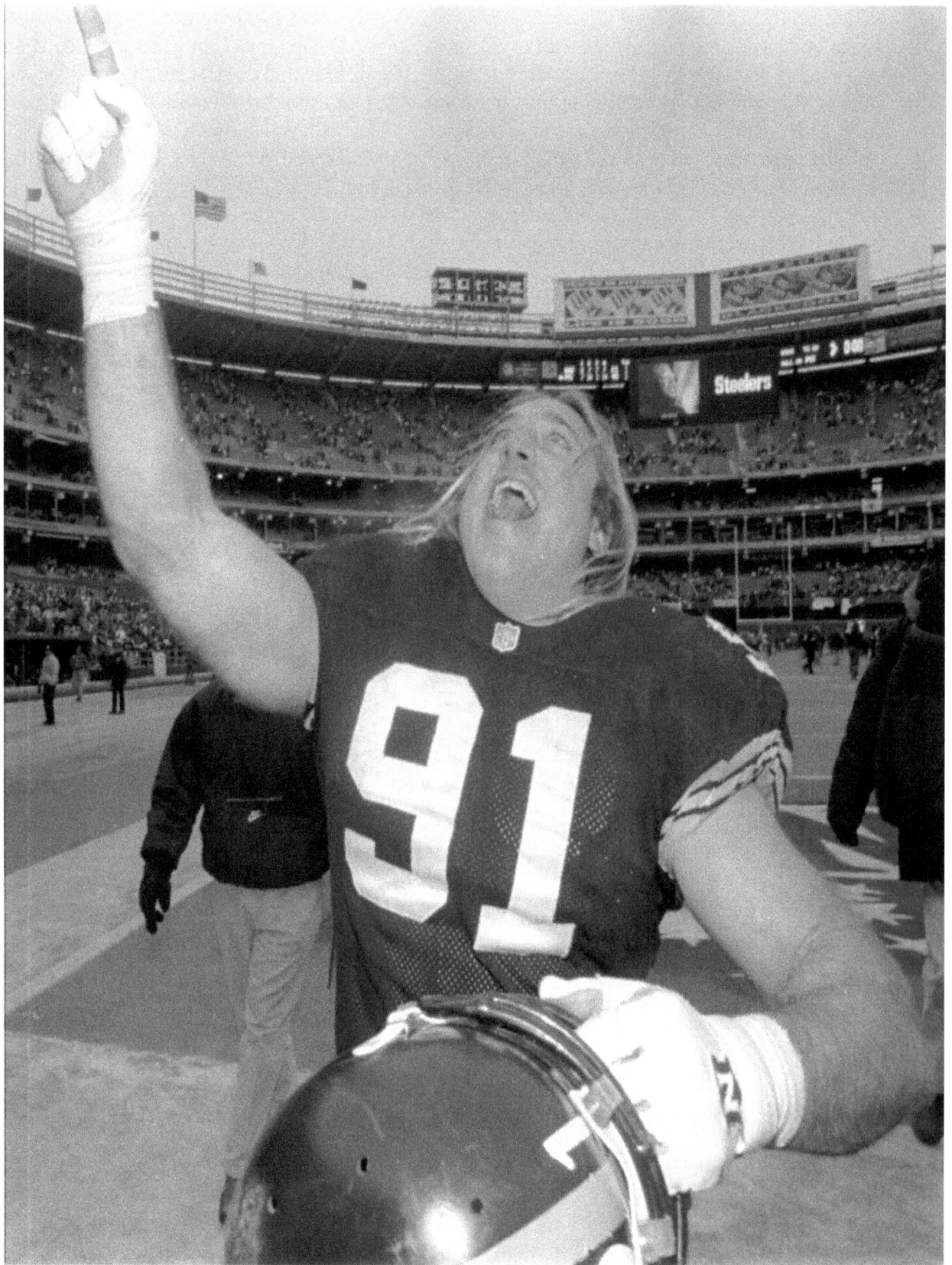

Photograph copyright Associated Press

Chapter 122

Bruce Smith

College:
Virginia Tech

Career History:
Buffalo Bills (1985–1999)
Washington Redskins (2000–2003)

2009 Inductee Pro Football Hall Of Fame

College Choice
There were a number of different factors that convinced me to attend Virginia Tech. Mainly, I wanted to stay in the state of Virginia, I wanted to be a part of something special, and I wanted to be close to my father who was ill at the time. Those were important factors for me. I wanted to be able to get home at a relatively quick pace if something happened to my father.

Ohio State, Michigan, you name the school, they were recruiting me. I had never been a great distance away from the state of Virginia and the city of Norfolk before, and I was really gun-shy about leaving the area.

Virginia Tech
As a kid growing up in Norfolk, Virginia I had never been on a plane before. Because I lived in a small town, I didn't know the world was so vast and worthy of being explored. So my first of many experiences was going to Virginia Tech. The first time riding on a plane, I was scared to death. Just the whole college experience was amazing—getting an education, being a student athlete and playing football at a level that I had never experienced before, and just making a lot of my dreams come true.

Virginia Tech was remarkable. Once again, I was part of something special. At that point, we were in an independent league and didn't get a great deal of respect, but it was big time college football; the atmosphere, the environment, the surroundings, the excitement of football, and some of the best athletes in the country. To be a kid who grew up and played sports in Norfolk, Virginia at Booker T. Washington High School, to be able to attend a major university, and become the number one pick in the 1985 draft after leading the nation in sacks two years in a row in 1983 and 1984, that speaks volumes. I accomplished this via goals that I set out to accomplish. I wanted to be a part of something special.

Winning Outland Trophy
Winning the Outland Trophy was certainly the icing on the cake after being a consensus All-American, on every All-American team that existed. It was certainly special winning the Outland Trophy.

When I went out to [I believe it was] Seattle and received the Outland Trophy, they had lost it. They could not find the Outland Trophy and years later, they had to make a replica and get it to me. It was the darndest thing I had ever heard of in my life. I was at the award ceremony and prior to that they had told me that they didn't have the actual trophy. Being a 20-year-old kid, I didn't understand how in the hell could you lose the Outland Trophy. Now that some years have passed Virginia Tech has a replica of the Outland Trophy sitting in their trophy room.

Draft
The Buffalo Bills were deciding between Ray Childress, who eventually went to the Houston Oilers, and me as the first pick in the draft. I think about two months prior to the draft they sat me down with my agent and said they were going to make me the number one pick in the NFL draft in 1985. It was a foregone conclusion on draft day. My walking out on stage and being announced as the first player picked, was just a formality. It was certainly something that was worked out well ahead of time, although the contract wasn't worked out.

The USFL's Philadelphia Stars tried to get me to come out of college after my junior year. They had my rights but it just wasn't enticing to me. I wanted to stay in school, continue my education, and finish out my senior year, which ended up being very enjoyable. It was just an exceptional time for me with my teammates, assistant coaches, and coach Bill Dooley.

Things were happening so quickly. I didn't understand the process of being drafted and all the expectations and the pressure that's placed on someone in that position. I was just happy to have the opportunity to do something I loved to do. I didn't realize the work ethic and the commitment it would take until my first year playing in the National Football League, My first year I had Kay Stephenson as head coach. We had six weeks of training camp. I never worked that hard and that long before in a training camp period.

Later that season, Hank Bullough came in and took over for Kay Stephenson. It was just an eye-opening experience for me. It helped to build my character and make me the person that I am today. I appreciate that opportunity, the hard work, and the lessons that were learned. I truly believe it's helped to put me in the position that I'm in today.

Marv Levy
When Marv Levy arrived it was like a breathe of fresh air. He wanted us to act like men and he treated us like men. He was very soft spoken and very rarely raised his voice. I probably can count on one hand the number of times he used a few choice words to get his point across. He was a constant professional, the perfect gentleman. I always tell people, Marv taught us how to be successful on the football field, but more importantly, he taught us how to be successful in the game of life. Those are the things that stick with you throughout your life. Your career in football is relatively short, but life itself and paying attention to details and the values is not. He taught us to not be late for meetings, to put in an honest day's work, to make sure we are prepared for any challenge or task, whether it is on Sunday or going to work on a day-to-day basis. It was just an incredible experience and learning lesson that I was taught by Marv Levy, and quite frankly, the whole coaching staff. I learned a great deal from MarvLevy.

Mentors With Bills

There were a number of guys. One gentleman who stands out is Ben Williams. He was very encouraging; he took me under his wing. One of the first things that I remember he told me was about the offensive lineman. He said, "If he can't grab you, he can't hold you." I took that, literally, to heart and I started working on things. I started to emulate the way he used his hands to keep an offensive lineman from holding him. I think that was one of the things that made me successful.

There was also Lucius Sanford, Darryl Talley, and a host of older guys taking the younger guys they saw had great potential, under their wings. It was a process for me, and I had to be committed. I had to work diligently and extremely hard. There was a nucleus of guys, coaches, teammates, and Rusty Jones, who handled the nutritional and conditioning aspects. When you put all those pieces together, in addition to my desire to be the best, that's when you create something special.

Playing In A 3-4 Defense

There was a constant double and an occasional triple team on pretty much every play. Teams can scheme against a 3-4 dominant defensive lineman a lot easier than they can in a 4-3 defensive system.

In a 3-4 defensive system, defensive front guys aren't known for getting a lot of sacks. They're known for getting a lot of tackles. It's rare a defensive end is able to get a lot of sacks and a lot of tackles for a long time in their career playing in a 3-4 defensive system. You just get beat up because there are double teams coming from all different angles and it just creates a lot of wear and tear.

First Mini-Camp In Buffalo

It was an eye-opening experience for me. It was roughly May 15, and I was walking out to the first mini-camp practice. The stadium is in the middle of the Snowbelt, right off of Lake Erie. I noticed the clouds in the distance and within 15 minutes it started raining, then it started hailing, then it snowed, and then the sun came out about 20 minutes later. I thought to myself, "What in the hell have I gotten myself into?" That was the lake effect snow in that particular region, and to be quite honest, I became quite fond of it after a short period of time because I enjoyed playing in the cold weather. I enjoyed playing in the elements. We used it to our advantage and it became a state of mind over matter. When we used to get teams from down South or out West that came to play against the Buffalo Bills, we knew we had that advantage.

Favorite Game

I think there are a number of games that actually stand out, but probably my favorite game was against the Houston Oilers. It's a great experience to watch that game to this very day and see the resilience, the overcoming of obstacles, and a group of guys who just would not quit. We were losing 28-3 at halftime. When we went into the locker-room, I remember Darryl Talley stood up and said to the guys, "Yeah, they think they're hot shit right now, but we've got them right where we want them." After halftime was over, we went back out and I believe the Houston Oilers only scored one touchdown and one field goal. We scored the remainder of the points. We ended up winning that game 41-38.

Buffalo Bills Transformation To Super Bowl Contender

The first sign of that was in 1986, when we were able to acquire Jim Kelly. The ownership and the front office made a committed effort to make a run. In 1985, they drafted Andre Reed and me. They already had Darryl Talley so we had a few bright stars. We needed to get a few more, and management was committed to doing that. In 1986, they went and got Jim Kelly. In 1987, they traded for Cornelius Bennett, and in 1988, they got Thurman Thomas. That was pretty much the nucleus of the team they would build around and we were off to the races. I think we all thrived and wanted to be a part of something special. We wanted to make the Bills something to cheer about and be proud about. Our mindset was to make this an enjoyable experience for western New Yorkers.

First Super Bowl

It was an incredible experience. The country was at the height of the Gulf War and there was a heavy military presence at the game. Whitney Houston sung the National Anthem. It was just an incredible atmosphere, one in which we thoroughly enjoyed. I wish we had come out on top. I wish we could have made the field goal, but it was still an incredible experience

That game could have gone either way. The first one is always the sweetest, so to speak. We had the ball in our court, but just missed the field goal. We win as a team and we lose as a team.

Comparison With Reggie White

My body of work speaks for itself; what I meant to the team, the contributions that I made, being the all-time sack leader against the odds of the double and occasional triple teams. I guarantee you that no one on that defensive line was double-teamed more than I was under that system. You can go to the 4-3 system or whatever type of system it is. I've even had conversations with Reggie White when he was alive and he said, "Bruce, if you ever played in a 4-3 system you would have never gotten touched," because he thought that highly of my athletic ability and the way that I was able to run.

We were two totally different players. Reggie was just a man-child. He was a powerful giant that had brute force. I was more on the athletic side. I could run, I used finesse, I had some power, but not as much as Reggie. Reggie was 295-300 pounds. I was more of a player that used my quickness, my speed, and my agility. We were two totally different players, but I have a great deal of respect for Reggie.

Deacon Jones Honoring Me

Deacon Jones had an event out in California to recognize me as being the All-Time NFL sack leader. Deacon and I were very good friends. I called him one time when I was in a slump. I hadn't had a sack in about five or six games. When I talked to him, he gave me advice and encouragement. I was honored to be among the greats in Bills history

I had a great relationship with Deacon. Certainly he didn't have to concede. I respected Deacon both on and off the field. He did acknowledge that I was the all-time sack leader.

Pro Football Hall Of Fame Induction

I was on cloud nine knowing that it wasn't necessarily just about me, it was about all the other people who played with me and took part in my reaching the pinnacle in my career. It was about my mother, father, sister, brother, my high school football and basketball coaches, Cal Davidson and Zeke Avery, and all of the other individuals who saw more in me than I saw in myself. They encouraged me, guided me, and taught me. It was just an incredible experience and opportunity for me to say, "Thanks to those individuals who believed in me and kept giving me the opportunities to succeed, and to Virginia Tech and Booker T. Washington High School." It was an opportunity to pay homage to them for what they did for me.

Bills Wall Of Fame Induction

That was exceptional as well, to be among the greats in Bills history. On the wall is Thurman Thomas, Ralph Wilson, Marv Levy, Jim Kelly, Bill Polian, Andre Reed ... the list just goes on. I'm just happy to have my name etched in stone in Ralph Wilson Stadium.

Photograph copyright Associated Press

Chapter 123

Charles Haley

College:
James Madison
Career History:
San Francisco 49ers (1986–1991)
Dallas Cowboys (1992–1996)
San Francisco 49ers (1998–1999)
2015 Inductee Pro Football Hall of Fame

College Choice
Initially my options were Liberty or James Madison. After the East-West All Star Game that I played in, other colleges wanted me. A big school middle linebacker was on the All Star team. I was also a middle linebacker, so I had to go play at my second position, which was tight end. I lit the other team up in the All Star Game, so schools were looking at me to play offense after that game. I wasn't gong to do that because I didn't like getting hit.

I'm one of those guys who didn't like being exposed on the field where I was going to get rocked. I took some big hits during that game and held onto the ball. I was ecstatic about going to James Madison. I think for me, a small town guy, going to James Madison was the perfect fit.

NFL Draft
People told me the 49ers and the Giants came down and looked at me. One thing I had going for me, was my 40-yard dash time. I was 6'4½" and weighed 200 pounds at the time, so I guess they saw something more than I saw.

As the draft came on, people were saying I was going to be drafted in the second or third round. When those two rounds finished, my girlfriend and I biked down to the movie theater and watched a movie. Then my roommate came down and said, "You've been drafted by the 49ers." I had no idea who played on the 49ers. All I knew was that I had to travel across the country and that was kind of frightening for me.

Bill Walsh
Bill Walsh was amazing. I still remember him up on stage giving a boxing analogy, telling us they hit the champ a couple of times but in the end, the champ knocks them out. When we go play, the other team is going to make some plays just like boxing champs, but we will win in the end.

The other thing that he did was, bring in great people who were winners, like Olympic gold medalists, singers, etc. They would talk about their journey and how they became great. For me, that was better than having somebody stand there, talking about things he had never done. When those people get up there and talk to you, it inspires you to be great.

He also brought back former players who had won a Super Bowl. I never thought that you weren't supposed to win playing football, because the expectation was always to win.

George Seifert

George Seifert micromanaged, but I loved him for that because he made me study. The Monday after every game, we studied for two and a half hours. We would go over everybody's position and everybody's responsibility. After about the third game, I sat there and learned every defensive alignment, as well as everybody's position on the field. That gave me the opportunity to take chances. Plus it empowered me. The more you know how other people are going to play, the better you can play.

Training

Ronnie Lott was fiery and led by example. I've never met anybody like that, or that intense. He took me under his belt and showed me the way. We did karate. He would show me how to do a lot of the drills and stuff. The best part about it was that I didn't train with the linebackers, I trained with the defensive backs. I trained with people who were faster than me and who had more of a skill set. My goal was not to get to that skill set, but to get as close to it as I could. Each time I did that it made me better.

I worked out with Roger Craig and Jerry Rice once. After about 30 minutes, I went home. They had flight jackets on, weights on, and they were just running. I was thinking, "Oh my God." I thought I could run, but nah, that wasn't for me. So I went back to doing the things that I could do to be great.

Nothing is easy. Every year I tore something or hurt myself. I never lifted weights. I don't know if that was the cause of it, but every year I played with pain. After a while, I could control the pain mentally. I didn't need pills or anything like that to control the pain. What I believe is, the more you can control your mind and control your breathing, the more you can be explosive and the longer you can stay on the field.

First Super Bowl

My first Super Bowl against Cincinnati was amazing. With about three minute left, we were losing, but we got the ball on the 8-yard line. The first play we got a holding call, so we were backed up farther. I was sitting over there thinking, "God, why did you bring me here to lose?"

I forgot that we had Jerry Rice, Roger Craig, Joe Montana, and Brent Jones. I was sitting there moping and ready to cry, and I heard the fans start cheering. I looked up and within about five or six plays, we were dancing and were the champions of the world. From that day on, I always believed in my teammates.

Joe Montana

Joe Montana was great. What made Joe great? Joe was not like any of the other quarterbacks who were stuck up, stuffy, and didn't want to talk to other players. Joe was an everyday guy. He played jokes on people did all kind of crazy things. He didn't make anybody feel small. We were all on the same line. He would get in the huddle when we were losing and tell jokes. He would get everybody's mind off of losing, and then we would go and win. One time he threw the ball and somebody hit him hard. The only thing he asked was if the player caught the ball. I've seen quarterbacks just go off because they got hit. I loved him, man. He was the best quarterback I've ever played with.

Edward DeBartolo

Eddie DeBartolo treated us like family. He took us to Maui. He's done many great things for players when things get rough for them. He takes care of them. I don't think anybody can ever measure up to Eddie D. Jerry Jones comes close to Mr. D, but Mr. D is in a class all by himself because of the way he treated players. He took care of them. His word meant something. When he said yes, it meant yes. I respect a man who makes a decision and is willing to stand behind it. That's the kind of man he is.

Trade To Dallas Cowboys

I was dejected. At one point I wanted to leave the 49ers and then when it came time for me to go, I had buyer's remorse. I didn't know what to expect. The best thing ever happened was Jerry Jones picking me up from the airport. He told me the vision that he had for the team. He told me what his expectations of me were. I never had an owner do that before. I bought in right then and there. He did not make you feel like you were beneath him. He is a great man.

When I walked into the practice facility, I saw Troy Aikman and Coach Jimmy Johnson. Troy was out on the field throwing the football. I said, "Troy, you ain't no Joe Montana." He was throwing the ball in those little three-hole things, way out there. He stepped back and threw it in the hole the first time.

I said, "Man, lightening can strike once." He went back and threw it right down the middle into the hole again. I shut up after that. I've said things to guys just to get underneath their skin. Sometimes you needed extra motivation to go out and do your job. I tried to provide that for guys.

I went out and did my job. I didn't need to talk trash. I let other people do it because that's what helps motivate some people. Nothing that somebody says can motivate me because I believe in who I am. I motivate myself. Whatever goals anybody set for me, I reached even higher. I don't believe that anyone should set a goal for another person. We should always over achieve.

I had great coaches. I was the luckiest guy in the world to have Bill Walsh, George Seifert, Jimmy Johnson, and Barry Switzer. It doesn't get any better than that.

Jimmy Johnson

Jimmy Johnson was great for me. He kept his foot on the guys' necks. I think he should be in the Hall of Fame because he took the youngest team to the Super Bowl twice and won. He might have done it three or four times if he continued as coach, but it didn't happen like that. Jimmy's motto was, "Repetition is the mother of learning", and we did a lot of repetition. If things didn't go right, he started the whole practice over. He trained us to be disciplined.

The bottom line is, the great Jimmy Johnson went out and the great Barry Switzer came in. You can't slight Barry because he's not Jimmy. Barry inherited the talent that Jimmy had left, but you still have to know how to deal with players and to motivate them year, after year, after year. After you win two Super Bowls, most of the time, guys lose their focus or you lose most of your talent to free agency.

Super Bowl XXX

I came back two weeks after major back surgery and played in Super Bowl XXX. I told the defense I'd never forsake them and I had to be a man of my word. I couldn't just leave them out there. I had to be a part of it. When I look back, maybe that was a selfish thing to do; maybe I should have taken the game off. My career would have lasted longer. I'd rather do what I did and have my career shortened than to sit there and watch my teammates lose, or not be a part of the winning.

Decision To Retire

If I had known then what I know now, I would have never gone back to the 49ers and played that year. The repercussion of that was that I had to get a back fusion. I had to get cages put in and that was probably the worst surgery I ever had. But, it was also the best surgery I ever had because I don't have the back pain any more. I'm happy the doctor performed it on me.

More Pressure Playing For Dallas Than San Francisco

The game is a game, is a game. Whether it's the Super Bowl, a playoff game, or the fourth game of the season, for me all of them are the same. It doesn't matter what team you play for, it's the standards that are set from the beginning. If high standards are set from the beginning, then they can't be lowered, they can only be raised higher.

Coaches dictate how players play. When you've got a fiery coach, you know you're going to have a team that is very determined. You have to look back at those things.

Bill Walsh was not a yeller. He didn't get on guys. He made guys become men by letting them make their own mistakes and their own choices. I don't like people telling me what to do, and he never did that. I would do dumb things to get in trouble and I would say, "Coach, why don't you just tell me what to do." He'd say, "You never ask."

I never thought about that. I never thought that all I had to do was ask somebody. I was always just doing it and taking control of my own destiny. I said, "Coach, that's all I've got to do?" And he said, "Yeah."

From that point on, I was not afraid to ask. I was never afraid to ask my D-line coach what I needed to do to be great. Most people are afraid to ask a coach what they need to do because they don't want to hear the answer.

Being In Cowboys Ring Of Honor

I never expected that. For me, I never expect anything and then the next thing I know I get it. Jerry said he couldn't spell Super Bowl without Charles Haley, so I guess he put his money where his mouth is when he put me in. Jerry is a man of his word. I don't know why he did it. It's like I tell people, I don't know why a lot of great people help me, but they do.

Not Wearing Super Bowl Rings

I'm not a flashy guy so I don't put my rings on. During my playing career, I never put them on because I always wanted to win another one. Now that my career is over, I want people to see me for who I am now, not just see me as a football player. I want them to meet the real Charles Haley. I want to be judged on what I'm doing now in my life and how I'm impacting the community, how I'm helping others. That for me, that's what it's all about.

Favorite Moment

Having my kids was my favorite moment. Just being there with them and taking them from California by myself, back home to Virginia. Just spending that time with them. That is the most important thing for me, family. It's always been family.

Toughest Offensive Lineman

Jackie Slater was the toughest offensive lineman I faced. I always did two things. I would always speed rush to get by guys, and would beat them on the inside. Then I would power rush in that combination.

One game during my rookie year I played against Jackie. I did a couple of speed rushes on him, and then I went to the power rush. When I power rushed Jackie, he hit me with his head and my head went backward. My knees hit the ground and I saw Jesus Christ in all three forms. I went to the sideline and sat down on the other side of the bench. I put my helmet where I couldn't find it. I did not want to go back out there. I was sitting down evaluating whether I should be in this game or not. That gave me a little time, five or six minutes, to get myself together. I went back on the field.

The thing I learned to do is use my speed. I just put my speed on Jackie because he couldn't handle that. I didn't try to muscle him anymore from that day on. I picked my poison. Guys that did the head butt stuff … I didn't power rush those guys, I used quickness.

That time I got hit, I went on my knees to pray, "Good Lord, God help me." He said get off the field then, and I ran up off of it.

San Francisco 49er Charles Haley rushes Falcons quarterback Chris Miller. Photograph copyright Associated Press

Chapter 124

Andre Reed

College:
Kutztown University

Career History:
Buffalo Bills (1985–1999)
Denver Broncos (2000)
Washington Redskins (2000)

2014 Inductee Pro Football Hall Of Fame

College Choice
Coming out of high school I just thought I'd go to school locally. Kutztown University had a pretty good football program and was a good academic school. I was a homebody. I look back on it now, and it probably was the best thing for me. I could have gone to a bigger school and tried to walk on the football team, but you never know what could have happened.

Kutztown University is in eastern Pennsylvania. It's about an hour and a half to two hours outside of Philadelphia. It's a small Division 2 school. If you look at a lot of NFL rosters now, there's a lot of D2 kids on NFL rosters. Back in the day it wasn't like that, you just didn't see them on NFL rosters. Some former D2 players are NFL Pro Bowlers.

Draft
I was projected to be drafted between rounds 3-6. Back then there were twelve rounds in the draft instead of the seven that they have now.

On the first day of training camp, there were 125 guys on the practice field. I think now you can only have 90 players. So that's thirty-five more players that were on the field, which diminished players' chances of making the team. But, times change, things change, and that's how it was.

Position Change From High School Quarterback To College Wide Receiver
When I got to Kutztown they had a pretty good quarterback there that was an All-American. He was a senior and they had a guy behind him that was a junior. Coming in as a freshman who knew if I was going to get any playing time or not. I got some great advice from people at Kutztown. They saw me in high school and saw that I could handle the ball, and do all of that stuff. They wanted to know if I could catch the ball. I said, "Yeah, anything to help the team. If I can get on the field and play, I would love to contribute any way I can." The offensive coordinator at the time, asked me if I would make the switch to wide receiver and I said, "For sure." That obviously was the best switch I ever made.

Marv Levy

The Bills were in transition and they just had back-to-back 2-14 seasons. They hadn't been in the playoffs since the 1981 season, and there was a change being made. I think bringing Marv Levy in as head coach that fourth game of the year was the change that the team needed.

Marv was just a good guy. I think he was more than a coach, he was kind of like a father figure. He really had a great rapport with his players and that was the good thing about it.

Jim Kelly

Jim Kelly had a great career with Houston Gamblers. He was a very feisty guy. From day one, when he was in the huddle he demanded respect. You knew that he wanted to get stuff done. You look at some quarterbacks in their eyes, and it's like a deer in the headlights. Jim was a guy confident in his ability. You need that in a guy that's pulling the trigger. We believed in him. We had a bunch of good players around him in Thurman Thomas, Bruce Smith, and Darryl Talley. We just had a lot of good players at the right time.

No-Huddle Offense

The Bills coaches saw what Jim Kelly did in the USFL, how he threw for all those yards and had all those weapons. Ted Marchibroda was very instrumental in us starting to use the no-huddle offense.

One game we were losing and we just started saying, "Hurry up, hurry up." We ended up scoring a lot and almost won the game. We came back the next week and Ted was asked, "Why don't we do this all the time and put people on their heels all the time?" That's when all that started. We started running teams out of the stadium because they couldn't keep up with the pace.

Sometimes the defense hated the no-huddle. They said, "Man you guys are scoring too quick. We just rested for five minutes and we're back on the field." My response was, "Well, our job is to score, and your job is to stop them from scoring."

Success Running After The Catch

There are a bunch of keys why I was successful running after the catch. As a high school quarterback, we ran an option type of offense. I was able to handle the ball a lot and run with the ball. My college coaches saw that and when I went to college, they wanted to try and get the ball in my hands as quick as possible. That's when it all started. When I got to Buffalo, they gave me even more chances to do that.

I really worked on being strong, breaking tackles, and all that kind of stuff. It was really important to me the way I trained in the offseason to get ready for that. Our offense changed when Tim Marchibroda came. I had to be in the middle a lot and take a lot of hits. I had to be physically fit to do all that stuff. Again, I had some great teammates, great people behind me that made me better and vice-versa. What it comes down to is they gave me the opportunity to do everything. Again, just really taking pride in what I like to do and never being satisfied. That was a big key, definitely.

"The Comeback" (Houston Oilers vs. Buffalo Bills Playoff Game)

I think we had to get something going because we had a great crowd. Our 12th man was probably one of the best, if not the best, in the game. We figured if we got a little bit going and the crowd got into it, we would start to make something happen. Plus, the Houston Oilers were making some mistakes. It's how you capitalize on the other person's mistake. We capitalized on every mistake the Oilers made and we turned it into points. The Oilers got a little complacent and that's what happens, you end up losing the game.

Toughest Cornerback

I can't say one guy or another, all of them were tough. You wouldn't be there playing that position if you weren't a pretty good player.

Playing Last Season For Redskins

I was with the Redskins for one year, the bulk of my career and accomplishments were in Buffalo. I always will be a Bill and remember that. I'm sure if you ask some of these other Hall of Famers, like Joe Montana who played the bulk of his career in San Francisco and he ended up in Kansas City. He's probably a 49er for life. I'm no different.

Not Winning A Super Bowl

Unfortunately we didn't win a Super Bowl. That's the way I look at it. That's what you play the game for, to get to the Super Bowl and win it. Some guys haven't even gotten to a Super Bowl, or to a playoff game, so that's really what your goal should be. When you step on that field in July, you want to be playing in that last game, at the Super Bowl.

I was blessed to be on that stage four years in a row, I don't think that is ever going to happen again. The outcome didn't turn out the way I wanted it to. If you look at those games, we have five Hall of Famers from those games. Obviously they think that the team was, not only individually what we did, but they think the team was very, very instrumental in changing the game at that time. We were pretty hard to contend with at the time. Opposing teams had to go through Buffalo most of the time during those years.

Pro Football Hall Of Fame Induction

The emotion was very, very ... it was a long wait, put it that way. I've told people, I'm very humbled by the accolade. I was only as good as the people around me. I respected the process of the Hall of Fame and how they pick people. It's so hard to pick five guys out of, what do they start with, one hundred twenty-five guys? It's hard to pick five and say, "Okay, these five are better than those one hundred twenty." I think if you're nominated you're just as deserving as anybody else. I'm glad to be with my teammates and to be part of the greatest team ever assembled, and that's the Pro Football Hall of Fame. If you were to ask me in high school if I would be a Hall of Famer in the NFL, I would have probably laughed at you a few times.

This is what God made and God gave me the ability. I tried to work it and I think I worked it pretty good for him. Now it's time to be an Ambassador for the Hall of Fame, and be an Ambassador for kids and say, "Hey, you can do it. There's no limit to your ability. If you work hard, you can achieve the goals you want."

<u>Reason Chose Marv Levy As His Presenter For Hall Of Fame Induction</u>
Marvin Levy was my presenter. He's done a few. I thought about Bill Polian who is a great speaker and a heck of a GM. Jim Kelly was another possibility. It's not that Marv beat those two guys out. I think Marv is such an eloquent guy and really knows me as a player, what I'm made up of, and how I went about things. I'm honored to have him, not only as a former coach of mine, but he's a Hall of Famer too, so he knows what that's about.

Buffalo Bills wide receiver Andre Reed and teammate Keith McKeller celebrate Reed's third touchdown during the fourth quarter of "The Comeback" playoff game against the Houston Oilers. Photograph copyright Associated Press

Chapter 125

Randall McDaniel

College: Arizona State Career History: Minnesota Vikings (1988–1999) Tampa Bay Buccaneers (2000–2001) 2009 Inductee Pro Football Hall Of Fame

College Choice
I was born and raised in Arizona. I always figured if I ever had the opportunity to go to college and play football at the school, it would be at Arizona State. They gave me that opportunity and I took it and ran with it.

There were other colleges more interested in me playing basketball than football, because I played both in high school. All I wanted to do was stay at home and go to Arizona State. So when Darryl Rogers gave me a call and said they were going to offer me a football scholarship, I immediately jumped on that.

Arizona State Tradition
There have been a lot of great players who came through ASU. It was nice to follow in that tradition and get an opportunity to play there and continue the tradition the Sun Devils have out there.

Position Change At Arizona State
When I went to college I was a tight end. I played my first year as a tight end. Then during my second year, I switched from tight end to guard and started from game six on. When the offensive line was struggling, they were holding tryouts for spots along the way. I just wanted the opportunity to play and show what I could do on the field. I threw my hat into the ring and it worked out for me. I got in there, started playing, and I never looked back from that point on.

Changing positions wasn't that bad. The tight ends at ASU caught passes a lot, but they did a lot of run blocking also. My strength as a tight end at that time was run blocking. I thought I could block just about anyone they put in front of me. Then, I had an unfair advantage when I moved from tight end to guard because I was a lot quicker than all of the defensive linemen around. My speed helped out there too. I did power lifting along the way through high school and college. So I was just as strong as everybody else. I just wasn't as big as everybody else, but I could still get the job done.

Playing Basketball At Arizona State

I thought about playing basketball at ASU for a little bit, but when you've got Byron Scott out there on the team and some other guys, I figured football was going to be the better sport for me.

I knew all the guys who played on the ASU basketball team. I'd be out there playing pick up games before their practices and before our practices. I thought about doing both, but I figured I should concentrate on just football and get that done.

Transition To Minnesota Vikings

I had somewhat of an idea what it was going to be like to play in the NFL. ASU had guys who were drafted before me, like David Fulcher and some of the other guys that I played with. So I had an idea about it. I knew it wasn't going to be easy. I knew I had to work at it. I knew I had a lot of studying to do and had to learn to watch film. The transition went pretty smoothly.

I had a lot of great veterans on the offensive line when I came in. Kirk Lowdermilk, Gary Zimmerman, Tim Irwin, and all those guys who were the veterans back then, worked with me. They would tell me, "You're going to do it our way until you can do it better." They taught me a ton. I was very fortunate to join an established group. I just had to mesh with them, and I did.

Back then, first round picks didn't start a lot. You had to earn your way into the starting lineup. Even with all the expectations on you, you still had to earn it. I remember sitting on the field one day and my coach was chewing me out. He offered me a bus ticket, a road map, and an apple. I thought I was gone.

You really knew when you got in there you were prepared. You knew what to expect. You knew the defenses. You knew what was going to happen if they shifted, before they shifted. So when I got that opportunity to step in the second game of that year, I never looked back. Once I got an opportunity to get in, I knew it was my job to lose and that's the way I played for all 14 years. It was my job to lose, so I went out and made sure I kept it.

Minnesota Vikings Defensive Line

We had some great defensive linemen; Keith Millard, John Randle, Henry Thomas, and Al Noga were there. I started with Doug Martin who was there toward the end of his career. Practice was like playing a game. So when you got to the game, it was like, I can take a breath now and have a little more fun.

Keith Millard and all those guys used to try to watch film of our practice so they could beat you in practice. In turn, we watched film on them and thought about what I needed to do to make sure Keith Millard, then later on John Randle, didn't have a good day in practice.

That was a nightmare. I actually told John after I retired that I hated practicing against him. I did whatever it took to make sure he couldn't get a rush or beat me in anything. If he were going to beat me, I would literally hold him and yank him down, and be like hey, you're never going to get there. It made the games so much easier. I give John and all those guys credit. They made practice fun. The work that I put into practice made the games a lot easier for me.

I think a lot of the guys used to wait to see John Randle and I go against each other at practice just to see what would take place. It got heated at times. At the end of each practice, we would both walk off the field and talk about it. We knew all we were going to do was make each other better, so we'd do it again tomorrow, and every day after. It just made both of us better.

There were times that there was no talking between us after plays. It was like okay, I got to get back at him for what he just did or he'll do the same thing. So it made for a rough day at practice sometimes, but when the games rolled around, whoever I was playing against, whoever he was playing against, we both kind of went okay, it's not against each other anymore so let's just take it out on somebody else.

John Randle's Trash Talking
I had an unfair advantage over him because I established myself early in practice against him during his rookie year. It was probably during one of those times when we got in a heated moment and I just made sure he knew I was in charge. I think that kind of stuck throughout our careers, but he never talked trash on me.

I know when I went to Tampa Bay for the last two years of my career, I thought he would talk trash, but he didn't do it. I tried to play head games with him telling him that I didn't have to hold back anymore. I said, "We're not teammates. I can finally just let it loose and finally go after you without holding back." He took it out on the other guard on the other side so it worked out.

Playing In 12 Straight Pro Bowls
I wasn't thinking about making the Pro Bowl when I made it after my second year in the league. All I was thinking about was the play at hand and doing well. When it happened, then it was okay, can I do it again? Can I put the work in to do it one more time? Each year it was always, can I get better to get back?

My wife said since I brought her to this arctic tundra Minnesota, I had to take her to some place warm every year in return. At the Pro Bowl she said, "You got to get me back to Hawaii." I could say I was playing for my wife, to make sure she got back to Hawaii every year.

I made a lot of friends along the way in Hawaii. I met a lot of people in Hawaii whom I still keep in contact with today. It was a good vacation. It was a good time to go see friends. It was always fun to play in the Pro Bowl.

Jerry Burns
Burnsy? I love him. He reminded me of Burgess Meredith. He was the Vikings head coach when I first met him. I learned a ton from him those first pro years. To this day, I owe Burnsy for taking a chance on [drafting] me. I was called the undersized lineman, and I was brought inwhen they didn't want to bring in a lineman. I owe Burnsy a lot for my career—giving me a start and an opportunity.

Dennis Green

Dennis Green was my head coach for eight years. The team did well. I finished my career in Tampa Bay with Coach Tony Dungy. I had a few different coaches along the way. You pick up what you can from each one and take it with you, and that's what I did.

John Michels

My first offensive line coach with the Vikings was John Michels. When I went into the Hall Of Fame, I'd made sure Johnny was there with me. I would say that he's the one who offered me the bus ticket, the roadmap, and the apple. I could've sworn I was going to be cut every day. Even when I started playing, I was still the person who took the brunt of the criticism in the meeting room because I was the young guy on the line. Johnny would go to battle for you, though. No one could talk about his offensive line. No one could yell at his offensive linemen, no one could get in his offensive line.

Basically, Johnny would just step up and do the job, but he made you learn. You had to know every defense against every situation and what the play could be. To this day, I still call him up and we talk. He actually chews me up for the first five or ten minutes of our conversation just to let me know he can still do it. He is amazing. Johnny, his wife Ann, and all his kids … I still do stuff with his daughters who live here in Minnesota. John Michels is the coach that I owe a lot to.

Toughest Defensive Lineman

Besides my teammates, Jerome Brown was the toughest defensive lineman. He used to give me headaches. He is probably the one player I would watch even more film of than I normally would, just to make sure he wasn't going to have the upper hand on me. He was the first big guy inside, but he'd be considered small today. He was about 300 pounds, but he had size, speed, and quickness. He reminded me of John Randle, just a little bigger, and he used to give me headaches. I would never tell him that. After the game we'd talk and everything, but during the game it was all business.

Rich Gannon

Rich Gannon was a good player. He was a good student of the game too. He was that way when he was with the Vikings. He just didn't get the opportunity in Minnesota with everything going on.

When he went to the Raiders, he did what I knew he could do all along. He just got that opportunity and he ran with it. Gannon was fun. He ran when he was with us. He used to take off with the ball a little more. He was a student at the game, always studying, and always prepared. So it didn't shock me when he went to the Raiders and did what he did.

Prefer Run Blocking Or Pass Blocking

I preferred run blocking. I loved it when I could impose my will on the other guy. That's how you wear them down. You get to go out and pound defensive lineman for 70 or 80 plays a game. By the end of the of the game, if you were run blocking more than pass blocking, it took a lot out of the defensive linemen. You had to be able to pass block, but if I had my choice, I'd rather run block any day of the week.

I'll admit it now, I held on every play. If the defensive linemen were foolish enough to let me get my hands inside and put them where I needed to, I'd really put my hands in there.

It is easier to work with your hands a little more in run blocking because you've got more body, more surface. You try to get the defensive linemen to go where they don't want to go, but you can work the hands a lot more on the run blocking.

Favorite Running Back To Block For

I loved blocking for Robert Smith, Smitty. I don't know how fast that guy really was. It was like he was never going all out with the stride that he had. Robert was a great one to block for. I enjoyed it. I knew that if an offensive lineman opened a hole up, and in that brief moment, if Robert got through it, no one was going to run him down. Robert was fun to watch for that.

I loved watching Terry Allen for his toughness. He'd bang it in there between the tackles and he tried to punish people. Between those two though, I'd go with Robert Smith.

Randy Moss

It didn't have to be an open field, Randy Moss just ran by everybody. I don't think anyone was quick enough to keep up with him. He came out in his rookie year in 1998, and introduced himself to the world. The guy was fun to watch. He had about 17 touchdowns as a rookie. He was just amazing.

I think that was the same year we set the scoring record. Moss changed the game. We had power receivers with speed. They could go deep. Moss was a game changer.

Pro Football Hall Of Fame Induction

I experienced a little bit of all the emotions: I was excited, humbled, and honored when I found out I was selected. It's something you don't plan for and never expect. You just go out and play and do what you do. I enjoyed my 14 years playing in the NFL, but to get that phone call on that day was something else. It still feels like it just happened yesterday.

Being in the Hall, I'm in a place where I don't think I belong. I can sit down and ask Tom Mack questions about what he did with Ram's back in the day. He can tell me all about Deacon Jones, if Deacon's not there to say it himself. I get to hear all the stories about Merlin Olsen. Then I can sit with Gale Sayers, Earl Campbell, and all those guys.

What a thrill it is just to be sitting in a room with all that history there and listening to their stories. It's been quite an honor. I still can't believe that I'm there, and I'm in there with them. You sit there with guys you played with and guys you sat and watched play with your dad beside you.

When I was inducted, my dad got to come to the Hall with my family. The most fun was when my dad was in the hotel with me, and all of the other Hall Of Fame players. My dad and I would meet every morning at six a.m. after I had my workout. I would ask him if he got the autographs that he was looking for. He would say, "Yes." I then asked, "Did you get them to sign twice?" He responded, "Yes. I got yours, too." My dad was collecting autographs for me too, and the guys did realize it. Some guys told me, "Your dad keeps asking us for two autographs." I responded, "Well, yeah, one's for me."

It was fun. It's fun to be around those guys. Any opportunity I have, whether it's a charity event or somewhere where there are more than five or ten Hall Of Famers, I just sit back and listen to them tell stories. It's fun to hear how they played and what they did. They're the ones who paved the way for all of us, and the young kids now playing. I owe them a ton for what they did and what they sacrificed to make the game what it is today.

Offensive Linemen Are The Smartest Players

Everybody says it's the quarterback who is the smartest player, but a lot of times the quarterback can't make his calls until the center and the line set the blocking. The quarterback can point everything out, but the linemen have to know just as much as the quarterback. We have to know who's blocking whom. We have to know where the help's coming from, where the help's not coming from. We have to see it before they see it. Then we have to do it all as one guy, five guys moving as one. It's fun seeing five guys who don't have to talk, working together. Sometimes you make your calls for the other guys so they know where they're supposed to go, but then nothing needs to be said from that point on. It's snapping the ball and everybody is working in unison. When you get a line that's been together, you can do that. It's just a fun thing to watch.

Decision To Retire (Next Season Tampa Bay Buccaneers Win Super Bowl)

I've always been one of those guys who once my decision is made, I don't look back. Playing in the NFL for fourteen years was good enough for me. I was ready to go. My body was ready to go. I told myself I was going to walk away while the game was still fun, while I could still do the things that I loved to do, and that's what I did. I have no regrets.

I called Jeff Christy the night they won the Super Bowl and left him a message. I got a phone call the following day at three in the morning, with him screaming and yelling. He said, "I know I woke you up, but I just had to let you know, you should've been here." I said, "Jeff, I'm not supposed to be there. I'm where I'm supposed to be right now." I let him know I enjoyed what he did. I got to play with those guys for that long, so I had no regrets I walked away when I walked away.

When I retired, I told the team they should go ahead and win the Super Bowl. They had a good team coming back. Jon Gruden had come in as head coach and they were changing some things around. I told them they had a great opportunity, so they shouldn't waste it. They went on and did what they were supposed to do.

Favorite Player Growing Up

I'm going to get in trouble. When I was a tight end in high school and during my first year of college, I loved watching Kellen Winslow. Then, I got to meet him and do events with him. That was fun.

When I was in middle school, I did a book report on Gale Sayers. Now, I'm sitting at a table with him, poking Tom Mack, and telling him, "That's Gale Sayers sitting next to me!"

I have done some events with Earl Campbell. One time I was in Austin, Texas, expecting to take a cab to the next event. Here comes Earl with his brother-in-law. They picked me up themselves.

Bob Lilly, Mr. Cowboy, is one of my dad's favorites. I've gotten to do stuff with him and John Hannah, the guard of all guards. I really don't have one particular favorite. There are a lot of favorites, but if I had to pick one, I'm going to get me in trouble, I'll go with Earl Campbell. It's been fun just getting to know him and the things that he did, as well as the things he's doing now. It's just a thrill to be around him.

Starting 202 Consecutive Games
I thank the good Lord above for looking out for me. I was a kid who never missed a day of school, from kindergarten thru 12th grade. When my brother and I would go out and play games we could both run into a wall, but I was the one who would get up and laugh about it. The good Lord is looking after me. I have been fortunate and I worked hard. I loved working out, I loved being prepared, and I loved being ready. I still workout now. I'm just blessed. I have been fortunate to have the right opportunities and things with my wife. There were times I didn't think I was going to be able to play, but somehow someone was looking out for me and I was able to play.

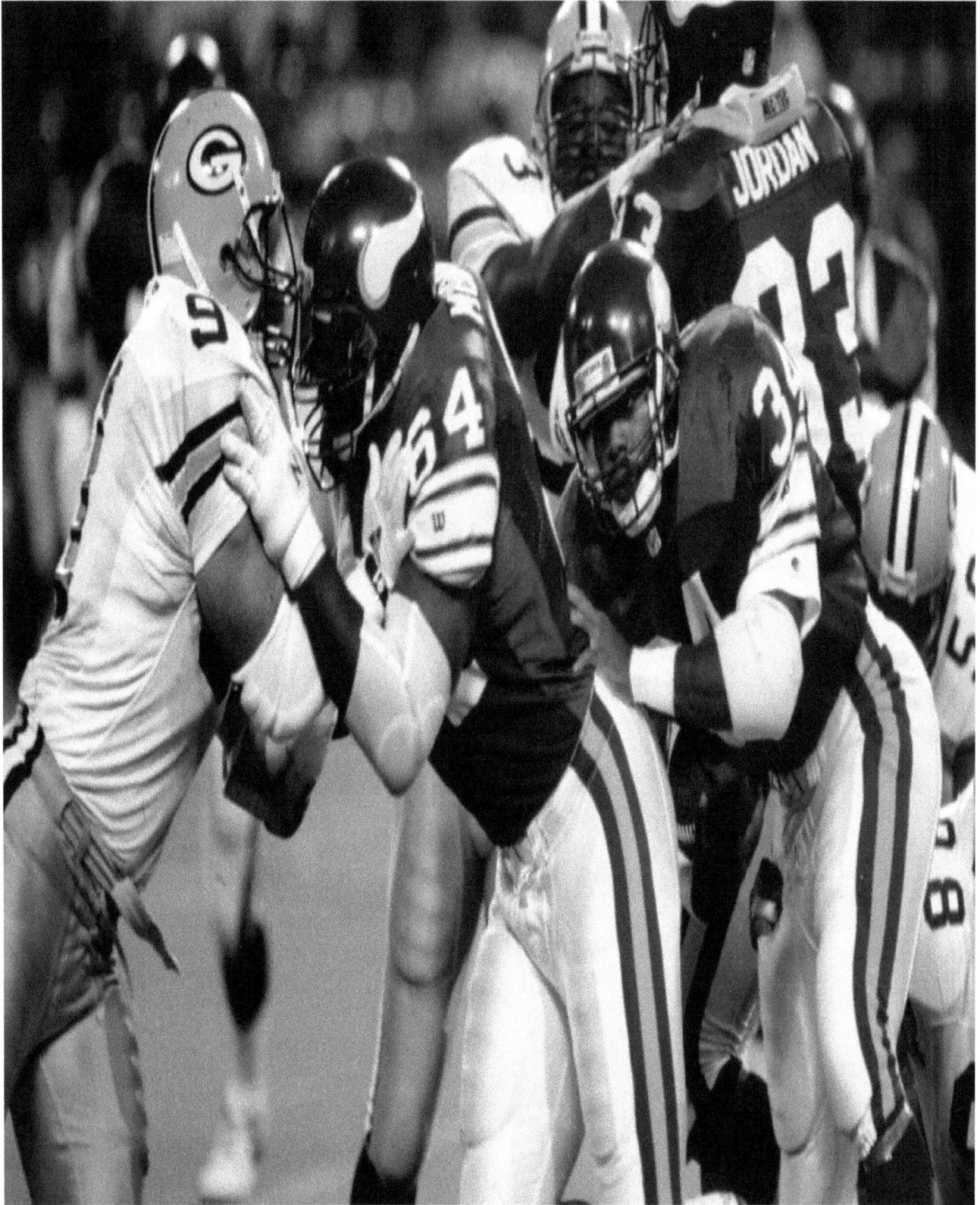

Minnesota Viking guard Randall McDaniel blocks for running back Herschel Walker.
Photograph copyright Associated Press

Chapter 126

Dermontti Dawson

College:
Kentucky

Career History:
Pittsburgh Steelers (1988–2000)

2012 Pro Football Hall Of Fame Induction

Bryan Station High School Football

I played football during my ninth grade year. I was on the team, but I didn't play in any games. I was basically a practice dummy. I really didn't care too much for football. Of course, after that I said, "No football for me."

Right before my senior year, Steve Parker was hired as the football coach at my high school, Bryan Station Senior High in Lexington, Kentucky. I was coming out of chemistry or biology, and he had mistaken me for an adult or one of the parents. He said, "Sir, can I help you?" I said, "I attend school here." He said, "Huh?" He put his hands on my shoulders and said, "Where have you been all my life? Son, you need to play football."

He was the one who convinced me to go out for football. Then he had two of my buddies who were on the track team with me, Marc Logan and Cornell Burbage, convince me to go out and try out for football. I did and the rest is history. Marc and Cornell played in the NFL as well.

We lost in the state playoffs against Christian County. They went on after they beat us, and won the state championship. We had a pretty good team. It's just we were outmanned against Christian County because they had so many players on that team. They had separate everything, separate special teams, separate defense, and separate offense. They were like a college team when they came to our school to play us in the playoffs. I couldn't believe it.

College Choice

Like a lot of us in high school, we have somebody that we are in love with—a girlfriend. I was a year ahead of my girlfriend in school. We wanted to be together. I said, "The only way it's going to work out is if we both go to Kentucky." So, that's how I ended up at Kentucky. We were married for 23½ years, and then got a divorce a few years ago.

Reason Named Dermontti

My dad's younger sister had naming rights of all the kids. She was the biggest influence on my mom. All my brothers have DD as initials. I'm the oldest, Dermontti Dawson, then Demarcus Dawson (four years younger), Deshawn Dawson (ten years younger and born on the same day as me), and then there's Deaaron Dawson (eleven years younger).

Kentucky
The football, track, and baseball teams all stayed in the same dorm. We stayed in the low-rise Kirwan Complex. We didn't have the walk-in lodge. That was for the basketball team. They had a pretty laid out little pad there on campus. We weren't privy to that.

I was redshirted as a freshman at Kentucky. The biggest difference that I saw between high school and college football was the physical part of it. I was about 250 pounds and the college guys were much larger, stronger, and faster than me. It was just a much faster and more physical game than what I was used to in high school, and the athletes were much better.

Replacing Mike Webster At Center
I was drafted as a guard and ended up starting in the fourth game of my rookie year beside Mike Webster. During the off-season after my rookie year, Coach Chuck Noll came up to me and said he wanted me to try me at center. He wanted Chuck Lanza, a third-round draft choice in 1988, and me to fight it out, to see who was going to take over Mike's position. We battled it out in mini-camp and training camp. At a certain point in training camp, I was named the starter.

I really didn't have time to think about the pressure in replacing Mike. I think the media made more fuss about it than I did. Mike was in his 15th year in the league, and was a legend in Pittsburgh. Of course, those are big shoes for anybody to fill.

I really didn't put any pressure on myself. I kept telling the media, "Just give me time to learn the position and go from there. Let me get settled in and just go from there." I did not put any pressure on myself because there was already enough pressure on me from everybody else. Why should I have put more pressure on myself? All I was going to do was learn the offense, learn the center position, and just go from there.

Playing Center For Different Quarterbacks
The voice inflection of all quarterbacks is different. It's just something that you get used to the more you work with the guy. Your hand position, the way they like the ball delivered to them, all of that stuff is a factor. Making the switch from one quarterback to another is a simple fix and not a hard transition. As long as the quarterback knows how you snap it, then you can accommodate him. It's not a big transition to a new quarterback.

Chuck Noll
I look up to Chuck Noll in awe because of who he was and what he accomplished as a coach. He was a very knowledgeable man about various subjects, and a great guy. He was one of those guys who had accomplished everything football-wise, in his life. I was just in awe and very, very proud that I had the chance to play under his coaching for four years.

Bill Cowher
The difference between Coach Cowher and Coach Noll was that Coach Noll had pretty much accomplished everything. Coach Noll was calm and relaxed. He would get upset every now and then, and let you know about his displeasure. Coach Cowher came in and he was much younger, not too much older than I was at the time. He still had that fire in his belly for the game. Not to say Coach Noll didn't have that fire, but it was a different kind of enthusiasm. Coach Cowher

was right in the mix with all of the guys. He was running sprints right in the middle of a drill, yelling and screaming. He was just into it. He was a great coach to play for. I had the pleasure of playing nine years for Coach Cowher. All I can say is, it was a pleasurable nine years.

Uniform Number Not Reissued
The Steelers don't officially retire uniform numbers, but my number hasn't been reissued since I retired. It's a great honor for somebody not to have been assigned my number after I finished. That says a lot about the Steelers organization and how they embrace guys who have done well over their career. It's a big honor that nobody has been issued my number, but I wouldn't be mad if someone wore it.

To have your number not reissued to another player, is a sign of respect for the player who gave his all throughout his career. It's a big honor.

Favorite Moment In NFL
My favorite moment in the NFL was after we won that AFC Championship game against the Colts and we were going to play in Super Bowl XXX. It was always a dream of mine to play in the Super Bowl. Even though we lost the Super Bowl, we made it there. We didn't accomplish what we wanted, which was to win, but we made it there.

I thought that we would get back to the Super Bowl, but it was so hard. I don't care how well or how much success you have during a season, there is no guarantee that you're going to make it. There are so many different variables that play a role in making the playoffs or Super Bowl.

I was surprised we didn't play in another Super Bowl because we had a good run and played in AFC Championship Games. We lost two AFC Championship Games, then we finally won the one against the Colts. I thought we had a chance to make another run, unfortunately, it didn't happen.

Pro Football Hall Of Fame Induction
I found out I was selected for the Pro Football Hall Of Fame right before the selection show. The protocol was you needed to be by your phone right before the show came on. They would call you and let you know that you made it as an inductee.

I didn't find out until the selection show itself, after Jack Butler's name was announced. Stephen Perry, the President of the Pro Football Hall of Fame was announcing the inductees and then he announced me. I was in pure shock. I just couldn't believe it and then my phone went haywire— phone calls, texts. I had a massive amount of calls and texts coming in.

Canton was special the year I was inducted. It was great to see all the Steelers fans out there. It was even more special for Pittsburgh, since there were four guys associated with Pittsburgh in one way or another who were inducted. That year, Curtis Martin, Chris Doleman, Jack Butler, and I were inducted. There was a ton of black and gold at that Hall of Fame induction.

Being enshrined is not something that you deserve. It's something that is rewarded to you based on your play, longevity, and consistency. It's an honor to be named and enshrined in the Pro

Football Hall of Fame with some of the great players that I looked up to, and some of the guys that I respect to this day. It's just a great honor.

Technique Of Pulling From The Center Position
It really makes me feel old when guys say, "Our coach used to show us tapes of you playing to teach us how to pull from the center position." It's flattering that they use my tape as an example of what they want to accomplish on offense. It's a humbling experience and an honor as well.

Decision To Retire
It's always tough when you consider playing for another team. I think it's even tougher when it's not on your own accord. I had to retire due to an injury. Even after the Steelers cut me, I still had trainers who knew about my condition say, "We just want you to play on Sundays. We're not worried about you practicing in training camp." I said, "That's flattering, but I just don't think I can do it anymore."

At that time, I wasn't going to move my family. I didn't want to go thru all the pain and stuff that I'd suffered through with the hamstring tendon. To this day, my hamstrings still hurt and ache 24/7. I didn't want to have that be a burden on another team.

Photograph copyright Associated Press

Chapter 127

Thurman Thomas

```
College:
Oklahoma State

Career History:
Buffalo Bills (1988–1999)
Miami Dolphins (2000)

2007 Inductee Pro Football Hall Of Fame
```

College Choice

Growing up in Texas, I wanted to go to the University of Texas. At the time, Fred Akers was the head coach. When I walked into his office and we started talking, his exact words were, "We're all set at the running back position. We'd love for you to play defensive back." I knew being 5'9½" there was no way that I was going to play defensive back. I left that meeting scratching my head because my idol, Earl Campbell, went to University of Texas and I followed them throughout my years in junior high and high school.

So, I went to Texas A&M next, where Jackie Sherrill was the head coach. I felt this has got to be the place in Texas for me. Jackie said the same thing, that he wanted me to play defensive back. So, I was thinking I have to go somewhere where they want me to play running back.

I got a call from Jimmy Johnson at Oklahoma State asking me to take a visit. I went there and Jimmy said to me, "I heard that Texas and Texas A&M want you to play defensive back. Well, I'll tell you what. If you come here you're going to be 6th in line for the running back position, and it's up to you to work your way up." I said "Coach, you've got a deal. I'm coming to Oklahoma State." That's how it happened.

I'm just thankful that I was there a couple of years before Barry Sanders got there. He ended up winning the Heisman Trophy the year after I left. The two years I that I spent with Barry, I really didn't know that he was going to be that explosive. Once he broke through in college and went to the Detroit Lions, he just burst on the scene. He had an outstanding, fabulous career.

Pat Jones

Even though Jimmy Johnson recruited me, Pat Jones ended up being the head coach at Oklahoma State University when Jimmy went to the University of Miami. Pat was just a great guy. We used to run up the middle the entire time. I probably carried the ball about 35 times a game and 30 of the rushes would be right up the gut between the two guards.

He was just a tough individual. I think the first thing he said to us when he became head coach was, "We may not be the most talented football team in the NCAA, but we will be the most in shape guys in the NCAA." We knew at that point we were going to be running our tails off. He was a big proponent of being conditioned and being conditioned for the 4th quarter. He was just a great guy to be around.

Favorite Game In College
The 1987 Sun Bowl and the 1984 Gator Bowl, I would probably put 1 and 1A as my favorite college games. The 1987 season was the first 10 game season Oklahoma State ever had. We went down and beat South Carolina that year. We were nationally ranked and finished ranked 5th or 6th in the country that year. I was a freshman at the time.

When I was in the Sun Bowl back in my home state of Texas, I had a lot of family come down for that Bowl game. We went up against West Virginia. I think the Gator Bowl and the Sun Bowl were probably running neck and neck for my favorite games I ever played in an Oklahoma State uniform.

NFL Draft
I had no clue that the Buffalo Bills were going to draft me. I thought I might be drafted in the first round, but it didn't happen. The Buffalo Bills running backs coach Elijah Pitts, came to visit me at Oklahoma State, but so did a lot of running backs coaches from around the league. I actually thought I was going to be drafted by the Los Angeles Rams, Atlanta Falcons, or my hometown Houston Oilers. After I dropped down to the 2nd round, I got a call from the Buffalo Bills and they said, "If these next two teams don't pick you, we're going to pick you at number 40."

Being from the South, I had never been farther north than Oklahoma. I thought it would be pretty exciting going to New York. I'd be close to the Knicks and Yankees. I got to Buffalo and it was just a total culture shock. It is just so far away from New York City.

Weather In Buffalo
Sometimes during mini camp there was snowfall. It wasn't just flurries that would hit the ground and go away, they would stick. We had some mini camps where there was snow on the ground for a couple of days. It was kind of a culture shock for a lot of the young players.

Marv Levy
Marv Levy was awesome. He was just a genuine, great guy. He was a history major at Coe College. A lot of the stuff he said to us was regarding American History. He let his coaches, coach. Marv would come up to you after a game and tell you how great you did, or things that you needed to work on. More importantly, he was a guy who always asked how your family was doing. He was more concerned about how your family was, how you were doing, and how everything was going on and off the field. He was just an awesome coach and a guy who deserved to go into the Pro Football Hall of Fame.

Origin Of Buffalo Bills No-Huddle Offense
Jim Kelly and Ted Marchibroda, who was offensive coordinator at the time, said we work really well in the two-minute offense, why don't we try to do it for the entire game. Marv really didn't want it to do that, but we started running it, and were really effective at it.

Marv said, "Okay, if that's what you guys want to do, you go ahead and do it." Sometimes we would score within 30 seconds with one or two plays. Sometimes we would have drives of 10-12 plays, but we were still continuing to run the no-huddle.

There were some times where Bruce Smith and Darryl Talley said, "Hey man, can you give us a break? You are all scoring too fast." That was the pace we wanted. That was the pace that even the offensive linemen wanted. They liked the up-tempo offense, because they knew what they were doing, and the defense had to get set. The defense had to substitute and things like that. It was part of not just the two-minute drill, it was the entire offense.

Jim Kelly and Ted Marchibroda worked really well together. Even during the week, sometimes Jim would always call his plays. When we were out on the football field, it was all Jim. Ted had nothing to do with the plays that Jim called. Jim had a great feel for the game. If we were running the ball effectively, Jim was going to stick with the run. If we're passing the ball effectively, Jim was going to stick with the pass.

Jim had a great sense of what we needed to do at certain times. Our center, the late Kent Hull, was a big factor in it, too. Sometimes Jim would call a running play and it might be the wrong play to run. Kent would look back and say, "No, you can't run that. You've got to run something else." Jim would call all the plays 95% of the time. The only time Ted even got to call plays was when we were in a short yardage goal line situation.

Houston Oilers vs. Buffalo Bills Playoff Game (The Comeback)
Being down 35-3 to Houston at that point in time, you want to maybe score a couple of touchdowns, and make the game a little bit closer. Darryl Talley got as many guys as he possibly could on the sideline, and looked everybody in the eyes and said, "Now we got them right where we want them." Everybody was like, really? It's 35 to 3.

We started coming back, and all of a sudden the momentum shifted. The crowd really got into it. People who had left were trying to get back into the stadium. Once we got that momentum, man, it was something to be around. You could tell the Houston Oilers were kind of in shock by what was happening. I was just happy to be a part of it.

The one guy that I really felt bad for was Warren Moon. Warren had been a great friend of mine for the first couple years that I was in the league and living in Houston. We used to work out a lot together and I really felt bad for him.

They had an outstanding team. They had a lot of Pro Bowlers and a lot of guys who knew how to play the game. You could just see Warren's reaction after the game. It looked like a lot of the players really wanted to cry. They really wanted to know what happened, how did we not win this football game?

It was a great game for us, and a bad game for them. You feel bad for those guys. Even though we won the game, you feel bad for them for not putting us away. We were able to come back and win the football game.

Favorite Of Four Super Bowls

When you play in four Super Bowls and lose four, there really is no favorite. You only think about what you could have done differently to try to win one. That was the mindset of our whole football team. We talked about it after every Super Bowl. It's just not a good feeling to have when you lose the Super Bowl, or any game. You try to come back the following weekend to correct things. With the Super Bowl being the last game of the season, we knew that we had to wait a full off-season to come back and try to get back to the Super Bowl and win.

The good thing is that the players became closer friends. We really cared about each other and our families. Anytime you lose a big game like the Super Bowl, and lose four Super Bowls in a row, you're obviously going to be hurting not only for your teammates and your family, but you're also going to be hurting for the fans of Buffalo, too.

People Saying Thurman Thomas Should Have Been MVP Of Super Bowl & Not Otis Anderson

A lot of people have said that, but I don't think that would have been any consolation to how I feel about not winning the game. Sure, it might have been nice, but you still would have had that L next to your team name after the Super Bowl. If I had a fail and a loss with my team, even if I would have got the MVP, it still would not have been a very good feeling.

Pro Football Hall Of Fame Induction

Obviously it was great to be inducted into the Pro Football Hall of Fame, and be in there with some of your heroes that you watched over the years. I got to meet Joe Greene, another hero of mine growing up. I try to go back for the enshrinement every year. I got inducted in 2007, and I've only missed two years since then. One year I missed was because my daughter graduated from the University of Florida. It's exciting to go back and see the returning enshrines and the new inductees.

My favorite part is going to the Ray Nitschke Luncheon which is just for Hall of Famers—no outsiders, no reporters, nobody. A couple Hall of Famers get up and talk. Willie Lanier, the great linebacker from the Kansas City Chiefs, leads the luncheon. They do a great job of organizing everything. We sit in a room for about 2½ hours and just talk football, really welcome the guys who are going in that year. It's great to go back and see guys that you grew up idolizing and guys you grew up watching on TV.

Ralph Wilson

Ralph Wilson was great. He was an owner who loved football, knew football, and knew stats. He knew about the weather where we were playing and the history of other teams. He was just a great guy.

Throughout the '90s, he met us on the road for away games. He would come down from Detroit Thursday or Friday, and spend nights with the team at the hotel. He always congratulated whether we won or lost.

I remember after every Super Bowl he would come in the locker room and shake everybody's hand. I got to know Ralph really well. Ralph got to know some of the other players really well, too. They would say, "Mr. Wilson just came up to me and said hey, great game. We wouldn't have got here without you." He told that to almost every single player on the football squad. He wanted to make sure that every player knew that he was behind us. He was just a great owner to be around.

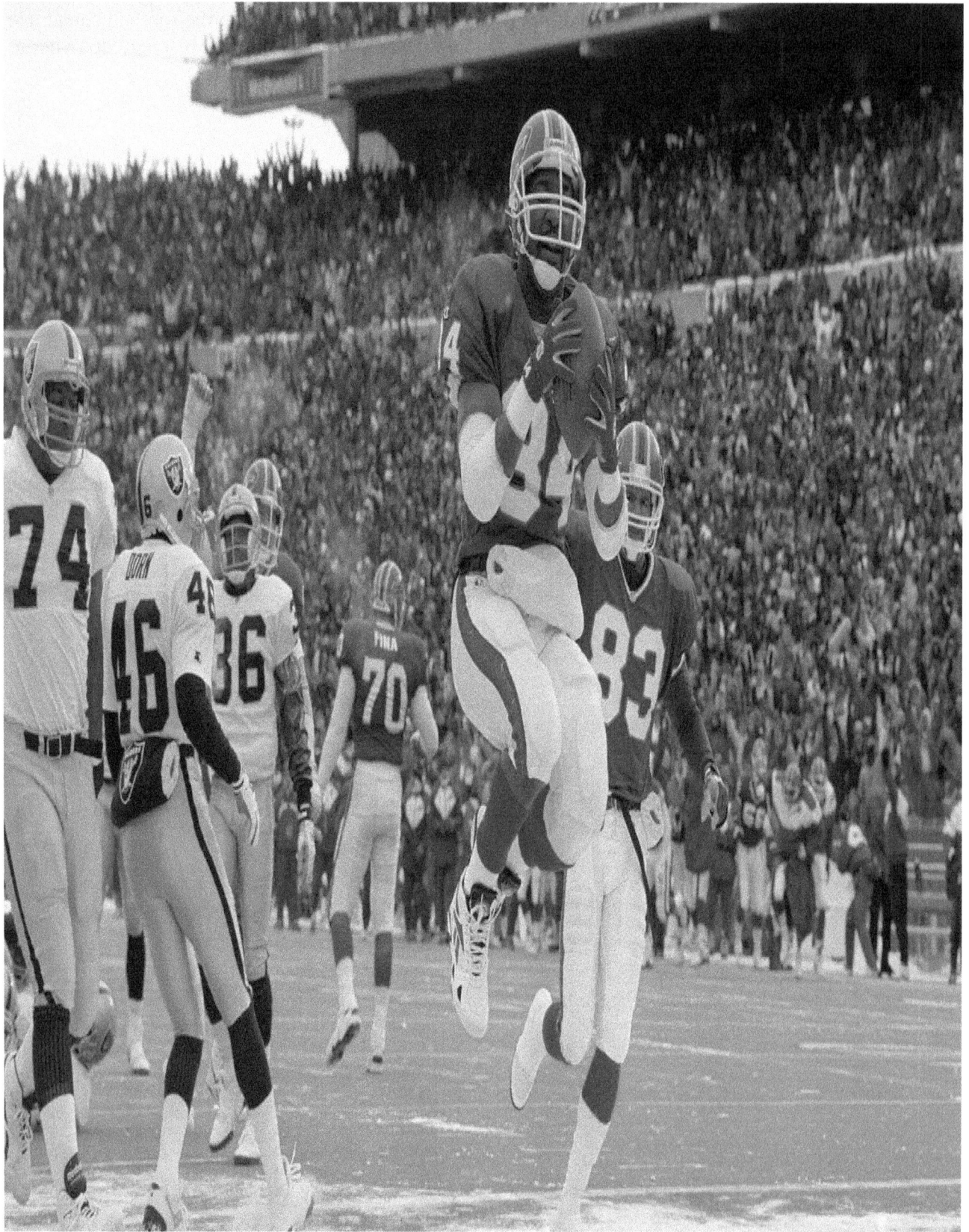

Photograph copyright Associated Press

Chapter 128

Tim Brown

College: Notre Dame Career history Los Angeles / Oakland Raiders (1988–2003) Tampa Bay Buccaneers (2004) 2015 Inductee Pro Football Hall of Fame

College Choice
My parents and I were looking for a place where I would get a great education. The only school that came to the house talking about education, was Notre Dame. My parents were pretty impressed with their track record of graduating over ninety-eight percent of their athletes at the time. We didn't think I had a future in football so it was all about getting that education and coming back home and getting a good job.

SMU was attractive because I wanted to stay home and it's a great academic school. I knew if I went there, I would do well. With all the potential issues regarding SMU football that people were talking about then, my parents and I knew that it probably wasn't the best place for me to go. I graduated from high school when I was seventeen and I wanted to stay home. I wasn't ready to go fifteen hundred miles away to school. It came down to SMU and Notre Dame. With SMU and their potential problems, I really didn't have a choice but to go to Notre Dame.

First Two Years At Notre Dame
It was a pretty bad situation with the football team my first few years there. I told people I didn't go to Notre Dame for football. I went there for the academics. We had a tough two years. I think we went five and six both years. We just weren't a good football team. Unfortunately, they got rid of Coach Gerry Faust. He was one of the greatest coaches I've been around as far as his ability to deal with players. On the field, it was just something totally different.

Lou Holtz
I knew right away that Lou Holtz knew exactly what he wanted to do and how he was going to get it done. The team felt as if we were a much more complete football team.

I think that his first year we went 6-5, but we really felt as if we had gone ten and one. We were really excited coming into my second year because we thought we had a chance. We were 8-1 until we met Penn State, and had a chance to go for the tie. We chose to go for the win and didn't get it. That knocked us out of the National Championship race.

Coach Holtz left it up to the captains and the seniors. It was our choice, whatever we wanted to do. If we wanted to go for the two points, we could. If we wanted to kick the extra point and tie the game, we could do that too. If we had tied, chances were we were going to be out of the National Championship race. Coach Holtz called the right play. Tony Rice just didn't pitch me the ball.

We were a great football team. Lou said when he first got there, that in three years he was going to win a National Championship, Sure enough, the next year after I was gone, they won it.

Touchdown Timmy
I believe it was the Notre Dame announcer who started calling me Touchdown Timmy. I think it was during a game when I scored that he said, "Touchdown Timmy". That was it; it stuck. It stuck with me throughout my NFL career too.

Winning Heisman Trophy
When I won the Heisman Trophy it was one of those moments that you really don't believe that it happened. I think by the time I got to the ceremony, I knew I had a good shot.

One of my teammates told me, "Well if somebody votes you third, then they shouldn't be voting anymore. You know everybody is going to vote you at least second. Don McPherson may win the East and Gaston Green may win the West, but you're going to be second in all those regions. You're going to win this on second place votes alone."

That actually made a lot of sense to me but going into it, I still had no clue what was going to happen. It was an incredible moment, no doubt.

I don't know if playing at Notre Dame helped me win the Heisman or not. Jim Nantz asked me that question and I told him, "Look, I went to Notre Dame for one reason, and one reason alone—to get a great education. If it turns out that it helps me on the football field, then so be it."

I'm not apologetic for that. That certainly wasn't the reason I went there, but if it did help me with that, then God bless Notre Dame.

NFL Draft
I was hoping the Raiders would draft me. I was trying to get to them so I did everything I could to get to that pick. Once it got to the Raiders pick, I was hoping they would take me. They ended up taking me and it ended up being exactly what I wanted.

Early Seasons With Los Angeles Raiders
My rookie year I led the team in receptions because James Lofton and everybody else got hurt. I got hurt in my second year and missed fifteen games. I came back the next year and I was the third down guy and punt returner. I did that for two years and going into 1992, my fifth year, I was set to do the same thing. Then, Mervyn Fernandez got hurt the second or third game of the year. I ended up starting the rest of the year and the rest of my career.

Playing With Different Quarterbacks Throughout Time With Raiders
It was tough, but at the same time you knew that they had some ability. You just had to find out what that was and play to their strengths. That's what I was able to do.

Al Davis

Al Davis was great at times, and not so great at other times. I think that his overall legacy is going to be one of greatness and one of excellence, because he won three Super Bowls and there are many Hall of Famers who played for him. You can't help but to be great, and he's in the Hall of Fame himself. So, from that standpoint it's a legacy of greatness and that's the way it should be.

Fred Biletnikoff & James Lofton

Fred Biletnikoff was my coach for fifteen years, so obviously I learned a lot from him. My rookie year, James Lofton stayed after practice with me and helped me get ready to play wide receiver.

Freddy and I spent many, many, many hours together in the classroom and on the field. Every once in a while, Freddy would drop nuggets of what he did when he played, or suggest to me what I should be thinking. He was very, very helpful.

Toughest Cornerback

Probably Dale Carter and James Hasty. Going against those guys twice a year was pretty tough. They were incredibly difficult guys to play against, but I managed to have some success against them. They sort of brought out the best in you.

Jerry Rice Signing With Raiders

I was really excited about Jerry Rice signing with the Raiders. I remember getting the call from Bruce Allen saying that they were going to do that. I said, "Do it yesterday and bring him in."

The next thing I knew, I saw Jerry Rice on CNN running routes with the Raiders. It was the right move. It was great for my career. I think we may have even have extended Jerry's career a couple years.

Playing In Super Bowl

It was great playing in the Super Bowl. It was year fifteen for me in the NFL when I got an opportunity to play for the World Championship. It was an amazing feeling.

We definitely had the better team that season, no doubt about it. We had the number one offense that year and our defense was ranked in the top ten. Everything that could go wrong just went wrong, and it ended up being what it was. It was still an incredible experience.

Defining Moment In Career

I don't know if there was a moment. I think for me, just being consistent for all those years was the thing that I may be known for rather than having one incredible, great year. I think I'm the only receiver in the history of the NFL that had ten years with seventy-five catches. I think that's good enough.

Waiting Six Years To Be Selected For Pro Football Hall Of Fame

The selection process is gut wrenching, and I wish there was a different way the Pro Football Hall of Fame could do it. I guess there isn't. If there were some kind of parameter list, I think it would make it a lot easier. Then guys would understand if you hit this number, it's going to take you two years. If you hit this number, it's going to take you five years. There needs to be something because this process is grueling, no doubt about it. I'm glad to see Charles Haley get in. I'm hoping that Kevin Greene (enshrined following year) gets in pretty soon. Kevin has been waiting nine or ten years. Haley waited eleven years. That's just way too long to be on the top fifteen list every year.

The wide receivers position is a tough position for the voters for some reason. I think it's only going to get tougher with all the guys becoming eligible. If they are having a problem deciding because of us playing in what they call the "Passer Era", I don't know how they're going to be able to navigate around these guys when they become eligible. We'll see what happens. It's just a tough deal. It took six years, but at least we got it done.

Photograph copyright Associated Press

Chapter 129

John Randle

College: Texas A&I–Kingsville Career History: Minnesota Vikings (1990–2000) Seattle Seahawks (2001–2003) 2010 Inductee Pro Football Hall Of Fame

College Choice

It was called Texas A&I Kingsville when I got there. My junior college coach, Keith Waters, was hired at Texas A&I as the linebackers coach. I followed him down there a year later.

Describing the City of Kingsville, I will put it in the words of Tom Moore, the former offensive coordinator for the Indianapolis Colts. He went down to Texas A&I one time and said, "If a man had six months to live and he went down to Kingsville, Texas, that would be the longest six months of his life."

It's a town of about 2,000 people down in South Texas. There wasn't anything to do but play basketball, lift weights, and watch cars pass by.

Visiting Brother Playing For Tampa Bay Buccaneers

Going down to Tampa and seeing my brother, who played for Tampa Bay, at camp was kind of like a high school moment. I faced the same thing in high school. My brother started high school before me and everybody was telling me, "This is where your brother did this, this is where your brother did that." It kind of reassured me that going down there wasn't the right idea for me.

Basically they did me a favor by telling me I was too small to play defensive line. I went down to Tampa Bay and said, "I want to play defensive line." They responded, "No, you're going to play linebacker like your brother." I said, "Okay, I can see why you guys are putting me in his category." But, I knew in my mind I was a defensive lineman. It didn't take long for me to make up my mind and leave.

I thought I would be drafted. Coming out of a small school, you don't really know what teams are thinking about you, especially in the late '80s. I thought I had a chance to be drafted, though. I sat around for two days, all day, waiting for somebody to call and tell me I was drafted. At some point, I felt embarrassed. I just said, "You know what, if it doesn't happen, it doesn't happen."

My first contract was about $50,000 before taxes. They gave me a signing bonus of about $5,000, which was basically $3,000 after taxes. It wasn't all about the money, it was just being able to make it. I knew in the back of my mind that I wanted to give it a try, because I said to myself, "If I don't try this, I will regret this for the rest of my life." I've said that to myself a few times in life, but this time I said, "You know what, starting today, I'm going to change. I'm not going to be that kid who grew up in a town of 150 people. I'm going to be a guy that all of a sudden says you know what, I'm going to stand for something." I'm going to at least try out.

Transition To NFL
It was a huge transition, because the year before, I was watching some of these guys on TV. These guys played at schools with their names on the back of their jerseys, and I'm a Division II player coming into this big place, not a draft pick, but as a free agent. I thought that I was going to a new school on the first day. I just felt completely out of place.

I knew one place that I kind of felt everybody had a decent shot was on the football field. I had faced that when I went to a junior college, then when I went to Texas A&I. I felt out of place at those two places, but the one place that I felt comfortable at was on the football field. On the football field, it didn't matter where you came from or who you were, your athletic ability and your talents would give you a better chance of playing. It didn't matter where you came from, it was just about who you were on the football field.

Vikings Defensive Line
When I got to Minnesota, they had Keith Millard at defensive tackle, Henry Thomas at nose guard, Chris Doleman at defensive end, and Al Noga. These guys would sit around with each other like they had known each other for 10 years.

The two things I looked up before going to Minnesota were the guys' weights and heights. Al Noga was about 6' tall, Henry Thomas was around 6'2", Chris Doleman was 6'5", and Keith Millard was about 6'6". They all weighted about 260, and I said to myself, you know what, I can at least kind of fit in with these guys' weights. When I got there and saw those guys, I knew I had a long way to go.

Goals As Player
I see things differently than most people do. Most people sit around, calculate, and say, "I accomplished this; I accomplished that." At the end of the 1993 season, I was looking forward to 1994. I wanted to prove that I was the best defensive tackle in the league. Every year I wasn't looking back, I was looking forward. I said to myself, "What can I improve on from 1993, to make 1994 even better?"

John Teerlinck, our defensive line coach, had similar thoughts about always looking forward and getting better. Just because the guys that are in the room one year, doesn't mean all of those same guys are going to be the next year. That was kind of how I was looking at things.

Practicing Against Randall McDaniel
In practice all I did was go against Randall McDaniel. In games teams were going against both Randall and Gary Zimmerman. My mindset was if you can't do it in practice, there's no way in

hell you can do it in a game. My mamma taught me this saying, "Responsibility starts at home." So my thing was, it starts at home practice, everything starts there.

I remember my first year with Paul Wiggin, the Vikings defensive line coach. I was going against Randall and maybe once every two weeks, I would win a drill against Randall. Paul Wiggin came to me and said, "What are you doing? Why are you going against Randall?" I said, "He makes me better." He said, "But you're not beating him." He told me to go against one of the other guys. I did and I just clobbered them. I just started taking these guys and tossing them to the side, left and right. Paul Wiggin comes back over and says, "Go back to going against Randall McDaniel. I see what you're doing and I like it."

That was what I was doing, I was always looking to get better. Going against Randall, I didn't win a lot. I knew if I could do something against Randall that was very productive, in the game it was surely going to work.

Playing Against Green Bay Packers
The state of Minnesota and the state of Wisconsin are side by side. I still live in Minnesota. Every year during Packer week, you see people driving from Green Bay with Packers flags on their cars. That just pissed off my teammates and me. To me, it felt like they were almost invading our state. When we played against Green Bay, it was almost like that Texas-Oklahoma rivalry coming up again. When we played the Packers, it was the bright lights and the State of Minnesota versus the State of Wisconsin.

When I went in the stadium every time we played against Green Bay, I got booed, but I liked it. I liked getting booed by the Packers fans because that just made it even more special for me. Here I am, a kid from Mumford, Texas with a population of 150 people, and I'm walking onto Lambeau Field and they're calling my name. I'm going, "Wow, they know who I am." To me it was like being the villain in Wisconsin.

Reggie White and I used to talk about it all the time. Reggie would tell me, "Take it easy on our quarterback." I would respond "Reggie, if you were back there, I would take you down." I'm sorry, Reg, you're a Packer, I'm a Viking. We're not supposed to get along. That's the way it is."

I always loved going against Brett Favre because he was a true competitor. He was like the neighborhood kid who was always beating everybody. You always looked forward to going against that guy, trying to take him down since he was that good; he was that talented.

Trash Talking
I didn't really trash talk a lot on quarterbacks. I got Trent Dilfer kicked out of a game at the Metrodome one year because we kept messing with him and talking trash to him. Trent thought we were trying to hurt him. Somebody tripped me (or something) and all I could do was just try to reach out and grab his shoe. He thought I was trying to take his leg out. He dropped down on the ground and started punching me, and they kicked him out of the game.

My way of thinking was to get in the head of the offensive linemen. I would say little things to get him unfocused. I knew offensive linemen have a tendency of not listening to everything that's going on, especially when the quarterback is calling out the cadence.

Every Monday, the opposing team's media guides would come out. The team would give you a stack of 200-300 pages containing stories about the team you were going against. I would sit there and read the stories about the offensive linemen. I would take the information and put it in my memory. I could remember all the stuff about these guys. As the game was going on, I could bring it up at the right moment. You could tell a guy something, and all of a sudden he would seem like he was in total shock that you knew his wife's name, his kid's name, his dad's name, the name of his car, and where he got his car from. All of a sudden the offensive lineman is asking you questions like, "How do you know that?" I'd just look at him and smile. The lineman would keep asking me, "How do you know that?" All of a sudden the quarterback is trying to pull the offensive lineman in the huddle, and the offensive lineman is shoving the quarterback, telling him to get out of the way. The next thing you know, those two guys are fighting or arguing in the huddle, and I would go, "Hey, my job is done." I would do things like that. It was fun to do stuff like that.

For example, a guy said in the media guide that his wife goes to every game and sits at the 50-yard line. This guy's playing really physical and I would say, "Nice job, really nice job. I can really tell that you really have been practicing all week, anticipating me coming out here and playing against you. I can also see that your wife Susan is over there at the 50-yard line, and she's really enjoying it. You know what? If I beat you on one play, Susan is going to be disappointed. What do you think Susan's going to think about that?"

All of a sudden he's going, "How do you know my wife's named Susan?" I'd say, "Don't worry about that." Again he's asks, "How do you know my wife's named Susan?" In would respond, "I don't know, maybe because ... she grew up in ... what was that town? She grew up in Michigan, right? She went to the University of Michigan. You know what, I spent some time up at the University of Michigan, hanging out there." Then the quarterback is trying to get him back in the huddle. He's saying, "No, no, no. I want to know how he knows my wife is named Susan and that she went to the University of Michigan." I was like, "I'll tell you later. I'll tell you later."

Every couple of weeks, you'd get a guy who says, "You're not going to get in my head." "Okay. No. I'm not trying to get in your head. I'm not trying to get in." He was like, "You can't talk to me." I would be already in his head.

It was just getting guys pissed off. The quarterback sometimes wouldn't want to give up a sack and he'd just throw the ball and throw an interception. The quarterback would say, "I didn't give you a sack." I would respond, "No, you didn't, but it was an interception, so thank you anyway."

First Career Interception
When I was running after intercepting the ball, my teammate Eddie McDaniel, was yelling, "Toss me the ball." He yelled again, "I told you to toss me the ball." I said, "Dude, listen. This is my first interception, and you want me to toss the ball to you? No, no. I don't get many of these,

so I'm not going to toss this." I got run down, and I told the guy I was going in slow motion. I felt like I was in quicksand. It was the most unusual feeling in the world.

Best Running Back
The best running back I played against was Barry Sanders. Monday morning was when you went into the team's facility for film review. Everybody would hope they didn't make Barry's highlight tape. You'd have a guy do a 360, trying to keep up with Barry.

Barry could be backed up on the goal line, and all of a sudden run 25 yards. It was as if Barry was running to classical music, his shoulders would move and it was just ... it was like the guy with the flute and the cobra. Barry's running style would almost lull you to sleep.

Emmitt Smith had a great offensive line. Emmitt wasn't a pushover, but his offensive line was devastating. Dallas had Larry Allen, who bench pressed 692. I'll never forget that. When I read that in those media guides, I said, "This dude bench pressed 692 pounds." Then we were talking about Nate Newton. I said, "Man, Nate Newton. He's big, but Nate can't bench press 692 pounds."

Daryl Johnston, the Dallas fullback wasn't any joke either. If Barry had Dallas offensive linemen, Barry would be still running today.

Pro Football Hall Of Fame Induction
The Pro Football Hall of Fame Induction was unbelievable. Growing up in Texas, Sunday was a day of going to church and then watching football. It was unbelievable. To be inducted was a dream come true for a kid from Texas. It's hard to explain, but it's unbelievable, because I have found myself among my childhood heroes. When I want go back for inductions now, most of the older guys sit up front and talk about old times. Sitting there with Roger Staubach, Dick Butkus, Earl Campbell, and those guys, it's almost like going back in time.

For me, I grew up loving the game and appreciated watching the game. It's like when a person goes to Disney World and they're walking around, looking at everything and they're going, "My God." To me, being around those guys is almost the same thing, because they're all sitting over there. I was sitting there one year with Franco Harris, John Madden, and Lynn Swann. All of the guys are talking. It's like going back in time. I'm a history guy, so I am fascinated with history. Going to Canton and sitting around with these guys, is like a childhood dream.

Chris Doleman
Chris Doleman taught me a lot my rookie year. He taught me how to respect the game and be professional. He was almost like my big brother on the football field because he taught me so much. I have so much respect for Dole. I was lucky to be around Chris Doleman, Henry Thomas, Keith Millard, and Al Noga when I came into the league. It was like business on Sundays with those guys, but any other day, we were having fun. Later on in my career, I tried to teach and show the younger guys who I played with, the same thing.

Playing For Seattle Seahawks

It was completely different. I had to get used to drinking a lot of coffee and just being in a different world. At the same time, I had so much fun out there and met so many people. The organization was great to be around. I was welcomed with open arms. I still talk to a lot of guys out there in Seattle. That's even where my wife learned to cook. I just had to get used to the rain. It was so different, but at the same time, my wife and I had a chance to discover Seattle together, and it was fun.

Mike Holmgren

Mike Holmgren had so much respect for me. When I got to Seattle, he said he couldn't believe that Minnesota let me go. I said, "One person's junk is another man's treasure."

I had just gotten married, and he taught me a lot about being a dad. It was great to see, because I had always wondered what he was like from watching him on the other side of the field. Being there with him, I got to see what he was all about, and I was lucky to get the chance to do that.

Comparing Playing Defensive End To Defensive Tackle

When a defensive end gets double-teamed, he's getting double-teamed by a tight end and the offensive tackle. When you're a defensive tackle getting double-teamed, it's by the center and the guard or it's the guard and tackle. I don't want to make anybody mad, but it's definitely harder to get a sack inside than it is outside.

Photograph copyright Associated Press

Chapter 130

Aeneas Williams

College:
Southern University

Career History:
Phoenix/Arizona Cardinals (1991–2000)
St. Louis Rams (2001–2004)

2014 Inductee Pro Football Hall Of Fame

College Choice
I started playing football when I was four years old, playing all the way through high school. After I graduated high school, I immediately started summer school at Southern University. The reason I didn't play is because my brother Achilles, who was two grades ahead of me, wasn't playing football. My entire goal was to get to Southern and really just follow and do everything that my brother did. He graduated with his degree in accounting in three and a half years because he went to school year-round, attending summer school. I was on pace to graduate in three years.

After Achilles graduated, he called me and said, "Little brother, slow down. You'll be working the rest of your life." It was then that I began to attempt to discover whom in the world I was. Prior to that time, I was Achilles's little brother and I was satisfied with that.

Two things happened that were instrumental in my life at that time; number one, I ended up committing my life to Jesus Christ. In that commitment, I began to understand the nature of [my] purpose as it relates to human beings and other things that are in the world. I also realized, in my heart, I always loved playing football.

The second thing that happened was it entered into my heart, to go walk on the football team. So a week before the season started, I joined the team. The coach allowed me to do it, and the rest is history.

Tying NCAA Record For Most Interceptions In A Season
It was studying, working hard, and working on catching the ball. My second year playing in college I had seven interceptions. The first year after walking on, I had two. I always loved catching interceptions and the impact of how it changed a game.

Joining Cardinals
When the Cardinals drafted me, I knew what to expect. I graduated high school in 1986. Maurice Hurst graduated in 1985, and was one of my mentors. Maurice also played at Southern. He was drafted in the fourth round, as a cornerback by the New England Patriots. Kevin Lewis,

valedictorian of the class 1984, the same graduating class as my brother, signed with the 49ers as a free agent cornerback.

Every summer, I got to train with those guys and all the players who were in college or playing in the pros, because they came home to New Orleans during the summer. We would all train at Tulane University. I would compete against professional players. I spent the most time around Maurice and Kevin. They helped acclimate me to the climate and speed of the NFL.

When I got to the Cardinals, it wasn't a culture shock for me at all. It was actually an environment that I was already familiar with.

I didn't understand the magnitude of all the draft choices in 1991. Our first round pick was Eric Swann, who was one of the more dominant interior defensive linemen during the time that he played. Larry Allen, who's a Hall of Famer, told me how difficult it was for him when he had to compete against Eric Swann. Our second round pick was Mike Jones, a defensive tackle from NC State. We wanted to be a draft class that would come in and make our mark, and more importantly be the best that we could be individually, and hopefully collectively.

Focus Not On Money
Money, honestly influences a lot. I learned quickly that if I worked to develop my potential, understood what I was doing, was an asset to my team, helped us win or did whatever I could to help us win, and exceled, the money would come. So if I developed my potential and became one of the best and reliable players, I always knew the money would come. So my focus was never the money.

Having Two Interceptions Against Troy Aikman In A Playoff Game
My number one goal was to prepare myself, and prepare our team, to beat one of the best teams of our day who had beaten us, literally every time. We had to win the last four games of the season to get in the playoffs, and we weren't expected to win against Dallas. So all I wanted to do was to compete. I knew my assignment was to be matched up on Michael Irvin the entire game. If he went to the restroom, I had to go to the restroom with him.

I knew what my assignment was, and I just wanted to make sure my teammates could trust that I would be able to compete with Michael. It wasn't that he wouldn't make some plays, but when I had the opportunity to make plays, I was able to. We were able to upset Dallas in that game. Then everybody was on notice. That's just the natural bi-product of excellence.

So my goal or my thoughts were never, "Man, now people are going to recognize me." That never was a conscious thought in my mind. It was a conscious thought in my mind to reach my potential, and that was what you were going to see.

Gill Byrd
I had some mentors, particularly Gill Byrd who played cornerback for the San Diego Chargers. He had already played for ten years when I befriended him my second year in the league, after we played the Chargers. I asked Mr. Byrd (I called him that at the time) if he would help me learn how to play the cornerback position. From that time on, my wife Tracy and I would go to

San Diego every off-season, and stay at their home. He would take me to the Chargers facility and help me understand how to play the cornerback position at an excellent level.

Hit On Steve Young That Ended Steve's Career
The first thought that occurred to me was to pray that Steve Young would get up and be fine. Even today, from what I've been told, it still would have been called a clean hit. I knew the competitive nature of Steve and more importantly, the great player that he was and I always respected that.

Pat Tillman
I knew Pat Tillman and was a part of the leadership structure that was in place, when the Arizona Cardinals drafted Pat. I spent time with him as he transitioned from college to the pros. Knowing the type of person Pat was, I wasn't surprised he went to the military, fought for the country, and was willing to leave the NFL.

His life ended much too early. Our military is fighting wars that allow us to have the freedom that we have in this country, including playing football. That was a sad moment for me. I get tears in my eyes knowing that Pat won't have the opportunity that I have, to have his children raised by their father.

I know his children and family know, as well as the NFL and teammates, what type of true hero he was. People sometimes call us heroes. I don't think we're heroes at all. Pat and all the servicemen are true heroes.

Playing For Cardinals During Losing Seasons
It wasn't hard. Certainly you want to win, but I always try to keep things in perspective. I would hear people say, "Aeneas, you're playing for the bad Cardinals, on a bad team." One thing I know, I was a part of one of the 32 teams, and it was an honor to be on one of them. I knew what my responsibility was, and I wanted to make sure that I was doing my job and I wasn't part of the reason we were losing.

Trade To St. Louis Rams
When I got traded to the Rams, I realized they already had a winning structure in place; they were already winners. Their team was the second worst team of the decade of the nineties. Dick Vermeil came in, built the foundation, and had got the organization and all of management turned around.

I came in to a team that had already won a Super Bowl, had just come off the playoffs, and was now restructuring the defense with new coaches and new players. I was excited because I knew this wasn't something starting from the ground up. It was a part of something that was already structured and built. I had an expectation that we weren't trying to make the playoffs. Our goal was to win the Super Bowl.

Having Two Interceptions Against Brett Favre In Playoffs
Unfortunately whenever I see a Packers fan, they haven't forgotten it. It was certainly a moment in the history of my career, as well as the history of the St. Louis Rams. The Packers came in our

dome, and I think we picked off Brett Favre six times in that particular game. It was a tremendous blessing and a tremendous game. I was proud of how we played collectively as a defense and an entire team.

Favorite Coach

My favorite coach was Lovie Smith, when he was my defensive coordinator. I played in the Senior Bowl coming out of college, and the staff that coached our team was the Kansas City Chiefs. Marty Schottenheimer was the head coach and the defensive backs coach was Tony Dungy. I experienced Tony's demeanor, his expectations, and his ability to communicate with players. Because of that, I always wanted to play for Coach Dungy.

When the Rams hired Coach Lovie as defensive coordinator and I found out that they were implementing the defense that I always wanted to play in under Coach Dungy, and that Coach Lovie was a disciple of Coach Dungy, I wanted to play there. Then I met Coach Lovie, and it was like I finally got a chance to play for Coach Dungy. Coach Lovie was just a spectacular, accountable person, and he helped my career. Coach Lovie is just one of the best that I've ever been around.

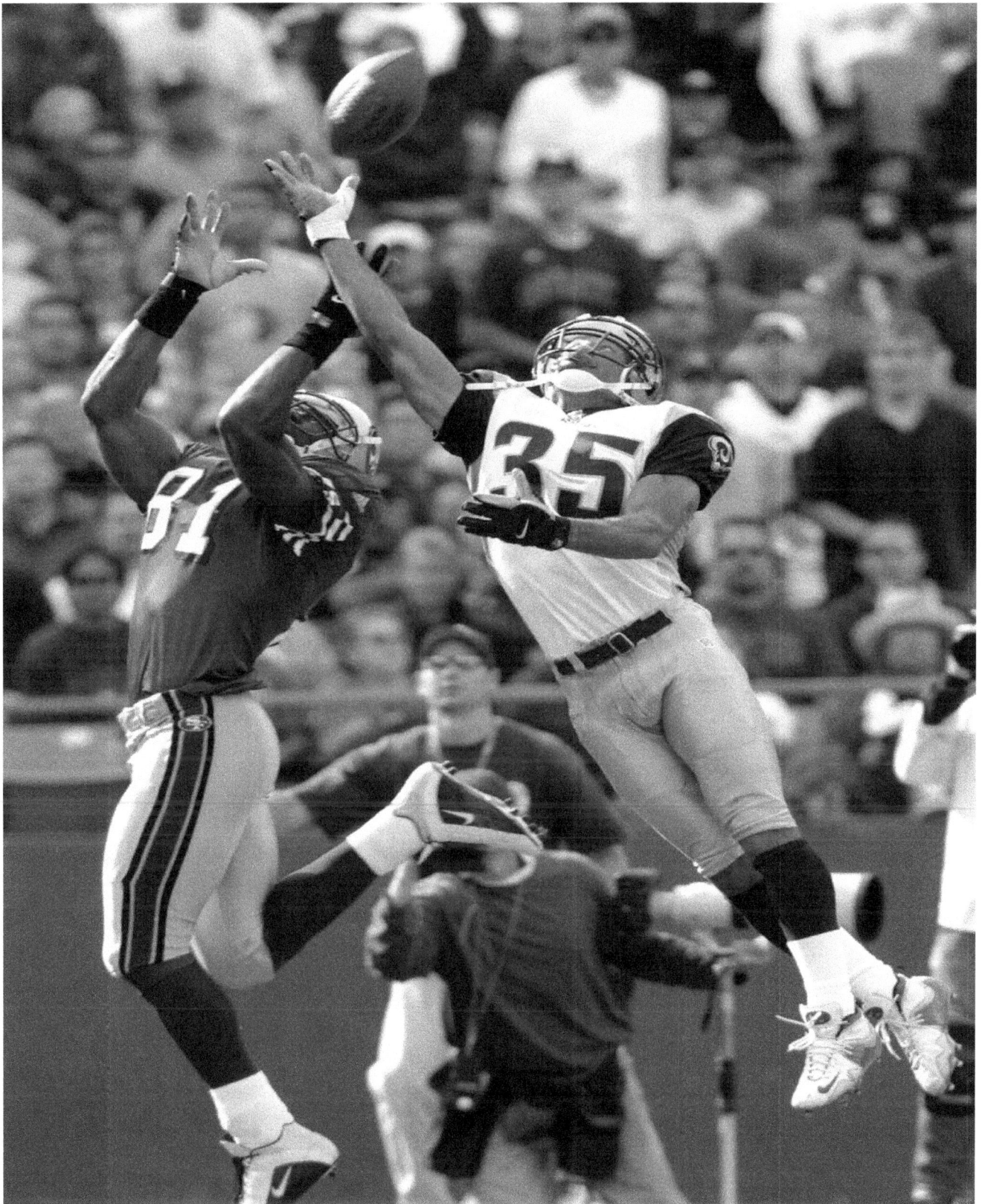

St. Louis Ram Aeneas Williams breaks up a pass in the end zone intended for San Francisco 49er Terrell Owens. Photograph copyright Associated Press

Chapter 131

Willie Roaf

```
College:
Louisiana Tech

Career History:
New Orleans Saints (1993–2001)
Kansas City Chiefs (2002–2005)

2012 Inductee Pro Football Hall Of Fame
```

College Choice

Back then, the Arkansas Razorbacks were kind of rebuilding. I'm from Pine Bluff, Arkansas, the same hometown as Torii Hunter, the baseball player. What happened was we had three guys who were very good football players go to Oklahoma. There was a quarterback named Eric Mitchel, Danny Bradley, and Curtice Williams, a defensive tackle. When those guys did that, Arkansas got a little bit pissed off with the program and didn't recruit us as heavily. My problem was I was playing basketball and weighed about 225 coming out of high school, and had big hands and big feet. I didn't get recruited very heavily.

My bloodline was definitely football. I was kind of raw at basketball and had some potential. I probably had a little more of a love for basketball, but things happen for a reason.

I went to basketball camp and there were about 400 campers there. I was a real good rebounder. They named me 'Mr. Rebound' at camp. I was offered a scholarship to UCA.

One of the biggest All-Star games in the country was called the King Cotton Classics and that was on ESPN. Back in '87 and '88, a couple of games were televised on ESPN. Dick Vitale came and broadcast the tournament in Pine Bluff. We even got to meet him at our luncheon.

We played the King Cotton and got a lot of exposure. Teams from all over the country played in it. Jason Kidd, Dennis Scott, and JR Reid played in that tournament. It was a huge high school basketball tournament. I started playing basketball in seventh or eighth grade. I started playing street ball. I don't know how old I was when I started playing that. When I was about 10 years old, I started playing organized football. I'm maybe 6'5" and I thought it was better just to take the football scholarship and go down to Louisiana Tech. It ended up being a blessing in disguise.

I got a letter from Connecticut when basketball coach Jim Calhoun got there. I guess they had heard about me at the camp in 1988. My basketball coach eventually let me know that he didn't show me all of the letters I had gotten, so I don't know how many offers I had in basketball. My dad knew that I was really a football player, so they didn't give me the letters I got for basketball. So, I took the football scholarship.

Louisiana Tech

I ended up going down to Louisiana Tech. Joe Ferguson was on the staff there. We ran a pro sets offense, so we flip-flopped. I had to know how to play both tackles, and we passed the ball a lot. That system was basically the perfect situation for somebody with my skill set. My basketball skills helped my foot movement. I blossomed in the football program.

Hokie Gajan was with the Saints and asked about me when I was a redshirt freshman. They always told me, "If you do what you're supposed to do, you'll be wearing diamonds." Coach Joe Raymond Peace always told me, "Willie, you've got a lot of potential." When I first got there, they knew I had a lot of potential. I didn't understand it. I said, "Man, I'm 235 pounds. I'm never going to be 300 pounds."

During my redshirt sophomore year, we played against Maryland in the Independence Bowl. We were 8-3, and they had a really good team. They had Larry Webster, Scott Zolak, and Clarence Jones, who ended up playing with me on the Saints. They had three or four pro prospects on that team. We ended up tying them in the Independence Bowl. I think at that time, I was maybe in the Top 40 tackles, and I was 20 or 21 years old. I realized that if I do what I've got to do in school and stay in college, I'm going to have a chance to go pro.

After my junior year, I accepted an invitation to play in the Hula Bowl. Eddie Robinson, the legendary coach from Grambling, and Lou Holtz were my coaches in the Hula Bowl. Eddie Robinson and I became real good friends.

Going into my senior year, there was Todd Perry, Brad Hopkins, and a couple of more guys; all bunched up together after Lincoln Kennedy on teams draft boards. My deal was to go out, establish myself, and work my way up the ladder. The beginning of the year, I couldn't get an insurance policy from Lloyd's of London for $500,000.

We played Alabama and they had top ten prospects in George Teague, Antonio London, Eric Curry, and all of those guys on defense ended up going pro. After the game I had against Eric Curry, my stock went up. The next week in practice there were 10 scouts following me around practice just watching me on the practice field. After that game, I got an insurance policy and my stock went up. Louisiana Tech ended up having four guys drafted because we were ranked the number two defense in the country, behind Alabama. We had a real good program, so it was a lot of fun back then. I didn't realize I had a chance to go pro until my sophomore year, but it was during the course of my senior year when my stock rose.

NFL Draft

Prior to the draft, I was sliding from being drafted anywhere between fifth and eighth in the first round. It was either going to be Tampa Bay, Cincinnati, the Bears, or Detroit drafting me. What happened was Detroit traded their pick to the New Orleans Saints. That's how I ended up becoming a Saint.

Jim Mora

Jim Mora pulled up to his house and there was an intruder in his house. I don't even know if he called the police. Jim went into his house and his wife was there. Jim confronted the intruder and got the intruder out of the house. Jim Moore was a tough, hard man, and had that marine mentality.

We were going to be in shape when we got out of training camp. It is hot and humid in New Orleans. If we got back and we were being a little lackadaisical in practice, he wouldn't even stop to say he didn't like what was going on and start over. We would start practice up from scratch.

We would also practice long and hard with Dick Vermeil in Kansas City. It was tough. We were in shape.

The only problem is when you do a lot of banging and you use your body like that, it gets you in shape and ready to play, but for the first couple of weeks of the season you're tired. You're trying to get your legs back underneath you when you're playing.

Mike Ditka
We worked hard with Mike Ditka, but I don't remember it being as hard as it was with Jim Mora. By that time, I had been in the league for four or five years. I was used to the routine, but it was hard. We had tough years in 1996 and in 1997. Jim Mora left during the 1996 season. The losing gets to you. In 1996, we were three in 13. Then, Mike Ditka came on as head coach.

For me, 1997 was a tough year. I wasn't in the best shape. It was a transition year for me. I either had to get myself together and really become a pro, or I was going to be out of the league. I needed Ditka and I needed 1997. The old legendary coach Dick Stanfel was on that staff in 1997 and 1998. He would get in there and run on the treadmill. I would see him working out. The way he pushed his body and the shape he was in was incredible. He was a real clean-cut man.

In 1998, I played a lot of basketball and was doing a lot of running. I got in real good shape and played really hard. I really didn't want to let the team down. I wanted Coach Stanfel to be proud of me after that 1997 year.

Ricky Williams
It was tough when Ricky came in 1999. It felt wrong when the Saints traded the whole draft for Ricky and then he was in that wedding dress. Master P. had him sign the worst contract in NFL history. Then Ricky was saying, "I'm going to reach these numbers …", which were crazy numbers to get those incentives. Those were astronomical numbers they put on him. Ricky got a lot of money upfront so he wouldn't think he got picked.

After watching Ricky play college football and the way he was perceived on TV, I thought Ricky was a lot more mature than what he was. Ricky was a very immature, sensitive kid, and got himself in a situation where he was lashing out. The whole time he was there, because of the contract, he was lashing out, doing stuff, and acting aloof. He realized what had been done. What was he going to do about it?

He really couldn't do anything about the situation with the contract. They had him and it was bad. You try to take a positive spin on it, but they put that kid in a real tough situation.

In 1999, before Mike Ditka left, was another tough year. I do remember going to Baltimore and playing against Michael McCrary. Johnny Unitas was standing on the sideline and I was excited to be playing in front of him. That was a circus, a whole lot of hoopla.

Ricky had a good year in 2000, and then he got hurt. I think he had 1,000 yards in 10 games. He was having a hell of a year. We went to the playoffs and won the first playoff game that year. We had really good offensive and defensive lines that year, and they carried our team. We had taken Darren Howard from Kansas State in the draft that year. La'Roi Glover had 17 sacks that year, and we also had Joe Johnson. I don't think Ricky really became a pro until he got to Miami.

It was a tough deal for that kid. I use to go check on him because he lived close by. He would have people over at his house, driving his cars. He just wasn't ready for the pros.

Trade To Kansas City Chiefs

I was in a tough predicament in 2002. There were some innuendos about some family situation going on. I had been with the Saints for nine years and we won a playoff game, but I think that was the best thing for me. With the situation the way it was, I wasn't going back to New Orleans and playing football. I kind of forced the Saints hand. They paid $500,000 to trade me, and I had to go take a new contract with incentives from the Kansas City Chiefs. I went from close to signing a three-year $13 million contract with the Saints, to a three-year $8 million contract that was mostly incentive based. I wouldn't have it any other way.

I had to start over in Kansas City. I saw Dr. James Andrews, and had ACL surgery. I just felt blessed to come out of that surgery. I had a knee scope in 1998, and came back in 12 days. The scope was a little different than ACL surgery, but I knew I came back from the knee scope pretty quick. I was looking forward to that challenge. I knew I didn't want to end my career limping off the field, trying to play with a bad knee. I knew I didn't want to end my career like that in 2001.

I just was looking forward to an opportunity. I think playing on grass in Kansas City helped me play a couple more years. So, it was a blessing in disguise that I went to play in Kansas City. We had one of the best lines in the NFL. I think over time, we were the best line in the league.

I was very fortunate that the Houston Texans took Tony Boselli that year in the expansion draft, and not me. They said they didn't want to take anybody over 30 years old. I was over 30 and coming off a knee surgery, so they didn't take me.

Being Named To All-Decade Teams of 1990s & 2000s

I didn't know if I was going to make the All-Decade team for the '90s. I was anticipating getting a chance to make it. Someone from ESPN called my agent and let him know that I made the 1990s First Team All-Decade Team. I was just so ecstatic that I made it. You have to come in at a certain point early enough in a decade that you get to play most of the decade. Then you have to play a long time so you get to play in the next decade.

If I hadn't gone to Kansas City, I wouldn't have made the Second Team All-Decade Team for the 2000s. I had four really good football seasons in Kansas City.

Kansas City Offensive Linemen

The Kanas City starting five offensive linemen didn't miss a game the first two years I was with the team. John Tait left and went to the Chicago Bears as a free agent. So next year, the other four of us didn't miss another game for three straight years. I got hurt my last year with the Chiefs in 2005.

My teammate in Kansas City, Will Shields, beat me for the Outland Trophy my senior year in college. He didn't miss a game for 14 years after he got in the lineup his rookie year. Casey Wiegmann started 10 or 11 years without missing a down between Kansas City and Denver, and then back to Kansas City. Brian Waters made the Pro Bowl six times with the Patriots and the Chiefs.

Treating His Body

I took anti-inflammatory shots during the week and on game day. My body hurt after the game. I got on a routine. I would go to the practice on Wednesday, and had a massage every Wednesday night. If we played on the road, it would be on Friday night. If I played at home, I would have a lighter massage on Saturday.

My first four or five years, I looked at teammates going to the chiropractor and I remember saying, "Why do these guys need to go to a chiropractor to get massages?" I could just bounce back then. As I got older, I started to realize why they want to get that done every week. I didn't understand it when I was young, because I was blessed with so much ability. As I got older, I realized that your body starts hurting, and you need this. Those massages are key for you, especially when you get older.

Photograph copyright Associated Press

Chapter 132

Will Shields

College:
Nebraska
Career History:
Kansas City Chiefs (1993–2006)
2015 Inductee Pro Football Hall of Fame

College Choice

I had a couple of colleges that were looking at me. I actually had a hard time qualifying to play college football because of my ACT scores. I had different schools that sort of dropped out of recruiting me. A coach from Oklahoma told me that I could use a combination of ACT scores to qualify. Big tests were not my forte. I ended up qualifying and there were four or five schools recruiting me. Nebraska was one of the top schools on my list of what was going to be the best fit for me as far as where I wanted to go to school.

The schools all had the same regulations of what you needed to get in. I was always close enough to qualifying that schools knew I could qualify. They maybe saw me as being a kid who wouldn't leave the Midwest or wasn't as talented as some of the guys that they were looking at. Nebraska fit what I wanted to do and how I played the game.

Coach Dan Young and Coach Milt Tenopir were the two Nebraska assistant coaches who recruited me. Coach Young came down and spent some time talking to me about different things, and then Coach Tenopir came down and talked a little bit. Coach Tom Osborne came down of course on that last visit to talk.

The thing that was really unique is that they were already ahead of the game as far as the academic side of it. That was very important for me since I felt like I was struggling a little bit to get started. I discovered Nebraska already had academic support in place that would help me get to where I needed to be.

Nebraska Offense

Nebraska was the best option for me. I already knew their offense, because my high school had put in the same offense as Nebraska in my junior year. So that gave me a leg up. And, it wasn't that hard of a transition as going somewhere else and basically learning things from scratch.

Playing Both On The Offensive & Defensive Lines At Nebraska

I like playing on both the offensive and defensive lines. The thing I really liked is that I could play on both. My first year at Nebraska, I actually spent the preseason practicing pass rushing and playing on the defensive line during scout team.

After practice I was helping a teammate rehab his knee. The coach had me pass rushing the rehabbing teammate, and things of that nature. That gave me an opportunity to play on the other side of the ball.

Tom Osborne
Coach Tom Osborne was a lot of fun to play for. The thing most people don't realize is that Coach Osborne let his coaches coach. You really developed a relationship with the coaching staff because of this. Coach Osborne never really sat down and went through the Xs and Os with you. He had meetings with the assistant coaches and they talked about things, and then the assistant coaches came back and implemented everything.

Adjustment To Living Away From Home In College
It was fairly easy. At home I was sort of a homebody, so it made it easy to be a homebody on the college campus. There are always some growing pains here and there, just getting used to being away for a little bit, that kind of stuff; nothing really difficult. The simple fact is I saw my team as my family.

Draft
I was projected to be drafted in the third round. I was hoping that I might be drafted in the first or second round. At one point, I was thinking I am the Outland Trophy Winner. I should be drafted in the first two rounds since I won a prestigious award. That's not necessarily the case and I learned that fairly quickly when I talked to scouts and agents. It's not where you go in the draft; it's what you do after you get drafted.

I got skipped for two rounds and then was drafted in the third round. I got an opportunity to go in and prove what I could do. I thought, now it's time to provide for my family.

I looked at it as a job. I did not want to be a flash in the pan. It was good that I had good coaches when I first came in. They sort of set the tone of what it was going to be like to be a Pro.

I had great players around like Joe Montana and Marcus Allen. I had a chance to sit and watch them prepare, and to see how they did things. I thought, "You know what? I want to be like those guys." I want to be able to say, "Hey, I had a good career." I had a coach who actually brought that up one of the first meetings we were ever in. He said, "If you can make this a true career, that means you've done something right." From that point forward, I was always looking for that next goal and that next round, so that I could keep performing better and better on a higherlevel.

Joe Montana
Joe Montana was very cool and relaxed in the huddle. That was the one thing about him, you never knew if he was rattled or if anything bothered him. He was the same regardless if we were down by 21 or up by 21.

There were times he would walk in the huddle and all he'd say is, "Give me a little more time." That's when you knew he saw something the last play, and that he was going to make something happen.

I liked having guys who understood the game from the inside out because they saw certain things and were be able to say, "You know what, give me two more seconds and I know this guy will beat that guy, and we'll make it happen."

When Realized Could Play In NFL
It wasn't until right before we went into training camp. We had a couple of mini-camps, and my first mini-camp was terrible. I had no idea what I was doing. I was sort of lost trying to catch up. The game was so fast at that point, and I was trying to figure out how could I get better.

Then one of my agents came out and we played one on one basketball. He explained to me, "You know you're making this way too complicated." I said, "What do you mean?" He said, "The goal is the quarterback and you're going to keep me away from him. Just like you play basketball, you're going to play football." He sort of made it simple. I said, "Is that how easy it is? It's not complicated? I don't have to stay focused and do this and do that?" He responded, "Nope."

I show up to the next camp, show some flashes, and the coach started giving me some tips and different things to work on when I went home. At that point I said, "You know what? I think I can do pretty well in this league if I just can keep moving forward and keep working on what I need to do to get better."

Toughest Defensive Lineman
John Randle was tough and gave me fits all the time. Next was Trevor Pryce. Trevor's rookie year, our line coach said, "I hope nobody teaches that kid how to pass rush because he's going to be something special." Lo and behold, guess who ends up leaving? My line coach ends up leaving, going to Denver, and teaching this kid how to pass rush. He could tell what guys could do just by seeing them on film.

John Randle tried to talk trash to me, but I had enough problems with him physically without even worrying about the mental part. I really didn't care what he was saying. I was more or less worried about the physical part. He would say, "Oh, you're not going to talk to me now, huh, you're not going to be my friend. You're not going to …" You can fill in the blank. I just looked at him like he was crazy. John is a great guy. What's really cool is you hate playing against him, but off the field talking to him, he is an awesome guy to be around.

Marty Schottenheimer
Marty Schottenheimer and I had a couple of meetings but we really didn't have a relationship. Marty is a defensive coach, so he was very tied into his defensive players and things like that. We got along but I ended up becoming closer with a couple of the other coaches.

Key To Success
I think it's constantly working on your game. I think you've got to work on different things. Also, learning what everyone else is doing really helps.

You need to push yourself. You've always got to be your worst critic so that you know you're always working to get better. If you can see where your downfalls are before somebody else does, that's always a better thing than waiting for someone else to tell you what you're doing wrong. You need to be open enough to take other people's criticism, and use it to make yourself better.

Not Missing A Game In 14 Seasons
Luck was one of those keys to me not missing a game in 14 seasons. I never thought, "I don't think I'm going to play." I also had a great staff around me, with a great chiropractor. The chiropractor would try some things that would get my body back on track. With that and the training staff we had at the Chiefs on top of that, it was amazing some of the things they could do to get you to be able to perform that next week.

There is a threshold of pain of what you can and can't do, but it's also recovery time; being able to recover enough to say okay I can push through it. You want to be able to get through it, one way or the other. On the other hand, you don't want to be a detriment to the team because you can't do what you need to do to help the team. That's the key. There's a difference between being hurt and being injured. If you're just hurting, you push your way through. If you're injured, you need to sit down and let somebody else in, who will play and perform at a higher level.

Derrick Thomas Dying During NFL Career
Derrick Thomas dying was hard on the team. He was a key player to what we were trying to do and what we were trying to accomplish.

We had a future built around him and what he did as a player. When we lost him, it was tough. The simple fact is that the guy was in the locker room with you, showed up to your charity event and things of that nature, and now he's gone. It leaves a void.

Herm Edwards
Herm Edwards didn't shout while coaching. He liked to talk and was very boisterous in a sense. You knew when he was coming down the hallway.

When I first met Herm he was really quiet. He was here when I was a rookie. He was a defensive back coach at that point, and didn't say a whole lot.

Then for him to come around full circle and be a head coach, it was different. He was a very nice guy and did a great job. Some players liked him and some players were not sure how to take him. I'm one of those guys in between. I liked him; he's a great guy. It's part of fitting the right scheme and the right people in the right place.

Decision To Retire
I knew it was time to quit when they said they were going young. I was sore every week and fighting to get back every week. That was one of those tough years that we fought through, and then when they said, "Hey, we're going to go young." I was like, "Yeah, it's time for me to move on." My knees hurt and my back hurts. For me to keep fighting a battle and we're not looking for a championship, I really didn't have that time on my body to keep fighting that old thing called age.

You always think you've got one good play left in you. As long as you can still walk, talk, and move, you've got that one good play in you. That's just sort of the mentality that you have; that's what kept you playing as long as you played. That's what kept you being the person that you are, the competitive nature of it.

Photograph copyright Associated Press

Chapter 133

Larry Allen

College:
Sonoma State

Career History:
Dallas Cowboys (1994–2005)
San Francisco 49ers (2006–2007)

College Choice
I went to a junior college in Chico, California until I had the grades to transfer to a four-year college. I was sleeping on my mom's couch when the Sonoma State coach, Frank Scalercio, called to say that he could get me into school. I took recruiting trips to the University of Texas at El Paso, Weber State, and UCLA.

Playing In The Senior Bowl
When I played in the Senior Bowl, I wanted to show my best to get noticed by the NFL teams.

NFL Draft
It was great when I found out I was drafted. Jerry Jones called me up when he drafted me. I was happy. I just ran out of my apartment and jumped into the swimming pool with all my clothes on.

Learning To Play Offensive Line In The NFL
With Mark Tuinei, Nate Newton, Ray Donaldson, and Erik Williams being on the offensive line, it was a great learning experience for me coming from such a small school.

My first day of Cowboys training camp, I got into a fight with defensive lineman Leon Lett. I was just tired and getting frustrated, and Leon and I just got into it I guess. After that day, he just took me under his wing. He said I was a fighter and a scraper. He felt I could help the team win.

My father always told me the Charlie Chaplin saying, "Never get mad; get even." Do it the right way.

Hardest Defensive Lineman To Block
During my rookie year, Reggie White was the hardest player to block. He was just a strong man. After playing against him, Reggie told me I had to get in the weight room and get stronger.

A Lot Of Turnover In Dallas Cowboys Head Coaching Position During Career
Even though there was turnover in the Dallas Cowboys coaching position during my career, I still had my offense line coach, Hudson Houck with me for eight years. He was such a great

coach. He taught me everything I needed to know. The head coaching changes really did not bother me much.

Induction Into Dallas Cowboys Ring Of Honor

Being inducted into the Dallas Cowboys Ring of Honor was great. I grew up, watching the Dallas Cowboys on Thanksgiving. I have been a big Cowboys fan since I was a young kid. Being honored with all those guys like Roger Staubach, Troy Aikman, and Emmitt Smith, was a great feeling. Tony Dorsett was one of my favorites growing up.

Preference Run Blocking Or Pass Blocking

I had no preference of run or pass blocking. Both were fine for me. I was just as aggressive a pass blocker as I was a run blocker. So it really did not make a difference to me.

I liked playing guard. You can be more physical at guard than tackle. With tackle, you have all those fast, quick guys you're blocking and you have got to control yourself a little bit more. I just wanted to keep my job. That is the reason why I played so well.

Emmitt Smith

Emmitt Smith was a great running back. People give him a lot of credit. He was a smart back. He was durable. I was happy to play with him.

Troy Aikman

Troy Aikman was a great leader. I did not want to disappoint him.

Leader Of Dallas Cowboys

A whole group of guys were the leaders of the Cowboys. They were Troy Aikman, Emmitt Smith, Michael Irvin, Nate Newton, and Charles Haley.

Michael Irvin Sleeping In Pro Football Hall Of Fame Gold Jacket After Receiving It

I slept in mine too.

Pro Football Hall Of Fame Induction

It is a great feeling being inducted into the Pro Football Hall of Fame. I am not a big public speaker; so giving my enshrinement speech was a little rough for me. I cannot describe the feeling. It is a great feeling.

Favorite Moment In NFL

My favorite moment in the NFL was winning the Super Bowl. I was young. Most guys do not even have a ring. For me, just to get a ring was amazing. It was a great game and a great feeling to win.

Photograph copyright Associated Press

Chapter 134

Jerome Bettis

College:
Notre Dame

Career History:
Los Angeles/St. Louis Rams (1993–1995)
Pittsburgh Steelers (1996–2005)

2015 Inductee Pro Football Hall of Fame

College Choice

My choice of which college to attend was between Notre Dame and Michigan. What it boiled down to was I played fullback. Michigan had just signed the number one tailback in the country. I knew he was going to have to get the football. I was a fullback and could run the football, but Michigan's office was based around the tailback running the football. So, I knew that my best opportunity was going to be at Notre Dame where Lou Holtz's system was really predicated on the fullback having success. Notre Dame was the perfect fit for me and who I was.

Lou Holtz

Lou Holtz was amazing. Coach was a dictator; make no mistake about it. If you got on his wrong side, you were in big trouble. He expected you to be disciplined, play with respect, and give one hundred percent. He helped develop me into the player that I became. He was great, but if you got on his bad side, watch out.

I never got on his bad side because I always knew I had to be on time. That was the number one rule. Being late was the quickest way guys got in big trouble. I always knew I had better be early to ensure my success. Because if you are late for a meeting, you'd better believe it's going to affect your football performance. That was the last thing I wanted to do. I was always smart enough to know I had better be sitting when he closed the door, or else I was in trouble.

Only Carrying Ball 15 Times During Freshman Season

I knew as a freshman I wasn't going to get too many opportunities. I understood what the hierarchy was and how everything went. I knew I was a freshman and Lou Holtz hated freshman carrying the football. Coach Holtz told us, "I only do it if I have to do it." He did this because we had veteran players, and at that time, we had All-Americans at every position. I was playing behind some great fullbacks already. I knew that I was going to have to be patient. The fact that I was able to crack into the starting lineup as a freshman, spoke volumes as to what he thought of me. In the bowl game, he gave it to me a couple of times, and that made a big difference.

Sophomore Season

Coach Holtz made up for it my sophomore year, by giving me the football every which way possible. He had the ball thrown to me, had me rush from the fullback position, and also put me at tailback sometimes. When he wanted to go with three wide receivers, I became the tailback. He gave me a lot of opportunities to carry the football starting my sophomore year.

I weighed about 250 pounds in college. I understood that it was best for me to keep it on the ground and not be a receiver. Also, I couldn't jump that high. I knew it was in my best interest to run it every chance that I got.

Notre Dame Rivalry Against Michigan
Notre Dame and Michigan was a big rivalry. It was usually the first game of the season, so the games were very heated, not only because it was the first one, but also because if you lost, you pretty much lost your chance of winning the national championship. They were huge games.

Coach Holtz was always in an uproar when it was Michigan week because he understood the significance of the games. As 18-20-year-old players, we never truly understood the significance of that game.

Convincing Lou Holtz To Allow Me To Tape My Shoes
I put that into the deal when Coach Holtz was recruiting me. I told him that in order to get me to go to Notre Dame, I wanted to have the ability to tape my shoes like I did in high school. It took a little while, but Coach Holtz finally decided to let me do it. So, I was able to tape them up before every game.

Nobody ever really said anything to me about it, and it actually never became a huge issue. It was something I wanted to make sure I had in the deal, that's for sure.

Decision To Forego Senior Year To Declare For The NFL Draft
It wasn't that hard of a decision to forego my senior year and declare for the NFL Draft. After my junior year, Coach Holtz wanted to meet with my parents and me. So, they came to Notre Dame and we all met. Coach Holtz told me that I had done all I could do in college football, and that I should go and test myself in the NFL. He gave us his blessing and that was the end of it.

NFL Draft
There were only two teams in the top ten picks of the NFL Draft who wanted a running back. The two teams were the Arizona Cardinals and the Rams. The top two running backs were Garrison Hearst and I. I had an idea once Arizona took Garrison Hearst, that I was probably going to the Rams.

I didn't know much about either franchise because they are in the western part of the country. I didn't really follow either team, so I didn't know much about either one. I really had no preference at that point.

Team Followed Growing Up
I was a Dallas Cowboys fan growing up. I didn't watch a lot of football because I grew up as a bowler. I didn't play football until high school. So the only games I really watched were on Thanksgiving, and it was either the Lions or Dallas playing. Dallas usually won so I watched them as opposed to watching the Lions.

Rams Change In Head Coach From Chuck Knox To Rich Brooks

It was a big adjustment from Chuck Knox to Rich Brooks. The adjustment was more in Coach Brooks' philosophy than on the field. Coach Brooks came in and he felt as though I had lied to him. You see, he had asked all the veteran players to come to training camp early, because he was putting in a new system.

I was in the middle of a contract dispute with the team, so I held out. He felt that I had lied to him, because I didn't come to camp on time while I was going through the hold out. At that moment, that was pretty much the end of our relationship.

So, he would pretty much put me in the game for a series, or two series, and take me out for the rest of the game. He pretty much ended the relationship I had with the Rams.

Trade To Pittsburgh Steelers

I was hoping a trade would come about. I had told management that if I didn't get a trade, I was going to retire. I was serious about that. I had re-enrolled in school and was committed to not coming back. Once the Rams management saw I was serious, they gave me permission to seek a trade, and that's how I ended up in Pittsburgh.

It was a great move for my career. The Steelers had just come off losing a Super Bowl to the Dallas Cowboys. I was going to a Super Bowl caliber football team. I just felt that it was going to be great for me and for my career. As it turned out, it was. It made a big difference.

Bill Cowher

Bill Cowher was great. He was a player's coach. He was the kind of coach who related to the players well. He knew what we were thinking, and he also gave us leeway to go out and take care of business. He was definitely a championship coach. They've also mentioned his name for the Pro Football Hall of Fame. He is somebody that I'd vote for.

Being Demoted From Being Starter With Pittsburgh Steelers

I'll never forget what I said when I found out I was demoted. I said that I had been on the other side of most of Coach Cowher's decisions. This time I was not on the positive side, but I handled it like I handled the other times. I thought, I'll deal with it, and I'll work my way to hopefully change his mind. By the end of the season, I was able to change his mind and become a starter again. I was patient, but I also understood that you deal with the ups and the downs with the same humility. I think that's what makes you a professional.

Thanksgiving Day Overtime Coin Toss Mistake By Referee (Caused Rule To Be Changed, Now Team Makes Call Before Toss & Not During)

I guess he misunderstood, or didn't hear what I called on the coin toss. I wish I could tell you what happened. What I do know is the referee gave the Detroit Lions the ball. The Lions went down, kicked a field goal, and won the game. After that, Coach Cowher fired me. That was the last time I ever called the coin toss.

It had never happened before where the referee misheard the call, so they didn't have a protocol for that. They took the referee's word for it and that was the end of it, which I can understand. It was devastating for us, because we lost that game and I believe the rest of the games that year. That was the sad part.

Ben Roethlisberger Convincing Me Not To Retire After 2004 Season

Ben Roethlisberger promised me that he would get me a championship. We were talking on the sidelines after we lost the championship game during the 2004 postseason, and Ben said to me, "Give me a chance. You come back, give me one more year, and I'll get you to a championship." He was a man of his word. We won a championship.

2005 Steelers Win Versus Chicago Bears

The 2005 win versus the Chicago Bears was a great game because it really propelled us to winning the championship. We went on a four game winning streak and went into the playoffs hot. We then won four playoff games, and became the champions. The Bears game was like a playoff game. If we lost, we were out of it. We won and then we kept winning. Next thing you know, I was holding the Lombardi Trophy in my hometown of Detroit.

Being A Finalist Five Consecutive Years For Pro Football Hall Of Fame Induction

I was hoping that I would be inducted into the Pro Football Hall of Fame. It is a very, very exclusive club to be in and so I understood that it was a process. I was just hoping that my time would come soon.

I was patient and I understood that if I didn't get in, it just wasn't my time. It wasn't that I wasn't worthy, it just wasn't my time, and that's how I was able to keep my sanity about it. I understood that there were some great players who went in before me who deserved to be in. Every guy that went in ... when you look at those lists, they all deserved to be on there. When I look at the group I went in with, there were also another ten guys on that list that deserve to be in. It's just not their time yet, and that's how I had to look at it.

It's difficult waiting every single year. Make no mistake about it, that's the difficult part but you have no choice, it's out of your hands. If I could score a touchdown and make getting inducted happen, you better believe I would've been through the hole and there wouldn't have been anybody to stop me. Unfortunately you're not in control of it. You can't determine the outcome, so you have to hang on and hope that it happens.

Photograph copyright Associated Press

Chapter 135

Terrell Davis

College: Long Beach State Georgia Career History: Denver Broncos (1995-2002) 2017 Inductee Pro Football Hall Of Fame

College Choice

I played so many positions in high school. I played five positions; nose guard, linebacker, fullback, kicker, and tight end. I really wasn't a standout athlete in high school. Because I played so many positions, it gave me a great sense of every aspect of the game, from running to tackling to kicking the ball.

My high school, Lincoln High School, was a small school. We only had about 25 players, so we had to play both defense and offense. Prior to that, I had grown up playing running back my entire life. That's the only position I played from Pop Warner until I got to high school. I couldn't get on the field because Lincoln already had two running backs that were starting. I had to find a way to get onto the field and I did that. I enjoyed playing the game, trying to make a difference, and not getting credit for it. That was fun. Then when it was time to find a college, it kind of counted against me, because I didn't have a position.

My brother was at Long Beach State. Long Beach State came around. They had just gotten George Allen as their head coach. I think my brother had mentioned to them that there was a kid in San Diego they should look at. They didn't know we were brothers, because my brother's last name is Webb. George Allen called because he liked what he saw. He said, "Hey, just come here. We can't promise you anything, but we will promise that if you work hard, we will try hard to take care of you." I guess that meant give me a scholarship. The other schools that were in the picture were Utah State, Pacific, and Cal State Fullerton. No real big schools were recruiting me. Those schools were my only options.

George Allen

George Allen was a defensive minded coach. He spent most of his time on that side of the ball. When I redshirted all I was doing was scout team stuff. That's really where I got back my running back position. I was on the scout team, and Coach Allen wanted the scout team offense to be as good as the starting offense. He thought that was the way you prepare your starting defense. He fell in love with me. He even gave me the nickname, Secretariat. The way he ran special teams, scout team, and meetings, everything was the first taste of a professional team that I had experienced. He had wisdom and knowledge. He was real big on playing together. He had a sign when you walked into our building, which said, "Togetherness: 53 men playing together, you can't lose."

I got a chance to work with him very closely because of the fact that he wanted his scout team offense to be extremely good against the defense. I remember times at a Thursday practice when the defense was trying to get off the field, but I'm making them repeat the plays because I'm running so hard. The members of the defense would be getting upset, telling me to slow down and stop running so hard, but George Allen respected that. That's what he taught me, how to practice and play at a certain level all the time. I have a profound respect for George. I learned a lot from him. Although he passed away the year after my redshirt freshman year, I tried to take what I learned from him and use that when I went to Georgia, and then when I went into the pros.

Recruitment After Long Beach State Program Disbanded
There were three schools that were recruiting me after Long Beach disbanded the football program. The first school that had contacted me was Hawaii.

UCLA contacted me, but they weren't serious. They had a lot of running backs that they were trying to give scholarships to. They invited me to come down on an unofficial visit, and I did. I was excited about UCLA; I loved UCLA. I thought I was going there.

As a kid growing up in southern California, the big schools were USC and UCLA. I loved UCLA and I loved their colors. I was thinking man, UCLA, that'd be perfect, but they weren't committed. They never offered me a scholarship.

Then I'm sitting there trying to think, should I stay at Long Beach State, should I go to UCLA, or should I go to Hawaii? I didn't really want to go to Hawaii, I just didn't.

When I was thinking about what I should do, I got a call in my room from Bob Pittard from the University of Georgia. He left a message that said, "Hey, give me a call. We'd like to bring you down for a visit." I heard that phone call, and I was shocked. I didn't know much about Georgia at the time, but I knew they had a big program. I did some research. I was telling people about the call, and they were like, "Man, Georgia called you?" Everybody was surprised, even more so than me. They sent me their media guide, so I looked at the players they had in the past, the bowl games they went to, and what conference they were in. It was a no-brainer. I called them and I went there on a visit. I fell in love with the place. I had never seen anything like it. When I was going back to the airport to go home, they pulled me off the shuttle bus and offered me a scholarship. I accepted immediately.

I was a little nervous about going to Georgia because I was a west coast kid. I hadn't really left the west coast and was a little concerned about that. I took a chance and stayed there. It was exciting taking a chance to go to a place not really knowing what to expect. At that time I was 18 or 19 years old. I felt like it was good for my development just go somewhere different. If I didn't like it I, could always go back home. That's kind of how I thought.

Getting Hurt Early In Senior Season In College

I thought there was no way I was going to play in the NFL when I got hurt my senior season in college. I missed a substantial amount of games my senior season and I hadn't had a great college career. Things weren't looking good for me. I remember reflecting on my career while I was sitting in the stands watching the team at one of our home games. I was thinking there's a good chance that I might not ever get a chance to play again for Georgia. Not that I wouldn't come back from my injury, but even if I came back from my injury, there was no guarantee that I was going to play. Hines Ward was our running back at the time and he was playing well. I didn't think I was going to be able to get back on the field once I was healthy.

I thought if I ever get a chance to play again, I've got to play this game differently. It wasn't to make it to the pros. I wanted to finish my college career where I could be proud, where I could look back and say I ended my career on a high note. That was my only goal at that point. I thought the NFL was gone. I didn't think there was any chance I could play in the NFL. I just wanted to try to do it for myself, to just play the game and leave on a high note. It really gave me some motivation. When I got back, I just gave it my all. I didn't care. I just played the game as if I was never going to play the game again. That was kind my mentality for the last four games.

Two of those last games, I played fullback. Hines was the halfback. Before the Auburn game, my coach pulled me into a room and said, "Hey, we've been seeing something different from you, and we like what we see. We're going to put you back as the starting tailback."

Auburn was undefeated at the time. I had two more games to play, Auburn and Georgia Tech. Those last two games were probably the two best all around games I had in my college career. I don't know if those two games got me drafted, but I think they got me into the Blue-Gray game. The Blue-Gray game was important because it kept my college career and football career alive. The draft came, and Denver drafted me.

Ray Goff

Ray Goff and I had a difficult relationship. It was not the type of relationship that I would have loved to have with my head coach. For whatever reason, maybe because he was a young coach and I was a young player, we just butted heads. We were like oil and water. We just did not get along.

Some scouts told me things that he had said about me. They said he was attacking my character by saying I wasn't tough. They also said that he was withholding tapes of me. It wasn't stuff that I was making up; these were things I was hearing from scouts. I was upset. At the time, I couldn't understand why a coach would do that. You would think a coach would try to promote you to the pros, so the program looks good and he looks good.

We had a nasty relationship in college. It's been a long time, and Ray and I have spoken a number of times since college. We're actually pretty good friends now. We talk a lot on the phone now. He'll be in Canton for my enshrinement.

We've had a chance to talk, and understand what happened then, and why it happened. I had reached out to him just to let him know that my heart was heavy with what happened, and I didn't feel right carrying that. I had already forgotten about it, really, and then people would bring it up. I'd say, "You know what, I don't feel the same way about Ray. That was years ago. How I felt then and how I feel about him now … I don't feel the same way."

I actually thanked him. I said, "I didn't think about it at the time, but sometimes when somebody's put in your life and they're doing things that in the end make you better, like being hard on you, you may not accept it at the time. You don't like it because you think they're just being hard on you. I believe in God, I believe there's a purpose for everything, and I believe when someone does something, it's for a reason. It's to build character; to make you into the person that you are meant to be. We've gotten past that. College, from that standpoint, was difficult.

NFL Draft
I had no idea the Denver Broncos were going to draft me. I had never heard of the Broncos coming to a pro day for me. They may have come, but they certainly didn't contact me. I didn't hear from an agent or anybody saying they had an interest in me. I don't remember interviewing for the Broncos.

The two teams I thought that showed the most interest in me were the Browns and Cowboys. I had thought maybe one of those teams would draft me. I was hoping the Cowboys drafted me, but they drafted Sherman Williams in the second round. There weren't a lot of pro teams that showed interest.

Starting For Denver Broncos In First Game Of Rookie Season
What's even more unbelievable than my starting my first game of my rookie season with the Denver Broncos is that every place I've been, I've had the same route. When I went to Long Beach State I was at the bottom of the depth chart and had to fight my way to the top. I end up starting my redshirt freshman year.

I go to Georgia and I'm sixth or seventh on the depth chart. During training camp I'm behind Garrison Hearst. Then, I'm starting during my junior year.

I've always loved playing running back. I think I was a natural tailback. When I got to Denver, I decided I was going to play this game as if it was the last time I was playing it.

At Georgia, the coach changed the entire offense my junior year. We changed the offense from a more running offense to a more passing one. I was catching the ball out of the backfield more than I was running it. I had to pick up the blitz and I had to catch the ball out of the backfield. It helped me to become a more well-rounded back.

When I got to Denver, their offense suited me well since I could do it all. We played the West Coast Offense, so I had to block, catch, and run. I had to be able to look up and see what coverage the defense was in, their fronts. I thought I had a bit of an advantage because of my college offense.

I was willing to do whatever it took. I did whatever I had to do. When I got my chance to play, it was running down on a kickoff and having to tackle somebody. I felt that I did that and showed I was willing to do anything; they would give me a chance at what I really want to do which was play running back. That was my approach, and it worked.

Timing was everything for me with Denver. I can't say that if I had gone to a team that had an established coach, staff, and running back, that I would have been given a shot at starting at running back. For Mike Shanahan to come in and have this open competition during his first year as Broncos head coach, and not just peg one guy as his starter helped. He was looking to build the team, and didn't have a lot of guys at that time that were already set in positions. He had a few guys, but not enough. He obviously gave me a chance to work my way up. I just liked his approach. He didn't care whether you were a free agent, a low round draft pick, or a first round draft pick. They were going to play the best person. That's all anybody can ask for. That's why I respect Mike Shanahan for that. He nurtured an environment that allowed us to compete, and the best player won. That's all anybody can ask for.

Super Bowl XXXII Denver Broncos vs. Green Bay Packers
Going into the game we were heavy underdogs. Green Bay had Brett Favre, Reggie White, and the NFC had won 13 straight Super Bowls. Here we were, a team that nobody thought had a chance. We felt different. We felt like we were built a little bit more like a NFC team. We had gone through enough adversity and didn't think that anybody could beat us if we played our game. That season we played Pittsburgh and Kansas City in their home stadiums and won. We felt if we could win in those two places, which were the toughest venues to play in, we could play anybody on a neutral field. We liked our chances.

Going into the game we felt confident. I knew that the game hinged on my performance. That's a lot of pressure for anyone, but I was prepared and excited for the opportunity. I felt comfortable with the game plan since we were going to run the ball 40 times. That told me a lot. When a coaching staff puts together a game plan which involves using you that much, as a competitor and as somebody who wants to be able to control the outcome of a game, you can't ask for anything better than that.

The night before the game, I slept like a baby. People ask me, "Man, weren't you nervous?" I respond, "Yeah, but I was prepared, and more excited than anything." I'd much rather go to sleep knowing we're going to run the ball 40 times than go to bed knowing we're going to throw it 50 times in a game. That would have been unsettling. I wouldn't have been able to affect the game like I wanted to.

The game starts and we are down seven-nothing very quickly. No one panicked. Everybody looked around and said, "Okay, they scored. We've got to score." We did that. We knew it was going to be a tough game. It was not going to be an easy game by any means. Our feeling was if we don't screw up, we're going to win the game.

Then I got a migraine in the first quarter. That was devastating, because I thought I had let everyone down. I thought I had let my teammates, fans, and myself down because I had to leave the game. I was sick thinking about the next day's headline of Denver losing this game and me not being able to help out. That hurt me.

I tried to get back as fast as I could. I end up coming back in the third quarter. Fortunately, I was able to come back when we were either tied or leading. I fumbled the first snap of the third quarter, which was not good.

It was a back and forth, very exciting game. I just stayed focused and tried not to think about the outcome. I was trying to think about my job and my responsibilities. I was trying to play my role as best as I could. I felt if I did that, then we had a great chance of winning the game. I tried to stay in the moment, and was able to do that. At the end of the game I looked at the scoreboard and saw we won 31-24.

The thing that stands out to me a lot is when John Mobley knocked down a pass that Brett Favre intended for Mark Chmura. I still replay that play in my head a lot because that was the culmination, the exclamation point on a season that we had fought our asses off during. To beat Green Bay, and to upset that team was exciting. I was exhausted at the end of the game. I will always remember that final play.

Suffering From Migraines

I've had migraines since I was eight or nine years old. I remember playing football with a migraine when I had no idea that I suffered from migraines. I was not diagnosed at the time. I was so ashamed, because I couldn't explain to anybody what was going on. I felt guilty about telling somebody how I felt, because I couldn't explain it. I played in a couple of high school games with full-blown migraines with no medication whatsoever. It was probably the most difficult thing that I had ever had to do.

In college, I was diagnosed with migraines. They would come every so often, and I could take medication. The medication would at least numb the headache. The headache wouldn't be as intense.

I played a few games with migraines in the pros. Against Tampa Bay I got hit in the head by Hardy Nickerson during the first quarter. I missed the second quarter and came back out and played in the third quarter. With that history, when I got the migraine in the Super Bowl, I knew that there was a chance that I could come back. Thank God the halftime shows are super long, because it allowed the medication to kick in. I knew I was going to be able to come back. That was the hope. My saving grace was I knew I would come back; it was just a matter of when. What would happen during the game while I was away was what I was concerned about.

When I got back, my vision was clear. It's like you have a hangover. Your head is still a little sensitive. I had no choice though; I had to play. If it was a regular season game, chances are I would have sit out. I couldn't in this case. I wouldn't have been able to forgive myself for not going back into the game, especially if we had lost the game. I was like, hey, do it now, go through the pain and suck it up. I can rest tomorrow, the next day, the next day, and a whole six months from now. Today you got to go.

John Elway Utilizing The Running Game More Later On In His Career
John Elway has never said this but I imagine behind the scenes it was tough for him to hand the ball off more because I think it's a sign that maybe he was not the same quarterback he used to be. That's tough for anybody to swallow. I would feel the same way if the roles were reversed. If we were a running team, then we get a quarterback and we start to throw it, I would feel the same way.

It wasn't like we were running the ball and we weren't successful. It wasn't like we were just running the ball a lot and he was not getting a chance to throw the ball. John still threw the ball a lot. We still had game plans where we threw a lot since we knew we couldn't run the ball against a team like we want to. It was important for John to be able to throw the ball, because we needed that to keep the opponent from putting extra defenders in the box, or doing things to slow down the running game. The balance we had in Denver was perfect. If the defense put too many people up there in the box, we knew John was going to kill the opponent throwing the ball. I don't know if John has ever said it publicly, but I just know that if it were me and we were used to being a running team and all of a sudden we were a passing team, deep down inside it would kind of hurt. You want to be the person that the team relies on. The way I look at it is we didn't take anything from John; we added something to what he was doing which allowed us to be a better team.

Not Breaking Eric Dickerson's Single Season Rushing Yardage Record
I probably could have broken his record. I didn't care about records at that time. I only cared about one thing, and that was if we were winning games, in the playoffs, and playing for the Vince Lombardi Trophy. That's the only thing I cared about. I cared less about 2000-yard seasons and whatnot.

This shows I didn't care, because there was one against Philadelphia and one against Dallas where the coach asked me if I wanted to stay in. I got pulled at halftime against Philadelphia and early in the third period against Dallas. I think in both of those games I had over 150 yards rushing. I didn't care about the record. I just wanted to be as healthy as possible so that I could help the team win a championship. That's really all I cared about.

1999 NFL Playoffs
We felt pretty confident about Atlanta. We were probably a little bit more concerned if Minnesota had made the Super Bowl. We were watching Atlanta play against Minnesota in the NFL Championship Game as we were preparing to play the New York Jets in the AFC Championship Game. When Minnesota lost we got pretty excited in our locker room. Everybody was like, "Oh, Minnesota lost, wow."

We were thinking it's going to be an easy AFC Championship Game. Somebody forgot to tell us we had a game to play. The Jets came in and we were down 10-0 early in the third quarter. We woke up and came back and won the game.

When we got ready to play Atlanta in the Super Bowl, we felt we matched up well against them. We felt like Green Bay did the year before when they played us in the Super Bowl. Knowing how the media was pumping us up, we had to really check our way of thinking. Our thinking was we knew what happened last year when Green Bay was favored by double digits against us. Now we're being favored. We have to make sure we stay focused, and don't believe the hype. We know we're good, but we've got to make sure we don't buy into all that stuff and think that we just have to show up to win the game against Atlanta.

We played a hell of a game, so I was proud of us. We went out there and played a good game.

John Elway's Decision To Retire After Super Bowl Win Against Atlanta Falcons
Man, we tried to convince John Elway not to retire after winning the Super Bowl against Atlanta. What people don't realize is he was beat up. John missed a lot of practice time. He was constantly in rehab, icing shoulders and knees. He gave us all he could give us. We appreciate him giving us that. We were trying to do everything to convince him not to retire. I was hoping that Mike Shanahan would say, "Hey John, sit out training camp, relax, we'll see you in early September. You just play in regular season games." We needed to have him back. It's hard when someone walks out after you win two Super Bowls, and you don't really give yourself a chance to win three in a row. You've got to go for it!

We understood his decision. We didn't like it, but we had to go forward. Obviously things didn't turn out too well after that. That flame burned out real quick.

Numerous Injuries Sustained After 1998 Season
It was a constant struggle trying to fight injury. I never regained my health. It's hard to be an elite athlete when you're fighting injuries and just trying to become a healthy player, let alone a player who was trained to play on a different level. It was mentally draining, more than anything. That was rough.

Mile High Salute
The Mile High Salute started in training camping in 1997. We had lost to Jacksonville the year before in the playoffs. I was just trying to think of something where we had to have a mentality for that year. The mentality that I was looking for was that of a soldier. This was for the running backs in particular. I was saying, "Hey guys, when we're on the field we have to adopt a mentality that is nasty, that is physical; you've got determination, you've got to do all this stuff." I was thinking about who represents that. A Soldier.

Being a soldier is not like being a football player where you go play football and then you walk off the field. Soldiers go out there and they put their lives on the line. Out of respect, I thought this is what we're going to do. When we score, we're going to salute each other. That's our Mile High Salute to each other, out of respect as soldiers.

We did it in the preseason and started doing it during the season. It just took off. Everybody on the team started to do it.

Selection To Pro Football Hall Of Fame
From what everybody was saying, they thought my career was too short to make the Pro Football Hall Of Fame. Then I made the semifinalist list for the Hall Of Fame. That was the first year I actually got excited. I was thinking maybe there's a chance I make the Hall Of Fame. I made it

again as a semifinalist and got excited again. I felt maybe there were people talking about me making the Hall Of Fame again.

The following years there weren't a whole lot of conversations about me making the Hall Of Fame. I'd see my name on the list, and when I would watch sports shows, people would talk about everybody else on the list except me. They might ask somebody, who on this list do you think deserves to be in the Hall Of Fame? No one would say me. Then I thought, I guess I'm not going to make it.

About year seven I really felt like, maybe this is where I'm going to be all the time. Maybe I'll just make the list of semifinalists, and that's it. Not that I was okay with it, but I was like, okay, that's where they're going to put me. You can't do anything about it. You can't go play any more, and you can't control it, so I tried not to worry about it.

Then, in 2014 they called me while I was driving with my wife and told me that I had advanced from the semifinalist list to the finalist list. I was fired up. I pulled over and told her, "You won't believe what happened." She's like, "What, what?" I said, "I just made the finalist list for the Hall Of Fame." We screamed and hugged each other on the side of the road. It was big. That kind of got me rejuvenated. That kind of got me thinking maybe there's something to it.

The following three years, it started to feel like there was more momentum behind it. More people were talking about it. When I would watch a show, I would see guys who didn't endorse me early on, change their opinions about me. It was great to see that. It was a good feeling to see people stop looking at the length of my career, and start to look at the substance of what happened.

I couldn't control whether I played seven or 20 years. The one thing I could control was the effort I gave when I played. I think people can look at that and say, "Damn, when he played, this dude gave it his all. My teammates will say, 'TD gave everything, TD played his ass off when he played.'" To me, that's the biggest compliment I can get. Knowing that I got your back, no matter what it is, I'm going to show up; I'm going to be there and show up. It was great to see the selection committee looked at that. It's a tough process, and it should be tough, because it's more rewarding when it happens.

I had so many emotions running through my head when Dave Baker, President of The Pro Football Hall Of Fame, told me I had been selected to the Hall. I was relieved, excited, and had jubilation. My mind was flipping the channel on what this all meant. I was thinking about things I wouldn't have to say anymore. I was like, thank God. I was thinking about the people that I had seen with these gold jackets on, and thinking that now I am one of them.

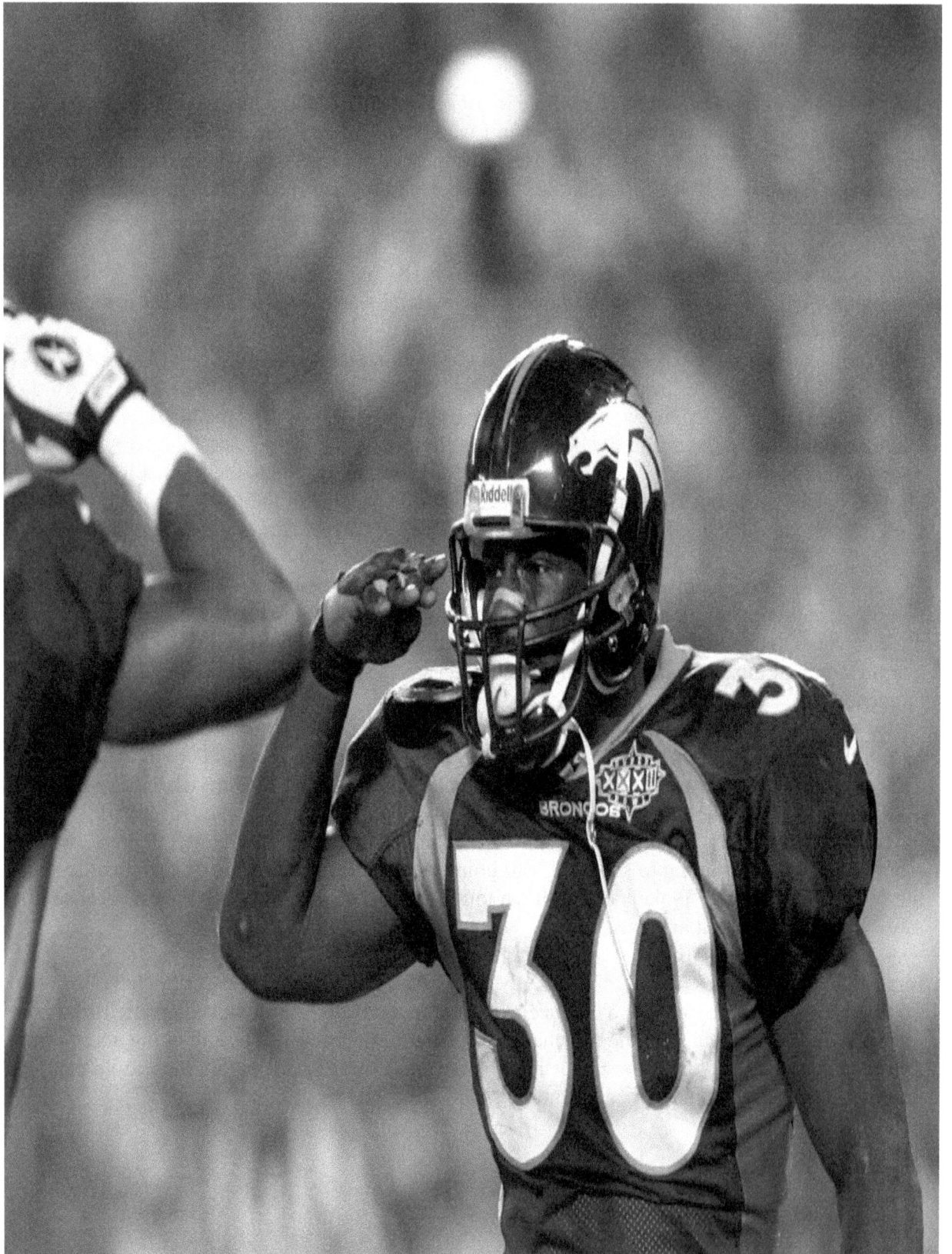

Photograph copyright Associated Press

Chapter 136

Derrick Brooks

College: Florida State Career History: Tampa Bay Buccaneers (1995–2008) 2014 Inductee Pro Football Hall Of Fame

College Choice
Florida State was my primary choice for a college when I was being recruited. When I was being recruited, so many colleges were starting to sound the same. I said no matter where I go I need to get a good education.

I was laying down one day and I thought, 'If something happens to me, my parents need to be able to get to me. So the closest university to Pensacola, Florida was Florida State and that's why I ended up at Florida State.

Miami was on my list to visit, but at the end of the day when it got down to it, Miami was 10-11 hours away. Florida State was only two hours and 10 minutes away. So, that helped me boil it down to Florida State, too.

Bobby Bowden
Florida State Head Coach Bobby Bowden was awesome. He had the principles to live his life with religious faith in the industry of college football for 50 plus years. That is amazing. He set the tone for the team thru his principles. Playing for Mickey Andrews, the Florida State defensive coordinator, allowed me to develop the mental toughness that I have today. That was awesome. I had fun there with the linebacker coaches, Wally Burnham and Jim Gladden. I really enjoyed my time at Florida State with all the coaches.

Winning National Championship Against Nebraska
Winning the National Championship against Nebraska wasn't bad either. That's another thing that I'm grateful for. I was on the team that brought Coach Bowden his first National Championship after he coached for so many years. It was great to be a part of that team and be able to say, "We did it for Coach Bobby. We were part of his first championship team." All of those things are important to me. I was blessed to obviously win it and to be a part of it.

We were heavy favorites in 1993, against Nebraska. Going into the game most people had us blowing them out. We knew it was going to be a lot tougher game than what people were projecting. Nebraska was a tough opponent. We made plays down the stretch to win, but we knew going in how tough the game was going to be, and we didn't take Nebraska lightly at all. I played to win and at no point did I doubt that we were going to win that game.

NFL Draft
Was I the 28th best player in the first round? Not in my mind. Obviously I was expecting the best, but I just wanted an opportunity to play and go in and prove myself. I thank God that the Tampa Bay Buccaneers moved back into the first round to draft me at number 28. I'm grateful that I was able to play my entire career in the state of Florida.

At that time, I was just thankful that I had got drafted. I wasn't a guy who was bitter, saying I should have been this pick or that pick. I was drafted where I was meant to be drafted, and I embraced the opportunity that was before me.

Tony Dungy
Tony Dungy was tough. He coached us tough, but yet it was fun. He brought discipline, consistency, and a way of doing business that changed the Buccaneers culture. He came in talking about changing our community and making us all winners on and off the field. Coach Dungy set the tone for my attitude towards making a difference in the community.

Tampa Bay Buccaneers Lack Of Success Until Late '90s
That's the intriguing part of the position that we were in to turn the franchise around. Now, I can say that was part of my Hall of Fame resume.

Tampa Bay Defense
The defenses architect was actually Chuck Noll of the Pittsburgh Steelers. Tony Dungy obviously put his principles on it and installed it, and he brought it to Monte Kiffin. Monte Kiffin and Tony Dungy had worked together before being with the Buccaneers. I like to think it was honestly the head coach's influence, and trusting the coaches to get the teaching over to the players.

When Coach Dungy talks about the Tampa defense, he always gives credit back to Chuck Noll and what the Steeler defense was able to do. Obviously, he changed things out depending on the talent level we had at Tampa. It all dates back to Chuck Noll when you talk about some of the principles that Tony Dungy ran defensively for us.

Leader Of Tampa Bay Buccaneers Defense
Each position had its own leadership within its position. At times, different leaders spoke up. Generally my teammates looked at me asking who was the leader. Then, I stepped up and embraced that role. I was the type of leader where the stage was big enough for everyone to shine. I like to think we did it together, to be honest.

Toughest Opponent
There really wasn't just one guy. I had my battles with all of my opponents. I looked at tough battles as an opportunity to shine. I embraced the joy in going up against the likes of Marshall Faulk and Barry Sanders, and determining how could I step my game up. Going against my opponent, I used that as motivation to bring out the best in me.

Personal Stats

My stats were pretty good every year. To be honest, I wasn't asked to sack the quarterback, so that's why I don't have a lot of sacks. I like to think that I had a complete game, and whatever the defense asked me to do, I believe I had the skill set to do it.

Playing Philosophy

I modeled my game after myself. I try to get better every single year. "Stay in the moment" was my playing motto, and it still is today. When I first came into the NFL, Junior Seau was in the league and as far as 4-3 linebackers go, you looked at him. Hardy Nickerson was on my team and set a standard for my position. At the end of the day, I wanted to make my game, my game and just try to get better every year.

2002 NFL Defensive Player Of The Year

I like to celebrate 2002, because when I received that individual award for being the best defensive player, we won the Super Bowl. That's special to me.

Winning Super Bowl vs. Oakland Raiders

I think the Super Bowl win gave validation to the Tampa Bay Buccaneers and the Tampa Bay area. The Buccaneers went from 0-26 when they first started in the league, to Super Bowl champion years later. I think it was a combination of a lot of hard work, a lot of disappointments, and obviously a lot of joy. I think the Tampa Bay area celebrated the championship because that's how much it meant to our city.

Feelings On Tony Dungy Not Winning A Super Bowl With The Tampa Bay Buccaneers

I felt bad every year we lost in the playoffs and didn't go further. Coach Jon Gruden came in and brought a different dynamic to our football team. Obviously, that dynamic helped us win a championship. At the time, we were blessed with the challenge of looking forward, not backward. I think Coach Dungy went on to have a pretty good career after Tampa.

Lee Roy Selmon Not Getting A Chance To Play In A Super Bowl

That's part of the Tampa Bay Buccaneers' history. It's overcoming those types of moments. Everybody doesn't get a chance to play in the Super Bowl. There are other Hall of Fame players who never played in the Super Bowl. So, you just understand how special the opportunity to play in the Super Bowl is, and when you win, it's even more special.

Favorite Play In Career

I didn't have a favorite play. I tried to appreciate all the plays I made individually. Obviously, some plays meant more in the game than others. You tend to gravitate toward those and I do that as well. But, I kind of appreciate them all. I was blessed to play a lot of football in the NFL, and I don't want to take any play that I made or didn't make for granted.

Decision To Retire

I just knew it was time to retire. I got some calls from teams after I was released from the Buccaneers, but I was just trying to wait for the right situation for me. There were situations that came close, but there was never one that I felt comfortable accepting as a total package.

It wasn't really one moment or one day when I decided to retire. It was just things added up over time while I started transitioning into life after football. Before I knew it, I had a full schedule. I had no regrets. It was time to move on.

Being Named Walter Payton Man Of The Year
Winning the award recognizes not only me, but also the work of a lot of people behind the scenes who are making changes in the community, and making life better for people. I was just grateful that we won the first year they renamed the award after Walter Payton. I was one of the co-recipients. That is life's work. That's where I feel the game gives you a platform to make a difference, and I thank God that I was able to do it.

Pro Football Hall Of Fame Induction
I was joyous, ecstatic, and emotional all at once. Sometimes you experience emotions that you can't describe. That was one of those moments.

I'm blessed that I was a first ballot Hall of Famer. I'm also blessed that I got a chance to be a part of history. I was enshrined with Ray Guy, the only full-time punter in the Hall of Fame. Claude Humphrey is one of the best defensive ends, and I saw how appreciative he was to be enshrined the same year as me. Whether you get in on the first ballot or you get in after many years, doesn't matter. The fact is they went into the Hall of Fame, and I got a chance to sharethat with them. I appreciate that I was a part of the 2014 Hall of Fame Class. God blessed me to be a part of it with those guys.

Photograph copyright Associated Press

Chapter 137

Walter Jones

> College:
> Florida State
>
> Career History:
> Seattle Seahawks (1997–2009)
>
> 2014 Inductee Pro Football Hall Of Fame

College Choice

Being from Alabama people ask me about my college choice all of the time. "Why didn't you go to Alabama?" I joke around and say, "Florida State's check was bigger." When I was being recruited, Florida State was one of the dominant teams in college football.

I went to Florida State for a visit and I said, "This is where I want to play my college ball." I was going to do whatever it took for me to get there and play at Florida State.

I was an Alabama fan growing up. Alabama was the team everybody in Alabama loved. When I was attending junior college, it was hard to choose Florida State because I still had an opportunity to go to Alabama. I had to go where I thought there was a better opportunity for me to get into the NFL.

Coming out of high school, I think everybody has a story of not doing as well in school I they would have liked. I had a high school coach that kind of got me on track. He took me around to college games and stuff.

I made a visit to Florida State and other colleges and went to major college football games. Coming from a small town, I figure, "This is my way out. This is something that I want to do, this is something I want to be a part of."

I'm not saying that it was a lot different, but there are more people. You get to meet all types of people. For me, that was something I wanted to be a part of. I wanted to be part of a big time school, playing football. I did everything I could to get to that point. I think the transition was more like I can't wait to get there. It was something that I had been working hard for. I worked through high school and junior college to get to Florida State. I wanted to be walking on that campus and I wanted to be a part of the whole school scene.

I came from a small rural town and didn't have much. I watched football and thought, "I got the potential to be good at this." For me, I just decided that football was something I wanted to pursue, so I kind of put all my marbles in one basket and said, "Hey, this is what I want to pursue."

Before I got into football, I wasn't doing that well in school. School wasn't something that was important to me. Once I got into football, I realized that I had to improve in school. I should have been doing my schoolwork, but I wasn't. I was doing other things. I had to put the other things that weren't helping me out, behind me and I had to concentrate on school. I was ineligible to play my senior year of high school. That's why I had to go to a junior college.

I had to do all my own recruiting. I had make all of my videotapes, send them out to teams, and let teams know that I was out there because I wouldn't be playing football my senior year.

I had to go the junior college route. At the junior college, my recruiting started all over again. Colleges found out I was from the state of Alabama, and I had already said that I was going to go to Florida State when I was in high school.

Bobby Bowden
Bobby Bowden is a hometown favorite. For me to get a chance to play for a great coach like that was fine. He was very family-oriented, where he knew everything about your family. Florida State had become a big powerhouse, so Coach Bowden was relying more on his assistants to make his team accomplish his goals. For him, it was more about getting to know you as a player.

Now that I think about it after being in the NFL, it was more like he was preparing you for the NFL. In the NFL, you don't see the head coach as much as you see the assistant coaches and the guys who are relaying the information down to you. You have to get it done on the football field. At Florida State, players were kind of getting that feeling of how things are done in the pros.

Florida State's Biggest Rival
That's tough, but when I was playing, it was Florida. Miami was their biggest rival back in the early '90s. I got a chance to play against Florida twice. My first year at Florida State, I was a redshirt, so I didn't get a chance to play. That game was so good. We came back and tied the game up. Just being on the sidelines and seeing that game was great.

Then the next year I played against Florida. Florida was the number one team in the country going into the game and we were number two. That game was so hyped, and we came out on top. That was our last regular season game and we had to see who we would play for the championship.

Florida went on and won the SEC championship, and we ended up playing those guys again for the championship. In that two-year span, Florida was the team that we knew we had to beat. We shouldn't have played them in a championship game since we had already beaten them, but those guys kind of figured out what we were doing to them. Danny Wuerffel kind of showed why he was the Heisman Trophy winner. He threw the ball all over the field and stuff. The game kind of got out of hand pretty fast, and we lost.

Redshirting
It's one of those situations where I learned a lot. I was doing everything except playing in the game on Sunday, so it kind of humbled me a little bit. I just had to wait my turn.

A lot of classes that I had taken at the junior college weren't transferring. There was so much paperwork to do to get those classes transferred, and making sure those classes counted with the Division I schools. I was preparing myself to play by practicing every day, doing everything, and hoping I would get in the game. It was about game six of the season when all my classes from my junior college had cleared. I sat down with the coaches, and they told me the best thing for me to do was to redshirt and it would be a learning year for me.

In the grand scheme of things, it helped me out a lot. I was able to play with great guys every day in practice, and hone my skills and preparing myself. The next year I was ready, prepared, and able to go out and play at a high level.

NFL Draft
I didn't know the Seattle Seahawks were going to draft me. When I was coming out in the draft, there was a list of the six elite guys coming out in the draft, and I was on that list.

I didn't think Seattle was going to draft me. Prior to the draft, I went to Seattle on a scouting visit. Even though they were showing interest in me, they just didn't say, "If you're available, we're going to pick you."

I was watching the draft with my family. Once Seattle picked Shawn Springs with the third pick in the draft, I figured I was going to be drafted by Oakland. Then some trades happened, and all of a sudden it was Seattle drafting with the number six pick. With probably a minute left on the draft clock for Seattle to make a pick, Seattle Head Coach Dennis Erickson called me and said, "How would you like to be a Seattle Seahawk?" I said, "I would love to be a Seattle Seahawk." They made the pick, and the rest is history. At that time, all I wanted to do was to get into the NFL and prove that I could play at the NFL level.

First Training Camp
The coaches put me at left tackle and said, "You're our left tackle. The only way you'll lose your job is if you don't play well." I realized that it was my job to lose, so I put everything into it. I said, "I'm not going to lose the job. I've been working for the last five years to get to this point."

For the Seahawks to draft me that high, I knew that they were pretty confident that I could come in there and be a starter for them. Once they gave me the job, I was thrown into the fire. When quarterbacks are that high of a draft pick, sometimes people say they should not start for a year. But, I think as an offensive lineman playing at that high level, at that high of a pick, you have to take the good and the bad and let the offensive lineman learn the system, learn the plays, and learn on the fly instead of sitting on the sideline. I think as an offensive lineman, you can learn so much by playing and getting a lot of reps at practice and in the game.

Seattle Seahawks Defensive Line
Phillip Daniels gave me fits every day. Phillip and Cortez Kennedy were true professionals. Those guys worked me every day. As a rookie, you have to earn your respect with those guys, so you want to go out there and prove that you can play at the NFL level. Those guys had been playing for a couple of years. For me, it was great work. I wanted to be a part of it, and this is where I wanted to be. I was going to do everything I could to gain their respect, and go out there

and prove to them that I could play. It was not just about going against them, going out there on Sunday, fighting and showing that I could fight. I wanted to show why the team picked me and wanted me to be their left tackle.

Realization Could Play At A High Level In NFL

I think the blessing for me is that we ran one offense for about ten years, so that made everything a lot easier for me. A lot of times the game plan for me was, "Hey, block the defensive end." That made it easier for me to go out there and say, "I know I can play this game. Now all I have to do is study the guy I'm going against, and do everything I can to take that guy out of the game."

That made my game plan easy, so all I had to do was go out there and focus on that guy. I'm not saying that wasn't a tough job at times, but as a player you want that competition. You want to go out there and shut a guy out. That's when things started to open up for me.

When I was growing up, Anthony Muñoz was probably one of the best left tackles out there. In high school the offensive linemen watched tapes showing techniques for lineman. Anthony Muñoz was shown as an example of how left tackles should play the game.

There were some great guys who were playing the game at that time. If you go back and look, there was Erik Williams, Jonathan Ogden, Orlando Pace, and Tony Boselli, before he got hurt. I wanted to play just like them. I wanted to be persistent just like those guys.

I had a lot of guys that I could watch and see what made them great. They would go in a game and shut their opponent out. That's how I wanted to be. That's the way I played every year. I wanted to be consistent and be at the top every year. That was something I strived for every year from that point on.

Favorite Running Back To Block For

I didn't really have a favorite running back to block for. Warrick Dunn made a lineman's job a lot easier because he was so small. He knew how to set up blocks, and he knew how to get behind the offensive lineman.

If you've got a great running back, all he wants you to do is to block the guys in front of you and get him to the safety. As an offensive lineman, that's what you want to do. You want to get him to the safety, or get him to the odd block guy. Most of the time, the running back can make those guys miss him. Once those guys get to the second level, they can make a lot of yards and a lot of plays. I never looked in the backfield to see what running back was in the huddle. I knew that the running backs out there understood the offense and knew what we were trying to do.

Mike Holmgren

Mike Holmgren came to the Seahawks and showed us that we could win and be in the big games. He said, "If you do it this way, we can win." I think that's where the Seattle Seahawks 12th Man started and all that. Mike Holmgren went in there and showed the city that this team could win just as well as the Green Bays of the world. He came in with a lot of respect.

For a team that wasn't doing that well, he came in and showed us the way we could become better—how we could be consistent and play at a high level. If you do that, you can be in games, or you can be in the hunt to win a Super Bowl. Getting the chance to play in the Super Bowl was awesome. He told us if we did what he said, and we did it right, we could play for a championship. We did, and it happened. We didn't bring home a Super Bowl victory, but everything that he said to do we did, and we had an opportunity to win the game in the end.

Toughest Defensive Lineman

When I first got into the league, I went against Derrick Thomas, who was playing for the Kansas City Chiefs. Going up there, probably before the 12th Man, I think we experienced the loudest stadium. As a rookie going up there, Derrick got the crowd going. I was thinking, "Oh my God, this is what I signed up for."

I went against great guys all the time. Those guys gave their A game every game, so I had to be out there and stay focused. I had to try my best to not go out there and be lackadaisical and give up a sack. That's part of the game. You don't want to give up a sack, but once you get let down one play, that's when things go wrong.

What A Quarterback Typically Does When Sacked

A lot of times, the quarterback will take on the responsibility and say, "That was my fault. I should have got the ball out." The quarterback understands how tough it is to go out there and block those guys.

A lot of quarterbacks feel that if a lineman gets beat for a sack, then the lineman shouldn't come and help the quarterback up. Most of the time, you see linemen once they give up a sack, go back to the huddle, because the quarterback is probably pissed off. If you got just completely physically beat, and the quarterback got hit, the quarterback doesn't want to see the guy who got beat helping him get up. Most of the time if that happens, the offensive lineman feels, "Well, I don't want to go back and pick him up after that." A lineman has the mindset, "Okay, I don't want to be that guy who goes to pick him up, so I'm trying my best to keep that guy from hitting my quarterback."

Mike Holmgren Said Walter Jones Best Offensive Player He Ever Coached

I love Coach Holmgren for saying that. When I played, I got a chance to be in one offense for ten years, and it made my game a lot easier. It made me say, "Okay, this is what I have to work on." I knew the offense, so it made it a lot easier for me. I wanted to go out there and be dominant and be consistent at what I did. I wanted to set the standard on how a left tackle should play the game of football. For him saying that, and for me now to be inducted into the Pro Football Hall of Fame, I can sit back and I can feel good that a young kid can look at me and say, "That's the way I want to play the game of football." I was honored to hear Mike Holmgren say that I went out there and played the game the way it is supposed to be played.

Pro Football Hall Of Fame Induction

In 2014, the Pro Football Hall of Fame brought the 15 finalists for the Hall of Fame to New York City. I was sitting in a hotel room for 30 minutes trying to figure out if I was going to get in or not. That was a very raw emotion, because at that point, I couldn't do anything. You've got all of these voters picking out five guys from the top 15. All 15 guys deserve to be in. I was sitting with my son, waiting on that phone call to say I got in.

When I found out I was selected, it was very emotional for my son and me. It was great for the city of Seattle. It was incredible. I played my whole career in Seattle. I was consistent during my football career, and then I ended my career as a first ballot Hall of Famer. I will never, ever forget all of the emotions I felt.

Only Penalized 9 Times For Holding In 13 NFL Seasons
If referees don't call it, it's not holding. I think it's a situation where referees always tell you if you keep your hands inside, it's not holding. Most of the time, if the referees call holding, it's because the offensive lineman's hands are outside the shoulder pads of a defensive lineman. For me personally, I tried my best to keep my hands inside. I am not saying that I wasn't grabbing cloth or grabbing pads, but as an offensive lineman, I think you have to learn how to get away with stuff that's part of the game. There's no way you can go out there and say you're not holding, because you probably can get called for holding on every snap. It's all about working on your techniques, and making sure you've got your hands in the right place.

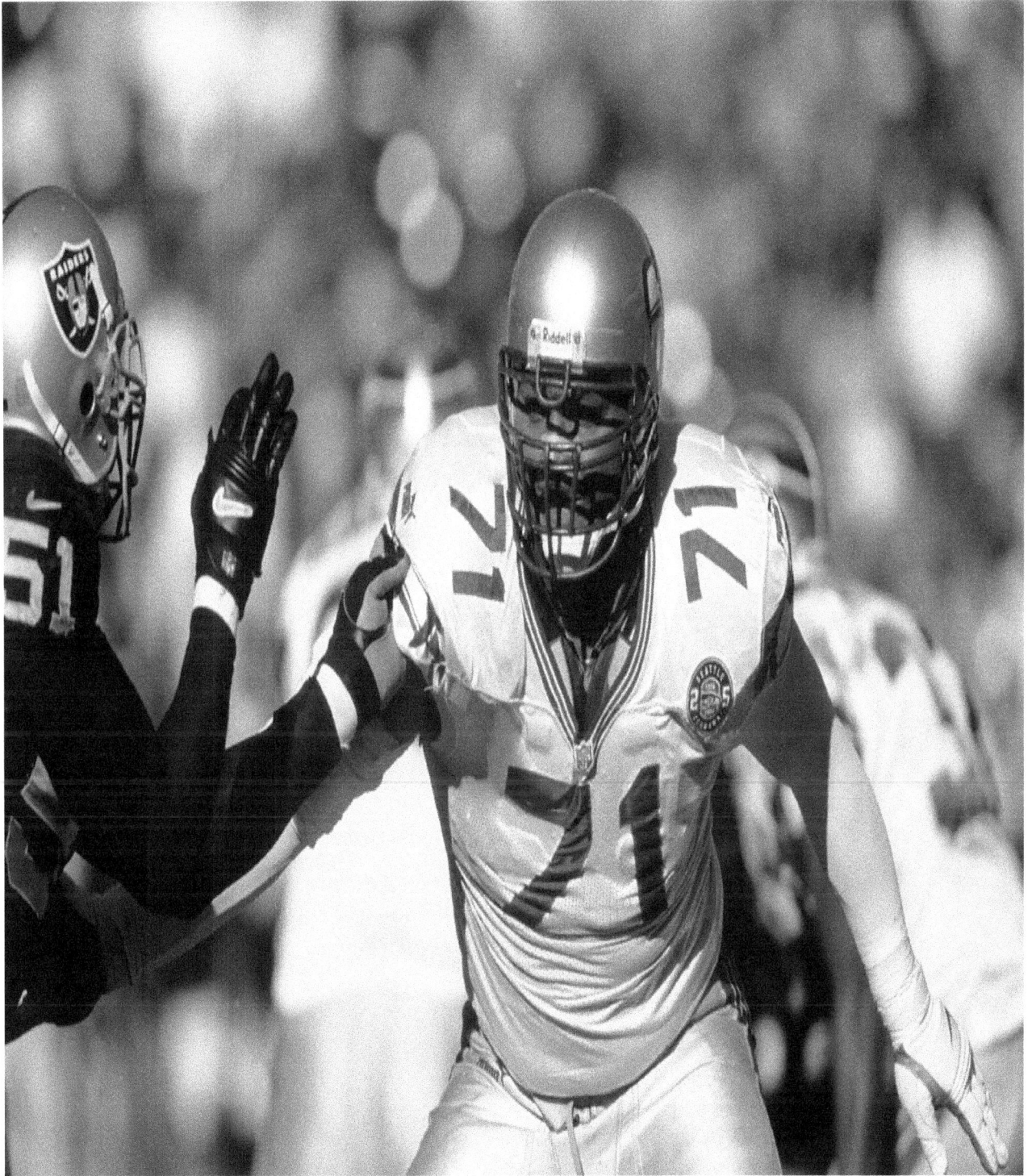

Photograph copyright Associated Press

Chapter 138

Orlando Pace

> College:
> Ohio State
>
> Career History:
> St. Louis Rams (1997–2008)
> Chicago Bears (2009)
>
> 2016 Inductee Pro Football Hall Of Fame

College Choice
Choosing a college was a tough choice. I hate to say it, but it came down to Michigan and Ohio State. I'm from Sandusky, Ohio, which is close to Michigan. You have Michigan fans in Sandusky. Of course there are a lot of Ohio State fans, too.

When I visited Ohio State University, I met some incredible people there like Korey Stringer, who was a great player at the time. Korey took me under his wing a little bit. That kind of sealed the deal for me. It was a great choice for me. Probably one of the best choices I've made in my life.

John Cooper
John Cooper was great. He treated us like young men. He was one of the guys who recruited me really hard. He wanted me to come to Ohio State. The biggest thing he offered me was an opportunity to play as a freshman. That's what I was looking for.

Being Only Second True Freshman To Start Opening Game
I immediately saw the speed of the game was a lot different from high school. The coaches kind of threw me in there with the big boys to see if I could handle it. The first game was a little rough, just because of the speed of the game. Everybody's big and everybody's strong. Being a freshman, I still had some growing up to do and had to develop my game. You kind of learn as you go out there. Each week got better for me. It was a good experience.

Rivalry With Michigan
When you go to Ohio State, you know that the Michigan game is "The Game". The game is played at the end of the regular season, and normally there's something on the line in that game. You really go to Ohio State to be in the atmosphere and be around that rivalry.

Winning Awards In College
All the awards are really special in their own right. Just to be acknowledged is special. I was the only guy who won two Lombardi Awards in college. I'm not sure if there will ever be another

lineman who will duplicated that. I was Ohio State MVP, Big Ten Offensive MVP, and finished 4th in the Heisman Trophy voting. You just don't see offensive lineman finishing 4th in the Heisman voting. You just don't see offensive lineman get that kind of acknowledgement. I was really fortunate and I worked really hard to get those awards.

Key To Success In College
I wanted to be the best. I really did. I wanted to do something that separated me from so many other linemen. I was 30 yards down the field blocking defenders. That was my way of saying "Hey I want to separate myself from any other linemen."

Also, I wanted to break the will of guys. It's an offensive lineman's dream to break the will of the defender. One of the things I really wanted to do was put something on tape where the guy playing against me the following week would experience some fear in his heart.

NFL Draft
I didn't know the St. Louis Rams were going to draft me. To be honest, I only took three scouting trips. I visited the New York Jets, who had the number one pick. I also went to visit the Oakland Raiders and the New Orleans Saints, who had traded up prior to draft day. I thought I was either going to go to the Jets, or at worst, not going to get past the third selection. Then the Rams traded up to the first pick.

I don't even remember the interviewing process with the Rams. Coach Vermeil had broadcast a ton of our games at Ohio State. I think he was familiar with the type of player I was. So as soon as the Rams made that trade, I got a phone call from Coach Vermeil that they would be selecting me with the number one pick.

Missing First Training Camp With St. Louis Rams
I missed the first training camp with the Rams. I was in contract negotiations. The second year training camp was tough. Coach Vermeil was an old school coach who believed in really tough training camps. He wanted to find out who his guys were and what they were made of. The training camps were tough, really tough. The physicality of the camps, the hours on the field, and everything he demanded of us was really tough.

Missing the first training camp wasn't by design. It kind of worked out that way. I didn't know how tough it would be at the time. Looking back on it, I could have missed a couple more training camps and I think I would have been fine.

When I started practicing with the Rams, it was tough for me. When you go in as a rookie and are the number one pick in the league, the expectations are high. The guys are saying, "Hey, where is this guy?" I bought my teammates a lot of breakfasts and dinners. They accepted me once I was practicing with them. Those guys were really great.

Kurt Warner
When Kurt Warner first started, for anybody to say Kurt was going to be an NFL MVP and a potential Hall of Famer, they would be lying. Kurt worked extremely hard, but no one new he

would be that good. When he got under center when Trent Green went down, he was phenomenal. He had his opportunity and he made the most of it.

Preference Run Blocking Or Pass Blocking
I came out of Ohio State, the pancake blocker trying to smash defenders. I didn't give a sack up in two years there. I could pass and run block. It didn't make a difference. Mike Martz was named the offensive coordinator in 1999. Mike Martz liked to chuck the ball down the field, so I had to have my pass technique correct and ready to go.

Pancake Block
I saw Korey Stringer play against Alabama in the Citrus Bowl, and he just crushed this guy. I could see the defenders were scared of him. At that point, I realized I wanted to impose my will on guys as well. I wanted to be able to finish blocks and really separate myself from guys. Guys always block to the man. I really wanted to block through the man. Once the "pancake block" took off and people started noticing it, then you obviously want to do it more.

Realization St. Louis Rams Offense Could Be Special
Going into training camp in 1999, we felt good with Trent Green being the starter at quarterback. Kurt got in there when Trent got hurt. Marshall Faulk had just come in and the guys were healthy. We knew this offense could be special when we beat San Francisco the third game of 1999. San Francisco had beaten us 18 times in a row, I believe. Once we beat San Francisco, we knew we were a pretty good team.

The great thing about that team was everybody was unselfish. They are all good guys. Nobody wanted the credit. Kurt Warner is an awesome guy. Marshall Faulk, Isaac Bruce, and Torry Holt are really good people. Offensive linemen always take pride in their team winning ballgames. That's just the mindset of offensive linemen. We don't really need the credit. We just want to go out there, do our work, and win ballgames.

Playing In First Super Bowl
As a kid, I dreamed of one day running out of the tunnel playing in the Super Bowl. To win that game the way we did, not knowing if the ball crossed the goal line or not, was really special. The first quarter I felt like I was walking on air because I was so excited to get out there and play. I couldn't wait to get out there. I felt faster. Everything felt great at the time.

Dick Vermeil Retiring After Winning Super Bowl
I didn't realize that Coach Vermeil was going to retire after we won the Super Bowl. I was thinking that we could continue our success for the next two or three years. The difficult part was Offensive Coordinator Mike Martz was so hot at the time. It was impossible to keep him as the offensive coordinator for the following year. Everyone thought he was going to be offered him a head coaching job. If he had been, I think he would have taken it. Coach Vermeil realized that he had the ultimate prize—winning the Super Bowl. He probably felt at that time, he could step away. Had Coach Vermeil stayed on another year, we probably would have won a couple Super Bowls.

Dick Vermeil

Dick Vermeil was great. He was an old school coach who really believed in his players, not as just the football player, but the actual person. His former players from the Philadelphia Eagles would come to our meetings. Coach Vermeil would cry about everybody, but it was genuine. That's one thing I really appreciated about him. He was genuine.

When he said we would rally around Kurt Warner, Coach Vermeil truly believed that. He also believed we were going to be a great team. That year everybody bought into his system. That's really the sign of a good coach. If you have a good coach who the players believe in, you'll have success.

Losing To New England Patriots In Super Bowl

The team felt confident going into the Super Bowl against the New England Patriots. The Patriots were playing with a backup quarterback in Tom Brady, and we thought we would run over the Patriots.

Patriots Head Coach Bill Belichick had a great game plan. They were really stopping our passing game. Had we run the ball, the outcome may have been different. The Patriots dropped a lot of guys in coverage to stop our passing game and we needed to make adjustments.

John Randle's Trash Talking

I played against John Randle a couple of times and the things he would say were just flat out hilarious. I couldn't believe it. He read player bios. He was talking trash to the offensive guard as I was in my stance next to the guard, literally laughing. I'd think, "Oh my gosh, this guy is hilarious." He talked so much trash. It was unbelievable. He told one of my guards the guard's wife's name. I thought, "How in the world does John know the guard's wife's name?" My guard got pretty pissed off about it.

Favorite Game In NFL

Every player will say that the Super Bowl was his favorite game. There were so many good games. One game that stands out is the game against San Francisco, and being able to get that monkey off our backs having lost 18 games in a row to them. When you play for 13 years, there are a lot of games that really stand out in your mind. The NFC Championship game against Tampa was a tough game. It was really tough getting to the Super Bowl.

One special game that really stood out, now that I think of it, was our first playoff game on the run to that Super Bowl against Minnesota. I can remember the city of St. Louis being really excited because the Rams had never been to the playoffs before. The first play of the game we scored. That's the game that really sticks out because the Edward Jones Dome in St. Louis was really rocking. It was good to be in the playoffs. I remember, wow, this is a great feeling to be in the playoffs.

Pro Football Hall Of Fame Induction

Being selected for the Pro Football Hall of Fame was great. That last hour when the decision was being made, was really tough. You try to visualize scenarios where you get in. You just never know how the process will shake out. I had a little nervousness. My initial feelings and reaction after finding out I was going to be inducted, were relief and excitement. Being one of the youngest guys in the Hall of Fame makes it even more special.

When you look at how many guys have actually played in the NFL and realize that there are only 300 guys who are in the Pro Football Hall of Fame, and you are part of that elite group, it's really hard to describe the feeling. It means so much as a player. The ultimate goal as a player is to be known, one day, as one of the best of all time. I'm humbled by the honor.

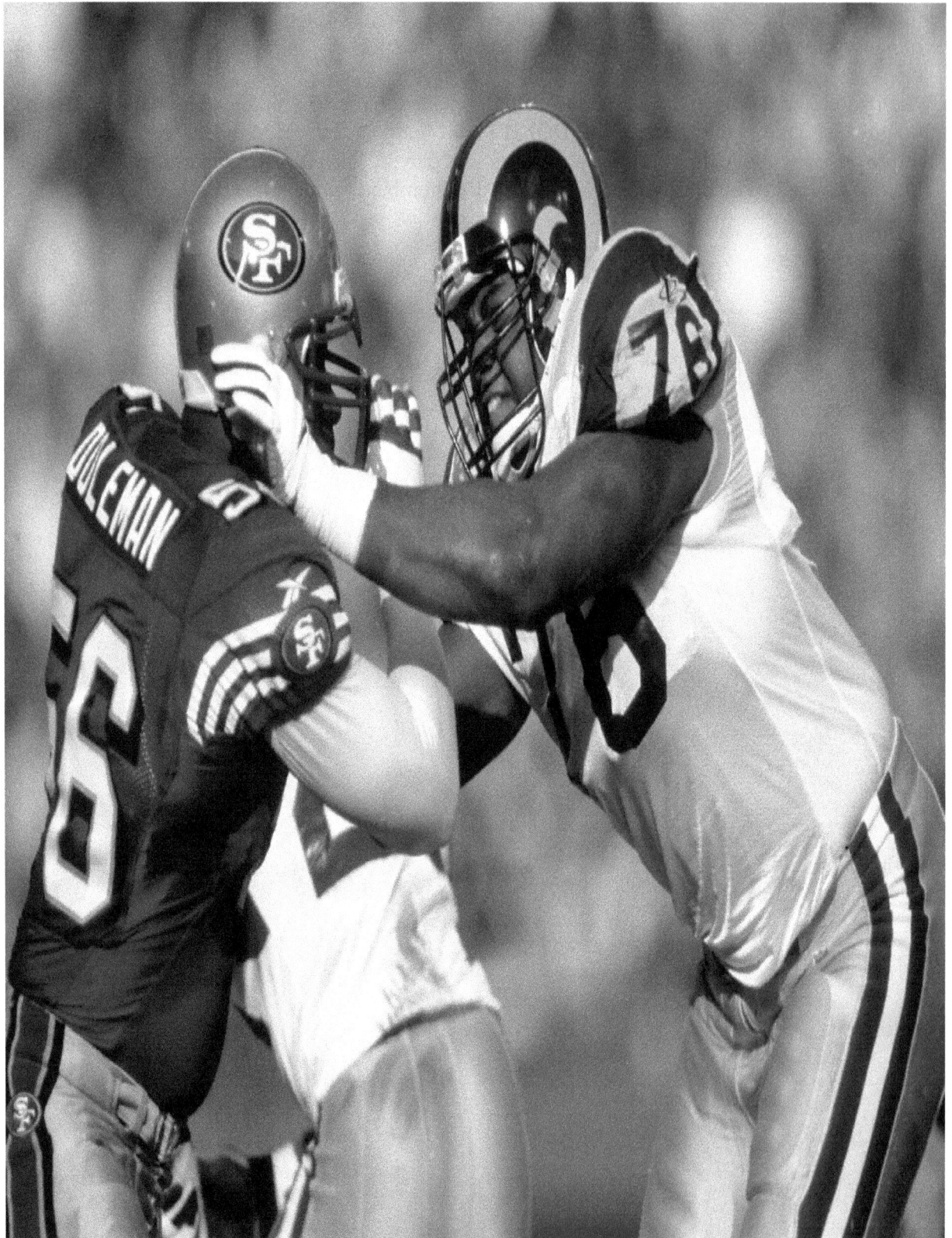

St. Louis Ram offensive lineman Orlando Pace pass blocks San Francisco 49er Chris Doleman during an NFL game. Photograph copyright Associated Press

www.ingramcontent.com/pod-product-compliance
Lightning Source LLC
Chambersburg PA
CBHW062021090426

42811CB00005B/920